ASSERTIVE RELIGIOUS IDENTITIES
INDIA AND EUROPE

ASSERTIVE RELIGIOUS IDENTITIES

India and Europe

Edited by

SATISH SABERWAL

MUSHIRUL HASAN

MANOHAR

2006

First published 2006

ISBN 81-7304-673-5

Published by
Ajay Kumar Jain for
Manohar Publishers & Distributors
4753/23 Ansari Road, Daryaganj
New Delhi 110 002

Printed at
Lordson Publishers Pvt Ltd
Delhi 110 007

Distributed in South Asia by
FOUNDATION BOOKS
4381/4, Ansari Road
Daryaganj, New Delhi 110 002
nd its branches at Mumbai, Hyderabad,
Bangalore, Chennai, Kolkata

Contents

Preface

The idea for the volume before you originated in a conversation between Professor Satish Saberwal and me, in early 2003. We have both been concerned over processes, sustained over several generations now, by major institutions—some Hindu, some Muslim—whose consequences have been *socially separative.* While these institutions' ostensible functions are 'religious' or 'cultural', which seem innocent enough, these have worked out low cost forms of organization and activity—which have given them a rather formidable expansive dynamic. Furthermore, their activities and campaigns have served, sometimes unintentionally, to provoke each other, thereby providing the other side with justification for *its* own activities, as if in collective self-defence. The mutual provocation has, over the decades, confirmed for both sides, a sense of their own victimhood.

We saw here a social mechanism which has had significant social and political consequences but which has remained largely off the radars of the social sciences. We proposed initially a half-day discussion of the theme; but as we worked on it, we were drawn into its complexity—and we found numerous colleagues who have been working on its many facets from different angles. The three-day seminar considered the processes at issue from a long-term historical perspective; and also a comparative one, reaching out to another important region where the mutual relations between major religious traditions have also been problematical for a very long time.

Fortunately, we were able to persuade three scholars to write on Europe's experience. Professor Michael Brenner, through the good offices of Mr Heiko Sievers, Programme Director, Goethe Institut, New Delhi, and Professor Gurpreet Mahajan and Dr Michael Dusche, both from Jawaharlal Nehru University, New Delhi. Mr Sievers and Goethe Institut helped us bring in Dr Jan Peter Hartung too, and we greatly appreciate their help.

We are able to publish this volume with unusual speed, thanks to exemplary cooperation from our contributors and from Mr Ramesh Jain, our publisher. We are grateful.

I am particularly grateful to Professor Satish Saberwal for his untiring efforts in organizing the seminar, persuading the contributors to revise their papers, and editing them with care. Without his active intervention, this book would not have been published. Let me add that he has been a great asset as a Visiting Professor at the Academy of Third World Studies.

New Delhi MUSHIRUL HASAN

Introduction

SATISH SABERWAL

The rising tide of chauvinism in South Asia, especially of the religious nationalist sort,. presents the social sciences with an exceptionally acute challenge. Numerous religious identities have been assertive in the subcontinent; but extraordinary vehemence, and violence, have come to be associated with groups claiming to speak for 'Hindus' and 'Muslims' in South Asia since the early twentieth century. We can now look back to earlier and crucial horizons. The later of these is in the nineteenth century, arising, first, in a particular mix of colonial political, administrative, and documentary practices and, second, in the availability of novel institutional models, and technologies, especially for communication. The earlier horizon lies in the medieval centuries. These latter may be seen as a time both for insulation and for mixing at the levels of ideas and social relationships, a time both for myriad cooperation and for contestation.

Of that ambiguous legacy, it is the insulating and the oppositional traces of memory and attitudes that found fresh energy through the nineteenth century initiatives, preparing the ground for a more determined re-carving of social spaces. The social sciences in India have not taken much notice of this ongoing social reconfiguration, not to mention its implications. This blindspot seems to have been overdetermined from several directions.

Clearly, to be able to comprehend the processes at issue required an openness to historical connections as well as to the inner lives of social and religious groups. A great deal needed to be considered: ideologies, social organisation, politics, interpretations of texts and of the past, and everyday activities and relationships in the localities.

*I thank T.N. Madan and Raghurama Raju for reading an earlier version critically, and Pradip Datta for his advice. I am grateful also to Shereen Ratnagar for her sage and beneficial advice.

Further, Sudhir Kakar, Hansen, and others have argued that the psychological implications of these diverse, pervasive experiences have been re-shaping categories in the unconscious too. That is to say, all this demanded of scholarship a simultaneous interest in multiple disciplinary traditions and perspectives: sociology, history, religious traditions, the unconscious. Here was a process too large and diffuse to be apprehended at one go.

Social sciences in India have had difficulty generating stamina of this order. There has been a certain reluctance to examine the domain of religion in modern India—and even more so the patterns of interactions between the major religious traditions. There was the preliminary difficulty over the categories 'Muslim' and 'Hindu'. Given the long implication of these categories in social and political conflict, 'secularists' have tended to eschew their use altogether, foregoing the possibility of grasping their antagonistic interactions in society. Yet the ongoing re-structurings of religious traditions, and re-structurings of their mutual interactions—sometimes provocative interactions—have been central to the history of modern India (Madan 1997).

Furthermore, our universities function with a division of labour where an interest in history is assigned to historians. The other social sciences, and especially sociologists over the past fifty years, have shown very limited interest in history. On the other side, only a few historians have cultivated a feel for complex social processes.[1] Consequently, there was no effort to put together the bits and pieces that began to become available through monographic literature in the 1980s, with key monographs from Francis Robinson, Rafiuddin Ahmed, Barbara Metcalf and others.

With something like the movements for Pakistan and Ayodhya, the outcomes have tended to be attributed to immediately preceding activities, campaigns, negotiations, and the like. Only recently has scholarship begun to locate these outcomes in their larger contexts, taking in their prehistories concerning the prior reconfiguring of the social ground on which the later mobilizations could work.

These notes will review the logics that prevailed along these several horizons and along those governing the transition from one to the next: the medieval legacy, the transition to colonialism, and the rise of contrastive identities since the mid-nineteenth century.

THE MEDIEVAL LEGACY

The caste order has long enabled society in India to carry social complexity in unparalleled measure; and this would hold for the diversity from one locality to the next during the medieval period too. There was a matching diversity in the patterns of relations between groups that might be classified as Muslim and Hindu in various domains. Here I can indicate only the range of variation on this limited issue: in their distinctive religious institutions, in their regional variations which sometimes mingled with other traditions variously, in the everyday life of neighbourhoods especially in north India, and in the culture of the Mughal ruling class.

Religious Institutions

There were the various religious specialists, living in institutions of the kind that continued to flourish in the twentieth century.

We read of Madhva Brahmin monks living—studying, praying, teaching, preaching—in a cluster of monasteries in Udupi in coastal Karnataka in the late twentieth century. This is a fairly exclusive social universe; in the anthropologist's account (Vasudeva Rao 2002), the monks' contact with Muslims is scant. They are passive sympathisers of the Hindu nationalist ideology espoused by Vishwa Hindu Parishad (VHP) and Bharatiya Janata Party (BJP); one of their seniors is active in VHP councils. The scene has been no different at centres of Islamic learning: the early Farangi Mahall (Robinson 2001), the latter day Deoband (Metcalf 1982), or the Barelvis (Sanyal 1996). Nor should we forget the ability—and the availability—of men of religion, during the medieval period, to bear arms: some Sufis and some orders of Hindu celibate monks could be found in military camps (van der Veer 1996).

Religious Crossings

Sufi centres of piety have sometimes been more open, as may be seen in the following instances which I have arranged along a continuum—from close relationships in the first case to seemingly complete separation in the last:[2]

1. For Sindh, Thapan (2005) notes that since the late nineteenth century a few Sufi pirs have had Hindu disciples, authorising some

of them, in turn, to be Sufi masters—without having to become Muslim. The range of contacts, however, is limited: 'Hindu individuals have contact with the sacred person of the pir and not with the rest of the Muslim community in Pakistan that may also venerate him' (personal communication 19 June 2003).

2. An 1833 visitor to the shrine of the Sufi Baba Farid, at Pakpattan, Punjab, now in Pakistan, found both Muslims and Hindus participating in a salvation-oriented ritual. At a succession ceremony at the same shrine in 1935, however, Hindu participation was peripheral (Eaton 2000: 241f).
3. The spread of Islam (and Christianity) in south India over the centuries took the form of locating Islamic (and Christian) elements in pre-existing frames of belief and practice (Susan Bayly 1989: 73-86). Narayanan (2002) offers an illustration for the process: in a Tamil composition on the life of the Prophet, Cirappuranam, *c.* 1700, the characters and the settings show the deep impress of those in a ninth-century Tamil *Ramayana*.
4. The course of Islam in medieval Bengal was somewhat divergent. Illustratively, Saiyid Sultan, a prolific, early seventeenth-century author, wrote a 'comprehensive history of all prophets, culminating in Muhammad' in Bengali (Roy 1983: 12). This, and other texts located Muhammad's birth and triumph, and other initial Islamic victories, in a milieu where they had to contend against powerful Hindu rulers and gods. These authors projected on to the moment of Islam's origin a significant opposition between the then nascent faith and its allegedly Hindu environment. Yet Bengali Muslims and Hindus continued to share textual forms, myths, rites, and festivals until well into the nineteenth century.
5. Behind what may seem to be a shared tradition, the meanings and the significance of the 'same' terms could be almost wholly mutually exclusive. Stewart (2002) writes of 'Satya Pir', the subject of two sets of texts that have spread through eastern India over the last five centuries. In one, *purana*-like set, Visnu/Narayan appears in the *avatara* of a Muslim-looking Satya Pir, who reveals his true identity when necessary. Faithful devotion to Satya Pir is thought, in this set, to facilitate general welfare and access to wealth; negligence can bring misfortune. In the other set, Satya Pir the Sufi aids the spread of Islam, demonstrating his (Islamic) powers to non-Muslims, commoners and kings alike. Two kinds

of identity, and two kinds of literary genre, converge on a single figure. (Roy 1983: 214-17 gives another account of Satya Pir.)

6. A sternly Islamic attitude among leading Sufi masters, as in Sheikh Ahmed Sirhindi (1564-1624) would, for example, have denied significant government employment to non-Muslims (Damrel 2002).

How is one to account for all this diversity in attitudes and in the patterns of relationships? Clearly, on one side there is the profusion of castes and sects, each a niche, together accommodating an infinite diversity of belief and practice. On the other, as we saw, Sufis did at times have a wide outreach, turning on the adept's personal qualities and grace; and, by and large, cordial relations between religious communities were in the state's interest, and were often encouraged by the state, whether in pre-colonial Malabar (Arunima, in this volume) or in Awadh (Fisher 1987; Alam 1996). Together, these elements could foster a certain sense of shared space.

This possibility was, however, contingent on rather particular circumstances, namely, that the arrangements would continue to enjoy immunity from critical scrutiny and reflection, and from demands for conformity to scripture and other texts held to be binding. Such immunity, however, has had no guarantors. Religious crossings could arise in local choices and these were short on doctrinal and institutional buttresses.

In contrast, the 'great' religious traditions, at their core, carry relatively coherent—comprehensive, usually taken-for-granted—complexes of texts, beliefs, practices, and institutions. For these reified complexes, the respective traditions have long proclaimed divine inspiration, prophetic quality, and other marks of transcendence. Their scriptural bases permit only limited discursive resources for articulate communication with bearers of other scriptures and religious traditions. This would have consequences, as we shall see.

Neighbourhoods

Reports on everyday life in medieval *neighbourhoods* are sparse but, reading back from the early colonial period, there are indications of different kinds of sharing, especially in the smaller localities. In a Gujarati village in the early nineteenth century, A.M. Shah finds that village Rajputs, whose ancestors had taken to Islam some generations earlier, maintained close bonds with those castemates whose ancestors had not; but another group of Muslims, whose ancestors from outside had received landgrants in the village, continued to be regarded as outsiders—though accommodated in the caste order (Shah 2002: 58f).

For Bengali villagers, despite the contrasts coded into some of the mythology and practices (Roy 1983), being a Muslim did not disturb their belonging to village society—until the rise of several nineteenth-century reform movements (Eaton 1994, Ahmed 1981). The social gap between the Meo and their Hindu neighbours, south-west of Delhi, began to widen only in the second quarter of twentieth-century (Mayaram 1997).

The seventeenth-century autobiography of Banarasi Das, of Jain merchant background, points to urban residential arrangements where communities with 'a shared way of life embodied in social mores, moral norms, rules of behaviour, customs, institutions, beliefs and the like' lived in separate quarters (Lath 1981: iv-v). 'All that was humanly meaningful or significant [for Banarasi Das] lay for him eminently in the life of his community' (ibid.: viii). Though he taught the then Mughal governor of Allahabad 'Hindi versification and poetic usage', Banarasi showed little interest in Persian poetry or histories, or other strands of life outside the world of the Jains (ibid.: xxiii-xxiv).

The Mughal Ruling Class

The Mughal—and later the Awadhi—ruling class was 'open' (Man Singh, Akbar's nephew by marriage, had led the Mughal troops that brought Bengal into the empire) even though the non-Muslim elements in this ruling class came from, and remained embedded within, particular *jatis.*

As the imperial and, later, the Nawabi hold on power weakened and shrank, the sons of the indigenes—Rajput, Kayastha, Khatri, Brahmin—stayed back within their *jatis,* ceasing to look up to, or identify with, the erstwhile ruling class. The last Rajput wife in a Mughal palace was reclaimed by her father, Maharaja of Jodhpur, in 1718 or shortly thereafter (Taft 1994: 224). What had been the rather ambiguous links at the level of royal marriages finally faded away.

The sons of immigrants, needless to say, would not have been embedded in a local *jati.* They had more reason to wish to continue to identify with the former ruling class. During nineteenth century they alone would advance claims to descent from the Mughal imperial ruling class—which was also a claim to special privileges (Robinson 1975). The social space of the Mughal ruling class had in some measure been a shared one but, as the nineteenth century advanced, that shared political legacy was to count for less and less.

THE TRANSITION TO COLONIALISM

Medieval 'shared spaces' were, in the main, working arrangements, a *modus vivandi.* The arrangements were 'opportunist', in the sense of lacking a rationalized larger design or articulated ideology. This can be seen again in the Non-Cooperation/Khilafat movement (1920-2): both these phases turned on immediate, pragmatic arrangements, not on integrating them into wider frameworks of visions, ideas, or practices (Hasan 1979).

It has been said that medieval identities had tended to be 'fuzzy'. Political affiliation, caste, occupation, and locality were some of the elements in the prevailing identities; and mixed in with these were other elements of the 'great traditions', propagated by the respective religious specialists over centuries past. These too, taken for granted, were part of the prevailing identities.

These identities and social arrangements had evolved in the course of everyday life. Arrangements happening to arise in this way tend to be weak in staying power: weak, that is, in the kinds of resources—ideological, organizational, ritual, symbolic—that would help withstand critical scrutiny or adverse circumstances. Such challenges to the shared arrangements in the middle ground began to gather strength in the late nineteenth century, from agencies which claimed to speak for their respective versions of the true faith and summoned the believers to shed their ignorance and abide by their faith and identity.

The impulse to constitute these agencies came ultimately from the uncertainties and the anxieties of colonial society.[3] There was the loss of power, as the British established a virtual monopoly in the use of force; in north India, this affected the old Muslim elite the more acutely. There were the Christian missionaries, insulting the several religious traditions in India and their texts, beliefs, and practices. There was an ongoing re-casting of the whole structure of opportunities—which men of Hindu castes, with traditions of learning, clerical work, and trading, were able to grasp more speedily than men of Muslim elite families, with traditions principally of governing. There were the consequences of this latter differential, as ascendant Hindu groups used the strength of numbers to challenge the older urban hierarchies over which the Muslim elites had often presided.

A slow reconfiguration of the social space was in progress. Efforts at coping with the attendant anxieties, and the local contestations pushed adversaries to reach out beyond the family or the *jati*. The consequent aggregations tended to congeal around 'religious' symbols, and oppositions—which had gained currency over the centuries—and these were increasingly identified, with distinctive religious identities, Muslim and Hindu, more often than with cross-religious networks in UP, like the Taluqdars, large land controllers. The older middle ground was beginning to cleave. Similar anxieties were at work in Bengal. With the coming of British rule in the late eighteenth century, Muslims had lost their hold on government and judiciary; and, in the flux over *zamindaris* that followed, there were net transfers from Muslims to Hindus, for the latter had a stronger presence in commerce, and therefore easier access to cash for buying the zamindaris that came up for sale (De 1974).

In this milieu, Muslim Bengali villagers received calls to complete their Islamization all through the nineteenth century—beginning with Shariatullah's labours, inspired by his long years as a young man in the sacred centres of Islam in Arabia, and aided by the tension of class difference between a largely Muslim peasantry and largely Hindu landlords (Ahmed 1981, Eaton 1994: 281-90). The working of the Bengali Hindu imagination, on the other side, was illustrated in, and influenced by, the writings of Bankim Chandra Chatterjee. It assimilated the experience of colonial humiliation with the experience of the earlier Muslim dynasties; and it cast the aspirations for liberation in an idiom that drew on Hindu religious imagery. And, whatever his intentions, Bankim's writings could be, and were, widely interpreted as anti-Muslim (Kaviraj 1995: 132-50, 186f n. 62). Nineteenth-century men of letters elsewhere, in Maharashtra and UP, were no less prejudiced (Sudhir Chandra 1992: 117-42).

RISE OF CONTRASTIVE IDENTITIES

Over the past century and a half, then, society in India—as elsewhere—underwent vast reconfigurations, in multiple keys. In these processes, religious identities loomed large; and there were multinodal efforts at accentuating *contrastive* religious elements in the prevailing mix of identities.[4] Thanks to these efforts, the distribution of mutual attitudes, stereotypes, and the like shifted towards greater polarization, especially across a 'Hindu-Muslim' line; and some of the subsequent political agendas would build on the hardening of identities under way.

To be sure there were rivalries on the ground, and numerous bones of contention: questions of local status, expressed in skirmishes over public spaces; of resources, by way of share of governmental work (should it be in Urdu or Hindi?), and therefore of government jobs; and of power (who should sit in elected bodies, on what basis?). Every society has its rivalries; those in northern India began to be cast increasingly in terms of religious identities. For these latter, the protagonists, began to claim overriding relevance, as they advanced comprehensive claims over individuals' allegiance. Religious identities became the framework of social categories through which common sense would do its daily work.

This polarization has followed complex rhythms over these generations, replete with reversals. Focussing on Bengal in the early twentieth century, Pradip Datta (1999) has disentangled a vast skein that separates out the consequences of (mis)interpreting census data, the shaping of the perception of economic interests and aspirations in terms of communal identities, the diverse political strategies emerging from the debris of Non-Cooperation and Khilafat, the social strategies of ambitious lower castes, the (more numerous) Muslim experience of discrimination by (the socially and economically dominant) Hindus, the fertile uses of potent symbols like 'music before mosques' and *go-kurbani* in a surly civil society, communal riots in hardening identities and antagonisms, and much else. Numerous subjectivities have been at play, at different levels, pursuing varied trajectories.

Tracking the myriad, everyday cross-currents over large space-time wholes is necessary. No less important, however, is the imperative to abstract, if possible, major processes ranging over still larger space-time wholes. We seek here to highlight one such long-term process. It concerns the convergent outcome of snowballing activities associated with well-known 'religious' and 'cultural' institutions from the late nineteenth-century—Deoband *madrasa*, the Arya Samaj, the RSS, the Tablighi Jamaat, and several others. These movemenets began to generate numerous ideologically driven activities and activists in the localities. Common to them has been their ability to embed, in localities, men motivated to foster distinctive (contrastive, separative) identities, and to carry these far and wide. These men were maintained economically, largely with resources found within their host localities. Their activities had a cumulative consequence: a 'de-composing' of society and culture, tending to arouse, sharpen and propagate religious identities on separative courses. The process has had three moments:

A. *Orientation* began with simple calls to religious truths, and to pull away from false doctrines. These sought to orient persons away from those who could be presented as bearers of 'other' religious identities and towards those of one's 'own' identity working more or less explicitly for contrastive identities. There were corresponding re-arrangements of social space and of what children learned while growing up.
B. *Mobilization* in a milieu of exceptional uncertainty, where customary hierarchies, and forms of legitimate action, were being challenged. There were few competing social visions in the field, and a sense of overriding relevance of religious identities tended to prevail by default. As this happened, these identities provided the foci for diverse efforts at mobilization of material resources (say for institution building, as in Arya Samaj or at Aligarh) and (exclusive) solidarities (as in RSS or Tablighi Jamaat), or to bid for power (as with Muslim League or, later, BJP).
C. *Collateral*: A separative move on one side provides a reason, an emotional justification, for separative pulls on the other side, and vice versa. Sectoral mobilization aroused anxieties across the hardening line of separation, and this elicited initiatives on the other side, which the protagonists would justify in terms of their own anxieties. A reciprocally provocative dynamic has been operative.

We proceed now to consider some of these institutions, and the snowballing processes each has devised.

INSTITUTIONS AND MOVEMENTS

Within a shared historical setting, the categories 'Muslim' and 'Hindu' have served as loci around which to consolidate memories of the past, and identities in the present and for the future. The dynamic in the two spaces being so constituted has been distinctive, yet mutually interacting.

In the Punjab the Arya Samaj was led by merchants and professionals. Establishing schools in the emerging mainstream was an early ambition; and when it did establish an analogue for the Deoband *madrasa* (see below)—Gurukul Kangri—its statement of intentions in 1900, included the teaching of 'English language and literature' (Jones 1976: 221). Yet, the Arya Samaj had only a limited geographical reach. The Arya Samaj rejected idol-worship and related activities stridently, so there was no question of the Gurukul's graduates simply taking over established temples. The Arya Samaj concentrated instead on building its own centres for congregational worship.

Some Gurukul graduates found jobs within Arya Samajs, performing *havans*, marriages, etc. The Arya Samaj was centred on Punjab,[5] present-day Haryana,[6] and UP. Elsewhere it had difficulty in overcoming the entrenched local matrices of religiosity—and of the challenges to such religiosity rising on other social bases, for example, the lower castes. It has had very few activists in the field, nothing like the Deobandi momentum. Nevertheless, it has sought the mantle of being the protector of Hindus, and some of its initiatives have contributed powerfully to separative outcomes along other channels. The Arya Samaj can claim credit for making *go-kurbani* an enduring bone of communal contention, and it has been willing to press the music before mosques issue (see Pradip Datta 1999: 248, 253). Specifically, some of its activists tried their hand in Malabar after the Mapilla uprising in the 1920s (Sikand 2002: 32; Haridatt 1984: 487-91), in Hyderabad in the late 1930s (Haridatt 1984: 594-605), and, most infamously, in Alwar, south-west of Delhi, against the Meo in the 1930s and 1940s (Mayaram 1999: 64-9, 189-91).

The most fateful Arya Samaji activity, perhaps, was its *shuddhi* campaign, seeking to re-convert Muslim communities which had continued to live with a large measure of their pre-Islamic beliefs and practices. This campaign was pressed especially vigorously in the 1920s, in the wake of the Non-Cooperation and Khilafat movements. Led by the Arya Samaji Swami Shraddhananda, who drew the more orthodox Sanatan Dharmis also into the campaign, it was dramatic in its success in western UP. Since a large majority of Muslims in India shared much of their neighbours' beliefs and practices, the *shuddhi* drive sent shockwaves through Muslim elites: if the campaign could succeed in one region, what would hold it back elsewhere, say among the Meo? (For north India and Bengal, Sikand 2002.) Among the responses to this threat was the rise of Tablighi Jamaat discussed below.

Deoband: a large *madrasa* was established in this small town in western UP in 1867. Men who studied the Koran and other Islamic religious texts and practices there, spread out to various localities as maulvis and the like. To foster 'pure' Islamic lives was one of the few skills in which these men were trained—other than calligraphy and Unani medicine (Metcalf 1982: 103). They would be sustained by the host community—and were able sometimes to establish their own *madrasas* for the further propagation of Islamic education. The central doctrine being advanced from Deoband was to Islamise more thoroughly people who continued to be engaged actively in traditions they shared with their neighbours, which were pronounced as un-Islamic. Families integrated into the local caste systems were drawn into a more exclusive Islamic social frame.

The Deoband *madrasa* and its graduates, and the numerous further institutions inspired by them, worked hard to foster a sharply defined, distinctive identity for Muslims in India. This reached inescapably into social separativeness and has been somewhat obscured by a contrapuntal theme at play between 1920 and 1947. The *ulama* took the lead in the Khilafat movement, entering the domain of the organized anti-colonial movement for the first time; they dominated the Khilafat campaign to the point of pushing the Muslim League and its politics into the shadows—while the issue lasted. To coordinate their efforts, a large body of *ulama* formed themselves into an organization, Jamiat Ulama-i Hind (JUH). JUH co-operated with Gandhi during the movement. Until 1947, under the influence of Maulana Abul Kalam Azad, the JUH tended to support the politics of the Indian National Congress rather than that of the Muslim League.

The JUH stance in favour of a united India, even as the politics of the Muslim League caught on rapidly, rested on several considerations (see Hardy 1971); these need not detain us. By the 1920s, however, distinctive identities and separative attitudes had come to pervade the prevailing common sense, too ingrained by then to be reversed easily. In the run up to the 1946 elections, despite the reservations of many JUH *ulama*, the wave of popular support for the demand for Partition covered large swathes of custodians of Sufi shrines, and numerous *ulama* too (Gilmartin 1988: 213-22 on Punjab; Sanyal 1996: Epilogue on Barelvis in the then United Provinces).

The Arya Samaj and Deoband had arisen, independently, amidst partially shared anxieties of post-1857 north India but did not initially react to each other. Both summoned the respective faithful to distinctive, contrastive, ways of life, shaped around particular religious observances; and the corresponding religious identities were already beginning to enter a dynamic of mutual provocation. The introduction of separate electorates in 1909 gave institutional political support to a growing social separation. The Non-Cooperation and Khilafat movements (1920-22) seemed to reverse that separativeness dramatically; but their collapse cut sharply into the levels of mutual trust between Muslims and Hindus in the mid-1920s Bengal (Pradip Datta 1999: 255-9). This was the time when the Arya Samaj-led *shuddhi* drive moved into high gear. This turns out also to be the time when RSS on one side and the Tablighi Jamaat on the other start their own powerful innings.

One of the mechanisms powering the spread of the RSS since 1925 has been the *shakha*. The RSS has long claimed to be only a cultural organization but never tires of proclaiming that it seeks to consolidate 'Hindus', by way of training for stronger physical bodies, greater social solidarity, and a pride in their past. Alleged deficiencies in these areas are thought to have exposed Hindus historically to recurrent humiliation. Laying the blame for these humiliations on the conquerors' religious identities, RSS directs its venom especially at Islam and Muslims, Christianity and Christians.

Even as RSS activities have spread far and wide, the core social module remains the *shakha*, a local group of volunteers whose daily routine includes meeting at a designated place for physical exercise, minor games, and indoctrination (Andersen and Damle 1987; Basu et al. 1993). From its initial social base among Brahmin and other upper caste, middle class men, especially merchants, it has spawned a string of subsidiaries since the 1950s, reaching out effectively to some other social categories such as upper caste and middle class women, separate organizations for lower caste men and women, and tribal people. Its subsidiaries have diversified into other areas of activity: carrying the RSS ideology through educational institutions, large scale symbolically charged pre-political spectacles, and electoral politics (Hansen 1999).

The RSS pattern of funding has remained undisclosed, though it has always had a sizeable base among (Hindu) traders (Hansen 1999: 117 notes Marwari support for RSS in Pune). Funds have been garnered partly through the annual *guru dakshina*: a traditional term for an offering from disciple to *guru* in gratitude, which casts the RSS in the role of *guru* to the member. This collection has been a resource base for wholetimers or pracharaks. A pracharak's brief, as Kanungo shows in this volume, includes spotting and grooming potential wholetimers among volunteers in *shakhas* under his charge, and organizing new *shakhas* elsewhere, in a snowballing process. Some pracharaks are delegated to oversee one of the many RSS subsidiaries. In recent times, a subsidiary, the VHP, has built up networks among sections of Indians living in Europe and north America, raising large funding there (Hansen 1999: 116-26, 156).

Alarmed at the threat of *shuddhi*, the Tablighi Jamaat (TJ) was founded at about the same time as the RSS. Drawing ideological inspiration from Deoband, it has sought to accelerate the process of Islamization. To this end it devised an extraordinary format, explored by Zainuddin and Anindita Chakrabarti in this volume: (1) to make ordinary Muslims responsible for persuading others to abide by Islamic religious routines more thoroughly, (2) to enjoin them to travel in small bands frequently, from one locality to another, one home to another, propagating a minimalist Islamic doctrine, alongside distinctive Islamic dress, appearance, and everyday routines, and (3) to persuade others to form similar bands of Islamic religious travellers. It must be remembered that TJ originated in acute anxieties over the prospect of large numbers of Muslims apostatizing to Hinduism. Hence its one point agenda, to reinforce Islamic identities.

The TJ's agenda has avowedly been 'religious', non-political; yet it has been potent in intensifying consciousness of a distinctive religious identity. This has separative implications, spreading a predisposition towards availability for communal mobilization in political and other domains (see Mayaram in this volume). From its initial campaigns in late1920s among the Meo, in districts south-west of Delhi, directed from its headquarters in Nizamuddin in New Delhi, the TJ has spread globally, to wherever Muslims live. It is said to have become the most influential Islamic movement in recent centuries. A travelling band's core activity, as we noted, has included that of getting men in its host locality to organize their own travelling group, which would then go on to spread its simple meassage and to raise Islamic consciousness elsewhere. The founder had a vision of Tabligh: 'It was self-propelling, with an inbuilt mechanism for expansion at little cost. All Sunni Muslims could participate in tabligh tours, and there was no formal membership' (Sikand 2002: 79; Mayaram 1997: 154-6; Ch. 7).

The list of agencies in this section could be expanded. One thinks, for instance, of the Shiv Sena in Maharashtra and elsewhere, and sundry Muslim militant groups. Overall, the Muslim-Hindu interface has borne the brunt of multiple agencies, on both sides, whose agents have worked vigorously since the mid-nineteenth century in ways that go to harden the separation between the two categories. One cannot say which side has contributed more to this hardening: the culpability has shifted over time and region. Reciprocal aggravation has been a major tendency. Both sides have mustered innovative strategies, pursued with recklessness, expressed in various forms: one need only counterpose the vast scale, often of aggressive activities of RSS and its affiliates, against the international operations of Islamic militants centred in Pakistan.

CONSEQUENCES

Seen another way, these institutions and movements have generated widespread networks which have served to promote contrastive modes of living. The contrasts prescribed differ but are wide-ranging; they can include lifecycle rituals (in some cases from birth through marriage to death), a particular 'community' to identify with, how to live this life to secure one's hereafter—coming down to particulars of one's bearing, one's clothing, the pots used in cooking, and so forth.[7]

The ideologies and agendas carried by their activists have exercised widespread, growing, and cumulative pressure, re-shaping grassroots attitudes at considerable social depth. The early shared spaces had difficulty in resisting pressures for beliefs, practices, and lifestyles for which support was claimed from scriptures or other authorities. It helped contrastive identities to take firmer hold, making these available for other uses, especially political ones.

The mobilizational potential demonstrated around the issue of cow protection in north India, and around Ganapati and Shivaji in Maharashtra in the nineteenth century, and later around the idea of Pakistan, have in recent decades been pressed around the mosque-and-temple at Ayodhya and a host of other symbols. Seen thus, in the fostering of separativeness, the role of these institutions has been primary, that of political actors secondary. Insofar as political, and especially electoral, mobilization turns around the distinctive identities and associated symbols, however, the emotions aroused in these contests have also aided in the cleaving of shared spaces. One climax to this process came in the violence at Partition; another, in 2002, in Gujarat, with lesser ones at other times.

* * *

I have argued that, over the past century and a half, South Asia saw the spread of what might be called the 'hard' versions of several religious identities. Numerous agencies have spurred a great deal of labour to achieve their objectives. It has all been seen as the work of God, or on behalf of something held to be equally transcendental, like the 'nation' or 'Bharat mata'—and who can find fault with that? Attending these campaigns, however, has been a certain recklessness, and an inability (perhaps a reluctance) to anticipate and consider the likely long-term consequences. Implicit in these campaigns has been the premise that if you do God's work, however mindlessly, the results can only be beneficial.

Large and complex societies like India's store up serious trouble for the future if they do not develop the skills for appraising where such wideranging processes are likely to lead over the long run. We need to develop a sense of historical judgement, and that can arise only from learning to review, continually and habitually, a wide range of historical experiences, past and current, our own and the experiences of other civilizational settings. It is our hope and prayer that this volume will provoke ideas, and stimulate initiatives that would help prepare us for making responsible choices for the future.

NOTES

1. Romila Thapar has pointed out to me that our universities take it for granted that students in social sciences are fluent in the modern vernaculars. This is not always the case; and the deficiency has been especially serious for Urdu.
2. I omit from this series the case of the Sufi warriors. Eaton (1978: Ch. 2) sees them as accompanying, and splintering off, the Sultanat expeditions to the south, in the late thirteenth and early fourteenth centuries, prior to the founding of Bahmani kingdom, 1347-1498. There was little of religious 'crossing' at that time though their successors in later centuries engaged closely with indigenous languages and traditions.

3. The processes have been worked out for present-day Uttar Pradesh at some length by C.A. Bayly 1983 and Freitag 1989.
4. This would have implications ultimately for reconfiguring political geography too.
5. In Punjab, Arya Samaj built an extensive range of institutions in the late nineteenth and early twentieth centuries. Managing these institutions tended to absorb the bulk of its energies (Jones 1976).
6. Nonica Datta (1999) has examined how and why the Jats in latter day Haryana took to the Arya Samaj, and the subsequent rise of antagonisms with their Jat neighbours seen to be Muslim.
7. Kalberg (1994: 58) has pointed to Max Weber's use of the concept of 'social carriers', 'cohesive bearers of action'. Their example, teaching, and activities, and certain repetitive ways of behaving, give weight to a body of ideas—making these ideas 'sociologically significant'.

REFERENCES

Ahmed, Rafiuddin, 1981, *The Bengal Muslims 1871-1906: A Quest for Identity*, New Delhi: Oxford University Press.

Alam, Muzaffar, 1996, 'Assimilation from a distance: confrontation and Sufi accommodation in Awadh society', in R. Champakalakshmi and S. Gopal, eds., *Tradition, Dissent, and Ideology*, New Delhi: Oxford University Press, pp. 164-91.

Andersen, Walter K. and Shridhar D. Damle, 1987, *The Brotherhood in Saffron: The Rashtriya Swayamsevak Sangh and Hindu Revivalism*, New Delhi: Vistaar/ Sage.

Basu, Tapan, et al., 1993, *Khaki Shorts and Saffron Flags: A Critique of the Hindu Right*, New Delhi: Orient Longman.

Bayly, C.A., 1983, *Rulers, Townsmen and Bazaars: North Indian Society in the Age of British Expansion, 1770-1870*, Cambridge: Cambridge University Press.

Bayly, Susan, 1989, *Saints, Goddesses and Kings: Muslims and Christians in South Indian Society 1700-1900*, Cambridge: Cambridge University Press.

Chandra, Sudhir, 1992, *The Oppressive Present: Literature and Social Consciousness in Colonial India*, New Delhi: Oxford University Press.

Damrel, David W., 2002, 'The "Naqshbandi reaction" reconsidered', in David Gilmartin and Bruce B. Lawrence, eds., *Beyond Turk and Hindu: Rethinking Religious Identities in Islamicate South Asia*, New Delhi: India Research Press, pp. 176-98.

Datta, Nonica, 1999, *Forming an Identity: A Social History of the Jats*, New Delhi: Oxford University Press.

Datta, Pradip K., 1999, *Carving Blocs: Communal Ideology in Early Twentieth-Century Bengal*, New Delhi: Oxford University Press.

De, Amalendu, 1974, *Roots of Separatism in Nineteenth Century Bengal*, Calcutta: Ratna Prakashan.

Depres, Leo A., 1968, 'Protest and Change in Plural Societies', Presented at 1968 Annual Meetings of American Anthropologial Association.

Eaton, Richard M., 1978, *Sufis of Bijapur 1300-1700: Social Roles of Sufis in Medieval India*, Princeton: Princeton University Press.

———, 1994, *The Rise of Islam and the Bengal Frontier, 1204-1760*, New Delhi: Oxford University Press.

———, 2000, 'Court of Man, Court of God: Local Perceptions of the Shrine of Baba Farid, Pakpattan, Punjab', in his *Essays on Islam and Indian History*, New Delhi: Oxford University Press, pp. 225-46. Reprinted from Richard C. Martin, ed., *Islam in Local Contexts*, Leiden: Brill, 1982, pp. 44-61.

Fisher, Michael H., 1987, *A Clash of Cultures: Awadh, the British, and the Mughals*, New Delhi: Manohar.

Freitag, Sandria B., 1989, *Collective Action and Community: Public Arenas and the Emergence of Communalism in North India*, Berkeley: University of California Press.

Gilmartin, David, 1988, *Empire and Islam: Punjab and the Making of Pakistan*, Berkeley: University of California Press.

Hansen, Thomas Blom, 1999, *The Saffron Wave: Democracy and Hindu Nationalism in Modern India*, New Delhi: Oxford University Press.

Hardy, Peter, 1971, *Partners in Freedom - and True Muslims: The Political Thought of Some Muslim Scholars in British India, 1912-1947*, Lund: Scandinavian Institute of Asian Studies.

Haridatt, Vedalankar, 1984, '*Dakshinbharat men Arya Samaj ka prachar*' [Propagation of Arya Samaj in South India] (1894-1947), Ch. 17; and '*Hyderabad ka dharmayuddha*' [Crusade in Hyderabad], Ch. 22, in Satyaketu Vidyalankar, ed., *Arya Samaj ka Itihas* [History of Arya Samaj], vol. 2: *Arya Samaj ka Prachar-Prasar* [Expansion of Arya Samaj] *1993-1947*, New Delhi: Arya Swadhyaya Kendra [In Hindi].

Hasan, Mushirul, 1979, *Nationalism and Communal Politics in India*, New Delhi: Manohar.

Jones, Kenneth W., 1976, *Arya Dharm*, New Delhi: Manohar.

Kalberg, Stephen, 1994, *Max Weber's Comparative-Historical Sociology*, Cambridge: Polity.

Kaviraj, Sudipta, 1995, *The Unhappy Consciousness: Bankimchandra Chattopadhyay and the Formation of Nationalist Discourse in India*, New Delhi: Oxford University Press.

Lath, Mukund, ed. (tr., intro. & annotation), 1981, *Ardhakathanaka: Half a Tale. A Study in the Interrelationship between Autobiography and History*, Jaipur: Rajasthan Prakrit Bharati Sansthan.

Mayaram, Shail, 1997, *Resisting Regimes: Myth, Memory and the Shaping of a Muslim Identity*, New Delhi: Oxford University Press.

Metcalf, Barbara Daly, 1982, *Islamic Revival in British India: Deoband, 1860-1900*, Princeton: Princeton University Press.

Narayanan, Vasudha, 2002, 'Religious Vocabulary and Religious Identity: A Study of the Tamil Cirappuranam', in David Gilmartin and Bruce B. Lawrence, eds., *Beyond Turk and Hindu: Rethinking Religious Identities in Islamicate South Asia*, New Delhi: India Research Press, pp. 74-97.

Rao, Vasudeva, 2002, *Living Traditions in Contemporary Contexts: The Madhva Matha of Udupi*, New Delhi: Orient Longman.

Robinson, Francis, 1975, *Separatism among Indian Muslims: The Politics of the United Provinces' Muslims, 1860-1923*, New Delhi: Vikas.

———, 2001, *The 'Ulama of Farangi Mahall and Islamic Culture in South Asia*, New Delhi: Permanent Black.

Roy, Asim, 1983, *The Islamic Syncretistic Tradition in Bengal*, Princeton: Princeton University Press.

Sanyal, Usha, 1996, *Devotional Islam and Politics in British India: Ahmad Riza Khan Barelwi and His Movement, 1870-1920*, New Delhi: Oxford University Press.

Shah, A.M., 2002, *Exploring India's Rural Past: A Gujarat village in the Early Nineteenth Century*, New Delhi: Oxford University Press.

Sikand, Yoginder, 2002, *The Origins and Development of the Tablighi Jamaat (1920-2000)*, New Delhi: Orient Longman.

Stewart, Tony K., 2002, 'Alternate Structures of Authority: Satya Pir on the Frontiers of Bengal', in David Gilmartin and Bruce B. Lawrence, eds., *Beyond Turk and Hindu: Rethinking Religious Identities in Islamicate South Asia*, New Delhi: India Research Press, pp. 21-54.

Taft, Frances H., 1994, 'Honor and Alliance: Reconsidering Mughal-Rajput Marriages', in K. Schomer et al., eds., *The Idea of Rajasthan: Explorations in Regional Identity*, Vol. II: *Institutions*, New Delhi: Manohar, pp. 217-41.

Thapan, Anita Raina, 2005, 'Sufism and Sikhism: Understanding the Dynamics of Tradition and Change in the Religious Beliefs and Practices of Sindhi Hindus', in Satish Saberwal and Supriya Varma eds., *Traditions in Motion: Religion and Society in History*, New Delhi: Oxford University Press, pp. 205-29.

van der Veer, Peter, 1996, *Religious Nationalism: Hindus and Muslims in India*, New Delhi: Oxford University Press.

THE PRE-MODERN WORLD

The rich papers in this section open with G. Arunima writing of pre-colonial Kerala, host to bearers of diverse traditions. She explores the 'origin myths' of Christians, Jews, and Muslims who moved along ancient, oceanic trade routes around the Arabian Sea and South-East Asia, and found comfortable niches in Kerala. Significant in each myth is the moment of the group's arrival in Kerala, when it found welcome and acceptance, and access to crucial resources—symbolic and material—even as it retained a distinctive, at times contentious, religious identity. The Brahmins' origin myth, incidentally, is more aggressive than that of any of the other immigrant groups. Alongside the contention between groups, in course of participating in diverse economic and political activities, there have emerged the shared language, Malayalam, and a shared regional affinity, together constituting a Malayali identity. This parallel evolution of religious and ethnic identities has configured the various groups' assertiveness, mutual tolerance, and shared practices.

The rhythm of Islam in northern India has been rather different and Raziuddin Aquil addresses the issues through the largely neglected Sufi sources from the Sultanate period. Their world was unstable: the kingship was unsteady; Mongol advance sent refugees from the north, and threatened northern India directly; and non-Muslim chiefs bided their time—their victory could be bad news for Muslim lives and religious places. In this milieu though the rulers were wary of the ulama's stern Islam, in a country overwhelmingly un-Islamic, the bonds of Islam did hold the ruling class together. The rulers needed the Sufi masters' support, but the latter's response was variable, ranging from zealously maintaining a distance, to providing active support in military campaigns. Sufi otherworldliness notwithstanding, our sources are full of their worldly difficulties with various others: Sultans, ulama, rival Sufi masters, Hindu kings, and the masses of unbelievers. Received memory credited them with 'paranormal powers'—an ability to hold them all at bay.

The Sufis responded to their predominantly Hindu milieu equally variably. In spite of the difficulties, the masters received widespread homage, stretching across social status and religious affiliation. Their popularity rested on their easy accessibility and use of vernacular languages. For drawing converts to Islam, their charisma received much credit in oft-repeated hagiographies. Even a master who might employ yogic practices in his own religious experience, however, could advise lesser men to stay clear of Hindu mystics: the latter's conception of God might be acceptable, but they were not Muslim. And given the uncertain political scene, some were clearly hostile to Hindus.

In a comparative vein, Michael Brenner gives us a broad brush review of the long histories of Jewish experience, principally in Christian Europe and in Islamic societies. All through the middle ages, the wheel kept turning between being at the margin, being expelled from one country, and being welcomed in another; early modern western Europe saw struggles with ideas of assimilation and citizenship; but also frustrations, leading to Zionism and the Holocaust, the making of Israel, and the persisting conflict over Palestine.

Certain themes stand out: the great diversity in experiences within such a category, responding to an area's economic needs (as for extensive credit), or a dominant group's ideology, welcoming or expelling diversity, or enforcing a uniform citizenship, and seeking to restrict differences to things like places of worship. There is also the long duration of images that come to adhere to particular groups, like that of the 'outsider' to Jews. The status of the Jews as autsiders used to follow from their not being Christian, a matter of religion. By the nineteenth century, the religious difference was losing importance; but the Jews continued to be seen as outsiders, now on grounds of race.

1

Who is a Malayali Anyway? Language, Community and Identity in Precolonial Kerala

G. ARUNIMA

INTRODUCTION

This preliminary statement is part of a larger study of the history of Kerala from the perspective of its four different religious groups.[1] For more than a thousand years Jews, Christians, Muslims and Hindus have lived together in Kerala. By the twentieth century, the term Malayali was used to designate all these people across community and caste difference. Today, the Christians and Muslims constitute more than 20 per cent each of the Malayali population. No history of Kerala addresses the fact of its rich religious diversity, or indeed the fact that this has not led to the kinds of communal conflict that have been the staple of north Indian history. By locating Kerala within a wider social geography of the Indian Ocean, and problematising the idea of the 'region', I raise questions about insider and outsider, about belonging and identity.

If we examine Kerala's history as the history of groups that are an integral part of its social fabric, what is immediately evident is that such a cultural mix was possible only because Kerala was connected to a much larger world. This extended from the Arab world on the west towards China on the east, with large parts of present South-East Asia linked to it through established networks of trade. This connection did not simply mean that Kerala had a vibrant commercial culture: that was certainly the case, but it also meant that it became home to people from various parts of this world, with their different cultural practices and belief systems. From religion and ritual, dietary and culinary practices, and new technological inputs, to a rich history of loan words that are an integral part of present-day Malayalam language, today's Kerala is shaped by the history of its geographical positioning. In brief, my argument is that many of the categories that we consider stable by the twentieth century (community, language, region, ethnicity) may not be adequate for understanding the past of a group or an area. This is particularly true in the context of communal conflict, where the frightening conditions of the present may become the filter to study the past. Such presentism, I would suggest, can neither address the complexity of the past, nor intervene in any meaningful way in the current contest over history.

People's histories of their own past become important in understanding the creation of ideas like 'community' or 'identity'. In this paper I explore a few representative narratives or 'origin myths' (I use this as a generic term for narratives of the arrival of the groups—the Jews, Syrian Christians, Mappilla Muslims and Nambudiri Brahmins—to indicate an 'origin' in a new locale) who came and settled in Kerala somewhere between the fourth and ninth centuries. By juxtaposing conventional histories of Kerala with these stories of arrival and settlement, I attempt to both problematize the understanding of this complex past, as well as hope to isolate moments and contexts that were indicative of 'assertive religious identies'.

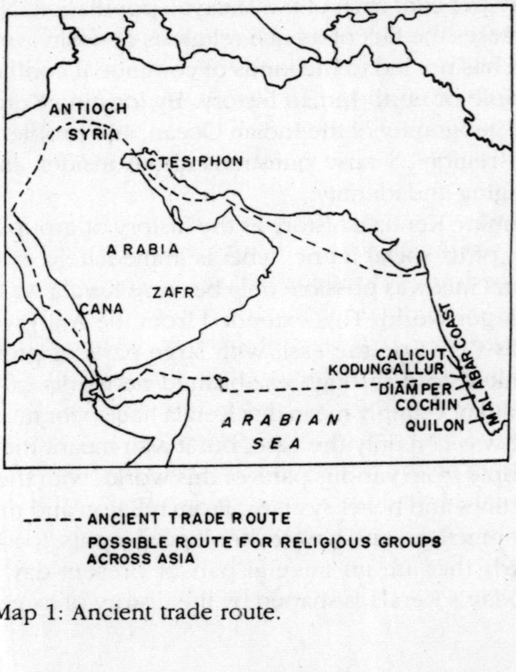

Map 1: Ancient trade route.

HISTORY

Kerala's history has been shaped by the presence of at least five of the world's major religions. From conventional histories we know that, from the early decades of the first millennium perhaps the ninth century, Buddhists and Jains, Jews, Christians, Muslims and Brahmins migrated into the territory of Kerala. By the twelfth century virtually no trace of the earlier Buddhist or Jain religious practice seems to have survived; either it was effaced, or incorporated into a broader 'Hindu' pantheon, by the inroads of Brahmanical Hinduism in Kerala. Hinduism, henceforth, as with other parts of the subcontinent, had both a popular and a Brahmanical aspect. Though there are pockets of Nambudiri Brahmins all over Kerala, they are predominantly found in central Kerala (around Kochi) and south Malabar.

Within the Jewish and other historiography there is an internal difference amongst the 'white' and 'black' Jews of Kerala. This is often confused as an issue of colour (or race), but has more to do with internal dissensions amongst them about points of origin and the time of immigration than with possible racial differences.[2]

Christianity too has had a rich and complex history within Kerala. By 1900, almost all the major Christian schisms and sects had found a presence there. Here I shall focus only on the Syrians, whose traditions claim two broad divisions, Western (who claim Apostolic descent from St. Thomas) and Eastern (Christians who trace their origins from Thomas of Cana). Unlike the Portuguese Jesuits who arrived on the west coast in the sixteenth century, the Syrian Christians were not 'missionary' and do not appear to have been proselytisers. In fact, they see themselves as the descendants of the first settlers. It is of course perfectly possible, especially when examining the degree of shared life-cycle rituals, that many original residents in the region would have become followers of this new religion.[3] In fact, one of the earliest periods of 'religious crisis' that we find on the Kerala coast was provoked by the Portuguese who targeted all three groups—Jews, Christians and Muslims—but the Syrian Christians most of all. However, in the history of religions in Kerala, with the arrival of the Portuguese one finds the establishment of the Latin church too, and until the mid-nineteenth-century arrival of the Protestant missions from England and Germany, Christianity in Kerala was primarily 'Nestorian' or Roman Catholic.

The history of Islam in Kerala is somewhat better known owing to the interest in the nineteenth- and twentieth-century rebellions in Malabar (north Kerala) known as the 'Mappilla *lehela*'. Here I shall not focus on the *lehela* (even though it displays the character of an assertive religious identity in which a small section of the Muslim peasantry attacked the Hindu landlords of the region, invoking the language of *jihad*)[4] but will examine instead the history of Islam within Mappilla historiography, looking specifically at the narratives about arrival and settlement of the early Muslims. Contact with the Arab world probably predates Islam, which would mean that Islam must have come to Kerala by the eighth century. Mosques (or the history of mosques) in Kerala date back to the early decades of Islam and are meant to have been located in seven key spots that map the coast from north to south (Gokarnam to Kanyakumari). Islamic groups in Kerala therefore were Arabic and came on the well-established trade routes. The Mappilla are ethnically the descendants of Arabs who settled on the coast and married local women, though by the sixteenth century we do know of the Zamorin (or Samuthiri) at Kozhikode encouraging fisherfolk to convert to Islam. The Samuthiri's closeness to the Muslims in this period was legion, so much so that he was 'known to the West as a Moorish prince'.[5] Predominantly Sunni Muslims, following Sha'afi law, the Mappilla have always been devout Muslims.

Like the Jews and the Christians, the Mappillas too share many social customs and practices with the various 'Hindu' groups, and sometimes with Cananite Christians, Jews, and other groups,[6] depending upon the geographical area that they inhabited or the point of origin in West Asia from where they traced their origin.[7] Of these, the one issue that concerns us here is the emergence of a shared (yet separate) linguistic domain—or how and when Malayalam becomes the language of the people of Kerala and whether this, along with a regional affinity, can be seen as constituting a Malayali identity.

I shall re-examine the conventional history in the light of the different communities' own perceptions of their past. The history of religion and religious communities is intrinsically tied up with the history of remembering. As Daniele Hervieu-Leger argues in the case of religious memory, 'the normativity of collective memory is reinforced by the fact of the group's defining itself, objectively and subjectively, as a *lineage* of belief'.[8] This 'lineage' is constituted by the religious act of recalling a past that both defines the present and heralds the future.[9] This is particularly true in the case of Semitic religions, all of which have particular foundational events that constitute the moment from which their genealogy can be traced. Additionally, all of these also have a variety of events, places and people that can be incorporated as mnemonics within this genealogy of belief that help believers to remember the story of arrival. Needless to say, there are inconsistencies and elisions within these narratives,[10] which, over generations, give religion as a 'chain of memory' its depth and texture. Moreover, it is this collective memory that constantly qualifies and renders conventional historical narratives more complex.

One of the significant foundational moments for each of the three Semitic religions in Kerala seems to have been the moment of arrival. For the Jews, Christians and Muslims, their arrival in Kerala is remembered as part of a momentous welcome. Therefore, unlike the mnemonics of trauma and repression (especially within the Judaic tradition, and persecution in their homeland in the case of the Cananite Christians) that might be part of their historical memory in their lands of origin, what we witness in Kerala is a reversal of this 'historical consciousness'. The Jewish example is particularly illustrative. One of the 'origin myths' of the Jewish community in Kerala dates its arrival to the year 70 CE, following the destruction of the second Temple in Jerusalem and the dispersal of the Jews living in Judea and Galilee.[11] As we will see below, their arrival in Kodungallur in central Kerala converts the historic memory of the Diaspora into a narrative of acceptance, almost akin to a homecoming.

In marked contrast to the 'origin myths' of the Jews, Syrian Christians or Muslims in Kerala is the Parasu Rama myth, the story of the arrival and settlement of the Brahmins. Here the story is structured more in terms of a claim, rather than a welcome or an invitation as in the other narratives. Moreover, in the particular version of the Parasu Rama myth discussed here (each legend, irrespective of community, can have several versions) it is significant that they are defining themselves as the creators of government and as law makers.

For the moment, in my attempt to understand religion through these origin myths, I wish to point to one or two issues. One, each of these myths encapsulates within it an apparently cohesive notion of group identity. Therefore, within these narratives, the 'religious' or 'caste' identity of the group—as Jews, Syrian Christians, Muslims or

Brahmins—exists prior to the foundational moment of arrival. Even though not explicitly stated as such, it is this prior identity that allows for the continuation of two complex processes, the incorporation of Kerala into the wider social imaginary of the Indian Ocean, and the subtle transformation of these older religious identities, forged in an earlier time and a different place, in the new milieu. Therefore there are two slightly different processes in the history of identity formation in medieval Kerala. One, as stated earlier, is the reconfiguration of older religious identities in new ways. The second is the evolution of an identity—Malayali—with linguistic and regional dimensions, and would have derived from participation in other areas of social experience, like the economy (namely the agrarian or trading systems) and the political milieu (the sphere of interaction of courts or the military).

It is significant that these are not mutually exclusive processes. I would suggest (though at this stage of my research it would not be possible to flesh out the details of the argument) that the refiguring of religious identities of all the groups is not inimical to the creation of an ethnic identity that will eventually incorporate these groups within a broader framework of being 'Malayali'. The histories of 'assertiveness', 'co-existence' 'mutual tolerance' and indeed, shared practices—all of which are manifest in the history of Kerala—must be studied against the backdrop of the simultaneous evolution of religious and ethnic identities.

When we examine the 'origin myths' we witness certain repetitive themes and motives: the place of origin, reasons for travel, arrival, and initial settlement. Here my aim is not to determine the veracity of the dates and places given but to explore how these were knitted together to create a 'community' identity for each of these groups in Kerala.

In the Jewish narrative(s), a king of Kerala gave a copper-plate grant to Joseph Rabban, the leader of the Jews, in 379 CE. This grant gave him privileges that placed him on a par with the indigenous elite: the use of a parasol and elephant; sounding of a trumpet salute; and the commercial prerogative to levy duties and tolls. One of the translations of the Jewish grant by the Tamil scholar, Kanaka Sabhai, says

> [the king] Bhaskara Iravi Varmar gives the principality of Anjuvannam to Joseph Rabban . . . the right to levy tribute in money and in kind, the

revenue of Anjuvannam, the light by day, the spreading cloth, the palanquin, the umbrella, the *vaduca* drum, the trumpet, the sandals for the feet, ornamental arches, awnings and presents carried on poles, balanced on the shoulders, along with the seventy two privileges of a noble man. We have exempted him from paying the land tax and water rate [and] we have enacted with this copper deed that when the other inhabitants pay taxes to the palace, he shall not have to pay, when they receive [presents], he shall also receive.[12]

The dates and meanings of certain terms used in this grant have been analysed several times in the last two centuries. Scholars more recently have argued that Anjuvannam, for instance, was not a principality but denoted instead the guild-like status of the Jews, who were an artisanal group.[13] Using Nicholas Dirks' model of a 'little kingship', Katz and Goldberg argue that what appears to be of interest in the grant is that it established the overlord/little king relationship between the maharaja and the leader of the Jews.[14] What is interesting is the symbolic meaning of the copper plates for the Jewish community rather than a mere detailing of the information in it. What is striking is that this is the 'origin story' of the Cochin, the 'white' (*paradesi*) Jews who may have come to Kerala later than the 'black' (*Malabar*) Jews, in which they claim that it was their leader Joseph Rabban who was given the copper plate by the king of Kodungallur. Elamkulam Kunjan Pillai's important insight, that there may have been a number of rulers in the second Chera empire who could have borne the title 'Cheraman Perumal', becomes relevant here as all the Cochin Jewish narratives retell the story of Joseph Rabban receiving the copper plate grants from Cheraman Perumal.[15]

References to the copper plates come up not only in the 'origin myths' and histories of the Cochin Jews, they also do in Malayalam Jewish folk songs.[16] What do the copper plates then symbolize within the Jewish collective memory? For the Cochin Jews these connote both a genealogy of their cultural presence within Kerala, as well as a special relationship with the rulers of Kerala. The symbolic significance of this 'first' encounter, which is akin to a royal welcome, means that within the Cochin Jewish tradition every Jew becomes Joseph Rabban, and every ruler, Cheraman Perumal.[17]

Alternatively, P.M. Jussay's reading of Malayalam Jewish folk songs suggests that the Cochin (or *Paradesi*) tradition might be different from the Malabari one. In the *Song of Evarayi*, a young man called Evarayi (Ephraim) begs his father for permission to visit

'Malanad' (Malabar). On route to Malabar, Evarai stops in Egypt and then in Yemen. Here he hires the 'best carpenter' to build his ship; as a reward the carpenter is given a silk shawl and a gold bracelet (the signs of royal appreciation in Kerala). Whilst in Yemen the learned Rabbi Avaroh (Abraham) joins him and they continue the journey. Nearing Persia they are frightened and they move out to Paloor bay in north Kerala. Here they are frightened once again and flee to 'Shibushu', where the locals flock around the 'learned visitor'. Once again the best available carpenter is summoned—this time to build their synagogue. Avaroh blesses it and Evarai studies the *midrashim* and becomes a Rabbi.[18]

Jussay's analysis examines four important issues: (1) The route—from Israel to Egypt to Yemen and then on to Kerala via Persia, which was perfectly viable as a sea route. (2) Paloor as a kind of temporary stop before moving down the coast to settle within the dominion of the Cochin kings. This too, as he suggests, could have been plausible as the Jewish tradition claims that there were temporary settlements to the north of Kodungallur. (3) The movement from there (because of fear)—this he attributes to the growth of the power of the Samuthiri by the fifteenth century—who patronized the local Mappilla Muslims. The move away from Paloor could have been motivated by this reason (we shall explore the tensions between the Samuthiri and the Cochin state, and its implications for inter-community relations a little later). (4) He identifies *Shibushu* of the song with the present-day Chennamangalam, which is east of Kodungallur. Historically, the hill in Chennamangalam had a synagogue, mosque, church and temple located not far from one another. Moreover, his analyses suggest another significant difference with the Cochin Jewish tradition. While the latter emphasizes the Joseph Rabban-Cheraman Perumal dyad, for the Malabari (or black) Jews it was the relationship between Evarai Moliaru (or Mudaliar) and Paliath Achan, the Nayar chieftain of Chennamangalam that was important.[19]

What is significant is that while the two traditions differ from each other, and thereby testify to internal differences amongst the Kerala Jewish community in terms of points of origin and racial genealogy, collectively they locate themselves as an honoured (or high status) group within the locality, akin to a Hindu upper caste group, possibly the higher sub-castes of the Nayars.

In the *Syrian Christian* narratives of origin the most important is the Apostolic genealogy. Referred to originally as the St. Thomas Christians (as a result of the tradition that the church was set up by the Apostle, St. Thomas), these followers of the Eastern Church claim to be the descendants of upper castes (principally Brahmin) converted to Christianity by St. Thomas himself. The point of entry of the Apostle in India is also debated within ecclesiastical histories; some claim that the Kerala coast was the original point of entry whereas others say that he lived and died on the Coromandel coast, and that the people were the descendants of those Christians who migrated westwards from there.[20] However, the more important issue here is that as the original Christians, these people claimed a presence in India from a period almost contemporaneous with that of Christ. The next critical event in this tradition is contact with the Eastern Syrian church with the arrival of Thomas of Cana, known as Cnai Thoma or Thomman in the Christian narrative. He appears variously as a merchant, a traveller, and a pilgrim, and is meant to have brought a group of Christians with him at a time when clearly there were waves of anti-Christian persecution in the homeland. According to the Cnanite legend, Thomas set about transforming Kodungallur, organizing it as a Christian community around a church. These two divergent points of origin within the collective memory of the St. Thomas Christians are probably responsible for their endogamous divisions: *vadakambhagakkar* [Northerners] and *tekkumbhagakkar* [Southerners].

An early eighteenth-century tradition is recorded by a Jacobite priest named Mathew. It states that after 93 years of being without a priest (after the death of St. Thomas) a non-Christian magician called 'Manikkabashar' attempted to wean Christians in Mylapore away from the faith. Those who were faithful fled to Malabar and were received by their brethren. But these 160 odd families had no priests or leaders. At this time the Metropolitan of Edessa had a dream about their plight, which he narrated to the catholicos of the East, who then addressed a great multitude of the faithful, of whom many were bishops and merchants. A certain Thomas from Jerusalem said that he had heard of Malabar and was sent by the catholicos to visit the place and report back. Upon hearing his report, the catholicos sent him back with priests and deacons, men, women and children from Jerusalem, Baghdad, and Nineveh. They landed in Maliamkara in 345. The Christians in Kerala welcomed them and all of them proceeded to meet 'Sharkun', the king of all Malabar. The latter gave them royal honours and conceded all their wishes; these grants were recorded on copper plates. As a part of the grant, the Christians proceeded to build a church at Kodungallur, and a township emerged there with 472 families.[21]

A late eighteenth-century anonymous account has a slightly different version of this story: St. Thomas had ordained priests from four principal families of the region—Sankuri, Palamittam, Kali, and Kaliave—whom he had baptized. This was in 52 CE. However the community began to decline as it lacked successors to the bishop. This was remedied by the 'rich and zealous' merchant Cnai Thoma [Thomas of Cana] who returned to his homeland in Babylonia and brought with him a bishop and two priests well-versed in the languages (Syriac and Chaldaic) of the Rite.[22]

This version deals more with how the St. Thomas Christians came to be within the dominion of the Eastern Syrian church. While it is not clear when East Syrian prelates began to come to India, certain reconstructions of Church history in Kerala date it back to the third century CE. From then, until about the ninth century, it is possible that there was a steady flow of prelates from Eastern Syria to India, even as the rest of the Church hierarchy would clearly have been Indian, as attested by the Portuguese.[23] The complex history of the development of the ancient Syrian Christian church, described pithily by Podipara as 'Hindu in culture, Christian in religion, and Syro-Oriental in worship',[24] cannot be discussed in the space of this paper.

In a third account documented in the early nineteenth century by Ward, an officer of the survey department in Travancore, the story is almost completely transformed. This narrative is said to have been in the Lebbi (probably Syriac) language but was explained to Ward in Tamil as follows:

> At a former time seven persons of a strange religious persuasion came to Travancore; among whom the name Mar Thomas occurs. The king of the country had previously received some admonitions respecting them in a dream. They called on the king to embrace their system, and to allow them to build places for their mode of worship. The king demurred to their claims and said these must be proved. He also summoned a council of *Brāhmans*, enquiring if the new system ought to be received: who replied most certainly not. The foreign persons ascribed to themselves the faculty of retaining the soul (when departed from a body) in the air above, and of recalling it, so as to reexamine the body; and, as stated, gave the proof of this power in the case of one among themselves. The

king, however, resisted their claims. Soon after the king's younger brother died; whereupon the recently arrived strangers told the king that if he would build seven churches in different places they would restore their brother to life. The king made the promise, and the body of this brother became re-animated, awaking as if out of a sleep. In consequence both the king, and his brother, adopted the new system, and along with them 64 householders with their families received the initiatory rite of baptism.[25]

After this is a detailing of disputes within the community; and an account of the building of the first seven churches. This account too mentions *Manicavasavar*, referred to as a 'person who chanted panegyrics' who came to 'Malayalam' and 'disseminated the *Saiva* five-lettered system; teaching to swallow the *Saiva* compound of five substances; and to use the *Vibhuthi* or sacred ashes. He drew away several families'.[26] It goes on to say that the head of the Christians received various privileges and immunities from Cheraman Perumal, who always directed the election of the *Metran.*[27]

As with the Jewish narratives, the traditions of the St. Thomas Christians point to a history of unconditional acceptance and the grants of extended privileges that covered religious (church building) and economic (land grants; establishing of a town) interests.[28] The relationship is established between the king and the leader of the community; while in these narratives, the king is not often mentioned (or else has an unidentifiable name), in the third narrative one encounters mention of Cheraman Perumal. Kodungallur once again is [one of] the principal sites of settlement.

The two instances that could suggest sources of threat to the community are both interesting: (1) *Manicavasavar* (or the Shaiva saint Manicavaccacar) attempting to win converts to Christianity back into the Shaivite fold and (2) Brahmins refusing permission to the king to convert (in the third narrative) both point to interesting symbolic and historical issues that shall be discussed later.

The narratives of the origin of the third Semitic religion in Kerala, *Islam*, share many features with those of St. Thomas Christians and the Jewish Diaspora in Kerala. In the most commonly discussed version, from Zain-ud-deen al-Maburee's *Tohfut-ul-Mujahideen,* the last king of Malabar was Cheraman Perumal who ruled at Kodungallur. Cheraman Perumal dreamed one night that the full moon appeared on the night of the new moon at Mecca in Arabia and split into two, with one half remaining up and the other descending to the foot of a hill where the two joined together again. Soon after, a group of Muslim pilgrims arrived, after visiting the footprint shrine at Adam's peak in Sri Lanka, and came to the Perumal. On being asked of news of their country they spoke of the miracle of splitting the moon that the Prophet had performed (of which the Perumal had dreamt) which had converted many to the faith. Hearing this the king set about setting his affairs in order and after eight days, dividing his kingdom into different parts and assigning them to different chiefs, set sail for Arabia to meet the Prophet. They passed Pantalayini Kollam and Dharmatam in north Malabar, and finally landed at Shahr on the Arabian coast. Soon after the king fell sick, and so he asked those accompanying him (Shiuff-ben-Malik, Malik-ben-Deenar and his nephew Malik-ben-Habeeb and others) to go back to Malabar and to spread Islam there. But as they were uncertain of where Malabar was, he wrote, 'in the character and language of the place' [Malayalam], a description of his territories and kindred. Then he asked them to proceed to 'Cranganore (Kodungallur), or to Durmufutun, or to Fundreeah, or Quilon'. Soon after Malik-ben-Deenar and the entire party landed at Cranganore and after the chief there had been informed of the dead king's wishes, proceeded to build a mosque. Before dying, this king had converted to Islam (which according to Zain-ud-Deen, many believe took place in the time of the Prophet but he does not believe that). However, he says that it was well known that in Zafr there is the tomb of this king, called As-Samuri, who came from Malabar, converted to Islam and died there.[29]

Y. Friedman discusses another tradition regarding the introduction of Islam to Malabar, the *Qissat Shakarwati Farmad* [could be an adaptation of Chakravarti Perumal] which, he says is rejected by historians but was popular among the Mappillas themselves.[30] The beginning of this story is set in Mecca before the hijra. The Prophet is commanded by Habib b. Malik, the 'king of the Quraysh', to perform the miracle of the splitting of the moon, which he does, and all gathered convert to Islam. At that time, Allah caused an Indian king to see this miracle. As he was so astonished by it he wrote down the date of the miracle. His astronomers could not explain it, but he dreamt that the Prophet had performed this and henceforth became keen to convert to Islam. In this period, a group of Jews and Christians came with their families in a large ship to his kingdom in Kerala. He asked them where they had come from, and they said from Mecca where a man named Muhammad was trying to convert them by magic. When the king asked what the magic was about, they describe the miracle of the splitting of the moon. The king realises that they are Muhammad's enemies and does not tell them of his secret. A few years later a group of derwishes came to India on their way to visit the footprint of Adam in Ceylon. The king honours them and asks one of them, Shaykh Zahir al-Din, about the splitting of the moon, who explains the whole story to the king. The king then tests the knowledge of the Jews and Christians with the Muslims and concludes that the 'Quran is superior to the Tawrat and the Injil'.[31] Then the King leaves with the derwishes from Kodungallur and arrives at the port of al Shihr. This he does after dividing his kingdom into several parts and handing them over to different people. On reaching Arabia they hear that the Prophet is in Jidda and they go there. There the king prostrates himself in front of the Prophet who embraces him, and then teaches him the *shahada*. This is in the presence of Abu Bakr who asks about the identity of this man, and Muhammad changes his name from Shakarwati Farmad to Taj al-Din al-Hindi al-Mulaybari. The rest of the story is about how Habib b. Malik and others then proceed to Malabar to spread the word, and how it was decided that they would land at Kodungallur. The king died in Arabia (probably Zafar) on the first of Muharram and was buried with great honour. The story ends with the ten mosques that were built by the first proselytisers at Kollam, Kodunkallur, Shaliyat, Fandarina, Darmafatan, Jurfatan, Hayli, Knjrakut, Manjalur, and Fakkanur. (Friedman makes a convincing argument that Zain-al-Deen must have depended on the *Qissa* for his own narrative.)[32]

The third narrative about Islam that I discuss here is from the *Keralolpatti*[33] (Origin of Kerala), an undated manuscript of the seventeenth or eighteenth century. The interesting difference here is that as the *Keralolpatti* was most certainly a Brahmin (or at least an upper caste Hindu) narrative, this version of the origin of Islam in Kerala is from the Brahmanical point of view. In this story the Brahmins bestow the 'Kayrala rajah' with the dignity, or 'avakasa', which confers the following privileges—coining, making of gun powder, catching of elephants, wearing brown and golden chains on the legs—after this they set him up in Aloor palace. At this point the Mappillas came and saw the Perumal and 'made known to him all the precepts of their scriptures'.[34] The Perumal believed them and ordered that all the subjects of Malanadu obey their law. 'Upon which they all lost their senses . . .' Meanwhile, the Brahmans become 'deeply afflicted' because of the arrival of the Mappillas and begin a special prayer to Brahma to 'cease' this affliction. Then they ask the Perumal why he has done this, and he says that this is the Truth. 'Upon which these persons learned in the shastras said if we argue with the Mappoolas and be worsted in the argument, cut out our tongues and banish us from the country; but should they be overcome in the controversy, cut out their tongues and banish them.' 'The Mappoolas argued, their countenances fell, being worsted in the controversy they became ashamed. Their tongues were cut out and they were banished from the country.'[35] Then the Brahmins gave some property to the Perumal who believed in the Mappoola scripture and threw him out from the caste. He put another in his place and went to Mecca. 'The Mappoolas therefore say that Cherooman Payroomal went to Mecca and not to Horaver. The Payroomal who went there was not Chayrooman Payroomal for he was Kayrala Rajah.'[36] After this it goes on to add that as the kings knew that the Mappillas who were coming in large numbers would 'create confusion', to avoid unanimity amongst them, the Kulashekhara Perumal divided the kingdom up; this was so that the 'carmaboomi' (or land of sacred works) must not be destroyed and for that the Brahmins must never abandon the land.[37] This is the only version of the origin myths of any of the three 'outside' religions that has been developed within a hostile framework. We shall examine the features of this version below.

If we examine the principle themes and motifs in these traditions, especially with reference to religious identity, we see that these knit together narratives of unopposed arrival and prosperous settlement, as well as moments of stress and conflict that affect the internal ordering of communities as much as the relations between them. In almost a parallel to the Mosaic tradition in West Asia, of which the three religions were inheritors, in Kerala too, the origin myths of the Jews, Syrian Christians and Mappilla Muslims share repetitive motifs in terms of travel, arrival at the same city (Kodungallur) and a royal welcome granting them economic and religious freedom. The difference with the Mappilla tradition is that it converts the 'little kinghip' logic of the other two by making Cheraman Perumal, 'the king of all Kerala', convert to Islam. If one examines the elements of the *Shakarwati Farmad* tradition, this is not simply a statement about a Malabar king converting (which may well have occurred), or even a story about a very propitious entry into Kerala. It is also a story that attests to the presence of Islam as the third religion of the Book, and one that had a higher status than the other two (in Kerala, the Mappillas refer to the Koran as the *Nalam Vedam* or the fourth Veda, the others being the Jewish and Christian texts).[38] By explicitly situating the origin myth of Islam within the existing tradition of origin of Judaism and Christianity (and a similar arrival in Kerala), and then ousting them from royal favour, we find an assertion of Islam, directed towards the other two Semitic traditions that had already found space within Kerala. If we examine this in the light of the contest for shared space (for instance in Kodungallur), or favours (as part of the royal court or army—both of which mention soldiers and courtiers from all three religious backgrounds), then this element within the *Qissa* can be seen as an attempt to associate the Mappillas with the complex patronage network within which the religions co-existed with each other.

The second moment of 'anxiety' in the Christian tradition concerns the 'magician *manikabhasar*' or 'the *saiva manikavasavar*'. On the face of it, it is clearly the fear that a small community probably had in its early days of being engulfed in a larger, pre-existing cultural matrix. The *saiva* details are of interest as they point not simply to 'Hinduism' but also of a *particular kind* of Hinduism that was prevalent at a *particular historical time.* This period in the history of Kerala predates the more structured Brahmanical Hinduism. It is significant that this version also has the Brahmins advising the king not to allow the Christians to build their churches—but that is miraculously rectified. Both *dreams* and *miracles*, that constitute such an important part of the collective memory and experience of the Semitic traditions, find space within their origin myths in Kerala too. Here however these also provide the space for transcending historical time. Within the space of 'dream-time' the different stages of state formation collapse. Moreover, in reconstructing a narrative of welcome, the Brahmin-opposition-that-is-rebuffed-by-the-kingly-welcome becomes a claim for a collective history of high social status. Therefore, the complexity of these different symbolic systems points to different kinds of histories as well as multiple time frames.

The *Keralolpatti* tradition about Islam in Kerala, on the other hand, represents a more aggressive rendition of the older traditions. What is important here is not simply the response to Islam, which is violent and hostile ('cutting off of tongues' and expulsion), but also what it did to the indigenous social order that Brahmins themselves claimed to have created. Unlike the mutually welcoming, symbiotic relationship between the Perumal and the Arabs, the king's welcome being tantamount to a conversion (we already find a similar representation of that within the Lebbi account of Christianity discussed above), by 'expelling the king from the caste' and throwing him out of his kingdom, the Brahmins were asserting their role as 'kingdom' makers. The Brahmanic 'assertiveness' is directed both horizontally against other religious groups, and vertically against competing 'Hindu' castes. It is tempting to think that this account was possibly written at a time when jati formation was becoming more evident in Kerala.

Here the origin myth of the Brahmins, the *Parasu Rama* legend, and their introduction into Kerala, is also illustrative. While many versions of this myth exist in Kerala (and all along the west coast of the Peninsula), I shall examine only one. This is from one of the many versions of the *Keralolpatti* in the Mackenzie Manuscripts. Briefly, Parasu Rama was required to expiate the sin of having killed Kshatriyas, the enemies of the Brahmins. At the end of a protracted series of twenty-one expeditions, Varuna grants him, after much penance, some land to dwell on. He throws his mace (the *parasu*) to determine its extent: it stretches from Gokarnam to Kanyakumari, creating Kerala Desam. Then Brahmins were brought and located in 64 villages, and they were divided into different classes and had different offices. The Brahmins at first conducted the government on the principles of a republic; but because there were differences amongst themselves, Parasu Rama determined that the place be governed by a king. One was selected born of a Brahmin father and a Kshatriya mother; and he was first settled in Kerala—therefore the name Kerala Desam. Later the whole Malayalam country was divided into four districts—Tuluva, Mushica, Keralam, and Cuva. The story continues, speaking of the coming of the '*baudd'has*', a term used particularly for the Muslims in Malayalam, and how they are initially driven away and later manage to return. In this version in fact it is stated that Cheraman Perumal's son was made to take an oath that he would never allow the Mappillas to enter the land.[39]

Throughout this narrative what is emphasized is the pre-eminent part that Brahmins played in the state formation of Kerala. Here, from almost being designated the original residents of Kerala, they also determine the nature and function of state systems, and the nature of social ordering. This version of the *Keralolpatti* must have been written in the seventeenth or eighteenth century; and it is significant that, apart from the wider landscape of an original Kerala created by Parasu Rama, the specific details concern northern Kerala. As this was the Samuthiri's domain, and these kings had openly patronized the Arab traders and later the Mappilla merchants, it is not surprising that it is only the Mappilla Muslims who find a space within this tradition as disrupters of a divinely ordained social order. This is particularly relevant when several sources attest that, apart from involving the Mappillas in the political, economic, and military functions of their state (the Nediyiruppu Swarupam), the Samuthiri also encouraged conversion of the coastal fisherfolk to Islam.

Other than questions of community and history, there are other issues about collective memory, religious reception, tradition and social interaction. I turn now to matters of community and identity.

INTERACTION

For the most part, the spheres of interaction between the different social groups were structured around commercial, military, political and religious realms. Both the Jewish people and the Mappillas were integrated into Indian Ocean trade routes; both of them, as well as Christians, found places within the courts of the Cochin and Samuthiri rajas. We also have mention of all three groups being recruited as soldiers by these kings; by the time of the Portuguese arrival on the Malabar coast, these groups were well entrenched within the local militia. This dimension makes for yet another important reconsideration. Much of the work on matrilineal kinship in Kerala claims that the Nayar were the militia (hence absent men and women-centred households). The fact that the medieval armies had a significant representation of all the other religions (not all of whom were matrilineal—though by nineteenth century there is evidence that some Christians in Travancore and some Mappillas in north Malabar were matrilineal) would mean that such a functional interpretation for a kinship system holds very little credence.

Other than the ports, markets and courts, a very significant social space for interaction between the different communities were the shrines. Susan Bayly's (historical) and Susan Visvanathan's (anthropological) work on the Yakoba in the twentieth century are the most important in this under-worked area; from both these perspectives we see the symbolic consequences that result from interaction around shrines, especially jati formation amongst the Christians, and other ritual and ceremonial borrowing. Similarly, the fact of matrilineal kinship extending across community boundaries stresses the development of ethnic solidarities (*Malayali?*) alongside religious ones. This is not to suggest that medieval Kerala had no community boundaries or that they were 'fluid' as has sometimes been rather vaguely suggested. On the contrary, the discussion above on the origin myths testifies to quite the opposite. I would prefer to use, for the moment, the distinction made by Katz and Goldberg between assimilation and acculturation, where the former means a loss of identity and the latter an ability to retain it while beginning to adopt certain practices of the new region. Developing on this, I suggest that 'becoming Malayali' (an ethnic identity), would incorporate these different strands of history, memory, social difference and community variation. It would not be a uniform amalgam but a more layered notion of identity, one that could lend itself to a variety of interpretations depending on who invoked it. What, then, was the prehistory of the 'Malayali' in medieval Kerala? Let us turn briefly to one last set of issues—that of understanding language as a source of identity formation.

LANGUAGE

As yet the history of the Malayalam language, its evolution as spoken, and its transformation into a written script, are understudied. Broadly, the consensus has been that Malayalam, a member of the Dravidian family, developed as a distinct dialect of Tamil in the eighth to the tenth centuries. It later diverged by the increased use of Sanskrit derivatives, leading to the evolution of a high literary tradition called *manipravala*. The pan-Brahmi script or *vattezhuthu*, a round writing, is evident by the thirteenth century. In fact, a seventeenth-century Dutch account makes a distinction between Tamil, 'real Mallabar' and 'Samscrudonis', and says that the 'real Mallabar' alphabet has 51 characters, 16 vowels, and 35 consonants. It also says there are two writings: 'Mallabar Samscrudonis and Mallabar Tamul'.[40] Literary Malayalam is an amalgam of at least three distinct traditions: Tamil *pattu* (song); *manipravala*; and folk songs. Spoken Malayalam has significant regional variation across the state and has remarkable external influence on literary forms. For instance, loan words from English, Syriac, Latin and Portuguese abound in the Christian dialects, and those from Arabic and even Urdu in the Muslim ones. The influence of Sanskrit is most prominent in the Brahmin dialects and the least in the Dalit ones.

There are two broad, yet different, kinds of phenomena. The first is the presence of different language speaking groups on the Malabar coast and the formation of linguistic communities. The second is the spoken Malayalam 'tongue' becoming the written language, thereby changing the relationship between language and ethnicity, and community formation. For the moment I shall be able only to indicate certain key issues and the kinds of questions that these suggest.

The notion that a single language marks the linguistic identity of a region often takes away not only from the multiplicity of languages in use, but also the different social uses, or internal hierarchies, that these could have implied. In the case of Kerala, while it seems that there was a 'vulgar' spoken language drawing on Tamil and Malayalam from very early on, the earliest written script would have been a classical Tamil. By the early medieval period (beginning with the coming of the four outside religious groups discussed above), the religious (liturgical) languages included Hebrew, Syriac, Arabic and Sanskrit. Malayalam Jewish folk songs attest to the development of a kind of 'Malayalam Yiddish'[41] with at least Hebrew, Spanish and Dutch words included. The linguistic community of Malayalam speakers in this case managed to accommodate a cultural variation that points to the religious and geographic diversity of the Jewish Diaspora (many of the Cochin Jews came from Spain and Holland in the later medieval period when they were persecuted in Western Europe).

Similarly, the Mappillas evolved a creolized Malayalam with a significant Arabic component. More importantly, they created a new written language, Arabi-Malayalam, where Malayalam was transliterated into Arabic. This process was true of the Syrian Christians too; while the liturgical language was Syriac and the spoken Malayalam, they evolved a transliterative system called *garshuni*. In the period of the Portuguese persecution of the Syrian Christians, especially after the *Udayamperoor Sunahados* (Synod of Diamper), they were known to have kept their records in Malayalam but written in Syriac.[42]

By the nineteenth century this rich diversity of 'Malayalams' was steadily being streamlined across and within communities (I am not suggesting that this was imposed, nor that liturgical and religious languages were shared democratically across priest/commoner divide). By the early twentieth century there seems to be a much sharper distinction between what constituted a religious and a 'modern' spoken language. The Malayalam that emerged thereafter has been shorn of this rich cultural texture and has become standardized across communities. Significantly, it is this standardization that attests to the 'coming of age' of 'Malayali'.

CONFLICT

In the medieval period the most significant period of conflict was with the arrival of the Portuguese on the Malabar coast. This conflict had political and communal dimensions that are not always easy to extricate. The history of the conflict is retold within each community's traditions, with some differences. For the Jews, it marked the flight from Kodungallur to Cochin and elsewhere. For the Muslims, there was a movement away from the central kingdoms under the Cochin raja to supporting the Samuthiri in the north. Both Jews and Muslims were attacked and their properties destroyed. The Portuguese attack weakened the Cochin raja in an unprecedented manner. Yet, the Samuthiri, with the help of the Mappillas managed to repulse them quite effectively. Hence, within the Jewish tradition this period is seen as an attack by the Muslims and the Portuguese on them. Whereas the Portuguese are portrayed as a brutal political force, the Mappilla (though clearly the political allies of the Samuthiri) were seen as a belligerent political religious force. It was the Syrian Christians who were possibly the worst affected in this period. For them this marked a fundamental turning point, their having to accept the suzerainty of the Pope and the Latin Church in place of allegiance to Antioch. In the centuries to come, the St. Thomas Christians had not only to accept the overlordship of Rome but were tyrannized by the Portuguese Jesuits who destroyed their libraries and condemned many of them to the Inquisition. The *auto da fe*, or the Inquisition, that continued in Goa until the early nineteenth century was believed to have claimed many St. Thomas Christians from Kerala as its victims.[43]

I am not in a position to examine the details of how the Portuguese are represented within the medieval texts of this period, or the changes that resulted from their attack on the Malabar coast (especially for the Syrian Christians). What is significant however is that it is this threat from a Western political power, whose aggression combined aspects of religious, political and economic aggrandizement, that had the maximum impact on re-ordering the internal structure of their own co-religionists, the Syrian Christians. The conflict between Western and Eastern Catholicism in Europe was being replicated in Kerala. The Counter-Reformation in Europe finds a resonance in the history of India, and in a discussion on religious conflict in India, it is well worth considering the significance of this for understanding the ideas of 'community' and 'boundary'.

An equally serious issue that deserves much greater attention from historians is the development of a markedly hierarchical caste system in Kerala. My earlier work on the Nayars of Kerala has shown that the category of 'Nayar' was much more inclusive, and vague, in the medieval period than in the nineteenth century. This is probably true of other groups too. However, by the nineteenth century, most accounts (colonial, official, indigenous) portray an immutable system, with the worst practices of pollution (touch and sight) firmly in place. The question then is, how 'cohesive' were the Hindus as a religious community? In the light of the discussion above, I would suggest that possibly the worst kinds of 'assertive' identities that developed in Kerala by then would have been those of caste—especially of the Brahmins and their allied upper castes (*Samanthar* and the richer *Nayar*). If that were indeed the case, and we also know of a history of shared cultural practices centred on shrines (Bayly), then who were the 'Hindus' who participated in these?

POSTSCRIPT

I have attempted to problematize the idea of 'religious community' and inter-religious interaction in the context of the collective memories of the different sections of the Malayali population. The questions that emerge create a frame within which one can address the problem of the history of religion and caste. For instance, whilst looking at the 'origin myths' of Jews, Syrian Christians, Mappilla Muslims, and Brahmins, what is striking is that, for the first three, their identity is inextricably linked to a story of arrival. This arrival is transformed into belonging only through a royal welcome, one that transforms immigrants into highly honoured members of the political community. The Brahmins on the other hand are neither 'accepted' nor do they 'accept' anyone else; on the contrary their myths see themselves as creators—of region, authority and community codes. While there is an awareness of a certain religious identity in the origin myths of the Jews and Christians prior to their arrival in Kerala, they also have a sense of internal difference. This is not true in the case of the Muslim or Brahmin narratives that I have seen. In both these cases there appears to be a sense of cohesiveness about who they were, except that in the case of the Brahmins there is also the display of a power difference between them and the kings. Apart from the kinds of issues regarding 'assertiveness' that I have discussed earlier, the Parasu Rama and other myths from the *Keralolpatti* relating to Brahmins are about their own cohesiveness, not about a larger Hindu identity.

However, when one locates the mnemohistory of these different groups within a wider context it is clear that while religious boundaries were reasonably well defined for the four groups discussed above, they did not foreclose the creation of a wider, more inclusive, *ethnic* identity.[44] This, the identity of a *Malayali* as one who lives in Kerala wherever one's ancestors came from and speaks Malayalam is something, though yet unnamed, that seems to be unconsciously developing, through the medieval period. It seems to develop more in an experiential sense and finds place within the collective memory of different social groups in Kerala by the 1900 or so, when the idea of a Malayali is one that is very clearly tied to language and place, cutting across boundaries of caste and community. What appears to me, at least at the moment, is that these are not structured as oppositional categories (Mappilla or Malayali; Nayar or Malayali) Nor does it appear that any group has a greater claim on this identity even though the idea of a 'settler' population remains strong in some of the early twentieth-century Mappilla writing. In fact, the ability to see 'identity' as something that is layered, and multiple, was what probably at that time allowed for a greater space for inter-religious interactions in Kerala.

Today, as with other parts of the country, we find the presence of both communal clashes, albeit low grade, and the growth of communal propagandist groups like the RSS and the Muslim fundamentalist groups . The electoral weakness of the BJP often masks the steady growth of assertive religious identities in Kerala. Given the history discussed above, it becomes that much more germane that we understand the complex social forces that have made this growth possible.

NOTES

1. I wish to thank Professor Satish Saberwal for the opportunity to present a part of my new work on religion in Kerala, and for his comments and suggestions in the course of revising the paper for publication. An earlier version of this paper received the careful scrutiny of V. Sanil, K. Saradamoni, Udaya Kumar, Vijay Pinch and Javed Majeed, and I thank them all for their detailed comments.
2. Rev. J. Henry Lord, *The Jews in India and the Far East*, Westport, Connecticut: Greenwood Press, 1976, pp. 74-7.
3. For details of life-cycle practices that were shared between the Syrian Christians and Hindu upper castes, like the Nayars, see A. Mathias Mundadan C.M.I., *Indian Christians: Search for Identity and Struggle for Autonomy*, Bangalore: Dharmaram Publications, 2000, p. 18; for a detailed and theoretical understanding see, Susan Visvanathan, *The Christians of Kerala: History, Belief and Ritual among the Yakoba*, Madras: Oxford University Press, 1993.
4. Stephen F. Dale, *Islamic society on the South Asian Frontier: The Mappilas of Malabar, 1498-1922*, Oxford: Clarendon Press, 1980.
5. M.G.S. Narayanan, *Cultural Symbiosis in Kerala*, Calicut: Mathrubhumi Press, 1972, pp. 39-40.
6. Shalva Weil, 'Symmetry between Christians and Jews in India: the Cnanite Christians and the Cochin Jews of Kerala', in Thomas A. Timberg, ed., *Jews in India*, New Delhi: Vikas, 1986, pp. 177-204.
7. Ibid. See also Susan Bayly, *Saints, Goddesses and Kings: Muslims and Christians in South Indian Society, 1700-1900*, Cambridge: Cambridge University Press, 1989, and Susan Visvanathan, *The Christians of Kerala*.
8. Daniele Hervieu-Leger, *Religion as a Chain of Memory*, Cambridge: Polity Press, 2000, p. 125.
9. Ibid.
10. For a complex discussion of the mnemohistorical process, Jan Assman, *Moses the Egyptian: the Memory of Egypt in Western Monotheism*, Cambridge, Mass.: Harvard University Press, 1997.
11. Benjamin J. Israel, *The Bene Israel of India: Some Studies*, Bombay: Orient Longman, 1984, p. 1.
12. Quoted in S. Venkatarayan, *A History of Cranganore*, Madras: Loganadhan Brothers, 1912, p. 18.
13. Narayanan, *Cultural Symbiosis*, p. 29.
14. Nathan Katz and Ellen S. Goldberg, *The Last Jews of Cochin: Jewish Identity in Hindu India*, Columbia: University of South Carolina Press, S.C., 1993, 43.
15. Barbara Cottle Johnson, 'The Emperor's Welcome: Reconsideration of the Origin Theme in Cochin Jewish Folklore', in T.A. Timberg, ed., *Jews in India*, p. 164.

16. P.M. Jussay, 'The Songs of Evarayi', in Timberg ed., *Jews in India*, pp. 145-60.
17. Katz and Goldberg, *The Last Jews of Cochin*, p. 46.
18. Jussay, 'The Songs of Evarayi', pp. 145-51.
19. Katz and Goldberg, *The Last Jews of Cochin*, pp. 50-1.
20. Mundadan, *Indian Christians*, pp. 1-6.
21. Ibid., pp. 8-9.
22. Ibid., pp. 10-11.
23. Ibid., pp. 11-15.
24. Ibid., p. 22.
25. Report on Mackenzie Ms., Ms Book, No.12- Countermark 905, quoted in *Malabar Journal of Literature and Science*, April 1839, pp. 358-9.
26. Ibid.,pp. 359-60.
27. Ibid., p. 360.
28. The Syrian Christians too have copper-plate grants of ninth century given by the governor of Kollam, which, extended 'seventy two privileges' to them, many of which are reminiscent of the rights enjoyed by the Hindu upper castes. For a detailing of some of these, see Mundadan, *Indian Christians*, 20.
29. Sheikh Zain-ud-deen al-Maburee, *Tohfut-ul-Mujahideen: an Historical Work in the Arabic Language*, trans. by M.J. Rowlandson, London: Oriental Translation Fund of Great Britain and Ireland, 1833.
30. Y. Friedman, 'Qissat Shakarwati Farmad: a Tradition Concerning the Introduction of Islam to Malabar', *Israel Oriental Studies*, vol. V, 1975, pp. 233-45.
31. Ibid., p. 237.
32. Ibid., pp. 237-41.
33. *The First Part of the Malabar Pooranam entitled Kayralolpatti or History of Malayalam*, Mackenzie Collection General, vol. V, no. 6, Oriental and India Office Collection (henceforth OIOC), British Library, pp. 197-248.
34. Ibid., p. 229.
35. Ibid., pp. 229-31.
36. Ibid., 233.
37. Ibid.
38. The first three are the *Taurat* or the prophecy of Moses, the Law; the *Zabur* or the prophecy of David, the Psalms; and the *Injil*, the prophecy of Jesus, the Gospels. Roland E. Miller, *Mappilla Muslims of Kerala: a Study in Islamic Trends*, Madras: Orient Longman, 1976, p. 48.
39. 'Kerala Ulpatti', in Report on the Mackenzie Manuscripts, in *Madras Journal of Literature and Science,* No. 13, October 1836, pp. 41-4.
40. Annotation about the Language, Science and Art of the Mallabar made

by Johan Adam Cellarius Little Merchant and Commander at Cranganore, 9, Mackenzie General LXXII (72), pp. 475-504, OIOC, British Library.

41. Katz and Goldberg, *The Last Jews of Cochin*, p. 46.
42. Jonas Thaliath T.O.C.D., *The Synod of Diamper*, Roma: Pont. Institutum Orientalium Studiorum, 1958, p. 176.
43. *The Works of the Reverend Claudius Buchanan Comprising his Christian Researches in Asia*, New York: Whiting and Watson, 1812, p. 113.
44. For instance, for trading groups in the medieval world, trade and religion were not hermetically sealed categories; the former often flourished where a network of co-religionists existed. See S.D. Goitein, *Letters of Medieval Jewish Traders*, Princeton: Princeton University Press, 1973, p. 7. However, ethnicity was equally important, and this often coloured the way in which a person might observe others, even if they were 'co-religionists'. For an extremely thought-provoking paper, see Richard Eaton, 'Multiple Lenses: Differing Perspectives of 15th century Calicut', in *Essays on Islam and Indian History*, New Delhi: Oxford University Press, 2001, pp. 76-93.

[illegible]

[illegible] Library.

[illegible]

[illegible]

[illegible] Letters of [illegible]

[illegible] p. 59.

2

From *Dar-ul-Harb* to *Dar-ul-Islam*?: Chishti Sufi Accounts and the Emergence of Islam in the Delhi Sultanate

RAZIUDDIN AQUIL

This paper aims to study the material in early Sufi literature, chiefly Chishti *malfuzat*, conversations of a Sufi shaykh, and *tazkiras,* biographies, celebrating the role played by Sufis in the emergence of Islam in the subcontinent. Sufi masters of the Sultanate period in upper north India figure in this paper. In particular, the focus will be on their role in politics and their interactions with non-Muslim religious leaders. The latter included yogis, gurus, Brahmins and *sannyasis.* The sources also employ the categories *kafir,* infidel, *ghayr-Muslim*, non-Muslim, and Hindu. In this paper, I shall use phrases such as non-Muslim, Hindu and infidel keeping this usage in mind. Further, Sufi narratives may not accord entirely with those originating outside their circles. Non-Muslim traditions have a very different representation of this period, including reports of encounters with Muslim mystics.[1] Within Islam, many people, especially the 'official' *ulama* (Muslim religious scholars), were ready to denounce the Sufis. The moderate amongst them criticized the 'bad' quality of Islam practised and occasionally preached, by the Sufis. Moreover, Muslim mystic movement was far from homogeneous. The Chishti construction of their religious ideas and the social roles of their *khwajagan* (leading preceptors) in the past may not have had many takers amongst the Suhrawardis, and later the Naqshabandis. Within the Chishti order (*silsila*), the attitude of individual Sufi masters differed on many important aspects such as the importance of *sama*

* I am grateful to Muzaffar Alam, Rimi Chatterjee, Rosinka Chaudhuri, Anjan Ghosh, Sanal Mohan, Tilottama Mukherjee, and Janaki Nair for reading an earlier draft and suggesting ways to sharpen it. The usual disclaimers apply.

(music), as part of their mystical practice of *zikr* (remembrance of God), as also their attitude towards conversion and Islamization. What follows then is a tentative attempt at making sense of a portion of Sufi literature pertinent to the history of the Delhi Sultanate.[2]

The study of the Sultanate period has been marginal to the concerns of the historians. A common explanation for this neglect is an alleged lack of sufficient source material, but there have been other factors. The lack of attention has also stemmed from certain basic assumptions, which have been shaped by contemporary ideological issues. For instance, the celebration of the achievements of Mughal emperor Akbar, in the dark medieval ages of 'intolerance' and 'fragmented' polities, meant that the history of the earlier, Sultanate, period be de-emphasized.[3]

The few studies on the Sultanate are largely based on court chronicles. These accounts are resolutely centred on the activities of the sultans, presenting a 'top down' view of history.[4] The Sufi literature offers rich data on societal and mental structures and political power and process, while presenting a view from below—of disgruntled elites and depressed commoners. A valuable portion of this literature, which was in circulation in the mid-fourteenth century and was subsequently used by authorities such as Amir Khwurd, Shaykh Jamali and Abdul Ḥaqq Muhaddis Dehlawi, is now dubbed 'forged', and denied historical value.[5] The abundance of miracle stories attributed to the Sufis is an important reason for the neglect of one set of sources. But then such tales are to be found in the so-called genuine texts also.[6]

Most historians prefer to put this literature aside in the belief that the Sufis, in general, and Chishtis, in particular, kept themselves aloof from the politics and government of their times.[7] Finally, for nearly four decades, the history of religions or ideas was a neglected stream, because of the dominance of Marxist historians in the field of medieval Indian history. The latter saw the Sufis as 'parasitic' on the political economy and hence their literature was considered to be of little value. We shall appraise such observations below.

II

A new chapter in the history of the subcontinent begins with the eastward expansion of Islam in the last decade of the twelfth century and the establishment of a series of Islamicate Sultanates. The Ghurid forces of Muiz-ud-Din bin Sam, referred to as the *lashkar-i-islam* in the early sources,[8] overran Ghaznavid Punjab. The Rajput resistance was smothered at Tarain in 1192.[9] The Muslim army went on to occupy large swathes of territory in northern India.[10] It eliminated the symbols of Rajput power and prestige in the region. Remarkably, there was no general massacre and no major demographic dislocation. Much as the chroniclers celebrated the conquest of new territories, the conquerors themselves preferred a minimum use of force and violence. Though iconoclasm may have been a motivating factor for some soldiers, the places of worship were generally plundered for their wealth. Alternatively, their despoliation was aimed at hammering home the point that the old regime was overthrown and could no longer protect the people and their religious places.[11] The general public was thus made aware that the Turks and their sultan had established a new Islamic order. Indeed, the minaret attached to Delhi's congregational mosque, and later known as the Qutb Minar, was subsequently perceived as a victory tower. Among the prime targets of Ghurid campaigns were Muslim Ghaznavids as well, but the Muslims of the Sultanate period particularly liked to remember the defeat of the infidels.

In their misplaced understanding of the Sultanate as an Islamic state, the *ulama* wanted the sultans to confront the Hindus of the dominion with the alternative of either death or Islam. In a measure, which speaks of the rulers' attempts at rapprochement with non-Muslims, they ignored the pressure of the *ulama* sodality. The Turks had realized that it was difficult to rule a population mainly non-Muslim through a narrow interpretation of *shariat*. Instead, they evolved a broad, 'secular' or non-theocratic state law, the *zawabit-i-mulki*,[12] with public protestations of respect to Muslim divines and their institutions.

The enthronement of Sultan Qutb-ud-Din Aybak (1206-10) in Lahore happened to coincide with the election of Chenghis Khan as the great leader of the Mongols.[13] The Mongol expansion brought large-scale devastation to Central and Western Asia in the next fifty years. Major centres of Islam, such as Bukhara and Baghdad, were sacked. The subcontinent was yet protected, though Punjab and Sindh were exposed to the threat. Escaping the wrath of the Tartars, Islam prospered in the Sultanate with the name of the caliph included in the *khutba*, Friday sermons, and the *sikka*, coins. The period witnessed a large-scale immigration of Muslims. A number of Sufis also came to settle down.

Sufi institutions such as the *khanqah* (hospice) and *dargah* (shrine), have contributed a great deal to the shaping of the harmonious culture of the subcontinent. In particular, the presence of Chishti Sufis ensured that force was not used for converting the general population to Islam. Much as Islamic 'orthodoxy' strove for a total annihilation of *kafirs*, the seemingly liberal approach of the Sufis proved to be more appealing to the early sultans.[14] The rulers themselves detested the arrogance of the *ulama*, and felt that the Sufis' position on the treatment to be meted out to Hindus, and generally on matters related to the *shariat*, was correct. The Sultanate was thus to have a 'secular' [see above] and broad-based polity, though religious ideas and institutions did play important roles. Controversial religious issues, which had the potential to create difficulties for the realm, occasionally came to the fore, but in the end sanity prevailed. The sultans were careful to avoid violence. (It remains to be explored as to what extent there was theoretical support for Muslims to live in peace with others.) Hindus were given the status of *zimmis* or *ahl-i-kitab*, People of the Book, like Jews and Christians and later Zoroastrians, as in the demand of the *jizya* (tax), from them, but they were often condemned as *kafirs* as well. Theoretically, *zimmis* were to be protected, *kafirs* eliminated. In grappling with the seemingly contradictory reports in this regard, we need to know the authors and the context in which they wrote. Ziya-ud-Din Barani (a companion of Muhammad Tughluq and disciple of Nizam-ud-Din Auliya) eventually emerging as a major historian and political theorist, took an extremely provocative position on these questions. He not only wanted the *kafirs* to be subdued and humiliated, but even 'low-born' Muslim converts to be suppressed. Apparently, not all his ideas were taken seriously even in the circles wherein he moved.

In a way it augured well for the history of Islam in India that the earliest Muslim reportedly born in the capital city of Delhi after the Turkish conquest went on to become a Chishti Sufi with a reputation for syncretistic proclivities: Shaykh Hamid-ud-Din (died 1274),[15] a disciple and *khalifa,* spiritual successor, of Muin-ud-Din Chishti Ajmeri.[16] Muin-ud-Din, in turn, was said to have been directed by Prophet Muhammad in a dream in Medina to go to Hindustan. The Khwaja's arrival coincided with the Turkish conquest. Sufi tradition claims that Muin-ud-Din had prophesied Ghurid victory in the second battle of Tarain. The Chauhan ruler Rai Pithora or Prithviraj was said to be harassing the shaykh and his disciples at Ajmer. Later traditions also claim that the Sufi shaykh had to display miraculous powers to subdue the Chauhan ruler. Amir Khwurd wrote in the mid-fourteenth century that when Muin-ud-Din reached Ajmer, Rai Pithora was ruling from there. The ruler and his officials resented the shaykh's presence in the area, but the latter's power to perform miracles is said to have prompted them to hold their hand. A disciple of the shaykh, who was in the service of the Rajput king, began to receive hostile treatment from the ruler. The shaykh sent a message in his behalf. Pithora refused to accept Muin-ud-Din's recommendation and resented the reports of the shaykh's alleged claims to understand the secrets of the Unseen. When the Sufi master, '*badshah-i-islam*', says the biographer, heard this, he commented: Pithora has been captured alive and handed over to the army of Islam. About the same time Muiz-ud-Din's army arrived from Ghazni and defeated the Rajputs.[17]

Amir Khwurd also utilized the material in *malfuz* collections which highlighted the personality of Muin-ud-Din as a preacher and Islamiser with considerable charismatic power. He wrote that infidelity and idol-worship were widespread in Hindustan before the arrival of the shaykh. The people worshipped stones, trees, animals, and even cow-dung. Their hearts were sealed in the darkness of infidelity. The author claimed that with the coming of the saint the dark clouds of ignorance gave way to the spiritual light of Islam. Addressing the Sufi master as the true *mu'in* or helper of the faith, the Chishti biographer claimed that the credit for conversion of the people of Hindustan goes to the shaykh and to those whose further preaching transformed this enemy land, *dar-i-harb*, into the abode of Islam, *dayar-i-islam*.[18]

Theoretically, *dar-ul-islam* is the territory where *shariat* prevails as the supreme law of the land, guaranteeing a privileged position to the members of the community of Islam (*umma*).[19] Others like the *zimmi* could stay in the dominion with assurance of protection of their lives and some amount of freedom to practice their religions. In the Indian case, the position of the Hindus in the Sultanate remained ambivalent even as the Sultanate was far from a *sharia*-driven Islamic state. Occasional rhetoric notwithstanding, no concerted effort for a complete political and religious transformation was undertaken. Sufis were also satisfied with the respect and spiritual authority that they enjoyed in the dominion. The veneration showed by the people, even if they did not formally convert to Islam, was gratifying enough.

We shall return to the question of Sufi attitudes towards conversion below, but Muin-ud-Din's popularity amongst non-Muslims may be mentioned here. The fact that infidels visited the shaykh's tomb every year and offered large sums to the keepers of the shrine is much extolled by Sufi biographers. In early Muslim perception, however, the shaykh brought the faith to the region of Ajmer. This image of the shaykh is also reflected in non-Sufi literature of the period. Referring to the visit of Muin-ud-Din's tomb by Sultan Muhammad Tughluq in the second quarter of the fourteenth century, chronicler Isami, in his *Futuh-us-Salatin*, called the shaykh the refuge of the faith.[20] Evidently, the shaykh's charisma, both as living master and when he lay in his grave, won him a large following, and his *khalifas* spread in different directions. Hamid-ud-Din, the child of Delhi, went to live in a village near Nagaur. He cultivated a small plot of land, became a vegetarian, and seemingly led a life conforming to the Hindu environment.

Muin-ud-Din Chishti chose a more sophisticated Qutb-ud-Din Bakhtiyar Kaki (died 1236) for the cosmopolitan *wilayat* (spiritual territory) of Delhi.[21] Bakhtiyar Kaki was born in Ush in Jaxartes in Central Asia. He is reported to have met Muin-ud-Din in Baghdad, and became his disciple. Following his *pir* or preceptor, Muin-ud-Din, 'the Sultan of Hind', Bakhtiyar Kaki reached Delhi in the reign of Shams-ud-Din Iltutmish (1211-36). The sultan welcomed the shaykh and invited him to live in the city. Though hesitant initially, he agreed. Bakhtiyar Kaki had to compete for a space in the spiritual geography of the city. Besides the *ulama*, quite a few eminent Sufis of various lineages had come to settle there. Many had just arrived following the Mongol invasions in Central Asia and Iran. Bakhtiyar Kaki found his most powerful antagonist in Shaykh-ul-Islam Najm-ud-Din Sughra, a Sufi of his own order. Najm-ud-Din and Bakhtiyar Kaki's *pir* Muin-ud-Din were disciples of the same shaykh; Usman Harwani Najm-ud-Din did not welcome the growing popularity of Bakhtiyar Kaki and his influence in political circles.

To prevent the tension from escalating, Muin-ud-Din, on a visit to Delhi, asked his disciple to accompany him to Ajmer.[22] The news of the departure of the saints was perceived as a sign of calamity by Sultan Iltutmish and the people. They followed the shaykhs for miles — crying and wailing. Touched by the grief of the ruler and the ruled alike, Muin-ud-Din allowed Bakhtiyar Kaki to remain in Delhi.[23] As a patron saint of the city, Bakhtiyar Kaki enjoyed prestige and authority, and in a measure influenced the sultan's style of governance.

The weakness of the rulers and the supremacy of the nobles were two important features of the period following the death of Iltutmish. Within a decade of his death, the nobles put four of his descendants on the throne and removed them at will. The next twenty years saw his slaves exterminating his dynasty by executing all the male members of his family. One of his slaves, Ghiyas-ud-Din Balban, ruled from Delhi for over forty years from about the middle of the thirteenth century. Acting first as *naib*, deputy, of the puppet Sultan Nasir-ud-Din Mahmud (1246-66)[24] he subsequently ascended the throne of Delhi as sultan (1266-87) in his own right. When Balban came to power, the Mongols had ravaged the major part of the Muslim world. Having sacked Punjab, they were threatening to take Delhi. Balban's aggressive Mongol policy protected the Sultanate from Mongol depredations.[25]

The suppression of 'rebellious' elements in the regions and the protection of trade routes were other achievements of Balban, which brought great prestige to the throne.[26] If Ziya-ud-Din Barani is to be believed, the king also thwarted political upheavals in the capital by providing a veneer of divinity to his rule. He called himself the shadow of God on earth, *zillullah*, and proclaimed that kingship was the vice-regency of God (*niyabat-i-khudai*). Tracing his genealogy to the mythical Afrasiyab, the sultan emulated the customs and ways of life of the pre-Islamic Sassanid rulers of Persia. Elaborate court rituals, including *sijda*, prostration, and *paibos*, kissing of feet, were introduced and forcibly implemented. Given the anarchy following the death of Iltutmish, Balban's measures restored the authority of the crown.[27]

Balban was a devotee of Farid-ud-Din Ganj-i-Shakar, *khalifa* of Bakhtiyar Kaki.[28] Ali Asghar, himself a descendant of Farid-ud-Din, recorded in the early seventeenth century that the saint had married Balban's daughter Bibi Huzaira and had six sons and three daughters from her.[29] Earlier, Amir Khwurd had noted that the shaykh had several wives and had five sons and three daughters.[30] The saint's favourite son, Nizam-ud-Din (not to be confused with his *khalifa*, Nizam-ud-Din Auliya) had joined Balban's army and died fighting the Mongol invaders in Punjab.[31]

Farid-ud-Din was succeeded by his illustrious disciple Nizam-ud-Din Auliya, who eventually turned Delhi into a major Chishti centre.[32] Nizam-ud-Din is an important member of the first cycle of the Chishti saints, following Muin-ud-Din Ajmeri, Qutb-ud-Din Bakhtiyar Kaki, and Farid-ud-Din Ganj-i-Shakar. Nizam-ud-Din's successor, Nasir-ud-Din Chiragh-i-Dilli (d. 1356),[33] completes the chain of the 'great' Chishti tradition, which is known to have played a crucial role in shaping the political and cultural traditions of the Delhi Sultanate. They are particularly known for their religious tolerance and broad-mindedness. It is their seemingly liberal attitude and their perceived ability to perform miracles and their consequent popularity that brought them into conflict with Islamic orthodoxy, and in the case of Nizam-ud-Din with the rulers as well.

Though Nizam-ud-Din's differences with the powerful Delhi sultan Ala-ud-Din Khalji (1296-1316) were amicably resolved, the saint's encounter with Qutb-ud-Din Mubarakshah Khalji (1316-20) and Ghiyas-ud-Din Tughluq (1320-25), is particularly celebrated in Chishti memory. Even as Nizam-ud-Din was concerned about the political instability of the period, the rulers were evidently angry over his indifference towards the court (*darbar*) and its rituals. For the saint, to visit the court would have amounted to accepting the superiority of the ruler over his own claim to authority in his *wilayat.* Indeed, Şufi claims to power and authority in society were a continuous irritant for kings and *ulama* alike. In such a situation, the Sufis had to defend their actions in the light of *shariat.* Early biographical accounts asserted that they also occasionally resorted to paranormal powers to defeat their opponents. Their reported victory in such cases contributed to their authoritative position in the society.[34]

In Nizam-ud-Din's case, he had to defend the legitimacy of his interest in music, *sama/qawwali*, in the light of the traditions of Prophet Muhammad. Conservative *ulama* insisted that he follow the Hanafite interpretation, which forbids listening to music.[35] In such a condition, the shaykh was reduced to cursing his detractors. In Chishti memory, the saint's righteousness was established when the sultans and their supporters were eliminated in quick succession. While a close confidante, Khusrau Khan killed Qutb-ud-Din Mubarakshah Khalji, Ghiyas-ud-Din's death in an accident on the outskirts of Delhi was suspected to be the handiwork of his own son, who enthroned himself as Sultan Muhammad Tughluq. Ghiyas-ud-Din was returning from a campaign in the east and had sent a *farman* (imperial order), asking Nizam-ud-Din to leave the city. The saint responded in his characteristically humorous way: *hunuz dilli dur ast*, that is, Delhi is yet far away (for the ruler).[36] The king never did return to the city. In Chishti memory, Nizam-ud-Din had already cursed Ghiyas-ud-Din and bestowed kingship on Muhammad Tughluq.[37] A number of scholars have thus shown that the Sufis, including the Chishtis, of the Sultanate period did take part in politics.[38] Some of them avoided visiting the sultan's court perhaps because they considered it below their dignity.[39] Some may have also felt that a tactical distance from rulers would help them deal with a hostile non-Muslim population.

Three of the five 'great' Chishti saints—Farid-ud-Din's preceptor Qutb-ud-Din Bakhtiyar Kaki, his successor Nizam-ud-Din Auliya, and the latter's disciple Nasir-ud-Din Chiragh-i-Dilli—settled down in Delhi. Other strategic places they chose to stay were on much-trodden trade routes. Ajodhan (renamed Pakpattan), where Farid-ud-Din established his hospice, was on the Multan-Delhi road. Caravans and armies passed through it and carried the saints' fame far and wide. Certainly, the Chishtis were against the idea of settling in forests or in lonely places. They were supposed to stay amongst the people in their *wilayat* and look after their welfare.

The Sufis accepted cash grants from the rulers and prayed for their success. Shaykh Farid-ud-Din received money from Ulugh Khan, later known as Balban, even as it was immediately distributed amongst the dervishes.[40] Farid-ud-Din's successor Nizam-ud-Din took five lakh tankas from the usurper Khusrau Malik and distributed the sum amongst the public.[41] Often during a campaign, soldiers would take a detour to visit a Sufi hospice or shrine and seek blessings. The sources refer to Nasir-ud-Din Mahmud's army visiting Farid-ud-Din at Ajodhan.[42] Also the shaykhs were asked about the fate of the Muslim army campaigning in the region. Ala-ud-Din Khalji, it is said, sought Nizam-ud-Din's help to know the fate of his army campaigning in the south—and victory was predicted.[43] Later, the latter spoke to his audience about the enormous booty collected by Malik Naib and suggested that it be used for public welfare.[44]

Some Sufis even aided Muslim control of newly conquered territories by sending their *khalifas* with the army.[45] Others allowed their sons to join the army and fight a *jihad* against infidels, as with Farid-ud-Din's son, Nizam-ud-Din. Yet others went to report on events of the campaign.[46]

Most Sultans, members of the royal family and court officials, were *murids* (disciples) of the shaykhs, who, it is said, bestowed kingship on a person of their choice and snatched it when dissatisfied with his performance. Also, there are a number of anecdotes in the texts concerning the opposition, disrespect, and abusive epithets used by rulers, *ulama* and other notables, provoking the shaykh's wrath. A saint's curse would cause the antagonists' sudden and often painful death.

Such episodes from the life of a Sufi saint like Nizam-ud-Din Auliya, narrated with embellishments over time, have contributed to his popularity. Chishti hagiographies highlight Nizam-ud-Din as a healer and protector of people in times of crisis, his charitable endeavours and his broad world-view drawing people across institutionalized religions. Later *tazkiras* and Chishti oral tradition may have helped spread the charismatic image of the shaykh; yet the saint *was* a living legend. His hospice in Delhi was a continuous source of sustenance for the people. In his death in 1325, the people lost a messiah. In course of time, his shrine emerged as a major pilgrimage centre.

While Nizam-ud-Din's successor Nasir-ud-Din Chiragh-i-Dilli followed his preceptor's instruction to stay in Delhi and 'serve' the people, a number of other fellow Chishtis were struggling to establish the order in various parts of the subcontinent, including Bengal[47] and the Deccan.[48]

III

Sufi tradition claims that its leading masters continued to play an important role in shaping the character of Islam and of Muslims under Afghan rulers and smaller regimes in the regions.[49] Abdul Haqq Muhaddis Dehlawi recorded that a number of infidels and sinners accepted Islam just by having a glimpse of the spiritual accomplishments of a Sufi of Uchch in Sindh, Abdul Qadir Sani.[50] Sufi sources also narrate cases when non-Muslim visitors or antagonists resist the temptation to convert to Islam, even as the paranormal powers of shaykhs are appreciated. Here is an incident recorded by Abdul Haqq. Listening to music in his home, Shaykh Muhammad of Mallawa, near Qannauj, went into a trance. The Hindu chief of the area, who happened to be passing that way with a companion, heard the sound of the music and peeped through the window. What he saw inside sent him into a trance, but his companion pulled him out of the window. When he regained consciousness, he told his companions that he had seen the Musalman dancing with his God in his lap;[51] and if he had not been pulled out, he would have gone to the Musalman, fallen at his feet and accepted his religion.[52] However, according to Abdul Haqq, nobody could resist Saiyid Kabir-ud-Din Hasan's invitation to convert. A peripatetic Sufi, later settled in Uchch, Hasan was well known for his miracles.[53]

Such anecdotes did not emerge suddenly in the Afghan period. Early Chishti literature records a large number of miraculous encounters between Sufi shaykhs and non-Muslim miracle-workers or mystic power-holders. The arrival of a Muslim mystic in a non-Muslim environment, and his decision to settle there, was considered in certain cases to be an encroachment on the authority of the incumbent priest, or the ruler of that territory. The Sufi shaykh's authority in such instances was established only after his victory in a combat. While due recognition was given to the supernatural power of non-Muslim religious leaders, according to the hagiographical accounts, a Sufi's victory proved his superior spiritual stature and thus convinced the local challengers, the yogi or the ruler, of the finality of the Sufi's faith. The yogi would become a *waliullah*, friend of God, and the ruler a pious *badshah*. The conversion of the yogi and the ruler was also sometimes followed by mass conversion in the territory. The accounts further say that if an adversary refused to convert to Islam even after defeat, there were two possibilities depending upon whether the loser recognized the superior miraculous ability of the shaykh. Either he was allowed to leave the place and settle elsewhere, or eliminated by a curse.

Our sources thus have some fantastic stories of conversion at the hands of miracle-working shaykhs,[54] notwithstanding earlier beliefs to the contrary.[55] Sufi shaykhs' laudatory narration of these accounts to their audience in their hospices helped their extensive circulation. In highlighting the 'achievements' of Sufi shaykhs in a non-Muslim environment, or in relation to a visiting yogi in their *wilayat*, the sources chiefly project them as disseminators of Islam.

There are a number of theories concerning conversions to Islam in the medieval period, inspired mostly by the political and ideological concerns of our time. These include claims about large-scale immigration of 'foreign' Muslims, about conversion at the point of a sword or political patronage, and about the social liberation of low-caste Hindus, said to have been attracted toward the egalitarian Islam practised by Sufis. These explanations have been questioned in recent years.[56] Even on the Sufis' role here, there is no single opinion. Some scholars see the attitude towards conversion in terms of the general outlook of a particular Sufi order. Thus it is suggested that the Chishtis were disinterested in formal conversion because they were tolerant and accommodative. On the other hand, Suhrawardis are considered to be orthodox and uncompromising and, therefore, intent on converting non-Muslims even by force.[57] This difference is said to be connected with an ideological difference. It is argued that those who believed in *wahdat-ul-wujud*, monism as a reality, sometimes glossed even as 'pantheism', were open-minded towards the Hindus and cared little about their formal conversion to Islam. For them the difference between the creator and the created is annulled; everything becomes God; all is God. By contrast, for those following *wahdat-us-shuhud*, 'feeling of monism as a reality', the difference between God and his creations remains; all is from God, but not all is God. They tended to be hostile towards the Hindus and would favour even forced conversion.[58] An alternate, more instructive position would move away from ideology to historical process, treating conversion as a long process of Islamic acculturation.[59]

On the other hand, reports of Muslims adopting 'Hindu' practices, and the call for reforming them, were also current. Though the Sufi shaykh himself was sure of his righteousness, and of his spiritual power being recognized in the wake of an encounter, he was often concerned about the yogi's 'bad' influence on his disciples. Farid-ud-Din Ganj-i-Shakar is reported to have asked young Nizam-ud-Din Auliya not to take interest in the yogi's knowledge of matters of worldly interest.[60] An anecdote in *Lataif-i-Quddusi* says the Chishti Shaikh Abdul Quddus Gangohi (d. 1537) told a disciple, Dattu Sarwani, an Afghan soldier, in a dream to avoid the company of a *sannyasi,* Anant Guru.[61] Apparently, Dattu was troubled in his conscience — which manifested itself in the dream. The soldier knew that though the *sannyasi* spoke about the unity of God, he was not a Muslim. Senior Afghan nobles had also not paid any heed to the *sannyasi's* preaching and his offer to pray for their victory against the Mughals. Further, Dattu must have been conscious of his loyalty towards his *pir* Abdul Quddus, and aware of the latter's attitude towards yogis. The Hindu mystics are condemned by him in the course of a discussion of *wahdat-ul-wujud* recorded in the *Lataif-i-Quddusi.*[62] Abdul Quddus letters to the Afghan and Mughal rulers also bring to the fore his hostile attitude towards non-Muslims in general. In his letter to Babur, he suggested that *kafirs* be excluded from high office, particularly in the revenue department; important revenue posts in the provinces should be given only to pious Muslims, who should assess and realize the tax in strict conformity with *shariat*. Hindus were to be forced to accept a status inferior to the Muslims' and to be prevented from dressing in the same way.[63]

And yet Abdul Quddus Gangohi was a noted Chishti shaykh, whose own mystical practices and beliefs seemed to be heavily coloured by Hindu spiritual traditions, as we shall see. So it is not entirely accurate to say that, unlike the other Sufi orders such as the Suhrawardis, and later the Naqshbandis, the Chishtis were always tolerant and accommodative, and cared little about conversions because they believed in *wahdat-ul-wujud*.[64] The saint's position may be understood in the light of his own troubles on account of the changing political scene. Indeed, the attitude of the Muslims, kings, courtiers or Sufis, kept varying with the ever-changing fortunes of political power throughout the medieval period. Both court chronicles and Sufi sources testify that the campaigns of the Muslim army for conquering areas hitherto controlled by non-Muslim chieftains, or pacifying them, were portrayed as *jihad*. Numerous Sufis participated in such campaigns as sword-wielding warriors—or for moral support and legitimacy: their *barakat* (blessed presence in the army camp) encouraged soldiers to fight with greater zeal.

Once the conquest was over, Muslims felt secure and safe. The earlier fanaticism gradually gave way to a more open-minded attitude towards non-Muslims. They were willing to appreciate and absorb from diverse sources of tradition: politics, but also language, religion, and culture, as we shall see. As long as the 'others' were politically submissive, there was no harm in borrowing from non-Islamic sources. It was also pragmatic not to alienate the subjects, the majority of whom remained outside Islam. The need for integrating the chieftains for lasting control over various regions notwithstanding, rulers were frequently advised, as by Chishti saint Abdul Quddus in the above letter, not to appoint Hindus to high positions, as their rebellion might cost dear. Instances of their revolts were, indeed, neither few nor far between.

Thus, while the rulers exploited the symbols of Islam to legitimise their campaigns, the *ulama* and occasionally even Sufis—showed their adverse attitude towards non-Muslims. The *ulama* dreamt of a strong Muslim dominion where their interpretation of *shariat* would be the law of the land. The Sufis also felt secure in a territory controlled by a Muslim governor, and so they supported Muslim rulers even if they flouted *shariat* in their personal lives and in governance. The sources refer to several instances when Sufis had to migrate when a non-Muslim chieftain rebelled and began persecuting Muslims. Abdul Haqq's *Akhbar-ul-Akhyar* notes the capture of the fort of Ajmer by the Rajput Rana Sanga, who allegedly martyred a large number of Muslims there. Following a vision, in which Muin-ud-Din Chishti warned of the impending calamity, Shaykh Ahmad Mujid Shaibani left the place with a small party of Muslims; this was seven days before the Rana captured Ajmer.[65] Abdul Haqq also records that during this period the *kuffar* had converted the tomb of Muin-ud-Din Chishti into a temple, and had placed an idol inside. Sultan Bahadur of Gujarat, then a prince, had visited Ajmer at this time. The prince had prayed that if he were blessed with the crown, he would wreak vengeance on the infidels for desecrating the Chishti shrine. On hearing this, Bayin Majzub, who is said to have been present there, indirectly announced the bestowal of kingship on the prince. Later, having assumed sovereignty, Sultan Bahadur marched to Ajmer and fulfilled his vow.[66]

The narration of the episode of attack on the shrine and its recovery may also be read along with Abdul Haqq's reference to Pushkar, a Hindu pilgrimage centre about 8 miles from Ajmer. In the course of his account of Muin-ud-Din's career and his settling down in Ajmer, the foremost Sufi biographer noted that every year for six days at the time of the passing of Scorpio the Hindus congregate at Pushkar and bathe in the reservoir there, wasting both their lives and their children's lives in futile religious rituals.[67]

Contestations for spiritual superiority between the Sufis and non-Muslims were not always cordial. Political intervention could hot things up. Threat to life and desecration of religious places in the wake of rebellions led by non-Muslim chiefs compelled the Muslims to support the idea of a strong Muslim Sultanate. Evidently, Muslim memory was haunted by reports of persecution in a hostile Hindu environment. One particularly ghastly incident narrated by Abdul Haqq was the cold-blooded massacre of Muslims engaged in a congregational Id-prayer at Narnaul.[68] There were however also instances of Hindu-Muslim coordination and reconciliation in the medieval period.

IV

Despite the conflicts, Islam's interaction with other religio-intellectual traditions in India has facilitated syncretism and synthesis in religion and culture, since at least the thirteenth century. Scholars particularly highlight Sufis in this connection. It is said that the propagation of the belief in Sufi circles that an individual's soul could achieve union with God, the doctrine of *wahdat-ul-wujud*, brought Sufis close to certain non-Muslim mystical traditions such as the Natha Yogis. Amongst the votaries of the doctrine was the leading Chishti shaykh of the Afghan period, Abdul Quddus Gangohi.[69] Though the shaykh's political approach could be similar to that of his contemporary *sharia*-minded *ulama*, his *Rushdnama* not only defended his belief in *wahdat-ul-wujud* but also attempted to establish the mutual compatibility of Natha Yogi and Sufi ideologies. Since the *ulama* and the rivals of Chishtis denounced learning from non-Muslim saints, Abdul Quddus explained that his discussion of the theory of *wahdat-ul-wujud* and other Sufic principles was based on the teachings of Shaykh Ahmad Abdul Haqq Rudaulwi (d. 1434), and that he had learned of them by mystical intuition. His son, Shaykh Rukn-ud-Din, also suggested that his father's attitude towards the Natha Yogis was based on Koran and *hadis* (traditions of the Prophet). Abdul Quddus, however, was less apologetic. He asserted that spiritual truths were common to all religions.

Modern authorities have studied, in detail, the influence of yogic elements in the religious teachings and practices of Abdul Quddus.[70] Though the Natha influence on Abdul Quddus' understanding of *wahdat-ul-wujud* is somewhat over-emphasized, there were indeed some significant parallels in the thought of the shaykh and that of Gorakhnath. At least the Hindi verses of the shaykh in support of *wujudi* doctrine clearly reveal that the shaykh used Natha idioms and metaphors to express his thought, even as it was rooted in Islamic tradition.

Further, Abdul Quddus' treatment of yogic ideas and techniques of ecstasy, probably passed on to him in the *khanqah* at Rudauli, may be seen as an attempt to adapt an unorthodox, non-Muslim tradition within the confines of a learned, though profoundly Indianized Islam. The official *ulama* may not have appreciated an uncritical borrowing of yogic ideas.[71] Yet, the shaykh emphasized two aspects of the mystical discipline, *salat-i-makus* and *sultan-i-*

zikr, which reflect the influence of Natha practices. *Salat-i-makus* or *chilla-i-makus* consisted of hanging upside-down in a well, with legs tied to the branch of a tree.[72] In the Chishti tradition, the practice can be traced to Farid-ud-Din Ganj-i-Shakar who was said to have performed it in thirteenth century, and even earlier to Shaykh Abu Sayid bin Abil Khair, and before him, to Prophet Muhammad himself.[73]

Abdul Quddus and fellow Chishtis were not alone in wishing to learn from Indian spiritual traditions. The Shattari exemplar Saiyid Muhammad Ghaus Gwaliari (d. 1562),[74] popularised Hindu mystical practices through his translation of the yogic treatise, *Amritkund*, and drew attention to the similarities in the mystical terminology of Muslims and Hindus. In fact, several versions of *Amritkund* in Persian and Arabic known as *Hauz-ul-Hayat* or *Bahr-ul-Hayat* were already in circulation in medieval Indian Sufi circles. Abdul Quddus had extensive knowledge of this text and imparted its essence to his disciples.[75]

In contrast with the fanaticism in Abdul Quddus' approach towards Hindus, Muhammad Ghaus treated everybody, including the *kuffar*, with honour and respectfully stood before them.[76] This was a cause of discomfiture for orthodox Muslims and even some fellow shaykhs denied him the status of a true ascetic. Mulla Abdul Qadir Badauni, the author of our source, was also defensive on this issue, as he wrote that God alone knew what the shaykh's motives were in venerating the infidels.[77]

Unsure of its own yardstick over norms of behaviour, Islamic orthodoxy, indeed, occasionally refrained from passing judgement on certain acts of saintly persons that appeared objectionable. The case of Kabir is illustrative. Though later Sufi tradition appropriated Kabir as a disciple of Shah Taqi of Kara-Manikpur, hardly any discussion on his life and ideas is to be found in early Sufi circles. Kabir, who probably lived in the early-fifteenth century,[78] has left an enduring impact on the religious attitude and culture of the subsequent period. His case is particularly relevant for understanding how Islam interacted with non-Muslim religious traditions at the popular level. His trenchant criticism of idol-worship and the caste system, and his emphasis on monotheism, clearly influenced religious leaders like Guru Nanak.

Sikhism's later shift from syncretism to hostility towards Islam, and the followers of Kabir separating into Hindu and Muslim Kabirpanthis, did not stop syncretistic borrowings across religious traditions. Despite assaults from Hindu and Muslim reformist and revivalist movements, syncretism in popular beliefs has survived in India. A common feature in most of the existing syncretistic cults is the worship of a galaxy of saints—legendary or otherwise. The lasting appeal of Muslim mystics of the medieval period can also be attributed to their willingness to mix with 'all kinds of men', often criticised by the *ulama* as in the case of Muhammad Ghaus.

The popularity of the Sufi saints was also due, in a measure, to their willingness to adopt the vernaculars for communicating with the masses and for expressing their own mystical experiences. Most early references in Indian Islam to the use of Hindvi, or regional languages, come from Sufi circles. Already in the thirteenth and fourteenth centuries, Hindvi couplets sung in Sufis' musical assemblies were popular. For some Sufis, poetry in Hindvi, rather than Persian, helped attain a higher level of ecstasy. Vernacular poetry was more popular in the Sufic fraternities of the late-fifteenth and early-sixteenth centuries, a period important in the growth and development of Hindi literature.[79] The Sufi poetry of love, in Hindi, is a significant example of cultural cross-referencing in medieval India. From the perspective of a purist, however, it symbolizes the secession of a Muslim mind from its 'own' culture and choosing self-expression in the rival Hindu culture.[80]

V

The *ulama* sodality did not always remain indifferent to such developments. Though at times 'covering up' some heterodox behaviour and practices, or dismissing them as aberrations, the *ulama* countered any statement or action which they saw as a source of *fitna*, disturbance in society. In such a situation, the need to check the degeneration of Islam was also strongly felt. Indeed, several reformist and revivalist movements emerged in medieval Islam in India. The leaders of such movements wanted to reform or purify Islam by reviving the model of Islamic society that existed at the time of the Prophet and during the reigns of the four rightly-guided caliphs. They all tried to bring contemporary Islamic practices in line with Koran and *hadis*; their impact was anti-syncretistic.

Cultural faultlines did appear in the pluralistic fabric of medieval India in the wake of an 'exclusivist' religious project emerging occasionally. Feelings of community identities, based on religious lines, could then be noticed. Persian sources pertaining to periods of hostility contain urgent calls to Muslims to dispatch the infidels to hell. At the other end, in times of peace, a great many Muslims could be intoxicated by the devotional poetry of the same Hindus. It was the context which determined the divergent attitudes of Muslims — Turks, Afghans, later the Mughal nobility, or converted Hindustanis— towards non-Muslims in medieval north India. Pragmatic politics demanded that hostility and violence be avoided, at least minimized, even as the questions of religious identities and control of political power remained matters of contention.

The sources are clear, too, that in conflicts over the political control of a territory, religious symbols were frequently used for mobilization. Muslims seemed to be engaged in a long-drawn *jihad* against the *kuffar*. Even though, at times, they were extraordinarily magnanimous towards Hindus, it is clear that the Muslims, at least the elite who have left their works in Persian, were conscious of the presence of an 'other' in the person of the Hindu. Even if these writings are rhetoric aimed at pleasing the rulers (for instance, accounts of conquests by Amir Khusrau, a close disciple of Nizam-ud-Din Auliya) they are important for understanding the context in which they were recorded. The fear of the overwhelming presence of an often dangerous 'other' provides one such context; the felt imperative to suppress it, another. It is in these contexts that the formation of community identities of Indian Muslims needs to be understood. Available sources permit us to examine closely Hindu-Muslim interactions in medieval India, thick with both discord and harmonious coexistence. Our discussion suggests that the accounts of the relations of the Sufis with the rulers and *ulama*, on the one hand, and their divergent attitudes towards non-Muslim traditions, on the other, can be of some help in understanding these issues in context.

Secular and pluralist historians either deny the existence of separate Hindu and Muslim identities, or highlight examples of communal harmony, in 'pre-colonial' India. They ignore the point that if religious 'identities' had not been competitive, and often combative, the question of 'communal harmony' would not arise. Also, it is hard to believe that a Chishti such as Ziya-ud-Din Barani — or his friend Amir Khusrau, and their spiritual master Nizam-ud-Din Auliya — were not conscious of their identity as Muslims.

Whereas some theoretically sophisticated studies have tried to explain relevant themes in the modern context in relation to colonialism, there has hardly been any serious and comprehensive study for the earlier period. Our ignorance of this aspect of our medieval past does not prove its non-existence. Not that we should harp on the incidents of violence and bloodshed, like separatist and communal writers tend to do. The latter also insist that Hindus and Muslims always constituted separate 'nations': again a presentist agenda dictating to scholarship, wholly false to the sources for the period.[81] A more balanced and empirically sustainable approach is necessary.

NOTES

1. For a thought-provoking counter-narrative, see Zelliot (2003).
2. For the existing literature on the Delhi Sultanate, see Habibullah (1945); Nizami (1961); Siddiqui (1961); Lal (1967); Halim (1974); Habib (1974); Husain (1976); Habib and Nizami (1992); Jackson (1999).
3. For criticisms of Mughal-centrism in north Indian historiography, see Perlin (1985); Subrahmanyam (1992); Alam and Subrahmanyam (1998).
4. Hasan (1968); Mukhia (1976).
5. Habib (1974: 385-433). Subsequent scholars like M. Mujeeb, K.A. Nizami, and S.A.A. Rizvi, among others, have reiterated Habib's position.
6. 'Aquil (2003a).
7. For a review of secondary literature, see Aquil (1995-6).
8. *Tabaqat-i-Nasiri*, 397, 399-400; *Siyar-ul-Auliya*, 57.
9. *Tabaqat-i-Nasiri*, 400.
10. Ibid., 400-1.
11. Eaton (2002).
12. *Zawabit,* regulations, rules, precepts, +*mulki,* of, or relating to, empire or government. The expression appears in the mid-fourteenth century text, *Fatawa-i-Jahandari* of Ziya-ud-Din Barani. The author insisted that *sharia* law was inadequate for running the Sultanate. A new extra-religious law should be evolved. *Zawabit* were indeed of secular nature, they were certainly not theocratic.
13. For Qutb-ud-Din's enthronement, see *Tabaqat-i-Nasiri,* 417.
14. The term 'orthodoxy' is being used here for the Sultanate *ulama*, often referred to as the *ulama-i-su*, who insisted on implementing the Sunni Hanafite interpretation of Islam, and sought to use political power for the purpose.
15. For the life of the saint, see Faruqi (1963).
16. For biographical material, see *Siyar-ul-Auliya,* 55-8. Also Currie (1989).

17. *Siyar-ul-Auliya*, 56-7.
18. Ibid., 57.
19. For Islamic theoretical positions on *dar-ul-harb* and *dar-ul-islam*, see Abel (1991a); Abel (1991b).
20. For this and other references to the visit to Muin-ud-Din's tomb at Ajmer in the fourteenth century, see Digby (1983).
21. For biographical material, see *Siyar-ul-Auliya*, 58-67; *Siyar-ul-Arifin*, 31b-43a. Also see, Rizvi (1978: 133-8).
22. *Siyar-ul-Auliya*, 64.
23. Ibid., 65.
24. Ziya-ud-Din Barani notes that Sultan Nasir-ud-Din was a mere *namuna*, as the reins of power were in the hands of Balban then known as Ulugh Khan, *Tarikh-i-Firuzshahi*, 12b-13a.
25. Ibid., 23b-24a.
26. Ibid., 26a-28a, 38a-45a.
27. Ibid., 13b-17b.
28. *Siyar-ul-Auliya*, 89-90; *Siyar-ul-Arifin*, 56b-57a; *Jawahir-i-Faridi*, 204, 214-15. For Balban's religiosity and his veneration of the Sufi saints generally, see *Tarikh-i-Firuzshahi*, 21b-22a. For biographical material on the shaykh's life, see *Siyar-ul-Auliya*, 67-101; *Siyar-ul-Arifin*, 43a-65b. Also see Nizami (1955); Eaton (2003); Aquil (2003c).
29. *Jawahir-i-Faridi*, 215-18. Also see *Khazinat-ul-Asfiya*, I, 301.
30. *Siyar-ul-Auliya*, 76, 195.
31. Ibid., 100, 200.
32. For an early biography of the saint, see, Muhammad Jamal Qiwam, *Qiwam-ul-Aqaid*. Also see the collection of his conversations in *Fawaid-ul-Fuad*, compiled by Amir Hasan Sijzi; *Siyar-ul-Auliya*, 101-65; *Siyar-ul-Arifin*, 75b-100b; Nizami (1991a).
33. For an authoritative collection of Nasir-ud-Din's *malfuzat*, see *Khayr-ul-Majalis*. For early *tazkiras*, *Siyar-ul-Auliya*, 246-57; *Siyar-ul-Arifin*, 126a-130b. Also see Nizami (1991b).
34. Aquil (2003a).
35. For the practice and defence of *sama* in Chishti circles, see Ernst and Lawrence (2002: 34-46).
36. For an early-fifteenth-century recorded version of the saint's remark (*dehli as tu dur ast*), see *Tarikh-i-Mubarakshahi*, 96-7.
37. The episode of bestowal of kingship to Muhammad Tughluq is recorded in a Chishti hagiography, *Qiwam-ul-Aqaid* (compiled *c.* 1350), 96.
38. Eaton (1978); Digby (1986); idem (1990); Alam (1996); Zilli (2003); Aquil (2003a).
39. Digby (1986); idem (1990); Aquil (2003a).
40. *Siyar-ul-Auliya*, 89-90.

41. *Siyar-ul-Arifin,* fols. 97b-99b.
42. *Siyar-ul-Auliya*, fol. 89.
43. *Tarikh-i-Firuzshahi*, fols. 153a-b.
44. Nizami (1991a: 110).
45. Nizam-ud-Din Auliya sent Wajih-ud-Din Yusuf with the army of Ala-ud-Din Khalji for the conquest of Chanderi, a strategic place on the route to the Deccan. Yusuf stayed at Chanderi after its conquest, *Siyar-ul-Auliya*, 296-7.
46. Nizam-ud-Din Auliya's leading disciples Amir Khusrau and Amir Hasan Sijzi participated in the campaigns. Khusrau's reports reflected the mood in the army.
47. Haqq (1975); Latif (1993); Eaton (1994).
48. Eaton (1978); Ernst (1992).
49. Several reports of the veneration of the Sufis, including the Chishtis, by Sultan Bahlul, the founder of the Lodi dynasty, are to be found in the sources, Aquil (2000: Ch. 5).
50. *Akhbar-ul-Akhyar*, 184b.
51. That is, the Hindu chief imagined that the Sufi was so powerful that he could even have his God in his lap. He was seemingly ignorant about the impossibility in Islam of Allah taking a physical form.
52. Ibid., 160b.
53. Ibid., 194a.
54. Aquil (1997-8).
55. See, for instance, Nizami (1955: 107). Also see Lawrence (1984).
56. Ernst (1992: 156-7); Eaton (1994: 113-19); Aquil (1997-8).
57. Nizami (1961: 177-80); Rizvi (1978: 215-26).
58. Rizvi (1993: 54-6); Mujeeb (1985: 297-8).
59. Mujeeb (1985: 22); Eaton (1994).
60. Aquil (2003c).
61. Quddusi (1961, 257-9); Digby (1965).
62. Digby (1975).
63. Quddusi (1961: 453-6); Digby (1975); Khan (1977).
64. For a discussion of different views on the Sufi attitude towards non-Muslims and more specifically the question of their role in conversion, see Aquil (1997-8).
65. *Akhbar-ul-Akhyar*, 171a.
66. Ibid., 243a.
67. The above reference is taken from the account of Muin-ud-Din's life in *Akhbar-ul-Akhyar*, translated in Ernst and Lawrence (2002: 152). Ernst and Lawrence have, however, ignored the value of this information. Indeed, they believe that the question of Sufis' relations with non-Muslims become important only from the colonial period and not before that.

68. *Akhbar-ul-Akhyar*, 46a.
69. Quddusi (1961, 234-42).
70. Digby (1975); Rizvi (1978).
71. Digby (1975).
72. Quddusi (1961: 196-8).
73. *Siyar-ul-Auliya*, 78-80.
74. Muhammad Ghausi Shattari, *Gulzar-i-Abrar*, 290-302.
75. Rizvi (1978: 335).
76. Mulla Abdul Qadir Badauni, *Muntakhab-ut-Tawarikh*, III, 5.
77. Ibid., III, 5-6.
78. Vaudeville (1993).
79. Halim (1957). Cf. Alam (1998).
80. Ahmad (1964: 241).
81. Numerous writings may be cited on these issues. 'Liberal' scholarship is represented by M. Habib, K.A. Nizami, S.A.A. Rizvi, and M. Mujeeb, among others. For a 'communal' Muslim position, see Qureshi (1985a); idem (1985b). For the 'Hindu' opinion, Lal (1992). For a more balanced approach, see Alam (1989).

REFERENCES

Abel, A., 1991a, 'Dar-al-harb', *Encyclopaedia of Islam* (New Edition), vol. 2, Leiden: Brill, 126.

———, 1991b, 'Dar-al-Islam', *Encyclopaedia of Islam* (New Edition), vol. 2, Leiden: Brill, 127-8.

Ahmad, Aziz, 1964, *Studies in Islamic Culture in the Indian Environment*, Oxford: Clarendon Press.

Akhbar-ul-Akhyar, n.d., Shaikh 'Abdul Haqq Muhaddis Dihlawi. Ms., IO Islamic 1450, OIOC, British Library, London.

Alam, Muzaffar, 1989, 'Competition and Coexistence: Indo-Muslim Interaction in Medieval North India', *Itinerario* 13 (1): 37-59.

———, 1996, 'Assimilation from a Distance: Confrontation and Sufi Accommodation in Awadh Society', in R. Champakalakshmi and S. Gopal, eds., *Tradition, Dissent and Ideology, Essays in Honour of Romila Thapar*, New Delhi: Oxford University Press, 164-91.

———, 1998, 'The Pursuit of Persian: Language in Mughal Politics', *Modern Asian Studies* 32(2): 317-49.

———, 2002, '*Shari'a* and Governance in the Indo-Muslim Context', in David Gilmartin and Bruce B. Lawrence, eds., *Beyond Turk and Hindu: Rethinking Religious Identities in Islamicate South Asia*, Delhi: India Research Press, 216-45.

Alam, Muzaffar and Sanjay Subrahmanyam, 1998, 'Introduction', in idem, eds., *The Mughal State, 1526-1750*, New Delhi: Oxford University Press.

Aquil, Raziuddin, 1995-96, 'Sufi Cults, Politics and Conversion: The Chishtis of the Sultanate Period', *Indian Historical Review* 22 (1-2): 190-7.

———, 1997-8, 'Conversion in Chishti Sufi Literature (13th-14th Centuries)', *Indian Historical Review* 24 (1-2): 70-94.

———, 2000, 'Aspects of Religion and Politics under the Afghans in North India (*c.* 1450-1550)', Ph.D. thesis, Jawaharlal Nehru University, New Delhi.

———, 2003a, 'Miracles, Authority and Benevolence: Stories of *Karamat* in Chishti Sufi Literature of the Delhi Sultanate', in Anup Taneja, ed., *Sufi Cults and the Evolution of Medieval Indian Culture*, New Delhi: ICHR and Northern Book Centre, 109-38.

———, 2003b, 'Reconsidering Sovereignty and Governance under the Afghans: North India in the Late Fifteenth and Early Sixteenth Centuries', *South Asia* 26 (1): 5-21.

———, 2003c, 'Episodes from the Life of Shaikh Farid-ud-Din Ganj-i-Shakar', *International Journal of Punjab Studies* 10 (1-2): 25-46.

Currie, P.M., 1989, *The Shrine and Cult of Muin-al-Din Chishti of Ajmer*, New Delhi: Oxford University Press.

Digby, Simon, 1965, 'Dreams and Reminiscences of Dattu Sarwani', *Indian Economic and Social History Review* 2 (1): 52-80 & 2 (2): 178-94.

———, 1975, 'Shaikh Abd al-Quddus Gangohi (A.D. 1456-1537): The Personality and Attitude of a Medieval Indian Sufi', *Medieval India: A Miscellany,* 3: 1-66.

———, 1983, 'Early Pilgrimages to the Graves of Muinuddin Sijzi and other Indian Chishti Shaikhs', in M. Israel and N.K. Wagle, eds., *Islamic Society and Culture: Essays in Honour of Aziz Ahmad*, New Delhi: Manohar, 95-100.

———, 1986, 'The Sufi Shaykh as a Source of Authority in Medieval India', *Purushartha,* 9: 55-77.

———, 1990, 'The Sufi Shaikh and the Sultan: A Conflict of Claims to Authority in Medieval India', *Iran,* 28: 71-81.

Eaton, Richard M., 1978, *Sufis of Bijapur, 1300-1700, Social Roles of Sufis in Medieval India*, Princeton: Princeton University Press.

———, 1994, *The Rise of Islam and the Bengal Frontier*, New Delhi: Oxford University Press.

———, 2002, 'Temple Desecration and Indo-Muslim States', in idem, *Essays on Islam and Indian History*, New Delhi: Oxford University Press.

———, 2003, 'The Political and Religious Authority of the Shrine of Baba Farid', in idem, ed., *India's Islamic Traditions, 711-1750*, New Delhi: Oxford University Press, 263-84.

Ernst, Carl W., 1992, *Eternal Garden: Mysticism, History and Politics at a South Asian Sufi Centre*, Albany: State University of New York Press.

Ernst, Carl W. and Bruce B. Lawrence, 2002, *Sufi Martyrs of Love: The*

Chishti Order in South Asia and Beyond, New York: Palgrave Macmillan.

Faruqi, Ihsanul Haq, 1963, *Sultan-ut-Tarikin*, Karachi: Dairah Muinul Maarif.

Fatawa-i-Jahandari, Ziya-ud-Din Barani, ed., 1972, Lahore: Afsar Salim Khan.

Fawa'id-ul-Fu'ad, conversations of Shaikh Nizam-ud-Din Auliya' compiled by Amir Hasan Sijzi, 1990, Persian text with an Urdu translation by Khwaja Hasan Sani Nizami, Delhi: Urdu Academy.

Gulzar-i-abrar, Muhammad Ghausi Shattari, AH 1395, Urdu translation by Fazal Ahmad and known as *Azkar-i-Abrar*, Lahore: Islamic Book Foundation.

Habib, Mohammad, 1974, *Politics and Society During the Early Medieval Period, Collected Works of Mohammad Habib*, vol. 1, ed. K.A Nizami, Delhi: Peoples Publishing House.

Habib, Mohammad and K.A. Nizami, eds., 1992, *A Comprehensive History of India*, vol. V, Part One, *The Delhi Sultanate* (first published 1970), Delhi: Peoples Publishing House.

Habibullah, A.B.M., 1945, *The Foundation of the Muslim Rule in India*. Lahore, 2nd edn., 1961, Allahabad: Central Book Depot.

Halim, Abdul, 1957, 'Growth and Development of Hindi Literature During the Sayyid-Lodi Period', *Journal of the Asiatic Society of Pakistan*, 2: 69-89.

Haqq, M. Enamul, 1975, *A History of Sufi-ism in Bengal*, Dacca: Asiatic Society of Bangladesh.

Hasan, Mohibbul, ed., 1968, *Historians of Medieval India*, Meerut: Meenakshi Prakashan.

Husain, Agha Mahdi, 1976, *Tughluq Dynasty*, Delhi: S. Chand.

Jackson, Peter, 1999, *The Delhi Sultanate: A Political and Military History*, Cambridge: Cambridge University Press.

Khayr-ul-majalis, conversations of Shaikh Nasir-ud-Din Chiragh-i-Dilli compiled by Hamid Qalandar, ed. K.A. Nizami, 1959, Aligarh: Aligarh Muslim University.

Khan, Iqtidar Alam, 1977, 'Shaikh Abdul Quddus Gangohi's Relation with Political Authorities: A Reappraisal', *Medieval India: A Miscellany*, 4: 73-90.

Khazimat-ul-sfiya, Maulwi Ghulam Sarwar, n.d., vol. I., Kanpur: Newal Kishore.

Lal, K.S., 1967, *History of the Khaljis*, Delhi (rev. edn.) 1980, Delhi: Munshiram Manoharlal.

———, 1992, *The Legacy of Muslim Rule in India*, Delhi: Voice of India.

Latif, Sk. Abdul, 1993, *The Muslim Mystic Movement in Bengal, 1301-1550*, Calcutta: K.P. Bagchi.

Lawrence, Bruce B., 1984, 'Early Indo-Muslim Saints and Conversion', in Y. Friedmann, ed., *Islam in Asia,* vol. I, *South Asia*, Jerusalem: Max Schloessinger Memorial Foundation.

Muntakhab-ut-Tawarikh, Mulla Abdul Qadir Badauni. 1864-9, ed., Ahmad Ali, Kabir al-Din Ahmad and W. Nassau Lees, 3 vols., Calcutta: Bibliotheca Indica.

Mujeeb, M., 1985, *Indian Muslims*, Delhi: Munshiram Manoharlal.

Mukhia, Harbans, 1976, *Historians and Historiography During the Reign of Akbar*, Delhi: Vikas Publications.

Munis-ul-Arwah, Jahan Ara Begam, 1991, in Qamar Jahan Begam, *Princess Jahan Ara Begam: Her Life and Works*, Karachi: S.M. Hamid Ali.

Nizami, K.A., 1955, *The Life and Times of Shaikh Fariduddin Ganj-i-Shakar*, Aligarh: Aligarh Muslim University.

———, 1961, *Some Aspects of Religion and Politics in India During the 13th Century*, Aligarh: Aligarh Muslim University.

———, 1991a, *The Life and Times of Shaikh Nizamuddin Auliya,* Delhi: Idarah-i-Adabiyat-i Delli.

———, 1991b, *The Life and Times of Shaikh Nasiruddin Chiragh,* Delhi: Idarah-i-Adabiyat-i Delli.

Perlin, Frank, 1985, 'State Formation Reconsidered', *Modern Asian Studies* 19 (3): 415-80.

Qiwam-ul-'Aqa'id, Muhammad Jamal Qiwam, Urdu trans. Nisar Ahmad Faruqui, Rampur: Idarah Nashar-o-Isha'at, 1994.

Quddusi, Aijazul Haq, 1961, *Shaykh Abdul Quddus aur un ki Ta'limat*, Karachi: All Pakistan Educational Conference.

Qureshi, I.H., 1985a, *Ulema in Politics*, Delhi: Renaissance Publication House.

———, 1985b, *The Muslim Community of the Indo-Pak Subcontinent, 610-1947*, Delhi: Renaissance Publication House.

Rizvi, S.A.A., 1978, *A History of Sufism in India,* vol. I, *Early Sufism and its History in India to 1600 A.D.*, Delhi: Munshiram Manoharlal.

———, 1993, *Muslim Revivalist Movements in Northern India in the Sixteenth and Seventeenth Centuries*, Delhi: Munshiram Manoharlal.

Rushdnama or *Alakhbani*, Shaikh Abdul Quddus Gangohi, 1971 Introduction, translation into Hindi, and annotation by Saiyid Athar Abbas Rizvi and Shailesh Zaidi, Aligarh: Bharat Prakashan.

Siyar-ul-'Arifin, Shaikh Jamali, n.d., Ms., IO Islamic 1313, OIOC, British Library, London.

Siyar-ul-Auliya, Amir Khwurd, 1978, Islamabad: Markaz Tahqiqat-i-Farsi Iran wa Pakistan.

Subrahmanyam, Sanjay, 1992, 'The Mughal State: Structure or Process? Reflections on Recent Western Historiography', *Indian Economic and Social History Review* 24 (3): 291-321.

———, 2001, *Penumbral Visions: Making Polities in Early Modern South India*, New Delhi: Oxford University Press.

Tabaqat-i-Nasiri, Minhaj-us-Siraj, 1963-4, ed. Abdul Hayy Habibi, vol. 1, Kabul: Historical Society of Afghanistan.

Tarikh-i-Firuzshahi, Ziya-ud-Din Barani, n.d., British Museum Ms. 6376, OIOC, British Library, London.

Tarikh-i-Mubarakshahi, Yahya bin Ahmad bin Abdullah Sarhindi, 1931, ed. M. Hidayat Hosain, Calcutta: Asiatic Society.

Vaudeville, Charlotte, 1993, *A Weaver Named Kabir—Selected Verses with a Detailed Biographical and Historical Introduction,* New Delhi: Oxford University Press.

Zelliot, Eleanor, 2003, 'A Medieval Encounter Between Hindu and Muslim: Eknath's Drama-Poem *Hindu-Turk Samvad*', in Richard M. Eaton, ed. *India's Islamic Traditions, 711-1750*, New Delhi: Oxford University Press, 64-82.

Zilli, I.A., 2003, 'Early Chishtis and the State', in Anup Taneja, ed., *Sufi Cults and the Evolution of Medieval Indian Culture*, New Delhi: ICHR and Northern Book Centre, 54-108.

3

Conflict and Coexistence: Jews in Europe under Muslim and Christian Rule[1]

MICHAEL BRENNER

PREMODERN ROOTS: JEWS IN CHRISTIAN AND MUSLIM SOCIETIES

The history of Jews in Europe under cross and crescent is a history of enormous success and achievements, and at the same time a history of unparalleled tragedy and suffering. It is this seemingly contradictory picture, which makes this history so fascinating and of interest much out of proportion to the actual size of the small Jewish minority. I hope to view Jewish history in the Middle Ages and the early modern period not exclusively through the glasses of our own time. The Holocaust and the State of Israel have so much dominated the perspective through which we view Jewish history that we sometimes lose sight of the diversity of its experience in previous centuries. But I should also say that neither the Holocaust nor Israel can be fully understood without a basic knowledge of the history of the Jews in the preceding centuries.

Jews have been a tiny minority over many centuries, and today they constitute much less than 1 per cent of the world population and the European population, which once used to be their centre. Yet, all over the world, Jews and their state loom large in the media, in publications and in a variety of stereotypes from old Europe to the Far East. The reason cannot only be sought in the dramatic events of our times: the Holocaust is seen today as the worst instance of genocide in human history, while the establishment of the State of Israel after 2000 years of statelessness also lacked a precedent in the history of nations. Even before that, however, the Jews attracted disproportionate attention for such a small group. The reason for this is quite simple.

The two religions that were to become the dominant religions in the world—Christianity and Islam—were each connected in their own way with Jews and Judaism. Both in the New Testament and the Koran, Jews figure prominently, though not always favourably. Thus, both Christian and Muslim attitudes towards Jews and Judaism relate to the genesis of those two religions and to their foundational texts. Both exhibit an ambivalent relationship towards the Jews: on the one hand, they are seen as precursors whose ancient traditions and texts are well respected, on the other hand they are accused of being blind or stubborn since they were not ready to convert to the new religions, be it Christianity or Islam.

Despite this basic common factor, there are also significant differences. Christianity has a much closer relationship with Judaism than does Islam. After all, not only was the founding figure of Christianity a Jew, in Christian tradition, Jews were also held responsible for his death. It is this closeness which proved extremely problematic throughout the centuries. The New Testament and other early Christian writings were nothing but documents of a fight among brothers: Jews who rejected Jesus as the Messiah *vs.* Jews who accepted Jesus as Christ. Hence the harshness of language, which for later generations was almost incomprehensible without its original context. At the same time, this closeness also helped Jews to survive: it was always the official position of the Church, especially the Popes, that Jews should be humiliated as those who are blind to their own scripture, but they should not be expelled or killed. After all, they were the people of Christ. There was, however, another logic to the Christian interest of their survival: only if they were around could they be humiliated in order to demonstrate which is the victorious and which the defeated faith. Thus, Rome, the Pope's city, was the only European city in which Jews lived without interruption for 2000 years—it was however also the city in which Jews until the late nineteenth century lived under extremely restricted and humiliating conditions.

This situation can be symbolized by two statues still to be seen at many medieval cathedrals. One of them, synagoga, signifies the Jews: it is a woman with blindfolded eyes and a broken stick in her hand. It is juxtaposed by ecclesia, the church, in form of a woman looking triumphantly with the crown on her head and the sceptre in her hand. Christians were well aware, of course, that they used at least partly the same Holy Writings as the Jews, and that those were indeed originally Jewish writings. The blindfolded woman, however, symbolized the fact that the Jews were unable to interpret their own writings in the correct way. They were blind as long as they remained in their old faith, but—according to the traditional Christian belief—they could be saved by converting to Christianity.

Thus was the basic position of Christendom towards the Jews. The picture in Islam is somewhat different: the closeness was there, but not as much as in Christianity. After all, Muhammad was no Jew. However, as we know, there were Jewish tribes in his region, from whom he probably took over some traditions and beliefs, including some parts of the Hebrew Bible integrated into the Koran. At the same time, he hoped—like the early Christians before him and Martin Luther after him—to convert the Jews. The Koran is full of this hope, which was in the end disappointed. But in general, Islam treated Jews not much different than other *dhimmi*, other followers of religions of the book, especially the Christian minority under Muslim rule. They had to wear special badges or clothes, they were not allowed to ride horses, build new synagogues, etc.

Islam also adopted part of the Hebrew Bible for its own tradition, and the accusation was slightly different from the Christian-Jewish one: the main line of accusation here runs that Jews distorted the original text of the Holy Scripture, not that they misinterpreted it. Thus the original text contained a different message, especially when it comes to the patriarchal stories of Isaac versus Ishmael.

Let me summarize the general background then: both Christians and Muslims over many centuries could draw on their Holy Scriptures and on many traditions built upon them in their attitude towards the Jews. Contrary to common belief, the closeness of their sources, traditions, and even religious practices was not a cause of better relations but rather of tensions. This closeness may have been the reason why the Jews as a tiny minority survived two millennia, but it was also the reason why they suffered discrimination and persecution, and expulsion to a larger degree than probably any other minority.

The few Jews who lived in societies with faiths other than Christianity or Islam, such as Indian or Chinese Jews, were never confronted with the same attitude of closeness resulting in theological tension. In India and China they did not constitute a very special minority, loaded with layers of theological meanings and of crucial importance to the majority's own religious traditions, but simply another minority. Although there were never large Jewish communities in those societies, their lives may have been somewhat easier.

This brief theological introduction is necessary to understand if we look at the fate of Jews in Europe under Christian and Muslim rule. Today, many Europeans tend to forget that Islam was a constitutive element in European culture for many centuries: in the west (Spain and Portugal), in the south (Sicily) and in the east (the Balkans). Jews lived prominently in all those areas, and in general it may be right to say that they fared better under Muslim than under Christian rule. I emphasize 'in general', because there were exceptions. There has been a myth of a 'Golden Age' of Jews in Muslim Spain—the co-existence in the tenth and eleventh centuries, which witnessed some exceptional Jewish statesmen, poets, and philosophers. Yes, it is true, there were Jewish ministers of high standing, such as Shmuel Ha-Naggid in Granada and there were poets who wrote in Hebrew and Arabic, such as Jehuda Halevi of Toledo, and there was a philosopher of high standing among all religions, like Maimonides of Cordoba. They all could not have been nearly as creative as they were had there not been a fertile soil.

But let us not forget: even in this Golden Age, our present idea of tolerance did not exist, and the life of everyone and especially someone who belonged to a minority had to be checked and rechecked every generation anew. And thus the son of the famous minister Shmuel Hanagid, Joseph, was murdered in the riots if 1066 in Granada; the poet and philosopher Jehuda Halevi left Spain to settle in the Holy Land; and even Maimonides was not safe in his part of Muslim Spain and had to flee to Egypt where he lived as the Caliph's physician. This last example shows also what should be very clear: it is a crude generalization to speak about Muslim rule *vs.* Christian rule, just as it makes no sense to confront Islam *vs.* Christianity. Maimonides lived in Muslim Spain under the rule of radical Berber tribes from north Africa who did not tolerate Jews (and many fellow Muslims!) and he fled to a moderate Muslim ruler in Egypt. Some Jews fled from the Christian Reconquista to the Muslim parts of Spain, while others, at different times, fled from more violent Muslim rulers to Christian Spain.

In other words, religious theory was one thing, its actual implementation by the respective rulers another. We saw before that, under Islam, Jews were not allowed to ride horses and to build new synagogues. But we have detailed descriptions of the installation of the new Exilarch, the Rosh Galutha or head of the Jewish community in the diaspora: he rode a white horse through the city of Baghdad and was officially greeted by all Muslim dignitaries. There can be no doubt that hundreds, if not thousands, of synagogues were built in Muslim countries despite the prohibition to do so. The same flexibility of implementation or not implementation of religious rules applies to the Christian world. The Popes represented the official position of the church by never expelling and never killing the Jews in their own territory. But many rulers who saw themselves as pious Christian rulers and used religious language did expel and kill Jews. Moreover, the masses of crusaders used the cross as a pretext for the elimination of Jewish communities flourishing on the Rhine river, while at the same time some bishops granted the Jews shelter (not without being financially compensated) from their own coreligionists. These movements began in the late tenth century.

England was the first country to expel the Jews already in 1290—France was soon to follow, and Spain and Portugal only concluded this development in the late fifteenth century. There were other Christian states who were eager to take the Jewish refugees in—Poland first and foremost among them. Poland was not less Christian than France or Spain, but the economic situation was different. By the Middle Ages, Jews had become an economically recognizable minority. They could not be the peasantry that most of the Christians were, because they could not own land; nor could they be artisans, because only Christians were allowed into the guilds. On the other hand, Christians could not lend money to other Christians for interest, a task which became more and more important in a more diversified society. Thus, a high proportion of Jews were merchants and moneylenders, and those societies which had more need for them found their religious justification to tolerate Jews, while countries in which Christians were taking to commerce and moneylending, and which therefore had less need for Jews, found religious justifications to expel them.

In this respect, the radical Berber tribes of the Almohades and Almoravides, who ruled Spain for parts of twelfth century, were rather exceptional among Muslim rulers. Usually, Jews were allowed to live in Muslim societies, though as a lower class. Thus, it is only understandable that the state to which most of the many Jewish refugees who left Spain and Portugal from the end of the fifteenth century migrated was the Ottoman Empire. There, they could live under much more favourable conditions than in Christian Europe. The largest Jewish communities in the seventeenth and eighteenth centuries were not in Prague, Frankfurt, and Warsaw, but in Istanbul and Salonika. As we know, a few of those refugees also found their way to India.

BETWEEN RELIGION AND POLITICS: CONFLICTING JEWISH IDENTITIES IN THE MODERN AGE

The new situation with which Jews in modern Europe were confronted was first expressed clearly by the Count of Clermont-Tonnerre in the French National Assembly of 1789: one should grant everything to the Jews as individuals, but nothing as a nation. In practical terms this meant that Jews as the only non-Christian minority in most European countries had to redefine their identity: in order to become French or German citizens of the Jewish faith they had to define Judaism only as a religion and get rid of all its ethnic components. They had to dress like all others, write the same letters, speak the same language, practice the same professions, and live in a non-Jewish environment. The only distinction allowed was that they would attend a synagogue and be buried in a Jewish cemetery.

The problem with such a definition came from both sides. Internally, in an age of increasing secularization, the difference was, as one nineteenth-century Jew put it, no longer that 'we attend the synagogue on Saturdays and our neighbours the church on Sunday, but that we don't go to synagogue and they don't go to church'. What then remains distinctive for a small minority like the Jews? While a few Jews went so far as to convert to Christianity, the broad majority did not want to give up a heritage that reached back 3,000 years or more. Thus they established a secular Jewish culture but at the same time became proud German or French citizens.

The external danger was the new nature of Jew-hatred, for which the term anti-semitism was created in 1879. Now it was no longer religion but race that counted. In former times, one could convert and thus avoid persecution, but now there was no way to escape. We see the consequence in Hitler's racial laws which required that even people whose forefathers had already converted to Christianity be now sent to concentration camps.

This was the situation in western Europe during the nineteenth century, but in eastern Europe, where the vast majority of European Jews lived, they never had the chance to be emancipated. They remained an ethnic and religious group, speaking their own language and being clearly distinguishable. It is thus not surprising that Theodor Herzl, the Western Jew and founder of political Zionism, found more supporters for his cause in eastern Europe. Only when the Jews of all Europe were persecuted by Hitler did Palestine become their last and only hope—a state of their own, like any other nation.

When we talk about the politicization of modern Jewry, we can start again with the Christian and Muslim societies in which Jews lived. Politicization began in 1860, when the Alliance Israélite Universelle was founded to support Jews in crisis throughout the world in reaction to the so-called Damascus affair of 1840 and the Mortara incident of 1858. The Damascus affair centred on an accusation imported from Christian Europe into the Muslim Orient, which contended that Jews in Damascus had killed a Christian child and used its blood for ritual purposes. This medieval legend, long consigned to oblivion, now induced severe riots against Syrian Jews, and was initially taken at face value even by French diplomats. Respected British and French Jews, notably Sir Moses Montefiore and the French Minister of Justice Adolphe Crémieux, hastened to point out the folly of accusations of this sort and to provide help to Jews who were threatened. The Mortara incident involved the forced baptism of a Jewish boy in Italy; this baptism was subsequently approved by the Catholic Church. The boy was seized from his family by papal officers and raised as a Catholic, never to be returned to his parents. The Alliance was formed to provide assistance in similar cases and ultimately also served to raise the educational level of the Middle Eastern and Northern African Jews by building up a network of French-speaking schools; it also provided the first modern international context for Jewish political activity.

The last decade of the nineteenth century ushered in a series of additional organizations dedicated first and foremost to the struggle against anti-Semitism. These organizations also had to explore the future outlook for Jews in a non-Jewish environment. The most notable example was the German Centralverein deutscher Staatsbürger juedischen Glaubens, founded in Berlin in 1893, which soon became the largest German-Jewish organization. The message was apparent from its name: the German Jews, who had acquired citizenship with equal rights when Germany was united in 1871, differed from their fellow Christian citizens only in the forms of their religious expression, which included visits to synagogues, cemetery statutes, religious instruction, and rabbinical training. We may wonder why they would found their own association if these areas were already handled by the religious administration. The answer can be sought in a new type of political anti-Semitism that was flaring up around 1893. The Centralverein was initially conceived as a protective association against anti-Semitism, which experienced a hitherto unprecedented wave of popularity in 1893 when sixteen resolutely anti-Semitic delegates were elected into the Reichstag. Anti-Semitism had found its way into the 1892 conservative platform of the conservative German party (the so-called Tivoli Programme) and into newly-formed mass organizations. It was therefore inevitable that a group that regarded itself as a religious community, in response to how it was viewed by others, would found an organization that was actually political. An increasing focus on questions of Jewish identity, rather than an exclusive emphasis on defence against enemies from without, was crucial to the internal dynamics of an organization of this kind over the course of the following decades.

In eastern Europe, secularization had resulted in the formation of a steadily growing intellectual class that was also seeking a new definition of its Jewish identity. This group was united by a common language and culture, as well as by rejection of Jews by the surrounding society. The Jewish Enlightenment movement (*haskala*) revived the Hebrew language as a new medium for secular Yiddish culture in eastern Europe; its first forums were magazines, publishing houses, and intellectual circles.

In the course of politicizing Jewish life, the battle over language now took on a political dimension. The 'Hebraists' were in accord with the assimilated Jews in at least one respect. Both condemned 'jargon', which is how they referred to the Yiddish that was spoken by the eastern European Jewish masses. They advocated the use of 'pure' languages, as had Moses Mendelssohn at the beginning of the Enlightenment movement.

A countermovement arose to promote the Yiddish language as the cultural language of the Jews. The representatives of this movement labelled the advocates of Hebrew as the vanguard of a small elite. Like the Hebraists, the 'Yiddishists' held their own language conferences, which were also political events. The Hebraists were typically in the Zionist camp, while the Yiddishists generally opted for more autonomy within the countries in which they lived.

Along these lines, the historian Simon Dubnov founded an

autonomy movement that advocated recognizing Jews as a national minority with commensurate legal protection. For the classic representatives of a national solution for minorities, such as the Austrian Social Democrats, the Jews were not a national minority because they lacked their own territory, but for Dubnov, this was all the stronger justification for a solution involving autonomy. The Jews, he argued, embodied a higher level of nationalism, since they, as the oldest nation in existence, had already transcended the early stage of territorial nationalism and had preserved their nationality for centuries in the Diaspora. Dubnov's *folkspartey* was one of the smaller Jewish political groups, but its tenets enjoyed success after First World War in the newly-founded states of east-central Europe. A Jewish minority status was legally instituted in Poland and the Baltic states.

The so-called Bundists, who considered socialism the solution to the Jewish question, carried greater weight within the array of Jewish parties. The Bund was founded in 1897 in Riga, even before Russian social democracy, and is therefore the oldest socialist party in Russia. For the Bundists, the Yiddish language was initially just a vehicle to communicate socialist ideas. However, they soon called for the recognition of the Yiddish language and culture as the legitimate Jewish form of expression, in the same way that Poles spoke Polish, and Ukrainians Ukrainian. Inevitably this demand fell on deaf ears in the socialist movement, which held that only nations with their own territory ought to be granted a national minority status.

One might see much of nineteenth-century Jewish history in terms of Emancipationist and post-Emncipationist societies. West European Jews tried very hard to be accepted as German, French or British of the Jewish faith, but were very often—not always—rejected. When it became clear that the legal Emancipation did not bring full social equality and integration into European societies and when a new, much more violent racial anti-Semitism developed later in the century, Zionism was born, not out of idealism, but out of desperation.

Theodor Herzl, the Viennese who convened the First Zionist Congress, serves as an example *par excellence* of a Jew who tried hard to integrate but would not be accepted. He wanted to be an Austrian, but the Austrians would not let him be one of theirs. The only solution, in his view, was therefore to found a separate Jewish society.

Deep in his heart, Herzl kept hoping to belong, right up to the point of his Zionist awakening. His diary opens with a look back to 1893, when he sought to 'solve the Jewish Question, at least in Austria, with the help of the Catholic Church' In a ceremony he pictured down to every last detail, the younger generation of Viennese Jews would be led into St. Stephen's Cathedral and be baptized: 'The conversion was to take place in broad daylight, Sundays at noon, in St. Stephen's Cathedral, with festive processions and amidst the pealing of bells. Not in shame, as individuals have converted up to now, but with proud gestures.' He soon abandoned any plans to convert, realizing that a change of religion would do little to help since anti-Semitism was being defined racially. Jews might become Christians, but not Germans or Austrians.

In order to assess Herzl's awakening from his dream of assimilation, we must fathom his profound pain at the recognition of its futility, as expressed in his pamphlet, *The Jewish State*:

> Everywhere we have sincerely endeavoured to merge with the national communities surrounding us and to preserve only the faith of our fathers. We are not permitted to do so. In vain are we loyal patriots, in some places even extravagantly so; in vain do we make the same sacrifices of life and property as our fellow citizens; in vain do we strive to enhance the fame of our native countries in the arts and sciences, or their wealth through trade and commerce. In our native lands where, after all, we too have lived for centuries, we are decried as aliens. . . . If only we were left in peace. . . . But I think we shall not be left in peace.

As a consequence, Herzl reversed the 'contract of emancipation', according to which Jews had to be defined only as a religion, while abandoning any (Jewish) national components of their identity. To the distress of most Western Jews he claimed, 'We are a people', and thus laid the foundation of a yet another modern Jewish identity, in which religion played at most a secondary role, but ethnicity was the central element. When there were Orthodox and Reform Jews, believers and agnostics, the Zionists claimed, religion was no longer a uniting element. But all were united by two elements: their common descent and history, as well as external pressure from anti-Semitism.

It is no coincidence that Zionism had its political breakthrough during the First World War, a decade after Herzl's death, when the British Foreign Minister Lord Balfour promised the Jews a homeland in Palestine. The First World War was, again and perhaps more than before, a decisive hour of change for Jewish identities and affiliations. It brought forward a different kind of nationalism in Europe, in which

Jews had no longer any role to play. The vast majority of European Jewry had so far lived in multi-ethnic states, namely the Czarist Empire, the Habsburg Empire, and the Ottoman Empire. With the fall of those empires, with the construction or reconstruction of nation states or at least states which pretended to be nation-states, such as Poland, the Baltic states, Czechoslovakia, Yugoslavia and Turkey, the role of the Jews was much less clearly defined than before—and much more threatened. At the same time, the new nationalism in Germany, Italy, Hungary and other existing nation-states of central Europe questioned their role in those societies. Only thus can the growing recognition of Zionism both diplomatically and as a political movement be explained.

A new concept, that of ethnic diversity within the modern nation state, was considered unavoidable already on the eve of First World War, as expressed by the British-Jewish diplomat Lucien Wolf in a letter to the British Foreign Office following the Balkan wars and the dispute over the role of Jews in Salonika. Wolf concluded that 'in the new conditions of mixed races and creeds which confront those states' Jews in the Balkans needed guarantees not only as a religious minority, but as an ethnic minority as well. Jews had to redefine themselves in an era characterized by nation states where ethnic majorities and minorities played an ever larger role, as formulated most clearly a few years later during the Paris peace treaties for East Central Europe.

EPILOGUE: INTO THE TWENTY-FIRST CENTURY

The dramatic events of the middle of the twentieth century profoundly transformed Jewish society. During the Holocaust and its aftermath, the Jewish population in Europe was reduced from ten million in the 1930s to just above two millions at the end of the century, with most of them in France, Britain, and the former Soviet Union. Today, the problem with which Jews were confronted from the eighteenth century onwards is a problem of all minorities in a much changed Europe. But there is one other big difference: they are just one among many more minorities in a multi-cultural Europe, and Europe sees itself increasingly as a union of nations. In this changing world, it is interesting to see how much identity one can show openly today. The Muslim headscarf, as well as the Jewish skullcap now serve as symbols of expressing a non-Christian identity in Europe. Are Turks in Germany, Algerians in France, or Indians in Britain bound to a situation similar to that of Jews in the Age of Emancipation? Are they to reduce their identity to attending religious services, to cooking recipes and maybe a darker skin colour? Or does Europe learn from the utter failure of Emancipation and become a more open and colourful society, a concept which the traditional immigrant nation, the United States, has adopted?

It is in the United States of America that the largest centre of Jewish life has been established after the Holocaust. Unlike European states, north America knew no history of restriction or discrimination against its Jewish minorities. In the society of immigrants, Jews were just one among many newcomers and enjoyed a place in society very different from the 'old world'. The danger of disappearance in such a society is different: successful integration may lead to complete assimilation. As demographic studies demonstrate, the number of Jews in non-traditional societies, relatively free of anti-Semitism, decreases steadily. Will American Jewry ultimately share the fate of Chinese Jews who have disappeared through assimilation?

At the same time, the transformation of Jewish societies also affected the Muslim world. The heart of the Muslim world experienced the establishment of a Jewish state—a development that could not take place without major conflicts. One direct consequence was the dramatic worsening of the situation of Jews in the surrounding Muslim states. By the mid-1950s most Jews had left, often by force, the countries that had been home to them for centuries, if not for millennia, from Algeria to Iraq, from Egypt to Yemen. The rich history of Jews in the Muslim world had come to a close by the end of the twentieth century, with small remnants remaining mainly in Morocco, Turkey, and Iran. With the continuity of the Middle East conflict and the radicalization of Islam among significant parts of the population, the image of the Jews in those societies may be worse today than it has ever been before. Traditional European and Christian anti-Jewish stereotypes, which are no longer to be found in the West, such as the myth of the Elders of Zion, are increasingly popular between Cairo and Kuala Lumpur. For the first time in history, Muslims have been under the jurisdiction of a Jewish state. While this episode started with some hopes for Israeli Arab citizens, the record especially after the 1967 war and the occupation of territories has been increasingly worrisome.

As has been shown, there have been periods in history when

Jewish-Muslim, just as Jewish-Christian, relations have been better and other periods where they have been worse. It is clear that without a solution to the Israeli-Palestinian conflict no improvement is imaginable. Only if the Muslim world is truly prepared to recognize the right of the Jews to their state and if Israel is prepared to concede the territories under its occupation for a sovereign Palestinian state, the complex and often-strained relations between Jews and Muslims have a chance for healing. It is clear that in the twenty-first century, religious quarrel is intimately tied to political conflict in the Middle East, just as in Northern Ireland or Kashmir. Unfortunately, the intimate relationship between the respective religious communities does not necessarily ease the political conflict. However, once the political conflict is resolved, the common ground of cultural and religious heritage may well constitute the fertile soil for a new dialogue, building on a long history of conflict but also coexistence.

NOTE

1. This paper is of a rather general nature and cannot be more than an introduction into a much more complex set of relations. It is supposed to lend a comparative perspective to the more specific contributions to this volume. Thus, instead of specific notes, I chose to provide a few suggestions for further readings on the various aspects of this paper. On the relationship between Jews and Muslims, the still most useful introduction is provided by Bernard Lewis, *Jews of Islam* (Princeton: Princeton University Press, 1984). There are also two source readers with long introductions on the topic by Norman A. Stillman: *The Jews of Arab Lands* (Philadelphia: The Jewish Publication Society, 1979) and *The Jews of Arab Lands in Modern Times* (Philadelphia: The Jewish Publication Society, 1991). As for the relationship of Jews in the medieval world between Christians and Muslims, see Mark R. Cohen, *Under Crescent and Cross: The Jews in the Middle Ages* (Princeton: Princeton University Press, 1994). The number of publications on Jews in the age of Emancipation is extremely vast. One suggestion for a comparative reading is: *Paths of Emancipation: Jews, States, and Citizenship*, ed. Pierre Birnbaum and Ira Kaznelson (Princeton: Princeton University Press, 1995). My section on Zionism is based on my book, *Zionism: A Brief History* (Princeton: Markus Wiener, 2003).

[illegible]

[illegible]

[illegible]

CURRENTS IN ISLAM

Our volume concerns religious identities, and their dynamic over the past couple of centuries. Protagonists of several religious identities in India, especially Muslim and Hindu, have felt impelled to assert publicly their own identity's exalted stature: campaigns to intensify interactions between co-believers, and claims to privileged public recognition. This section has four studies on such currents among Muslims; the next one, three around Hindutva. The opening paper in this section, however, tracks a counter-current.

Mushirul Hasan writes of a largely neglected group in Delhi, a group that embodied what he calls the spirit of Delhi Renaissance: historian Zakaullah and novelist Nazir Ahmad, but also educationist Sayed Ahmad Khan, poet Ghalib, and writer Hali. Generous, neighbourly relations of mutual care and understanding with non-Muslim neighbours were embodied in Zakaullah's everyday living and Nazir Ahmad's writings. They searched for arrangements that would 'reaffirm Islam's social values and cultural ideals in a world in which science and technology progressed'. While the range of their concerns included social reform, especially concerning the lifespace of Muslim women, even the more liberal leaders of Muslim thought wavered over their unequivocal emancipation. This hesitation converged with the colonial courts' reluctance to support a women's share in familial property, which suited the *ulama*. By the third and fourth decades of twentieth century, the orthodoxy's restrictive vision had edged out the more open, vitally nourishing, aspirations of the kind that had informed the men in Hasan's cluster.

The orthodoxy's reach was evident again in relation to a somewhat different late nineteenth-century impulse. An anxious activism had marked the Islamic theological response to Akbar's innovations; and Jan-Peter Hartung sketches its complex, multiple channels, whose markers have included Waliullah and the *shariat*-centred Deoband *madrasa*. Other winds were blowing too, however, including the attempt at Aligarh to absorb Western 'reason', and the Barelwi veneration of saints and their graves; and there was much bickering between the numerous rivals and fragmenting of Muslim communities. The 1890s then saw a move to foster an Islamic ecumene, by reforming the educational system through a new religious seminary, the Nadwat al-ulama—which would draw in all shades of Islamic thought, including the Shias, and open out to Western learning too. Hartung gives us a blow-by-blow account of the career of the projected Nadwa where, over a period of some two decades, the Deobandi *ulama* were able to peel nearly every alternate orientation away, turning the institution into a citadel of Deobandi thought—so much so that it has been among the ideological nurseries for the Tablighi Jamaat—which engages several later papers.

Yoginder Sikand's recent study marked a watershed for the public understanding of the history and functioning of the Tablighi Jamaat (TJ). We have three papers hereto take us further, Zainuddin, Chakrabarti, and Mayaram offering studies from Orissa, Gujarat, and two areas of Rajasthan respectively. In an insider's account, Syed Zainuddin shows us the TJ's benign face. Its ideology places 'the responsibility of calling people to Allah' on lay Muslims, individually and collectively, equipping them with a minimalist theology. Given its simple, otherworldly agenda, its formal organisation is minimalist too, relying on ample face-to-face consultations, and dispensing with hierarchies and written records. The heart of the movement lies in a small group, the *jamaat*, walking about in a locality, and calling all Muslims to the correct Islamic ritual and piety, acting out a model of egalitarian, purposive, mutual caring—and urging others to similar activism. As the TJ has spread globally, its simple flexibility has enabled it to continue to learn from experience and to adapt to circumstances while holding fast to its basic tenets.

Like Zainuddin, Anindita Chakrabarti too gives us a poignant insider's understanding of the TJ, summoning fellow Muslims to a more earnest piety; and attributing their plight in contemporary Gujarat to their own failure to follow the true path of the Prophet. The TJ has spread in Gujarat rapidly over the past decade, in the face of exposure of Muslims to violence, and their consequent search for solidarity. For all their stress on changing the self as the route to changing the world, there is also the resolute public marking of their identity, as in dress. 'Tableeghis' priority is to lead an exemplary life as Muslims, not as citizens. The exclusivity here is not merely in relation to non-Muslims; it reaches into schismatic conflict with other Muslim groups such as Barelwis and the Jamaat-i Islami. Taking difference and mediation as conditions of democratic life, Chakrabarti's central question is, how are the public ideologies of secularism, democracy, and pluralism going to accommodate groups which are avowedly exclusivist even though their primary concerns are otherworldly, and their ideology inculcates gentleness and non-violence to the point that Zainuddin calls Gandhian? (A later, less indulgent, paper by Shail Mayaram gives the competitive activities of the TJ and some Hindu groups a sharper look.)

4

Living Plurally: A Nineteenth-Century Delhi Intelligentsia

MUSHIRUL HASAN

> No one can fathom the mystery of another person.
> Each individual in the world is like an undeciphered manuscript.[1]

> Seldom is one allowed to see a pageant of history whirl past, and partake in it too. Ever since becoming the capital in the early thirteenth century, imbibing knowledge and ideas and imparting cultures, becoming homogeneous and cosmopolitan in spite of the origins and ethnicity of its rulers and inhabitants, [Delhi] had remained the embodiment of a whole country, free of the creedal ghosts and apparitions that haunt some of modern India's critics and bibliographers chased by the dead souls of biased historians of yesterday.[2]

Long ago, the British Orientalist H.A.R. Gibb (1895-1971) discussed 'the atomism, the discreteness, and the intensity of the Arab imagination, its resistance to synthetic constructions and, above all, its aversion to rationalism'.[3] His conception of the 'Arab imagination' is untenable, for the reformist and traditionalist strands are so mingled that any period in history must be considered and judged as a whole. This is best illustrated by the expression of deep-seated convictions by sections of the Muslim intelligentsia in nineteenth-century Delhi. Even though 1857 left indelible scars and ruins and the best men were seized with despair, the second half of the nineteenth century appears to be fairly creative in the evolution, articulation, and dissemination of 'modernist' thinking. While the cramped sphere in which its proponents moved stifled intellectual activism, the historian must recognize that it was due to them, and to their impressive scholarly output, that upper India's Muslim communities, notably in Punjab and UP, were held together.

The noteworthy point is that there was amongst them, with the notable exception of Hali and a few more writers, no quest for a lost or submerged past, or for images and exemplars that would serve as prototypes and models for social and cultural innovation. Whether it is the poet Ghalib or the historian Zakaullah, there is no attempt to establish the Mughal glory of the past to evoke in Muslims a parochial consciousness. Instead, the modernists explained the reasons for Europe's strength in order to demonstrate that Muslims could adopt European concepts and methods without being untrue to their faith. They stubbornly maintained, while exalting the place of reason and freedom in Islam, that true Islam teaches family virtues, the application of reason, and true equality. They argued that it was important to restore the rights, not of an outward and fossilized orthodoxy, but of the inward reason of Islam, and to reaffirm Islam's social values and cultural ideals in a world in which science and technology progressed. This could be done in such a way as to build a stable society endowed with a vigorous social order capable of playing an active and constructive role.

The breadth of the modernists' appeal lay in their ability to reflect the aspirations of their time, as much as of their own people and to speak in their own terms, both to Urdu readers in their thousands and to educated elites of the cities. Let us consider for a moment the kind of intellectual temper and inclinations that were widely diffused through the vast corpus of Urdu literature that Delhi alone produced.

There was no consensus on defining modernism, a term used by Muslim thinkers such as Muhammad Abduh and Western scholars like C.C. Adams and Gibb, or on delineating sharply the contours of a 'modern' way of life. Part of the problem lies in the philosophical predilections of those who regard themselves as *islahi* or modernists, their difficulty in seeing their own time in historical perspective, and the complexity of disentangling reform issues from the community's political entanglements and preferences. Under the circumstances, our protagonists' point of view, even when they rallied ordinary citizens to the banner of civic engagement to promote the public good, suffers from ambiguities. This is the burden of Sayed Ahmad's arguments;[4] in fact, there are certain respects in which his own stance, a hybrid of liberalism and reform, is avowedly elitist, authoritarian and indifferent to even friendly censure. Yet he and his colleagues, though maligned as apostates or unbelievers by some, read the signs of the times, and used their sound critical judgement with a nice historical sense. They moved with the times, uncontrolled by theology, attacked the mumbo-jumbo of Muslim theologians, nurtured a moral and transcendental vision of Islam, and responded to the conditions of modern life with a strong universalistic component in defining the Indian Muslim.

I shall not enlarge upon this question, as I have dealt with it elsewhere in the context of Awadh's qasbas.[5]

In another work[6] I have discussed certain prominent figures whose achievement differed so widely. They range from people like Sir Sayyid, who moved heaven and earth to convince his community of the importance of Western education; to historians like Zakaullah; to novelists like Nazir Ahmad; to writers like Hali; and to poets like Ghalib. While none of them achieved quite the recognition or gained quite the lustre that surrounded their counterparts in other regions, their scholarly output was indeed impressive, and of some originality. Without being reformers of the type who go to the stake for their convictions, they each significantly affected the thoughts, feelings, and actions of many in north India. In fact, even though historians have shown Sayyid Ahmad, Ghalib, Zakaullah, Nazir and Hali a condescension they do not deserve, they stand as principled and conscientious individuals with the promise and perils of a new colonial modernity.

Broadly speaking, each of them was unique in his background, thinking, and aims. In the final reckoning, though, the spirit of Delhi's renaissance was present in each of them. When placed side by side, they appear to be in tune with the newer tendencies, not out of sympathy with them. Yielding to necessity and pointing to how 1857 brought the Muslim communities to the precipice, they engaged with changing Muslim attitudes towards modern education, reforming the Muslims from within, and creating a viable moral structure to fortify their confidence in their heritage, their present, and their future. Despite being sometimes vague and evasive in their recommendations, they were strongly and consistently wedded to the ideals of abnegation, self-sacrifice, and service, the basis of *adab*.

What legacy did such men leave behind? What was the impact of their main beliefs and their general outlook on life? To this, the answer is many-sided. In the first place, moderation was an essential part of their outlook and without it they would not have survived. Their type of devotion was therefore well suited to become the model for thinkers and reformers and publicists whose members were increasing rapidly in the early twentieth century.

If we regard Muhammad Iqbal, the twentieth-century poet-philosopher, as their most prominent interlocutor, it will not take long to discover that some of his ideas represent not only a departure from the traditional methodological prescriptions but also contravene his previously declared principles. At the same time it is hard to dispute his stature or to deny his role as one of the key exponents of the most sweeping modernist reformulation of Islamic doctrine. Besides elaborating and refining Sayyid Ahmad's views on *ijtehad*, he talked of *ijma* or 'consensus', one of the bases (*usul*) of the Islamic religious law, to revive and give the legal system an evolutionary character, and stated that 'the claim of the present generation of Muslim liberals to reinterpret the foundational legal principles, in the light of their own experience and the altered conditions of modern life, is, in my opinion, perfectly justified'.[7] Author of the chronogram inscribed on Sayyid Ahmad's tomb in the University mosque at Aligarh, Iqbal set its great reformer apart 'as probably the first modern Muslim to catch a glimpse of the positive character of the age which was coming'. According to him, 'The real greatness of the man consists in the fact that he was the first Indian Muslim who felt the need of a fresh orientation of Islam and worked for it. We may differ from his religious views, but there can be no denying the fact that his sensitive soul was the first to react to the modern age.'[8]

In like manner, Nazir Ahmad and Ameer Ali shared certain views on polygamy, divorce and widow remarriage. They shed disquieting light on the seclusion of women, and on their soul-destroying burdens of joyless domesticity. Ameer Ali held that the Prophet secured to women rights they had not previously possessed,[9] and that he restrained polygamy by limiting the maximum number of contemporaneous marriages to four. He regarded polygamy not only as 'an unendurable evil', but hoped that a general synod of Moslem doctors would declare the practice, like slavery, to be abhorrent to Islam.[10] He drew comfort from the ninety-five men out of every hundred Indian Muslims who were monogamists, either by conviction or necessity, to conclude that polygamy did not find much favour among the educated classes.[11]

Purdah retarded Muslim advancement, observed Ameer Ali.[12] But this British-trained lawyer and jurist lapses into the familiar apologetic tone and rhetorical device with the remark that purdah had many advantages for the 'unsettled and uncultured communities'.[13] In the same narrative, though, he points out that, 'to suppose that [the Prophet] ever intended his recommendation should assume its present inelastic form, or that he ever allowed or enjoined the seclusion of women, is wholly contrary to the spirit of his reforms.' He concludes with the rhetorical flourish: 'The Koran itself affords no warrant for holding that the seclusion of women is a part of the new gospel.'[14] The truth of the matter is simple: in general, Muslim reformers wanted to unveil women's minds without unveiling their faces [15]

Although Ameer Ali did not strike a responsive note in the heart of his generation, for he was a Shia and that too an anglicized one, his arguments are far more advanced, if not progressive, than Sayyid Ahmad's (on Muslim women's education) or Iqbal's (on the modern Western woman as heartless and devoid of womanhood).[16] What is more, their followers construed the views of these two men, especially during the high noon of the Pakistan movement in the 1940s, in an anti-rational direction.[17] Even though some adamantly hold the opinion that amid the ups and downs of politics Iqbal's 'politics-mongering followers' distorted his perspectives, the crux of the problem, one that confronted the Muslim modernists generally, is their inability to formulate a basic synthetic attitude and resolve the contradictions between things 'Islamic' and otherwise. Shibli Numani mentioned this, though in general terms, while speaking at the Aligarh College in 1913.[18] A year earlier, he had been more explicit on his home turf in Nadwat al-ulama, when he told the assembled:

> If we remain inflexible in our attitudes rigidly and adhere to taqlid (*taqlid-i jamid*), we will be destroyed. In our trying times, we will not be able to compete with any one. Hence, we must take into account the changes in the world and, accordingly, the demands of religion. [We have] to consider the resources we can marshal to meet the requirements of the faith.[19]

The tension between the position of Iqbal, Ameer Ali, and the neo-modernists and that of the religious orthodoxy assumed, for the most part, different forms in different periods. Yet, common to their basic predicament was to decide what elements in the history of Islam they should emphasize and re-combine for an effective self-statement to the existing challenges; what should they modify and what should they reject?[20] Despite anxious heart-searching, reformers and thinkers like Sayyid Ahmad and Iqbal found it extremely tricky to decide. This, in part, explains their ambivalence on the status of Muslim women.

Unlike Turkish and Egyptian educators who placed changing the status, education and roles of women at the core of national advancement,[21] their Indian counterparts did not have the same degree of commitment. This is not all. Even when explored through the prism of nationalist educational discourses in other regions of India, notably Bengal and Maharashtra, one does not see the intersection of educational nationalism (not in the narrow but in its broad sense) and gender in north India's Muslim communities. Thus Muslim educators, reformers and creative writers quite often espoused traditional notions in terms of modesty, domestic centrality, self-sacrifice, and self-abnegation. The emancipation of women emerges in their writings and public stand as a lost option, a road tragically not taken.

Moving to a more recognizable and an ideologically more cohesive entity, the *ulama* created their own structures and had insulated themselves, at least on contentious issues, in their imagined world of piety. So long as they were not too visible in the public domain as agitators, as some had become in 1857, they were left alone within the confines of their theological seminaries. In addition to not disturbing the *status quo*, a lesson learnt from the 1857 experience and succinctly expressed in the Queen's proclamation, the colonial government even made concessions to religious sentiments or negotiated with the religious orthodoxies which the Deobandis and Barelwis embodied.[22] No longer a set of specific rights, no longer a privilege to be enjoyed by a body or people in specific circumstances, religious freedom now became an open-ended entitlement. This arrangement suited the men of religion, especially because it enabled them, from the time Deoband's *dar al-ulum* came into being, to define the frame of reference, and the terms of the religious discourse, with a view to controlling its outcome.

In general, the imperial policy on critical social issues stemmed from a broad consideration of how best to curb the influence of the traditional Muslim groups, particularly theologians, beyond their own self-defined boundaries. After the horrors of the 1857 uprising, the imperial aspirations towards social reconstruction in the Victorian image appear to have been discarded. No wonder, then, that the government usually lent its weight, as a tactical step, to a traditionalist interpretation of the *shariat.* To give one example, the courts' rulings very often worked to deny women access to property even though the Koran asserts that women are entitled to inherit a portion of their parent's or husband's wealth. Like the courts, the political arm of the raj pursued no consistent policy with regard to women's property rights. This suited the theologians, who took little or no interest in issues of women's property rights.

In sum, if a mark of modern society was improvement in the status and rights of women, then neither the administrative nor the legal arms of the colonial government were engines of modernization. What they gave to women with one hand, they often took away with the other.[23]

Being deeply sensitive to the religious susceptibilities even of those who were neither custodians of the *shariat* nor certified by any person, body, or institution as its 'qualified' interpreters, the government made concession after concession to muftis, mujtahids, and maulvis. Even before 1857, it had fought shy of modifying Muslim criminal law even when some of its features were demonstrably not suited to the notions of justice entertained by the British themselves.[24] Not only was there a dual court system, but Hindu and Muslim criminal law continued to operate, albeit often without British participation or permission.[25]

In this rather complex process, the government sanctified the men of religion, while secular intellectuals, public figures, and other Westernized elites encountered exclusion and denial of official recognition. Indeed, officials either ignored or discarded their concerns on the presumption that they were uninfluential, unrepresentative, and not quite attuned to the so-called Muslim/Islamic way of life. As in the case of specific social reform issues, such as widow immolation, so also in relation to the growing liberal opinion, they secured 'an insistence on their own view by ignoring, marginalizing, domesticating, and exceptionalizing whatever did not accord with their presumptions'.[26] To say the least, this had a devastating impact on liberal processes as well as the secular nationalist projects.

In the end, colonial perceptions of where the liberal intelligentsia stood influenced the sum and substance of the colonial agenda as well as its strategy towards the Muslims. This mattered more than anything else. Soon enough, public discourse was polarised, as evident from Sayed Ahmad's tortuous reform career, between a wide variety of perspectives that often converged on certain matters. Moreover, because their platform was gradually narrowed by the government and their stature lowered within imperial structures—executive and judicial—liberals and modernists of all hues felt inhibited fighting their battles on an enlightened plank. Some pressed on, as evidenced from the career of various progressive literary movements from the 1920s onwards; others joined the revolutionary struggles. To keep its head above water, the Communist Party of India acknowledged in the late 1930s (and ultimately yielded to) the growing demand for cultural self-determination in terms of a Muslim collective identity. This was a fatal mistake.

In a more general way, the Muslim public at large, especially in the 1930s and 1940s, was faced with only one choice: to shore up the variegated Islamist groups who presented themselves as the protectors and the authentic interpreters of the Islamic codes. As the decades rolled on, more and more reformers conceded the high religious ground to their opponents on education of women, their property rights, and purdah. This opposition came not so much from traditional thinkers as from those steeped in modern learning.

Thus the failure of Muslim modernism lies as much in colonial mentalities that retarded the flowering of liberal thought, as in the resistance to reform and innovation from Muslim orthodoxies: Shia, Sunni, the Ahl-i Hadis, led by Sayyid Nazir Husain of Delhi (d. 1902), the Barelwis and the Deobandis. This is probably what Shibli meant while decrying his community as 'blind', in the lifetime of Sayed Ahmad and his own (*Qaum haqiqat mein Sir Sayyid Marhum ke waqt mein bhi andhi thi aur ab bhi hai*).[27] Blind or not, large segments of it were decidedly ill-equipped to value or promote the democratic aspirations of the kind that became so central to the powerful reformist currents engendered by Brahmo Samaj in Bengal and Arya Samaj in Punjab.

LIVING IN A PLURALIST SOCIETY

> We have created you from a male and a female, and We have made you into peoples and tribes so that you may come to know one another. The noblest among you in the eyes of God is the most pious, for God is omniscient and well informed [Koran: vlix, 13].

In my forthcoming book on Delhi's intelligentsia in the nineteenth century, I have analysed the opinions of certain key figures that found expression on various issues. By and large, I have tried to show how best they took a crack at reconciling and integrating the religious and secular discourses, minimizing disharmony around them, and giving a secular twist to communitarian debates. I emphasize just a few points especially because of a certain analytical blindness or blockage in the learned world, especially in relation to Delhi's intellectual and academic discourses and their impact on north India generally. The points I draw attention to are not only among the most engrossing themes of the historians but are of the highest value to all who wish to know what advocates of pluralism were saying, and why their appeal diminished in the 1920s and 1930s.

First and foremost, Sayed Ahmad, Zakaullah, Nazir Ahmad, Hali, and Ghalib hardly ever dreamt of a unified society where everyone would share the same belief and practices. Without advocating the merging of religious traditions or the dissolution of religious boundaries, they were content to let the hundred flowers bloom. They found wisdom in numerous religious traditions,[28] built bridges of understanding and mutual respect between them, and balanced, on the strength of their reading of Persian *akhlaq* literature, notably the works of Nasiruddin Tusi, the interests of different religious communities. While Islam was a necessary cultural and spiritual ingredient of the national culture, they viewed religion as a matter of personal choice and disposition. Again, while adhering to the personality paradigm of the Prophet, they drew on non-Muslim religious figures so as to develop a conception of co-existence between religious institutions and the men of faith in different religions.

In this way, all five put across, despite dissimilarity in emphasis, a maximally inclusive notion to make the various segments of the two communities become parts of a whole.

Zakaullah's moral structure and his overall worldview served as a resource for engagement with other communities, and he extended the basic premises, conceptions, and values of Islam to them. These included moral education, kindliness, and a sense of justice. 'All men are equal, but it is the goodness of the person that makes him superior to the other,' he wrote.[29] Knowing full well that the world around him was charged with hatred and filled with sectarian animus, he explored the ways to move diverse cultural and religious traditions towards inter-community cooperation. He avoided theological controversies to become 'one of God's peacemakers who brought unity among the children of men by his goodness and love'.[30] In total contrast to the Arya Samaj tradition of exclusionary nationalism, he made cultural pluralism—an idea previously associated with Sayed Ahmad Khan and Ghalib—an article of faith. Delhi College, the main source of his early intellectual energy, may not have created a new form of liberalism, but it helped to invigorate liberal values, and to imbue its members with a more pluralistic understanding of north Indian society. Critics referred to Zakaullah disparagingly as a 'free-thinker', but, as Andrews put it:

> If the phrase 'free-thinker' means, that he thought freely and sincerely and with an open mind about religion, and regarded the spirit of his Islamic faith to be more important than the letter, then the phrase is nobly true concerning Zakaullah, and he well deserves the title. For it would have been hard to find a man more free from formalism and bigotry, more open-minded and tolerant. It was this fact that made him a close friend and associate of earnest Hindus all through his long life. It was this also which was one of the things that drew me instinctively to him from the first, and has remained rooted in my memory ever since.[31]

No wonder that when Pandit Tulsi Ram's family lighted the lamps to worship every evening, they included Zakaullah's name in their prayers, along with those of other close family members. Andrews amplified this viewpoint:

> What most struck the imagination of us, Englishmen, who used to be present (at the Reading Room in Delhi), was the exceeding kindliness of toleration, unsullied by a touch of religious bitterness—an atmosphere in which political wisdom could mature and social friendships ripen. In all the many years during which I knew Munshi Zakaullah (and during the last years of his life I used to see him almost every day) I cannot once remember hearing a bitter or uncharitable word spoken by him concerning any Hindu or any Hindu religious custom. On the other hand, I have continually heard him speak with a deep respect for those who differed from him fundamentally in matters of belief. Wherever he went his influence always made for peace and goodwill.[32]

Nazir Ahmad ascribed his own experiences to a senior, or *buzurg*, in his student days: 'in short, sometimes I was a Christian, sometimes a Muslim, and sometimes not at all'.[33] The source of Hindu-Muslim friction according to him lay in the values instilled in youth and in the phobias created in them. But it was still possible to resolve disagreements through education and reconciliatory methods (*sazgari aur sulahkari*). 'After all, the sweet maker does not object to the cloth merchant not producing sweets like him; nor does the cloth merchant get angry with the sweet vendor for not selling cloth.' He referred to Zauq,[34] the poet, to point out that differences were the essence of creation, the gift of God that created people with diverse social and cultural habits and religions. Nevertheless, divergences had to be reconciled with the aid of British structures and the secular educational curriculum, also a British gift, and not allowed to explode into violent conflicts.[35] In this, the great Urdu novelist tried shifting the self-image of the Hindu and Muslim ideologues to create new possibilities in which communal violence is not the core of the country's ethos. The choice had to be made, and then fought for.

If social identities and differences are constructed, fluid, multiple, and overlapping, then every group has a right to its own history and myth making that embodies and strengthens their identity. The key is to enable 'mythic structure and future dreams to embody the erstwhile enemy other in a benign way, even in loving embrace'.[36] A scholar writing on the long-standing Israeli-Palestinian conflict concludes with the plea:

> It is our job to enter into the damaged and strange world of enemies and enemy systems, to suspend judgement, to see truths on all sides, to see justice and injustice on all sides, to engage in a level of empathy that is enormously demanding, all to help evoke peace processes that resonate at the most profound level of human consciousness and experience. If enough of us, on all levels of intervention, do this persistently and patiently, I do believe that we can stimulate a fundamentally new path to peace.

Some of late nineteenth century Delhi's best men, Hindus and Muslim alike, reflected much the same sentiment. Nazir Ahmad, who was consistently impatient with demagogic religious leaders, did not want fellow-Muslims to demonize non-Muslims but to discover, through regular processes of self-examination, their own faults and weak points.[37] In *Taubat-an Nasuh*, he narrates the story of a missionary preaching and distributing books, like a member of a theatrical cast, at the Chandni Chowk bazaar. This was not an uncommon occurrence. The missionaries not merely read the Bible to their listeners, but rather demonstrated its purpose. In their street sermons they took the Bible with them and used it to emphasize the truth of their message. On that fateful day, so runs the story, a boy used an opprobrious epithet for the preacher. This agitated many of the bystanders, but not the preacher. He did not want the boy to be hurt by anyone. This act charmed Uleem [Alim], Nasuh's second son. He approached the same missionary for the Bible, which he read with great interest. Unlike his elder brother who disapproved of such reading habits, Uleem was struck by the fact that if Christians followed the teachings in that religious text, they could not be as wicked as his people had painted them. Nasuh, who listened to this story, remarked:

> There is no doubt some opposition between the doctrines of Islam and Christianity, but then no two religions have so much in common. The Koran speaks well of Christianity and its professors, and their Gospel is held to be the word of God. The Mosalman may lawfully eat and intermarry with the Christian, and the alienation which now characterizes their relations is not sanctioned by the canon law. The best of our religious books could hardly have benefited you more than the missionary's volume. But you said just now you had learned sympathy for others from its maxims. Tell me, have you ever put this teaching into practice?[38]

The performance by the missionary, almost like a rehearsal of a text rescued from the Biblical records somewhere, and the reaction of the audience, opens for us a panoramic window into the world of that Delhi, and encapsulates an entire culture that was so much more tolerant than it was to be in the following decades.

As detailed above, the process of entering into other cultures is daunting in any period of history and in any situation, but Zakaullah and Nazir Ahmad showed an appreciation of what they read of Hindu and Christian texts. The former, having spent a lifetime of intellectual friendship with Hindu scholars, held, right up to the day of his death at the advanced age of eighty-seven, that harmony and reconciliation [between Islam and Hinduism] were always possible.[39] 'Reconciliation', he contended, 'sustains faith [*iman*] and brings in its wake generous [*fayyazana*] behaviour.'[40] No wonder, Nazir Ahmad fervently applauded him for being 'far-sighted', in avoiding painful religious disputes. The fact is that Zakaullah observed toleration in every detail, in spirit as well as in letter, in religious matters.[41] 'What is the use of argument and controversy?' he told Andrews. 'Tell me your beautiful Names for God, and I will tell you mine.'[42]

The account sketched above suggests that the dialogical element signalled a crucial step towards avoiding paradigms of encounter, undermining religious violence. The point is not to exaggerate its limitations or to debate whether or not such men were authentically modern, but to highlight their inventiveness. As people who had no conception of pacts and unity conferences that became the métier of peace in the 1920s for the sake of immediate political goals, they talked of building on the overarching shared ethical values and practices, and acknowledging each other's common visions. Andrews, who was moved by such thoughts, concluded with a paean of praise to Zakaullah's kindness, courtesy, confidence and friendship. He deserved a place among the great Indians of the nineteenth century, so he wrote, as a 'singular and beautiful example of the combination of the past and the present, of the East and West', and also as a 'true prophet of the future'.[43] He owed something more to Nazir Ahmad—an idea of the power of Islam at its best, in moulding character and creating an atmosphere of reverence.[44]

Zakaullah's outward manners and customs were so much a part of Delhi's sharif ethos. His dress, his habits, his domestic life, and his religious life—all that he valued most dearly—remained unchanged.[45] *Makhzan*'s editor, Shaikh Abdul Qadir, who knew him well during 1907-8,[46] wrote that while sticking to the old-fashioned style in dress and manner of living, he held 'progressive' views. Progressive or not, he remained true to the same social and cultural ideals that informed many others in his generation. While Islam provided them a universal frame of identity and considerable freedom to retain their regional, linguistic, and class identities, the historically conditioned symbiosis between region, language and faith enabled the educated elites, if not the masses, to pursue a high degree of cultural and historical continuity to transform it into a modern national identity.

Whatever their differences in emphasis, Sayed Ahmad, Ghalib, Zakaullah, Nazir Ahmad, and others planted the seeds of a pluralist vision that could eventually become a touchstone of a liberal and secular polity. With Hakim Ajmal Khan and Mukhtar Ahmad Ansari, another prominent Dilliwala, providing depth and acceleration to the process in the early 1920s, their homes—Sharif Manzil in Ballimaran and Dar-us Salam in Daryaganj (now Ansari Road)—became powerful and living symbols of a new awakening.

This paper will have served its purpose if the sagacious and memorable admonitions of such men stimulate writers to reconstruct this heritage in South Asia. Moreover, it would be intellectually fruitful to foreground the submerged story of social and cultural invigoration and not just concentrate on, as is often the case, the inadequacies, contradictions, and paradoxes of the Muslim intelligentsia and plumb the deep and hidden meanings of their 'failure'.

The wind has blown away the dust of men
unnumbered from your lane:

Yet your true lovers are not daunted: men
come to your threshold still.

Reasonable as these conclusions are, we cannot escape the consequences of serious Hindu-Muslim disputes in the lifetime of Zakaullah, Nazir Ahmad, and Andrews. Indeed, it was their misfortune that the prospect of inter-faith dialogue was to chill and then freeze. Yet, as the new century begins, the peoples and countries of South Asia are striving towards greater cooperation in shaping their destinies. Nobody can predict the ultimate fate of such trends. All one can hope is that studying Delhi's past would be a source of knowledge of a cultural and intellectual heritage that belongs to all of South Asia. When the history of ideas of the countries of the subcontinent is better explored and better known, the historian will recognise the currents of influence which, from Pakistan to Bangladesh, constitute the very fabric of the history of Islam in the region. We may not have it in our power, as Thomas Paine (1737-1809) proclaimed in 1776, 'to begin the world again'. But we can provide an adequate language for comprehending the twenty-first century; and we can decide for ourselves the importance of living together, understanding each other, and interpreting each other's lifestyle and value systems. Arnold Toynbee sums up this message candidly in the following words:

> In order to save mankind we have to learn to live together in concord in spite of traditional differences of religion, civilization, nationality, class and race. In order to live together in concord successfully, we have to know each other's past, since human life, like the rest of the phenomenal universe, can be observed by human minds only as it presents itself to them on the move through time. . . . For our now urgent common purpose of self-preservation, it will not be enough to explore our common underlying human nature. The psychologist's work needs to be supplemented by the archaeologist's, the historian's, the anthropologist's and the sociologist's. We must learn to recognize, and as far as possible, to understand, the different cultural configurations in which our common human nature has expressed itself in the different religions, civilizations, and nationalities into which human culture has come to be articulated in the course of its history. . . . We shall, however, have to do more than just understand each other's cultural heritages, and more even than appreciate them. We shall have to value them and love them as being parts of mankind's common treasure and therefore being ours too, as truly as the heirlooms that we ourselves shall be contributing to the common stock.[47]

NOTES

1. Ghalib, cited in M.A. Sadiq, *A History of Urdu Literature*, Delhi, 1984, 2nd edn., p. 203.
2. Ahmed Ali (1910-94), *Twilight in Delhi*, Delhi, 1940, 1991 rpt., p. viii.
3. H.A.R. Gibb, *Modern Trends in Islam*, Chicago, 1947, p. 109.
4. He wrote:

   What a great pity it is that the Muslims of this age have not only failed to discover any way to preserve the exercise of intellectual scrutiny, but have even discarded those methods that had been discovered in the past! In acquiring every kind of knowledge the condition of Muslims for a long time has been such that they hardly read in any area of learning in order to find out the reality and truth in it. Their purpose is simply to know all that is written in a given book, regardless of whether it be true or false. . . . If discussion occurs, it is not on the question of whether a principle written in a book is true or false, but simply on whether that particular principle is recorded in the book or not. . . . This method has destroyed freedom of opinion and broken the way of life that used to afford protection against falling into error. All their learning and wisdom has fallen into error.

   Sayyid Ahmad Khan, 'Azadi-i Rai', M. Moaddel and K. Talattof (eds), *Contemporary Debates in Islam: An Anthology of Modernist and Fundamentalist Thought*, London, 2000, pp. 119-20.
5. *From Pluralism to Separatism: Qasbas in Colonial Awadh*, Delhi, 2004.
6. *A Moral Reckoning: Muslim Intellectuals in Nineteenth Century*, New Delhi, 2005.
7. Muhammad Iqbal, *The Reconstruction of Religious Thought in Islam*, Oxford, 1934, pp. 159-60.
8. Speeches and Statements of Iqbal, Lahore, 1945, p. 131.
9. 'If Moslem woman does not attain in another hundred years, the social position of her European sister, there will be time enough to declaim against Islam as a system and a dispensation. But the Teacher who in an age when no country, no system, no community gave any right to woman, maiden or married, mother or wife, who, in a country where the birth of a daughter was considered a calamity, secured to the sex rights which are only unwillingly and under pressure being conceded to them by the civilized nations in the twentieth century, deserves the gratitude of humanity. If Mohammad had done nothing more, his claim to be a benefactor of mankind would have been indisputable. Ameer Ali, *The Spirit of Islam*, London, 1967 rpt., 1st edn. 1922, p. 256.
10. Ibid., p. 232.
11. Ibid., p. 231.
12. Ibid., p. 248.
13. Ibid., p. 249.
14. Ibid.
15. Gail Minault, 'Other Voices, Other Rooms: The View from the Zenana',

in Nita Kumar (ed.), *Women as Subjects: South Asian Histories*, Charlottesville, 1994, p. 119.

16. For Sayyid Ahmad Khan, *Tahzibul Akhlaq*, vol. 1, pp. 71-4.
17. Fazlur Rahman, *Islam*, London, 1966, pp. 225-6.
18. Sayyid Sulaiman Nadwi (ed.), *Khutbat-i Shibli*, Azamgarh, 1965, p. 185.
19. Ibid., p. 131.
20. Rahman, *Islam*, p. 235.
21. Barak A. Salmoni, 'Women in the Nationalist-Educational Prism: Turkish and Egyptian Pedagogues and their Gendered Agenda, 1920-1952', *History of Education Quarterly*, vol. 43, no. 4, Winter 2003.
22. For Deoband, Barbara Metcalf, *Islamic Revival in British India: Deoband 1860-1900*, Delhi, 2002 edn; Usha Sanyal, *Devotional Islam and Politics in British India: Ahmad Riza Khan Barelwi and his Movement, 1870-1920*, Delhi, 1996.
23. Gregory C. Kozlowski, 'Muslim Women and the Control of Property in North India', *The Indian Economic and Social History Review*, vol. 24, no. 2, 1987, p. 181.
24. M.P. Jain, 'Challenges of Indian Legal System', cited in K.L. Raman, 'Utilitarianism and the Criminal Law in Colonial India', *Modern Asian Studies*, 18, 4, 1994, p. 746.
25. David Skuy, 'Macaulay and the India Penal Code of 1862: The Myth of the Inherent Superiority and Modernity of the English Legal System in the Nineteenth Century', *Modern Asian Studies*, 32, 3, 1998, p. 522.
26. Lata Mani, *Contentious Traditions: The Debate on Sati in Colonial India*, Delhi, 1998, p. 193.
27. Shibli to Abdul Majid Daryabadi, 15 November 1913, *Makatib-i Shibli*, vol. 1, p. 292.
28. *Jitne mazahib duniya mein hain waqt aur maqam ke lihaz se sab ke sab aadmi ki islah aur uske faide ke liye chale hain aur har ek mein kuch na kuch faide aur sadaqat aur neki ke ansh maujood hain.* Nazir Ahmad, *Lekcharon ka Majmua*, Agra, 1918, vol. 2, p. 154.
29. Zakaullah, *Mahasinul Akhlaq*, vol. 1, Delhi 1891, p. 209.
30. C.F. Andrews, *Zakaullah of Delhi* (with introduction by Mushirul Hasan and Margret Pernau, Delhi, 2003, p. 98.
31. Ibid., p. 109.
32. Ibid., p. 107.
33. Oesterheld, 'Nazir Ahmad and the Early Urdu Novel', *Annual of Urdu Studies*, 16, 2001, p. 40.
34. *Gulha-i rang rang se hai raunaq-i chaman/Ai Zauq is jahaan ko hai zeb ikhtilaaf.*
35. Nazir Ahmad, *Lekcharon ka Majmua*, vol. 2, pp. 420-1.
36. M. Gopin, *Holy War, Holy Peace: How Religion can Bring Peace to the Middle East*, Oxford, 2002, p. 91.

37. Speech at Anjuman Himayat-i Islam, Lahore, December 1888, Nazir Ahmad, *Lekcharon ka Majmua*, vol. 2, pp. 117-18.
38. Nazir Ahmad, *The Repentance of Nasuh* [tr. from original Hindustani by M. Kempson], London, 1884, pp. 33-5.
39. C.F. Andrews, *The True India: A Plea for Understanding*, London 1939, p. 198.
40. Ibid., p. 199.
41. Andrews, *Zakaullah of Delhi*, p. 10.
42. B. Chaturvedi and M. Sykes, *Charles Freer Andrews: A Narrative*, London, 1949, p. 40.
43. Andrews, 'Munshi Zakaullah: A Great Educationist', *Modern Review*, April 1911.
44. Ibid., *North India*, Oxford, 1908, p. 135.
45. Ibid., p. 92.
46. For Abdul Qadir's career, see *Auraq-i Nau*, Lahore, 1951.
47. Arnold Toynbee, *A Study of History*, quoted in Richard C. Martin (ed.), *Approaches to Islam in Religious Studies*, Oxford, 2001, p. 105.

5

Standardizing Muslim Scholarship: The Nadwat al-ulama

JAN-PETER HARTUNG

It seems reasonable to believe that Muslim scholarship in India gained new momentum after the uprising of 1857. Whether or not the shock of the so-called 'Mutiny' was indeed the watershed, as, for instance, Francis Robinson has suggested,[1] will not be answered in this paper. However, what has to be acknowledged is that almost all the so-called reformist scholarly movements in India rose up just after 1857. Bearing that in mind, one nevertheless needs to be aware that Muslim scholars' understanding of imminent political and social crisis goes back to the eighteenth century at least. Thus, the 'Mutiny' might have only been the necessary spark that animated scholarship. Following this assumption, it is useful to first outline those tendencies of the eighteenth century that proved to be preconditions for the reformist movements in the nineteenth century and, finally, for the attempt to standardize Muslim scholarship by establishing a 'National Council of Muslim Scholars', the Nadwat al-ulama.

THE LEGACY OF THE SEVENTEENTH AND EIGHTEENTH CENTURIES

Muslim intellectual elites based in cities, especially in the administrative centre of Delhi, perceived the breaking apart of the once centralist Mughal empire as a moment of cultural and political crisis. The threat to Mughal political sovereignty was located, on the one hand, in the growing strength of revivalist movements in other religious communities in the eighteenth century, namely the Sikhs in the Punjab and the Marathas in Maharashtra. On the other hand, there were separatist movements among Muslims such as Jats, along with the military campaigns of Iranian and, later, Afghan rulers. All these tendencies were—from the perspective of the centre—

interpreted as the cultural disintegration of a normatively understood Muslim community that had to be counteracted.

These tendencies can be traced back even to the seventeenth century, when Sufi orders played crucial roles as social vehicles for reformist ambitions. The Qadiri Abd al-Haqq Muhaddith Dehlawi (d. 1642) is regarded as the prime driving force in systematizing *hadith*-scholarship in India.[2] His famous contemporary and theological opponent, the Naqshbandi Ahmad Faruqi Sirhindi (d. 1624), stood for a return to an Islamic religiosity in strict conformity with the *sharia*, while protesting against syncretistic tendencies at the courts of Akbar and Jahangir.[3]

Among the Sufi orders, the Naqshbandiyya became the prime vehicle of a traditionalist renaissance in the eighteenth century. Within its two dominant chains of transmission, the Ahrariyya and the Mujaddidiyya, attempts were made to counteract the process of cultural disintegration. Its major exponents in Delhi were Mirza Mazhar Jan-i Janan and Shah Wali-allah Dehlawi. Even though they offered different approaches to solve the social and political crisis at hand, they, nevertheless, emphasized the assertion of religious orthopraxy as a precondition. According to Mirza Mazhar Jan-i Janan, the only way out of the crisis had to be the strict observance of the *sharia* according to its codification in the Hanafi *fiqh* by each single individual. He himself believed that that aim could best be realized by withdrawing as far as possible from all worldly affairs and by constant recollection of God [*dhikr*]. This rather apolitical attitude was later elaborated into a core-teaching of the Mujaddidiyya by Jan-i Janan's prime *khalifa*, Ghulam Ali, who pleaded for avoidance of all contact with the British colonial administration.[4]

In contrast, the traditionalist reformism that revolved around Shah Wali-allah was oriented more towards a collective renewal that was to set out from the political superstructure. Firm political rule was, according to a canonical Prophetic tradition, the fundamental condition for a moral reform of each single member of the polity. Already Wali-allah's father, Shah Abdal-Rahim Dehlawi (d. 1719), reacted to the political decline of the Mughal empire with a turn towards the traditionalism that proceeded from the already mentioned Abd al-Haqq Muhaddith Dehlawi. His Madrasa-yi Rahimiyya in Tughlaqabad became famous as a centre for the study of traditional sciences, the so-called *manqulat*, that proved a traditionalist pendant to the Lucknow-based Farangi Mahall,[5] which shall be elaborated upon below. In his major work, the *Hujjat allah al-baligha*, Shah Wali-allah argued for placing more emphasis on *hadith*-studies and intuition-based Sufism and against the dominance of the *ratio* as the predominant mode of cognition. The *ratio*, so he pointed out, refers only to exoteric [*zahiri*] knowledge and is, thus, only an analytical tool. The aim is, however, a synthesis of all knowledge that finds its expression in the cognition of the fundamental oneness of God [*tawhid*].[6]

THE POST-1857 QUEST FOR APPROPRIATE MUSLIM REFORMIST EDUCATION

Rooted in the Delhi-based traditionalist scholarship of the eighteenth century, the early nineteenth century brought forth three trends which all drew their legitimacy from a selective reception of the works of Shah Wali-allah. The first trend strongly emphasized *fiqh* as an attempt to put the insights of the sciences of *hadith* into practice. The second opted for a rather militant activism to push through a 'reformed' Islamic society. Finally, the third trend emphasised the Sufi approach and tried to combine the norms for action set in the Prophetic *sunna* with popular religious practices. The legalist trend was prominently represented by Shah Abd al-Aziz Dehlawi, the son of Shah Wali-allah and his successor as head of the Madrasa-yi Rahimiyya. Shah Abd al-Aziz Persian *fatwas*, compiled only between 1893 and 1896 and published as *Fatawa-yi Azizi*, were 'his major tool for disseminating instruction in shari'at beyond the circle of his students and disciples'.[7] According to Metcalf, the medium of the *fatwa* considerably widened its scope of influence during the nineteenth century. Having traditionally been a point of reference for a *mufti* appointed from the court for concrete juridical decisions to be made by a judge [*qadi*], it now became a point of reference for individual Muslims in their efforts to decide upon ways of conducting themselves that were in accordance with the religious norms. The authorization to issue *fatwas* by a worldly ruler was not required any longer; its reinforcement relied more on approval by the Muslim community.

The resurgent emphasis on independent decision-making based on a critical analysis of Koran and *hadith*—i.e. *ijtihad*—instead of following the opinions developed in one of the canonical schools of law [*taqlid*], altered the role of *fiqh* as well. Jurisprudence was no longer only a means for decision-making within the frame of effective law, but became more and more interwoven with the ethical concept of *adab*—'shared norms of personal cultivation'.[8] As *mujtahid* [one who is entitled to practice *ijtihad*] in his father's tradition Shah Abd al-Aziz's *fatwas* emphasized the *hadith* as prime source of reference, using the opinions of the canonical schools of law only as secondary references. A whole chapter of his *fatawa* is devoted to methods of *hadith*-critique and their application in *fiqh*.[9] For our purpose, his famous and momentous *fatwa Masala-yi dar al-harb shudan-i dar al-islam* need only be mentioned because it inheres the potential for conformist as well as a non-conformist activism.[10] While conformists have derived from this *fatwa* the strategy of a purist execution of religion as a means to maintain and preserve cultural identity within an only hypothetical *dar al-islam*, non-conformists emphasized that British India actually belonged to the *dar al-harb*, against which even militant action was legitimate in order to return to the *dar al-islam*.[11]

A pupil of a grandson of Shah Abd al-Aziz Dehlawi, Nadhir Husayn Dehlawi (d. 1902), revived the tradition of the Madrasa-yi Rahimiyya in Delhi, after the school was razed by the British in the course of the uprising of 1857. He emerged, besides the Bhopal-based Yemenite *hadith*-scholars Husayn b. Muhsin al-Hudaydi (d. 1909) and his brother Zayn al-Abidin (d. 1879), as the leading authority for *hadith* and as a central figure in the formative phase of the traditionalist scholarly movement of the *Ahl-i hadith*.[12] At the very same time, Nadhir Husayn became influenced by representatives of the above-mentioned activist trend, namely Shah Ismail Dehlawi (killed 1831), another grandson of Shah Wali-allah, and Sayyid Ahmad Barelwi (killed 1831). Their interpretation of the intellectual heritage of Shah Wali-allah, again, became manifest in their so-called movement of the *tariqa-yi muhammadiyya*, and their militant *jihad* against the Sikhs, beginning in 1826.[13]

Another traditionalist reform movement which perceived itself in direct spiritual descent from Shah Wali-allah and Shah Abd al-Aziz came into being in 1867 in the north-Indian town of Deoband. Muhammad Qasim Nanawtawi (d. 1877) and Rashid Ahmad Gangohi (d. 1905) set up a *madrasa* with a curriculum that—in regard to its *hadith*-centrism—certainly showed some affinity to the *Ahl-i hadith*.[14] Over the course of time, they set up a network of Deobandi seminaries all over the subcontinent and even beyond; of special importance for the history of Muslim reformist scholarship in India are the *Mazahir al-ulum* in Saharanpur, from which the leading figures of the missionary movement Tablighi Jamaat emerged.[15] In the case of Deoband a structural change took place since, after the massive intervention of the British in Delhi during 1857, the Muslim scholars turned away from the administrative centre and shifted their traditionalist activities to the *qasbas.* While towns and cities became places of increasingly fast social, political, and economic changes, the *qasbas* remained relatively unaffected by the colonial presence. Moreover, here the traditional patterns of the establishment and consolidation of religious authority—such as the family, teacher-pupil-bonds, and *piri-muridi*-relations—were of major importance. Thus the *qasbas* became elevated as the ideal space for a pious religious lifestyle in accordance with the commandments of the normative sources.[16]

This elevation of the *qasba* has to be seen as a feature of the emancipatory process of former vassal states from the Mughal centre in the eighteenth century. A prominent example that has been given much ink by Francis Robinson and Jamal Malik, was the *qasba* Sihala in Awadh, where a learned dynasty rose to be of great importance for the establishment of Muslim scholarship in the new capital of the former imperial province and now more or less independent princely state of Awadh, in Lucknow.[17] The tradition of Mulla Nizam ad-Din Sihalawi (d. 1749), who, after his father Qutb ud-Din was murdered in 1692, was given an estate for teaching and habitation by the Mughal ruler Aurangzeb in Lucknow's Farangi Mahall. Here some factors came together that proved decisive for Nizam ud-Din's success as scholar: first he managed to integrate into the learned setting in Lucknow by using the personal network of his Qadiriyya-murshid Shah Abd ur-Razzaq Banswi (d. 1724), who was most influential in the region. Second, the Nawab required competent specialists to set up and effectively run an administration that took the socio-structural particularities of the state into account. In exchange, the Nawab was generous in offering those scholars social prestige and, by way of fief [*madad-i maash*], economic independence. Thus education in Farangi Mahall focused on the crucial aim of sharpening the intellect of the students and stimulating reflexive thinking regardless of religious confession. Nizam ud-Din set up a teaching canon, named the *dars-i nizami,* that incorporated shorter texts on logic, mathematics, and *usul al-fiqh*, and fewer religious texts than those taught at around the same time in Delhi. After all, the study was primarily designed to have methodical skills and, only in a subordinated way, to obtain knowledge of the traditional sciences.[18] It seems as if the *dars-i nizami* proved quite practical at this time, because it was widely employed also outside Awadh, when the Mughal empire broke apart and the former vassal states became autonomous. In the nineteenth century, however, this emphasis on the practicability of the teaching receded. Colonial expansion weakened the princely states and the regents tried to come to terms with the British instead of having their own rule legitimated by religious scholars. It seems that it was mainly because of this that centres of the rational sciences lost their social and political importance when a good part of the scholars drifted into scholastic debates, a fact that was heavily criticised especially by the Naqshbandiyya-affiliated traditionalists who after 1857 made a massive entry into the *qasbas*.[19]

There remains to discuss two major reformist scholarly movements of the nineteenth century. One of them, the Aligarh movement, substantially initiated by Sir Sayed Ahmad Khan (d. 1899), who took up the idea of a rather rationalist curriculum by incorporating Western thinking without much reservation, in order to enable Muslims to assert themselves against the Hindu majority.[20] The other movement had its social base in the rural areas of Rohilkhand and combined Islamic legalism with the popular custom of venerating saints and their graves. The Barelwiyya was centred around the Hanafite *mufti*, Sayyid Ahmad Rida Khan Barelwi (d. 1921); in an interesting theology he made the veneration of the Prophet Muhammad and his grave at Medina a crucial issue and that is most probably why they took up the classical expression 'People of the (Prophetic) Sunna and of the Community' (*Ahl-i sunnat wa jamaat*), to name themselves.[21] But before elaborating on the Barelwiyya within the context of their involvement in the Nadwat al-ulama, we shall dwell a little more on a few particularities of the Aligarh movement.

Bringing a Western style positivist rationalism, as was dominant in the European scientific landscape at around that time, into the reformist concept of the movement led not only to a reassessment of the importance of the *ratio* as mode of cognition, but also produced a social stratum of intellectuals [*mufakkirun*] distinct from the *ulama*. The education of these intellectuals did not aim at integrating them into the traditional religious establishment, but rather at enabling them to act at the multiple interfaces of the traditional and colonial sectors.[22] The original background of the founders in traditional education was overlaid by ideas from the Western fund of knowledge imparted by the European colonial presence. In this sense, they constituted hybrid personalities that inhered a social integrative potential.[23] At the very same time, however, they were prime targets for polemics by the Muslim scholarship. Now it was rationalism of the Western kind [*aql parasti*] much more than the Islamic rationalism fostered by the Farangi Mahallis, that became increasingly the object of fierce criticism by traditional and traditionalist scholars. This 'ideologization' marked a decisive turn in a learned discourse on the proper mode of cognition, because now the debate was taken outside the store of an Islamic system of religious sciences. 'Rationality' in this new stage of argument became a topos for a modernism that set out from the West and that was considered by the traditionalists as being aimed only at the disintegration of the Muslims by infiltrating their intellectual culture; thus, the adversaries in this argument no longer stood within Muslim scholarship as treasurers of Islamic knowledge, but outside of it.

There was a great need among Muslims in general to counteract the fragmentation of the Muslim communities under colonial conditions and, particularly in India, to do so in an integrative way. That is why representatives of both the modernist and the traditionalist camps agreed on the necessity of a platform for all the current streams of Indo-Muslim scholarship, in order to sort out their differences and to finally work out a concept of reform that could harmonise diverse opinions. Since Muslim scholars regarded themselves as upholders of religious identity, it seemed common sense to them that an up to date Muslim identity could only be generated and maintained by a reform of the Muslim educational system. As Jamal Malik has put it, 'Only a reform of the scholarship and the educational system related to it, that has transported the so far valid norms and values, could lead to a fundamental change, could mobilise the masses, and could integrate the polarised realms of society that were expression of a far-reaching split of the complex Islamic public.'[24] Such a platform, the Nadwat al-ulama, was set up during a large gathering of representatives of most of the brands of Indo-Muslim scholarship at the Madrasa Fayd-i amm in Kanpur izn April 1893.

QUEST FOR MUSLIM SCHOLARS' UNITY

It was a civil servant, a deputy collector named Abd al-Ghaffur, who first proposed an Anglo-Oriental Educational Conference, a body heavily dominated by the leaders of the Aligarh movement including Sayed Ahmad Khan, in 1891 in Kanpur. After the agreement to form a national body of Muslim scholars was achieved, the next two years were spent in mobilizing *ulama* for this project. This almost coincided with the travels of Shibli Numani (d. 1914), one of Sayed Ahmad Khan's most important companions, to centres of Muslim religious education in the Ottoman Levant in 1892, the impressions of which he published a year later *Safarnama-yi Rum wa Misr wa Sham*. His assessment of the state of Muslim religious education in renowned and highly reputed centres of learning, such as al-Azhar in Cairo, was quite sobering: Shibli was satisfied only with the teachings there of *fiqh* and Arabic grammar, but complained about the teaching of other disciplines, the absence of the rational sciences, and, above all, the lack of a visible system of education that could set standards for achieving progress.[25] This assessment—a fair one—was neither Shibli's alone, nor was it only a temporary impression. Similar criticism was pronounced as late as 1917 by Ali Surur uz-Zankaluni (d. 1940), an Egyptian scholar who taught at the famous al-Azhar, and for whom the system of religious education in India had set standards for the entire Muslim world.[26] Shibli, however, after returning from the Middle East, became a major driving force in the endeavour to standardize Muslim scholarship in India with the aim of enabling Muslims to cope with the conditions of modern times without being forced to abandon their distinct religious identity. He emerged as one of the most important figures in what has been called the Nadwa movement.

This movement, emerging from the 1891 convention of the Anglo-Oriental Educational Conference in Kanpur, attempted to gain popular support by approaching especially the religious élites in the *qasbas*, since, as already outlined above, traditionalist scholarship had massively retreated after 1857. Using different kinds of networks, the initiators of the movement were able to gain support from renowned north-Indian scholars of different traditions already in the run-up to the convocation of the Nadwa in April 1893.

It was only in March 1893 that Abd al-Ghaffur had an epistle circulated among the *ulama* in north India that outlined a proposal for the reformation of Indo-Muslim scholarship, to be discussed at the Kanpur congregation a few weeks later. His letter opens with the statement that religion is absolutely necessary for the progress of a people, since it brings forth universal laws and, thus, determines a people's rise, as well as its fall. Muslims had deviated from that path, and this deviation finds its vivid expression in the manifold quarrels within the Muslim community. The letter continues by stressing the crucial role of the *ulama* in the guidance of the people. They wanted reforms, so the epistle says, but were not convinced which way to choose. But a thorough reformation of the people could only be brought forward by a religious community able to achieve consensus, because success is only granted in mutual action. That is why Abd al-Ghaffur's epistle goes on, a common goal is needed to establish harmony among the *ulama*. The goals of all the current religious schools are, however, the same at the core, and that is why only different ways of education need to be reconsidered. The *ulama* must learn the languages of other cultures, just as scholars of other religious groups have already done, and are ahead of the Muslims only because of that. Abd al-Ghaffur then turned to the effectiveness of missionaries of other religions: Indian Muslims would fall easy prey to Christian and Hindu missionary efforts for lack of effective knowledge, for which the *ulama* were responsible.[27]

It seems as if the epistle had the desired effect. Renowned *ulama*, among them the influential Deobandi Mahmud al-Hasan (d. 1920) and two Farangi Mahallis, agreed with Abd al-Ghaffur's stock-taking and his urgent appeal to reconcile the differences within the various factions of Indo-Muslim scholarship. Consequently, it was agreed that a convention of representatives of all the factions would be called and a National Council of Muslim Religious Scholars, the Nadwat al-ulama, would be set up. The initiators of the meeting managed to bring together a large number of scholars and intellectuals—as well as merchants, entrepreneurs, and publishers to secure a material base for the council in its initial phase. They did indeed succeed in assembling 62 *ulama* of all the different branches of Muslim scholarship, even those who were opposing each other: Deobandis, Barelwis, Shiites, Ahl-i hadith, Farangi Mahallis, and Aligarhis. Among the latter was the already mentioned Shibli Numani. The congregation at the Madrasa Fayd-i amm was presided by its own head: Sayyid Muhammad Ali Mongiri (d. 1928), a regionally known traditionalist and shaykh of the Qadiriyya-Mujaddidiyya and Naqshbandiyya-

Mujaddidiyya.[28] Moreover, already in the run-up to the gathering in Kanpur, it was decided to entrust him with the presidency of the to-be-founded Nadwat al-ulama for strategic reasons. In order to reconcile the different, partly even diametrically conflicting, views and interests of the various factions within the council and to be able to represent the body to the outside, a personality was needed that would be acceptable to all groups because of his charisma. Due to a number of reasons, such charisma was attributed to Sayyid Muhammad Ali Mongiri; this claim was, moreover, consolidated over time through hagiographic texts written by Nadwi scholars. The best known and most widespread of these texts was written by Sayyid Muhammad al-Hasani (d. 1979) and published in 1964 as *Sirat-i Mawlana Sayyid Muhammad Ali Mongiri*, subtitled *Bani-yi Nadwat al-ulama* (*The Path of Life of Mawlana Sayyid Muhammad Ali Mongiri—Founder of the* Nadwat al-ulama). It is this subtitle in particular that might be taken as a hint that the contribution of Abd al-Ghaffur to the establishment of the Nadwa was being step by step marginalized in favour of Mongiri. Why that happened will be addressed in the following section.

STANDARDIZING BY MARGINALIZING: THE DEVELOPMENT OF THE NADWAT AL-ULAMA

Already in the first general meeting of the council, a year after its inauguration, it became obvious that the tension among the different factions was not easy to overcome. When a senior member of the Nadwa proclaimed the leading role of the *ulama* in the guidance of mankind in accordance with the revelation, he was interrupted by the Mujtahid Ghulam al-Hasanayn Kinturi, the representative of the Shia communities. The latter noted the decay that most of the religious sciences have experienced, and questioned whether the Muslims could be saved from their downfall anyway. Others retorted that only a limited number of sciences was necessary for the reform. Emphasis was to be placed on the unity of knowledge and action.[29] This rhetorical exchange foreshadowed the formal exclusion of the Shia from the council soon after the second general meeting and reduced the initial aim of the Nadwa—to be an umbrella organization for all brands of Indo-Muslim scholarship—to absurdity. The Shia, firmly established in Lucknow from Nawabi times, had been perceived as a threat to the Sunni Muslim scholarship in town, prominently represented by the scholars of the Farangi Mahall. It seems as if the Farangi Mahallis played a vital role in driving Shiite scholars out of the Nadwa and establishing themselves more firmly within. The Shia religious establishment of Lucknow succeeded in working out its own strategies to deal with the colonial situation: With the explicit support of the British colonial administration, they opened the Shia College in the Chawk of Lucknow in 1917, a few hundred metres away from the Farangi Mahall. The Nadwa, meanwhile, had now turned into a purely Sunni Muslim enterprise.

The next group that could not withstand the theological differences with other factions in the council, which had grown over the preceding decades, was the Barelwiyya. Already by the second general meeting of the Nadwat al-ulama, which took place in Lucknow in January 1895, there were no representatives of the Barelwis among the delegates. The third general meeting in 1896, when almost 700 delegates gathered together in Bareilly, however, saw a final row sparking off. Only less than a third of the delegates belonged to the *ulama*. In this meeting, it became apparent that the leadership of the council around its head, Sayyid Muhammad Ali Mongiri, with its Naqshbandiyya-Mujaddidiyya ties and strict orthopraxy was not willing to compromise with what it called superstitious popular beliefs and practices.[30] To have such a large gathering held in the geographical centre of the Barelwiyya and, moreover, despite repeated protests, to openly attack what constitutes the core of Barelwi belief, was considered by the Barelwiyya too offensive to be tolerated any longer.

What commenced from here was a bitter argument between the urban, strictly orthoprax Nadwa, and the Barelwiyya, that found its major clientele in a rural environment where the Qadiriyya proved even more influential. This debate between the two groups was even turned in the following years into a transnational debate: Both sides sought the backing of eminent Muslim scholars in the Hijaz and started a fierce battle of *fatwas* and counter-*fatwas* that rage until today.[31] What should be of concern here is, that by this *de facto* exclusion of the Barelwiyya from the council—even if this has never been formally announced—the Nadwat al-ulama had made the next step towards becoming a body that represents only a particular section of Indo-Muslim scholarship.

The third group to be effectively marginalized at the end of the Nadwa's first decade of existence was the faction of the so-called

Modernists, led by Shibli Numani. This, the traditionalist turn of the Nadwa, is considered the major turning point in the early history of the council. Jamal Malik, who has presented the most thorough analysis of the matter so far, points out that this clash had a number of driving factors, such as the different clientele of each faction and their respective points of reference. The *ulama* represented the traditionalism preserved within the *qasbas*, whereas the modern scholars, the intellectuals or *mufakkirun*, referred rather to the towns and cities with all their inherent norms and institutions. The first group was represented by the head of the council, who was to symbolize the advocacy of traditionalist interests by the leadership of the Nadwa.

The charismatic Shibli, as the leading representative of the second group, lacked the backing of an office within the Nadwa, and thus seems to have been in a much more unfavourable position, despite his greater competence in addressing questions about the reform of a religious educational system. Accordingly, the conflicting interests of the two major factions within the Nadwa became most apparent in the discussion on a reform-oriented curriculum.

Shibli used the insights he gained in his travels to the Middle East as major arguments in the debate on the curriculum. To put it briefly, he emphatically stressed the necessity for studying the English language, a new scholastical theology [*kalam*], and, finally, a new historiography.[32] It was especially the last field that gained Shibli lasting fame: he was and is considered the first modern Muslim historiographer in India who tried to use Western historical methods, as can be seen from the expansive preface in his biographical work *al-Faruq* on the Umayyad caliph Umar b. Abd al-Aziz (1898).[33] The quest for a new theology might have been influenced by Shibli's knowledge of similar considerations by the Egyptian Grand-*mufti*, Muhammad Abduh (d. 1905) and his companions at around the same time.[34] The demands made by Shibli were perceived by the traditionalist wing of the Nadwa as questioning their self-understanding as well as their authority regarding religious learning. The opinion of the finally succeeding traditionalists on Shibli and his associates was expressed in a number of ways: the biography of Muhammad Ali Mongiri by Sayyid Muhammad al-Hasani, as a good example, accused Shibli of a hot temper, partly due to his origin from the vivacious Rajputs and partly due to his admiration for the rational sciences that lack a spiritual dimension. Shibli, according to the text, had improper intentions because of his socialisation. He did not see, as Mongiri did, that the goal of education was to establish a spiritual relationship to God, and therefore his ideas were not designed to make the Nadwa an integrative institution.[35]

We skip the intriguing developments of the next decade and move right to the year 1903, when Muhammad Ali Mongiri resigned from his office. This event is depicted as a great surprise in the official history of the Nadwa, but it cannot have been as unexpected as the source would like us to believe, because, already in 1895, three years after the inauguration of the council, Mongiri asked for his release from office due to his state of health and heavy workload. His request was not granted by the council, and he was awarded an assistant, Sayyid Abd al-Hayy al-Hasani of Rae Bareli (d. 1923) who was at that time only twnety-six.[36] Abd al-Hayy, a fierce traditionalist, shared with Mongiri an allegiance to the same Sufi-shaykh, the Naqshbandi-mujaddidi Fadl ar-Rahman Ganj Muradabadi (d. 1895),[37] and he received his education from eminent traditionalist scholars, among them the two already mentioned intellectual fountainheads of the *Ahl-i hadith*, Nadhir Husayn Dihlawi and Husayn b. Muhsin al-Yamani.[38] His aversion to a modernist rationalism had openly been expressed in 1894 in a letter to Sir Sayed Ahmad Khan, wherein he urged Sir Sayed to orient the teaching at Aligarh much more towards the study of Arabic and the traditional sciences.[39]

When Muhammad Ali Mongiri resigned from office, the vacuum was first filled by splitting the office between three secretaries, two of whom were Shibli and Abd al-Hayy. The argument between the two factions, however, became exacerbated and, in a board meeting in 1913, Abd al-Hayy proposed the abolition of the secretary that was Shibli's office. In July 1913, only a year before his death, the disappointed Shibli resigned and left for nearby Azamgarh, where he founded the Dar al-musannifin to realize his own ideas of reformist Muslim education.[40] Two years later, in April 1915, Sayyid Abd al-Hayy was appointed head of the Nadwat al-ulama. His appointment can be regarded as the final triumph of the traditional faction in the council over the so-called modernists. Moreover, it proved decisive for the future fate of the Nadwa, which has reached its peak so far under the presidency of Abd al-Hayy's second son, Sayyid Abul-Hasan Ali al-Hasani Nadwi (d. 1999), commonly known as Mawlana Ali Miyan.

THE 'TRADITIONALIST TURN': THE NADWAT AL-ULAMA IN THE TWENTIETH CENTURY

Already during the presidency of Sayyid Abd al-Hayy, the 'traditionalist turn', marked by a strong emphasis on Arabic as a medium of religious instruction and a much more traditional historiography than the one advocated by Shibli, was reinforced by a specific personnel policy that heavily relied on different kinds of loyalties. Muhammad b. Husayn al-Yamani (d. 1935), for example, was appointed teacher of Arabic and the sciences of *hadith* immediately after Abd al-Hayy's election as head of the Nadwa; he was the oldest son of Abd al-Hayy's own teacher in *hadith*, Husayn b. Muhsin al-Yamani.[41] Besides this particular staffing policy, however, there was the much more influential prevalence of nepotism within the al-Hasani-family, evident not only in the office of the head of the Nadwa, but even more so in the assigning of most of the male family members to different teaching positions at the Dar al-ulum of the Nadwat al-ulama, established already a few years after the inauguration of the council as a paradigmatic institution for reformist Muslim higher education. The Dar al-ulum soon became the crucial institution for the Nadwa—meanwhile shifted to Lucknow—where the impact of Deobandi scholarship is clearly visible.

In this regard, it has to be remembered that, under the label Deobandiyyat, a number of sometimes even conflicting positions and attitudes were brought together;[42] not all of these were formally supported by the scholars of the Nadwat al-ulama. The Jamiyat-i ulama-i Hind, for instance, founded by an influential section of Deobandi scholars in the wake of the Khilafat movement that collapsed in the early 1920s, allied itself with the Indian National Congress in order to have a learned Muslim body involved in day-to-day politics and, at the same time, to counterbalance the separatist attitude of Jinnah's All-India Muslim League after the 1937 elections. The Nadwis of Lucknow, however, seemed not to have supported such a vivid interest in practical politics: A look at the lists of participants of the Jamiyat-i ulama-i Hind's annual general meetings reveals that the scholars of the Nadwat al-ulama were represented only in a marginal way. Even in the annual convention in 1949, for example, which was held on 16-18 April at the Nadwa's Dar al-ulum, not a single representative of the Nadwa was present.[43] Even though the head of the Nadwa at that time, Sayyid Abd al-Ali al-

Hasani, participated two years earlier in a working session in Lucknow, it seems as if this was only a one-time affair.[44] There was, however, a strong personal relationship between Sayyid Abd al-Ali al-Hasani (d. 1961) and the then president of the Jamiyat-i ulama-i Hind, Husayn Ahmad Madani (d. 1957),[45] so that one can assume that there was some exchange between the Nadwa and the Jamiyat-i ulama-i Hind, albeit probably on a rather informal level.

Another offspring of Deobandi scholarship proved to have more of a formal impact on the Nadwa than the politics-oriented Jamiyyat-i ulama-i Hind: The manifold relations of the council with the missionary movement of the Tablighi Jamaat that took off in the 1920s and understands itself explicitly as an apolitical enterprise, became the most vivid expression of the 'traditionalist turn' of the Nadwat al-ulama. Even though the contacts between the council and leading Tablighis can be traced back as far as Sayyid Abdal-Hayy's term of office, it reached its climax during the presidency of Mawlana Ali Miyan. At least from the 1950s, when Sayyid Abdal-Hayy's eldest son Sayyid Abdal-Ali al-Hasani presided over the Nadwa, the council's estate in Lucknow became the scene of large annual gatherings of the Tablighi Jamaat.[46]

In the later decades of Ali Miyan's presidency as well, these gatherings clearly reflected the close relation between Nadwa and Tablighi Jamaat. This institutional affinity, expressed in a learned axis between the Dar al-ulum of the Nadwa in Lucknow and the Mazahir al-ulum in Saharanpur—the intellectual centre of the Tabligh movement—was supported by personal networks between leading Nadwis and Tablighis, as the case of Mawlana Ali Miyan himself illustrates.

Ali Miyan came to know of the Tabligh movement during his own personal search for proper religious guidance through an article of Sayyid Abul-Ala Mawdudi (d. 1979) in the latter's journal *Tarjuman al-quran*.[47] The connecting link, however, was the Deobandi scholar Muhammad Manzur Numani (d. 1997) of Lucknow, who was at that time already a *murid* of one of the spiritual leaders of the Tablighi Jamaat, Abdal-Qadir Raepuri (d. 1962). When Abdal-Qadir came to Lucknow on a missionary tour in 1948, Ali Miyan took the *baya* and, thus, became part of a Sufi network that was very much instrumental in spreading the Tabligh movement all over India and even beyond. Leading Deobandi scholars, such as the already mentioned Husayn Ahmad Madani, who was—apart from being the *murshid* of Sayyid

Abdal-Ali al-Hasani—also a teacher of Ali Miyan, belonged to this network, giving it additional weight.[48] After the demise of Abd al-Qadir Raepuri, Ali Miyan seems to have employed the very same strategy of using *piri-muridi*-relations to spread the movement. His own reputation in the Arab speaking world, mainly gained from his famous work *Ma-dha khasira l-alam bi-nhitat al-muslimin* from 1947, became the major vehicle for spreading the movement in a number of Arab speaking countries. On the other hand, with his international reputation and self-confidence rising, Ali Miyan seems to have begun to contest the leading role of the *Mazahir al-ulum* at Saharanpur as intellectual centre of the Tablighi Jamaat and, instead, attempted to have drawn this position to the Nadwat al-ulama.[49] This endeavour is embodied in the so-called Academy of Islamic Research and Publication—*Majlis-i tahqiqat wa nashriyyat-i islam*—founded in May 1959 on Ali Miyan's initiative within the institutional frame of the Nadwa.[50] The Academy seems to have been established to counterbalance the publishing houses of the Tablighi Jamaat in Delhi and Saharanpur, such as the 'Institute for the Distribution of Religious Writings'—the Idara-yi ishaat-i diniyyat—opened in 1950 in Delhi's Basti Nizamuddin.[51] Alongside the establishment of the Academy of Islamic Research and Publication and supporting its activities, Ali Miyan initiated the foundation of the fortnightly *Tamir-i hayat* as the new Urdu-periodical of the Nadwa. Already its title—Establishment of the [pious] Life—points towards the aim of religious call [*dawa*] in the way of the Tablighi Jamaat, and, in this programme it somehow constitutes a break with its predecessor. In the editorial in the first issue the editor Sayyid Muhammad al-Hasani Nadwi, son of Ali Miyan's elder brother Sayyid Abd al-Ali al-Hasani, highlighted the connection between the journal and the new emphasis on religious *dawa* within the Nadwat al-ulama. First, he explicitly stressed the relation with the Majlis-i tahqiqat wa nashriyyat-i islam in terms of its programme as well as its institutional structure. Second, however, he pointed towards the ultimate goal of the periodical, the presentation and propagation of the temporally and spatially invariable Islamic message.[52] Consequently, the *dawa*-activities of Ali Miyan and the Tablighi Jamaat occupied a central place in the first volumes of *Tamir-i hayat*. At the same time, the editor of this journal emphasized the crucial importance of the Nadwat al-ulama and its institutional support for advancing these aims through the special position of the council and its numerous bodies in relation to a general Islamic reform.[53] That, again, relates to Ali Miyan's own idea of the central role of the *ulama* as the only legitimate administrators of religious knowledge, especially within the realms of the Islamic Law. Because the *ulama*, so he imagined, had to bear an extraordinary responsibility in this regard, they had to be awarded a leading position. The argument finally comes full circle and meets the historical outline with which we started.

CONCLUSION

The establishment of a National Council of Muslim Religious Scholars in India was already rooted in the ambivalent role Muslim scholarship played in relation to political rule in the seventeenth and eighteenth centuries. The decline of the Mughal state alongside the emancipation of its former vassal states to *de facto* autonomous territorial states, found vivid expression in the increasingly diverse perceptions of the political and religious situation in the land. Muslim scholars developed different strategies of dealing with it, depending on their views which were, again, determined not least by their perspective, be it from the centre of the Mughal state or its periphery.

The colonial encounter of the early nineteenth century first provided more or less a shared situation by levelling the differences between what had been the administrative centre and the periphery of the Mughal state. The aftermath of 1857 seems to have provided a new impulse for evaluating the state of Muslim communities in India, and for developing strategies to overcome what has been perceived as religious and political crisis. These strategies, however, exhibited great variety, owing to different religious traditions and the need to address different social clienteles. What appeared was a heterogeneous picture of conflicting scholarly traditions that seemed able to provide neither a firm nor a common base for Indian Muslims to orient their lives to the commandments of the normative sources of Islam, the Koran and the Sunna. As a final attempt to solve this problem of representation of different strata of the Indian Muslim communities and to enable the intellectual élites to act as advocates of Muslim interests in their difficult social and political situation that followed the breakdown of the Mughal empire, a National Council of Muslim Religious Scholars was convened. This council's initial task was to settle internal differences and to work out strategies to deal with the present situation.

As we saw, the Nadwat al-ulama became in fact rather a battlefield in which different factions sought to push through their specific interests, claiming them to be the common interests of Indian Muslims. The plurality of opinion gathered by its initiators, in order to consensually come to a balance in an almost Habermasian discourse, was soon undermined by either expelling certain factions from the council, or by forcing them out, as seen in the case of the 'Modernist' faction led by Shibli Numani. What remained in the National Council of (now exclusively Sunni) Muslim Religious Scholars was a traditionalist institution, dominated by Deobandi (and, although to a lesser degree, *Ahl-i hadith*) scholarship, even though it still claimed to represent a national consensus of scholarly opinion. In the course of the 'traditionalist turn' of the Nadwa, officially marked by the election of Sayyid Abdal-Hayy al-Hasani as head of the council in 1913, it became increasingly affiliated with the missionary movement of the Tablighi Jamaat, an offspring of Deobandi scholarship and, to this day, heavily interrelated with it. What remained at the core of the Nadwa was a religious missionary institution, competing with other learned entres of the Tablighi Jamaat—above all the Mazahir al-ulum at Saharanpur—for religious leadership within the scope of religious *dawa*, and an internationally acclaimed centre for the Study of the Arabic language and (religious) literature.

This development, however, seems to follow the logic of the predominantly inward gaze of Muslim religious scholars in times of accelerated economic, social, and political change. This logic differs considerably from the more politically-minded and, in this sense, more outward orientation of the new functional élites, the so-called *mufakkirun*. The Jamiyat-i ulama-i Hind may seem to be an exception to the rule, but final conclusions have to await a more thorough analysis of this body. Although the Nadwat al-ulama was initally meant to harmonize all prevailing viewpoints in Indo-Muslim scholarship by involving intellectuals as well as different factions of the *ulama*, it soon became apparent that the competing notions of 'appropriate' Muslim reformist education as the crucial issue for a Muslim cultural identity for the age were not equally in play. The role of the intellectuals with their more politically-oriented gaze faded out quite early, leaving the field almost entirely to a particular tradition of South Asian Sunni Muslim scholarship that claimed legitimate representation of Indo-Muslim interest. The inward gaze of a large number of these South Asian *ulama* leads to a certain conservatism, which, in turn, is reflected in the assertion of a particular Muslim religious identity by constantly narrowing the variety of interpretations of 'Muslimness' that in fact co-exist at one particular time within a certain spatial and social frame.

NOTES

1. Cf. Robinson (2000: 142-4).
2. Ikram (1957: 343-89); Rizvi (1983: II, 84-96); id. (1995: 148-75); Voll (1980: 265).
3. Ikram (1957: 223-342); Rizvi (1983: II, 196-223); id. (1995: 202-60); Friedmann (1971).
4. Qurayshi (1995); Fusfeld (1981: 154-241); Algar (1991: 135); Damrel (1991: 275); Malik (1993: 56f.; 2003: 83f.).
5. Thubut (1374sh/1996: 63-76).
6. Dehlawi (1986: 24-6); Khan (1992: 210-13).
7. Metcalf (1982: 47).
8. Ibid. (1984: 6).
9. Dehlawi (1321/1902-3: II, 53-83).
10. In this paper the terms 'Conformism' and 'Non-Conformism' refer to the position of an individual towards an existing political structure. These positions lead to the adherence to different paradigms of action that might be perceived similar to the Weberian distinction between 'ethics of conviction' [*Gesinnungsethik*] and 'politics', as the execution of rule by power.
11. Ibid. (I, 30f.).
12. al-Hasani (1991: VII, 212f.; VIII, 122-6, 523-7); Siyalkoti (1995: 425-35).
13. al-Hasani (1991: VII, 66-71); Ahmad (1994); Malik (1997: 190f.).
14. Metcalf (1982: 265, 273f., 294); Ridwi (1976-7: I, 12, 92-5); Athari (1415/1995: 66-76).
15. Metcalf (1982: 125-37).
16. Ibid. (36, 209-11).
17. Robinson (2001); Malik (1997).
18. Ibid. (151-68, 522-9); Robinson (2001: 46-55); Thubut (1374sh/1996: 29-48).
19. Malik (1997: 530-5).
20. Ibid. (214f.); Troll (1978: 144-70, 215-22); Lelyveld (1978: 204-52); Metcalf (1982: 320-4).
21. Sanyal (1996: 132-5, 151-65, 255-64). In classical use, however, this phrase constituted a code for the Hanafite approach in jurisprudence, backed by the theology of the *Maturidiyya* (on this cf. the remarks of Wilferd Madelung in his 'Religious Schools and Sects in Medieval Islam', London: Variorum Reprints, 1995).

22. On the sector model Schulze (2000: 103-7).
23. On the problem of the dichotomy of scholars and intellectuals cf. Hartung (2001: 191-3).
24. Malik (1997: 223), translation mine.
25. Numani (1999: 156-60, 172-6); S.S. Nadwi (1993: 213-18); Jalis Nadwi (1407/1983: 76-86).
26. al-Majdhub (1983: I, 196).
27. Malik (1997: 232f.). On the missionary efforts of Christians on Muslims cf. Powell (1993). On the missionary activities of Hindu organizations, over and above all the reconversion movement of the Arya Samaj culminating in the first decades of the twentieth century, cf. Fischer-Tiné (1995).
28. Jalis Nadwi (1407/1983: 95-100).
29. Anonymous (n.d.: 96f.). Typically enough, neither the official protocol of the meeting, nor the official history of the Nadwa mention the speech of Ghulam al-Hasanayn Kinturi. The latter, moreover, attempts to rather draw a picture of harmony between the different factions. Jalis Nadwi (1407/1983: 104).
30. Ibid. (165f.).
31. Hartung (forthcoming).
32. Troll (1993: 1-19).
33. Numani (1898: I, 9-21).
34. Hourani (1962: 144-58, 161-92).
35. al-Hasani (1964: 272-84).
36. Nadwi (1390/1970: 136-8).
37. Ibid. (93-103).
38. Ibid. (64f.).
39. Ibid. (72-81).
40. S.S. Nadwi (1993: 690-701).
41. Khan (1404/1984: 91, 118, 127); Nadwi (1414/1994: I, 210f.).
42. This variety, that culminated so far in providing ideological and also logistic backing to the Afghan *Taliban* by a certain brand of Deobandi scholarship, has been impressivly analysed in Metcalf (2002).
43. Anonymous, *Minute Book of Jamiate Ulma-e-Hind* [*sic*] *1925-51 (Exec) 47-67 (Admin)*, MS on Microfilm (Urdu), New Delhi: Jawaharlal Nehru Memorial Library, No. R-1934., pp. 75-9.
44. Ibid., pp. 33-5; Nadwi (1390/1970: 377f.).
45. Ibid. (369f.).
46. al-Hasani (1420/1999: 340-2, 349f.).
47. I.A. Nadwi (1992: 42).
48. A.H. Nadwi (1404/1984: I, 279, 352-4); id. (1994: 166-98).
49. As a vivid expression of the tension between Ali Miyan and Muhammad Zakariyya (d. 1982), for a long period of time the

intellectual driving force behind the Tablighi Jamaat, cf. Zakariyya (s.t.: I, 12).

50. Anonymous (1963: 17).
51. On this publishing house cf. Metcalf (1993: 583f.).
52. al-Hasani (1963 (2): 1).
53. Ibid. (1963(1): 1f.).

REFERENCES

Ahmad, Qeyamuddin, 1994, *The Wahhabi Movement in India*, New Delhi: Manohar (Revised Edition).

Algar, Hamid, 1991, 'Political Aspects of Naqshbandi History', in: Marc Gaborieau, Alexandre Popovi, Thierry Zarcone (eds.), *Naqshbandis. Cheminements et Situation Actuelle d'un Ordre Mystique Musulman*, Istanbul: édition Isis, pp. 123-52.

Anonymous, 1963, 'Majlis-i tahqiqat wa nashriyyat-i islam—maqasid', *Ta'mir-i hayat* 1:1, p. 17.

Anonymous, n.d., *Madrasa-yi Fayd-i amm Kanpur 1308*, Kanpur.

Athari, Irshad al-Haqq, 1415/1995, *Pak wa Hind men ulama-i Ahl-i hadith ki khidmat-i hadith*, Maunath bhanjan: Markazi maktaba-yi Ahl-i hadith.

Damrel, D.W., 1991, 'The Spread of Naqshbandi Political Thought in the Islamic World', in: Marc Gaborieau, Alexandre Popovi, Thierry Zarcone (eds.), *Naqshbandis. Cheminements et Situation Actuelle d'un Ordre Mystique Musulman*, Istanbul: édition Isis, pp. 269-87.

Dehlawi, Shah Abd al-Aziz, 1321/1902-3, *Fatawa-yi Azizi*, 2 vols., Deoband: Kutubkhana-yi Rahimiyya.

Dehlawi, Shah Wali-allah, 1986, *Hujjat allah al-baligha*, Deoband: Maktaba-yi Thanawi.

Fischer-Tine, Harald, 1995, 'Die suddhi-Bewegung des Arya Samaj und ihre Rolle bei der Konstituierung einer Hindu-Identitat', unpublished M.A. thesis, South Asia Institute, University of Heidelberg.

Friedmann, Yohanan, 1971, *Shaykh Ahmad Sirhindi: An Outline of His Thought and a Study of His Image in the Eyes of Posterity*, Montreal: McGill-Queen's University Press.

Fusfeld, Warren Edward, 1981, 'The Shaping of Sufi Leadership in Delhi: The Naqshbandiyya Mujaddidiyya, 1750 to 1920', unpublished Ph.D. thesis, University of Pennsylvania.

Hartung, Jan-Peter, 2001, 'Affection and Aversion: Ambivalences among Muslim Intellectual élites in Contemporary South Asia', *South Asia Research* 21: 2, pp. 189-202.

———, forthcoming, 'Wahhabis and Anti-Wahhabis: The Learned Discourse on Sufism in Contemporary South Asia', in: Sìren Lassen (ed.), *Tradition and Renewal of South Asian Sufism*, Würzburg: Ergon.

al-Hasani, Abd al-Hayy, 1991, *al-Ilam bi-man fi tarikh al-Hind min al-alam yani nuzhat al-khawatir wa-bahjat al-masami wa-n-nawazir*, 8 vols., Rai Bareli: Darat ash-shaykh Alam-allah (rpt.).

al-Hasani, Muhammad Thani, 1420/1999, *Sawanih-i Hadrat Mawlana Muhammad Yusuf Kandhalawi*, Lucknow: Majlis-i sahafat wa nashriyyat.

al-Hasani, Sayyid Muhammad, 1963 (1), 'Tajdid-i ahd—kuchh yaden kuchh azaim' , *Tamir-i hayat* 1: 1, pp. 1f.

———, 1963 (2), 'Tamir-i hayat ka maqsad', *Tamir-i hayat* 1: 5, p. 1.

———, 1964, *Sirat-i Mawlana Muhammad Ali Mongiri: Bani-yi Nadwat al-ulama*, Lucknow: Maktaba-yi Dar al-ulum-i Nadwat al-ulama.

Hourani, Albert, 1962, *Arabic Thought in the Liberal Age, 1798-1939*, London, New York, Toronto: Oxford University Press.

Ikram, Shaykh Muhammad, 1957, *Rud-i kawthar. Islami Hind wa Pakistan ki madhhabi wa ilmi tarikh, ahd-i mughaliyya se pahle*, Delhi: Matiya Mahall.

Jalis Nadwi, Muhammad Ishaq, 1407/1983, *Tarikh-i Nadwat al-ulama. Hissa-yi awwal*, Lucknow: Daftar-i nizamat-i Nadwat al-ulama.

Khan, Shams-i Tabriz, 1404/1984, *Tarikh-i Nadwat al-ulama: Hissa-yi duwum*, Lucknow: Daftar-i nizamat-i Nadwat al-ulama.

Khan, Hafiz A. Ghaffar, 1992, 'Shah Wali Allah: On the Nature, Origin, Definition, and Classification of Knowledge', *Journal of Islamic Studies* 3: 2, pp. 203-13.

Lelyveld, David, 1978, *Aligarh's First Generation. Muslim Solidarity in British India*, Princeton: Princeton University Press.

al-Majdhub, Muhammad, 1983, *Ulama wa-mufakkirun araftuhum*, 3 vols., al-Qahira: Dar al-itisam.

Malik, Jamal, 1993, 'Islamic Institutions and Infrastructure in Shajahanabad', in: Eckart Ehlers, Thomas Krafft (eds.), *Shahjahanabad/Old Delhi: Tradition and Colonial Change*, New Delhi: Manohar, 2003, pp. 71-92.

———, 1997, *Islamische Gelehrtenkultur in Nordindien. Entwicklungsgeschichte und Tendenzen am Beispiel von Lucknow*, Leiden-New York-Cologne: Brill.

Metcalf, Barbara Daly, 1982, *Islamic Revival in British India: Deoband, 1860-1900*, Princeton: Princeton University Press.

———, 1984, 'Introduction', in: id. (ed.), *Moral Conduct and Authority, The Place of Adab in South Asian Islam*, Berkeley-Los Angeles-London: University of California Press, pp. 1-20.

———, 1993, 'Living Hadith in the Tablighi Jamaat', *Journal of Asian Studies* 52: 3, pp. 584-608.

———, 2002, *'Traditionalist' Islamic Activism: Deoband, Tablighis, and Talibs*, ISIM-Paper 4, Leiden: ISIM.

Nadwi, Hakim Khwaja Iqbal Ahmad, 1992, *Mawlana Mawdudi awr ulama-i karam: Ek tajziyya*, Lahore: Islamik Pablikeshanz.

Nadwi, Sayyid Abu l-Hasan Ali al-Hasani, 1390/1970, *Hayat-i Abdal-Hayy. ma' damima*, Delhi: Nadwat al-musannifin.

———, 1404/1984, *Karwan-i zindagi*, 7 vols., Lucknow: Maktaba-yi islam.

———, 1414/1994, *Purane ciragh*, 3 vols., Lucknow: Maktaba-yi Firdaws.

———, 1994, *Sawanih-i Hadrat Mawlana Abdal-Qadir Raepuri*, Lucknow: Maktaba-yi islam.

Nadwi, Sayyid Sulayman, 1993, *Hayat-i Shibli*, Azamgarh: Dar al-musannifin (rpt.).

Numani, Muhammad Shibli, 1898, *al-Faruq yani Hadrat Umar—radiyya llahu anhu—ki mufassal sawanih umri*, 2 vols., Azamgarh: Matba Maarif.

———, 1999, *Safarnama-yi Rum wa Misr wa Sham*, Azamgarh: Dar al-musannifin (rpt.).

Powell, Avril A., 1993, *Muslims and Missionaries in Pre-Mutiny India*, Richmond: Curzon.

Qurayshi, Abd ar-Razzaq (ed.), 1995, *Makatib-i Mirza Mazhar Jan-i Janan*, Patna: Khuda Bakhsh Oriental Public Library.

Ridwi, Sayyid Mahbub, 1976-7, *Tarikh-i Dar al-ulum Deoband*, 2 vols., Deoband: Idara-yi ihtimam-i dar al-ulum Deoband.

Rizvi, Saiyid Athar Abbas, 1983, *A History of Sufism in India*, 2 vols., New Delhi: Munshiram Manoharlal (rpt.).

———, 1995, *Muslim Revivalist Movements in Northern India in the Sixteenth and the Seventeenth Centuries*, New Delhi: Munshiram Manoharlal (rpt.).

Robinson, Francis, 2000, 'The Muslims of Upper India and the Shock of the Mutiny', in: id. (ed.), *Islam and Muslim History in South Asia*, New Delhi: Oxford University Press, pp. 138-55.

———, 2001, *The Ulama of Farangi Mahall and Islamic Culture in South Asia*, New Delhi: Permanent Black.

Sanyal, Usha, 1996, *Devotional Islam and Politics in British India. Ahmad Riza Khan Barelwi and his Movement, 1870-1920*, New Delhi: Oxford University Press.

Schulze, Reinhard, 2000, *A Modern History of the Islamic World*, London: I.B. Tauris.

Siyalkoti, Muhammad Ibrahim Mir, 1995, *Tarikh-i Ahl-i hadith*, New Delhi: al-Kitab Intarneshnal.

Thubut, Akbar, 1374sh/1996, *Madaris-i islami-yi Hind dar tul-i tarikh wa jaygah-i farhang-i Iran anha*, Tihran: Bakhsh-i tahqiqat.

Troll, Christian W., 1978, *Sayyid Ahmad Khan: A Reinterpretation of Muslim Theology*, Karachi: Oxford University Press.

———, 1993, 'Muhammad Shibli Numani (1857-1914) and the Reform of

Muslim Religious Education', *Islam and the Modern Age* 24:1, pp. 1-19.

Voll, John O., 1980, 'Hadith Scholars and Tariqahs: An Ulama Group in the 18th Century Haramayn and their Impact in the Islamic World', *Journal of African and Asian Studies* 15, pp. 264-73.

Zakariyya, Muhammad, n.d., *Ap biti: Khud-niwisht sawanih-i hayat*, 2 vols., Saharanpur: Maktaba-yi Shaykh Zakariyya.

6

Local Roots of Tablighi Jamaat in Orissa

SYED ZAINUDDIN

This paper focuses on the organizational structure of the Tablighi Jamaat (hereafter TJ). It is based on fieldwork experience and participation in the programmes and activities of Tablighis in the coastal districts of Orissa between April 1994 and December 1996.

I begin with some observations on the state of the literature on Islam and the TJ. Recent years have seen a resurgence of interest in Islam, but scholars have found it difficult to resist the temptation of projecting Islam in homogeneous and essentialized terms, with regional variations either sidelined or presented as a deviation from the norm.[1] Imtiaz Ahmad has since long been protesting against the marginalization of Indian Islam, and the general tendency among scholars to deny it an authentic status of its own.[2] Indian Islam is not a pale imitation of the Islam of some other Islamic world; it has evolved through centuries of interaction with the non-Muslim people of India.

Within the framework of an essentialized Islam, most works on Muslim religious organizations, including TJ, tend to paint them in broad strokes, endowing them with an immanent and quite immutable ideology and organization.[3] There is also a tendency in these works to emphasize their pan-Islamic, 'extra-territorial', connections, largely bypassing details of their activities in India.[4] Thus one important scholar of Indian Islam has described the TJ as a 'transnational religious movement'.[5] My objective in this paper is to study the activities and organization of TJ in a regional and local context. In order to do so, I reject the pan-Islamic, decontextualized frames of reference within which much work on contemporary Islam has been undertaken. But we can go a step further to deconstruct, as it were, even the category of pan-Indian Islam, taking local conditions as the primary context of analysis.

The area of my study is the coastal districts of Orissa: Cuttack, Puri, Balasore, Kendrapara, Jajpur, and Jagatsinghpur. According to

1991 Census, Muslims constitute 1.83 per cent of the total population of Orissa. Their concentration is higher in Balasore (4.3 per cent), Cuttack (4.14), Sundargarh (2.62), and Puri (2.32). The majority of Muslims are engaged in agriculture and related occupations. Being a minority community in an industrially backward state, their poor representation in various modern sectors of the economy is easily understandable.

Unlike north India, Muslims in Orissa are deeply integrated in the regional culture of Orissa and, economically, pose no threat to non-Muslims in trade, commerce, business, or government jobs. Therefore Orissa does not witness a high incidence of communal tension and violence.[6] However, within the context of uneven development and relatively poor access of the minorities to its gains, they are becoming more and more conscious of their deprivation, which leads to the sharpening of identity. Their identity articulation is visible in the construction of new mosques, the renovation and expansion of old mosques, the establishment of *madrasas*, increased attendance in mosques, and the celebration of religious festivals.

IDEOLOGY OF THE JAMAAT

No study of the organizational structure of TJ would be complete without outlining its ideology. Like any other Islamic movement, the TJ is premised on the lives of Prophet Muhammad, his associates, and the teachings of the Koran and Hadith. As Prophethood came to an end with Prophet Muhammad, the responsibility of calling people to Allah, according to Tablighi ideology, falls squarely on the shoulders of the Muslim community.

The secret of success for Muslims in this world and hereafter, it is believed, lies in practising and recreating the teachings of Prophet Muhammad and his associates which were revealed by Allah. Any deviation from the path of the *Sunnat* (the Prophet's practices) is deemed to be a failure. Maulana Ilyas diagnosed the predicament of Muslims as a deviation from the path of Prophet, especially from his practice of preaching about Allah's commands. In order to regain their lost glory, it is believed, Muslims must take to the work of Tabligh, call people to Allah, and show the right path of success. This practice of calling people to Allah is viewed as the prime mission of all the Prophets from Adam to Muhammad. In their preaching they should follow the Koranic teaching to call people to 'the way of the Lord with wisdom and fair exhortation and reason with them in the better way'.[7]

Thus the collective success of the Muslim community is believed to depend on activities such as internalizing the missionary spirit, acquiring basic knowledge of Islam and its dissemination to Muslims through mutual cooperation so as to call upon the believers, within the Koranic injunction to 'command what is amicable and forbid what is indecent'.[8] Unlike Maulana Maududi, Maulana Ilyas did not seek conversion, but stressed on purifying Muslims into better Muslims who would set practical examples of Islam before other communities. Maulana Ilyas's strategy was aimed at winning the hearts of the Muslims for seeking favour from Allah.

The fundamental principles of Tablighi ideology come out vividly in *chhe baten* (six points) developed by Maulana Ilyas, which are discussed in the following paragraphs.

First, *kalimah* (the profession of the faith) is the most fundamental aspect of faith obligatory for all Muslims. It consists of two parts. The first part is *tauhid,* that there is no one worthy of worship except Allah, the second part is known as *risala* that Muhammad is the last Prophet of Allah. There is a great deal of emphasis on reciting the *kalimah* properly and understanding its meanings fully and practising them in everyday life, so that the faith in Allah and His Prophet is deeply entrenched in the mind and heart of the believers and manifested in thoughts, actions and outlook. After all when a person recites *kalimah,* he or she submits to the will of Allah. The participants are asked to erase the faith in all other beings except the trust in Allah. This is because, it is believed, all creatures, all human beings are dependent upon Him and He is dependent on none. The Tablighis are further taught that Allah can do everything without depending upon any means whereas human beings cannot do anything in spite of the requisite means unless Allah blesses it. The success and failure of human beings is entirely at His disposal. He is also capable of ensuring success under distressing situations and failure in apparently favourable circumstances. The second part of the *kalimah* refers to the belief that Muhammad is His last Prophet. His way of life and teachings are to be considered as the guidelines for every believer. Moreover, the prevailing lifestyles are believed to be false and improper for the believers. The success of the believers in this world and Hereafter is linked to conformity to the ways of the Prophet, which faces threat in the present time. Therefore, the recitation and practice of *kalimah* is expected to be repeated so often that, 'its spirit permeates all our beings, our soul is filled with the burden of its music and all our actions are performed with the total submission of our will to Allah'.[9]

The second fundamental point of *Tabligh* is the five times daily *namaz* (canonical prayer). If *kalimah* is the pledge that binds the believer with Allah, namaz is its demonstration and evidence in the everyday life of Muslims. The offering of namaz by all adult males and females five times a day at specified times is obligatory. Its importance in Islam is explained through the metaphor of the 'head'. As there cannot be any human being without a head, so there could be no Muslim without namaz. Of all the rituals in Islam, namaz is considered the most important. Its importance is expressed as the 'gateway to all other practices', 'mother of all practices', etc. Unlike other practices, namaz is the only practice which solely concentrates on the realm of the profane. This is explained with reference to *roza* (fasting), *zakat* (alms giving) and *haj* (pilgrimage to Mecca), as the believer constantly shuttles back and forth from the 'profane' to the 'sacred'. What is expected from namaz is the total submission of the believer to the command of Allah. This enables him to realize that he is nothing but a slave of Allah. In namaz, all parts of human body like tongue, hands, fingers, eyes, legs, etc., are engaged in the obedience of Allah and His Prophet. Maulana Ilyas elaborates this as:

> What we have professed in *Kalimah* has to be proved by employment of our 'self' and 'resources' in the service of Allah. By offering *Salat (*namaz) at the appointed hours of day and night as an obligatory duty we, in fact, practice the employment of our 'self' in Allah's service. *Salat* should, therefore, not be merely a ritual but be so full of earnestness that it may influence our whole life by refining and improving all our habits. It should be imbued with the spirit of constant service to Allah.[10]

The believer can seek solutions to his difficulties in this world and the hereafter through namaz. Namaz is believed to be the most effective protection against all sinful acts. The benefits of namaz have been much emphasized and explained with reference to Koran and Hadith. This has been a point of criticism. The critics of tabligh point out that Tablighis have reduced Islam to namaz.

The third fundamental of Tabligh is *ilm* (knowledge) and *zikr* (remembrance of God). The adherents of Tabligh are exhorted to acquire basic and working knowledge which would enable them to perform religious practices like namaz, *roza, zakat, haj,* etc., and other-worldly engagements in consonance with the commands of Allah and His Prophet. The purpose of knowledge is also to inform believers about the virtues of various Islamic practices and warning and admonitions about negligence. If *ilm* is looked upon as a path to come closer to Allah, then *zikr* is seen as the light leading to that path. The activists of Tabligh are trained to remember Allah in all spheres of their lives. Through continuous and repeated remembering of Allah, it is believed, Allah becomes part of the consciousness. There is no time limit for performing *zikr* as it can be performed in one's spare time. But to inculcate the habit of engaging in *zikr,* every believer is advised to recite every morning and evening three Arabic verses such as *kalimah tamhid* (glorification of Allah), *darud* (salutation on Prophet Muhammad and invoking Allah's blessings on him) and *istighfar* (seeking forgiveness of Allah from one's own sins), a hundred times each. Furthermore, adherents are also exhorted to memorize various *dua* (Koranic verses) and to recite them on various occasions such as dining, travelling, retiring for the night, etc.

The fourth fundamental of Tabligh refers to *ikram-e-Muslim* (respecting every Muslim). This fundamental quality is cultivated to show respect and concern to their co-religionists irrespective of their merits. Members are taught to treat all Muslims not only as equals but also as superior to themselves. They are further trained to ignore distinctions of class, status, power, race, and nationality. This finds vivid expression during the course of Jamaat in action. The *Amir* (leader) allocates various roles in Jamaat right from preparing food, looking after the belongings of members, and delivering discourses, irrespective of their status, class, and power. Moreover, during the course of Jamaat, the novices are never put to embarrassment for their errors and are looked after well. Volunteers carry their own baggage on their shoulders, irrespective of social status.

Apart from showing respect to every Muslim, the other aspect of the fourth fundamental of Tabligh is *akhlaque* (civility) and *huquq-ul-ibad* (the rights of human beings) which are not confined to Muslims alone but extend to all humanity. Volunteers are exhorted to offer their services to all the creatures of Allah, without expecting a return. The minimum level of Tablighi is not to harm anyone and to do good to all, irrespective of religious affiliations. This dictum is used with the belief that Islam could spread only through moral values and character building. The experiences of performing various religious activities like namaz, *roza, haj,* and *zakat* remain confined to Muslims, and do not go beyond their community. It is only the moral values and character building which could be experienced by non-Muslims as well, in the public domain. These experiences, it is believed, would attract non-Muslims to the fold of Islam. The rights incorporated in *huqul-ul-ibad* include, among others, the right of the non-Muslim neighbours, the sick, poor and old. Muslims are also expected to learn the habit of fulfilling the rights of others and forgetting their own rights even if they are violated. This disposition could be acquired, the Tablighis believe, by moving out and seeking people's help in preaching, so that the art of seeking blessings from Allah and bringing benefits to people at large could be attained.

Ikhlas-e-niyat (sincerity of intention) is emphasized as the fifth fundamental of Tabligh so that every act by a Muslim is performed with the sole objective of earning the pleasure of Allah rather than attaining name and fame. The followers of Tabligh are constantly forewarned that if their acts are performed for any purpose other than pleasing Allah, they would not qualify for any reward, and instead it will amount to indulging in *shirk* (polytheism).

The sixth fundamental is *tafrigh-e-waqt* (sparing time). It is strongly emphasized among the adherents that their lives and resources belong to Allah and they are not free to use them as they wish. Adherents are taught to make limited use of these things in this world as per His commands and spend the rest in calling others to Allah so that they would be rewarded in both worlds. Nevertheless, the question of the extent of time and resources the believers would spend on their own necessities depends on the model of the Prophet. It may be clarified that the purpose of sparing time does not mean giving up the duty of earning one's livelihood and looking after familial and other necessities. A member should allocate a period of four months in his lifetime, in addition to forty days every year, for work beyond his locality. The schedule for his residential locality is to hold *mashwarah* (consultations) every day in the local mosque with the people living in and around the mosque; organizing one *talim* (reading of excerpts from *Fazail-i-Amal*) at the neighbourhood mosque and another in one's residence everyday; organizing every week two *gasht* (taking round), one in the locality and another in a neighbouring locality; going out for three days in Jamaat in every month to nearby areas and spending two and a half hours every day in the mosque in *zikr*, recitation of Koran, etc. TJ's ideology does not have any explicit and elaborate social and economic agenda like that of the Jamaat-e-Islam, and has so far remained confined to the six-point programme discussed above.

ORIGIN OF THE TABLIGHI JAMAAT

The TJ began as a reform movement in the late 1920s in the Mewat (Haryana) and its neighbouring areas. The ideology of the movement resembled several other early twentieth-century Islamic movements that endeavoured to revive 'True Islam' in response to the cultural onslaught of the colonial occupation. Maulana Muhammad Ilyas, the founder of the TJ, constantly highlighted the threat which a non-Islamic society posed for those who had only superficially internalized the Islamic faith. He laid stress upon certain routine imperatives taken from the Koran and Hadith for the daily affirmation of Islamic identity.

From its early mobilization in a Muslim population that was a minority and lacked power and privileges, the TJ gained credibility in many other areas where Muslims enjoy political power and are in majority. Indeed, there is enough material to support the view that the TJ has today emerged as a salient trans-national religious movement throughout the Islamic world.[11] Its influence has been reported in north Africa, Pakistan, and Bangladesh as well as among Muslim immigrants in western and eastern Europe, and north America.

ORGANIZATIONAL STRUCTURE

I had the opportunity to collect in-depth data through participation in several three-day Jamaat. Interviews were also conducted with those Tablighi volunteers whose exposure to the Jamaat experience ranged from one *chilla* (40 days) to three *chillas*. The interview questions were guided by three broad considerations: (1) the nature and content of processes and networks which bring volunteers from the community to mosque (2) from the mosque to the Jamaat's formation, spanning from three days to three *chillas* and (3) how the TJ continuously reproduces allegiance to its programme among its active and casual members. In other words, how conformity is secured and control is exercised in the Tablighi community.

To a casual observer the TJ does not seem to possess a clear formal organization, yet from the elaborate level at which the movement operates today, involving regulation of programmes and activities, and formulation of strategies of the movement in different countries, it is difficult to believe that it can operate without an organization of some kind. Yet, the organization does not embody explicit rules and regulations and has no fixed schedule and offices for its personnel. It is this feature to which Maulana Ilyas referred when he said:

> We have no party, no formal type of organisation, no office, no register. Our work is to be shared by all Muslims. That is why according to the times, we have not formed our people into a separate Jamaat (party). We are just working on the pattern of the mosques where people come together from different walks of life and after having said their prayers return to their daily chores. In the same manner we ask you (Muslims) to spare some time to train yourself and then go back to your daily duties. Once you have imbibed religion in its true spirit, the people of the world will approach you to acquire knowledge from you and Insha Allah, one of these days, the leadership of the world will be conferred upon you.[12]

To get a feel for how this functions, we need to understand the working of a Jamaat consisting of 10-12 persons, the various activities undertaken therein, their regulation and organization, and the allocation of specific roles to its members.

The working of TJ is centered on the community around mosques. In the early days of Islam, mosques played a key role in religious as well as community life. A mosque was the centre for *talim* (education) and *mashwarah* (consultations), for training individuals for social life, and for forming preaching groups. Over time, the mosques have lost their traditional functions.[13]

ORGANIZATION AT MICRO LEVEL

TJ has revived some of the original functions of a mosque. When a Jamaat is formed around a neighbourhood mosque with the help of responsible Tablighi volunteers, it is reported to the zonal mosque, the Jam-e-Masjid. The zonal mosque in its weekly *mashwarah* appoints an *amir* (leader) and decides *rukh* (direction of a place) for every mohalla's jamaat coming under its jurisdiction. For a three-day programme, the *rukh* is confined to nearby colonies and places. But a *chilla* (for 40 days or more) takes more time and money.

Hence the *rukh* of the Jamaat is decided in accordance with the amount of money members are willing to spend on their travel and daily expenses. The *amir* and the programme decided, the Jamaat starts its journey from its *mohalla* mosque. All members bring their bag, baggage and money.

To maintain unity and ensure smooth functioning, the Jamaat is given some instructions, which are to be followed by all members. The first and foremost among these is obedience to *amir's* instructions and sensitivity to his intentions. The importance of cooperation and obedience is stressed by invoking examples from the Prophet's life.

Other instructions relate to the best use of time during preaching. Members are requested to spend more and more time in the mosque and refrain from discussing current affairs and other irrelevant topics, spending minimum time in the bathroom or on meals. They are expected to avoid debate and controversies, refrain from making comments on different denominations of Islam, etc.

To avoid unpleasant and embarrassing situations, members are instructed to do their work by themselves, not to use other members' belongings without permission, nor expect financial help from other members.

Before setting out on their journey all Jamaat members, led by their *amir,* supplicate together that they are embarking on a noble task of the Prophet for which they are not worthy. In anticipation they seek forgiveness from Allah for possible laxity or mistakes in their work and seek His help in inviting people to the right path of religion. Throughout the journey the amir exhorts them to keep themselves busy in *zikr* and abstain from useless and unnecessary conversation. Upon reaching their destination (usually a mosque in another locality), all of them again offer *dua* together for the success of their work. Next they offer an individual prayer known as *Tahiyyat-ul-Musjid* to mark their stay there. After this prayer they gather to hold *mashwarah* for the allocation of roles the members are going to assume.

The *amir* instructs a member of the Jamaat to explain the importance, necessity, virtues and etiquette of *mashwarah* to all members. The significance of *mashwarah* derives from three terms: Allah*'s* will, the Prophet's Sunnah, and the characteristic style of *maumeneen* (believers). The perceived virtues of *mashwarah* are:

a. The *mashwarah* ensures the well-being of its participants. Allah remains the source of all the best things in the world.

b. It burns the lamp of deliberation, spreading light from one person to the other.
c. *Mashwarah* protects people from having to repent mistakes, if any, for the failure of a collective decision is seldom blamed on an individual.

ETIQUETTE

i. *Mashwarah* is initiated with the permission of the *amir,* who presides over the deliberation.
ii. All members sit with rapt attention. It is not necessary for each member to give his opinion on every matter. However, they are expected to engage with devotion.
iii. The participants are supposed to extend their opinion without considering personal gain and preference. The individual opinion is expected to lend strength to the purposes of *deen* (religious pursuits).
iv. During *mashwarah* extreme care is taken not to criticise or to outrightly reject on opinion or sentiment. This is to avoid hurting the feelings of other participants.
v. Members are persuaded to air their views without fear or favour.
vi. As the *mashwarah* draws to a close the *amir* takes stock of all suggestions but turns to Allah for the final resolution. He is not bound by the opinions of either the minority or the majority. He enjoys the freedom to draw upon the intuition that Divinity is believed to provide.
vii. It is held that differences of opinion before a mashwarah concludes have an element of goodness about them. But it is considered a source of malaise if the differences persist after the mashwarah. Members are enjoined to regard the collective resolution as their own and to remain committed to it and defend it whenever necessary.

When roles are being assigned, all members show willingness to take up any role given to them by their *amir* in the *mashwarah,* especially offering oneself for *khidmat* (service involving physical labour) of Jamaat, such as preparing and serving food to the members. Each member is expected to show his readiness for *khidmat,* irrespective of social status. Such a manner of allocation assumes special significance in a society where mental labour is valued higher than physical labour. Jamaat activities are planned to avoid this kind of inequality.

Each role is valued in the work of Tabligh. Members doing *khidmat* are told that they will get a double reward in return, one for rendering *khidmat* to their companions, the other for freeing the companions from their worry, letting them do Tabligh work without constraints. The assigned role is discharged with a great deal of sincerity, with an understanding that it is being done for the pleasure of Allah for which they will be rewarded in this world as well as in the hereafter.

Mashwarah is held everyday, and role allocation changes every day or every other day. The importance and benefit of every role is traced to examples from the Prophet's life, which needs to be emulated by all members. However, the role of an *amir* is fixed for a given Jamaat. Generally, an amir takes up the role of a *dai* (preacher). But, he may take on any other role as thought necessary during a *mashwarah*. Sometimes the *amir* may offer himself for *khidmat* that does not require special skills.

ACTIVITIES

KHIDMAT (SERVICE)

The work of *khidmat* is allocated to two or three members, who will be responsible for preparing and serving food to all others.

ELAN (ANNOUNCEMENT)

A member is entrusted to make announcements after namaz about the arrival of the Jamaat and to request everyone to stay in the mosque for a while after prayer and to sit through a talk on some important and necessary matters of religion.

TALIM I (READING OUT BOOKS)

There are two sessions, one after *namaz-e-zohr* (afternoon prayer), another one after *namaz-e-isha* (late evening prayer). Designated members read out some passages from different books of Tabligh (*Fazail-i-Amal*).[14] All members of the Jamaat are expected to sit together in this programme with full concentration, in a state of *ba wadu* (ritual purity). It is explained to members that when people sit together in *talim,* angels surround them and inform Allah about the programme.

During the general session of reading out these books for an hour and half, the Jamaat is split into two or three sub-groups depending upon the number of people. In these every one practises the recitation of *kalimah* (profession of faith) and the verses of Koran which are read in namaz. They recite these aloud, one by one, so they can learn and correct one another freely, but with a caution that the mutual corrections neither lead to shame nor humiliation of the erring reciter. If someone is not able to recite, others help him so that he may memorise those verses in spare time. If someone helps others in memorizing these verses, it is considered virtuous.

After this programme, all members practise repeating *chhe baten* (the six fundamentals) of Tabligh. Every member is required to name these in serial order and explain each briefly to others. In addition, they are advised to practise these fundamentals in their daily life.

TALIM II

The incidents and stories relating to the Prophet and his companions are read out from the book entitled *Hikayat-i-Sahaba* by a member of the Jamaat, and others sit together and listen with devotion.

GASHT (TAKING A ROUND)

Before going for *gasht* a member is assigned the work of explaining its meaning, purpose, importance, and code of conduct to other members. *Gasht* is believed to be the main pillar of the Tabligh. It is an act believed to have begun with the Prophet and other messengers of Allah.

The meaning of *gasht* is to visit Muslims door to door and invite them to attend the talk of the preacher. There is a great deal of emphasis on performing this act with devotion and care. It is performed with the understanding that it seeks to replicate the practice of the Prophet and his companions.

Members follow some other norms during their *gasht.* They remain busy in *zikr* and walk together on one side of the road. While walking, their eyes are downcast in order to screen out worldly distractions like shops, buildings, etc. When they go to market to invite Muslims for Tabligh, the temptation for worldly goods is resisted by a constant reminder that these have their origin in dust and will return to dust on the day of resurrection.

With these instructions, some roles are allocated by the *amir* to members who are ready for *gasht*. The task of the *amir* is to remind all members to busy themselves in *zikr* and maintain unity in the group. Another member is assigned the role of *mutakallim* (speaker) who invites the people of the *mohalla* to join them in their *gasht*. If someone is busy, he is requested to join the prayer in the mosque and attend a talk on religious matters after prayer. The *mutakallim* briefly explains the transitory nature of this world and importance of *akhirat,* life hereafter, and reminds people of the basic tenets of their religion. When the *mutakallim* speaks, others are expected to listen in silence and total attention.

In order to take the Jamaat to every house of the neighbourhood, a local person is assigned the role of *rahber,* guide; he introduces the Jamaat to people of the neighbourhood.

There are two types of *gasht: umumi* (general round) and *khususi* (special round). The purpose of the second is to involve the old workers as well as influential persons in the Tabligh—*ulama,* educated people, traders, etc. If the neighbourhood is large, groups are formed . The *gasht* is usually held after *asr* (late afternoon prayer) or *maghrib* (prayer after sunset) and completed ten minutes before the next prayer.

BAYAAN (TALK)

After completing *gasht* the congregation offers namaz together in the mosque. The next task is to offer *bayaan* to the people. The speaker would have been designated in the *mashwarah*.

The speaker is generally an experienced volunteer of the Tabligh. Many a time the *amir* takes up this role, but he prepares others to take up this role too. The speaker is expected to make his presentation brief and simple, not an oration or speech. He avoids a tone of command and superiority. The main objective is to make people aware of the temporary nature of worldly objects, and the greatness and eternity of the rewards and enjoyments in the life hereafter. This world should be treated as a temporary place and a testing ground for following the dictates of Allah. The speaker may also dilate on what happens in the grave, the rewards and punishments associated with this world and the world hereafter, and refer to the spiritual and religious benefits of Tabligh.

Sometimes, the talk arouses emotions among the listeners to a point where some people burst into tears. This creates an atmosphere wherein individuals begin relating to another and realising their ultimate purpose. This inculcates among listeners the motivation to do well, for it speaks of the authority of a supreme power, all-comprehensive and all-pervasive.

Tashkil (To Form or Organize)

This concerns inducting people into the Jamaat. After his talk, the speaker requests people to spare some time for Tabligh and places before them the minimum time required for the purpose. They are asked to give three *chillas* in their lifetime, one *chilla* in every year, three days in every month. The people are persuaded to come forward to opt for a Jamaat of whatever duration depending upon the time they are willing to spare. The Tablighi members in the audience also persuade others to volunteer for a Jamaat. A member of the Jamaat notes down their names. If no one offers for three *chillas* or even one *chilla,* people are persuaded to offer themselves for three days. In this way the new members are recruited. The list of these new members is given to responsible volunteers of the Jamaat of that mohalla mosque who make programmes for this new group in consultation with volunteers of the zonal mosque.

At the end, people are requested to organize two *talims* everyday, one in the *mohalla* mosque, the other in their homes. They are also required to attend the weekly *ijtema* (congregation) of their zonal mosque. This weekly *ijtema,* though not common in every zone, is held regularly in some.

Adab-i-Taam (Etiquette of Taking Meals)

All sit together on the floor to eat. While explaining the etiquette, stress is laid on the fact that every action of Muslims should follow in the footsteps of Prophet Muhammad. The Prophet has laid down the etiquette of every action for Muslims in every day life. If an individual acts according to Prophet's teachings, he will get rewards for his actions, be they mundane or religious.

All members must take meals together, two or three eating from a common plate. The important norms at this time includes washing hands before eating, reciting a particular *dua*, eating food from one's own side of the plate, eating it in a manner that the other person does not feel offended, cleaning the entire plate and not leaving food. Any negative comment on the quality of food is avoided. At the end, a *dua* is recited in gratitude to Allah for taking care of hunger and thirst.

Adab-i-Naum (Etiquette of Going to Bed)

Before going to the bed, a member will occasionally repeat to all others the etiquette of going to bed, to be done according to the practice of the Prophet: it comprises going to bed with *wadu* (ablution), cleaning the bed thrice, lying in bed rolled over on one's right side, putting the hand under the cheek, reciting particular verses of Koran, and reciting another verse when waking up.

Bayaan (Talk)

There is another *bayaan* after the Namaz-e-Fajr (before sunrise prayer). This talk also concentrates on six fundamentals of Tabligh and is delivered by a member as decided in the *mashwarah*.

The above-mentioned activities constitute the daily routine of a TJ of ten or twelve persons. In addition to these compulsory activities, others are optional and may be carried out individually: *tahajud* (after midnight prayer), special *zikr* as instructed by the shaikh, and recitation of Koran and reading selected religious books.

Members are expected to involve people from all walks of life, all classes, all *beradaris* (clan groups). Moreover they should visit the *ulama*, pious and distinguished people of the locality, and seek their favour and guidance in order to involve them in Tabligh. All it requires is sincerity of intentions. Members are reminded to seek forgiveness from Allah in their actions, to realize their duties and be ready to correct their shortcomings.

STRUCTURE AT THE MACRO LEVEL

We move now to consider the organizational frame of TJ at different macro levels. Every district is divided into three to four zones depending upon the size of the district and density of Muslim population. The zone is again divided into four to five sub-zones, each with several mosques. A mosque has its own neighbourhood with varying number of volunteers, usually between one to fifteen.

When the Jamaats is formed for three days, the amirs are selected and rukh determined for all Jamaats in zonal mosques. In case of Jamaats of three and one *chilla* the approval of the national and international centre, in Nizamuddin, New Delhi, is sought. The zonal mosque decides the rukh on the basis of *taqaza* (demand) and requirements from various places in the district and state but it is also brought to the notice of headquarters. Sometimes the latter may suggest changes. This is the organizational style of Jamaat in every district.

All efforts are coordinated into an inter-district network at state level. For that purpose, *mashwarah* of volunteers are held quarterly. Three *mashwarahs* are held in three different parts of the state and one *mashwarah* is held at *markaz* where two to three hundred volunteers are called to participate from every state once in a year. Invited volunteers stay in the *markaz* for three days and discuss their *karguzari* (accomplishements) and *masail* (problems) in Tablighi work. They are asked to send people where a national or international *ijtema* is being organized.

In order to maintain uniformity in Tablighi work, two or three volunteers from each district undergo a two-months stay for training at *markaz*. They are also educated in their training period on various aspects of Tablighi work.

The *markaz* at Nizamuddin, New Delhi, is primarily oriented to developing a shared understanding. It relies on the socialization process to mould behaviour in such a way that volunteers become self-regulating. The *markaz* tends to promote decentralization of operational rather than strategic levels of control. In other words, the *markaz* sets in motion two principles of organization: decentralization of operations, and centralization of command. Consequently the *markaz* can set the strategies to be pursued from time to time, prioritising policy matters, and above all generating the shared culture of Tablighi Jamaat.

ORGANIZATIONAL STRATEGIES

To widen the base of the movement, expand its horizons and strengthen Tablighi work, the Jamaat adopts various strategies from time to time according to changing conditions. The main organizing strategy devised recently revolves around the formation of groups with reference to mosque in different localities. It is possible to delineate certain features of the strategy:

FIKR (DELIBERATION)

The first salient motif is *fikr*, attention to the means and strategies which could transform the prevailing ethos among Muslims in a manner that an ordinary Muslim comes to recognize the mosque and the schedule of namaz as the central axis of his life. To describe the desired ethos which a *tablighi* upholds with affectivity, the image of the Masjid Nabavi (Prophet's mosque) and the neighbourhood of Madina is invoked. The other elements of *fikr* involve reviewing the tasks carried out until the previous day for planning the next day, and holding *mashwarah* every day after any namaz as per the convenience of members. Following the review, the group meets absentees in their homes to enquire what prevented their coming. The members of Masjidwar Jamaat are also expected to visit the homes of volunteers who have gone out to enquire about the well-being of members of their family, especially if it has no adult male present. Jamaat members are further expected to visit the sick and the ailing of the neighbourhood and extend necessary help. Other occasions when members are expected to offer their services include giving a *ghusal* (ablution) to the body of a deceased Muslim in the *mohalla*.

How someone is invited towards Islam depends on his level of religiosity. If a Muslim does not offer namaz, then the Tablighi strategy is to extend invitation for namaz. For a namazi not yet introduced to *talimi* session, the invitation may be for *talim*. Another important element of *fikr* involves welcoming jamaats visiting the *mohalla* (neighbourhood) and extending them help and cooperation.

TALIM

There are two *talim* daily, one for the mosque, another for one's own household, usually for half-an-hour each. The volunteer reads from all nine books in the two volumes of *Fazail-e-Amal*. However, in the months of *Ramadan* and *haj*, greater emphasis is laid on reading out the virtues of *Ramadan* and *haj*. The objective is to make volunteers familiar with *fazail* (virtues) only and not on *masail* (*sharia* rules) as it involves a member of controversies among different schools of thought.

The talim session for the household is organized by women under the supervision of male members. It seeks to make all family members learn *masail* of namaz, *sunnat,* Koran, etc., along with their virtues and create the spirit of *amal* (practices) which would go a long way in constructing the religious ethos. These *talim* sessions are conducted on daily basis.

GASHT

As with talim, two *gashts* are to be organized every week. One *gasht* is expected to be organized in one's own *mohalla* around the mosque, another in an adjoining or nearby *mohalla* within *panch kosa* (15 km.). The purpose of *gasht* in nearby *mohalla* is to prepare the people to organize their own weekly *gasht* on their own and form their own Masjidwar Jamaat.

SAHROZA JAMAAT (THREE-DAY JAMAAT)

The most important task of Masjidwar Jamaat is to launch a three-day Jamaat every month. These Sahroza Jamaat work in nearby localities within 15 km.

SPENDING TWO AND HALF-HOURS IN THE *MOHALLA* MOSQUE

Every member of Masjidwar Jamaat is expected to spare the stipulated time as per his convenience to engage in *amal-e-dawat.*

The *amal-e-dawat* includes inviting people to religious activity; engaging in individual prayers like namaz, tasbih, and recitation of the Koran; engaging in *khidmat* of sick and needy persons of the *mohalla*; and welcoming tablighi volunteers coming from elsewhere.

The foregoing discussion highlights two purposes of the Tablighi movement. The first is to sustain and hold together those already in the Jamaat fold, the second, on the basis of the emergence of common values and practices, is to recruit new volunteers.

Early in the movement, the strategy of personal approach was stressed. The ijtema (congregation) strategy was adopted later to introduce the movement to large groups of people. A number of large *ijtemas* was held in different parts of the state where thousands of people participated and formed several jamaats for one year, three *chillas* and one *chilla*. These *ijtemas* played a key role in spreading the movement far and wide. The organization of an *almi ijtema* in Orissa on 7-9 December 1996 assembled approximately two lakh people, capturing the attention of the entire Muslim community and even the government and non-Muslims.

To broaden the impact of the movement further, the strategy of involving and mobilizing women is beginning to be emphasized, for socialization of the younger generation begins in an early period in which mothers play a key role. Moreover, it creates a conducive environment in the family so male members can more often stay away for Tablighi work. Experienced male volunteers often address these women who observe strict *purdah*. Sometimes women Jamaat from outside Orissa visit for ten days along with their husbands or a *mehram* (a person with whom marriage is prohibited). Women volunteers from USA and UK at times visit women in Orissa in connection with Tabligh. These women are predominantly Indian emigrants.

In order to widen the base of the movement, the strategy of involving people from all backgrounds and all walks of life is emphasized. One of the strategies in this regard is to involve influential people who command respect among the masses: *ulama*, educated sections, traders, etc. The involvement of *ulama* in Tabligh is held to be crucial because of their widely accepted authority.

In the case of educated people, volunteers are required to attract them by discussing solutions to the various existential problems of society in general and Muslims in particular. The discussion concentrates on the widespread prevalence of Western and materialistic culture which is rapidly disrupting, and threatening to destroy, the Islamic patterns of life through the effects of global economy.

The rules and regulations of Tabligh are sometimes relaxed for educated volunteers, so they can participate in spite of their pressing schedules. For example, a three-days Jamaat in Orissa, of teachers and students, sent to nearby places after Friday prayer, is permitted to come back for a few hours on Saturday in connection with work commitments. In the afternoon they return to the Jamaat, concluding its work by Sunday evening.

In case of the volunteers going out for longer durations, the volunteers of their home locality help take care of their families, freeing the outgoing volunteers from family worries and enabling them to concentrate on Tabligh. When a person is away from the family, it was observed that his wife and children were looked after by local volunteers, in matters like shopping for everyday provisions, medical treatment if required, or any other exigency.

In countries outside India, the strategies adopted for the movement are adapted to local conditions. In countries that are hostile, or do not encourage Tabligh, such as Saudi Arabia and Kuwait, volunteers adopt a low profile and do not use mosques. At the time of *haj* the jamaats are formed from these countries to visit India and other places for training and education.

Due to political considerations, volunteers from Pakistan do not visit India often for *mashwarah* and training. Instead, a few responsible persons of the *markaz* visit Pakistan. The Tablighis in Pakistan are in any case in touch with the *markaz* through letters, telecommunication, etc.

While sending Jamaats from South Asian countries to the Western and Islamic world, the *markaz* carefully checks the bonafides of the volunteers. Only volunteers who have completed three *chillas* and who are recommended by some responsible volunteers of their own locality are considered for going to other countries. This screening is to ensure that volunteers do not misuse these visits for personal ends.

SALIENT FEATURES OF ORGANIZATION

Certain organizational motifs can be identified:

1. In drawing people to the Tablighi fold active volunteers employ several ways of persuasion. One is to use local knowledge regarding individual biographies. The networks of an individual's peer group, ethnic affiliation, kinship, and family ties, occupational identity, etc., are mobilized, wherever possible, to bring him to the mosque and to draw him into the Jamaat. The already existing social ties in the community are employed to form bridges between the Jamaat programmes and the routine life of the individual.

   Tablighi activists often find their persuasive methods unsuccessful. Such cases are discussed in weekly *mashwarah* of the mosque. With zealous Tablighis, confident of their strategies, other elderly Tablighis explain to them politely that it is not for them or their strategies to decide whether an individual would come to the fold of *dawat*. Surely, it is Allah and none other who decides when the door of *hidayat* would open in the heart of an individual. This helps convert the active voice of the volunteer who has faced failure into a passive voice, where his role is confined to that of a person who simply invites the listener but does not worry about the latter's response. In addition the quality of endurance among the *sahabas* (Prophet's companion), whose efforts in the spread of Islam never flagged in the face of failure is emphasized. The activities of the Tabligh, as well as its organizational relations, are thus constantly imbued with ideological content. This is conspicuous when the sagging morale of an active volunteer is restored lest he drop out.

2. All activities and programmes are discussed through *mashwarah* before being implemented. *Mashwarah* precedes allocation of roles, holding of *ijtema*, or any other matter relating to the activities of the movement.

The role allocation pattern is very striking in TJ. There is no fixity of roles. Every role is considered important and is defined with reference to how it was enacted by the Prophet and his companions. There is not a single member of the Jamaat who is not involved in each of the activities in one way or the other.

The allocation of various roles does not flow from a functionary in power. Nomination/election to a role is accompanied by an elaborate explanation of its character and significance. It is understood that in accepting a particular role, a person accepts the entire repertoire of beliefs, emotions, concerns, etc., of the Tablighi movement. Interestingly enough, a role is never divorced from its ideological thrust with respect to the precepts and practices of the movement. For instance, *khidmat* in a mundane sense involves cooking food for all members of a Jamaat; when this concrete activity is linked to biographical details of Prophet Muhammad and his companions, even such mundane role becomes ennobling. *Khidmat* is seen as an activity which earns one proximity to Allah and makes one a co-sharer in the virtues gathered by others of the Jamaat in their *gasht*, *talim* or any other activity (which the *khidmatgar* has to forego). During fieldwork, I noticed that every member showed eagerness to volunteer for this particular role.

This should not create an impression that the controls exercised in the Tablighi organizations are only internal and have no external elements. I wish to stress that, unlike modern bureaucracies, the organizational style of TJ is deeply rooted in a system of common legitimization and internalized symbols and commitment.

3. The rules of Tablighi are not clear-cut guides to action. Instead, they are used more as starting points or background assumptions about what might be feasible and congruent in specific situations. The actual action starts with the way in which volunteers use, change, and elaborate the rules to create altogether new rules or radically restructure existing ones. Within the Tablighi format, a space is created where the stringent rules and regulation of conduct are relaxed. During fieldwork I observed several deviations, relaxations and reinterpretation of rules. For example, rules relating to *Sheh roza* Jamaat were relaxed in case of employees, students, businessmen and others to ensure their involvement. Similarly, rules (completion of three *chillas*, being married, etc.) are sometimes relaxed for volunteers going abroad.

There are other rules whose observance is practically beyond the capacity of volunteers, but these are seen as ideals practised by the Prophets, *sahabas, hazratjis* (*amirs* at *markaz*). Volunteers are urged to follow these rules in their lives. They are reminded that they are *gunahagar* (sinner) and can never come to those expectations, thereby keeping a sense of imperfection and incompletion alive in them. The rules are also partially relaxed keeping in view the amir's perception of the dispositions and aptitudes of a volunteer.

The rules of TJ are not written, rigid, or arbitrary. Many are part of the oral tradition of the Jamaat which gives discretion to volunteers to use them as they judge specific situations, and develop ways of dealing with practical problems, rather than simply abiding by the rules.

Sometimes rules are reinterpreted to suit the needs of the volunteers. Taking leave from one's job on medical grounds to do Jamaat activities creates a sense of guilt; one does not embark on noble work on false grounds. Volunteers rationalize this guilt by claiming that the medical leave is on grounds of spiritual illness, not physical ailment.

Certain rules are nevertheless essential, unchanging and reified, like the six fundamentals noted earlier: kalimah (the profession of faith), namaz (canonical prayer), *ilm-o-zikr* (knowledge) and the remembrance of Allah, *ikram-e-Muslim* (respecting every Muslim), *ikhlas-e-niyat* (sincerity of intention) and *tafrigh-e-waqt* (sparing time).

4. The contradictory principles of centralization and decentralization have been incorporated in the organizational structure of the movement in such a way that these become mutually reinforcing. The organizational structure does not stipulate at the *markaz* how strategies are to be put into practice. It is driven by the belief that the periphery is closer to the people, and that it is here that valuable local learning takes place. However, decentralization does not necessarily weaken the role of the centre. Indeed, it can be argued that effective decentralization requires a strong and confident centre. The centre gives strategic direction and promotes the creation of 'shared culture' involving all peripheries.

In TJ the centre does not control the peripheries by drawing tight boundaries. Instead, it assigns greater freedom within a set of flexible but clear boundaries. The relationship between the centre and peripheries is based upon mutual trust. According to this belief, the members will be guided by the value system that they share with the centre. Members exercise freedom within the agreed framework of conduct. The rules are applied in situations where such boundaries fail to contain behaviour which deviates from the 'shared culture'. The centre relies heavily upon the power of socialization process, based on the principle of freedom within boundaries, to ensure that people become self-regulating. The devolution process has been shaped to have an impact primarily upon operational rather than strategic levels of working.

The organization combines strong, confident, strategic guidance with radically decentralized peripheries. The centre is less concerned with specifying courses of action than with being an initiator and facilitator to local learning from the experiences of others in different peripheries. The opportunity for learning arises especially in various sessions of *karguzari* (accomplishments) where the peripheries meet the centre. The role of the centre in this regard is to take account of the significant shifts in operational details at the peripheries, and to pay explicit attention to the emergence of ideas in novel currencies. The process of learning in Jamaat is as much from periphery to centre, as from centre to periphery.

5. The Tablighi movement interprets all problems as emanating from a distorted practice of Islam. The solution is understood to lie in a return to the pristine past of Islam as inscribed in the Koran and Hadith. In effect, this movement has strengthened 'High Islam', but weakened 'folk Islam', which carries the imprint of local social and ecological conditions of different regions.[15] Returning to 'High Islam' becomes difficult in reality and is seen as a never ending process. Thus the need for reform is kept alive for all time to come.
6. An important paradox that is presented by the TJ is that even as it is averse to institution-building, it enjoys a social network that goes far and wide. Some scholars have argued that the TJ is able to manage this apparent contradiction by an obsessive otherworldly attitude.[16] There is, of course, some justification for this argument. Its founder Maulana Ilyas is reported to have said:

> Life is a moving train. The hours and minutes are its bogies (carriages) and our engagements (the way we spend our time) are the traveling passengers. What has happened is that our worldly and materially-base engagements have crowded the bogies of the train to such an extent that they do not allow the ineffable and otherworldly commitments to enter in. Our task is to seat, with determination, the exalted schedule (which pleases Allah and ensures our security in the *akhirat*) and make the degenerate passengers move out.[17]

However, it needs to be borne in mind that asceticism and rejection of the world is not the primary objective of the preaching. Discourses on the 'other-world' are, in fact, deeply entangled with the concerns of this-worldly existence. The Tablighis emphasise the value of productive work and equate work with spiritual pursuit. Furthermore, the construction of the 'other-world' is millenarian and utopian, and is invoked to mobilize followers towards the improvement of the world of here and now. The concept of *jannat* (heaven) is invoked not with a view to encourage renunciation but to create a world in which a conflict-free, egalitarian social order could be made possible. The concept of the 'other-world' is, therefore, both political and ideological in the sense that it is invoked to challenge widespread social inequalities, modern materialism, mindless consumerism, acquisitiveness, individualism, etc. The Tablighis seek to create a world order like Gandhiji's concept of 'Ram Raj' that is communitarian, spiritual, and egalitarian.

7. The aversion to institutions in TJ, it seems, emerges from their reticence in accepting modern forms of communication, in particular, the written medium. In the dissemination of their beliefs, the emphasis is always on orality, on face-to-face communication. It has rightly been pointed out by Walter Ong that oral cultures are usually antithetical to institution-building, because discourse in oral communication relies primarily on face-to-face interaction and participation for its intended impact on the audience.[18] Therefore they do not repose trust in institutions for the dissemination of their messages, because propaganda through institutions is distant, non-participatory and based on the separation of speakers from audience. An absence of institution-building and formal organization enables TJ to reject and eliminate modern forms of inequalities based on class, caste, status, power, etc. These inequalities, generated through differential access to material and political resources, are not only absent but vigorously resisted in the ideology and organization of TJ. This is, however, not to suggest that TJ functions in an entirely harmonious, egalitarian and conflict-free environment. In its style of functioning and ideological orientation, it generates its own forms of inequalities based on gender, age differences and differential access to symbolic and spiritual resources.

NOTES

1. Francis Robinson, 'Islam and Muslim Society in South Asia', *Contributions to Indian Sociology*, 17, 1983.
2. Imtiaz Ahmad's four edited volumes: *Caste and Social Stratification Among Muslims,* New Delhi: Manohar, 1973; *Family, Kinship and Marriage Among Muslims in India*, New Delhi: Manohar, 1976; *Ritual and Religion Among Muslims in India*, New Delhi: Manohar, 1981; *Modernization and Social change Among Muslims in India*, New Delhi: Manohar, 1983 and 'The Islamic Tradition in India', *Islam and the Modern Age,* 12: 44-62, 1981.
3. S. Anwar-ul Haque, *The Faith Movement of Maulana Muhammad Ilyas,* London: George Allen and Unwin, 1972; Barbara D. Metcalf, 'Remarking Ourselves: Islamic Self-Fashioning in Movement of Spiritual Renewal', in Martin Marty and Scott Appleby (eds.), *Accounting for Fundamentalism: The Dynamic character of Movements*, Chicago: University of Chicago Press, 1994; Shail Mayaram, 'Hindu and Islamic Transnational Religious Movement', *Economic and Political Weekly,* 3 January 2004, pp. 80-8.

4. Metcalf, op. cit.
5. Mayaram, op. cit.
6. Major communal riots took place in 1961, 1968, 1992. Due to the recent political activities of Sangh Parivar, Orissa witnessed some isolated incidents of communal violence in Mayurbhanj district. The burning of Australian missionary and his two children there received worldwide condemnation. Another incident reported recently from the same district was the brutal killing of a Muslim shopkeeper.
7. *The Quran* (XVI: 125).
8. Ibid.: III: 110.
9. Maulana Mohmmad Ilyas, 'A Call to Muslim'—A Message of the Maulana to an All India Conference of *Ulama* and the Muslim Political Leaders in Delhi, April 1994. The English translation of this message is in *The Teachings of Tabligh* (tr. Ehteshamul Hasan and Ashique Ilahi), New Delhi: Idara Ishaat-e-Diniyat, 1985, p. 13.
10. Ibid., pp 12-14.
11. Ziaur Rahman Faruqui notes that TJ has spread to 165 countries. See his *Ulma-i-Deoband Kawn Hain, Kya Hain?* Deoband: Darul Kitab, 1992, p. 43. The other works on Tabligh in Europe and north America include Felice Dassetto, 'The Tablighi Organization in Belgium', in Tonus Gerholm and Y.G. Lithman (eds), *The New Islamic Presence in Western Europe,* London: Mansell Publishing, 1988; John King, 'TJ and the Deobandi Mosque in Britain', in Steven Vertovec and Ceri Peach (eds.), *Islam in Europe: The Politics of Religion and Community,* London: Macmillan, 1997 and S.H. Azmi, 'An Analysis of Religious Division in the Muslim Community of Toronto', *Al-Basirah,* January 1989, 1: 2-9.
12. Quoted in Wahiduddin Khan, *Tablighi Movement*, New Delhi: Maktaba Al-Risala, 1986, p. 41.
13. Imtiaz Ahmad, Mosques, 'Mobility and Mobilization', *The Statesman* (Delhi), 25 March 1990, p. 5.
14. Maulana Mohammad Zakriya Kandhlawi, *Fazail-i-Amal,* vols. I and II, New Delhi: Idara Ishaat-e-Diniyat.
15. For the distinction between 'High Islam', and 'Folk Islam' in India, see Imtiaz Ahmad, 'Orthodoxy in Indic Islam: A comment', *Islam and the Modern Age,* August 1979, pp. 88-94.
16. Yogender Sikand, *The Origins and Development of the Tablighi Jamaat (1920-2000): A Cross-Country Comparative Study,* New Delhi: Orient Longman, 2002.
17. Quoted in Mohammad Talib, 'The Tablighis in the Making of Muslim Identity', *Comparative Studies of South Asia, Africa and the Middle East,* 17: 35, 1997.
18. W.J. Ong, *Orality and Literacy,* London: Methuen, 1982.

7

Assertive Religious Identities, Secular Nation States and the Question of Pluralism: The Case of the Tablighi Jamaat[1]

ANINDITA CHAKRABARTI

Despite expectations during the Enlightenment, religion has shown no sign of leaving the public arena. The aim of the paper is to look into the challenges that religious movements like the Tablighi Jamaat (henceforth TJ) pose to the practice of secularism and pluralism in the context of democratic nation states. The TJ is a transnational, non militant Islamic reform movement. In its world-view, those Muslims who have fallen from the path of true Islam are a cause of problems and hence the target of reform. From its beginnings in the 1920s in northern India, the TJ has grown to be the most widely followed religious movement in contemporary times.[2] It should be noted that this movement addressing Muslims across nations was gaining momentum at a time when separate nationhood for Muslims of the Indian subcontinent was at the forefront of the political agenda. Today, the TJ works in all types of socio-political environments and countries where Muslims are in a majority (Bangladesh, Pakistan) as well as in countries where they are in a minority (India, United Kingdom, Belgium).

The objective of this paper is to analyse how movements like the TJ that assert a religious identity function in the context of a secular, democratic, nation state and plural society. The TJ claims to forward the correct interpretation and practice of true Islam. But it is aware that there are other movements too, which claim the same. Looking at the movement in the context of Gujarat, I shall show that it believes in changing the world by targeting and changing the individual rather than the state or any institution of public life. But even as the TJ holds back from participating in the public or political sphere, it asserts its presence in the public domain. In a context of violence, the TJ's quest for internal purification of the religious community, marked by a process of Islamization, is imbued with multiple meanings/possibilities and should not be seen only as a step towards militancy and counter-violence. It should be stated at the very outset that this study being exploratory in nature, its task is to raise questions rather than answer them. It explores how, from time to time, 'critical events' have brought the concepts of secularism, democracy, and pluralism under scrutiny. The Partition of India in 1947 on the basis of religious identity has complicated the question of nationhood for Indian Muslims, and transnational movements like the TJ bring this tension to the forefront.

TABLIGHI JAMAAT AND ITS MISSION OF CHANGING THE WORLD BY CHANGING THE SELF

In the first section I shall focus on certain aspects of the movement as studied by different scholars and on the basis of my fieldwork in Gujarat.[3] The TJ was started by Maulana Muhammad Ilyas (1885-1944), who initially tried to Islamize 'nominal' Muslims by establishing a network of small-scale *madrasas* to promote Koranic education among the local population of the Mewat region. Disillusioned with the *madrasa* approach to Islamization, he realized that Muslim society needed a new type of reform movement. This was to be organized in the pattern that the Prophet and his companions had followed in the early days of Islam. Z.H. Faruqi writes that the TJ's only innovation was its methodology, which had not been adopted by any other contemporary Islamic movement (Faruqi 1971: 67). The aim was not to convert others to Islam but to persuade Muslims to follow six main principles or *chhe baten*: *kulimah* (the profession of faith—there is no other deity but Allah and Muhammad is Allah's Messenger), namaz (prayer), *ilm* and *zikr* (knowledge and prayer in glorification of Allah), *ikram-i-muslim* (kindness and respect for Muslims), *ikhlas-i-niyat* (sincerity of intention), and *tafrigh-i-waqt* (sparing time). The movement works through volunteers rather than full-time, paid cadres. It has consistently used vernacular works based on translation of the Koran and especially the *hadis*.[4]

At the outset, I would like to clarify one important characteristic of this movement. Very often the TJ is seen as being against the Sufi tradition. But on closer inspection this opposition seems to be false. Actual TJ practices are based on the Sufi notions of *dua* (appeal) and *baya* (oaths of spiritual initiation). Conflict arises mainly from the challenge posed by the TJ against the traditional custodians of charisma. Rafiuddin Ahmed had also noted in the case of 'fundamentalist' movements such as Faraizi and Tariqah in early nineteenth-century Bengal, that the reformists' principal opposition to the *pirs* (religious preceptors who lead a Sufi order) was not simply doctrinal; much of it was directed against the economic exploitation of the masses by the *pirs* who derived considerable material benefits from their profession. Moreover, the Sufi tradition on which these movements were based came to the forefront over a period of time when the son of the founder of the movement, namely Dudhu Miyan (1819-62), allowed himself to be referred to as a *pir* (Ahmed 1981: 60). According to Maulana Wahiduddin Khan, the TJ is based on the Sufi tradition. 'Whatever is there in the Sufi tradition, you will find them in the TJ. It is all about *barakat* (blessings), *zikr* and *baya*. It is not based on rationality or the spirit of the modern times.'[5] Metcalf also notes that Sufism has in no sense disappeared in the TJ. In fact, the holiness associated with the Sufi *pir* was now associated with the Jamaat itself (Metcalf n.d.). The Sufi orientation of the movement has been pointed out by Ebrahim Moosa in his study of the TJ in South Africa. According to Moosa, many aspects of the TJ attempt to bring about a synthesis between the esoteric tendencies of the orthodox Sufi orders (*tariqah*) and the exoteric juridical practices (*shariat*) (Moosa 2000: 216).[6]

THE FIELDWORK

After starting my doctoral work on a Hindu religious movement called Swadhyaya, in 2000 I travelled to Gujarat and spent about three months observing Swadhyaya projects and programmes and hunting for a suitable locale where I could settle down for further research. During one of these visits I met Tariqbhai, a TJ activist from Saurashtra, on a train journey from Delhi to Ahmedabad. He spoke on Islam and TJ for hours. I was struck by the organizational and methodological similarities between the Swadhyaya and the TJ and looked for an opportunity to observe the latter during my stay in Gujarat. In January 2001 I moved into the house of a local level Swadhyaya activist in village Harshupur near Surat city, Surat district.

After spending six months doing fieldwork on Swadhyaya, I started to interact with the TJ followers of a nearby village, which I shall call Ratanpur, who happened to be shop owners in the village.[7] Yoginder Sikand has mentioned in his book the near impossibility for non-Muslim scholars to make field investigations on the TJ (Sikand 2002: 9). In my case, it was further complicated by gender, since men are supposed to maintain *ankhon ka purdah*, a veil on the gaze, in relation to all women apart from one's wife, mother and sister. My fieldwork largely consisted of visiting the families of local level activists/followers and interviewing them in the shops. At the shops I was never turned down, even though sometimes the interviews were interrupted by business or prayer. Sometimes I had to wait long hours. I was told that they understood how I felt (arriving at their doorsteps, unsolicited) since they also feel the same way when they go on Jamaat! I interacted with the men primarily in public spaces whereas the interaction with the women was in their homes. I could attend a couple of sessions of women's *talim* (education).[8] My activity, I was informed by the TJ activists themselves, had been under observation, and were discussed in the *mashwarah* (consultation) at the mosque. The fact that I would be able to speak to the TJ followers in Ratanpur was a collective decision taken at a weekly meeting at Olpad mosque. My credibility rested on the fact that I lived with Jethamama's family—he used to be their milkman and was considered a man of integrity. Nevertheless, once one anxious relative of a TJ activist asked Jethamama whether I was a 'CID'. Much later, I came to know that they often wondered whether I was a Christian and had gone there to convert them to Christianity. Alternately, it was also thought that since I was showing so much interest in Islam, I myself was contemplating conversion to Islam. The reserve of the male public places was compensated by the children who would shout 'Anandiben' and invite me to their homes. Apart from these families I often asked Swadhyayis and other Hindu villagers about the TJ. Though initially the Swadhyayis would not acknowledge any similarity with the TJ, later they mentioned in informal discussions that while explaining their movement to Muslims during their religious tours (*bhaktipheris*), they were supposed to say that it was like going on their Jamaats. One young Swadhyayi from Harshupur told me that it was in this context that he had heard about the TJ for the first time. I left Gujarat in December 2001 and within a few months, the Godhra and post-Godhra violence took place.

The village 'Ratanpur' comes under Olpad taluka in Surat district. Ratanpur had a population of 12,856 in 2001, of which 7,258 were men and 5,598 were women. The *talati* (village accountant) informed me that about 5 per cent of the village population was Muslim. There has been out-migration of Muslims over the years. The residents also confirmed that the Muslim population would be about 650 in Ratanpur. The percentage of Muslims is 8.73 per cent in the state and 9.18 per cent in the district, according to the 1991 Census of India. In Olpad taluka, there are 104 villages, according to the 2001 Census of India. I was told that 13 villages have Muslim residents.

The Muslim communities of Ratanpur comprise endogamous groups such as the Multani, Fakir, and Shah who belong to the Other Backward Castes (OBCs); a few Pathan families in the village who, it is said, came to Gujarat from Afghanistan about 400 years ago; and Sunni Bohras who are a trading community, but also participate in agriculture. The latter owned considerable land but have sold out much of it.[9] (The older members pointed out that these days, the younger people were not interested in agriculture and preferred to go abroad. They migrate to African countries like South Africa and Zimbabwe.) Some people from Ratanpur go to Surat for government jobs. There is a secondary school in the village and two primary schools. There are five temples, three mosques and one *dargah*. Ratanpur has a railway station, a post-office and two banks. It has a primary health centre, a private hospital, and six private clinics. All my respondents were petty traders.

The TJ began its activities in Gujarat when Enam-ul-Hassan (Maulana Ilyas's nephew) became its *amir* (leader). It is said in the TJ circles that what Maulana Ilyas did for Mewatis, Enam-ul-Hassan did for Gujarati Muslims. Currently, it is the Gujarati trading community that is the most influential among the leadership in the Nizamuddin *markaz* (headquarters) in New Delhi. The TJ *amir* for the taluka resides in Olpad town. He is responsible for the TJ work in the taluka. The amir of Ratanpur was a fruit vendor by occupation. The activists confirmed that the TJ began to visit the villages in the late 1960s. A man in his fifties recalled going on Jamaat to Nepal when he was about ten years old. At the same time, I was told that it was only in the last ten years that the TJ had gained momentum in the region. In the following section, I shall discuss the correct path as envisioned by the TJ participants; a path that has to be followed by all Muslims.

THE PROJECT OF RECONSTITUTING THE SELF

> Tabligh is essentially about not more than two things, one material, the other spiritual.
>
> Maulana Ilyas's letter to A.H.A. Nadwi (1940, cited in Troll, 1985: 164).

In the TJ world-view the reconstruction of the individual self is a process both spiritual and material. Religion, Maulana Ilyas had pointed out, was a *zahir* or outer reality and *batin* or inner reality at the same time. Maulana recognized the crisis of religion as a result of neglecting to recognize the necessary connection between the two. Giving up of Jamaats, i.e. travelling preaching parties, which had marked early Islam, had been a mistake since this was as fundamental as any other inner spiritual experience. This material aspect, along with the spiritual or inner aspect of faith and self-examination, makes the project of Islam complete (Maulana Ilyas 1940, cited in Christian Troll 1985: 153-4). According to this perspective, preaching was not enough, the principles had to be put into practice and the way to do it was to go on Jamaats. The tour is the central feature of the TJ. It has an inner and an outer aspect. It takes people away from their immediate surroundings of family and neighbourhood in small groups of ten or twelve men. Within the group, one is stripped of one's status in the material world: a radical break from everyday life. This break, Maulana Ilyas believed, would transform the proselytiser more than the audience. During my fieldwork, *maulavi* of the village mosque, Ibrahimbhai, told me, 'We do not go to teach others, but to change and improve ourselves. We spend our own money to do so.' During these tours, they are at the risk of continually facing rebuffs, which instils humility in them. Barbara Metcalf notes that the *amir* allocates different duties among the members, such as cooking, looking after the belongings, and delivering discourses, irrespective of status, class, and social position. The key to accepting these roles is the concept of service or *khidmat* (Metcalf 1995). The tour is a significant means of putting the physical self through tests by giving up personal food habits and suffering humiliation. It provides an opportunity to purify the mind and body.

There is a strong sense of emulation of the Prophet and his life in the Tablighi ideology. The life of the Tablighi has to be so pure and impeccable that others would be inspired to imitate them. Metcalf has talked about how a Tablighi is supposed to consider his own life an example to set for others. I was told by a Tablighi worker, 'The honesty we talk about in the masjid, the same honesty has to be practised in our business. Our life has to be so pure, so good, that others would like to be like us. But what is the situation today? According to our religion, if a drop of alcohol falls on a dress that dress should be burned, but today in our area Muslims are involved in illicit liquor trade!' It should be mentioned here that group rivalry over the control of the trade in illicit liquor has been the immediate cause of several communal riots in Gujarat.[10] (Engineer 1982). As a TJ activist puts it, in the life of a Tablighi, *iman* (faith), *ibadat* (devotion), *ikhlaq* (exemplary conduct, morals), *muamilat* (business transactions) as well as family life—all these spheres have to be equally pure and correct. The Tablighis should be noted for their humility and non-violence. It is emphasized that one should not seek revenge even when one is humiliated. The TJ's egalitarianism lies in asserting that not just the *ulama* or the *shaikh* (Sufi spiritual preceptor), but any Muslim could be a teacher and a role model for others (Metcalf 1993: 603).

The Tablighi believe that in the project of changing the world by changing oneself, religious education or *dini talim* plays the most important role. This brings us to the TJ's relation with one of the institutions of mainstream society—education. Critics often point at TJ's lackadaisical attitude towards modern education. I was told by Farooqbhai, owner of an ice-cream shop in the village, that the kind of education I was pursuing had no value in their society. He explained to me that *madrasa* education had prestige and value and that his wife was an *alima* (Islamic theologian, a learned woman). I shall use a narrative in order to show how *madrasa* education is perceived by the community. Hanifbhai is the owner of a shoe shop and a local level TJ leader in Ratanpur. His daughter studies in a residential *madrasa* in Baruch. While discussing Islam in his shop, he once told me:

> My daughter used to go to an English medium school. She was a very bright student. But in this area there is no proper *madrasa* for women. So she was not getting any *dini talim*. I took her out of the school after her

tenth class and put her in a *madrasa* in Baruch district. The school-teachers were very upset. They thought that the father must be an illiterate person. When I went to her school, they tried to convince me that she should continue at school because she had the prospect of becoming a doctor or an officer. But I told them that while as teachers they were worried about her life in this world, which is, say, for sixty or seventy years, as a father I was worried about her life after death. That, undoubtedly, is much longer. I have to take care of that and not only worry about this life. That is why I took her out and put her in the *madrasa. Madrasa* education teaches you correct behaviour with everybody around you—elders, juniors, and equals. When she comes home during her vacation I observe her behaviour, ask her a few things from her course. Since she is very bright, she is doing well. You cannot study all these if you are dull. My son is a bit dull. He failed twice in ninth grade so I took him out of school and he is working in the shop.[11]

Though the importance of secular, economy-oriented education is not completely denied, it is given a secondary status. Ibrahimbhai's elder daughter was a school teacher before she went to South Africa with her husband. Ibrahimbhai is of the opinion that there is no bar on secular education, but one should not forget the truth (*hakikat*). When women complete their *madrasa* course, they are known as *alima*. These women have prestige in the community and it is definitely a qualification when marriage alliances are made. Hanifbhai's narrative also makes us understand that looking for the political implications of religious movements can often lead to over-interpretation and thus leads us to neglect the function they fulfil for their participants. Saba Mahmood, in her study of the mosque movement among Egyptian women, has raised this question in the following way: How do we understand, from a feminist/liberal perspective, a women's movement in which the pious subjects actively promote a kind of piety and virtue that leads to their own submission and subordination (Mahmood 2001).[12]

Metcalf notes that in the TJ, women are expected to conform to the rules of modesty and seclusion but at the same time their lives change through their involvement in the movement. Feminine qualities such as humility, generosity, piety, and bravery in the face of persecution are to be cultivated by men going out for Tabligh work Women in South Asia are discouraged from going to the mosque, but a *dawa* (invitation) meeting offers an opportunity for women to congregate religiously. A talk given at an annual meeting reminded men that women also owed responsibility to the Tabligh and that men should not only acknowledge this fact but also actively facilitate women's participation by providing child-care (Metcalf 1995). I was told by the women leaders that women should observe behavioural codes that were compatible with the TJ world-view—the correct path shown by the Prophet (*nabi*). Gender segregation, cooking food after saying some Koranic verses, practising the correct way of eating, i.e. on the floor, and performing other ablutions should be practised. Nevertheless, there were some women in the village who did not wear a *burkha*. I asked one of them, a divorced daughter of the *maulavi* who was staying with her parents, why she did not veil herself. She pointed out personal discomfort as a reason. Shail Mayaram has also noted that neither veiling nor any life-cycle rituals including dowry had undergone change in Mewat despite the TJ. What has undergone change are names, the mode of dressing and greeting, participation in community festivals like Holi and Diwali, and worship of the goddess (Mayaram 1997: 262-3). These, unlike kinship rules or life-cycle rituals, are all markers of one's public identity.

When a group goes to a neighbourhood to convince others to join them, individuals narrate the changes brought about in their lives through participation in the TJ: how they have given up vices like smoking, drinking, and gambling, to which they were addicted earlier. These public confessions regarding private behaviour make the TJ open to scrutiny by the larger community; the conduct of individual TJ activists is subject to public gaze. Yet, critics point out that the TJ's influence is limited. Their ritualism has become extremely tedious. Others say that they have reduced Islam to mere performance of the namaz. The TJ makes it difficult for Muslims to participate in the modern world and, through the process of Islamization, makes them detached from the local cultural context. Moreover, the organization is secretive in nature.

I shall conclude this section by drawing attention to some of the organizational aspects of the TJ. Despite its reticence vis-à-vis the media and the wider public, it should not be forgotten that the TJ is open to all Sunni Muslims. The activists are always looking out for new members and nobody is rejected. They even go to prisons to spread the message of the Tabligh. Mohamed Tozy has also noticed this 'easy availability' or 'relatively open character' of the TJ in Morocco (Tozy 2000: 164). The centre at Nizamuddin in New Delhi is the global headquarters of the TJ. The ultimate authority lies with a group based at Nizamuddin, centred around the Hazratji (chief *amir*) and the *shoora* (consultative body), but local level work goes on without their intervention. For example, the regular tours and programmes in which the TJ members in Olpad area participate are decided at their zonal headquarters at Panoli in Baruch district. The Nizamuddin centre's intervention is not needed in these decisions. The Jamaat from this area goes to south India, I was told. At the village level, the TJ followers keep a kind of census of the Muslims and review who are the ones not going to the mosque for namaz. Then they would go to them and ask them to come to offer namaz at the mosque. The names of the women are not mentioned in the census; only the number of women per family is mentioned. Women are approached through, and in presence of, the men of the family. Very often the TJ gets requests from families to speak to their young men who drink too much. It should be mentioned here that alcoholism is a big problem in rural Gujarat where buying and selling of alcohol is illegal.

The TJ activists might address one and all, but from the TJ's viewpoint there are three types of people in the world. An activist once explained this to me in the following way.

> I shall explain with examples. Suppose it rains on a rock. The water runs away and it has no effect. These are the first type of people on whom *ilm* has no effect. If it rains on a field, one could grow grains since the field gets nourished. These are the second category of people. And then there is the third type, who like a pond, not only get nourished from rainwater but they also become a source of nourishment for others.[13]

The TJ undertakes activities from the immediate neighbourhood to foreign countries in order to find new recruits who would, like the third category of people, carry forward its message. In her study of the TJ in Belgium, Felice Dassetto has attributed its success to a structural organization that allows the different groups to enjoy both a relative functional autonomy and a functional integration at the same time. There are a number of groups who work rather independently and on their own initiative, but the broader rules and regulations are set in Nizamuddin. 'This complex organization', writes Dassetto, 'capable of dealing with multiple segments of the environments, seems to give the Tabligh a major asset when it comes to survival and expansion' (Dassetto 1988: 170). In India, the TJ operates on the same principle. Wherever they are, for the TJ the mosque is the centre of activity. An important aspect of these group activities is that there develops strong social intercourse among the activists. (For details of TJ's organizational activities see S. Zainuddin's paper in this volume.)

A few Jamaats are especially organized for certain groups: students, sometimes occupational groups such as doctors and engineers, railway workers, etc. Women's Jamaats are usually smaller, involving five to six couples. The women are always accompanied by their husbands. In a women's Jamaat, the route (*rukh*) is never chosen spontaneously, it has to be decided at the headquarters at Nizamuddin. Women stay in houses with due arrangements for *purdah* and men stay at the local mosque. Jamaat, however, I was told, is not organized through the *biradari* (kindred).

The TJ relies on self-financing and the participants join those Jamaats, which they can afford. In fact, as Tozy has noted, the TJ does not employ any propaganda technique that requires significant financing (Tozy 2000: 162). Periodically, the TJ holds very big *ijtemas* (congregations) apart from the annual congregation at Tongi, Bangladesh, which is Islam's largest after the Haj. During these gatherings the TJ employs innovative techniques to raise resources. Zainuddin notes (2001: 172-3) that during the *ijtema* in Orissa, the slogan was *'lao, lagao, le jao'* (bring, use and take it back). The 300 odd pump-sets that were installed during the *ijtema* were auctioned off after the event. There were no written accounts of contributions and expenses. People contributed in cash as well as in kind—by providing fuel for vehicles, and arranging cars and trucks. As far as possible, organizational work is done orally and no written accounts are kept.

Such practices aim to spread the notion of a true Islam that would change the individual as well as the community. The changes are reflected in dress code, behavioural patterns, and finally a change of heart. Yet for the Tablighis, Islamization of the most intimate behaviour is not just a private matter. With their dress and manners, individual Tablighis become embodiments of the religious. It is through this embodiment that they lay claim on the public arena. Though the TJ might claim that they are concerned only about things that are either above the sky and below the earth (*aasman ke upar aur jamin ke niche ki baat*), we shall see that their assertion has deep political consequences.

GUJARAT VIOLENCE, THE TJ AND THE PUBLIC DOMAIN

> Last evening, at Kathod, a boy of about 12 or 13 years ran after a moving bus and latched on to the ladder fixed to the back of the bus. He was wearing a white *kurta-pajama* and a skull-cap. My companion said (in jest), 'Look at a future Osama-bin-Laden' (Fieldnotes, Kathod, Surat district, December 2001).

The only connection between the Gujarati boy and Osama-bin-Laden was their religion. A connection identified through the boy's attire. A university professor told me that when Vishwa Hindu Parishad (VHP) activists were asked how they recognized a follower of the TJ, they said, 'by their dress'. The Tablighis wear their 'elder brother's shirt and younger brother's pajama'. The professor added that the *kafni-pajama* was the dress of the Muslim traders of Gujarat. What does this strict dress code mean for the Tablighis? Sikand says that for the TJ members among the Meo, religion is not merely an inner spiritual experience but they believe that their religious identity must be publicly expressed through visible symbols; the explanation lies in the urge of the Meo to differentiate themselves from the Hindus who were increasingly seen as the oppressive Other (Sikand 2002: 130). But if the external markers' only purpose is to demarcate Muslims from the oppressive other, how do we explain its phenomenal rise in independent Bangladesh? According to Mayaram, the violence and trauma of Partition is an important factor why Meos' dress, names, patterns of belief, rituals and associations have undergone a change in accordance with the TJ injunctions. Also significant is the factor that the post-colonial, democratic state takes cognizance of electorally significant numbers (Mayaram 1997: 247). I would like to point out that the external markers of religion are much more than an electoral game, which one can very well play even without a beard or a *burkha*. Peter van der Veer has noted that in the European and American contexts, these expectations regarding dress code have complicated the question of assimilation, race and ethnicity (van der Veer 1994: 130). The question that arises is why do people in different socio-political and cultural contexts feel the need to publicly express their religious identity?

As the Tablighis become more inward looking, they become more prominent in the public space through external markers that set them apart. In times of communal violence (and in everyday life in Gujarat), these markers make them vulnerable. Yet, through these, the

Tablighis make a claim on the public sphere as a distinct community. Gulabmama (father of a local level TJ leader) pointed out to me that more and more people were wearing 'Islamic' dress these days. Also there were many more men who grow a beard. Only that which was 'natural' (*kudrati*) and 'correct' (*sahi*) would prevail, he added. What is popularly perceived as Islamic dress is the *salwar-kameez* (known as *punjabi dress*) for younger women, *frock-ijar* for older women and *kafni-pajama* for men. For men, their *pajama,* cut above their ankle, along with a cap and the beard make it recognizable.[14] But the *salwar-kameez,* recommended for Tablighi women, is worn by Hindu women too. What is exclusively Muslim for women is the *burkha* or at least covering of the head with the *odhni.*

A number of TJ activists told me that their organization had gained prominence in the area over the last ten years. This ten-year period coincides with the post-Babri Masjid demolition riots, in which Surat city was one of the worst hit. Violent conflicts strengthen a group identity that might not be combative from the actor's point of view but might be interpreted very differently by others. N. Jayaram and Satish Saberwal pointed out this lack of correspondence between actor's 'intention' and observer's 'interpretation' as a reason why social conflicts are suffused with unintended and unforeseeable consequences (Jayaram and Saberwal 1996: 19).

Some TJ activists have been implicated and arrested in connection with the fire in a coach of the Sabarmati Express at Godhra. But why and how the coach was set on fire will probably remain an unresolved mystery, given the political interests involved. The theory of 'Islamic conspiracy' fits in well with the government's rationalization of the violence that followed. While the Forensic Science Laboratory experiments showed that the fire could be started only from inside the bogie, the TJ has been implicated not only by the Sangh Parivar but also by the secular media (Swami 2002). With dangerous fluidity, terms like 'orthodox', 'ultra Right', 'fundamentalist' and 'militant' slip into each other in these 'secular' accounts of communal violence.

The post-Godhra massacre was backed by the ruling government, with the police mostly passive spectators. South Gujarat, however, had remained peaceful with the exception of Surat city, which saw some unrest in the early days (Yagnik 2002). The TJ, as before when the Babri Masjid was demolished or when Muslims were massacred in Mewat at the time of Partition, has maintained that Muslims were being punished for their own *karma.* Hanifbhai told me that none other than Muslims themselves were responsible for their plight today:

> Today the Muslims are at the receiving end and it means that there is something wrong with us. It is the result of our *karma*. We have deviated from the correct (*sahi*) path, the path of Allah, and that is why all this is happening to us. There are political processes and forces acting against the Muslims since the time of Independence but they are only the means. I will give you an example: it is as if you are beating a dog with a stick, and the dog thinks that the stick is beating him. Our belief has to be strong. And belief becomes strong only when they are put into practice and not just preached. If Praveen Togadia comes here, we would welcome him and speak to him the way I am speaking to you. Who is he? He is just the means, it is Allah who is punishing us. And even if someone eliminates him, there would be other Praveen Togadias in his place.

Hanifbhai explained at length how Paigambar—the Prophet—used to go to different people and they used to harass and sometimes even beat him. But he would not retaliate and instead asked Allah why was he angry (*naraz*) with him. 'For us Paigambar's path is the only right path. *Dini talim* gives us these enlightened thoughts (*jagruti*). Those who are against us know it, and therefore they are attacking the *madrasas*.' But Hanifbhai was clear about the fact that the problem facing Muslims was not a local or a national phenomenon. It is a worldwide phenomenon and he gave the example of Iraq. 'America claimed that there were weapons in Iraq but now everybody knows that there were no weapons. The truth will finally come before you. Dr. Kelly was part of this conspiracy but his conscience could not take it, and he committed suicide.' As we were talking, a Jamaat returned from a visit to Dharwar, Karnataka, and the participants informed us that it had been extremely successful. After they left, I asked Hanifbhai whether it had become more difficult to go on Jamaat these days. He said yes, but added that whatever difficulties they were put through were tests to their commitment. 'Whatever happens, we shall tolerate with fortitude (*sabar se bardast kar lenge*). Only Allah can redress what is happening.'[15] Yet as they wait with fortitude for better days, the fear in the heart of the community has a real basis. During the post-Godhra violence, several places, especially in rural areas, witnessed communal carnage for the first time. I was told that the Shiv Sena had been coming to the area in recent times and had even found a few followers in Ratanpur. Hanifbhai's shop name is barely visible behind a huge poster of a brand of shoes called 'Trishul Shoes'.

Describing the days after the burning at Godhra on 27 February 2002, a non-Tablighi man, Bilal, said:

In the evenings, all the boys would gather for prayer in the masjid. If you are at home, you watch all these terrible news on TV. How would the youth react? To calm ourselves, we would gather in the masjid, we would ask for *dua* and we would cry. All these would help us feel lighter. But then others would say that we are gathering in order to attack with our weapons. What weapons? There is not even a stick in our masjid.[16]

Bilal is no stranger to communal riots. His restaurant was looted and burned down in the post-Babri Masjid riots in Mumbai. He told me that after the demolition, he had met with Amir Eman-ul Hassan at Nizamuddin, who told him that counter-attack was not the answer. The solution of destruction is construction. In fact, in the TJ discourses, there is no language of retaliation. A Tablighi is supposed to be calm even in the face of insults, the TJ activists repeatedly told me. The *bayaans* (talks) that I attended (in Gujarat and Aligarh) were addressed to Muslims and centred on their duties. They put the self under strict surveillance, upon which the individual and the religious community are created and re-created through certain practices (daily routine as well as dress and manners). Thereby they make an anachronistic attempt to recreate time and history. But these features, the TJ shares with a number of other sectarian movements. And it is interesting to observe that very often sectarian movements provoke the suspicion of the authorities just because they defy the sanctity of the nation-state and dominant socio-cultural norms. The Falun Gong in China and the Branch Davidians in the US are examples of such mistrust and repression.

In the context of Gujarat, while some would go to court and may or may not get justice (the Best Bakery Case), others think that recourse to violence is the best way to bring about justice (Gujarat Muslim Revenge Force). But there are still others who ask for *dua* in times of trouble. I shall use Gulabmama's narratives to illuminate this point. Gulabmama is not involved in the TJ but his son is a very active worker. They belong to the Fakir community, which is traditionally a poor cultivating community also involved in miscellaneous trades (Misra 1964). Villagers often recall how Gulabmama has come up in life after going around selling betel leaves from village to village on foot. Once, he described the situation during the post-Babri Masjid riot in 1992. He said that at the time of the disturbance (*dhamal*) his younger son was away on a Jamaat tour. 'My elder son sat day and night in the mosque asking for *dua*. I was the only man in the house. I kept the door shut. They were difficult times (*mamla bahut tedha tha*).' At this point Gulabmama's five-year-old grandson came back from school. His name is Osama. Gulabmama introduces him to me, laughs and says 'These days he is in great danger.' Then suddenly he became serious and said 'My son asks *dua* for Osama all the time'.[17]

Faruqi recognized this aspect of the TJ when he wrote that the TJ was not an intellectual movement; by emphasizing *iman* and *dua* it showed its mystic approach towards reforming the life of the individual (Faruqi 1971: 67). A riot is a moment of breakdown of civil society and while we try to find answers to why and how they happen, for some people asking for *dua* is an important way of coming to terms with uncertainty and tragedy.

We learn that people sometimes decide neither to appeal to institutions of the democratic state nor take recourse to violence in order to bring about justice. They feel that the only solution lies in going to their co-religionists and strengthening their collective identity, which lies in the public domain but outside the domain of the power of the nation state. Thomas Blom Hansen has also noted two distinct responses among the Muslim communities after the 1993 riots in Mumbai. One is what he describes as a conservative quest for the internal purification and unity of the Muslim community with a return to the basics of the Koran and a withdrawal from political, legal, and economic dependence on the larger society. The TJ is such a group. But the other response, Hansen notes, has been the pragmatic strategy of 'plebeian assertion' linked to the 'underworld' and the Samajwadi Party. This claims detachment from the mosque and 'pious people'. The 'religious sensibilities' are with the Barelwis (Hansen 2000: 267). Sikand pointed out that it was only after the unprecedented violence of 1947 that the TJ actually took off as a mass movement in Mewat (Sikand 2000: 344). At that time, the *ulama* affiliated to the TJ and Deoband worked tirelessly to supply relief, helping the Meo to get their lands back from Hindus. I have already pointed out that in Surat district, the TJ has become popular over the last ten years, since the 1992 riots. After the post-Godhra massacre of Muslims in 2002, the TJ has been one of the main organizations working for relief and rehabilitation.

In the concluding section I shall draw attention to the fact that the

TJ's claim on the public domain and its refusal to accept religion as a private affair makes its relationship with secular democracy a strained one. The priority is to lead an exemplary life as Muslims, not as citizens. At the same time, the TJ is aware that what constitutes the exemplary life for Muslims is a contested question. There are others who work towards this end. Therefore, one needs to study the TJ within an inter-organizational framework as well. In some contexts all these groups come together, for example, at the time of relief and rehabilitation of the victims of Gujarat violence in 2002. But in other contexts they do not. Zainuddin's study of a TJ *ijtema* in Orissa in 1996 shows that the Barelwi Muslims not only opposed the *ijtema* but mobilized Hindu Right Wing organizations such as the Bajarang Dal, BJP, Hindu Jagaran Samukhya and RSS by providing them factually incorrect information which created an impression that the *ijtema* would bring about conversion of Hindus to Islam and large scale cow slaughter (Zainuddin 2001: 173-4). Hansen has noted violent conflicts between the TJ and Barelwis in Mumbai in 1998 (Hansen 2000: 263). It is said that Maulana Ilyas was of the view that the TJ and the other Islamic groups were complementing each other's work and therefore, there should be no rivalry between them. But despite such a view, a *fatwa* issued by one of the leaders of the TJ, Maulana Mohammad Zakariyya, against Maududi and his Jamaat-i-Islami has been a source of hostility between the two movements since the 1950s. Furthermore, the TJ leaders consider the Jamaat-i-Islami's approach to religion as politically motivated and devoid of any spiritual content (Ahmad 1991: 522). The local leaders in Ratanpur were aware of this tension between Zakariyya and Maududi.[18] Despite their claim that they are urging the people to follow the path of 'true' Islam, they acknowledge that various groups are working according to their own judgement (*vicar*) towards the same goal.[19]

CONCLUSION

The TJ is turning its head away from 'this world' and preparing for the next, but at the same time it is claiming its space in the public arena. Any process of secularization renders religion a private, not public, affair, but it is not yet clear what is considered religious and thereby unacceptable in the public domain. We also need to ask, where does the private end and the public begin in democratic nation-states? Emile Durkheim had recognized this problem when he discussed the demarcation between private and public laws. He argued that the demarcation is never very neat since all law is private in the sense that it is always about individuals who are present and acting. At the same time, all law is also public in the sense that all individuals are functionaries of society (Durkheim 1964: 68). Likewise, one wonders whether the individual Tablighi's 'religious' dress and manners embody private choice or whether it is a religious assertion in the public domain. Moreover, as Gurpreet Mahajan has noted, religion cannot be restricted to the private domain in any democracy. 'Religious liberty involves, at the very least, the right to worship collectively and build places where the congregation can meet and pray; this itself places religion in the public domain' (Mahajan 2003: 910). At the same time, it is difficult to ascertain how public religion could go. The debates in France on headscarves in public schools show that it is not easy to decide what exactly constitutes religious assertion in the secular public domain. The *zahir* aspects of religion are in palpable tension with the principles of secular nation states.

In India, both the secularists and the followers of Hindutva claim that the negation of multiple identities on behalf of the Muslims is the source of the problem. Groups like the TJ attempt to claim a monolithic identity, which defies history and the pluralistic local culture. Now the question is: how does our theory of pluralism understand and address groups which are not very open to multiple identities, at least ostensibly?[20] Does our notion of pluralism extend only to those who do not claim exclusivity and exclude those who want to remain exclusive? William. E. Connolly has explored this issue by raising the question, 'To what extent does a cultural presumption of the normal individual or the preexisting subject precede and confine conventional pluralism? What conceptions of identity (and difference) are taken for granted in pluralist celebrations of "diversity"?' (Connolly 1995: xiii). Critical appraisal of the concept of pluralism has caught the attention of political theorists but the most serious shortcomings in conventional pluralism are difficult to articulate, argues Connolly. In Gujarat, a man whose shop was burnt in the riot told me, 'I do not know whether it is right or wrong but my religion is the most important thing for me.' On the other hand, an RSS activist, who happened to be a university professor, claimed that the RSS has nothing to do with religion. 'One could be an atheist and still be a Rashtriya Swayamsevak Sangh activist. Hindutva applies to all those who live in this land. Why should it be intolerant to Muslims? We are willing to accept them as Muhammadpanthis! But they should be willing to change and become Indians first.'[21] And therefore arises the most important question: how does a believing, practising Muslim *become* an Indian?

The problem common to both conventional secularism and Hindutva is that groups like the TJ remain resolutely stubborn in upholding their exclusivity. But it is within the structure of the democratic state that such community identity becomes more complex. Commenting on the Indian paradox of persistence of democratic institutions as well as conflict along community lines, Stanley J. Tambiah points out that participatory democracy, competitive elections, mass militancy, and crowd violence are not disconnected factors (Tambiah 1996: 260). Communities in this context constitute the real or imagined 'vote-bank'. During the assembly elections in December 2002, the BJP argued that the Congress was a party for Muslims. A Hindu respondent told me about the 'wonderful speech' given by a national level BJP leader who said, 'I am not unhappy if the Congress wins. But I shall be unhappy about the fact that if the Congress wins, Muslims will smile (*mian muskurayenge*).' Mushirul Hasan has succinctly pointed out that the structure of governance created by the British, with its separate electorates, reservations and weightages, offered the Muslim League much scope for articulating a religio-political identity in the colonial image of being unified, cohesive, and segregated from the Hindus (Hasan 2000: 147). On the other hand, it should be noted that the TJ's claim to exclusivity is not only *vis-à-vis* other religions. Usha Sanyal has noted this aspect of the Islamic reform movements in the late nineteenth and early twentieth centuries where the 'Others' against whom these movements defined themselves were primarily fellow Sunni Muslims (Sanyal 1996: 3). The TJ's exclusivity is equally pronounced with other Muslim sects such as the Barelwis, Ahl-e-Hadis, and the Ahmadiyas, to name a few. These are contending parties claiming to represent 'true' Islam. Each is well aware that multiple groups occupy this contentious space and they are in cooperation and conflict with each other. One needs to see the TJ as one of the movements within the multiple traditions of Islam that emerge from time to time. Any attempt to unify also divides the community. Madan has rightly pointed out that the task of developing a well-argued ideology of religious pluralism on the basis of the religions of India awaits serious and competent attention (Madan 2003). The TJ in today's Gujarat offers an excellent opportunity for understanding that though equally desirable, secularism, democracy, and pluralism are not always unidirectional processes.

NOTES

1. I would thank Tulsi Patel, Deepak Mehta, J.P.S. Uberoi and the participants of the seminar for their comments on an earlier draft of the paper. Thanks to Satish Saberwal for providing the necessary intellectual challenge and an opportunity to present my work. I am grateful to S. Zainuddin for sharing his views and unpublished thesis with me and to Aparajita De for providing important contacts in Baroda city. Finally I would like to acknowledge the generosity and trust my respondents in Gujarat have shown towards me during these difficult years.
2. Zainuddin quotes Faruqui, who has reported that the Tablighi Jamaat has spread to 165 countries. In a list of addresses of Tablighi Jamaat centres on the internet 135 countries were listed. http://Tableegh.tripod.com/markaz.html
3. I have done fieldwork between December 2000 and December 2001 on a Hindu religious movement called Swadhyaya. During this time I had the opportunity to interact with TJ followers in a village in Surat district. I was in Mumbai and different parts of Gujarat in 2003 for three weeks, interviewing Tablighis, non-Tablighi Muslims, Swadhyayis and RRS activists. All the names of the people in the field have been changed to protect their identities.
4. Metcalf mentions Urdu, Hindi, and English as the languages into which the Arabic texts have been translated (1993: 584). I would like to add another phenomenon I had seen during my fieldwork in Gujarat where the TJ participants would be reading out Urdu written in Gujarati script.
5. Interview, New Delhi, October 2003.
6. Describing a similar tendency among the Deobandis, Kenneth W. Jones has found that the latter conceived of Islam as having two points of focus, *shariat* (the law, based on scriptures and religious knowledge) and the *tariqah* (path, derived from religious experience). Therefore, they accepted both the role of the *ulama* and Sufism with its forms of discipline. However, what was rejected were the numerous ceremonies, pilgrimages to saints' tombs, and the death rites of a particular saint (the *urs*) and authority of *pirs* who claimed sanctity by their descent rather than by their learning (Jones 1994: 59-60).
7. Ratanpur, since 1981 is considered as a town with a village *panchayat* by the civic administrative status parameters of the census.

8. In 2003 October when I visited Aligarh Muslim University I attended one such session. I went there with the wife of a university teacher.
9. While doing a household survey in Harshupur I found out that the richest Patidar farmer had taken considerable land on rent (*ganot*) from Muslims of Ratanpur.
10. This informant's father told me that after work, his son goes around trying to persuade people not to sell or drink alcohol. It will be important to find out what kind of intervention TJ has been able to make and/or the hostilities they suffer, vis-à-vis the alcohol trade in Gujarat.
11. Ratanpur, Surat district, November 2001.
12. I thank Amita Baviskar for drawing my attention to this paper.
13. TJ activist, Ratanpur, November 2001.
14. Journalists' accounts of the events on the 27 February 2002 on Godhra platform show that the Hindutva brigade chose its targets on the basis of the beard (Punwani 2002).
15. Interview, Ratanpur, September 2003.
16. Interview, Baroda city, September 2003.
17. This interview took place in November 2001, two months after 9/11.
18. Sikand has noted that the Jamaat-i-Islami activists pointed out that the Tablighis were deviating from Ilyas's central tenet of 'respect for all Muslims'. It has been alleged by Jamaat-i-Islami leaders that TJ activists generally believe that Muslims who do not go on Jamaat are 'misguided' and so they do not reply to their *salaam* (Sikand 2002: 105).
19. Interview, Ratanpur, October 2001.
20. Interestingly, in Britain, Sikand notes that Gujarati Muslims with whom the TJ leadership and following are associated, maintain strong familial and cultural ties with Gujarat and are acutely conscious of their Gujarati identity. They are thought to be a well-knit and closely integrated community, characterized by 'an insular almost caste-like mentality' (Sikand 2002: 228). Yet, in Gujarat, Tablighi credentials as Gujaratis are suspect.
21. Interview, Rajkot, October 2003.

REFERENCES

Ahmad, Mumtaz., 1991, 'Islamic Fundamentalism in South Asia: The Jamaat-i-Islami and the Tablighi Jamaat of South Asia', in *Fundamentalism Observed*, ed. Martin E. Marty and R. Scott Appleby, Chicago: University of Chicago Press, pp. 457-530.

Ahmed, Rafiuddin., 1981, *The Bengal Muslims 1871-1906: A Quest for Identity*, New Delhi: Oxford University Press.

Connolly, William E., 1995, *The Ethos of Pluralization,* Minneapolis: University of Minnesota Press.

Dassetto, Felice., 1988, 'The Tablighi Organization in Belgium', in *The New Islamic Presence in Western Europe*, ed. Tomas Gerholm and Yngve Georg Lithman, London: Mansell, pp. 159-73.

Durkheim, Emile, 1964 (1933), *The Division of Labour in Society*, New York: Free Press.

Engineer, Asghar Ali., 1982, Baroda Riots: Wages of Political Corruption, *Economic and Political Weekly*, XVIII, 46-7.

Faruqi, Z.H., 1971, 'The Tablighi Jama'at', in *India and Contemporary Islam,* ed. S.T. Lokhandwalla, Simla: Indian Institute of Advanced Study, pp. 60-9.

Hansen, Thomas Blom, 2000, 'Predicaments of Secularism: Muslim Identities and Politics in Mumbai', *Journal of Royal Anthropological Institute* (N.S.) 6, 255-72.

Hasan, Mushirul., 2000, '"Majorities" and "Minorities" in Modern South Asian Islam', in *Pluralism and Equality: Values in Indian Society and Politics*, ed. Imtiaz Ahmad, Partha S. Ghosh and Helmut Reifeld, New Delhi: Sage, pp. 141-55.

Jayaram, N. and Satish Saberwal (eds.), 1996, *Social Conflict,* New Delhi: Oxford University Press.

Jones, Kenneth W., 1994, *Socio-religious Movements in British India,* Cambridge: Cambridge University Press.

Madan, T.N., 2003, 'Religions of India: Plurality and Pluralism', in *The Oxford India Companion to Sociology and Social Anthropology*, ed. Veena Das, New Delhi: Oxford University Press, pp. 775-801.

Mahajan, Gurpreet, 2003, 'Secularism', in *The Oxford India Companion to Sociology and Social Anthropology,* ed. Veena Das, New Delhi: Oxford University Press.

Mahmood, Saba, 2001, 'Feminist Theory, Embodiment, and the Docile Agent: Some Reflections on the Egyptian Islamic Revival', *Cultural Anthropology*, 6 (2), pp. 202-36.

Mayaram, Shail, 1997, *Resisting Regimes: Myth, Memory and the Shaping of a Muslim Identity,* New Delhi: Oxford University Press.

Metcalf, Barbara Daly, 1993, 'Living Hadith in the Tablighi Jamaat', *The Journal of Asian Studies* 52 (3) 584-608.

———, 1995, 'Islam and Women: The Case of Tablighi Jamaat', http://www.webonthenet.com/Articles/JamaatByBarbaraMetcalf.htm (18 September 2003).

———, n.d. '"Traditionalist" Islamic Activism: Deobandh, Tablighis, and Talibs', Social Science Research Council (Online) http://www.ssrc.org/sept11/essays/metcalf.htm (18 September 2003).

Misra, Satish C., 1964, *Muslim Communities in Gujarat,* Bombay: Asia Publishing House.

Moosa Ebrahim, 2000, 'Worlds "Apart": Tablighi Jamaat in South Africa Under Apartheid, 1963-1993', in *Travellers in Faith: Studies of the Tableeghi Jamaat as a Transnational Islamic Movement for Faith Renewal*, ed. Muhammad Khalid Masud, Leiden: Brill pp. 206-21.

Punwani, Jyoti, 2002, 'The Carnage at Godhra', in *Gujarat: The Making of a Tragedy*, ed. Sidhharth Varadarajan, New Delhi: Penguin, pp. 45-74.

Sanyal, Usha, 1996, *Devotional Islam & Politics in British India: Ahmad Riza Khan Barelwi and his Movement, 1870-1920*, New Delhi: Oxford University Press .

Sikand, Yoginder, 2002, *The Origins and Development of the Tablighi-Jamaat (1920-2000)*, New Delhi: Orient Longman.

———, 2000, 'The Tablighi Jamaat in Post-1947 Mewat', *The Eastern Anthropologist*, 53 (3-4), 341-50.

Swami, Praveen, 2002, 'Godhra Question', *Frontline*, 16-29 March, 12-14.

Tambiah, Stanley J., 1996, *Levelling Crowds: Ethnonationalist Conflicts and Collective Violence in South Asia*, Berkeley: University of California Press.

Tozy, Mohamed, 2000, 'Sequences of a Quest: Tablighi Jamaat in Morocco', in *Travellers in Faith: studies of the Tablighi Jamaat as a transnational Islamic movement for faith renewal*, ed. Muhammad Khalid Masud, Leiden: Brill, pp. 161-73.

Troll, Christian W., 1985, 'Five Letters of Maulana Ilyas (1885-1944), the Founder of the Tablighi Jammat', Translated, Annotated and Introduced, in *Islam in India: Studies and Commentaries*, vol. 2, ed. Christian W.Troll, New Delhi: Vikas, pp. 138-76.

van der Veer, Peter., 1994, *Religious Nationalism: Hindus and Muslims in India*, Berkeley: University of California Press.

Yagnik, Achyut, 2002, 'The Pathology of Gujarat', *Seminar*, May (513), pp. 19-22.

Zainuddin, S., 2000, 'Economic Internationalization and Islamic Resurgence in India', *The International Scope Review*, 2 (4).

———, 2001, 'Some Aspects of Society and Culture in a Religious Movement Among Muslims: The Case of Tablighi Jamaat in Orissa', unpublished Ph.D. thesis, Department of Sociology, Faculty of Social Sciences, Jamia Millia Islamia, New Delhi.

Moosa, Ebrahim. 2007. [illegible] In [illegible] 2007. [illegible] *[illegible] Transnational Islamic Movement [illegible]*. Muhammad [illegible] pp. [illegible]
[illegible]. 2002. [illegible] *[illegible]*. New Delhi: [illegible], pp. [illegible]

[illegible]. 1995. [illegible] *[illegible]*. [illegible]
[illegible] University Press.

Sikand, Yoginder. 2002. *The Origins and Development of the Tablighi Jama'at (1920–2000)*. New Delhi: Orient Longman.

———. 2006. 'The Tablighi Jama'at' in [illegible]

[illegible]. *[illegible]*. Bombay, [illegible]

[illegible]. [illegible] University Press.

[illegible]. 2002. [illegible]

[illegible]. [illegible] University of [illegible] Press.

[illegible]. *[illegible]* [illegible] (ed.), [illegible]

van der Veer, Peter. 1994. *Religious Nationalism: Hindus and Muslims in India*. Berkeley: University of California Press.

[illegible]. 2002. 'The [illegible] of [illegible]', [illegible]
pp. [illegible]

[illegible]. 2000. [illegible] and [illegible] in India', *[illegible]*

———. [illegible] Movement [illegible] the Case of [illegible]
[illegible] Department of [illegible]
[illegible]

HINDUTVA

Our papers on the assertiveness of Hindu 'nationalists' turn on the laying of its ideological foundations by two mid-twentieth-century men, V.D. Savarkar and M.S. Golwalkar; on the extraordinary organizational pattern of Rashtriya Swayamsevak Sangh (RSS), the primary vehicle for the ideology of Hindutva; and on the recent campaign by the Vishwa Hindu Parishad (VHP), an RSS subsidiary, to distribute among its stormtroopers the *trishul*, an intimidatory, lethal trident—positioning it as an innocent religious icon.

In texts by Savarkar and Golwalkar, prime ideologues of Hindutva, and in their followers' continuing practice, Pradip Datta notes a deliberate erasure of the line between historical narrative on the one hand and legend, myth, and fiction on the other. For the resulting amalgam, Datta proposes the term 'myhstory', and he tracks its source to James Tod's work on Rajasthan. Hindutva practitioners deploy the potentials of myhstory to try to produce a new Hindu subject who will violently seek to recover mastery of his nation.

The inner logic of myhstory is not just to suppress some and invent other historical facts. It is to visualise/interpret/allegorise the present as a part of a long saga of battles between Hindus and Muslims inherited from the past and to seek to reverse this history in the present. Mhystory invents the past as a time of defeat and humiliation, the present offering a decisive, violent, near apocalyptic opportunity to recover Hindu pride and master the Muslims. In turn, this will produce, it is hoped, a new past that will no longer bear the stain of humiliation. Not just the course of history but the memory of the past is sought to be transformed.

For this ideology it is the RSS that has been the most potent vehicle since its beginnings in Nagpur in the mid-1920s. The core mechanism for its phenomenal spread has been the pracharak, the organizer or propagator, working principally through the *shakha*, the local branch which draws largely middle class young men into its daily routine. Pralay Kanungo explores RSS organizational arrangements around the *pracharak*: his starting as a young participant in the *shakha*, being drawn to the local pracharak's personality and ascetic lifestyle, his being selected, groomed, and indoctrinated for pracharakhood himself, and, after some years in the field, organizing and leading *shakhas*, either becoming a householder or joining the core (celibate) cadre, overseeing its farflung activities and its growing array of affiliated organizations. With its enormous diversification in recent decades, active political interest, and the taste of power through its front, the Bharatiya Janata Party (BJP), the RSS, and its pracharaks now face difficult dilemmas.

An entity in the RSS conglomerate, the Vishwa Hindu Parishad (VHP), has spread out into the Hindu diaspora, especially in north America, drawing large funds ostensibly for developmental activities in India. A major part of its energy and activities at home, however, has gone into organizing among poor, unemployed, youth, to make them the foot soldiers for Hindutva, prepared to assert themselves violently, say for building a Ram temple in Ayodhya. If the young men in RSS were trained to wield the six-foot staff, the youth in VHP and its stormtroopers, the Bajrang Dal, wield the *trishul* weapon. Amar Farooqui examines the uses of religious icons and practices for intimidating target populations, comparing the *trishul* with the Ku Klux Klan's 'cross-burning' in United States, intended to intimidate Blacks, and the judgements of the law courts thereon.

8

Hindutva Ideas of the Past

PRADIP KUMAR DATTA

I am grateful to the late K.R. Malkani for having solved the riddle of Hindutva history.[1] In an article that defended the Ministry of Human Resource Development from the charge that it was promoting myths in the name of history, he declared, 'The fact is that there is often more history in myths and more myth in history.'[2] My gratitude stems from the fact that Hindutva history had for long teased its opponents[3]—and possibly itself—with its now-you-see-it-now-you-don't play with facts and traditional memory. The Ramjanmabhumi claim could be seen as mythic and based on popular memory if one looked at it from the story of Ram, historical if seen from the vantage point of the Babur narrative. Correspondingly, Hindutva propagandists could claim that the conviction about Ram's birthplace was based on popular belief even as they strenuously appealed to facts to prove their case.[4]

Malkani's clarification that the Hindutva past consists of both history and myth has led me to call this phenomenon 'myhstory'.[5] At the risk of sounding tacky, I chose the neologism because it expresses the hybrid character of Hindutva's past. Also, it signals the paradoxical usage of myth by Hindutva. Sometimes, for instance, Hindutva propagandists use myth in the negative, rationalist sense of a fiction. An entire polemical exercise in public relations entitled *Ramjanmabhoomi: History versus Casuistry*[6] confidently dons the mantle of historical facts to denounce the 'myths' floated during the 'Freedom movement' that India possessed a 'composite culture' and that there was no serious Hindu-Muslim problem before the British arrived. Myth here is treated as the equivalent of lies—and is, in fact, dubbed 'mischievous'. While this notion of myth goes against the grain of the actual usage of the mythic by Hindutva—and Malkani does not provide a definition of myth that could clear up the confusion—what is more certain is that 'myth' indicates a place that constantly shadows the one occupied by history and facts in Hindutva narratives of the past. That is to say, Hindutva history never relies on facts alone to advance its claims about the past. Its history is always accompanied by 'living traditions' in texts of narrative, poetry, monuments, or popular belief and legends.[7] What all these non-historical phenomena share with the mythic is their transcendental nature: all of them are seen as manifestations of the overarching spirit of the Hindu nation.

Myhstory is crucial for the ideology of Hindutva because it is deeply entrenched in the past. Hindutva develops its world-view through the past: it is the past that gives Hindutva the vocabulary and structure to conceptualize the present. The record of battles between Hindus and Muslims is central to making Hindutva a political vision of the present. But this does not mean that Hindutva is traditionalist in its understanding of the past. Paradoxically, as I shall argue, it privileges the present in relationship to the past. This means that Hindutva has a double-need: it requires a flexible past that can explain and politically activate the present; at the same time it also needs a past that is stable so that it can preserve the steadfastness of political beliefs. It is this particular configuration of needs, arbitrariness and stability, that myhstory satisfies.

I may also add that it is important to look at the evolution of myhstory. Recent debates on Hindutva history have tended to conceptualize it as a part of a binary between modernity and what can be loosely called 'tradition'. Anti-secularists have regarded it as an expression of state rationality while secularists have understandably emphasized its non-historical and fictional dimensions. In contrast, myhstory cuts a complex trajectory across both these cultural formations; in addition it draws upon the constructivist elements of post-modernism. This is significant because often cultural-epistemological formations are equated with certain political values; for instance, it is often assumed that a recognition of the arbitrariness of factuality undermines the authoritative stability of 'facts' and encourages a more democratic orientation. The progress of myhstory indicates that political narratives can draw on a host of other cultural formations, completely changing the political associations of certain ideas, to produce its own autonomous reality. In short, a history of the myhstorical returns us to the question of specificity.

II

The hybrid genre of mythic history was not invented by Hindutva. Partha Chatterjee[8] and Sumit Sarkar[9] have demonstrated its existence in the nineteenth century. Such early histories, influenced by colonial requirements and Fort William scholarship, transit unproblematically from cosmic chronotopes to the more defined this-world paradigms of time and space. In this it can be seen to follow the narrative trajectory of Puranic stories which, Romila Thapar has argued, make a similarly easy narrative transition from cosmological origins to the more historically identifiable world of lineages.[10] Such simple, linear hybridity (in which the narrative takes the reader from cosmic to worldly time) is disturbed by alternate forms in the nineteenth century. I wish to mention two of these. The more significant one was developed by Jotiba Phule, the pioneering low caste ideologue of Maharashtra. In *Gulamgiri* (Slavery), Phule confronts the Brahmanical myths of the Puranas.[11] Proceeding from historical assumptions based on commonsensical, this–worldly ideas of how individuals and power relations operate, Phule attempts to show that the Puranic narratives conceal and dress up a terrible narrative of the colonization of the native dwellers of the country by Aryan foreigners who instituted the caste system to perpetuate their domination. These stories, according to Phule, legitimize a system that is unjust in the minds of its victims.

Mythic history is complicated by another approach that takes a literalist view of its stories. It was initiated by orthodox Hindus, such as Sasadhar Tarkachuramani, who wished to demonstrate the superiority of ancient Indian civilization to that of the West.[12] Reading myths as literal truths, Tarkachuramani tried to prove that the material and technological achievements of the West had been anticipated by the ancient Indians. While this exercise was to influence the formation of a household common sense of the past in which children like me grew up—and to put its impress on the nature of debates that Hindutva historians have on the historical truths of the *Mahabharata*, for instance—it failed to acquire intellectual respectability. A direct translation of the mythic into the factual tended to tear apart the two epistemes and offer itself to sceptical readings even by those such as Bankimchandra Chattopadhyay who approximated Tarkachuramani's position.

When we turn to myhstory, what stands out is that the latter is more integrated: at its most sophisticated, the historical references become a part of the mythic and both are shaped by the plots of Hindu-Muslim conflict. Indeed myhstory restores the power of mythic histories, the constituent elements of which, as I have hinted, had begun to fly apart by the end of the nineteenth century. Myhstory sometimes infuses history with a logic that makes it approach the fantasy of myth. We shall see how Golwalkar uses facts about the antiquity of the Hindus in a way that makes them into near-fantastic assertions. At other times history can be absorbed into an extant mythic framework, as the entry of Babur into Ram's legend in the Ramjanmabhumi story.

There are two other, productive, differences between the two genres. The first is the privileging of the past in the narrative of the present. The past poses an urgent issue. Second, myhstory has a performative orientation. While this is obvious in the case of the Ramjanmabhumi narrative which, as I will show, is designed for mass performance, it is also true—although in a less direct manner—for earlier practices of the myhstoric which strain towards the performative. That is to say, myhstory carries a strong aesthetic element that takes the form of theatrical perfomance.

The importance of the aesthetic prompts another look at Partha Chatterjee's suggestion that the emergence of a strict historical genre from the 1870s produced (along with other possibilities) the sense of a fundamental difference between Hindu and Muslim, motivated by the search for the Hindu origins of the nation. What this argument overlooks is that the past was not just the province of the historian. It was a larger cultural preoccupation of the intelligentsia and motivated a great deal of intellectual activity in many fields. Its wider influence is tangible in the field of aesthetic production. In order to demonstrate that it is this other lineage of the communal past that led to myhstory, I begin with James Tod's *Annals and Antiquities of Rajasthan* which co-opted myth and legend to reconstruct a past.[13]

Lt. Col. James Tod can be called a public historian. His *Annals* was a popular narrative that could lend itself to be used as a history by professional historians,[14] a mine of geographical and ethnographic detail, a source book of stories, and a foundational book for Hindu nationalism. Above all, Tod was a public historian in the sense that his work on the Rajput past was meant to influence British strategic policy as well as the British public, to that end. For Tod could be called a Rajputphile: he was convinced that Rajput nationalism demanded respect and encouragement.[15] It was this commitment that led him to scour the interiors of Rajasthan to collect legends and ethnographic information and that finally landed him in trouble with the authorities.[16]

Tod is the real parent of myhstory, on at least two counts. First, he justifies the use of myth and deploys it as if it were factual evidence. Second, he produces a distinctive combination: mythical history and martial Hindu nationalism.

For Tod, history is clearly the normative discipline for understanding the past. But he takes myth seriously as a part of the evidence. Tod suggests that myth is a sort of proto-history. According to him, legends are based on facts that are obscured by primitive irrationalism.[17] It may be noted, parenthetically, that for Tod, myth and legend existed on the same epistemic plane (the specific historical legends he relates have their geneaological origins in mythic events and are often informed by the mythic in their unfolding). They reflect things that had actually happened but which were given a mythical form—just as the changes of the seasons were what gave rise to the myth of change.[18] In practice he utilizes the genealogical information and the basic events that seem to be probable events 'encoded' in the myths. Till this point, Tod can be seen to follow—although walking in the extremities of the path—the Orientalist attempt to discover the truth of a common, original world civilization through treating ancient Hindu names as linguistic codes.[19] But interestingly, he also goes beyond them to concede a literal (and not just coded) status to improbable events on the ground that they form a part of popular belief. Thus he regards the Padmini legend as an unlikely one, but nevertheless adds that its truth lies in the fact that it is believed to have happened.[20] Mythic truth is literalized, although it is done so in deference to the claims of popular will.

The criterion of belief to assess evidence is a fateful move—for it is one that L.K. Advani, after 150 years or so, invoked to unleash one of the most divisive communal movements that the subcontinent has seen. While Tod sees popular belief as self-justifying, it is also true that he is not unaware of its uses for nationalism. This provides an additional, if implicit, reason for treating belief as evidence. Belief can be given the status of fact—which is Tod's conception of truth — since it expresses the true Rajput identity, that is, its nationalism.

Equally, the *Annals* makes another crucial move. Orientalist scholars had produced a national past basking in Hindu glory, but had placed it in an antiquity so remote that its impact on the present was palpable only through normative texts. As such this discovery of the past was useful for social reformers, since it offered a body of re-interpretable texts. These could be made to yield new sanctions and prohibitions: for instance Rammohun Roy referred to the shastras to argue for a ban on sati. True, the Orientalist conception of the Indian past as composed of Brahmanical texts encouraged the idea that Hindus were the real children of the land, while the hoariness of the Indian past allowed its votaries to claim cultural supremacy over the rest of the world on this ground alone. But it is also true that the dry research of Orientalist scholarship was not directly useful to militant Hindu nationalism for the latter required the past to be used as a banner for mobilization. What Tod demonstrated on the other hand, was that the fire of national glory was not just a matter of high cultural and philosophical attainments. It was tangibly produced in the not so distant past by a string of battles between Rajput princes and Muslim invaders. Rajputs battled to defend their Hindu religion—conceived as the heart of their patriotic devotion—against Muslim invaders who were engaged in spectacular acts of desecration, destruction, and humiliation.

The marks of the past survived in the present in the form of self-division. One the one hand the persistence of their religion and customs showed that the heroic qualities of Rajput nationalism remained. But there were also negative aspects, although these remained external to their character, being the consequences of Muslim invasions. Admittedly this is a structure that Tod has inherited from the orientalist division of ancient Hindu glory and medieval Islamic depredation. But the massive stress on the transformative impact of war opens out the possibility of a violent renewal of the past. It takes just another step in the argument to conceive of the past as the accumulated burden of invasions that could be redeemed by a series of counter-invasions in the present.

What is also consequential in the *Annals* is the idea that nationalism did not exist in a passive state. Its zeal still burnt in the present, being preserved in bardic and other traditions that recounted stories of Padmini and other such legends. The fact that Tod pieced together the national history of Rajasthan from these legends testified to the rich deposit of nationalism in them. Nationalism was something that animated the present through the recall of popular expressive forms. Here was another important implication that Tod bequeathed. For it is the assumption that expressive forms can be the vehicle of nationalism which explains the wealth of literary and other works that recirculated the stories of the *Annals* as their plots. Well over fifty texts of prose and poetry in Bengali were inspired by Tod's work in the nineteenth and early twentieth centuries.[21] And this included nationalist plays such as Rangalal Bandopadhyay's *Padmini Upakhyan* (regarded as one of the first works of high Bengali literature) and Jyotirindranath Tagore's *Sarojini* that featured a jauhar scene which many commentators felt marked an important moment in the development of (Hindu) nationalist consciousness. Another play, Rangalal Bandopadhyay's *Karmadebi*, actually prefaces the main action (taken from Tod) by a scene in which a bard in the present recounts the story of this nationalist romantic tragedy. Tod's influence was felt to be so powerful that Vivekananda asserted that two thirds of Bengal's modern nationalist consciousness was due to Tod's book on Rajasthan![22]

Tod's influence was not restricted to Bengal alone, as the popularity of the Padmini legend, which derives from Tod's work, testifies.[23] By the time Golwalkar wrote his *We* in 1938, he could treat this particular story as a certified emblem of Muslim oppression. Tales of Rajput valour circulated very easily across the country, together with and often as part of communally structured stories of Muslim lust and Hindu bravery. In addition, these stories allowed a synecdochal treatment of provincial histories that were already being compiled by the time the *Annals* came out in 1839. The history of Rajasthan via its generalized commitment to the Hindu nation, could be treated as a synecdoche of the Indian past. By extension, the formation of regional cultures could then be regarded at one and the same time as national. A symbiotic process can be seen in Bengal where numerous literary works were based on Tod's stories, and where Bengali pride dovetailed into a form of Hindu nationalism through the recall of Rajput valour. The imprint of this process is also visible in the way Ranade's *History of the Marathas* (1878)—published in a decade of intense nationalist self-consciousness—conceives of a pan-Hindu national awakening in the hundred odd years of Maratha dominance.[24] The importance of this ability to slide the provincial into the national is evident in the fact that only half a century later, Savarkar's narration of Maratha national history in *Hindu Pad-Padshahi* (hereafter *HPP*) drew on the basic structure of Ranade's work to argue for the persistence and ever increasing glory of Hindutva in general.[25]

III

Savarkar was a rationalist grounded in history. Indeed, as we shall see, he tried to follow such verification procedures as footnoting. However he was primarily a political theorist and activist of religious conflict. Consequently his understanding of the past had to draw upon myth and legend. But for the most part the obvious mythical references, such as the ones to Ram or to the origins of the land, tend to be inspirational, operating as cultural symbols/beliefs. But there is also another sense in which the mythic plays a part, and that is in the more general sense of providing a repetitive narrative. Savarkar's histories are structured by the story of repeated battles between Hindus and Muslims. However the ultimate objective of such a narrative pattern was not to perform the eternal order of time, but to encourage the decisive breakup of this pattern of repetition and to transform time.

In his short exegesis on history in *HPP*, Savarkar states that the aim of his 'great epic' of the Marathas is to show the ideal of 'Swadharma Rajaya', that is, the 'living ideal of Hindu empire dedicated to the service of Deva and Dharma . . . throbbing and pulsating throughout the mighty movement'.[26] Savarkar further spells out his historical assumptions in his gloss on Mazzini's comment on Carlyle's *History of the French Revolution*. He says that the 'fundamental principle' of the revolution is to be found in the 'innermost desire of those who brought it about'.[27] Clearly Savarkar's history is voluntarist in conception. It is the desire generated by the ideal of religious nationalism which provides the fundamental dynamic of history, and gives order to the apparently random multiplicity of motives and details that make up historical events. By implication the historian's task is to articulate the intensity of that desire, which means passing on the torch of that motivation to those in the subjugated present. Myth may possess transcendental authority, history may be processual, but both are ultimately subject to the desire of the nationalist subject. These assumptions, as we shall see, allow for massive innovations in the mythic and historical, evident in the Ramjanmabhumi movement.

The voluntarist conception of history has an elective affinity with Savarkar's moorings in revolutionary terrorism (his early life was largely spent in running Abinava Bharat, an organization that was terroristic in orientation). He says that history needs to have an apocalyptic effect on its readers. In the passage quoted above where he talks of the 'innermost desire' of historical writing, Savarkar goes on to state that, once this is discerned, not only will inconsistencies disappear, but also 'light appears where darkness is, what appeared ugly becomes fair and what looked beautiful is seen to be deformed'. Savarkar draws on the romantic relationship between beauty and truth to make the point that aesthetic transformation precedes a perceptual one. Light (the trope of knowledge) is redefined in this new condition. By enacting this change at the level of perception, historical narrative prepares for what is enacted in the apocalypse of revolution: 'crowns are destroyed and created, existing ideals are shattered and new ideals break forth, and for the sake of which vast masses of people think lightly of shedding sacred human blood'.[28]

Savarkar brings the desire for perceptual transformation and actual revolutionary enactment together through the narrative element of shock. Shock is used as a narrative equivalent of the physical ruptures of violence. It predisposes the mind to acts of violence by rupturing the sanctions against it and simultaneously preparing the ground for making it legitimate. Savarkar reiteratively narrates sequences of battles, glorying in acts of violence and remorseless vengeance—as if, by doing this, he can break the stubborn moral resistances to it by ceaseless waves of shocks, like a terrorist network carrying out a series of violent 'strikes' against its enemy.

The immediately transformative effect of violence, it may be observed, makes it an appropriate vehicle for a voluntarist and apocalyptic orientation to change. But Savarkar goes beyond revolutionary terrorism in his relationship to violence. Despite the ritual and rhetorical celebration of violence, the early twentieth-century revolutionary terrorist strategy had seen it as a means of making colonial governance unworkable. And this violence was limited to individual acts of spectacular terror. In contrast, we do not get the sense that violence is instrumental and tactical with Savarkar. It is not something to be endured but perpetuated. Violence is a constitutive part of the desired transformation of the national collective called Hindus. At times violence seems to be the ultimate proof of the Hindutva revolution. Indeed, violence is so important a part of the philosophy underlying Hindutva's past that we need to consider it separately.

Savarkar's philosophy of violence is in a sense derived from the Social Darwinist thought of Herbert Spencer. Actually, "derived" may not be the best word to use here. For one, Spencer's thought is selectively chosen, a process that suggests a greater degree of initiative than the verb 'derived' indicates. Further, these selected elements interlock with other traditions, including those derived from Tod and revolutionary terrorism, to release an independent trajectory of praxis. In effect Spencer's thought can be located as a starting point in a grid of many points rather than an origin that determines a later trajectory.

The Social Darwinist idea of the survival of the fittest was one that entered the common sense of the Indian middle class and provided theoretical frameworks for communal thinkers such as U.N. Mukherjee.[29] Savarkar was probably introduced to Spencer's thought by his patron in England, an Orientalist scholar called Pt. Shyamji Krishna Varma. The latter was a follower of Spencer's thought and dedicated a special chair at Oxford in memory of Spencer on the occasion of the latter's death in 1903.[30] The references to Spencer's thought are scattered throughout Savarkar's writings; he treats Spencerian opinions as truths of existence. In *HPP*, Savarkar refers to the 'stern law of nature' according to which men and groups will be consolidated into 'larger social units'. This entails war with other groups, a process that tests out the moral fitness 'that entitles races and types to survive in this world'. The notion of existential corporate competition supplies the philosophical justification for unremitting Hindu-Muslim conflict in the historical narrative of Hindutva. At the same time, the Hindutva framework extends Spencer's idea of competition between corporate groups to that of direct physical battle.

In order to make this transition to physical battle, Savarkar draws on a key idea of Spencer, viz., the unity of the biological and the social.[31] This notion is deployed by Savarkar to treat the trope of social demise as a literal possibility. Expectedly, Savarkar replaces the category of 'society' that is foundational to Spencer with 'nation'. Among the consequences of this move is that it allows a persuasive rhetoric of the impending death of Hindu 'race' because of its religious and socio-cultural organization. But this rhetoric itself turns on an idea of competition so fierce that it is always a final one, for every axis of difference, every act of confrontation with the other, is loaded with the question of survival. Consequently, Hindu existence at every moment is caught in the stark binary of death or victory.

This re-orientation of Spencerian ideas leads—in a somewhat bizarre way—to the reproduction of history as a moral lesson. The emphasis on morality was (and remains) important for Hindutva because it had to proclaim the primacy of violence in a culture perceived, first, to be other-worldly (following from the Orientalist definition of Hinduism) and second, as non-violent and ethical praxis (a meaning given by Gandhi). To counter this heritage, Savarkar had to construct an alternate moral order[32] and Spencer's ideas helped him in this enterprise. Since Savarkar took group competition (reinscribed as physical combat) to be an absolute truth of human existence, morality was correspondingly divided between the values of survival and destruction. It was not a normative morality, but a necessary and relative one: whatever helped to survive was good. In *Six Glorious Epochs*, Savarkar claims that 'virtue' is not absolute. It is positive only when it helps 'the best interests of human society', a vice if it 'caused harm'.[33] History was necessary to spread the pedagogy of this morality, for it showed how human life had always been structured by its truth: the races that fought with determination and intelligence survived to dominate; the others just died. Further, it also revealed the values and strategies that permitted survival—or led to death.

Perhaps the most significant moral lesson of history for Savarkar is that it demonstrates the dangers of universalism. The devaluation of universalism springs from his radical attempt to weed out the legacy of Buddhism and its doctrine of *ahimsa* or non-violence, seen as a universalist position based on the sanctity of human life. In Savarkar's histories, this principle is seen to emasculate Hindus and pave the way for foreign invasions. Worse, universalism makes Buddhism develop affiliations with foreign cultures, such as the Greek, and actually leads to treachery against the Hindu nation. To counter universalism, Savarkar propagates the virtues of patriotism, militarism, and a ruthlessness so absolute that it converts human beings into semiotic entities no different from objects. Commenting on the 1857 uprising, he exults, 'The National Vengeance, awakened after a century, crushed down men, women, children, houses, stones, bricks, flesh, bones—anything that had any relation with the English!'[34] I may add that, unlike revolutionary terrorists who emphasise the readiness to sacrifice one's life, Savarkar emphasizes the enthusiasm to take the lives of others. Clearly, it was the injunction against killing that needed to be sacrificed, not one's own life, since survival was the all important virtue.

Spencer's ideas inflect Savarkar's other historical perambulations.

As may be inferred from the biological-social alliance, Spencerian thought had a strong unitary orientation, which Savarkar presses forward. His idea of the nation, seen as a comprehensive entity, has various elements: as primarily the coincidence of *pitribhumi* (fatherland) and *punyabhumi* (holy land),[35] but also consisting of (the interchangeably used) culture, civilization, race, and history. Savarkar seeks to make these equivalent terms. It is true that he does not fully succeed; for instance he cannot quite attribute pure racial lineages to the Hindu nation since he subscribes to the idea that Aryans had migrated to India from elsewhere. But he kicked off a process that allowed Golwalkar—who followed in his tracks and was less inhibited by the problems of historical research that constrained Savarkar somewhat—to assert blithely that Aryans originated in India, thereby inserting race as an equivalent of common origins and the other constitutive elements of the nation.[36]

This unitary orientation has another implication in its discreet silence about the state. Hindutva—especially Savarkar—deals with the fate of the nation. There is good reason for this. The history of the state is messy and would have plunged Savarkar into a story of historical development (instead of a preformed nation), internal wars between Hindu kingdoms, questions of authority and legitimacy, and the haunting problem of the internal repression of Hindus by other Hindus. Such a story would question the presumption of a unitary nation, complicate and finally marginalize it.[37] By focusing on the ideal imaginary of the nation on the other hand, not only is the possibility of maintaining the transcendental-mythical framework preserved, but also the very unitary nature of the national imaginary can be seen to demand a correspondingly centralized, all embracing state. Thus whenever Savarkar visualizes the state, it is as a Hindu empire; and when the state in the past is referred to, such as the 'Chakravartin' idea of the Marathas, it is as a unitary empire.

Finally, the unitary orientation manifests itself in Savarkar's conception of historical process. For instance, his mentor in Maratha history, M.G. Ranade, represents the story of Maratha religious nationalism as the rise of political power that is preceded by a spread of the Bhakti movement among the subalterns of Maharashtra. As against this, Savarkar presents the two—the religious and the political—appearing as an epiphanic unity, embodied in the simultaneous rise of Shivaji and his spiritual advisor Ramdas, a combine that leads the initiative for the establishment of the Maratha

Hindu nation. It may be remarked that a similar "epiphanic" visitation marked the eruption of the Ramjanmabhumi movement in the 1980s, constructed as it was by the 'spiritual' and political wings (that is, the VHP and the BJP) of the Sangh Parivar.

IV

I wish to enter into a brief dgression in this section. It concerns an apparently fundamental and inexplicable change in Savarkar's attitude to the Muslims, the prime object of his project of violence. It is commonly assumed that while Savarkar celebrated the unity of Hindus and Muslims against the colonisers in his first book, *The Indian War*, he soon—and inexplicably—shifted to communal Hindu nationalism.

It is true that there is a shift, but it is not a paradigmatic one. Savarkar makes it clear in *The Indian War* (and repeats it in *HPP*) that unity with the Muslims was only possible because the Hindus had already militarily humiliated them. Without this prior triumph the question of friendship would not have arisen. Savarkar's views on the matter may have shifted—as with other Hindu communal nationalists such as Malaviya—after the mass mobilization of Muslims in the Non-Cooperation/Khilafat movement and the Hindu-Muslim conflicts that followed. But equally interesting is the evidence given by his biographer, Dhananjay Keer, which indicates that Savarkar had made the transition earlier. While his childhood shows pronounced proclivities towards anti-Muslim violence, his antipathy hardened during his stint in the Andamans Jail. Keer relates how the British authorities, in a classic divide and rule strategy, probably the more potent in the harsh, paranoic condition of imprisonment, appointed only Muslims as warders. Hindus felt slighted and humiliated. It also produced a scare in Savarkar that Muslims were attacking the Hindu religion. Confronted with cases of Muslim warders taking on Hindu partners, Savarkar started a *shuddhi* movement for the moral reform of Hindus and their self-assertion, climaxing in a near riot situation over the privilege of playing music in jail.[38]

This little prison tale is an apt one to understand the location of Muslims and the idea of history. It is appropriate because it shows that hatred of the Muslims is not just a historical legacy or a simple bias; rather, it is a potent force that motivates the making of a new, empowered Hindu subject in conditions of subordination. This involves, first, creating an emotional drive for subjective change; and, second, it points to a new world of possibilities for violence.

Hindutva history inserts its readers into a binary between memories of humiliation and a thirst for power that is born of pride. Savarkar explains this apropos the terms of the appeal for rebellion in 1857 by Bahadur Shah, which he cites in full. He claims that this appeal was effective in mobilizing Hindus and Muslims because it appealed to their religion and its desecration by the British. He appealed not just for a defence of religion; it also made people feel they are complicit in the acts of destruction. According to Savarkar, it 'awakens the people to the fact that they are destroying religion' for, 'The command of God is, obtain Swaraj. . . .'[39] To publicise acts of humiliation is to make the public feel that it is participating in acts of humiliating itself. Conversely it awakens the necessity to fight for religion as an act of fighting for one's self-respect.

Clearly this is what history can do effectively, because it can narrate acts of humiliation repetitively. Yet a simple record of humiliation would not do. It could confirm the conviction that Hindus were fatalists. It is for this reason that humiliation has to be complemented by pride. The task of the historian therefore is to produce images of heroism that readers will 'adore'. Such images provide the sign of an 'ideal condition' that affirms a potential for change and at the same time point to the future, utopic destination of history.

This produces a line of thinking in which history strives towards the condition of myth. The mythic is sought to be presented not only in the visions of the 'golden age'. More profoundly, it is present in the patterning of the narrative on the cycles of ideal conditions of freedom, and the death-like condition of subordination, with human aspiration mediating the two. It is a cyclical structure that replicates the existential truth of victory or death, and the moral lessons that it offers.

Besides, violence is empowering. As commentators have observed, the Hindu nationalist imagination seeks to stereotype the Muslim in terms of qualities that the Hindu apparently lacks but which need to be appropriated and mastered.[40] History provides records of the efficacy of the Muslim qualities of power, organization, and ruthlessness. It was only after these had been mastered by Hindus that Hindu-Muslim unity in 1857 was possible. In short, subjectivity is a technology of power that needs the record of history to identify the objects of its aspiration.

The objects of emulation changed with time. In *The Indian War*, Savarkar had enthusiastically supported the alleged butchery of women and children by the sepoys, but had vigorously defended them against the charge (made by the colonial propaganda machine) of molesting women. But by the time he wrote *Six Glorious Epochs* over half a century later, Savarkar explained the need for Hindus to abduct Muslim women since the Muslims had expanded their numbers by stealing Hindu women. Just after the publication of *The Indian War*, indeed even before that, discourses had developed about the decreasing numbers of Hindus and the increasing population of Muslims. The resulting conviction about the vulnerability of Hindu women to Muslim maleness was consolidated by the Partition riots that actually saw mass abductions and violations of women.

The appropriation of the Other does not, however, completely replace the Self. It cannot, for while the Other belongs to the realm of history, the Self originates in the mythic time of the nation. What is produced in the encounter with the other is addition and paradox. The benign, universalist Hindu self, supposedly the sign of the original and distinctive character of Hindus, is retained. But it is now coupled with the aggressive and the violent. The imprint of this model subject can be seen in the VHP's iconography of Ram, the ideal subject. Ram has an *udar* face (liberal, a sign of innate Hindu temperament) even as he launches his arrows (a sign of the resurgent Hindu battling for his patrimony).[41]

The ambitious assumptions of this project are evident. While mounting a scathing critique of universalism, Savarkar still feels the need to hang on to the authenticity of the Hindu. His solution is to distinguish between 'absolute' universalism, as in the 'fanatical' Buddhist, and 'relative' universalism, of which he approves. He finds that the *Bhagavad Geeta* exemplifies the latter in Krishna's famous advice to Arjun that *dharma* of right action is contingent on the circumstances in which one finds oneself in war. This distinction is used to demolish universalism, while retaining it in a modified form. Yet Savarkar is still loath to relinquish the 'absolute' kind. He consequently refers to 'absolute' universalism as a condition that the Hindu aspires towards, for the Hindu is 'nothing if not universal'. But the precondition for this is that the Hindu must have taken care of the contingencies of historical antagonism—which is logically possible only if he gets to master the world. If everyone became Hindu there would be peace. 'A Hindu is most intensely so' Savarkar concludes modestly, 'when he ceases to be a Hindu; and with Shankar claims the whole earth for Benares. . . .'[42]

It seems to me that the logic of his ideas leads Savarkar into a serious problem about his ultimate goals. Briefly the problem is this. If the future utopia of Hindutva involves a golden age where identity will correspond to the self, and the physical world will provide a chrysalis for both, how, in this tightly integrated unitary world, will the necessity of history and violence be accommodated? For clearly the lesson of the past is that the golden age breeds dangers internal to it, such as Buddhism which sprouted much before the first invasion appeared. Golwalkar too talks of the sense of complacency that inevitably accompanies a world of security and contentment.[43] This fate can only be averted if the lessons of history are made a part of the utopic future. Only fear can make one cherish the possession of happiness and guarantee the continued reign of Hindu peace. But then who can be the antagonistic Other in a future utopia when everyone is a Hindu? Who else can it be but the self? Could a golden age ever be based on the fear of the self? A more apposite name for this condition is dystopia.

V

In his book *The Indian War* Savarkar compares history to a telescope. The obvious suggestion of the trope is that of a disengaged, objectivist history associated with rationalism. But in the specific practices of Savarkarite thought, it acquires a negotiated meaning. That is, Savarkar uses the telescope as the trope of participation from a distance. This produces some interesting paradoxes.

For Savarkar, participation involves active performance. The question is: what is the mode of performance available to the writer of history? Performativity is important for Savarkar for he seeks to make his readers participate actively in a project of change through his historical narratives. His history is designed to inspire them with new ideas and provoke acts of transforming their unfree present. In literary terms Savarkar is caught between the performative models offered by the novel and the proscenium theatre. While narrative is useful in that it can draw upon the novelistic resources of an omniscient author who aspires, through plot and characters, to remould the moral ideals of the readers (an aspiration common among nineteenth-century literary critics in India), Savarkar strains towards a more spontaneous and active connection with his audience which only theatre seems able to provide. His narrative can suddenly break off in the course of a historical description into a dramatic mode, with dialogue between the main protagonists. The theatrical affords a more direct relationship with the audience; and it complements terrorist assumptions about a divorce between the exceptional political actors—the terrorists—and the rest of society that would be inspired by their example. Both elements can be seen in a poem ('Historic Stage') written to his comrades upon his extradition from England in which he consoled them with the prospect of becoming a part of the theatrical afterlife of history:

> Thus actors we innumerable once more shall meet
> On History's copious stage before the great
> Applauding audience of Humanity.[44]

It is well known that Savarkar's literary reputation rested on his historical and his creative writings. Clearly his notion of history is moulded to a great extent by his aesthetic orientations. But he is also unable to fully reprocess history into a resource for aesthetic activism. The problem lies in a deep inability to fully renege on his historiographical commitments. Savarkar is not quite able to completely instrumentalize his relationship with the past. Ironically, he is too committed to the value of evidence and the procedures of verification. His two pronouncedly history books—*The Indian War* and *Six Glorious Epochs*, the first written at the beginning and the second at the end of his career—flaunt their mastery over evidence and footnotes. *The Indian War* bears the marks of his research in the India Office Library in London. *Six Glorious Epochs* may not contain many footnotes, but its publisher makes it a point to tell us that everything is substantiated by Savarkar's remarkable memory and that it was only his extreme physical condition and death that prevented the book from being fully footnoted.

This regard for evidence imposes a distance between present and past—a hurdle to making history a living and contemporary resource for the present. At times the historical narrative is thick with events and analysis. For instance, his description in *The Indian War* of the multiple ways in which the British took over Awadh absorbs the reader, through a tale of complex causes, in a world that cannot be fully familiar to the present. Also his regard for evidence sometimes makes him weaken his ideological structure. It leads him to accept Tilak's thesis regarding the Aryan migration into India. This of course creates a foundational self-division within the Hindutva national self, and it's privileging of origins, once it is acknowledged that most of its bearers originated from outside Bharat. The embarrassment is underlined by his treatment of the Aryans almost as if they were respectable nineteenth-century tourists using the natives as their guides.[45] The choice of this innocent mode of arrival by the Aryans, and its apparent acceptance by the natives, begs the question why this should be so, and why the other, later 'alien' migrations cannot be seen in the same way.

Golwalkar removes these marginal angularities in his brand of Hindutva. It is true that Golwalkar does not provide any new insights. He operates within the framework of Hindutva set by Savarkar, especially the central historical plot of Hindu-Muslim conflict. But by taking certain tendencies of Savarkarite ideas to their extreme point and deleting the more awkward ones, Golwalkar produces an even more unitary (and intellectually complacent) mode of Hindutva. More specifically, Golwalkar converts the past into a question of attitude. The past has to supply certain affirmative values for the present. I may add here that this seems, in part, to be the result of Golwalkar's own historical temper. In contrast to the strong, activist historian persona of Savarkar, Golwalkar's *We* possesses the measured distance of a political scientist. His attitude to history is not that of a participant whose extravagant commitment leads to internal fissures in argument, but that of a technician who treats history as raw material, selecting broad historical conclusions to support some generalized assertions and arguments on national existence. All these contributions of Golwalkar, in turn, prepare the ground for the complete dissolution of history into a political-aesthetic mass performance that can transform the present.

The writing of *We* was probably dictated by political exigencies. It was published in 1939. This was a period when Savarkar, who had been legally constrained in his actions by the British State for acts of terrorism, was finally set free to participate in public life. He now re-entered active Hindu Mahasabha (HMS) politics with great fanfare and immediately embarked on an all-India tour that consecrated him and the HMS as the undisputed leaders of Hindu communal nationalism. It may be recalled that the HMS had been forced to separate from the Congress organizationally in 1938. It was necessary for its continued existence to carve out a separate identity for itself as an umbrella organization of Hindus. But an independent HMS also involved a threat to the RSS, which had hitherto been regarded as a marginal but independent Hindu communal organization. The rejuvenation of HMS, especially under the charismatic Savarkar, threatened the RSS constituency.[46] It was possibly this conjuncture that led Golwalkar, the Sarsangchalak (Supreme Leader) of the RSS, to establish a separate lineage from that of its ideological founder.

An important shift that Golwalkar makes is to frankly and comprehensively subordinate history to culture: it becomes a supplement to culture. This is not a radical departure: the dividing lines between history and culture were not very clear in Savarkar but Golwalkar provides a more integrated relationship between the two. This has to do with Golwalkar's greater emphasis on cultural activism. Savarkar's natural tendency is confrontationist and his objective, like that of conventional terrorists, is of immediate destruction/seizure of power. The privileging of political power is what accounts for the importance he accords to history. On the other hand, Golwalkar and RSS emphasise the slow, cellular transformation of Hindu national subjectivity.[47] The Hindu must be slowly trained in body and mind to take on the Muslim and establish his mastery over the land. The emphasis on cellular growth was especially necessary in the period before Gandhi's assassination, when the RSS did not need to open up a separate political wing to stave off government bans or to expand its political influence. The RSS stressed the sphere of culture; it still proclaims itself to be a cultural organization[48] and announces an ostentatious distance from the political doings of the BJP, taking on the public role of an advisor (even as its tutoring influences are all too evident) and arbitrator. By culture the RSS means a transformation of the signifying practices of the nation and the subjectivity of Hindus, which are meant to accompany the establishment of Hindu Rashtra. Its politics may be badly defined but it has two clear imperatives: the rule of the Hindu majority and the suspension of direct, adult franchise based democracy.

The shift to culture as the site of struggle and transformation entails a corresponding change in the conception of history. The question of history becomes one of historiographical assumptions alone. For Golwalkar the main struggle is over how history is perceived. The framework of his historical understanding is structured by the opposition between 'colonial' and 'Hindu' perceptions of history. While the first denigrates the position of Hindu by subordinating his superior rights over the land, Hindu history must teach the Hindus that they were a martial and fiercely independent race born with an integral connection to the land of the nation.

Inevitably this maps on to the Hindu-Muslim war: the first version naturalises the cultural subjection of the Muslims, while the second provides the weapon of self-confidence to Hindus.

This does not mean that the category of evidence disappears. But it is now given an absolute status, undisturbed by and invulnerable to the needs of either verifiability or falsifiability. Consequently the weight of evidence rests upon the power of assertion alone. In short, Golwalkar implodes the category of 'evidence' from within, rather than dismissing it outright. The liberty this allows him is nowhere more apparent than in the opening paragraphs of *We*. These paragraphs claim—using a tortuous historical logic that I have discussed elsewhere[49]—that Bharat (India) has had an unbroken 10,000 years of civilization, although this is qualified by the opening statement that it is impossible to actually date the hoariness of the Indian civilization since it antedates history itself. More important than the details mobilized in this claim is the assumption that allows Golwalkar to formulate the assertion at all. It is the idea that a hypothesis is nothing but a conjecture and is thus without any truth value. This leaves Golwalkar free to 'reject all' hypotheses and 'positively maintain that we Hindus . . . are indigenous children of the soil . . . and are natural masters of the country'.[50] Involved here is the idea that evidence has to be based on absolute certitude alone; anything short of that is suspect and without value. There is no space for undecidability or for assessing the degrees of probability of particular events—leave alone the possibility of contradiction. Historical procedures are robbed of the powers of imagination, speculation and debate.[51]

Golwalkar adheres to a conception of history—shared in some extreme critiques of history today—which assumes that history is a matter of political representations and that there is little point to evaluating practices, categories, and evidence. Golwalkar places little store on evidence. Facts are used rhetorically, for the power of their truth-effects. Indeed, Golwalkar has little by way of historical writing *per se* and when he does try his hand at history, the results are more pathetic than embarrassing. More pertinently, Golwalkar's representational orientation to history sanctions the suppression of elements, such as the nuanced evaluation of evidence, that could complicate his political position and prevent the them-us binary from working at all levels of historical understanding. In short, the arbitrary invocation of historical procedures corresponds to an authoritarian stabilization of historical conclusions.

For Golwalkar, the most pressing need for stable historical facticity comes from his obsession with the pure Hindu origins of the nation. I may add here that this concern remains the crucial preoccupation of Hindutva historians today: the two issues that obsess them are those of the Aryan invasion and the Ram temple, both fundamentally related to the idea of pure Hindu origins of the nation. The fetishization of origins is important to Golwalkar for various reasons, both cultural and political. The cultural reason stems from his adherence to race theory. He draws on the notion that miscegenation tends to breed backwardness. He argues that Europeans seek to demonstrate their superiority by claiming that Aryans originated elsewhere and that their arrival in India led to racial mixture with the indigenous population. In contrast European blood remained pure. This was responsible for the backwardness of India as compared with Europe. Against this assertion, Golwalkar reverses Tilak's argument, to say that the Aryans migrated out of India when the Arctic circle broke away from the original landmass that joined it to India. This allows Golwalkar to assert the cultural superiority of Hindus over the West because of their more hoary antiquity and pure lineage.

The political reason for his emphasis on origins is inherited from Savarkar. The quasi-mystical fetish of the Hindu origins of the nation is crucial for Hindutva in order to distinguish Hindu nationalism from what Golwalkar calls 'territorial nationalism'. Golwalkar regards the idea that the country belongs to those who have settled in it (instead of those who originated in it), as an opinion encouraged by European historians. According to Golwalkar, the European argument that Aryans invaded India was advanced in order to prove to the Hindus that their country actually belonged to all those who had come from outside. While Golwalkar's assertion on this score echoes, on a more fundamentalist register, Savarkar's notion of *punyabhumi* coinciding with *pitribhumi*, he goes beyond his mentor by developing the anti-democratic implications of the Hindutva definition. For Golwalkar, democracy consolidates the evil effects of 'territorial nationalism' by equalizing everyone's sense of belonging and hence giving equal rights to all. It thereby appeases invaders and settlers (the British and the Muslims) and produces a loss of nationhood, implicitly attendant on the loss of a sense of exclusive possession of the land.[52]

I should mention here that Golwalkar's invocation of the superiority of Hindus over the West is new and not present in Savarkar. It has an important consequence besides the ones already elaborated. The use of 'Europe' as the master context of all ideas on origins is one that necessarily dictates the need to pose counter claims. It leads to the labelling of any assertion originating in the West as a conspiracy to humiliate; in turn this demands that the Hindu resort to his pride in order to construct a counter argument. In short the binaries of humiliation and pride become foundational for understanding any argument made by Hindutva. The binary explains the motivation of the argument and also provides the criteria for assessment. Incidentally, it also allows latter-day Hindutva to recover some of the conservative fantasies of Tarkachuramani, which was less possible for the more rationalistically oriented Savarkar. Any phenomenon originating in the 'east' commits one to claiming its superiority in terms of its antiquity; or even more extreme, anything recognized as valuable in the West (it could even be aeroplanes!) is seen to originate in the east.[53]

The final outcome of Golwalkar's discourse is that it produces new grounds for conceptualizing the past that are not confined to History—or, for that matter, to Myth. It uses categories from history even as it invokes mythic figures or mythic claims (especially related to origins), but both of these begin to operate with new meanings in a different terrain. The past becomes completely an attitudinal resource, unmediated by any existence apart from the needs of the present. The past exists as a pure representation, required for sustaining Hindu pride. Categories such as 'evidence' or 'history' are used but only if these affirm that pride. Following Golwalkar's footsteps, Hindutva spokespersons consistently prioritize belief (which gives positive self-representation, self-confidence and pride) over evidence in the Babri Masjid/Ramjanmabhumi controversy—without letting go of evidence if it suits their cause. Of course, when belief comes into conflict with evidence, the latter has to be dismissed: we have noted already Advani's infamous claim that Ram's birthlace was a matter of belief, not testable by evidence. Sumit Sarkar has also noted how the withdrawal of the 'Towards Freedom' volumes constitutes a new turn in Hindutva in that it is now actively engaged in suppressing historical documents.[54] To this may be added the popularization of this phenomenon during the 'Hum Sab Ayodhya' exhibition which was ransacked because a particular folk representation of the *Ramayana* did not agree with the tastes of its modern votaries; also the deletion of apparently critical references to the history of Sikhism and so on in the NCERT textbooks on the grounds that it offended religious 'sentiments'.[55] Deployed in these instances is an opposition wherein 'sentiment' is weighed against 'evidence' (which includes evidence of alternate representations of the 'great tradition') and found to be stronger, for it is claimed as part of popular belief—and is therefore sovereign.

The past is attitudinized. And this changes the idea and deployment of myth. Like evidence, myth becomes a narrative based on the fabrications and assertions of the present. Consequently myth loses its flexibility, being orchestrated as a simple, uncontestable truth, a hyper-stable facticity. Myth no longer forms interpretative communities. It is made to produce a nation-wide interpreted community that receives its hard and fixed self from the mythic narratives of Hindutva.

Ordinarily, a myth is respectful of the past, which is used as an authority to sanction and naturalise new interpretations and emphases. In Hindutva, as we will see, the mythic past is invoked instead as a burden that needs to be redeemed in the present. The present is privileged over the past. In the Prologue to *We*, Golwalkar states that there is little attraction in inhabiting the golden age of the nation, for it breeds complacency. It is really the present that is exciting, for adversity produces opportunities for heroism. In short, it is the present that is really active, that can achieve the larger-than-life status which is the stuff of myth and legend. The past requires invocation, not respect.

To sum up, it may be said that Gowalkar established the full contours of myhstory. He draws on both history and myth, shapes both by the criteria of pride and sentiment in order to produce an attitudinized past. Further, he uses the past solely as a tool of the present. He has no respect for the otherness of the past and hence no sense of commitment to procedures through which this respect is both embodied and evaluated—and certainly not for the norms that preserve physical signs of the past because it is the past.[56] The instrumentalization of the past is finally a means of controlling the other in the present. The past becomes a resource for the present because it helps to produce a need to master the Muslim, and the other others of Hindutva thought. This concern is of course equally present in Savarkar, but it is the shifts in Golwalkar that prepare the way for the classic moment of the myhstorical, that is, the Ramjanmabhumi (RJB) movement.

VI

The RJB movement was developed in the 1980s at a time when the nationalist idea was being increasingly shorn of its Congress-style social consensus of class and caste groups. Movements for secession, and affirmative action for disprivileged castes that roused the ire of the upper castes, were just two of the many political problems that had undermined the nationalist consensus. At the same time the cold winds of liberalization and the increased internationalization of the economy had also dealt Nehruvian economic nationalism a body blow, making it even more imperative to acquire the grounds for a new national identity. It was this particular need that the RJB movement sought to meet, promoting through its carefully rehearsed script a new founding myth for the nation.

But there was also another development in the position and nature of history itself in the same period. On the one hand, there was the introduction of the NCERT textbooks. On the one hand, the superior conceptual approaches of these books offended the Right. On the other hand, the overload of facts that these books had to bear made them less than popular among a generation of self-confident students whose impatience with history was compounded by the dazzle of technology and the call of the future. At the same time, paradoxically enough, there was an expansion in the popular preoccupation with the past. This had already been consolidated in the Amar Chitra Katha comic strip series that reached out to the different sections of middle class children. Another significant index was the popularization of history of the freedom struggle as the source of novelistic plots in Indian-English fiction beginning from Salman Rushdie's *Midnight's Children*. In these novels history is treated as a source of narrative signs that could be combined in different ways to produce alternate imaginaries of and critical commentaries on the nation. This exercise was obviously restricted to the English-speaking middle class, but what is more interesting is that this is a global Indian middle-class, a sector that first felt the pulls of identity in a globalized culture that encouraged the articulation of the signs of difference. The social power of this move may be seen in its spill over to Bollywood where a crop of historical romances such as *1942* established itself as a new sub-genre. Another significant development starting from the 1970s was the massive promotion of tourism which produced a literature about both historical and religious sites, inserting both of them into a larger concept of national culture. To sum up, the popularization of history opened it up to more flexible appropriations than what was sanctioned by professional historians. This condition was helpful to the legitimization of the myhstory of the RJB.

The necessities of, and support from, the late twentieth-century context also helped to resolve a problem that had dogged Hindutva. While Hindutva's past was envisioned as a resource for present action, was crucial to it, it could only move the converted. It simply provided an inspiration and a source of identity for members of RSS and its fellow travellers. The main problem was that it remained a textual resource: Savarkar and Golwalkar wrote myhstorical tomes, but these were not read by everyone. Hindutva remained marginal, with its ideas regarded by the uncharitable as a little over the top. More fundamentally, the scriptural elaboration of the past could not fully cancel out the fact of its death. The past remained enclosed in the deadness of letters and, hence could not be envisioned as an organic part of the present. Further, these works were not fully and obsessively focused on the real source of Hindutva's activist energy, that is, the Hindu-Muslim conflict: they also contained other themes that deflected attention from what was the primary contradiction in Hindutva's reckoning. These problems were resolved by the myhstory of the RJB.

The RJB movement makes the past live again. The past is joined to the present through a myhstorical story that is not simply retold but enacted. Savarkar's striving towards the condition of theatre in his historical narrative is now released from its scriptural confines and proscenium assumption. Hindutva's narrative theatre is now made co-terminous with the involvement of the nation as a whole. Also, it is aesthetic in the sense of recreating the past according to an expressive logic in order to produce a new structure of feeling and meaning about the very identity of the nation. This new structure, as I hope to show, has important consequences for the relationship between the past and present as well.

Let me briefly recall the salient points of the story. Ram's temple was built in the reign of Vikramaditya in *satyayug* (the golden age of truth) and existed in a glorious state befitting its status as the heart, the real capital, of the Hindu nation. All was more or less well until 1528, when Babur entered Ayodhya and demolished the temple there and erected the Babri Masjid in order to shame the Hindus and put on them a mark of subordination. This gave rise to various and repeated wars in which the divided Hindus threw themselves at the Muslims to restore the temple. But despite miracles and feats of courage the Hindus could not do anything important till 1949 when an idol of the baby Ram miraculously appeared in the inner sanctum. The movement in the 1980s was directed at reclaiming this patrimony by building another temple, but the Hindus were unable to do so because of a 'pseudo-secular' dispensation that appeased Muslims.[57]

This story is completely new. It embodies not only a new myth but also a novel conception of medieval history. And yet it resonates with the accumulated meanings of both existing myths and histories. Ram brings with him the story of the *Ramayana* and all its resonances to the birthplace; Babur may have featured in an event that most professional historians would have thought was insubstantial and petty, but his figure brings to bear all the historical implications of Mughal rule, especially its central significance for the syncretic Indo-Islamic culture. What RJB operates is a process that plucks these personages from their contexts, and reprocesses them as metonymic signs of those contexts. Once detached, they can be recombined in a new configuration of meaning that is meant to explain the present. Both history and myth are evacuated of their pastness, that is, the sense of difference that their contexts and narratives respectively demand. The past becomes simply a storehouse of signs, its contextual meanings made into a bouquet of resonances. Correspondingly, the present becomes the site of assemblage, where the past is reconfigured to suit its needs.

A more significant feature of the story—from the viewpoint of both praxis and the privileging of the present—is that it brings together non-material signs around the tangible presence of space. Birthplace is the crucial issue. The protagonist of this story is actually the plot of land occupied by the Babri Masjid and which the RJB protagonists would restore to Ram and his inheritors. The birthplace contracts time into itself. The collapsing of time is done through various moves. In the first, through the act of desecration, the mythic time of the *satyayuga* enters the world of history and Ram and Babur come to occupy the same period of time. The battles that then break out show that the mythic and the historical provide inspiration in different measures to Hindus and Muslims to dominate their common world in time. Finally, the continued existence of the Babri Masjid—the heart of all the quarrels—indicated that this war structures the present. The substantiality of the masjid and the land on which it stood makes the past a material part of the present. Without this particular space, the story would have become simply another legend of the past.

The past is even more integrated into the present through supportive mobilization. The birthplace becomes a synecdoche of the nation: it embodies the very identity of the Hindus that consists in an integrated relationship with their gods, the time of their antiquity, and the land itself. Videos compiled during the movement highlighted Ayodhya in an otherwise unmarked map of India, clearly indicating its central location. Further, the battle is an allegory of a cultural-political confrontation. It is a battle between the inheritors of Ram, born in the land and physically a part of it, with those who assume they belong to the land because they have invaded it and settled in it. The pretenders are encouraged by the pseudo-secularists who, inspired by Western ideas of secularism, conspire with the Muslims to obscure the identity of the nation to itself, preferring the badge of humiliation. In short this is a war between origins-based nationalism and 'territorial nationalism'.

The structure of this story gives a living form to Golwalkar's integration of the past into the present. Indeed, the RJB story goes beyond Golwalkar in its presentism. It actually features a battle about the present that draws upon the past. The present structures its self-understanding by converting the past into an allegorical resource. To repeat, Ram is not only the ancestor; he is a sign of Hindu national identity direly needed in the present. The Babri Masjid is not just a Muslim monument; this sign of historical humiliation has been preserved by 'territorial' nationalism, sanctioned by Nehruvian secularism. The present allegorises itself through the battles of the past in order to challenge the foundational cultural identity of the nation. The present then is also the point in time that will redeem all the humiliations of the past that are defined in a chain of religious, social, political and cultural phenomena: Buddhism, Mughal architecture, Nehruvian 'territorial nationalism', and so on. The building of the temple would ensure that the past would be regarded with only pride and positive sentiments. Hindutva will bring a new past into existence. In short, the RJB approaches an apocalyptic vision of the past.

Of course, the present exists only in a collective sense. The past had been characterized by the internal divisions of the Hindus and the organized mastery of the Muslims. The present transfers to itself the historical character of the Muslim (following the earlier move by Savarkar) by visibly demonstrating to the Hindus that they are a collective body united in a single movement. To do this the RJB produces a collective theatre. We have seen how Savarkar's myhstory strove towards the performative, but that it drew on a proscenium idea of the historical stage: it assumed that the exceptional would be the actors, while the rest would just applaud. In contrast, the RJB movement not only produced a theatrical spectacle, it also sought to insert the Hindu nation—and even its NRI offsprings abroad—into the performance. Actually the RJB movement is best described as a high-tech ritual theatre which consists of many participative forms. It is structured by a pilgrimage cum crusade (the *ratha yatras* that journeyed through the country, often coincided with the sacred ritual calendar, and followed by riots), collective sacred labour (*kar seva*) and donations (the bricks which were specially purchased all over the world and donated for the building of the temple), regular worship at neighbourhood temples, public signs of devotion (stickers of Ram that paralleled the chanting of the name) and of recall of the central story (paralleling the epic tradition through the dissemination of audio-visual material including the infamous Sadhvi Rithambara cassette) and so on.

Above all, the collective mastery over the past was palpably performed by the mastery over the bodies of the other. Riots have been with us for a long time, their presence especially marked during the last century and a half. But at no time, except during Partition, have they acquired such a degree of popular and sustained legitimacy as they have in the current RJB movement, especially in its Gujarat phase of 2001 (at least inside Gujarat). The reason for this, it seems to me, is that RJB has been able to create a narrative framework that legitimises riots by making them acts of cultural redemption. The 3000 odd persons who were killed after the first phase of Advani's *rath yatra*, the nation-wide riots in 1992-3 after the demolition of the masjid, the latest pogrom in Gujarat sparked off by the *kar sevak* programme of 2001, are all grounded on the idea that the bodies of Muslims are simply traces of a past war over national identity that continues to the present. The Muslim body carries the stain of past—and continuing—humiliation and has to be therefore savaged in the most brutal ways.

All that the myhstory of the past has repetitively invoked, the objective towards which each of its elements has striven, is fulfilled in the blood and gore of the riots. The abduction of women and the gruesome killings of men, women, and children fulfil a script that legitimized all this as national tasks, in works such as the *Six Glorious Epochs*. For Savarkar however, the objective had been to extract revenge and provide a warning, but the RJB movement aspired to reverse history itself. By doing to the Muslim what Hindus have apparently undergone, the RJB leaders thought they could wipe out the past that had existed as a record of humiliation. And replace it with one that would allow the Hindu to live in an uninterrupted condition of pride and mastery.

If Babri Masjid was positioned at one end of the spectrum of cultural signifiers of the past, the other end was occupied by the bodies of Muslims. The public dismantling of the Babri Masjid was matched by the spectacular violation and dismemberment of men, women, and children in Gujarat. They became objects to be dismantled, 'disappeared', flushed out if they refuse to be Hinduized—just as the masjid has 'disappeared' into rubble and open land since it was a *kalank* (sign of humiliation) of the past. The allegorical structure of the RJB removes the distinction between the inanimate and the living. This may seem obvious since all violence needs a prior act of dehumanization. But what is significant here is its extent. Pre-RJB riots (especially those preceding the Gujarat 2002 riots) had been characterized by certain redemptive stories, especially those concerning the way in which neighbours and friends rescued the victims.[58] However the Gujarat riots are known for the many encounters in which neighbours, intimate friends, actually participated in the killing of Muslims. Clearly the RJB movement—in its moments and places of intensity (Gujarat being a state ruled by the BJP for long)—can level out all cleavages of human recognition that interrupt the monolithic inhumanity of communal violence. Myhstory builds a coffin of signs that gives a new body to the Muslim. And holds out the hope that the rites of burial will reverse the Hindu past.

NOTES

1. I am also grateful—in solidarity—to the questions posed to me in the workshop on 'Assertive Religious Identities' hosted by the Jamia Millia Islamia, for Nonica Dutta's suggestion that I more rigorously historicize the process of history writing and for Satish Saberwal's support, editing and many kindnesses.
2. K.R. Malkani, 'History and Nationalism', *The Statesman*, 23 December 2001.
3. Brief summaries of the debate within the anti-Hindutva academics about the value and nature of the past in reference to Hindutva's past is available in my *Carving Blocs: Communal Ideology in Early Twentieth Century Bengal* (1999) and 'Hindutva and its myhstory', *Seminar*, 522, 2003, pp. 42-7.
4. Neeladri Bhattacharya was the first to recognize the mixed genre of the Hindutva past in his essay, 'Myth, History and the Politics of Ramjanmabhumi', *Anatomy of a confrontation: The Babri Masjid-Ramjanmabhumi issue*, ed. S. Gopal, New Delhi: Viking, 1991. See also my 'VHP's Ram at Ayodhya: Reincarnation through Ideology and Organization', *Economic and Political Weekly*, vol. XXVI, no. 44, 2 November 1991.
5. 'Hindutva and its Myhstory', *Seminar* 522, February 2003.
6. *Ramjanmabhoomi: History versus Casuistry: Evidence of the Ramjanmabhoomi Mandir presented by the Vishwa Hindu Parishad to the Government of India in December-January 1990-1*, New Delhi: Voice of India, 1991, p. vi.
7. See M.S. Golwalkar, *We or our Nationhood defined*, Nagpur: Bharat Prakashan, 1945, 1st pub. 1939, p. 36; also Navaratna S. Rajaram, David Frawley, *Vedic Aryans and the Origins of Civilization: A Literary Scientific Perspective*, New Delhi: Voice of India, 1997.
8. Partha Chatterjee, *The Nation and Its Fragments: Colonial and Post Colonial Histories*, New Delhi: Oxford University Press, 1994, pp. 76-87
9. Sumit Sarkar, *Writing Social History*, New Delhi: Oxford University Press, 1997, especially pp. 76-9.
10. Romila Thapar, 'The Historian and the Epic', *Cultural Pasts*, New Delhi: Oxford University Press, 2000.
11. 'Slavery' (1st pub. 1873) trans. Maya Pandit, *Selected Writings of Jotirao Phule*, ed. G.P. Deshpande, New Delhi: Leftword, 2002.
12. There are brief discussions of Tarkachuramani in English scattered throughout Amiya Sen's *Hindu Revivalism in Bengal 1872-1905: Some Essays in Interpretation*, New Delhi: Oxford University Press, 1993.
13. Ch. 5, op. cit., *Annals and Antiquities of Rajasthan or the Central and Western Rajpoot states of India*, New Delhi: K.M.N. Publishers,

1971, 1st pub. 1829. For an excellent—and different—reading of the text see Norbert Peabody, 'Tod's Raj'asthan and the Boundaries of Imperial Rule in Nineteenth Century India', *Modern Asian Studies*, vol. 30, pt. 1, February 1996.

14. Tod came to be known popularly as the 'modern *charan* (bard) of Rajputs'. Madhu Tandon Sethia, *Rajput Polity: Warriors, Peasants and Merchants (1700-1800)*, Jaipur/New Delhi: Rawat Publications, 2003. Tandon also states that modern historiography of Rajasthan originates with Tod.
15. In his dedication to George IV, Tod writes that 'it would suit our wisest policy to grant' to the Rajputs 'the restoration of their former independence'. *Annals*, op. cit., p. xi, Peabody rightly argues that Tod did not see any contradiction between Rajput freedom and colonial policy.
16. According to Bishop Heber, Tod's popularity in Rajasthan, where he was Political Agent, excited suspicion in the East India Company authorities who forced him to resign at the age of forty. Barunkumar Chakraborty, *Toder Rajasthan o Bangla Sahitya*, Calcutta: Pustak Bipani, 1399 (1981), pp. 8-9.
17. He declares, 'mythology may be considered the parent of all history', *Annals*, p. 445.
18. Tod prefaces the passage on the mythological parentage of history by the need to investigate into mythology in terms of 'a theogony typical of the seasons, their changes, and products', ibid.
19. See T.R. Trautman's discussion of Bryant and Jones in *Aryans and British India* (New Delhi: Vistaar Publications,1997), pp. 42-52.
20. Tod states that it does not matter whether this was 'a fiction of the past' or 'whether the scene was got up to animate the spirit of resistance', since 'it is consistent with the belief of the tribe', *Annals*, p. 213.
21. Chakraborty, *Toder Rajasthan o Bangla Sahitya*, op. cit.
22. Cited in Ibid., p. 14.
23. See my 'Questionable boundaries: abduction, love and Hindu Muslim relations in modern Bengal' (forthcoming), for a brief discussion of the representations of the Padmini story in Bengal.
24. See the discussion of Ranade's histories in T.V. Parvate, *Mahadev Gobind Ranade: A Biography*, Bombay: Asia Publishing House, 1963, Ch. XI.
25. V.D. Savarkar describes the theme of this 'great epic' as the exhibition of how the Nation 'evolves . . . as great characters men and women . . . pass crowding in thousands . . . and the action thickens in the ever widening stage of centuries.' *Hindu Pad-Padshahi or A critical review of the Hindu empire of Maharashtra*, Madras: B.G. Paul, 1925, p. 224.

26. Ibid., p. 223.
27. Ibid., pp. 2-3.
28. *The Indian War of Independence (National Rising of 1857)*, London: Mayuresh, rpt. date not given, 1st pub. 1909, p. 2
29. See my discussion of U.N. Mukherjee in Ch. 1, *Carving Blocs: Communal Ideology in Early Twentieth Century Bengal*, New Delhi: Oxford University Press, 1999.
30. Krishna Varma was an Arya Samaji, an ex-Dewan of a princely state who settled in London. See Dhananjay Keer, *Veer Savarkar*, Bombay: Popular Prakashan, 1966 (1950), p. 29.
31. I have drawn on both the Introduction and the selected texts of Spencer in *Herbert Spencer: Structure, Function and Evolution* edited with an introductory essay by Stanislav Andreski, London: Thomas Nelson, 1972.
32. See Purushottom Agarwal, 'Surat, Savarkar and Draupadi: legitimizing rape as a political weapon', in *Women and the Hindu Right: A Collection of Essays*, eds. T. Sarkar, U. Butalia, Kali for Women, 1995 for an insightful formulation of this morality.
33. Savarkar, *Six Glorious Epochs of Indian History*, tr. and ed. S.T. Godbole, New Delhi: Rajdhani Granthagar, 1971, p. 167.
34. *The Indian War of Independence*, op. cit., p. 104.
35. See T. Basu et al., *Khaki Shorts Saffron Flags*, New Delhi: Orient Longman, 1993 for a discussion of this central concept of Hindutva nationalism.
36. Savarkar, *Who is a Hindu?* Poona: S.P. Gokhale, 1949 (1923), pp. 4-9. Golwalkar, *We or Our Nationhood Defined*, Nagpur: Bharat Prakashan, 1945 (1939), p. 12.
37. Among its specific problems was also that of acknowledging the majesty of the Asokan state, since Savarkar was highly critical of Asoka for his propagation of Buddhism. See *Six Glorious Epochs*, pp. 246-8.
38. Keer, op. cit., For a more vivid autobiographical account, see Savarkar, *The Story of My Transportation for Life*, Bombay: Sadbhavati Publications, 1950.
39. *The Indian War*, pp. 65-8.
40. See Tanika Sarkar's observations on the figure of Krishna in 'Imagining Hindu Rashtra: The Hindu and the Muslim in Bankimchandra's Writings', *Hindu Wife Hindu Nation*, Delhi: Permanent Black, 2001 and the imagined figure of the Muslim in U.N. Mukherjee's *Dying Hindus* discussed in *Carving Blocs*.
41. See my 'VHP's Ram at Ayodhya', op. cit. for a more elaborate discussion of this as well as some of the points made in the last part of this paper.

42. *Six Glorious Epochs*, op. cit., p. 274.
43. Prologue, *We*, op. cit.
44. Keer, op. cit., p. 79.
45. *Who is a Hindu*, op. cit., p. 6.
46. Especially because Savarkar's 'militarise Hinduism' campaign begun in 1938 (see Savarkar, *Whirlwind Propaganda 1939-41*, ed. A.S. Bhide, Bombay, 1941) showed that the HMS was embarking on a para-military option which had hitherto been the distinctive province of the RSS.
47. See *Khaki Shorts*, op. cit. for a discussion.
48. Article 4 of its constitution says, 'The Sangh as such, has no politics and is devoted to purely cultural work'. Cited in Parvathy Appaiah, *Hindutva: Ideology and Politics*, New Delhi: Deep and Deep, 2003, p. 261.
49. *Seminar* 522, op. cit.
50. *We or Our Nationhood Defined*, op. cit., p. 12.
51. This is the inspiration behind Elst's contempt for the 'unscientific' temper of historians in favour of a scienticist approach. He dismisses Romila Thapar's arguments on the Aryan invasion theory as the outpourings of a 'bookworm from JNU's History Department' and not worthy of comparison with the authoritative findings of a NASA scientist such as N.S. Rajaram. Konrad Elst, *Update on the Aryan Invasion Debate*, New Delhi: Aditya Prakshan, 1999, p. 42. Incidentally Rajaram was accused of fraudulently deciphering the Indus Valley script and of manufacturing computer generated evidence about the existence of a horse seal in the Indus Valley Civilization. Michael Witzel and Steve Farmer, 'Horseplay in Harappa', *Frontline*, vol. 17, no. 20, 30 September-13 October 2000. If this is true (and I am yet to read a convincing refutation) then it very nicely brings together the point about the hyper-stability and arbitrariness of evidence that lies at the heart of myhstory.
52. *We or Our Nationhood Defined*, op. cit., pp. 18-19.
53. A contemporary example appears to provided by Rajaram, whose analysis of the Vedas is reported as follows: 'The Rigveda *rishis*, we find [in Rajaram's work], packed their hymns with occult allusions to high-energy physics, anti-matter, the inflational theory of the universe, calculations of the speed of light, and gamma-ray bursts striking the earth three times a day.' 'Horseplay in Harappa'.
54. 'Hindutva and History', in his *Beyond Nationalist Frames: Post-modernism, Hindu Fundamentalism, History*, New Delhi: Permanent Black, 2002, p. 256.
55. See an excellent rebuttal of sentiment as historical criteria in Rajeev Bhargava, 'Community Sentiment and the Teaching of History' *Seminar* 522, February 2003.

56. See Tapati Guhathakurta's incisive critique of the obsession with evidence (in both Hindutva and secularist spokespersons) and her upholding of the procedural norms of archaeology. Tapati Guhathakurta, 'Digging the Past', *The Telegraph* , 9 September 2003. I may add that it is the respect for the past which provides the moral grounds for upholding archaeological procedures.
57. See my 'VHP's Ram at Ayodhya', op. cit., pp. 2518-19.
58. *Carving Blocs*, Ch. 5.

9

The Navigators of Hindu Rashtra: RSS Pracharaks[1]

PRALAY KANUNGO

This story begins in the summer of 1941. Ram Dutt, RSS pracharak, visits Gojra, a *kasba* near Jhang city in western Punjab, and inaugurates there a *shakha* (local unit). Ram Prakash Katyal, a sixteen year old boy from a well-off Punjabi, upper caste Khatri family, who has just completed his matriculation examination, is curious, and comes to the *shakha* to play games and learn to wield the *lathi*. Quickly learns other things as well: 'Hindus are oppressed by the Muslims and need to be rescued; a swayamsevak should be ready to sacrifice his limbs (*baju* and *tang*) for the community.'[2] Ram Prakash becomes a devoted swayamsevak. He then visits Ganga Bishen, the district pracharak (propagator), a twenty-three year old postgraduate in science with second rank in the university. Ram is fascinated by his personality, educational qualifications, family background, and, above all, his decision to sacrifice a bright career for the sake of the Hindus. Bishen asks him to become a pracharak. Ram readily makes the promise and decides to quit his temporary job at the Imperial Bank. Sensing opposition from his father, he runs away from home to reach Layallpur and reports to Ganga Bishen who assigns him the duties of a pracharak. Ram's elder brother finds out his whereabouts, convinces him to return home to complete the formalities of resignation with the bank. On his return, his furious father beats him severely with a *lathi* but fails to beat his son's resolve. Ram returns to his assignment. His sympathetic brother sends him money for six months to meet his personal expenses. Ram works with dedication at various places in Punjab, expanding the RSS work. He serves sentence of six months after Mahatma Gandhi's murder. A few months after his release, he leaves the pracharakship, takes a private job, and starts family life. This is a fragment of the life-story of a RSS pracharak and there are hundreds of similar stories, which have never been scrutinized with any seriousness.

Unfortunately, though volumes have been written on the authoritarian/fascist ideology of Hindutva, scholars have, deliberately or otherwise, either evaded or underplayed some of the key factors behind its monstrous growth. While the instrumentalist looks at everything as contrived and power-driven, the naturalist unrealistically exaggerates the so-called 'given' differentiation almost as a divine dispensation. In this process, both fail to explain the ideological nuances of Hindutva, and more importantly, its multiple manifestations in practice.

This paper explores how an imaginative and innovative interplay of ideology and practice has led to the bourgeoning expansion of Hindutva, in which some committed practitioners—pracharaks, whom I call the navigators of the Hindu Rashtra—play a crucial role. I shall analyse the process of their recruitment and grooming, lifestyle, and commitment, and of course, the method they adopt and the message they disseminate to achieve their mission. In brief, the paper intends to provide a holistic understanding of the pracharak system of the RSS, which has been largely ignored despite its centrality to Hindutva.

THE LEGACY

In the religious history of India, perhaps the earliest evidence of organized missionary activity would be found in Buddhism, in its activities both within India and abroad. Among the Hindus too, there was a comparable process of cultural and religious dissemination within India and South-East Asia. In early medieval times, Adi Shankaracharya contributed towards the consolidation of a pan-Indian Hindu-Brahminical identity by setting up the first Hindu monastic order, which exists to this date. During the later medieval period, different Hindu religious sects propagated their beliefs through committed disciples.

Despite primarily being ascetics, these missionaries had always been active, exchanged views, at times acrimoniously, with other sects, and continued to interact with the larger society. However, nineteenth-century colonial India crystallized and sharpened their public role. Swami Dayananda founded the Arya Samaj, a strongly revivalist and proselytising organization, and its missionaries transmitted his message in India and abroad. The Arya Samaj propagation of *shuddhi*, cow protection, and replacement of Urdu by Hindi aggravated communal conflict in north India.[3] In contrast to Dayananda's divisive agenda, Swami Vivekananda's 'cultural counter-offensive' was emancipatory. He preached his own as well as his guru's gospel through a monastic order, the Ramakrishna Mission; missionaries went abroad and set up Vedanta Societies. Vivekananda innovatively projected the *sannyasi* as an active public figure rather than a traditional renouncer.[4] The *sannyasi* as a bearer of spirituality could emancipate the nation from its present degenerate state.[5]

Such emissaries and missionaries, right from the pre-modern to the colonial period, may or may not have been formally designated as pracharaks, but all of them performed the role of preachers—propagating the message or ideology of their sects and gurus, but more importantly, putting it into practice. All of them shared a common objective—the induction and indoctrination of new disciples and the expansion of their brotherhood.

EVOLUTION OF THE PRACHARAK SYSTEM

The RSS is not a religious organization, and it never claims to be so; it rather fondly and mischievously claims to be cultural, though its core ideology is political. However, it borrows vocabulary and verses from Hindu Shastras and Puranas and uses them liberally for purely non-religious purposes; though the term pracharak a religious association, the RSS pracharak has nothing to do with religion. For Curran,[6] the pracharak is an organizer, for Daniel Gold[7] a professional organizer, and for Hansen,[8] a Hindu nationalist *karma yogi.* I would prefer to call him the navigator of the Hindu Rashtra.

K.B. Hedgewar, a qualified doctor, decided to remain a bachelor and dedicate his life not to the medical profession, but to the Hindu Rashtra. He founded the RSS in Nagpur in 1925 and recruited young boys, primarily Maharashtrian Brahmins. After imparting a rigorous physical and ideological training, he dispatched a special corps of his recruits to different parts of India to initiate Sangh activities. These dedicated disciples, designated pracharaks,[9] reached their destinations, contacted notables and sympathisers, opened *shakhas*, recruited swayamsevaks, and preached the ideology of Hindu Rashtra. All these men[10] were personally loyal to Hedgewar, emulated his lifestyle, and devoted themselves to RSS. They remained in the assigned territories and travelled extensively to raise a committed cadre of swayamsevaks and pracharaks. Thus emerged the pracharak system of the RSS.

M.S. Golwalkar, Hedgewar's successor, concretized, systematized, and institutionalized pracharakship and incorporated it in the RSS constitution.[11] As the constitution states, pracharaks shall be full-time workers selected from amongst those devoted workers of high integrity, whose mission is to serve society through the Sangh, and who, of their own free will, dedicate themselves to the cause. They will receive no remuneration.[12] Thus only the highly committed members who can work full time for the RSS are chosen as pracharaks. They act not only as catalysts in its expansion, they are also entrusted to bind the entire organization in a uniform ideological mould, the Hindu Rashtra.

In common parlance, a pracharak is seen as a whole-timer; but in the RSS lexicon, these two terms are contrasted. The pracharak receives no remuneration; the unit to which he is assigned provides him with living expenses (maintenance), and travel expenses connected with his duties. Though pracharaks are supposed to be absorbed within RSS, they may also be 'loaned out' to affiliates; with the mushrooming of the Sangh Parivar, loaning out has become a routine. Narendra Modi is an example. The pracharak 'on loan' is supposed to be loyal to RSS as well as to the affiliate. However, his loyalty to the RSS remains primary.[13] At present there are about 3,000 pracharaks; 90 per cent of them are in the RSS, the rest with affiliates.

A whole-timer, in contrast to the pracharak, receives an honorarium (*mandhan*) and works for the affiliate. Though trained by RSS, he usually does not possess the ideological commitment and intense loyalty of a pracharak; and hence he does not enjoy similar prestige and status. Theoretically, the whole-timer follows the instructions of the affiliate, not the RSS, though in fact the affiliate too follows the *diktat* of the RSS despite the standard justification that it only 'consults' the mother organization on certain occasions.

All cadre-based organizations, including the Communist Parties,[14] appoint full-time workers to maintain organizational and ideological control. An interesting comparison may be made between the pracharak of the RSS and the member of a Communist Party. Though both have intense dedication and ideological commitment to their respective causes, but they usually differ in their personalities. The former, invariably, does not get easily provoked, usually avoids arguments and prefers a subtle demonstration of power. The latter, is as a matter of course more polemical and argumentative and tries to score points in open debate. However, of late, particularly since the Ramjanmabhumi agitation, one does notice an element of aggression amongst young RSS pracharaks.

Golwalkar reinforced the pracharak system as the steel frame of the RSS; it is the 'bedrock on which the Sangh stands'.[15] He sent the pracharaks to different affiliates of the Sangh Parivar[16] to maintain organizational control and ideological coherence. Balasaheb Deoras, Golwarkar's succeesor, expanded and strengthened the system further. For a long time, pracharaks were recruited mainly from Maharashtra and some north Indian states, most of them belonging to an urban, middle-class and upper-caste background. In fact, Maharashtrian Brahmins dominated the organization for many years. Deoras expanded the geographical as well as the social base of the system by recruiting pracharaks from different regions, castes, and social classes, thus consciously overcoming the Maharashtrian-upper caste-middle class barrier. Since then many pracharaks have come from rural, peasant, lower-middle class and backward-caste backgrounds. Known for his expertise in organization and management, Deoras also emphasized a systematic training for professional and managerial skill, in order to keep command and control over the burgeoning Parivar. Rajendra Singh and Sudarshan, the subsequent RSS chiefs, carried forward the Deoras strategy.

STRINGENT SELECTION

Right selection is the key to the success of the pracharak system. Talent-hunting is protracted; recruitment follows a prolonged scrutiny. The first criterion for selection is that a man should be an ideal swayamsevak, for whom regular attendance at the *shakha* has become a sacred duty. The latter, the basic unit of the RSS, is its chief instrument to organize Hindus. For Golwalkar, *shakha* was the 'living practice of principles' and not a bundle of dry preaching.[17] Practices are those modes of embodied doing through which personal, social and cosmological experiences and realities are shaped and negotiated.[18] Practices include both everyday practices[19] such as walking, driving, hygiene, etc., and there are also rituals, dances, theatre performances and martial arts which require the practitioner to undergo specialized physical training in order to attain a 'certain specialized state of consciousness, body, agency, power, and so on'.[20]

Golwalkar describes shakha activities as *sadhana* and an ideal swayamsevak must undertake it with apt devotion and regularity. These activities combine two types of training: *sharirik* (physical) and *bauddhik* (intellectual). Physical training consists of *Surya pranam*, *yogic asanas*, and games like kabaddi, kho-kho, and the use of the *lathi*. The objective is to make swayamsevaks courageous *vis-à-vis* opponents. Physical training also has a significant psychological dimension. *Bauddhik* teaching focuses on 'glorious Hindu history', 'Muslim invasion and oppression', 'Christian conspiracy', 'plight of Hindus', 'Hindu disunity' and the need for 'Hindu unity' or *sangathan*. The *shakha*, in Jaffrelot's words, represents 'an ideo-logical *akhara*'.[21] Making a sharp distinction between Hindu national-ism and 'wrestling nationalism', Joseph Alter[22] observes that while the former is sectarian, militant, political, and organizationally cohesive, the latter is non-sectarian, peaceful, moral and organizationally loose. Hence, the wrestling ideology is the antithesis of RSS ideology.

The *shakha* collects people and its activities include *loka samparka* (mass communication), *loka samskara* (inculcation of a new spirit) and *loka niyojana* (deployment of the people).[23] Thus, an ideal swayamsevak should not only be regular in the *shakha*, he must motivate others to be regular as well. Accordingly, he undertakes to awaken his fellow swayamsevaks in the morning and bring them along to the *shakha*. He is expected to visit those who have not turned up and enquire about their health and well-being and find out the reason of absence. He also actively takes part in the discussions (*charcha*) and meetings (*baithak*) and follows the instructions of his *adhikaris* (seniors) obediently, preferably without question.[24] The main objective of the shakha is to instil in its swayamsevaks the spirit of brotherhood, cohesion, discipline, reverence to authority and ideological conformity.

The second criterion in selecting a pracharak is to assess how much time he can devote to the organization. The RSS demands complete devotion. In fact, a willingness to devote his entire time for the Sangh, rather than intelligence and educational qualifications, becomes the basis of recruitment. However, with the expansion of the RSS, the supply of intelligent and talented swayamsevaks has increased, thereby improving the quality of recruitment. As the Sangh

Parivar has made its forays into different spheres of civil society, it has become indispensable for the RSS to recruit educated and intelligent pracharaks knowledgeable in different fields—from environment to e-governance.

Third, the pracharak must be willing to lead an ascetic life renouncing worldly affairs such as marriage and the possession of property.[25] Asceticism is not specific to Hinduism alone; it is common to all religious systems emanating from 'desire of self-humiliation before the Unseen Powers'.[26] An ardent desire on the part of the followers to imitate the life of the founder of their own religion or sect, such a founder being often an ascetic and having a contempt of the things in this world, influence the practices of self-denial. More than a century ago, John Campbell Oman found the condition in India 'very conducive to mental depression and gloomy religious speculations, leading naturally to abnegation and ascetic living'.[27]

Asceticism has two main themes: renunciation and celibacy. While emphasizing the need for strong men, Vivekananda defines this strength in terms of both renunciation and celibacy. Renunciation is perhaps the best-known cultural ideal of Hindu society; Dumont calls it 'a sort of universal language of India'[28] and further observes that what one is in the habit of calling Indian thought is for the very great part the thought of the sannyasi.[29] Renunciation, however, was traditionally restricted to twice-born males; the pre-eminent position of the Brahmin in Hindu society is based 'on his being the exponent of the values of renunciation'.[30] Neither women nor lower caste men were allowed to practice it. Since post-Vedic period, the prohibition on women and non-Brahmins studying the sacred Vedic texts or participating in Vedic rites has effectively barred their embracing sannyas except as members of unorthodox sects. While the Bhakti movement opened up possibilities for the lower castes to become renouncers, the women were never allowed into major religious Orders. As renouncer's wandering life is the very embodiment of independence, it was not considered 'appropriate' for women.[31]

Celibacy may be seen as a form of renunciation. Although the RSS constitution does not actually prescribe celibacy, most pracharaks remain unmarried. With tremendous value placed on marriage and family life in India, 'self-chosen celibacy is as dramatic a statement of commitment to a cause as one can make'.[32] Though RSS does not denigrate family life, it understands well that family obligations would not allow a pracharak to devote his time and energy to the job fully.

Hence, the pracharak often chooses to remain celibate. Incidentally, at the time of initiation, each pracharak takes the vow of 'brahmacharya', which 'stems from the ancient Hindu tradition that true service to the highest ideals of life can be given only by those who renounce worldly affairs'.[33] Mahatma Gandhi, an ardent advocate of *brahmacharya*, also understood its importance for the higher purpose of unfettered service to the community. He argued that the gratification of sexual passion vies with a man's obligation to enhance personal vitality and psychic power. A man 'who is unchaste loses stamina, becomes emasculated and cowardly'.[34] The RSS also believes so, while differing fundamentally with Gandhian notions of masculinity and cowardliness.

ENTICING TO THE FOLD

Various factors motivate an adolescent swayamsevak to become a pracharak. A prime motivator has been the personality of the senior pracharak. K.D. Jhari, who became a pracharak at the age of seventeen, was greatly impressed by Vasant Rao Oke, a Maharashtrian pracharak. As he writes: 'In 1944, when I first saw him I was immensely impressed by his personality. Till today my memory is engraved with the charm and fascination of his personality. At the time he appeared to me with the halo of god irradiating his head.'[35] Maharashtrian pracharaks, particularly the recruits of Hedgewar, because of their personalities, invariably attracted young boys.[36] Fascination may be any experience that captures our attention, without at the same time being amenable to our understanding entirely; it is a paracritical mode of attention.[37]

The pracharak's ascetic appearance makes a deep impact on the young swayamsevak and attracts him instantly. The first meeting between Hedgewar and Golwalkar was 'historic' and it established 'a subtle psychological relationship' between the two and they 'were drawn near to each other'.[38] After a couple of meetings, many boys join the RSS, being fascinated by the pracharak's personality and psychic power. Thus, fascination turns out to be an instrument of indirect control and domination. Ashis Nandy sees a danger in the ideology of asceticism being manipulated as a resource for authoritarianism.[39] In an impressionable age and with uncritical faculties, these youngsters make the pracharak their role model. The latter is mystical, celibate, renouncer of worldly pleasures, and above all, devotee of the mother nation.

Closely linked to the impact of a fascinating personality is adolescent anxiety. Different types of anxieties trouble a male adolescent, the crucial one being the quest for a personal identity. An important manifestation of this is his conscious as well as unconscious obsession with body imagery. The Indian body image conceives an intimate connection with the cosmos.[40] The Hindu body imagery gives rise to 'cultural diseases' such as *svapnadosh* (nocturnal emissions) in which young men develop feelings of fatigue and depletion of energy because of the loss of semen.[41]

The ideas on semen and celibacy are embedded in Indian culture. In its most popular form, as Sudhir Kakar explains, the Hindu theory of sublimation goes something like this: 'Physical strength and mental power have their source in *virya*, a word that stands both for sexual energy and semen. *Virya*, in fact, is identical with the essence of maleness. *Virya* can either move downward in sexual intercourse, where it is emitted in gross physical form as semen, or it can move upward through the spinal chord and into the brain, in its subtle form known as *ojas*.'[42] The Hindus regard the downward movement of sexual energy and its emission as semen as a waste of vitality and essential energy. If semen is retained, converted into *ojas* and moved upwards by the observance of *brahmacharya*, it can be a source of spiritual energy rather than cause of physical decay. 'Longevity, creativity, physical and mental vitality are enhanced by the conservation of semen; memory, will power, inspiration—scientific and artistic—all derive from the observation of *brahmacharya*.'[43]

At the time when an adolescent encounters these perplexing questions, the RSS offers him, if not all, at least a few answers. The celibate pracharak appears to be the man who has mastered his control over ejaculation through physical and mental discipline and has been able to convert it into *ojas* (spiritual power). The *shakha* appears to be an ideal training ground for disciplining body and mind under the tutelage of the pracharak. Projecting as its ideal Vivekananda, who successfully transformed sexual energy to spiritual power, the RSS further captures the imagination of the young. It preaches that the sexual energy of youth, if controlled, could be channelled into the devotion of 'Mother India'.

Besides possessing an impressive physique which supposedly carries spiritual energy, another vital aspect of a pracharak's personality that captures the imagination of an idealistic adolescent is his spartan lifestyle. The pracharak trained in the traditions of Hedgewar and Golwalkar leads an austere life with minimal possessions. He sleeps either on the floor or on a hard bed and eats simple vegetarian food with fellow swayamsevaks. From an ascetic point of view, eating and sexuality are linked; eating, especially meat and spicy food, is believed to stimulate sexual passion. Gandhi strongly believed that control of palate is very closely connected with the observance of *brahmacharya*. The Puritan Revolution of seventeenth-century England was also accompanied by a series of restraints on food, cuisine and consumption; desires were regulated by vegetarianism, dieting, exercise, fasting. RSS pracharaks wear simple clothes (cotton *dhoti* and *kurta*).[44] The clothes one wears indeed make a statement of one's socio-cultural identity. Clothing has its own grammar, syntax, and vocabulary.[45] Thus, the simple, self-denying and sacrificing life-style of the senior pracharaks has inspired many swayamsevaks to embrace pracharakship.

The over-awing personality of a senior pracharak is ideally supplemented by his power of story-telling. Stories are powerful means of effective ideological transmission to young boys. And most pracharaks are storytellers *par excellence*, narrating tales of brave, adventurous, courageous, mythical as well as historical, Hindu figures lucidly. Their words are seductive. Jhari, an ideal swayamsevak, got so mesmerized by the 'inspiring words' of his senior pracharaks that he decided to leave home to become a pracharak:

> They said to me in crystal words: why do you tie yourself up in domestic bonds? They are all futile and purposeless for a young boy of high patriotic aspirations. There is the call from Mother—the mother of us all. Who will listen to her call if not boys like you? Renounce your all for the RSS and serve the Motherland. Think of Tanaji. When Shivaji called him for conquest of Singh Garh, Tanaji left off the marriage arrangements of his son in the middle, and joined Shivaji. Service of the nation is above all mundane things. We should renounce our homes and other material pursuits and possessions for the sake of our nation. A Swayam Sevak has nothing to do with sub-lunary pleasures or pursuits.[46]

A swayamsevak has to become a renouncer not for his personal salvation, but for the service of the RSS and the Hindu nation. The example of Deendayal Upadhyaya, a prominent RSS ideologue, will further illustrate. He decided to opt for a pracharak's career, being influenced by idealism as well as the core ideological message of RSS.[47] A young man's concern is evident when he regrets: 'Every one of us is engrossed in his personal interests and is inclined to think about himself alone.'[48] At the same time, ideological indoctrination is clear when he explains that 'Hindu samaj' is disorganized, 'weak and degenerate, devoid of power and steeped in selfishness'.[49] That is why, 'Muslim goondas may, at a single stroke, besmirch the honour and reputation of the highest citizens'.[50] In pracharak stories and discourse the construction of the enemy 'other' is so convincing that it leaves an indelible imprint on an impressionable mind and motivates him to devote his life for the protection and promotion of Hindu nation.

HIERARCHICAL STRUCTURE

Once in the fold, the pracharak is placed under a hierarchical organizational structure. The procedure of recruitment and placement has been laid out on the principle of a well-defined hierarchy. The Sarkaryavaha (General Secretary) is in command and control of the entire pracharak system. He appoints the Akhil Bharatiya Pracharak Pramukh (all-India chief organizer), who with the consent of the Sarkaryavaha and in consultation with the concerned provincial chiefs (Prant Sanghchalaks), appoints the prant pracharak (provincial chief organizer). The latter, in turn, recruits pracharaks for the different regions in the province in consultation with concerned local RSS functionaries. Thus the hierarchy: national, regional, provincial, divisional, district, city, and so on; the lower level pracharak reports to the superior and takes his instructions.

Most of the pracharaks, usually college-educated, are recruited in their early 1920s and have been associated with the RSS since early adolescence. Further, they should have attended at least two Officer's Training Camps (OTC) as well as a number of other RSS camps. They usually know Hindi, English, and the language of the area in which they work. And they also have a flair for travelling. Pracharaks during their probation, which usually lasts for one or two years, are called *vistarak*. The potential of the probationer is assessed during this period, and his future tenure and placement decided.

Despite the fact that the state units assess their own manpower needs and have considerable discretion in assigning their own pracharaks, the ultimate power for their appointment, transfer and discontinuance of the service resides with the Sarkaryavaha. He may shift them to other states and affiliates, if needed.

THE MISSON: REINFORCING HINDUTVA

Organizational expansion and ideological indoctrination are the main tasks of the pracharaks. Hence, they are primarily engaged in recruiting new members and converting them to Hindutva. The local level functionary does the background work by portraying a magnified image of the pracharak as a wise, honest, sacrificing and dedicated nationalist before bringing a potential recruit for introduction (*parichay*). The pracharak is trained to work on the psychology of the young; appearing familiar and close, yet enigmatic and mysterious. He makes the young comfortable with his affectionate behaviour and elucidation of simple intelligible concepts. His choice of vocabulary further makes a positive impact; e.g. addressing a boy much younger to him with respect, as 'bhaya' (brother) or 'ji', raising his self-esteem.[51] And gradually he is roped in and starts coming to the *shakha*. Hedgewar visualized the construction of a selfless 'new man'—physically well-trained, 'manly', self-disciplined, courageous, and above all, loyal to the Hindu nation and RSS. Hence, a pracharak undertakes the responsibility of 'man-making' by guiding the activities—physical and mental—in the *shakhas* assigned to him.

Soon after his entry, the process of indoctrination starts; pracharaks impart ideological training at different levels as they are well versed with the ideology of Hindu Rashtra. Pracharak's discourse, through stories or otherwise, is full of negative projections of the 'other'—the enemies of the Hindu nation—Muslims, Christians, Communists, and, a recent addition, the pseudo-secularists. This discourse is usually silent on, or barely concerned with, social evils and practices among Hindus. For instance, swayamsevaks are hardly advised not to accept dowry and bribe; there is again no serious critique of the exploitation of Dalits, tribes, and women. However, with democratic upsurge and the explosion of identity politics, the RSS discourse now has some space for certain socio-economic issues and marginalized sections.

Pracharak discourse includes the rather simplistic RSS views on current national and international problems. A pracharak may appear to be the repository of knowledge to the saffron brotherhood; an average one is not really so. Jhari, who became a pracharak at the age of seventeen, admits: 'Like all pracharaks I vociferated volubly

PREDICAMENT

A pracharak's life becomes hard as he has to work within the physical and material space of the society while leading the life of an ascetic. The classical *ashrama* system, endorsed by Manu, allows men to become renouncers only at the fourth stage of life. By that time, they have fulfilled their domestic obligations, and their natural passions have subsided. But the RSS, for its own reasons, defies this prescription. Celebrating celibacy is one thing; practising it is tough for young pracharaks. Hence there is nothing unnatural about the reports of Govindacharya's love for Uma Bharti or Narendra Modi's quiet marriage. The young pracharaks pass through physical and mental agony. This repression, at times, leads to reported homosexuality.[59]

The RSS is conscious of these problems and takes various steps to keep morale high. The pracharaks are imparted continuous and rigorous ideological training reassuring them about the purpose of their mission. Examples from the lives of dedicated pracharaks are generously cited to inspire them. For instance, RSS literature glorifies the dedication of Babasaheb Apte, a dedicated pracharak, who refused to see his sister when he was working in the city in which she lived.

Despite these efforts, one could still notice elements of introspection, apprehension, uncertainty, and guilt among some pracharaks. At times they regret their decision to follow this course. Since many do so against the wishes of their family, they feel guilty. Those from middle and lower middle-class background never really forget their family responsibilities and obligations. The pracharaks invariably get apprehensive about their future as the prime of their life is dedicated to RSS. Many of them, in fact, leave on their own to resume normal family life. A senior pracharak hopes that this 'unusual system' will wither away when the RSS achieves Hindu Rashtra. But that is a distant dream.

POWER-POLITICS

The RSS pracharak tradition has undergone some visible transformation. The young generation of pracharaks looks different from their older counterparts despite both swearing by the same ideology. In life style, young pracharaks now wear western clothes, travel by motorcycle for easy and quick mobility, and more importantly, look for more comforts and privileges.[60] However, the real difference between the generations is with regard to their attitude towards political power. While the older ones, imbibing the traditions of Hedgewar and Golwalkar, put more emphasis on the ideal of Hindu Rashtra and consider political power as its derivative, the younger ones moulded in the traditions of Balasaheb Deoras, Rajendra Singh, and Sudarshan show a significant desire for political power. In comparison with the former, who are cool, restrained and temperate, the latter appear to be restless, assertive, and aggressive.

This metamorphosis could be understood tracing the RSS's political experiments, following the ban on it after Mahatma Gandhi's murder when some young pracharaks felt the dire need of a political front to defend and promote the interests of the RSS.[61] Golwalkar, after initial reluctance, concurred and launched the Bharatiya Jana Sangh (BJS) in 1951. He deputed some of the talented pracharaks to take organizational and ideological control over the party. The party slowly but steadily expanded and the 1967 elections provided the opportunity for some pracharaks to come to power in Uttar Pradesh, Punjab, Madhya Pradesh, Bihar, and Delhi.

Balasaheb Deoras's appointment as Golwalkar's successor in 1973 proved to be a turning point. A passionate propounder of power politics, he allowed the RSS to intervene in national politics by a strategic alliance with Jayaprakash Narayan against Indira Gandhi's Emergency. Veteran RSS pracharaks like Nanaji Deshmukh and Dattopant Thengadi constituted the backbone of the movement. The experiment paid off. The RSS emerged as an important political player, the BJS merged with the Janatà Party, and former pracharaks like Atal Behari Vajpayee and L.K. Advani became ministers in the central government. After the failure of the Janata experiment, the BJP emerged as the new *avatar* of the BJS. And the success graph of the BJP and the Sangh Parivar since the mid-1980s certainly could not have been charted without the pracharaks, the navigators of Hindu Rashtra. It then became imperative for them to have command and control over state power.

But political power has its own dynamics. The lure of the political world has been irresistible for some of these talented men; instead of remaining back-room boys they prefer to be part of the glitterati and chatterati. They love the glare of publicity and showbiz thereby deviating from Golwalkar's prescriptions of anonymity and quietude.

Some of these master organizers have turned out to be master manipulators. They have become so indispensable to the political affiliate that the parent organization dare not shift them. Being unable to stay above factional politics, they invite gossip and rumour. There have been slander and innuendoes, diminishing and devaluing this carefully-nurtured institution.

Cultural politics has its own advantages and limitations. If the pracharak could conveniently sell to the swayamsevaks his cultural brand image of pure personality and sterling character, now he finds it hard to explain the rationale behind his indulgence in the impure world of power politics. Old generation pracharaks deserve full credit for the enormous expansion of saffron brotherhood; they have certainly exercised an immense moral power over the swayamsevaks because of their self-less work—even though morality wears a strait-jacket in their scheme. As navigators of Hindu Rashtra, their primary objective has been to control and condition the body and mind of these young men and orient their immense energy against the 'enemies' of Hindu nation. But that was not their fault; as loyal disciples they single-mindedly preached and practised the world-view of Hedgewar and Golwalkar. On the contrary, their younger counterparts, while cruising along towards the same destination, occasionally dither in the maelstrom of power politics. As the likes of Ganga Bishen fade away, the RSS finds it difficult to attract the likes of Ram Prakash.

NOTES

1. This paper is based on my article published in *Contemporary India*. See Kanungo, 2002: 175-97.
2. Interview with Ram Prakash Katyal.
3. For a comparison between Arya Samaj and RSS, see Daniel Gold, 1991: 531-93.
4. Contrary to the time-hallowed custom of quietism and pietism of recluse life, the Sadhu in Ramakrishna order lived 'out of the society as well as in it'. See Indira Chowdhury-Sengupta, 1996: 135.
5. The RSS, incidentally, attempts to appropriate this legacy.
6. J.A. Curran, 1951: 55.
7. Gold, 1991: 561.
8. Thomas Blom Hansen, 1991: 96.
9. In the early years the RSS used the term *parivrajak* (wandering ascetic) instead of pracharak.

10. Prominent disciples of Hedgewar included Balasaheb Deoras, Madhavrao Mule, Eknath Ranade, Babasaheb Apte, Moropant Pingle, Bhausaheb Bhuskute, Yadavrao Joshi, Bhaurao Deoras, Bhaiyaji Dani and Dada Rao Parmarth (Dinanath Mishra 1980: 63; Bisheshwar Dwivedi 1990).
11. The RSS was banned after Mahatma Gandhi's assassination. The Government of India compelled the RSS to adopt a written constitution in 1949 before lifting the ban.
12. Article 17 of the RSS constitution.
13. Walter K. Andersen and Shridhar D. Damle, 1987: 87.
14. The number of whole-timers in the Communist Parties has declined sharply over the years.
15. Mishra, 1980: 63.
16. The first RSS affiliate Rashtra Sevika Samiti, the women's wing, was set up in 1936 during Hedgewar's time. But it was Golwalkar who thought out a strategy and founded some important affiliates: the ABVP (students) in 1948, the BMS (labour) in 1955, and the VHP in 1964. Deoras expanded the Parivar by setting up an affiliate in every possible sphere of civil society. There are over 150 RSS affiliates. See H.V. Seshadri, 1988.
17. Golwalkar, 1980 [1966]: 513.
18. Martial arts, like other overt techniques of disciplining the body . . . are 'incorporating practices' through which the body, and therefore experience and meaning are culturally shaped in its actual practices and behaviours (Zarrilli, 1998: 5).
19. Bourdieu, 1977.
20. Zarrilli, 1998: 5.
21. Jaffrelot, 1996: 35.
22. Alter, 1997: 261-3.
23. For details see Mishra, 1980: 55-7.
24. While addressing the participants of a RSS camp at Delhi, Dattopant Thengadi observed that an ideal swayamsevak is one who follows the instruction of his *adhikari* (officer) without any doubt; if he is asked to jump into a well, he should have no hesitation to obey.
25. Hindu scriptures repeatedly warn the renouncer to stay away from *kamini* (woman) and *kanchan* (gold).
26. Campbell, 1973 [1903]: 7.
27. Ibid., 15.
28. Louis Dumont, 1960: 52.
29. However, Madan (1996) argues that it is not the renouncer, but the householder (*grhastha*), who occupies the centre stage of Hindu society. For debates between asceticism and domesticity, see Patrick Olivelle, 1994: 533-46.

30. J.C. Heesterman, 1985: 44.
31. The Arya Samaj provided greater scope for women (Llewellyn, 1994: 462-72). Vivekananda also planned for a monastic order for women; see Bull 1997. The Sangh Parivar has brought to its fold *sannyasinis* like Rithambara and Uma Bharti and has used their passionate oratorical skill against the Muslims during Ramjanmabhumi agitation. While Uma Bharti opted for the world of politics, Rithambara presented the image of selflessness and purity—evoking the power of a virgin goddess among her audience and appealing to their fantasies. 'There is a subtle sexual challenge to the men in her audience to prove their virility (*vis-ã-vis* the Muslim) in order to deserve her' (Kakar, 1995: 199).
32. Embree, 1994: 626.
33. Curran, 1951: 55.
34. Quoted in Kakar, 1989: 97.
35. Jhari, 1970a: 35.
36. There are also exceptions; for instance, Dada Rao Parmarth, who was instrumental in the southern expansion of the RSS, did not have an impressive personality.
37. Abbas, 1999: 29-45.
38. See *Shri Guruji*, 1956: 11.
39. Ashis Nandy, 1993: 108.
40. Brenda Beck (1976: 213-14) looks at various ways in which human body form and concepts of cosmic structure are linked in southern Hindu traditions.
41. Substance-loss anxieties, however, 'are not schizophrenic but the natural (though pathological) outcome of a cultural vision of the body in ceaseless flux', Kakar, 1994: 234-5.
42. Kakar, 1989: 118-19.
43. Ibid., 119.
44. The pracharaks, wore cotton clothes, but did not use *khadi* for a long time as it was a strong Gandhian symbol.
45. Davis, 1992.
46. Jhari, 1970: 37.
47. See *Organizer*, 1968.
48. Ibid., 9.
49. Ibid.
50. Ibid.
51. However, this does not suggest that the pracharaks do not believe in hierarchy. It is a practice in the RSS to touch the feet of senior pracharaks.
52. Jhari, 1970: 37.
53. For instance, Deendayal Upadhyaya and Govindacharya.

54. Hitler understood that civilization is only skin deep, that primitive emotions lie very close to the surface of ordinary people, and that these instincts can be most effectively manipulated. For more on Hitler's manipulation of his brilliant oratory skills, see William Carr 1978: Chap. I.
55. Gold: 561.
56. For details of this strategy at a provincial level, see Kanungo, 2003: 3293-3303.
57. Kakar, 1995: 44.
58. Gossip articulates and bounds identity, group memory and legitimate group social practice. It 'represents the recreation *of* the structures of that group, and of society in general, at the level of consciousness.' Chris Wickham, 1998: 23.
59. Jhari, 1970a: 35.
60. Under the present system of mass consumption in contemporary capitalism 'asceticism is replaced by calculating hedonism'. See Bryan S. Turner, 1984: 4.
61. See Craig Baxter, 1971: Chap. IV.

REFERENCES

Abbas, Akbar, 1999, 'Dialectic of Deception', *Public Culture*, 11 (2), 1999, pp. 29-45.

Alter, Joseph S., 1997, *The Wrestler's Body: Identity and Ideology in North India*, New Delhi: Munshiram Manoharlal.

Andersen, Walter K. and Shridhar D. Damle, 1987, *The Brotherhood in Saffron: The Rashtriya Swayamsevak Sangh and Hindu Revivalism*, New Delhi: Vistaar Publications.

Baxter, Craig, 1971, *The Jana Sangh: A Biography of an Indian Political Party*, New Delhi: Oxford University Press.

Beck, Brenda E.F., 1976, 'The symbolic merger of body, space and cosmos in Hindu Tamil Nadu', *Contributions to Indian Sociology* (NS), vol. 10, no. 2, pp. 213-44.

Bourdieu, Pierre, 1977, *Outline of a Theory of Practice*, Cambridge: Cambridge University Press.

Bull, Wendy Sinclair, 1997, *Female Ascetics: Hierarchy and Purity in an Indian Religious Movement*, Surrey: Curzon Press.

Campbell, Oman John, 1903 (rpt. 1973), *The Mystics, Ascetics and Saints of India: A Study of Sadhuism, with an Account of the Yogis, Sannyasis, Bairagis, and Other Strange Sectarians*, Delhi: Oriental Publishers.

Carr, William, 1978, *Hitler: A Study in Personality and Politics*, London: Edward Arnold.

Chowdhury-Sengupta, Indira, 1996, 'Reconstructing Spiritual Heroism: The Evolution of Swadeshi Sannyasi in Bengal', in Julia Leslie, ed., *Myth and Mythmaking*, Surrey: Curzon Press.

Curran, Jr., J.A., 1951, *Militant Hinduism in Indian Politics: A Study of the RSS*, New York: Institute of Pacific Relations.

Davis, Fred, 1992, *Fashion, Culture, and Identity*, Chicago: University of Chicago Press.

Dumont, Louis, 1960, 'Renunciation in World Religions', *Contributions to Indian Sociology*, 4, pp. 33-62.

Dwivedi, Bisheshwar, 1990, *Sangh Nib Me Visarjit*, 3 vols. [in Hindi], Lucknow: Lokhit Prakashan.

Embree, Ainslie T., 1994, 'The Function of the Rashtriya Swayamsevak Sangh: To Define the Hindu Nation', in: Martin E. Marty and R. Scott Appleby, eds., *Accounting for Fundamentalisms: The Dynamic Character of Movements*, vol. 4, Chicago: University of Chicago Press, pp. 617-52.

Gold, Daniel, 1991, 'Organized Hinduisms: From Vedic Truth to Hindu Nation', in Martin E. Marty and Scott R. Appleby, eds., *Fundamentalism Observed*, Chicago: University of Chicago Press, pp. 531-93.

Golwalkar, M.S., 1980 [1966], *Bunch of Thoughts*, Bangalore: Jagarana Prakashana.

Hansen, Thomas Blom, 1999, *The Saffron Wave: Democracy and Hindu Nationalism in Modern India*, New Delhi: Oxford University Press.

Heesterman, J.C., 1985, *The Inner Conflict of Tradition: Essays in Indian Ritual, Kingship, And Society*, Chicago: University of Chicago Press.

Jaffrelot, Christophe, 1996, *The Hindu Nationalist Movement and Indian Politics 1925 to the 1990s: Strategies of Identity-Building, Implantation and Mobilization [with special reference to central India]*, New Delhi: Viking Penguin India.

Jhari, K.D., 1970, 'I was a swayamsevak—II', *Secular Democracy*, vol. 3 (1-2), pp. 35-7.

———, 1970a, 'I was a swayamsevak—IV: Revealing details of pracharak life', *Secular Democracy*, June, pp. 33-5.

Kakar, Sudhir, 1989, *Intimate Relations: Exploring Indian Sexuality*, New Delhi: Penguin Books India.

———, 1994, *Shamans, Mystics and Doctors*, New Delhi: Oxford University Press.

———, 1995, *The Colours of Violence*, New Delhi: Viking.

Kanungo, Pralay, 2002, 'Pracharaks of Hindu Rashtra', *Contemporary India*, vol. 1, no. 2, April-June, pp. 175-97.

———, 2003, 'Hindutva's Entry into a "Hindu Province": Early Years of RSS in Orissa', *Economic and Political Weekly*, vol. XXXVIII, no. 31, 2 August, pp. 3293-3303.

Llewellyn, J.E., 1994, 'The Autobiography of a Female Renouncer', in Donald S. Lopez, Jr., ed., *Religions of India in Practice*, Princeton: Princeton University Press, pp. 462-72.

Madan, T.N., 1996, *Non-renunciation: Themes and Interpretations of Hindu Culture*, New Delhi: Oxford University Press.

Mishra, Dinanath, 1980, *RSS: Myth and Reality*, New Delhi: Vikas.

Nandy, Ashis, 1993, *At the Edge of Psychology: Essays in Politics and Culture*, New Delhi: Oxford University Press.

Olivelle, Patrick, 1994, 'Ascetic withdrawal or social engagement', in Donald S. Lopez, Jr. (ed.), *Religions of India in Practice*, Princeton: Princeton University Press, pp. 533-46.

Organizer, 14 April 1968.

Seshadri, H.V., 1988, *RSS: A Vision in Action*, Bangalore: Jagarana Prakashana.

Shri Guruji: The Man and His Mission [On the occasion of His 51st Birthday], 1956, Delhi: Bharat Prakashan.

Turner, Bryan S., 1984, *The Body and Society: Explorations in Social Theory*, Oxford: Basil Blackwell.

Wickham, Chris, 1998, 'Gossip and Resistance among the Medieval Peasantry', *Past and Present*, no. 160, p. 23.

Zarrilli, Phillip B., 1998, *When Body Becomes All Eyes: Paradigms, Discourses and Practices in Kalarippayattu, A South Indian Martial Art*, New Delhi: Oxford University Press.

10

Trishul Diksha, Cross Burning and the Politics of Hate

AMAR FAROOQUI

Since the founding of the RSS, the Sangh Parivar's mobilization strategy has revolved around the twin themes of militant Hindu resurgence and hatred of the minorities, especially Muslims.[1] In this it has followed, and contributed to the development of, a pattern that has been common to similar movements throughout the world during the last hundred years or so. German Nazism is one obvious source of inspiration.[2] M.S. Golwalkar's endorsement of and admiration for the Nazi policies of anti-Semitism and ethnic cleansing is well-known.[3] Hatred, in a primeval sense, of an entire community is inseparable from the militant Hinduism that the Sangh Parivar espouses.

Further, violence, which in turn reinforces hate, is a crucial component of the parivar's project. From exercises in the RSS *shakha*, which at a very basic level include training in the use of the *lathi*, to the rifle-training camps of the VHP and the Bajrang Dal the emphasis is on violence and male physical prowess.[4] And this is what riots and pogroms are all about. Violence, after all, is participation. The extent of participation can be increased dramatically if the scale of violence is multiplied. Localized communal riots engineered in a secretive and underhand manner, something that the RSS has so often been accused of (and with good reason),[5] can only bring forth limited physical participation. The massacres of Sikhs in 1984 demonstrated

*This paper is a revised and expanded version of an article with the same title published in *Mainstream*, 3 May 2003: 19-21. I am grateful to Satish Saberwal for encouraging me to rework the article into a paper for this seminar. Discussions with K.M. Shrimali and Vishwa Mohan Jha on *trishul diksha* helped me to formulate my views on the subject. I thank them both for their suggestions.

the efficacy of the pogrom as a grand spectacle. It ensured both mass participation on an unprecedented scale as well as facelessness.[6] Hence the riots/pogroms of 1992–3 and the Gujarat carnage of 2002. In this situation the clandestine manner in which the RSS operates,[7] though otherwise a great asset,[8] can be an obstacle to the organization of violence on a qualitatively different scale.

Not surprisingly, there has been a shift in focus since the early 1980s with the VHP and the Bajrang Dal intervening actively and openly to mobilize the community that the RSS seeks to constitute.[9] Pralay Kanungo has outlined the various phases of this new strategy and drawn attention to its potential for violence.[10] He concludes his discussion on the *Ramshila Pujan* of 1989 that marked an important stage in the militant offensive of the Sangh Parivar, with the assessment that the *Ramshila* campaign was not only for mobilization but also confrontational. 'It became aggressively anti-Muslim and provoked communal violence.'[11]

The specialized role that the VHP and Bajrang Dal are expected to play has acquired particular significance with the formation of a BJP-led government at the centre. To put it crudely, the task of rabble-rousing violence has been left to them. This can hardly be achieved by organizing periodic congregations of sadhus or convening Dharam Sansads. It is the youth, often unemployed or with no steady employment, who have to be drawn into the movement on a mass scale, and the peculiar organizational structure of the RSS and its methods do not allow it to reach out, in physical terms, to large sections of such youth.[12] On the other hand organizations such as the Bajrang Dal and VHP can go in for a mass recruitment that is flexible enough not to be very demanding in terms of discipline. Their looser organizational structures give them a wider appeal, and ensure the right mix of commitment and lumpenization.

In the months leading up to 6 December 1992 the recruitment of *kar sevaks* constituted the principal method of declaring admission into the fold. More recently this has been replaced by intiation through the ceremonial presentation of a *trishul.* The VHP has been holding programmes in different parts of the country for the public distribution of trishuls, known as *trishul diksha* or initiation.[13] In many ways *trishul diksha* goes beyond recruitment of *kar sevak.* For one, its symbolism is more potent. The idea originated with the Bajrang Dal, formed in 1984 against the backdrop of militancy in Panjab.[14] The *trishul* was supposed to be the Dal's response to the *kirpan.*[15] The

Dal refers to its ceremony as *trishul dharan* rather than *diksha*, though the terms have become interchangeable.

The VHP and Bajrang Dal have constantly argued that the distribution of *trishuls* is essentially innocuous and that the possession of *trishuls* merely indicates Hindu identity:

> The trishul is the symbol of Lord Shiva and Goddess Durga and their spiritual, physical and divine forces. The Bajrang Dal worships Hanuman, the incarnation of Shiva. It is natural for it to worship, possess and carry the holy trishul, which is an ancient Hindu tradition. From the beginning, the Bajrang Dal adopted trishul diksha as a compulsory organizational activity. It is a sort of convocation function where workers take an oath to serve the nation and not to misuse the trishul.[16]

Parallels have sought to be drawn between *trishuls* and *kirpans*, completely ignoring the historical development of Hinduism on the one hand and of Sikhism on the other, curiously, even by the National Commission for Minorities.[17] Whereas carrying the *kirpan* has been an integral part of Sikh religious practice for several centuries, there has been no tradition of ordinary Hindus carrying trishuls around. The *trishul* is indeed one of the sacred symbols associated with Hinduism, but it certainly has never been an object which common people carry with them on a regular basis to announce their faith.[18] It is unlikely that one would come across a *trishul* in the average Hindu household in any part of the country. In this context D.N. Jha makes the pertinent observation that 'Till ten years ago, even five years ago, the *trishul* was associated with militant sadhus. It is a symbol of renunciation, not to be worshipped in homes'.[19]

The attempt by the VHP/Bajrang Dal to equate Hindu identity with *trishuls* is in fact an innovation. According to Shrimali,

> Epic-Puranic mythology is replete with examples of Shiva giving his favourite weapons to divinities, devotees and more often to *raakshasas*. Thus, Ravana, Madhu, Arjuna, Parashuram, and even Vishnu were recipients of Shiva's various weapons. Significantly, none of these allusions mentions trishul among Shiva's weapons. In the classic myth of the creation of Durga to kill the demon Mahisha (narrated in the *Devi Maahaatmya* of the *Maarkandeya Purana*), for which more than a dozen divinities gave their treasured weapons, Shiva gave his *shool* (not trishul), which is invariably translated as spear/lance rather than trident.[20]

That *trishul diksha* is an 'invented tradition' is obvious from the fact that the VHP/Bajrang Dal discourse on it is still evolving. Among the various arguments put forth to uphold its sanctity as an established religious practice is one that links it to *shastra pujan*, or ritual worship of weapons. Thus, while at one level its justification is derived from the *kirpan*, at another it is 'meant to inculcate respect among Hindus for a tradition of "shastra pujan"'.[21] It is also true that the purpose is not to make all Hindus carry the trishul but to give a sense of belonging through identification with the initiated. Not only is the possession of the *trishul* equated with Hindu identity, but it is supposed to symbolize the nation as well. In the words of a VHP functionary, 'The trishul has become the symbol of Hindu awakening, enlightenment and pride. *Diksha* has taken the place of Vande Mataram'.[22]

To reduce a religious tradition that is so rich in symbols, and so abundantly eclectic in the ways in which faith can be expressed, to just one form of representation—a form decided upon arbitrarily by the VHP—amounts to negating that richness. Moreover, it is not without significance that out of the vast array of symbols that it could choose from, it was the *trishul* that the VHP found the most suitable. The appropriation of this symbol is directly related to the VHP's hate-campaign against the minorities. The *trishul* can be made to suggest violence much more easily, and in so doing the VHP has invested it with a meaning that derives from the anti-minority agenda of the Sangh Parivar. The *trishul* has been re-invented as a symbol of intimidation. It is the misuse of the *trishul* (rather, the modified version of the *trishul* which is distributed by the VHP[23]) that needs to be taken into account.

The Indian state has by and large taken a lenient view of *trishul diksha*, explicitly condoning and implicitly encouraging the campaign. It has taken a strictly legalist view, concentrating exclusively on the question of whether or not the trishul can be used as a weapon. This has helped the campaign to continue unchecked. The only significant intervention so far has been the arrest of VHP international general secretary Praveen Togadia, on 13 April 2003, for defying a ban imposed by the Rajasthan government on *trishul diksha* programmes. Togadia was granted bail after being detained for eight days, on the condition that 'he would not defy the ban on distribution of tridents'.[24] However, soon afterwards a Jodhpur court granted anticipatory bail to five VHP activists who had been accused of displaying *trishuls*. The court was of the opinion that a *trishul* could not be considered an arm or an article for offence or defence.[25]

* * *

A landmark judgement concerning the use of a religious symbol for violence was delivered by the United States Supreme Court on 7 April 2003 (*Virginia* vs. *Black*). The judgement relates to convictions in two separate cases of cross-burning that occurred in 1998 in the state of Virginia.[26] Cross-burning has for long been associated with the notorious Ku Klux Klan. As is well known the Klan was formed soon after the American Civil War as an avowedly racist and anti-black organization.

Officially banned in 1870-1, the Ku Klux Klan continued to function as an underground secret society. There was a revival in the beginning of the twentieth century, partly due to the legitimacy that its racist ideology acquired through contemporary popular literature and cinema. The Klan was reconstituted in 1915 (in the state of Georgia) with a well-defined organizational structure and elaborate ceremonies. Although blacks were still the main target of the Klan, over a period of time its hate-campaigns extended to other minorities (including Jews and Catholics) and Communists.[27] It was from 1915 onwards that cross-burning became a prominent feature of the Klan's activities.

Members of the Klan prefer to designate cross-burning as 'cross-lighting'. It has been suggested that the idea was borrowed from a medieval Scottish practice whereby large crosses would be set ablaze on hilltops to mobilize a clan/community for warfare, but this origin remains doubtful. The Klan regards cross-burning (or 'cross lighting') as an act of purification. Nevertheless, given the racist ideology of the organization and the implications of cross-burning, it is perceived by the people generally, and blacks specifically, as an act of intimidation.

The ritual as performed by the renewed Klan was influenced by a detailed description presented in Thomas Dixon's racist novel, *The Clansman* (1905). Dixon's uncle, Colonel Leroy McAfee, who was of Scottish origin, was 'Grand Titan of the Invisible Empire, Ku Klux Klan', and the book is dedicated to him. The novel has a crucial scene vividly describing the ritual:[28]

> He looked on the prostrate negro lying in his uniform at his feet, seized the cross, lighted the three upper ends and held it blazing in his hand, while, in a voice full of the fires of feeling, he said: 'Men of the South, the time for words has passed, the hour for action has struck. The Grand Turk will execute this negro to-night and fling his body on the lawn of the black Lieutenant-Governor of the state.' . . .
>
> . . . 'In olden times when the Chieftain of our people summoned the

clan on an errand of life and death, the Fiery Cross, extinguished in sacrificial blood, was sent by swift courier from village to village. This call was never made in vain, nor will it be to-night in the new world. Here, on this spot made holy ground by the blood of those we hold dearer than life, I raise the ancient symbol of an unconquered race of men. . . .'

High above his head in the darkness of the cave he lifted the blazing emblem. . . 'The Fiery Cross of old Scotland's Hills! I quench its flames in the sweetest blood that ever stained the sands of Time.'

He dipped its ends in the silver cup, extinguished the fire, and handed the charred symbol to the courier, who quickly disappeared.

More than the novel it was the film based on it that popularized the notion of cross-burning in a big way. D.W. Griffith's controversial but highly successful film *Birth of a Nation*, released in 1915, was inspired by *The Clansman*. The film is regarded as a landmark in the history of American cinema both due to its immense popularity and the narrative techniques that it pioneered. Its popularity ensured that the racist message of the Klan reached a vast audience. The powerful visuals of the film made this audience sympathetic and receptive to the message and the Ku Klux Klan witnessed a revival in 1915, symbolized by a cross burning ritual. Throughout the 1920s and 1930s the Klan was a major political force in the southern states of USA.

Cross burning has been invariably linked to acts of violence against black people. It is with the burning cross that the Klan announces its presence in a particular locality, and following this 'ritual' there are systematic attacks against black people and their property. Thus, cross burning usually marks the initiation of a specific campaign. One can well imagine the terror that the symbol conveys.

It was against this backdrop that several American state legislatures imposed restrictions on the burning of the cross. One that took the lead in this matter was the state of Virginia. Through a series of legislative measures between 1952 and 1975, the Virginia General Assembly imposed a ban on this practice. As of today thirteen other states have similar legal provisions. However racial hatred is still so deep-rooted that there have been nearly 1700 recorded cases of cross-burning in the US in the past two decades.[29]

The Virginia law led to the conviction, in 1998, of three persons who were involved in two separate incidents in the state. In the first incident a number of teenagers burnt a cross in the yard outside the home of a racially mixed family. The family was so panic-stricken that it eventually shifted residence to another location. In 1999, two of the young men who had perpetrated the Act were convicted and sentenced to 90 days in prison and fined $2,500 each. In the second and more serious incident, a few months later, a person named Barry E. Black organized a rally in Virginia which culminated in setting on fire a huge cross. Black, whose surname is an interesting irony, is a member of the Klan. Black was convicted in 1999 and fined $2500. Incidentally this punishment was imposed by a jury consisting entirely of white people.

While Black was being tried the two men who had been convicted earlier went in appeal to the Virginia Court of Appeals on the ground that their conviction amounted to a violation of the First Amendment to the American Constitution which guarantees freedom of speech. Cross burning, it was argued, was a form of expression. The appeal was turned down unanimously by the court. In its judgement the court observed that cross burning was linked to 'sudden and precipitous violence—lynchings, shootings, whippings, mutilations and home-burnings', and that its connection with 'forthcoming violence' was 'clear and direct'. It concluded that the message that cross-burning conveyed was beyond the protection of the Constitution. Subsequently, the Court of Appeals also upheld the conviction of Black.

In 2001 the convictions were struck down by the Virginia Supreme Court. By a majority of four to theee verdict the court ruled that the laws which prohibited cross burning were a violation of the Constitution, especially the First Amendment. The judgement stated that 'Under our system of government, people have the right to use symbols to communicate. They patriotically wave the flag or burn it in protest; they may reverently worship the cross or burn it as an expression of bigotry.' Nevertheless, one of the dissenting judges, who happened to be black, noted that

> the majority opinion invalidates a statute that for almost fifty years has protected our citizens from being placed in fear of bodily harm by the burning of a cross. Without question, the framers of the First Amendment never contemplated that a court would construe that Amendment so that it would permit a person to burn a cross in a manner that intentionally places citizens in fear of bodily harm.

The State of Virginia filed an appeal in the US Supreme Court against this decision. The case aroused considerable interest throughout the country and several human rights groups mobilized public opinion on the issue. Some of these groups became party to the case by filing an amicus brief. In its majority (6–3) judgement delivered on 7 April 2003, the Supreme Court struck down the verdict of the lower court and upheld the Virginia ban on cross burning. According to the judgement, the history of cross burnings in the US 'shows that cross burning is often intimidating, intended to create a pervasive fear in victims that they are a target of violence'. Further, that, 'While a burning cross does not inevitably convey a message of intimidation, often the cross burning intends that the recipients of the message fear for their lives. . . . And when a cross burning is used to intimidate, few if any messages are more powerful.'

In his separate judgement Justice Clarence Thomas, the lone black Supreme Court judge, stated: 'In every culture, certain things acquire meaning well beyond what outsiders can comprehend. That goes for both the sacred and the profane. I believe that cross burning is the paradigmatic example of the latter'. Justice Thomas had in an earlier case related to the misuse of the cross by the Klan (*Capitol Square Review Board* vs. *Pinette*, 1995), declared that 'Although the Klan might have sought to convey a message with some religious component, I think that the Klan had primarily a non-religious purpose in erecting the cross. The Klan simply has appropriated one of the most sacred of religious symbols as a symbol of hate'.

This is precisely what the VHP has done by appropriating the trishul. The motives behind the burning of a cross and the distribution of the *trishul* are identical: intimidation. Given the track record of the VHP, its trishul distribution programme is anything but innocuous. The role played by the VHP in the state-sponsored pogrom against minorities in Gujarat is well documented. The BJP too has aggressively endorsed the *trishul* distribution campaign, realizing its potential for communal mobilization. The president of the party has gone on record to affirm that the VHP has the full backing of the BJP on this issue. So have the leading functionaries of the RSS. The BJP argues that the *trishul* is merely a religious symbol, and that as a weapon it is relatively harmless, while a fork could be much more lethal.[30] However the issue at stake is not the efficacy of the *trishul* as a weapon. The massacres in Gujarat did not require *trishuls.* The misuse of an important religious symbol such as the *trishul* for furthering the hate-campaign of the Sangh Parivar is the main question that has to be addressed.

Manufacturing symbols for use in the politics of hate has been an ongoing project at least since the first half of the nineteenth century, to which the colonial encounter contributed in no small measure. 'Divide and rule' might be a cliché, yet it was real for all that. Colonial rule had its own agendas but in so far as its strategy was based on perceiving Indian society in terms of antagonistic religious communities, principally Hindu and Muslim, elements of the strategy could be coopted by indigenous movements seeking to formulate exclusivist identities. The appeal of divisive symbols could be direct, with enormous propaganda value. One prominent example, namely the transformation of the Somnath temple into such a symbol, should suffice.

Romila Thapar has comprehesively shown how Somnath became a metaphor for Hindu–Muslim conflict in twentieth century India with the propagation of the myth that 'the raid of Mahmud created a trauma in the Hindu consciousness which has been at the root of Hindu–Muslim relations' for nearly a thousand years.[31] The process was already under way prior to 1857 and may be dated to the early 1840s, when Lord Ellenborough had the so-called 'Gates of Somnath' removed from Mahmud's tomb in Ghazni and ceremonially brought to India. The language of the proclamation issued on the occasion leaves one in no doubt about the intent: 'The insult of eight hundred years is at last avenged. The gates of the temple of Somnauth, so long the memorial of your humiliation, are become the proudest record of your national glory, the proof of your superiority in arms over the nations beyond the Indus'.[32]

A British officer, Captain William Herries, who accompanied the ceremonial procession from Ghazni to north India recorded his impressions of it in a series of personal letters which reveal the manner in which Somnath was being invented as a symbol as well as the synthetic nature of the symbol.[33] In a letter to his father, Herries mentions that 'Lord Ellenborough has written personally to the *Hindu* Princes thro' whose country we pass . . .' (emphasis added). Herries was rather sceptical about the tradition which associated the gates with Somnath and candidly remarked, 'I do not know that there is any authority, except the tradition among the people of Ghuznee for saying that they originally belonged to the temple of Somenauth'.[34] It would appear that the magnificently decorated cart carrying the 'trophy', drawn by twenty-four bullocks, aroused more interest than the gates themselves.[35] In any case the gates resulted in no religious fervour among the common people. The reaction was quite different from what Herries had been led to expect and he noted, with some disappointment, 'On the whole . . . the general feeling among the Hindus who visit our trophy is that of curiosity, and not of religion'. Eventually he was 'convinced that the procession might wander thro' the whole of India, without disturbance or creating any jealous feeling among the natives'.[36]

Herries's account is noteworthy because it tells us about the initial spontaneous 'Hindu' response, during the modern period, to this symbol in the making. Here we have the prehistory of the formation of an identity in which Somnath was to have a central place. There was no recognition in this first encounter, no familiarity with the meanings which came to be associated with the symbol. All these associations are much later. In these meanings a shared trauma is intended to define the community, legitimizing revenge and hate, rendering the place much more than just a religious site. It was with L.K. Advani's September 1990 *rath yatra*, which commenced from Somnath, that the full potential of the site as a symbol of intimidation was realized. The cumulative meanings with which symbols such as Somnath have been invested by the Sangh Parivar have given to *trishul diksha* its real intimidatory character.

NOTES

1. Cf. Kanungo, 2002: 21.
2. Marzia Casolari observes that 'In the 1920s and 1930s fascism was an international phenomenon. As such it was bound to influence the ideology and practice of similar movements all over the world', and referring to the Shiv Sena adds, 'Since many of Bal Thackeray's most outrageously anti-Muslim and racist statements are literal quotations of [V.D.] Savarkar's speeches and theories, it is legitimate to conclude that such influence is still alive in today's militant Hinduism'. 2002: 227.
3. See Golwalkar, 1939: 34-5.
4. Kanungo, 2002: 71-2; Editorial: *Indian Express*, 16 June 2001; 'VHP readies firearms for cadre', *Telegraph*, 6 May 2003.
5. Goyal, 1979: 151-73.
6. Facelessness of the crowd, and the implied anonymity, has been vital for subverting the legal process and ensuring that miscreants will remain unpunished. Simultaneously this has made the state and its organs an accomplice in the violence, thereby further legitimising it. On the stance of the RSS in relation to the 1984 massacres see Islam, 2002: 39-47.

7. Goyal points out that 'the RSS never decides to do anything nor does it ever put on record any orders or instructions given to its members. If a deed finds approval of the public it comes forth to claim the credit; if it is otherwise it is promptly disavowed without as much as batting an eye-lid'. Goyal, 1979: 148.
8. Cf. Goyal, 1979: 191.
9. It is no coincidence that this was precisely the period (*c.* 1979-84) when Indira Gandhi tried to play the 'Hindu card'. Kanungo remarks, 'In the context of Indira Gandhi's wooing of the Hindus, the VHP was perceived as an ideal instrument for the rival mobilization of Hindus, particularly in north India'. Kanungo, 2002: 193.
10. Ibid.
11. Ibid., 197 and n. 81.
12. This might seem a paradox, but reports suggest that there has been a decline in recruitment in the recent period (Chatterjee 2003). According to Chatterjee, 'Though the number of shakhas has registered a rise each year, the average number of attendants has been on the decline. RSS members are loathe to give out figures that do not suit them, but they do concede that not enough young people are being drawn to the disciplined life of the swayamsevak.'
13. The VHP claims that it has distributed 2,80,000 *trishuls* in Gujarat alone since the beginning of the programme. *Times of India*, 22 April 2003. Nearly 70,000 *trishuls* are stated to have been distributed in Rajasthan during the five years preceding March 2003, PUCL Report: 2003. It is likely that these figures are exaggerated. However what matters more than the number of recipients is the number of programmes organized for *trishul diksha*.
14. www.hinduunity.org/bajrangdal.html
15. Gopinath and Gupta, 1999.
16. Surendra Kumar Jain (2003) is secretary of the VHP. *Trishul diksha* is visualized as the first step towards training for violence at a higher level. According to another VHP functionary, 'The rules to gain admission to the [rifle] camps are rigid. Youths interested in firearms training should have undergone the *trishul diksha*. Those who have cleared the *diksha* get priority over other volunteers to the camps'. *Telegraph*, 6 May 2003. One is not certain what is meant by the phrase, 'cleared the *diksha*', but this could imply training in the use of the *trishul*.
17. Ghose, 2003.
18. On the history of the *trishul* and the concept of *diksha* see Shrimali 2003.
19. D.N. Jha quoted in Reddy, 2003.
20. Shrimali, 2003.

21. VHP Kendriya Margdarshak Mandal member Acharya Giriraj Kishore quoted in *Week*, 11 February 2003.
22. Jain, 2003.
23. Since the Arms Act (1959) and Arms Rules (1962) regard objects with sharp blades over 9 inches in length (6 inches according to similar laws in some states) as weapons, the VHP and Bajrang Dal have kept the size of the *trishuls* distributed by them in their *trishul diksha* programmes less than 6 inches (Reddy 2003). One might mention here that the *trishuls* routinely carried by VHP/Bajrang Dal activists, especially at rallies and meetings, are often much larger in size. At the Dharam Sansad held in Delhi on 24 February 2003 a huge *trishul* adorning the dias formed the backdrop (photograph in *Tribune*, online edition, 25 February 2003).
24. Reports in *Hindu*, 14, 15 and 22 April 2003.
25. *Times of India*, 8 May 2003.
26. The complete judgement is available on the website of the Legal Information Institute, Cornell Law School, USA, www.law.cornell.edu/lii.html; www.virginiavblack.com. It gives the background information and other details relating to the case. The following discussion on the case is based mainly on material obtained from these two websites.
27. Cf. Kennedy, 1990. Kennedy was an undercover agent in the Ku Klux Klan in the 1940s.
28. Dixon, 1905: 325–6.
29. Burek, 2002.
30. 'BJP defends "trishul" distribution', *Hindu*, 22 April 2003. The BJP spokesperson Vijay Kumar Malhotra is reported to have declared that, 'The fork has four spokes and it is more than four inches in size. You cannot injure anyone with a trishul, but the fork can be used with lethal effect' (Benedict, 2003).
31. Thapar, 1999.
32. The text of the proclamation, dated 16 November 1842, is reproduced in Thompson and Garratt 1935: 352-3. Bernard Cohn suggests that, given the rout of the British army by the Afghans in 1842, 'Ellenborough conceived of symbolizing the defeat of the Muslim Afghans by having what were thought to be the Gates of Somnath . . . returned in triumph to India . . .'. Cohn, 1996: 175.
33. MSS Eur C634.
34. MSS Eur C634, 18 December 1842.
35. In one of his letters Herries drew a coloured sketch of the cart, describing it in great detail. MSS Eur C634, 14 January 1843.
36. MSS Eur C634, 18 February 1843.

REFERENCES

Papers of Captain William Robert Herries, MSS Eur C634, Oriental and India Office Collections, British Library.

Benedict, Kay, 2003, 'For the BJP, fork is more deadly than Togadia's trishul', *Telegraph*, 22 April.

Burek, Josh, 2002, 'What are the Origins of Cross-burning?', *Christian Science Monitor*, 13 December.

Casolari, Marzia, 2000, 'Hindutva's Foreign Tie-up in the 1930s: Archival Evidence', *Economic and Political Weekly*, 35 (4): 218-28.

Chatterjee, Manini, 2003, 'Repackaging the RSS', *Indian Express*, 16 March.

Cohn, Bernard S., 1996, 'Representing Authority in Victorian India', in Eric Hobsbawm and Terence Ranger, eds., *The Invention of Tradition*, Cambridge: Cambridge University Press, pp. 165-209.

Dixon Jr, Thomas, 1905, *The Clansman: An Historical Romance of the Ku Klux Klan*, New York: Doubleday, Page and Co.

Ghose, Bhaskar, 2003, 'A New Logo for Hatred', *Telegraph*, 20 May.

Golwalkar, M.S., 1939, *We, or Our Nationhood Defined*, Nagpur: Bharat Prakashan.

Gopinath, Vrinda and Sharad Gupta, 1999, 'The Wrath Yatra', *Sunday*, 31 January.

Goyal, D.R., 1979, *Rashtriya Swayamsevak Sangh*, New Delhi: Radha Krishna Prakashan.

Islam, Shamsul, 2002, *RSS ki Rashtra-vinash Yatra*, Delhi: Media House.

Jain, Surendra Kumar, 2003, 'Symbol of Shiva', *Pioneer*, 4 May.

Kanungo, Pralay, 2002, *RSS's Tryst with Politics: From Hedgewar to Sudarshan*, New Delhi: Manohar.

Kennedy, Stetson, 1990, *The Clan Unmasked*, Gainesville, Florida: Atlantic University Press. Originally published as *I rode with the Ku Klux Klan*, London, 1954.

PUCL (People's Union for Civil Liberties) Report, 2003, Reproduced in *People's Democracy*, 27 (9).

Reddy, Sheela, 2003, 'The Origin of Trishul', *Outlook*, 27 April.

Shrimali, K.M., 2003, 'Trident Stridency', *Frontline*, 24 May.

Thapar, Romila, 1999, 'Somanatha and Mahmud', *D.D. Kosambi Memorial Lectures*, University of Bombay, reprinted in *Frontline*, 1999.

Thompson, Edward and G.T. Garratt, 1935, *Rise and Fulfilment of British Rule in India*, Allahabad: Central Book Depot, 1976 (rpt.).

POLITICAL ISLAM

Following the studies on Hindutva or political Hinduism we return to Islam, and especially the courses taken by political Islam during the twentieth century: Ranabir Samaddar on Bengal, and Nagendra Rao and Rekha Chowdhary on Jammu & Kashmir.

Asserting an identity, religious or other, is for Ranabir Samaddar a contentious act; and he explores the making of Islamic political consciousness in Bengal—before Independence, during the Pakistan phase, and after the emergence of Bangladesh—through the political thought of several ideologues, especially Maulanas Maniruzzaman Islamabadi, Akram Khan, and Bhasani. Each of them gave his campaigns various, and sometimes varying, thrusts: *Swaraj*, public service, anti-landlordism, cultural democracy, piety, the politics of the Muslim League, and, later, Bengali assertiveness leading to Bangladesh. Each ideologue acted in terms of his understanding of the (changing) setting and his sense of what was then important and necessary. In interpreting what we see as assertions of identities, Samaddar insists, 'The crucial thing is to treat identity as politics and *not* as a representation of something that can be managed by a juri-dical arrangement or by the boutique aesthetics of multiculturalism.'

While Jammu and Kashmir (J&K), like eastern Bengal, had predominantly Muslim peasantries, Nagendra Rao and Rekha Chowdhary explore a very complex terrain in J&K. Major internal processes of social, religious, and economic evolution have been buffetted by powerful external forces pulling in contrary directions. On the one side are successive Governments of India, committed to securing the country's borders whatever the cost in resources or other values. On the other side are relentless tugs at the bonds of Islam, not only from diverse forces in Pakistan, but also from developments in Central and Western Asia. Despite the prolonged stalemate between militancy and State violence, our authors hold that the 'plurality of society, the cultural and living ethos of people, the agrarian character of the economy and the ethnic, tribal and sectarian divisions do not allow any particular fundamentalist ideology to dominate.'

11

Identity Assertions as Contentious Acts

RANABIR SAMADDAR

Are assertive religious identities any different from other assertive identities? In view of the fact that such assertions overwhelm society, blinding us to the background with their shining light, it is understandable to want to know the context in which these assertions take place. One route to such an understanding is obviously a study of the religious and cultural institutions that have fostered assertive religious identities. Besides the sociological, there is a second route, a psychological route that tells us the dark secrets of identity and violence. This second route is a kind of roulette game, where you can start at any point and make your exit at another, a game played between four elements—identity, assertion, violence, and religion. You can also take a quasi-philosophical route of identity-discussion—the third. And, fourth, you can take a political route. That will tell you that the assertion of identity is an act in contentious politics. This route does not deny the insights of the other three, but its strength is in the fact that it helps us to understand the specific moments, the specific clash of interests, and the specific conflicts in which and by which politics takes shape, and assertion of identity—ethnic, religious, national—becomes above all a contentious act. Assertion is a political action, in the sense of contention, challenge, conflict, and at times war. Assertion is an act in a war that is going on most of the time without guns and swords; and such acts come as/at a conjunction of circumstances.

In this brief essay I shall explore the fourth route by trying to understand how contentious politics takes shape, and how the assertion of identities plays a crucial and integral part in it. My recounting of some known and relatively unknown tales of the pursuit of utopia in Bengali Muslim political thinking is the ground on which I want to state my argument about the assertion of identities, in this case religious, as contentious acts. Utopia as we know is the place where the purest of the identity is revealed and realized. But while utopia in political thinking is associated with a state at which you arrive, here I show emergence-as-utopia to be a contentious act, conflict-ridden, something that is in the happening, therefore once again a conjunction. In this connection, it is also necessary to point out that I draw here a distinction between the assertion of identities and assertive identities—that is to say, between an act as product of conjunction of circumstances and an adjective, which does not denote act, but a quality. The latter as I have indicated in the beginning belongs to other routes; it in a way belongs to the enterprise of explaining 'nature', while the former strictly belongs to the world of action, the world of the most radical anti-Platonism. That this is not making too fine a point, but something substantive, I hope, will be clear at the end of this essay.

I

Before we delve into accounts of Bengal, it is in order that we pose at the outset the issue of identity in the context of the juridical-political thinking that dominates this national universe of ours. The fragments that I shall present will then make sense. We shall see that the violent clashes and the contentious politics going on below the civic surface are effaced in an impersonal juridical order that legalizes the nation, presents the assertion of identities as a 'problem' to be tackled by the administration of politics and by methods of the state, and makes the nation-form perennially adaptable to assertive identities growing within and claiming the nation-form for themselves. Contentious politics and juridical serenity are the marks of a nation-world, which provides the context in which assertion of identities takes place.

In *A Biography of the Indian Nation*[1] I tried to raise the question that had animated Rousseau more than two centuries back, *what makes a people a people*? Placing the question in the context of nation-formation, and deliberately removing the question from the ambit of identity-discussion, I had tried to show that nation-form was a product of what Charles Tilly has termed contentious history, and I argued that nation's identity was not immutable, but subject to periodic revisions. Indeed, the fact that the nation-form survives is due more than anything else to its capacity to re-form and re-identify with certain marks, and its adaptability to circumstances that to say the least are marked by intense contentions, struggles, and conflicts. In that book, one of my inquiries was to find out how the national form of rule could co-exist with what we see as the two permanent problems, caste and communal identities. My argument was that the administrative strategies of managing inter-community and inter-caste relations sat well with the nation-form and the imperatives of a nationalizing state, which saw itself as an umpire—the nation as the guardian angel of society.

To give just a few examples of this juridical-administrative order: the Constitution of India provides for special status for certain states such as Jammu & Kashmir, Nagaland, Sikkim, Manipur, Arunachal Pradesh in Articles 370 to 371H. The Constitution also embodies the principle of non-discrimination in Articles 14, 15, 16, 19 and 29. It assures freedom of conscience in Article 25 and freedom to manage religious affairs in Article 26. Article 30 ensures the right of minorities to establish and administer their own educational institutions. Under the special protection clause in Article 371, tribal customary laws, procedures, and land rights are protected. Part XVI ensures special provisions for scheduled castes, scheduled tribes and other backward classes.

There is more to this unequal co-existence of nationalism, republicanism, and autonomy. For example, there is no uniform civil law, on the contrary a variety of personal laws, and linguistic autonomy in some measure. The Indian constitutional and political system has evolved through at least seventy years a range of forms of autonomy, administrative, cultural, religious, fiscal, and legal-juridical. Yet, demands for the right to self-determination ranging from autonomy to secession have arisen frequently, and if some have mellowed, others have persisted and have grown insistent notwithstanding massive state suppression and loss of life. It began with the Muslim demand for self-determination in the pre-independence time and continues in various forms and at various levels today. The constituent states have said that their legislative, administrative, and financial autonomy is inadequate or has diminished. Kashmir says its autonomy is fictive. Insurgents in the north-east have said that grant of statehood is a ploy to subsume them in the Indian polity. Religious minorities say that they are under unprecedented attack from fascist communal forces of the majority religion backed by the state. The scheduled castes and tribes say that their deprivation, poverty, and disempowerment have only grown. The legal-administrative measures for protection of autonomy such as the Minorities Commission, Human Rights Commission, Women's Commission, are severely limited in their powers, and their state counterparts are even more limited in power and function. So are weak and inadequate the commissions in the states for the protection of minority languages and cultures, and the interests of scheduled castes and tribes. In short, we have in the Indian instance the most extraordinary juxtaposition of measures of autonomy as the form of satisfying the assertion of group identities, and a relentless centralization; seen from another angle, the most relentless constitutionalism and the most insistent cry for the self to achieve recognition. It is also a narrative of how and when a group refuses at some historical moment to accept the status of a minority and claims that of a people, a nation.

In short, 'the Indian paradox', to borrow a term from the late Myron Weiner, has been most evident in the tortuous history of legal negotiation with the notion of autonomy on the basis of certain constitutional principles that have not been adequate for that purpose. Marc Galanter had commented thirty years ago,

> The modern legal system has transformed the way in which the interests and concerns of the component groups within Indian society are accommodated and find expression. In traditional India, many groups (castes, guilds, villages, sects) enjoyed a broad sphere of legal autonomy, and where disputes involving them came before public authorities, the latter were obliged to apply the rules of that group. That is, groups generated and carried their own law and enjoyed some assurance that it would be applied to them. In modern India we find a new dispensation: the component groups within society have lost their former autonomy and isolation. Now groups find expression by influence in the political sphere, by putting forth claims in terms of general rules applicable to the whole society. The legal system, then, provides a forum in which the aspirations of India's governing modernized western-educated elite confront the ambitions and concerns of the component groups in Indian society. In this forum the law as a living tradition of normative learning encounters and monitors other traditions of prescriptive learning and normative practice.[2]

We can argue that nationalism and democracy have broadened the public sphere and that the disadvantaged within the group now have access to justice previously denied them. In Galanter's argument only one kind of autonomy looms large. Primarily concerned with battles within 'Hindu' society for legal justice, he neglected the issue of the autonomy of other kinds of groups. But the predicament is clear. Do we have a differential system of justice, or an equal system of public justice with one or the other group dominating the public and turning its norm into its favour? The predicament further is, if we have a differential system, will it be competitive or cooperative? Since a modern constitution is based on the republican system of an equal public sphere that sees autonomy as an exception, how will such a basic law inhere autonomy as an integral principle of democracy? Also important is the question, how will that equality be pursued in a land of hierarchy?

The Indian legal system permits different family laws on religious lines, and even permits different public laws according to different religions on matters like religious trusts; it permits compensatory discrimination in favour of disadvantaged groups, and is sometimes extremely solicitous of religious sensibilities. The broad regulative powers that the state has ('subject to public order, morality and health' vide Article 25.1, and Article 25.2a) are rarely comprehensively enforced. The result is a paradox: we have on the one hand a publicly equal system with broad state powers to regulate practices of separate identity so that they do not go against equality, but we have also differential provisions to help the disadvantaged, and then we also have a public system accessible to a group determined to impose its values in large (or total) measure thereby almost equalizing the public and the group interest. In such a situation, as Galanter shows, the stress on the judiciary is excessive. Political failure is sought to be compensated by judicial activism to the extent where a judge is compelled to define 'who is a Hindu', or the boundaries of faiths.[3] Galanter goes further. In analysing what he termed as 'symbolic activism', he shows that compensatory measures sit unhappily with the broad doctrine of equality as a fundamental right. Should these measures be seen as defining equality, so that, faced with inequalities, the court should now force compensatory measures, or should they be seen as guidelines to the state towards making un-equals equals?[4] The implication is that, if we take the first view, a view that bifurcates Indian society into two broad groups—the scheduled castes and tribes, and other dispossessed minorities on one hand, and the rest on the other, we cannot have a republican constitution promoting public politics. If we take the second view, that is prescriptive policy to the state to provide succour to some disadvantaged groups, we herald an unending series of demands for classification on the basis of which the discrimination will be made. Both possibilities show the dilemmas of a liberal constitution trying to grapple with the issue of inequality and autonomy. This engenders what I term here as 'constitutionalism'; ironically this produces even more inequality, dispossession, and clamour for autonomy.

One can take also the case of caste as an example of the impossible politics of a constitution producing an enduring form of autonomy. Though the constitution did not include a whole series of draft enunciations relating to lower castes and tribes, which had aimed at defining them as minorities, clearly the text as we find it today aims to define the place of caste in Indian life and the role of law regulating it. The constitution takes a dim view of the place of caste in Indian life, is ostensibly not concerned with it, the ties of ascription remain beyond its domain; but it sees itself as the fundamental instrument to ensure that these ascriptions do not lead to hierarchy, inequality, and invidious treatment in public life. Caste, therefore, with its own internal orders and rules promulgating powers and functions, may continue as an autonomous association, but this autonomy is supervised so that it does not spill over into public politics. Doctrine, ritual, and culture all remain outside the juridical bounds unless these affect the constitutional mission of promoting equality. If they do, courts and the law become active. In such a perspective, caste becomes both a religious body in the sense that its own prerogative on such matters as marital rituals, devotional methods, or representation to various bodies is allowed, and a non-religious body in the sense that the constitution tries to detach it from the wider perspective of Hindu society and to determine its character (advantages and disadvantages) among Muslims and Christians as well. But with the institution of caste securely tied to the 'Hindu world', few can opt out of a caste-fold and receive protection. The entire controversy over the right to be converted to another faith shows the limits of constitutional safeguards of the right to choose faith.[5]

In short, the Indian instance shows that modern law is not a self-fulfilling prophecy working towards the satisfaction of the political subject. Faced with asymmetries of power, it can manage at best the co-existence of various normative orders, and at worst it can become a willing accomplice to the manipulation of the public principles by a particular group. It also shows that beyond the given territorial form of autonomy, South Asia by and large has not been able to discover other forms of autonomy that will combine spatial and spiritual dimensions. The resultant situation displays the existence of two political idioms. There is a liberal republican idiom of democracy originating in the constitutional exercises of 1946-9 in India (elsewhere in this region at different times) that tolerates autonomy and dissent to a defined extent. There is also a politics of recognition, fundamentally expressed in territorial form, pre-existing and now reinforced by the same liberal idiom, which threatens to break out and indeed sometimes does break out, of the imposed confines. The result is a renewed phase of constitutional frenzy. These two are the quarrelsome duo, one not being quite able to displace the other. Together they have produced the uneasy reality of accommodation, which is not tolerance, but an accommodation of competing realities until one succeeds in pushing the other out of existence.

We need to remember that the demands for self-determination, nation-formation, and partition have been always closely interconnected. Mohammed Ali Jinnah, invoking the principle of self-determination and claiming for the Muslims the right to self-determination, commented in his presidential address to the Muslim League in Lahore in 1940,

> Babu Rajendra Prasad . . . only a few days ago said, 'Oh, what more do the Musalmans want?' I will read you his words. Referring to the minority question, he says: 'If British would concede our right of self-determination surely all these differences should disappear.' How will our differences disappear?
>
> . . . The word 'nationalist' has now become the play of conjurers in politics.
>
> . . . The problem of India is not of an inter-communal but manifestly of an international character, and must be treated as such. So long as this basic and fundamental truth is not realized, any constitution that may be built will result in disaster and will prove harmful not only to the Musalmans, but also to the British and Hindus. . . .
>
> Musalmans are not a minority. . . . Musalmans are a nation according to any definition of a nation, and they must have their homelands, their territory and their State.[6]

In such a historical situation the element of conflict is inherent. On one hand we witness a sort of return to the age of natural rights, on the other hand there is a reinforcement of authority, for in the case of a right not defined, it is always best to leave it to the authority to define, sanctify, authorise, institutionalize and execute the right. As we know natural rights and natural law co-existed with absolutism—the contentious milieu in which the nation-identity flourished. Identities became actors in politics in that way. More important, they appeared in politics as products of conjuncture of contending forces and circumstances that mark the national and republican form of rule.

After all we know that the minority problematic arose only in the context of the modern nation state that survives on the unspoken tenets of what is today called 'majoritarianism'—a sort of fictive ethnic core that would form the essence of national identity, a process that also witnessed the marginalization of other elements and identities. Similarly all other individual and group rights, that define identity and site identity in very particular ways, were born of two simultaneous trends—one, towards constitutionalism, and the other, that which provided the basis of constitutionalism, namely natural rights and natural justice. Constitutionalism grew in the contentious milieu of contending rights, identities, and politics. One need only examine the wealth of material marshalled by Charles Tilly to see how the rights, contentions, identities, and laws grew together, and marked the career of the modern nation since the demise of the absolutist rule that, ironically, had given the state in country after country a definite identity in the first place.

My tales here go one century back, though in order to understand what happened to them we shall have to return and re-situate ourselves in our political-juridical time that this section has very briefly described—after we have recounted the past tales of utopia.

II

Writing on the political history of Muslim Bengal, subsequently Bangladesh, I have described in some detail the chronicles of morality in the making of the public. Morality is the road to utopia, and as we know, the story of a nation is not only the story of many modernities, but many utopias too.[7]

In Muslim Bengal the Anjuman movement at the start of the last century, primarily a pedagogic enterprise, owed above all to the efforts of Maulana Maniruzzaman Islamabadi, a preacher, organizer, and a publicist. He wrote profusely in Bengali on Islam in India, Islam's contribution to the development of the sciences, the message of freedom in the Koran, and on social reforms. His chronicles on the conditions of peasantry, published in the pages of two journals, *al-Islam* and *Mihir O Sudhakar*, helped establish his status as a leader of the peasantry. Born in Chittagong in 1875, Islamabadi's many years of wandering took him to Rangpur, Rangoon, Lahore, and parts of Orissa and Assam. His trail led him also to Kumedpur and Calcutta. He was a *maulavi*, a *moktar*, and sometimes an *imam*. He joined *madrasas* to teach there, founded new ones, gave *azans*, and began giving thought to the improvement of the quality of *madrasa* education. In Rangpur he received the *Wakil* (journal) from Lahore, and *Mihir O Sudhakar* (journal) from Calcutta. Till then well versed in Persian, Arabic and Urdu, his grasp of the Bengali language soon became thorough. As his biographer Shamsuzzaman Khan notes, Islamabadi could now discuss 'the lives of Sayed Ahmad Khan, Imam Gazzali, Mazzini, Jamaluddin al Afghani, Saiyad Ahmed Beralbhih, and Maulana Ismail Sahid'. He lectured differently from others. 'Politics, history, religion, ethics, geography mixed easily in (his) sermons. People would be happy at such lectures. They would donate money heartily' (*Maniruzzaman Islamabadi, 1875-1950*, Dhaka, 1988, pp. 18-19). With Ismail Hossain Shiraji and Muhammad Shahidullah, both of whom were to become noted figures in shaping Bengali Muslim cultural identity, Islamabadi founded the Bangiya Musalman Sahitya Samity (later on Bangiya Musalman Sahitya Parishad) in 1911. He was writing on issues such as the Hindu-Muslim problem, discrimination against Muslims, the quality of education, colonialism, Islam, the destiny of Islamic civilisation, the nature of imperial power particularly in Turkey, and the state of Bengali language.

He collaborated with Maulana Akram Khan and co-edited *al-Islam*. His campaign for the Hanafi sect created much bitterness. He himself was to later call this phase as one of 'idiocy and ignorance' (*aiyame jahaliat*). In any case he was now ready for politics—the politics of *Khilafat*, *Swaraj* (self-rule) and Islamic Mission (a missionary organization), the politics of non-communalism and tolerance, of piety, of independence and mass-activism. Both Islamabadi and Shiraji were pracharaks (itinerant campaigners). Shiraji had used the term and had defined the aims of a pracharak's life: to explain the principles of religion and to counter opposing arguments, to glorify the history of the Muslims, to invoke the past, and 'to think of the present'. They started campaigning on the falling price of jute and the depressed condition of the Muslim peasantry, and the havoc caused to the *ryots* (cultivating peasants) in Midnapore by Watson & Co. They propagated in their speeches the need for the unity of the Hanafis and the Muhammadis. Islamabadi proposed the establishment of an Arabic university for the education of Muslims now sunk in ignorance. To him, the nation, that is Muslim Bangla, was to be redeemed and *dharma* (Islamabadi used the word again and again) was the primary path.

Islamabadi soon joined the Bangiya Krishak Praja Dal and in 1937 was elected from Chittagong to the Bengal Legislative Assembly. But above all, his activities in setting up the Anjuman-e-Olema-e-Bangla had the greatest significance in the evolution of a Muslim nationalist leadership in Bengal. The Anjuman movement in Bengal had begun towards the close of the nineteenth century. The influence of Wahhabi ideology was on decline, even though as Abul Mansur Ahmed's autobiography, *Atmakatha*, reminiscing on his childhood in Mymensing testifies, many participants in the Wahhabi campaign were still alive in the villages of Bengal. Qazi Abdul Wadud, one of the prominent members of Shikha (a new enlightened group of Muslim intellectuals of Bengal), admitted that pan-Islamism was not a major influence in the Anjuman movement, and that it was more a creation of the newly-educated middle class Muslims emerging from the small towns and villages of Bengal. The National Mohammedan Association had become defunct and the new middle class Muslim intellectuals were more sympathetic to the problems and attitudes of peasant and semi-proletarian Muslims. Their motto, as Islamabadi often put it, was to 'awaken society from the lowest strata'. The Muslim League was elitist and the patriotic *ulama* had little in common with either what Amir Ali had done in Calcutta or Nawab Salimullah had done in Dhaka. Anisuzzaman has commented in his introduction to the anthology of Muslim periodicals *Muslim Bangler Samayikpatra* (1969), that the Anjuman movement sometimes echoed *tariq-i-muhammadia,* sometimes Sayed Ahmad Khan and Amir Ali (Anisuzzaman, ed., *Muslim Bangler Samayikpatra, 1831-1930* (Dhaka, 1969). However, from the point of the growth of nationalism, the Anjuman was unique in significance. The goal of the Anjumans was reform: of education, of rites and customs, but most importantly, that of the condition of the peasantry. Anjumans were being formed at the *thana* level also. Islamabadi became involved.

Maniruzzaman Islamabadi's activities in Rangpur brought him close to the Anjuman spirit. Himself a renowned cleric, he had now also Maulana Akram Khan as his colleague in the initiative. He knew Maulana Phulwari, Maulana Qadir Baksh, Munshi Meherullah and others who were regular visitors to the *alem-sammelani* or meetings of the *ulama*. In 1913, the Anjuman-e-Olema (to become famous later on as Anjuman-e-Olema-e-Bangla) was formed in Baniapara of Bagura and in 1919 the *alem samiti* was formed. *al-Islam* was the organ of the Anjuman. This was a different journey from the Wahhabi and other revivalist paths. Resisting communalism, organizing relief work among the flood affected and other distressed people, pleading the cause of the tenants, spreading Bengali language among the *ulama*, advocating the need to learn from the modern saga of the entrepreneur, bringing out newspapers and periodicals as organs, formed an agenda of a genre that was different from the call to return to the 'original' ('the golden age', 'the past')—the 'original purity' of Islam. These activities led the Anjuman to the Jamait-e-olema-e-Hind. The literary conference of the Jamait-e-ulema-e-Hind in Bengal was held in Chittagong in 1930. Maulana Maniruzzaman presided over the conference. The praja movement drew strength from the nationalist *ulama*, and the leader who represented this phenomenon most authentically was Islamabadi.

At the core of this Muslim nationalist identity there were ideas of anti-landlordism, cultural democracy, and a moral community of pious preachers invigorating the people with healthy thoughts, ideas, and actions, in short the ideal of a community of the *alem*. Characteristic of this ideal was the combination of utopia and modernity—the link-up of three elements—agrarian democracy, divinity realised through spiritual minds and acts, and new ideas about the claims of a community, which extended beyond the constitutional chamber politics typical of the comprador class of the colonial age. His impassioned submission to the *ulama* was that the Muslim League had not cared for the peasantry, had not fought against the landlords, and what was most repugnant, it had no religiosity, no piety, the Muslim League people were not true Muslims. The invocation of the democratic virtue of a 'true Muslim' was the critical element in his activism in the Anjuman movement. The Anjuman movement thrived heartily for twenty years more. Nonetheless it was to be soon caught in the paradox of nationalism. After all the Anjuman-e-Olema-e-Bangla or the Jamait-e-ulema-e-Hind could not be a modern political party. Too innocent of the reality marked by the dissociation of modernity and democracy, the movement lost its independent space by the 1930s, and most of its cadres soon merged with the Muslim League, a development symbolized by none else than Akram Khan. Islamabadi's became a lonely voice increasingly shrill and desperate.

If Maulana Maniruzzaman Islamabadi was a preacher who wanted to create a new modern identity of the Bengal Muslims by purifying the modern through invoking morality again and again, his colleague, Maulana Akram Khan, may be said to have created a 'politics of identity' by creating a public-political sphere of Muslim Bengal through a strategy of modernizing the utopia. As a publicist Akram Khan reached unprecedented heights in the public milieu of colonial Bengal.

It began in the form of writing in a magazine called *Ahl-e-Hadis.* For some years Akram Khan worked in several newspapers and journals in editorial and other capacities, until 1910 when he published his own newspaper, the *Saptahik Mohammadi.* Then other publications too commenced under his guidance like the *Dainik Jamana* (1920), *Saptahik O Dainik Sebak* (1921), *Dainik Mohammadi* (1922), *Masik Mohammadi* (1927), *Dainik Azad* (1936) and *Saptahik Comrade* (1946). He was also the first editor of *al-Islam*, the organ of the Anjuman-e-Olama-e-Bangla. Indeed he was soon recognized as the father of Bengali Muslim journalism. In 1905 he associated with the Congress and was involved in protest against the partition of Bengal. After the revocation of the partition in 1911 he gradually associated himself with Muslim politics and particularly the Muslim League and till 1928 was one of the important leaders of both Congress and the League, as well as a crucial supporter of the Bengal Pact initiated by C.R. Das between Hindu (in this case represented by the Congress) and Muslim leaders to ensure political unity and communal amity. But by 1928, fed up with the attitude of the Hindu leaders of the Congress who were determined to undo the Pact (revoked in 1926), he severed his connection with the Congress. In 1936 as the most important leader of the League in Bengal, Akram Khan set out to reorganize the League there. As the president of the Bengal Muslim League from 1941 to 1947, he became the most determined and consistent advocate of Pakistan and even after Partition remained a loyal champion of the Muslim League. Until 1962 he was connected with politics and journalism, apparently untouched by the surge of Bengali identity and the rise of Awami (popular) politics in East Pakistan. He died in 1968, after one hundred years of an active and contradictory life.

Akram Khan has been often compared to Jinnah for his unflinching commitment to the idea of Pakistan. Like Jinnah he was a believer in composite nationalism in his early phase. Like Jinnah, it is said that he was not a practising believer. In Anjuman-e-Olama-e-Bangla he translated some *surahs* into Bengali. In the presidential address to the third conference of the Bangiya Musalman Sahitya Parishad in 1919 he referred to the complexities in the Muslim mind regarding the question of language:

> There are many strange questions in this world. 'What is the mother tongue of the Bengali Muslims, Urdu or Bengali?', is the strangest of them. It is like asking whether coconut should grow on a coconut tree . . . if somebody approaches us with that query we shall have to raise money to send that person to Behrampur . . . Bengali has to be enriched with Arabic and Persian words . . . in the current style of written Bengali the idolatry of the Hindus is so apparent and the Musalman loses his way in this. First we need publication of our religious texts and our national history in Bengali. The alem should learn Bengali. It is his holy task to serve the mother tongue. Muslims have their distinct notion of nation or jati. This is the particular feature of Muslim nationalism and the amulet of the Muslim nation. . . . Muslim nationalism is completely religious. . . . to its great peril the Muslims can forget that their national language is Arabic. . . . Look what Persia did to Arabic . . . Urdu is neither our mother tongue nor our national tongue. However, for the protection and nourishment of Muslim nationalism we need Urdu. (Anisuzzaman, ed., *Muslim Bangler Samayikpatra, 1831-1930*, Dhaka, 1969, Introduction)

In engaging with modernity and designing a community's or a nation's own sense of the modern, he wrote in *Masik Mohammadi*,

> There is now a novel awakening in the many layers of Muslim Bengal with the arrival of different thoughts and influenced by the surroundings. On one side the hold of the old, on the other the lure of the modern. . . . The outlook of the first group is getting narrower increasingly, though it is not extinct. . . . And here on the other side though there is no dearth of light around the young group enchanted with modernity, they are totally blind today regarding Islam. . . . We have to tell the first group, 'open the door', and the second group, 'open your eyes!' (*Samayikpatra*, p. 504)

The venture of defining the Muslim nation in Bengal on the basis of a nationalist alliance of Hindus and Muslims that had consumed the preceding twenty-six years of his life failed finally in 1929. Akram

Khan could not but feel betrayed. He severed all his connections with the Congress and nationalist politics based on communal unity. The leader, who had been opposed by the clergy, particularly by the ulama of the *Ahl-e-Hadis* in the 1920s, as un-Islamic, now became the pillar of the political aspirations of the clergy.

The rest of his life is well known. Akram Khan's writings became increasingly concerned with the Muslim cause and not the cause of Muslim Bengal. He became in due course the president of the Muslim League in Bengal. He had arrived at the natural(ized) idea of Pakistan. The journey of the intellectual had come to an ironic end. After Independence he remained the League president in East Pakistan. Apart from supporting the language cause he showed no sympathy for the movement for autonomy. Awami politics was anathema to him. Even army rule was welcome. He extended support to Ayub Khan. The idea of Pakistan as the natural homeland of the Muslims of the subcontinent was not utopic, it had been achieved. Islam as the religion of the intellect (as opposed to the religion of the plough or the bazaar) had been vindicated. By primarily intellectual means Maulana Akram Khan had created a public, roused his followers, erected the intellectual framework of a nation, and almost 'conjured up a nation', the Muslim Bengal. He had begun his journey with a policy of alliance between Muslim Bengal and Hindu Bengal. He had then given shape to the idea of Pakistan as the natural habitat of this nation. And when linguistic nationalism was breaking this habitat, he was at a loss to understand how any such consideration like a claim on the basis of a language could disturb the natural journey of the Muslims on earth. Being a consistent Muslim meant to Akram Khan believing in the idea of Pakistan.

In that garden of identity, however, there was a snake. If Islam allowed in place of universal brotherhood a nation for the Muslims (Pakistan), where was the place of democracy in that argument? Akram Khan had achieved a solution in his own mind. And it was final. In the permanently unstable world of nationalist solutions, his intellect and austere style marked with certitude had proved unequal to the demands of the nationalist public of Muslim Bengal, a public that he had helped to create. His biography of Prophet Muhammad was an event in Bengal's intellectual history. Such intellectual history is in any case a battleground of legitimation or contestation. But ironically that which legitimates also contests. Akram Khan's *Mostafacharit,* a narration of Muhammad's life as well as an exercise in argumentation and refutation, was a demonstration of his 'belief in rationality'. It was the narration of a life that had to be rescued from myths as also neglect by the Muslims. It was indeed an elaboration of the supreme statement of Akram Khan that to be a believer was to be a rationalist also. Akram Khan had thought that with his intellectual writings on Islam, the Prophet, and on the political culture of the Bengali Muslims, he was achieving a settled disposition of the nation. But little did he realise that the identity of a nationalist public was a self-conscious projection, and involved the invocation of memory in various forms and stages and therefore could never be settled.

The trajectory of the anjuman movement in Bengal and the political careers of two of its prominent leaders point towards how utopia is a dream that always combines with reality, is fraught with conflicts and responses with contradictory pulls, and operates in the form of situations, ideologies, and institutions that are instrumental in 'creating' the public(s) of the nation. They are utopias because they can be dreamt in these sites (or, rather, in any of them) because utopia is never antithetical to 'heterotopia', but the 'heterotopic' character of public institutions has allowed utopias to flourish.[8]

Nothing illustrates this more than the way the Muslim League disintegrated in East Pakistan. In the conflictive politics of assertion, Maniruzzaman Islamabadi could have smiled in satisfaction, were he alive in 1949, to see how the Muslim Awami League was born to give the signal that utopia and modernity were combining again in the political space of Muslim Bengal. Utopia in any kind of nationalist thought, we must remember, is a complex thing, and unfortunately this has remained neglected in readings of Bengali Islamic political thought. In that thought, moral judgement was always crucial. It involved themes of divinity, critiques of present civil society and a demand that an ethical politics be sovereign—a form, it recognized, present only in the kingdom of the Almighty. Thus political thought dealt with the contemporaneity of the Koran, the injustices on believers in the reign of the colonial masters and their supporters—mostly 'the Hindus', and all that was relevant in explicating the ethical imperative of a homeland.

Utopia has a recursive legacy. Thinkers and leaders go back to the 'ideal' again and again. A thinker like Akram Khan had to rationalize the utopia, whereas another leader of Muslim Bengal,

Maulana Bhasani of whom we shall speak in a moment, found it self-evident. One relied on written words, the other on the spoken; one relied on organization, the other on instinct; one on logic, the other on proselytising and evangelical campaigns. Yet both were tied to the anchor of utopia. In creating the nationalist public, political ideas verged on being absolutely moral-utopian.

It has been pointed out that utopia makes politics, that is, noble politics, self-evident. In other words, contrary to the common idea, politics is not the field where power is contested and arrived at; politics presupposes the power of which it is only a mode. And this power is, above all, justice, and it flows from the capacity to do justice. Power, then, takes the form of justice—justice for the believers, for the common man, for the oppressed, justice against *jalims* (wrong-doers, evil people).

Thus, in Bengali Muslim political history, and more significantly, in its politico-religious discourse, utopia was invoked again and again (from mid-nineteenth-century Titu Meer's to mid-twentieth-century Maulana Bhasani's): power was presented as a capacity to do noble things and to punish evil acts and thoughts. Consequently, justice and power informed the core of a utopian vision of a Muslim land. In sermons to the faithful, the utopian vision had to be shared; the politico-religious discourse had to be congregational and open.

If the political had to be justified by the divine, the political emanated from the divine also. We must appreciate the break, as much as we appreciate the continuity. From 1949, the year of the birth of the Muslim Awami League, the politics of Muslim Bengal attained a dream-like quality. The opposition became the mainstream by harping on the self-evident, on the just, on the inevitable. Political contestation was successfully grounded in total moralism. Thus the national awakening in 1952 did not have to be 'secular'; it did not have to disconnect itself from a Muslim identity. The past of the Pakistan (movement) was to be rescued from the evil usurpers. If the Medinian golden age was unattainable fully, it was nonetheless there, as the standard, as the just, as the inspiration to overcome the dark period.

But here was the 'miracle of the modern'. For, it may be asked, if the utopian inspiration was the force behind such a dramatic change in leadership in Muslim Bengal in 1949-52, why did such inspiration not follow the celebrated path of utopia, that of the Wahhabis? Or, as was being enunciated at that time, the path of Maulana Maududi?

The creation of Pakistan had occasioned theological reflections on state, religion, polity, and moral human existence. It is important to note that Maulana Bhasani's quest in this situation bore little resemblance to that of Maududi. In Bengal the pursuit of the ideal took the modern form of open mass politics, democratic activities and anti-fundamentalism, so that many commentators have been deceived into typifying this period as one of the growth of 'secular consciousness'. It is difficult to go into the details of that discussion now, but we may note that the search for the pure, the just, the Medinian, and the divine never strayed from the path of toleration. Bengal, at once a colonized and plural land, produced as a resolution of the tormenting conflicts and contradictions its own utopia, which bore little resemblance with the principles of the Wahabite polity (though admittedly Wahhabi ideology had had its impact on rural Bengal in the nineteenth century and contributed to the evolution of the form of the pracharak so crucial in the politics of Muslim Bengal). For this, Abul Mansur Ahmed's description of his family memory and his childhood is crucial for any scholar of Muslim Bengali activism; we have only to read the available autobiographies such as his *Atmakatha* (Dhaka, 1978) to get a glimpse of that world.

The emphasis on the application of Islamic law, so characteristic of Wahhabis, was singularly absent in the denunciation of contemporary rule by the 'new' leaders. They certainly condemned the corruption of the state leaders. But the ideal of a pure life of the divine was irrelevant to them. Clerics were crucial for the 'new awakening', but as pracharaks, not as clerics. In this utopia the script (the scripture) was not the absolute; the spoken, the entire language, was the principal element. Until Akram Khan, the political was defined with the aid of canonical texts. But in the dense atmosphere marked by Partition, agrarian unrest, national awakening over the language issue, and the sudden loss of legitimacy of the ruling party, canonical texts lost their primacy to a significant extent. The result was Bengal's 'own utopia'. The inequities of the exterior were to be redressed not through a redefining of the interior. Redefining the exterior itself in the light of the 'natural' soul of Bengal was the way (it is remarkable that the language demand was often raised as the 'natural right' of a Bengali, the fight against the government was 'natural' for a populace which had fought for its homeland, Pakistan, and that the demand against the zaminders (landlords) was a 'natural' one of the peasants). Thus conceiving a new nationalist identity was contentious, marked by the moral and the ethical—the reinforcing of utopia as an inspiration for public politics. This was in effect an interrogation by the plebeian public of the aspirations of the ruling Muslim bourgeois political class. In this utopia, there was also a conflation of power and morality, of language and the entire range of civic culture, of democracy and the ideal of Pakistan; in short the interpreted past and the desirable future. And as every utopia suffers because the conflation of the two registers becomes impossible, this one too was to meet its nemesis.

The decline of Bhasani style politics in Bangladesh was the most marked instance of this. After the emergence of the comprador, crony-capitalist class as the ruler of the new nation, as he realized that his version of radical *darbesh* (the wandering mystic) style politics had lost out, and he was nearing the end of his life, he would ruefully remark that he was alone in his dreams. The utopian, evangelical, *darbesh* style of politics was not shared by others; this was a style with which the organized leftist peasant politics of nationalism could not co-habit comfortably for long. The passing of utopia was in any case marked in the politics of the time. In his last year the Army seized power and a helpless and desperate Bhasani could only watch and place his faith in its capacity to deliver. The Awami League era had ended within four years after it began, in ignominy and disaster. Above all, the events of 1971 had shown how ineffective 'pious opposition' was in the time of tanks, cannons, mortars, foreign help, intervention, and the Seventh Fleet.

To Bhasani, however, a combination of Islam, piety, Muslim nationalism, and pride in being a Bengali had not been unnatural. In his youth he had come under the influence of the writings of Saiyad Nasiruddin Bogdadi, Maniruzzaman Islamabadi, and Ismail Hussain Shiraji with whom he had campaigned jointly in North Bengal. His spiritual quest had taken him from Assam to Deoband seminary. He joined the Anjuman-e-ulema in 1915 in the Calcutta session, met Akram Khan and took *al-Islam* to Assam. He was now to educate and train the ulama. In 1915 he started relief-work among famine, flood and cyclone victims, this time in Pabna. This would become a life long vocation and symbolize, more than any other act, his politics amongst the peasants of Bengal. He became the president of the Assam Congress in 1916 and wandered in those years from one *charland* to another. Peasants and *murids*, religious disciples, addressed him as *huzur*. His biographer tells us the story of the formation of the Banga-Assam Praja Samity and the Banga-Assam Praja Sammelan in Phulchuri in 1929, both supported by the communists and leftists, and the envy that all this roused among the mullahs, and maulavis. The events of 1930 in Chittagong occasioned another outburst of activity. He was now founding schools in places like Shalmara in opposition to the zamindars, mobilizing peasants against the Gauripur landlord and the landlord of Santosh, and was 'enchanting the audience with magic oratory and a bull-dog voice'. In 1937 he had formed the Assam Chashi-Majur Samity (Assam Association for Peasants and Workers) and started agitation against the coolie line system. The same year he was elected from south Dhubri to the Assam Legislative Assembly and was now a recognized political leader besides being an organizer, agitator, *pir*, and *maulana*.

Rest of that political history is well known. The radical Left tried to infuse social radicalism into his politics of nationalist-religious identity, a desirable but often an illusory expectation. The moment Mujib came out of jail in 1969, the Bhasani-led National Awami Party's eleven-point charter lost its relevance. Federal autonomy, already a subterfuge for Bengali nationalism, became the main issue. Mujib became the first unquestioned supreme leader of the nationalist public. From an activist of a nationalist party and subsequently a nationalist leader, he had become within twenty-two years the chief tribune of Muslim Bengal and of the opposition to the reality and the idea of Pakistan. In this congealed form where all other elements of opposition politics had been pushed to the margin, no one had anything else to say or offer—not, particularly, Maulana Bhasani, burdened with a half-century long association with the ideology of 'pious opposition'. From then on, the personal story of Bhasani, now busy invoking moral politics, is inalienable from what we may call the sociology of mass upsurge.

The Left now found him inadequate, the Right found him unnecessary. His Islamic moralism was now arcane, possibly more suitable to the conditions of the early part of the century. One can read his speeches and short testaments after 1970—for example, *Amar Parikalpanaye Islami Viswavidyalaya* (1970), *Keno Islami Viswavidyalaya* (1971), *Islami Viswavidyalayer Rup O Katha* (1974), *Palanbad—Ki O Keno* (1973), *Rabubiyater Bhumika* (1974), and his last speech to the conference of the Khuda-i-Khidmatgar in Santosh in 1976, three days before his death on 17 November. After 1971 he had become a liability to the politics of the land. His 'return to Islam' in this period, if one can see this in his turning away from organized party politics to moral activism, was unsung. The public found his programme of achieving a fusion of religious moralism, democracy and the politics of nationalism too ambiguous a legacy to hold on to. Yet, one can surely say that, with increasing bitterness about the reality of the nationalist state that emerged through 1971—its corruption, and the ruthless private use of public power and wealth—the *darbesh* style politics would not be the only thing of memory for the public to preserve; the other passion in Bhasani's life, character building, would also be an equally abiding legacy. Pedagogy after all has always been one of the necessary conditions for a utopian project.

If these fragments have any lesson for us, it is this: assertion of identity will always remain an ambiguous venture. One can of course say that only by retaining ambiguities within assertions strategically does a nation come of age. Thus no wonder while nations want stable citizenry, large bodies of population can come to salute more than one national flag in their lifetime.[9]

III

Today when we witness paroxysms of terrorism, immigrants, minorities, and non-state people characteristically find themselves beyond the pale of the law. They are denizens of a shadowy world that inspires fear; and democracy, in order to secure itself, must draw for them elaborate and stringent restrictions and controls. Drawbridges are being pulled up; and a new type of racism, based on fictive cultural identities bordering on almost biological differences, marks the strangers out. This is a milieu in which religious identities assume assertive forms. Yet, as the foregoing tales suggest, these assertions exhibit ambiguities. If this was true when the Muslim public sphere was appearing in Bengal a hundred and fifty years ago, the ambiguity is equally evident in our time, when as I show in detail in *The Marginal Nation*, thousands and thousands of Muslim illegal immigrants from Bangladesh taking shelter on this side of the border flock to mosques, yet their main cry is not to evoke a new brotherhood of the believers, but to acquire citizenship that can entitle them to life-saving means in a world where states have less and less of the means and the will to care for them. New mosques, new charities, new networks, new dispensations, and new orders appear—yet in this growth of a huge amorphous mass of shadowy denizens, religious identity is a contingent product, being constantly predicated by the politics of democratic citizenship, that is, daily negotiations and transactions over rights and means.

Identities in this sense are contentious acts. Because they are so, even when they appear solid and autonomous, problems grip identity and the politics of identity from unexpected quarters. These problems can be immediately traced, as I indicated in the fragments narrated above, to their inherent ambiguous 'nature' which is due to the paradox of the particular nature of an identity and that identity's universal claim. Each identity in this world of contentious politics is 'micro-politics'; that is to say, it is ambiguous in relation to the majority-identity, always surviving in face of a majoritarian state by becoming 'minoritarian' by which I mean constituting itself into a minority, re-territorializing itself in face of a state, the majority, and the centralizing power bent upon erasing the territories of all others.[10] Identity assertion is the act of constituting a subject in contentious politics, 'which takes as its object the very violence of identities'.[11] Indeed, one can say, politics is taken to its extreme by the logic of identities, which cannot identify themselves without causing violence. The mission of identity is fulfilled only in a war of annihilation that ironically makes the politics of identity sit on its head, by ending at least one identity.

To be true, this violence as we know it can take extreme forms of cruelty, making people 'disposable'. The word 'neo-fascism' can barely describe the phenomenon, because in politics this survives only as epiphenomenon. Since identities as political subjects are in fact non-realizable, responsible politics today can only strive for historical conditions where such ultra-violence can be dispelled. On the other hand, under conditions of extreme violence, where no macro-politics can make a significant dent on the milieu, micro-politics covers the process of resistance at every level, rather than of identity, which 'is the product of an invariably uneven, unfinished process, of hazardous constructions requiring greater or lesser symbolic guarantees'.[12] Study of identification, which means a study of a process, enjoins us to take identities to be always over-determined, which means taking identities as performing several functions at the same time; certain identities do at times float freely between all roles and places—like the market of the global world.

Strangely, then, assertive and asserted identities are also floating, co-existing with many situations, just as the liberal identity at certain times in history co-habited, as it does today, with absolutism, royalty, bedchambers of queens, parlours of princes, and the patronage of the unsavoury dictators,[13] or as the modern assertive Hindu and Islamic identities co-habit with strange companions.

Seen another way, there are also the marginal masses, particularly youth who seek identification with values and roles that form fields of contention, spaces for opposing social forces. In order to understand the faultlines that characterize the theory of identity, we must go back to histories—past and current—of the kind I have considered in this essay. We have to study very closely not only the processes in which identifities arise and conflicts occur, but also the forms of micro-politics that seek to regulate the violence of identification through strategies of 'civility', democracy, and accommodation. This I repeat is not a theoretical choice, but a choice emerging out of a conjuncture; it is a question of the art of politics, which means contingencies, contentions, and roles dictating those strategies. The crucial thing is to treat identity as politics and *not* as a representation of something that can be managed by a juridical arrangement or by the boutique aesthetics of multiculturalism.

The story of how identities are fixed by juridical arrangements, or how juridical serenity denies the existence of the violence of identities, admittedly does not sit well with the other story, the other half of the matter of identity: namely its production as a result of contentious politics. But that is what the political world is, where identity, contentious politics, and juridical order are the constitutive elements.

NOTES

1. New Delhi: Sage, 2001.
2. Marc Galanter, 'Hinduism, Secularism, and the Indian Judiciary' *Philosophy East and West*, 21 (4), October 1971, reprinted in Marc Galanter, *Law and Society in Modern India*, New Delhi: Oxford University Press, 1997, pp. 237-8.
3. Galanter examines in this context a case (1966) that involved the Swaminarayana Sect and went to the highest court of the land where eminent jurists such as Gajendragadkar, Wanchoo, Hidayatullah had to decide who was a Hindu, and the various sects traditionally within the Hindu fold could opt out and claim the rights of minorities. Ibid., pp. 237-56.

4. R. Dhavan, R. Sudarshan, and S. Khurshid (eds.), *Judges and the Judicial Power—Essays in Honour of Justice Krishna Iyer*, Bombay: Oxford University Press, 1985.
5. On the legal complexities arising out of the position that caste occupies in public life, see, D.E. Smith (ed.), *South Asian Politics and Religion*, Princeton, N.J.: Princeton University Press, 1966; Marc Galanter, 'Law and Caste in Modern India', *Asian Survey*, 3, 1963, pp. 544-59; F.G. Bailey, *Caste and the Economic Frontier*, Manchester: Manchester University Press, 1957.
6. Reprinted in Mushirul Hasan (ed.), *India's Partition—Process, Strategy and Mobilization*, New Delhi: Oxford University Press, 1993, pp. 44-5.
7. *Paradoxes of the Nationalist Time*, Dhaka: University Press, 2002, Chap. 2.
8. The notion of 'heterotopia' made famous by Michel Foucault contains many meanings, many uses, and many transformations. The distinction with 'utopia' is evident as behind utopia there is a sense of one meaning, one vision, and one dream—a singularity that would mark the new city. Heterotopia indicates a new architecture, and a new ethos of the place. For this and many other meanings, see Michel Foucault, 'Different Spaces', trans. Robert Hurley in James Faubion (ed.), *Michel Foucault—Essential Works*, vol. 2, London: Allen Lane, 1994.

   While Foucault makes a distinction, I suggest a connection between utopia and heterotopia.
9. One can read in this context the fascinating autobiography of one of the most famous cultural chroniclers of Bengal Muslim mind, Anisuzzaman, who writes of a family, a person, and a people saluting three national flags in one life. Anisuzzaman, *Kal Nirobodhi*, Dhaka: Sahityaprakash, 2003.
10. I have drawn insights from Gilles Deleuze and Felix Guattari, *A Thousand Plateaus—Capitalism and Schizophrenia*, trans. Brian Massumi, London: Athlone Press, 1988.
11. Etienne Balibar, *Politics and the Other Scene*, trans. Christine Jones, James Swenson, and Chris Turner, London: Verso, 2002, p. 23.
12. Ibid., pp. 27-8.
13. Eric Hobsbawm alludes to this in *The Age of Revolution—1789-1848*, New Delhi: Viking, 1995, p. 3.

12

The Evolution of Political Islam in Jammu and Kashmir

V. NAGENDRA RAO AND REKHA CHOWDHARY

Interpretations of contemporary Islamic movements follow two dominant though opposite trends. In one, the rise of Islamic movements is attributed to the character and nature of Islam, treating it as ahistorical, irrational and opposed to modernity or the modernization process. In this kind of essentialist argument Islam is portrayed as a universal civilization or culture or community, and Muslim identity is reduced to a single religious construct, ignoring all cultural and political ones. In contrast, the second trend locates the emergence of political Islam in the contemporary social, political, and economic situation. In this view, the resurgence of religion in politics is a result of the interplay of social forces released by the modernization process. Assenting with the second view, this paper situates political Islam in Jammu and Kashmir in contemporary conditions, both internal and external, and traces its emergence in the modernization process.

This paper deals first with Kashmir's transition to Islam,[1] then with the emergence of political Islam in first half of twentieth century, and moves on to the rise of political Islam since the mid-twentieth century.

THE CONVERSION PROCESS

Kashmir's transition to Islam replicated, more or less, the process of conversion in its surrounding regions in the Indian subcontinent, in Central Asia and in Iran. The formation of Muslim Sultanates and the missionary work of Islamic Sufi saints played a major role in this process. However, the process of conversion in Kashmir also had its specifics.

There is general agreement among historians about the role of Sufism in the transition of Kashmir to Islam. As Prem Nath Bazaz notes, barring a few who came from outside as invaders or as adventurers, most Kashmiri Muslims are indigenous converts (Bazaz 2002: 248). Kashmir's proximity with Central Asia enabled many Sufi saints—from Sayyid Sharafuddin to Sayyid Husain Simnani and Mir Sayyid Ali Hamdani—to come and preach here frequently. In Hewitt's view, 'within Kashmir (as throughout South Asia as a whole) voluntary religious conversions have taken place because of shared culture, even if they have acted in the long term to divide that culture along confessional lines' (Hewitt 2003: 74).

One can point to the cultural specificity of Kashmiri Islam, especially the influences of mysticism, Islamic Sufism, and the Hindu Rishi tradition. Sheikh Nur-ud-Din, known as Nund Rishi, had followed an indigenous order of Sufism—the Rishi order—which combined Hindu asceticism and traditional Sufism. These rishis were popular among both Muslims and Hindus. Because of the Rishi tradition, argues Peer Gias-ud-Din, 'Kashmir gained a new position as the meeting place of traditional Hindu thought and culture and new Islamic thought and culture' (Gias-ud-Din 1994: 4).

Notwithstanding their agreement on Sufism's influence on Kashmir, historians remain divided over the nature of conversion process—between those who see it as voluntary and gradual, and those who view it in terms of force and conquest. Those who stress voluntary conversion attribute it to the greatness of Islam and its moral and ethical order, as compared to the Brahmanical and caste ridden character of Hindu society. For instance, A.B.M. Habibullah (1976: 280-3) and Ishaq Khan (1997) argue that it was not merely the Sufi's supposed miraculous powers, and the material prospects that Islam held out for converts, but his 'social values' that attracted non-Muslims, especially those who were suffering from 'Brahmanical caste-tyranny'. Therefore, for Ishaq Khan, the mystic order of the Rishi movement in Kashmir was the culmination of the mounting disaffection, tension and conflict generated over time in a particular section of the people who were in contact with Islam: 'The Rishi movement was thus not merely a movement of ascetics, but in reality, a manifestation of social protest against the caste taboos that cut at the very root of human dignity' (Khan 1997: 224).

Contrary to this view, many historians have documented the use of force in conversions. Specific mention is made of Sikandar (1389-1413) who invoked the power of the state to spread Islam forcibly: many ancient Hindu temples were destroyed; and many Hindus, fearing the option of death or exile, were forced to adopt Islam. In the words of R.K. Parimu (1969: 432), 'the Hindus accepted Islam simply as security against perpetual harassment'. Mention of such harassment has been made by Prem Nath Bazaz as well while analysing mass conversion in the villages: 'During the Muslim rule for about five centuries, the Hindus of Kashmir had to suffer far greater hardships than the Muslims. The lower classes of Hindus therefore considered it more convenient to embrace Islam and live a less miserable life' (Bazaz 2002: 248).

The process of conversion, therefore, was a blend of diverse forces that resulted in a predominantly Muslim society with a miniscule Brahmin minority. However, despite their minority status, the Brahmins formed a vital part of the elite, so powerful that no Muslim ruler could ignore them. It was due to this continuation of the elite position of a significant section of Kashmiri Pandits that the medieval state, though collaboration with the religious establishment, did not become theocratic. As Gias-ud-Din (1994: 4) observes, the 'medieval Muslim state in Kashmir was not a theocracy but a monarchy. The head was Muslim, but the state was not Islamic. The state did not follow the injunctions of Holy Quran. . . .'

However, as Gias-ud-Din (1994: 4) further points out, this is not to read perfect secularism. The state 'did derive part of its political support from a religious source', like other medieval states of the subcontinent. In order to legitimise power it had to go beyond religion, and command respect from those who were part of the power structure, both the Hindu and Muslim nobility. To that extent, the state identified with the interest and position of the elite rather than that of the people of a particular religion. Hence, it was 'difficult to distinguish the lower classes of Muslims from the lower classes of Hindus' (Gias-ud-Din 1994: 4).[2] At the same time, Sufism, following the local tradition of the Rishi order, did not disrupt the traditional bonds which constituted the social structure, though it converted large sections of society into Muslims. There emerged a composite culture that reflected the confluence of Islam with the Hindu tradition. As Ishaq Khan notes:

> Notwithstanding the popular movement against the Brahmans for turning temples and idols into agencies of exploitation in the name of faith, the Kashmiris did not totally reject their ancestral belief in the efficacy of temples and shrines (*asthapans*). That is the reason why in the newly constructed mosques and shrines (*ziyarats* or *asthans*) certain features of

the Hindu and the Buddhist monastic life were retained to a marked degree. (Khan 1997: 81-2)[3]

In similar vein, Walter Lawrence observes the tendency among Kashmiri Muslims to worship the saints: 'All the veneration in the Kashmiri character comes out as the Musalmans approach a shrine. . . .' Referring to Sheikh Noor Din as the national Saint of Kashmir as well as to scores of other rishis, babas and pirzadas, Lawrence notes that all these are connected with shrine-worship, and argues that 'their influence is far greater than that exercised by Mullahs in the mosque' (Lawrence 1996: 287).

THE SEEDS OF POLITICAL ISLAM, 1900-1950

Until the beginning of the twentieth century, the Muslims of Kashmir had not developed an Islamic identity in modern religious terms. The bases of self-identification were multiple, and for most of the people, the village or tribe remained as an important identity marker. 'Quite evidently, then', noted Mridu Rai, 'neither the Hindus nor the Muslims of Kashmir formed homogeneous social entities. For both groups the notion of *zator kram*, evoking the concept of birth into a common clan group, was a decisive factor in specifying and living out their identities' (Rai 2004: 39).

However, Kashmir witnessed a deliberate process of redefining religion and re-conception of Muslim identity in the late nineteenth and early twentieth centuries. This redefinition was based on the notion of a 'pure Islam' as against what was projected as a degenerate version of saint-worshipping. This process, a consequence both of modernization as well as the increased communications with the external world (i.e. the Indian subcontinent, as the princely state of Jammu and Kashmir had come under the control of British Empire), was reinforced by the institutionalization of the position of Mirwaiz.[4] In the early twentieth century, Rasul Shah, the Mirwaiz of the Jama Masjid of Srinagar, in his efforts to claim the leadership of the Kashmiri Muslim community, initiated a process of bringing all the religious figures and shrines under the institution of the Mirwaiz (U.K. Zutshi, 1986: 194; C. Zutshi, 2000: 110). Chitralekha Zutshi observes (2000: 110) that it was a process linked with the changing political economy in this period. She argues that due to the decline of flourishing shawl trade and land settlement, the socio-economic position of certain urban social groups, including the shawl merchants and the landed elite, was threatened. 'Hence they turned their attention to the control of shrines which had been repositories of wealth and which . . . besides being symbols of religious authority also enjoyed immense political power since the medieval times'.

Rasul Shah emphasized a 'pure' version of Islam and used education for that purpose. While establishing a number of schools, he emphasized the doctrine of *Tawhid* (oneness) based on the unified community of Muslims. He also condemned the local practice of saint worship as contrary to the orthodox tradition of Islam.

However, the authority of Rasul Shah as the Mirwaiz of Jama Masjid did not go uncontested. His detractors, more specifically the head preacher of Shah-i-Hamdaan[5] who also proclaimed himself Mirwaiz, labelled him a '*wahhabi*' and questioned his right both to represent the Muslims as well as to preach 'pure Islam'. He contested Rasul Shah's declaration that 'saint worship' is against the doctrine of *Tawhid* and hence un-Islamic. Each Mirwaiz, however, had his independent base of support. While Mirwaiz Jama Masjid had the support of the grain dealers among the petty bourgeoisie, Mirwaiz Hamdaani had the support of *mutawallis*[6] of the shrines. Frequent clashes between the supporters of the two Mirwaizes over various issues, especially over the right to preach in the shrines of the city, acquired such intensity that the state had to intervene, which resulted in a government order laying down the jurisdiction of the two Mirwaizes in 1910 (Zutshi 2000: 112-18; Bazaz 2002: 256). The institutionalization of the Mirwaiz and the intra-religious contestation and conflict led to the deepening of Muslim consciousness and defining community in religious terms. However, this process followed two different directions. On the one hand there was the claim of one-ness of the Muslims, as made by the Mirwaiz of Jama Masjid, that resulted in underscoring the boundaries between those who were Muslim and those who were not. On the other hand, owing to the contest between the two Mirwaizes, the differences within the community of Muslims were also being sharpened.

EFFORTS TO PURIFY ISLAM: *AHL-I-HADITH*

The endeavour to purify Islam and unite the Muslims was not restricted to the efforts of the two Mirwaizes of Kashmir. The *Ahl-i-Hadith* movement[7] disapproved of the practice of the worship and deification of saints and other holy persons and sought to provide

Islamic education based on texts to the common Kashmiris, especially the peasantry, whom it found ignorant of the real tenets of Islam. Commenting on the nature of the *Ahl-i-Hadith* movement, Ishaq Khan notes:

> For them [*Ahl-i-Hadith*] the great majority of the people in the Valley, though Muslims by faith, needed to be converted afresh in view of the dichotomy existing between the normative Islam and Islam as practised by Kashmiris, or for that matter by various other ethnic groups of subcontinent. . . . (Khan 1997: 27)

The *Ahl-i-Hadith* movement with its emphasis on purity coincided with the Jama Masjid Mirwaiz's efforts to consolidate his position as a representative of the whole community. His inclination towards this ideology, notwithstanding his neutrality towards this movement, sharpened the difference between his followers and those of the Mirwaiz Hamdaan. While both agreed with the idea of the unity of Muslims, the Hamdaanis also justified saint worship, arguing that it helped popularise Islam. They also argued that shrines, and all practices associated with them, had an Islamic origin (C. Zutshi 2000).

However, efforts at institutionalizing and purifying Islam and consolidating the Muslim community in the Valley achieved only partial success since the leadership did not adequately represent the concerns of the differentiated community. As C. Zutshi notes, the religious leadership's influence remained restricted to urban areas, 'leaving 78 per cent of the Kashmiri Muslim community, comprising largely of peasants, outside the ambit of their concerns and debates' (Zutshi 2003: 156). Hence rural Muslims remained aloof from the theological and other battles influenced by the puritanical movements of the urban elite. And yet religion acquired some prominence in the process of construction and articulation of identities in the late nineteenth and early twentieth centuries throughout Jammu and Kashmir, as this period saw the emergence of a number of social and religious organizations with nascent political orientations, eventually leading to nationalist movement.

Yet, the impact of British colonialism in defining identities in religious terms cannot be ignored. As the State of Jammu and Kashmir under its Dogra Maharaja became part of the British colonial set up, agrarian, administrative, and social reforms along with increased communications and commerce with British India, transformed the urban and rural landscapes of the State. This process of integration with British India also resulted in bringing Kashmir into mainstream Muslim politics. Many Muslim organizations of the subcontinent, especially the Muslim League and the Muslim Kashmiri Conference of Lahore, Ahmediyyas, and Ahrars began to pay greater attention to their compatriots in Jammu and Kashmir.

On the whole, the integration of the State with British India saw the redefinition and reassertion of identities in religious terms. This, however, was not an isolated process and in effect, formed a part of the overall changes taking place in the Indian subcontinent. Among the operative forces were constitutional changes, new educational institutions, and the influence of the press and publications. Like the rest of the subcontinent, modern education and constitutional changes led to the consolidation of separate religious identities. Meanwhile, increasing contact of Kashmiris with the outside world—via the educated class who attended universities in Lahore and Aligarh, the press and the publication market—had led to a renewed appreciation of their religious bonds and identities.

CREATION OF THE MUSLIM CONFERENCE

The process of articulation of the political aspirations of Muslims in Jammu and Kashmir began in the first quarter of the twentieth century, initially through the press, semi-religious organizations and groups of ethnic Kashmiris in Lahore.[8] Later on, the newly educated youth of the State (especially Aligarh graduates) started their own organizations like the Young Men's Muslim Association of Jammu and the Reading Room Party based in Srinagar which included many prominent leaders of the time such as Mirwaiz Yusuf Shah, Sheikh Abdullah and Choudhary Ghulam Abbas.

The political process gathered momentum in the 1930s when people of Jammu and Kashmir started a campaign against the autocratic rule of the Maharaja; this acquired an organized form of resistance following communal violence in 1931.[9] Underlying this violence was a popular struggle, led by the Muslim intelligentsia of Kashmir as well as Jammu, against political, social and economic oppression (Gias-ud-Din 1994: 9). The formation of the All-India Jammu and Kashmir Muslim Conference (referred hereafter as the Muslim Conference) in 1932 was the logical conclusion of this struggle.

While focusing on the problems faced by the Muslims of the State, especially those related to education and employment, those who organized the Muslim Conference aimed to represent a unified Muslim response to Maharaja's autocracy. However, such a unified response failed, due to three levels of political divergence: between the two Mirwaizes; between Mirwaiz Yusuf Shah and Sheikh Abdullah; and between the Kashmiri Muslim leadership and the Jammu leadership.

These divergences were reflected in Mirwaiz Yusuf Shah dissociating himself from the political movement led by the Muslim Conference in favour of the Maharaja[10] against whom the movement was launched.[11] However, the rival Mirwaiz of the Shah-i-Hamdaan remained with the Muslim Conference and used it to settle scores with Mirwaiz Yusuf Shah. For the four years that the former remained in the Muslim Conference, 'Muslim politics', says Bazaz, 'became a battle-field of politicians in which muck-raking and mud-slinging were the chief weapons' (Bazaz 2002: 260). The situation became dangerously communal as both Mirwaizes competed with each other to gain support of the people.

On the whole, the religious leadership played an ambiguous role in the political movement of Kashmir, especially during the initial period. While the lower clergy became the bed-rock of the anti-feudal movement, the upper clergy, along with the Muslim feudal elements, opposed the movement. This process was, writes Gias-ud-Din,

> not only confined to the political sphere but extended to the sphere of education and culture as well. The feudal elements in collaboration with religious Mullahs opposed modern trends in culture, education and social reforms. A generation of Muslim intellectuals throughout India and especially in Kashmir was reared in the Aligarh tradition. Many of them later turned their backs [on] religious sectarianism opposing Mullahism and adopted an Indian national viewpoint. (Gias-ud-Din 1994: vii-viii)

EMERGENCE OF THE NATIONAL CONFERENCE

As a result of interaction with subcontinental movements, the Muslim Conference was converted into the All Jammu and Kashmir National Conference (hereafter NC). This shift, aimed at realizing the progressive potential of the political movement in Kashmir and endowing it with a popular character, was initially supported by the Jammu-based leaders.[12] But with Sheikh Abdullah moving closer to the secular Indian National Congress, particularly Nehru, Jammu-based leaders such as Chowdhary Ghulam Abbas, Chowdhary Hamidullah, and Mian Ahmed Yar, influenced by larger currents of the Muslim elite politics of the subcontinent, started drifting away. Abbas, repudiating the principle of national unity, argued that Hindus and Muslims were two nations and that Islam did not accept their integration into a social and political unit. In 1941 he finally parted ways with Abdullah on the question of the Pakistan Resolution and joined Mirwaiz Yusuf Shah to revive the Muslim Conference.

The revived Muslim Conference, which eventually came out in favour of the movement for Pakistan, also got the support of Muslim leaders in Poonch, Mirpur, Kotli and Muzaffarabad districts of Jammu region. These leaders acclaimed the Pakistan Resolution and pledged their support for a separate homeland for Indian Muslims. Soon after its revival, this organization aligned itself closely with the Muslim League and joined the All-India States People's Muslim League. This, in a way, had the effect of crystallizing the politics of the NC further in the secular direction, with a pro-people programme. The *New Kashmir Manifesto* adopted by it in 1944 contained a radical agenda for the transformation of Jammu and Kashmir on the principles of equity and equality.

To counter the secular agenda of the National Conference, the Muslim Conference issued its own political manifesto *Azad Kashmir*, which committed the Muslims of Jammu and Kashmir to the Muslim League's struggle for a separate homeland, reiterating faith in one leader (Qaid-e-Azam Mohammed Ali Jinnah), one organization (the Muslim League) and one objective (the realization of Pakistan). While the NC gave the call of 'Quit Kashmir' against the Maharaja, the Muslim Conference opposed it and participated in elections to the Praja Sabha and won many seats as NC boycotted these elections.

The divergence in the Muslim political response further intensified in 1947 around the future of the State—with the leadership of Kashmir inclined towards joining India, though on negotiated terms, and that of Jammu favouring merger of the State with Pakistan. This division became more acute when Kashmir was invaded by infiltrators. While the Muslims of Jammu, particularly in Poonch, rebelled against the Maharaja, those of Kashmir became part of a spontaneous, semi-organized resistance against the infiltrators. The events unfolded at that time dictated the future course towards the division of the State. A substantial part (mainly comprising of Mirpur, Kotli, Muzaffarabad, Baltistan, Hunza and Gilgit and a major part of Poonch district) came under the control of Pakistan, and the rest of the State acceded to the Indian Union with a constitutionally guaranteed special status.

In this overview we see that the growth of political Islam was largely contingent on the prevailing social conditions and political context. In Jammu and Kashmir, the conditions were not conducive for political Islam to grow in the first half of the twentieth century, though some seeds were planted through consolidation of the otherwise fragmented Muslim society—to which both the Mirwaizes and *Ahl-i-Hadith* contributed significantly. However, as the economy was still agrarian and the cultural and material traditions of the peasantry were not conducive to a dogmatic religious ideology, it could not prevail. Moreover, as significant sections of the Kashmir elite came under the influence of secular and socialist ideology, an alternative vision helped isolate the religious factor from the polity to a large extent. This vision based on the concept of land reforms and the establishment of cooperatives was to consolidate the secular politics in late forties and early 1950s. However, those who lost their political and economic superiority owing to these developments waited for an opportunity to strike back.

THE EMERGENCE OF POLITICAL ISLAM

The rise of political Islam in Jammu and Kashmir during post-1950 period was due to the interplay of internal and external conditions. Partition on 'two-nation' theory influenced political events in the State in more than one way. Apart from increasing the religious consciousness of the people, it altered the composition of the State, both geographically and demographically, as significant parts came under Pakistan's control. It also led to a perpetual controversy over Accession, both within and outside the State, since Hindus and Muslims perceived it differently.

The context was complex. There was, first, the dilemma of the political elite, both the Maharaja and Sheikh Abdullah, regarding Accession, which bore on power relations. The central government too, due to internal and external developments, could not keep to its commitments with regard to a negotiated autonomous space for the State of Jammu and Kashmir. Contestation of the principles on which the NC had negotiated this autonomous space, also contributed to the Muslim consciousness. In Jammu, a Hindu Rightist party, the Praja Parishad, representing interests which had suffered consequent to changes in power structure, and the land reforms initiated by the newly installed NC government, launched a communal agitation challenging the special status of Jammu and Kashmir within the Indian federation and demanding the abolition of Article 370 of the Constitution.

The Political Economy of Jammu and Kashmir

The political context under which the economy and society of Jammu and Kashmir evolved aided the rise of political Islam. Partition violence and later political events made it difficult to sustain the initial relationship of trust between the Central and the State leadership. In 1953, Sheikh Abdullah, the popular leader of Kashmir, who had initiated momentous land reforms in the State, was dismissed from power and detained for a prolonged period. This resulted in an internal crisis of legitimacy in Kashmir: henceforth, democratic processes were made subservient to the politics of what was claimed to be the 'national interest'. Unrepresentative governments came to mark the polity, and appeasement and subsidies became parts of the economy. Writing about this politics of appeasement, Riyaz Punjabi notes:

> . . . a new machinery for the distribution of political and economic rewards was set in motion. The concessions included generous Central Government aid, setting up a highly subsidized economy, and the arbitrary and discretionary sanction of quotas, permits, licences and contracts. . . . The Government in the State did not devise schemes with the long term objectives of creating the avenues of employment; rather, the State itself became the major employer of the semi-educated and educated class of people. (Punjabi 1992: 142-3)

State interventions in agriculture and industry were constantly subjected to the pulls and pressures of various interest groups. The land reform programme was diluted due to increasing political interference. In the process, the distribution of land came to be linked with the political connection that the tenants could flout, and orchards were exempted from the ceiling on holdings due to the political clout of prosperous landowners. Cooperatives, channels for large financial loans, were also politicised (Prakash 2000: 322).

Riyaz Punjabi analyses the distortion in the economy from the perspective of emerging social contradictions. He notes the emergence of a new urban middle class—bureaucrats, businessmen and politicians—that cornered most of the advantages from the developmental programmes and the educational and employment opportunities provided by the state. 'This left', notes Punjabi, 'vast segments of the population—urban and rural, educated and illiterate, men and women—engaged in a fierce struggle for social and economic survival' (Punjabi 1992: 142-3). The resultant discontent was skilfully manoeuvred by the *nouveau riche* in such a manner that it held the Centre responsible for all the problems in Kashmir.

The impact of these forces was clearly felt in the 1960s. The Plebiscite Front, formed by the lieutenants of Sheikh Abdullah demanding Plebiscite to determine the future status of the State, and Mirwaiz Maulvi Farooq's Awami Action Committee came to a single platform to oppose the Centre as well as the State government. Incidents like the loss of a sacred religious relic from the Hazaratbal shrine in 1963 provided opportunities for the opposition to mobilize the people.[13] Though the alliance between the NC and the Awami Action Committee could not last long, it led to a popular religious response that demonstrated the spread of resentment to the countryside.

THE RISE OF POLITICAL ISLAM

Many scholars have interpreted 1975-83 as a 'Golden Period' in Jammu and Kashmir, mainly because Shiekh Abdullah returned to the centre of Kashmir's politics: power politics in the State acquired some legitimacy after a long time. With overwhelming support to the NC, recorded in one of the most credible and participatory elections in 1977, the two-decade old history of the governments 'imposed from above' was reversed. Yet everything was not normal. Some effects of the distortions in politics and economy since the early 1950s continued even in the changed circumstances. Specifically, the increasing Islamization of Kashmiri society gradually impinged upon the liberal and secular ethos of Kashmiri politics. Islamization had accelerated due to three developments in the mid-1970s: a more Islamized Pakistan under General Zia-ul-Haq intervening in the affairs of Jammu and Kashmir; the Iranian revolution spawning religious fervour in Kashmir; and the Afghan civil war generating an infrastructure of Islamic terror in neighbouring regions.

Internal discontent in the Valley, especially among the youth, provided a favourable atmosphere for the external forces to operate there. Such discontent, arising in the economic and social developments of the time, was aggravated due to the disillusionment with the return of Sheikh Abdullah.[14] New social groups were mobilized, but '*without a corresponding outlet for democratic expression*', thus channelling them in the religious direction (Pasha 1992: 369-72; emphasis added). In Riaz Punjabi's words:

> By 1980, on the one hand, in some urban elite pockets of the society, the bells of yuppie culture, with all the trappings of glamour, drugs and whisky, were ringing. On the other hand, waves of Islamic resurgence making their way through the mountain passes had touched the shores of the Kashmir Valley, and a large section of the youth appeared to be riding on them. . . . Sheikh Abdullah was a colossus, and it was through the sheer charisma of his personality that the above contradictions that had grown in Kashmir society could be managed, even if only superficially. But Abdullah was aware that he was sitting over a volcano. (Punjabi 1992: 144-5)

Sheikh Abdullah, despite his aversion to fundamentalist tendencies, could not stop politics based on religion. His moral authority was challenged by youth raised on his earlier politics of 'plebiscite'. Attuned to the tradition of contestation, they could not accept his politics of reconciliation and joined the forces of religion-based politics, especially the Awami Action Committee of Moulvi Farooq and the Jamaat-e-Islami, which had become the refuge of all those opposed to the Sheikh's new political incarnation.[15]

THE GROWTH OF THE JAMAAT-I-ISLAMI

The Jamaat-i-Islami had a branch in Jammu since 1940 and was operative in the State as a regional party since early 1950s, but remained aloof from active politics until it consolidated its position in the 1970s. By then it had a well-trained cadre for advancing Islamization in the State. As Gias-ud-Din has observed:

> Over the years since 1972, the Islamic fundamentalists carried on ceaseless and clamorous campaign for the Islamization of Kashmir. Their ideological influence had been greater than their actual support among the people. Though fundamentalism and secessionism complement each other, however, it is through secessionism that Jamaat not only forges links with broad masses but helps them in their mass mobilization. (Gias-ud-Din 1994: 63)

Having an essentially lower middle class base of traders, students and lower level government employees, the Jamaat was successful in mobilizing people who were frustrated with the politics of secular groups such as the NC and the Congress. With Sheikh Abdullah in detention, the NC led by Bakshi Ghulam Mohammad had lost its popular character, and the habits of power had shredded whatever democratic content it had earlier. To quell the consequent discontent, the ruling elite promoted all kinds of political and religious forces, generating a political space congenial for the Jamaat-i-Islami to extend its political constituency, and to start building its cadres in villages and towns through *madrasas* (Shah 2000: 142). Later, in the 1970s, it could also gather some political clout due to its collaboration with the Congress. With a view to distract Kashmiris from the influence of Sheikh Abdullah and the Plebiscite Front, Syed Mir Qasim, the then Chief Minister, facilitated the entry of the Jamaat into the electoral politics of the State in early 1970s. Although its electoral role was of not much consequence, it could use the electoral space for mobilizing the disgruntled people of Kashmir. By summer 1980, it had been successful in giving rise to a youth movement. Young people, especially students, were attracted to the Jamaat-i-Tulba, its student organization, which advocated an Islamic order in the State.

Being closely associated with the Jamaat-i-Islami of Pakistan, the Jamaat-i-Islami in Jammu and Kashmir opposes the idea of a secular order. According to it, the secular system as it operates in India neither allows Islam to flourish nor ensures the security of life of Muslims. Though ostensibly claiming to believe in non-violence, in practice the Jamaat tends to draw inspiration from militant tendencies. The youth wings and the organizations associated with it (like Jamaat-i-Tulba during the 1970s and 1980s, and Hizbul Mujahideen more recently) specifically believe in militancy and many a time instigate violence.

The growth of the Jamaat (especially since the 1960s) was linked with its educational and social roles. Its schools, combining modern and Islamic education, helped expand its influence; similarly its charity programmes. It could win support through its reformist agenda by publishing large amounts of literature.[16] It also raised its voice against what it considered the evils of society such as alcohol, the secular education system, the system of co-education and modern entertainment emanating from cinema, radio and television, etc.

Sheikh Abdullah, after resuming power in 1975, realized the danger that Kashmir was going to have from the popularity of the Jamaat and ordered closure of the schools run by it. He also took other steps to limit its influence. He banned a convention of Jamaat-i-Tulba planned for Srinagar in 1981.

> Sheikh's reaction to the Muslim influence in the schools of the Jamaat demonstrated his concern but the Jamaat-i-Islami had only won one seat in the 1977 elections and did not appear to be a significant political force. Neither he nor anyone else could have predicted the growth in support for the Islamic movement, which came in later years, especially after the Iranian revolution in February 1979. . . . (Schofield 1997: 220)

THE MUSLIM UNITED FRONT (MUF)

Political change came to Kashmir with the passing of Sheikh Abdullah in 1983. He was the tallest man in the Valley who brought disparate groups of Kashmiris together. He represented a tradition of secular politics, initiated when the Muslim Conference had turned into NC. After his death, his son, Farooq Abdullah was 'able to galvanize Kashmiris of all hues and shades, young and old, thereby absorbing dissent and contradictions in one huge momentum' (Punjabi 1992: 145). He could do this by identifying with the popular sentiment against the Centre in a secular manner. To channel discontent against the Centre, he joined with the anti-Congress oppositional parties and made the NC a part of the mainstream national oppositional politics.

However, the tradition of secular politics of Kashmir had faced a setback during the 1983 Assembly election, in which a subtle communalism surfaced as both the NC and the Congress used religion. While the NC exploited Muslim sentiments in the Valley, the Congress exploited Hindu sentiments in the Jammu region. Such communalism was further reinforced as the NC, facing the pressure of Congress, sought the support of Mirwaiz Maulvi Farooq, the religious and political leader.

The communal space thus generated by the 1983 elections was extended in the 1980s following a series of political developments. Of these, the first related to the dismissal of Farooq Abdullah's government in 1984 as a reproach to his anti-Centre politics. This incident not merely had the effect of hurting the political sentiments of people but also bringing about a phase of uncertainty in Kashmiri politics. G.M. Shah, who succeeded Farooq Abdullah as Chief

Minister, led a government comprised of defectors—and faced a perennial crisis of legitimacy, the consequence being that 'gradually but at an increasing rate, extremist parties became more successful in using region and religion as the basis for political mobilization' (Punjabi 1992: 146).

By 1987, secular politics was further jeopardized as the NC and Congress entered into an alliance. It was an unpopular alliance, imposed not only on the NC but also on people of Kashmir. In the vacuum arising out of the loss of the NC's autonomous political space, Islamic forces coalesced around a loose alliance, the MUF. The Jamaat was a key component of this alliance, and around twelve smaller Islamic parties also joined it. With these Islamic parties assuming some legitimacy in politics, the stage was set for centrality of issues based on religion. The MUF described politics as an inseparable part of religion, saw shrines as effective power centres, and declared the 1987 Assembly election a contest between 'Islam and Secularism'.

The MUF, however, was not a unified group and did not represent all the oppositional forces of the time. The Peoples' Conference led by Abdul Gani Lone, for instance, did not identify with its religion-oriented politics and contested election outside its banner. Many others like Mirwaiz Mohammad Farooq, wary of the politically abrasive language used by some MUF leaders, criticized it for its communal tendencies.

Notwithstanding this limitation, the coalition of religion-based political groups was able to make a mark in the electoral politics of the Valley, capturing as many as a third of the total votes polled during the 1987 Assembly elections. However, it could not win many seats; this led to allegations of widespread rigging but also to the eventual collapse of democratic politics. As the leaders of the MUF and other oppositional parties refused to accept the electoral verdict, the newly elected NC government faced a severe crisis of legitimacy which was intensified due to popular response against the State and the Central governments. Pakistan, meanwhile, used this situation to involve itself directly in the affairs of Jammu and Kashmir. All this led to a phase of 'militancy' in the State when many who had earlier been part of the electoral process, as candidates or as supporters of MUF, crossed the border to be trained for armed conflict against the Indian State.[17]

Militancy extended the space for religion in politics, initiating a new phase of political Islam in Kashmir. With the mushroom growth of militant groups justifying their political existence on religious grounds, people were exposed to Islamization as never before. Some of these groups enforced religious and moral codes like the veiling of women, closure of cinemas, video parlours and other such places considered to be un-Islamic. Separatism in itself had given a boost to politics based on religion as many militant groups, on grounds of religious proximity, had chosen merger of Kashmir with Pakistan as their ultimate goal. For these separatist groups, the basic issue underlying the struggle concerns the Muslim character of Kashmir and has to be located in the international political context of *jihad*. The whole phenomenon of *jihadi* militants, many of whom are 'guest militants' from other Muslim countries, is based on this presumption.

Religion, therefore, has not only entered the politics of Kashmir in a major way but has also left its mark on Kashmiri society. Compared to earlier, more secular times, politics based on religion now enjoys greater sanctity. Religion had played on the political fringes since 1930s; now it is often central to the separatist politics.

However, the politics of religion suffers from a number of limitations. With the strong cultural and inter-community bonds pulling the other way, the political ethos in the State continues to be based upon secular politics—as we shall argue in the concluding section.

CONCLUSION

As stated earlier, the resurgence of religion in politics is an aspect of the modernization process and is linked with the present-day social, political and economic realities. As many scholars of political Islam have pointed out, states that have not gone through the modernization process and have remained largely traditional have not experienced strong political movements based on Islamic ideology. Similarly, it is in urban, not rural, areas that Islamist themes are more admired. In rural areas people still follow popular Islam. To quote Henry Munson, 'generally speaking, the least educated and most traditional social strata were not active in the fundamentalist Islamic movements of the late twentieth century. Peasants have been conspicuously absent from such movements, as have the urban poor and blue-collar workers with regular jobs . . .' (Munson 1988: 103-4; as cited in Ayubi 1991: 159).

The confluence of Islam with politics began in Jammu and Kashmir in the early twentieth century. As a part of larger subcontinental phenomenon, its emergence coincided with the nationalist movement. Its rise also resulted from subcontinental influences. Of these, the most important include the Partition; the controversy over the Accession of the State to Indian Union; the arrest of Shiekh Abdullah and the installation of unrepresentative governments; tampering with democratic and electoral norms; the transnational *jihadi* forces with active support of Pakistan; and finally the collapse of all democratic institutions, including mainstream political parties, with the onslaught of militancy based upon separatism.

However, politics based on religion faces difficulties in a plural society like Jammu and Kashmir. Francois Nielsen argues that in a society where multiple identities overlap, individual decisions of participation in collective action are typically the result of a very complicated interplay of circumstances (Nielsen 1985: 138). Society in Jammu and Kashmir is differentiated along religion, region, ethnicity, language, caste, class and political affiliation and ideology. Not only are the descendants of immigrant Muslims different from those of converts (Syeds and Sheikhs), but also there are different categories of converts in terms of their social hierarchy. There are differences of sect (Shia and Sunni), of regional divide (Kashmiri and non-Kashmiri Muslim, or Dogra or Poonchi Muslim), and even of caste (Rajput or ordinary Muslim). Linguistically and culturally not much is common to the Kashmiri Muslim and the Muslim belonging to Jammu.

This differentiation, combined with the process of modernization, has led to competitive claims to resources and to a crystallization of differences among the Muslims—as can be clearly seen in the construction and assertion of political identity of *Paharis* in competition with the *Gujjars*. Though the two share a religion, a strong political rivalry exists between them over the privileges that the state can bestow by granting them Scheduled Tribe status, or by providing political reservations. Similar rivalry can be seen between Kashmiri and Jammu Muslims, the latter feeling that they are discriminated by the Kashmiri elite in the allocation of resources. And a predominantly agrarian, rural population has its differences from the urbanites.

The uneven influence of fundamentalist ideology in Kashmir, specifically its rural-urban divide, has been clear in the way the people have responded to religion-based politics, and the violence perpetrated in its name during last fourteen years. While the urban sections, particularly the elite, have thrived on militancy and violence, with more money coming in for various reasons, the material conditions of rural society have drastically deteriorated.

The rural areas have also been suffering from neglect. In the absence of the kind of protection provided to the people in the urban areas, the rural population has been extremely vulnerable to militant violence. Non-functioning of administration due to threats from the militants, meanwhile, has resulted in a drastic decline in their quality of life. As a result, there is a kind of aversion, not seen in urban areas, towards the *jihadi* forces and the high level of violence. This was clearly established during the 2002 Assembly elections. Whereas urban Kashmir chose to turn its back on electoral politics, rural Kashmir showed an inclination to take a fresh interest in it.[18]

More importantly, the principal hurdle to political Islam in Jammu and Kashmir is the secular character of its society. The notion of *Kashmiriat* in the Valley, and strong cultural links between various communities, are still intact, notwithstanding the mass exodus of Pandits from the Valley in the wake of militancy, and selective and targeted killings on a communal basis. The fault-lines based on religion are certainly there, but the human bonds established between various communities are still operating against communal agendas. Plurality here is so time-tested that it has not been affected by the communal violence that has been erupting elsewhere. Stories abound about the strong inter-community bonds and inter-communal relations—whether of lone Hindu families still surviving within a Muslim neighbourhood or of Muslims sharing the sorrows and the pleasures of these Hindus. The shared culture and traditions, the common shrines and pir babas, the nature of worship, and interdependence in daily life, are still strongly working against any fundamentalist ideology.

In the end one can argue that the religious resurgence in Jammu and Kashmir has dual implications. Internally, the plurality of society, the cultural and living ethos of people, the agrarian character of the economy and the ethnic, tribal, and sectarian divisions do not allow any particular fundamentalist ideology to dominate. This differentiation has clear implications for separatist politics, especially that resting on Islamist ideology. There are numerous organizations and militant outfits working not only parallel to but also in competition with each other. The All Party Hurriyat Conference (APHC) was organized with a view to bring them under one banner and to negotiate their contradictions, but it could not overcome its internal fragmentation. Its split in 2003 has been attributed, among other factors, to the lack of acceptability of its chairman Maulvi Abbas Ansari, a Shia leader, to the Sunni leadership of the organization.[19]

Yet one cannot ignore the indications of an extension of the role of religion in the politics and society of Kashmir. This extension may not be due only to internal socio-political factors, as delineated above, but also to external factors and events. A Salman Rushdie episode, the destruction of the Babri Masjid, events in Gujarat, the Palestine struggle, the war on Iraq by the USA––any of these events has the potential of bringing the entire Muslim community to a single platform, speaking with a single voice.

Political Islam, then, thrives on the negative forces released by economic and political conditions. Its emergence in Jammu and Kashmir is linked with the interplay of internal and external conditions: the resentment of people against successive governments in Delhi, as well as in the increasing transnational Islamic influences. The political and material forces underlying political Islam, however, have blurred its boundaries over the years, with the result that it has been manifesting itself through the politics of separatism. However, due to its elitist nature, political Islam in Kashmir has been witnessing reversal, as popular aversion against the fundamentalist forces is being expressed sharply, time and again.

NOTES

1. The princely State of Jammu and Kashmir that emerged in 1846 was a conglomeration of the smaller kingdoms of Kashmir, Jammu, Ladakh, Mirpur, Poonch, Muzaffarabad, Gilgit, Baltistan, Nagar and Hunza. However, our analysis of the transition to Islam is here restricted to Kashmir.
2. Prem Nath Bazaz (2002: 249) also substantiated this by stating that 'most of them [rulers] cared much more for their own glory than for the welfare of their subjects. A few courtiers and noblemen, mostly Muslims, shared in this luxury and enjoyment. The Muslim masses also suffered and . . . their economic condition was not enviable.'
3. Ishaq Khan further adds:

> Even now one notices bells fastened to the gates of some *ziyarats* in the Valley, belonging to the medieval period. The preservation of the relics of the Sufis, particularly, those of the Rishis, in their tombs and their public exhibition on special occasions speak of the assimilation of the local Hindu-Buddhist

practices in the Islam of Kashmir. It is also not be wondered at, therefore, that a mere sight of the relics at congregations specially on the eve of '*Urs*, causes the devotees to recite litanies and *munajat* in chorus. A special characteristic of the Kashmiri Muslims' social behaviour at such gatherings is the focus on the object of veneration with folded hands, which undoubtedly suggest local influence on their mode of prayer. From the architectural point of view too, the medieval *ziyarats* are representative of a curious blending of Hindu, Buddhist and Islamic art styles. (Khan 1997: 81-2)

4. Head preacher of the Jama Masjid, Srinagar. 'The title of mirwaiz had been used at least since 1901 and the position had gradually become a hereditary one, held by the same family to this day' (Rai 2004: 235).
5. Shah-i-Hamdaan is one of the most revered shrines of Kashmir established by Sayyid Ali Hamdaani, a sufi mystic who came to the Valley from Hamdaan, Persia in 1379. The latter is considered one of the most influential sufi saints who played a very important role in popularizing Islam in Kashmir.
6. He was the custodian or manager of a shrine who controlled the affairs of the shrine and who 'had access to revenues of villages attached to the shrine as well as alms received from visitors to the shrine, and had to dispense them according to the terms of the deed' (C. Zutshi 2003: 128).
7. The *Ahl-i-Hadith* was a subcontinental movement seeking to 'purify' Islam from its 'deviations' arising in the influence of earlier cultures or religions.
8. In the articulation of unified Muslim consciousness in Jammu and Kashmir, the role of the Muslims outside the Valley was significant. Outside the State, a lobby of Muslims was actively involved in voicing the problems of the Kashmiri Muslims. Kashmir has always been a sensitive issue in Muslim Punjab. To a substantial extent this has been due to the influence of the Kashmiri *Biradari*. It was these people of Kashmiri origin, in Punjab, who in the early 1930s started mobilizing other Muslims of Punjab, and with their help initiated an organized campaign in support of the Muslims of Kashmir (Samad 1995: 65-77).
9. On 25 June 1931 at a meeting organized in Srinagar to express resentment at the Maharaja's discrimination against Muslims, a non-Kashmiri, Abdul Qadeer, made a speech advocating violence against the Maharaja—and was immediately arrested. At his trial on 13 July 1931, violence broke out and 32 people were killed in police firing. That day, which became a symbol, 'Martyrs Day', also had a major role in the initiation of the political movement in Kashmir.
10. To quote P.N. Bazaz,

The Mir Waiz of the Jama Masjid . . . slowly but surely and steadily . . . went to the Government side. . . . He and his followers were encouraged in many ways. They were granted immunity from the provisions of any emergency regulations applied against the Muslims. In a notorious case when punitive tax was levied upon the Muslim residents of Maisuma in Srinagar *Usuf Shahi* Mussulmans were exempted. . . . In 1936 he presented on behalf of the public an address of welcome to His Highness on his return from Europe. He was presented a *jagir* by the Ruler in an open Durbar as a reward. (Bazaz, 2002: 257)

11. Highlighting the duplicity and opportunism displayed by Yusuf Shah at that time, Prem Nath Bazaz writes:

    When the movement was conducted on communal lines, he came forward as the champion of the cause of nationalism, condemned the Conference leaders as *Qadianis* and worst types of communalists, sided with Ahrars, invited Hindus to join him and started a progressive party known as the Azad Conference. When nationalism entered the portals of the Muslim Conference and the leaders broad-based the movement, the Mir Waiz became frankly and avowedly communal in outlook, repudiated all his previous slogans and declarations and charged his rivals with having proved traitors to the Muslim community. Significantly enough, on both the occasions, he pressed religion into service to prove the veracity of his assertions. (Bazaz 2002: 259)

12. In fact the day before its conversion into National Conference (on 10 June 1939), in the last session of the Muslim Conference, Ghulam Abbas, a Jammu-based leader of the organization, made an appeal in which he said, 'The garb in the shape of the Muslim Conference has become outworn and threadbare. Now we are in need of a Nationalist guise. The time has come when we should discard the old and decayed mantle and tear it to pieces' (quoted in Bazaz 1954: 171).
13. The accumulated discontent took the form of a spontaneous mass response to the theft of *Moi-i-Muqaddas*, the sacred relic of Prophet, from the Hazaratbal mosque. The situation became so volatile that the Government of India had to intervene to pacify the situation.
14. In the period between 1953 and 1975, especially after the formation of the Plebiscite Front, a whole generation of Kashmiris had been exposed to a kind of politics in which Sheikh Abdullah and his colleague Mirza Afzal Baig had contested the finality of Kashmir's accession and had raised the issue of plebiscite. After Sheikh's accord with the Central government in 1975 and subsequently his return to power left many young Kashmiris confused. Many of them were disillusioned with the leadership and were later involved in underground political activities in continuity with the politics of 'self determination'.
15. Alistair Lamb observes that

    The State of Jammu and Kashmir in 1975 was indeed very different from that to which Sheikh Abdullah had returned from Aligarh some four and a half decades ago. . . . By 1975 university graduates in Jammu and Kashmir had long ceased to be rare phenomena. What was becoming relatively scarce, however, was the suitably employed (and adequately remunerated) graduate.

Advances in education . . . had not been accompanied by a corresponding expansion of opportunity. There had been considerable economic progress: the Indian Government, indeed, had at times gone out of its way to push money towards the State for obvious political reasons. . . . However, as usual, the rich got richer and the not so rich became ever more disgruntled. (Lamb 1992: 310)

16. As per the statistics provided by Shah, as against 13,000 students in 1985 in schools run by the Jamaat, there were 33,000 in 1989 and 40,000 by early 1990. The estimated number of schools run by the Jamaat at that time was 2500, with 1,300 teaching staff (Shah 2000: 145). Sumit Ganguly's observation is interesting in this context: 'the growth of *madrasas* paralleled the expansion of the video-parlours. . . . In the emerging milieu, where traditional values were eroding, those most threatened sought solace in a form of revitalistic Islam (Ganguly 1997: 75).
17. The journey from 'militancy' to 'terrorism', and from the 'struggle for self-determination' to 'transnational jihad', and the emergence of All Parties Hurriyat Conference to negotiate these contradictions, is a complex one and needs separate analysis. However, a few things may be stated here briefly: first, the rise of religious and sectarian violence was part of a larger phenomenon observable throughout the world; second, the retreat of pro-independence Jammu and Kashmir Liberation Front (JKLF) from Kashmir's militancy in the 1990s, was largely due to the rise of transnational *jihad* forces; third, Pakistan aided the spread of the violence with active support from Western powers, especially US and its allies in West Asia; fourth, though the indigenous element is strong in the Kashmir conflict, the massive operations of militancy there would not be possible without the involvement of transnational actors and infrastructure; and finally, in Kashmir it erupted in the aftermath of the failure of all democratic institutions and in the retreat of mainstream political parties.
18. For example, the voting percentage in the city of Srinagar was as low as 7 per cent, whereas in the rural areas of Kupwara district, exposed more to *jihadi* forces than any other district, the voting percentage nearly touched 50 per cent.
19. There is earlier evidence of similar sectarian response in the recent history of Kashmir, as in the sectarian violence between Shias and Sunnis after the death of Zia-ul-Haq (see Schofield 1997: 234).

REFERENCES

Ayubi, Nazih N., 1991, *Political Islam: Religion and Politics in the Arab World*, London and New York: Routledge.

Bazaz, Prem Nath, 1954, *History of Struggle for Freedom in Kashmir*, New Delhi: Kashmir Publishing Company.

Bazaz, Prem Nath, 2002, *Inside Kashmir*, Srinagar: Gulshan Publishers.

Ganguli, Sumit, 1997, *The Crisis in Kashmir: Portents of War, Hopes of Peace*, Cambridge: Woodrow Wilson Press and Cambridge University Press.

Gias-ud-Din, Peer, 1994, *Kashmir: Islam, Ideology and Society*, New Delhi: Jay Kay.

Habibullah, A.B.M., 1976, *The Foundations of Muslim Rule in India*, revd. edn., Allahabad: Central Book Depot.

Hewitt, Vernon, 2003, 'An Area of Darkness, Still? The Political Evolution of Ethnic Identities in Jammu and Kashmir, 1947-2001', in Rajat Ganguly and Ian Macduff, eds., *Ethnic Conflict in Secessionism in South and Southeast Asia: Causes, Dynamics, Solutions*, New Delhi: Sage, 2003, pp. 59-98.

Khan, Ishaq, 1997, *Kashmir's Transition to Islam: The Role of Muslim Rishis*, New Delhi: Manohar.

Kosambi, D.D., 1956-57, 'Origins of Feudalism in Kaśmīr', *Journal of the Bombay Branch of the Royal Asiatic Society*, vol. 31-2, pp. 108-20. Reprinted in B. Chattopadhyaya, ed., *D.D. Kosambi: Combined Methods in Indology and Other Writings*, New Delhi: Oxford University Press, 2002, pp. 295-307.

Lamb, Alistair, 1992, *Kashmir: A Disputed Legacy*, Karachi: Oxford University Press.

Lawrence, Walter, 1996, *The Valley of Kashmir*, Jammu: Kashmir Kitab Ghar.

Munson, Henry, 1988, *Islam and Revolution in the Middle East*, New Haven and London: Yale University Press.

Nielsen, Francois, 1985, 'Towards a Theory of Ethnic Solidarity in Modern Societies', *American Sociological Review*, vol. 50, no. 2, pp. 133-49.

Parimu, R.K., 1969, *History of Muslim Rule in Kashmir*, New Delhi: People's Publishing House.

Pasha, Mustafa Kamal, 1992, 'Beyond the Two-Nation Divide', in Raju G. C. Thomas, ed., *Perspective on Kashmir*, Boulders: Westview Press, pp. 368-87.

Prakash, Siddharth, 2000, 'Political Economy of Kashmir since 1947', *Economic and Political Weekly*, 10-16 June, pp. 319-20.

Punjabi, Riaz, 1992, 'Kashmir: The Bruised Identity', in Raju G.C. Thomas, ed., *Perspective on Kashmir*, Boulder: Westview Press, pp. 131-52.

Rai, Mridu, 2004, *Hindu Rulers, Muslim Subjects: Islam, Rights, and the History of Kashmir*, New Delhi: Permanent Black.

Samad, Yunus, 1995, 'Kashmir and the Imagining of Pakistan', *Contemporary South Asia*, vol. 4, no. 1, pp. 65-77.

Schofield, Victoria, 1997, *Kashmir in the Crossfire*, New Delhi: Viva Books.

Shah, S., 2000, 'Jamaat-e-Islami of Kashmir: A Background', *Himalayan and Central Asian Studies*, vol. 4, nos. 3-4, July-December, pp. 142-50.

Widmalm, Sten, 2002, *Kashmir in Comparative Perspective: Democracy and violent Separatism in India*, London: Routledge.

Zutshi, Chitralekha, 2000, 'Religion, State and Community: Contested Identities in the Kashmir Valley, 1818-1920', *South Asia*, vol. xxiii, no. 1, pp. 109-28.

———, 2003, *Languages of Belonging: Islam, Religious Identity, and the Making of Kashmir*, New Delhi, Permanent Black.

Zutshi, U.K., 1986, *Emergence of Political Awakening in Kashmir*, New Delhi: Manohar.

COMPETITIVE CONVERSIONS

Earlier papers having featured the protagonists of contentious religious identities, some of whom have grown global, we next have studies of their confrontations—in regions which, before the twentieth century, had known but lightly of high religious traditions grounded in ancient scriptures. In Mewat, south-west of Delhi, and in Merwara in central Rajasthan, Shail Mayaram finds aggressive Hindu organizations and the Islamic Tablighi Jamaat in contention; and she explores their trans-national workings too. Pietistic campaigns in these localities are run under local leadership, yet Mayaram stresses the potently political implications—and expressions—of their pieties. Nandini Sundar's focus is local: the case of entrenched Christian, especially Roman Catholic, Missions in north-eastern Chhattisgarh, and the challenges to them, most tellingly by RSS organizations, with tacit or active support from one or other governmental level.

Central to these several bodies' campaigns is the drive to win souls for their respective faiths, to save them from the follies of their rivals. The intrusive, global, organizations often command vast resources—symbolic, textual, financial, institutional, political. By way of wedges, sometimes they use rivalries within hitherto shared spaces. Alternatively educational institutions, student hostels, sports and other entertainments, health facilities, loans, and legal and political help in securing land rights are mobilized in rural areas, where neither successive goverments nor other agencies of civil society have initiated the necessary facilities. Given the intrusive pressures, host communities do not know whether, or how, to defend their indigenous traditions, those of the Oraon in Chhattisgarh, and the local pools of belief and practice in Mewat and Merwara. The powerful contrary pulls, then, alter the local scenes dramatically; and this can include creating 'boundaries within communities', sometimes rending local fabrics apart, down to bonds between brothers.

13

Do Hindu and Islamic Transnational Religious Movements represent Cosmopolitanism and Difference?

SHAIL MAYARAM

We have become dramatically aware in our times of the growth, visibility, and reach of transnational religious movements (TRMs) that comprise a particular subsection of the heterogeneous universe of transnational civil society.[1] There has been a phenomenal intensification of transnational religious networks and of new international players and styles oriented to missionization, religiosity, spiritual rejuvenation, and creating and recreating community. The writing on globalization has tended to focus far more on capital and labour flows and on transnational, regional and global governance than on the global operations of religious movements. Only a fragment of this literature brings into relation religion, labour and other migration and capital flows. Work on civil society similarly presumes the secular character of civil society and the public sphere. This article makes some preliminary observations regarding the transformation of religion under globalization and new modes of transnationalism in the context of a discussion of the Tablighi Jamaat (henceforth TJ) and the Vishwa Hindu Parishad (henceforth VHP). It asks the question of the relation between the local, the national and the transnational and opens up for debate the question of their role and impact. Do these organizations foster an alternative cosmopolitanism as has been argued by van der Veer (2001)? Or do they exacerbate religious difference and distance between religious communities, as Saberwal maintains in his introduction to this volume? What do competitive conversion and religious transnationalism tell us about the historical processes of the growth or otherwise of cosmopolitanism and difference?

India as the 'home' of these two significant movements (as also of several others) is a key player in religious transnationalism suggesting the importance of the nonwest in global cultural flows. The discussion of transnational religion relates to Islam and Hinduism. This does not, however, imply that this subject is not also of central importance to new processes within other religions such as Sikhism, Buddhism, or Christianity.[2]

A note first on the acronym, TRM, a take on the NRMs, the New Religious Movements. Mandaville prefers the term, Transnational Social Movements (TSM) to characterise their work (2001). This misses the point for, to that extent, religion has always been social. The *religious* in the transnational movements, however, brings to mind the particular power of religious iconography and symbolism that is used to mobilize persons in diverse countries and continents as also the fact that their normative agendas are grounded in sacred rather than secular visions. The age of globalization has been one of energization of transnational religious movements, even though we know that religions have frequently crossed the borders of empire, state, and nation in the past as well. But the characteristics of these movements that Mandaville points to are useful: they occupy a particular political space but not necessarily a specific place; many of these movements operate across borders and without exclusive reference to a specific nation, state, or region. Further, that certain variants of these movements are often engaged in activities, which are explicitly critical of state regimes or traditional aspects of state sovereignty (Mandaville 2001).

It is only by identifying this transnational character that one can obtain a sense of the tremendous financial and other resources that organizations such as the TJ and the VHP are able to command, and of the audiences they address. The power of religious transnational organizations is potentially far greater because of the legitimacy these claim as interpreters of religious truth and the trust vested in them qua representatives of religious communities.

The discussion of the TRMs that follows draws upon the cultural universes of two communities that I have been privileged to access as ethnographer, those of the Meos and of the Merat. These are communities categorized as Muslim, but who actually accomplished a complex negotiation with respect to cosmologies that we refer to today as Hindu. Both communities relate to contexts that are paradigmatic with respect to diversity. I refer back to the 1890s and 1920s before returning to the 1980s and 2000s, periods that are crucial with respect to competitive conversion in the South Asian subcontinent. The attempt is to relate the micropolitics of household, neighbourhood, village and town with that of the nation, metropolis, and globe. Needless to say, only a preview of what is obviously a complicated theme is possible here. The research is based on archival sources, primary and secondary literature, and fieldwork carried out intermittently since 1990.

The question of selection of cases for comparison first needs to be addressed. Religious transnationalism includes a range of movements both modernist and radical, as also the more 'traditionalist'. Inasmuch as they belong to the larger phenomenon of transnational religion there is then a family resemblance between the TJ and VHP, but no more. Indeed, it might be argued that a comparison would be more appropriate between the VHP and the Jamaat-i Islami, or between the TJ and the Swadhyaya movement. Exercises in comparison also include the possibility of comparison by contrast. The two organizations considered here relate very differently to nationalism. While one organization clearly identifies with a single nation state and is concerned with state power, the TJ seeks to transcend the nation state and its narrow concern with worldly power and nationalism. Neither has it engendered a hatred for minorities that is associated with the VHP. Its domain has been largely the inculcation of spirituality and the inculcation of what it identifies as core Islamic values. Even die-hard Hindu nationalists acknowledge that their fear is not of Muslim but of Christian proselytism. In many ways, then, the VHP and TJ represent two contrasting models of religious transnationalism. There have been a series of situations where there is evidence that the VHP and its youth wing, the Bajrang Dal, have actively been involved in violence. With the TJ what is often worked out is a largely quietistic, peaceful model based on the idea of inner transformation. The VHP draws extensively on funding by the indigenous bourgeoisie both in the homeland and in the diaspora, while Tabligh parties are largely self-financing.

Two points need to be made with respect to the literature on the TJ. First, it has on the whole ignored the question of impact, the kinds of conflicts that TJ work has resulted in. Further, the issue of how jamaats are viewed by persons outside the circle of addressees has also not been addressed. The following discussion of the two areas of Mewat and Merwara, suggests that organizations such as the Arya Samaj, the VHP, and the TJ need to be approached by also examining the chemistry of interaction between multiple religious groups and the cordialities/animosities among groups that are being produced as a result.

The regions called Mewat and Merwara, adjacent to the cities of Delhi and Ajmer in northern India, have over the twentieth century become theatres of experiment in the redefinition of religious identity. In both areas a certain shared space between Hindus and Muslims has more often than not been transformed into a contested space following extensive conflicts over identity.

ARYA SAMAJ AND TJ AMONG THE MEOS

Regarding the Meos of the Mewat region the story goes back to the simultaneous arrival of Arya Samaj and Tabligh cadres in the 1920s. The Arya Samaj was founded in 1875 by the Gujarati Brahmin Swami Dayanand Saraswati (1824-83). This was a movement of religious and social reform that invoked *vaidik* authority and wanted to rid Hinduism of the messiness of *nonvaidik* and *pauranik* texts and practice. Arya Samaj activity relating to *shuddhi*—defined as 'purification' and reconversion—has usually been seen as motivated by the new census figures (Jones 1976). The role of colonial ethnographies that showed how several communities were both Hindu *and* Muslim and defied categorial classification has not been noticed as also providing a significant impetus. Groups with liminal identities soon became a major site of operation. *Shuddhi* that had already been undertaken sporadically became a central activity of the Arya Samaj following the Mapilla Revolt (1919-21) during which certain forced conversions to Islam had been made by Mapillas, the descendants of early Arab traders who had married local women. Mass *shuddhi* in the 1900s was directed at the Shaikhs of Larkana in Sind, Sabrai Labanas of Ludhiana, the Mair/Mer of Ajmer and neo-Hindu Ismaili groups all over Rajputana, Muslim Rajputs in Deeg and later Etawah, Kanpur, Meerut and Mainpuri (Khan 1997: 166; Sikand 2002: Chap. 3).

The Arya Samaj came to these Meo villages from Agra that had become the headquarters of the All India Shuddhi Sabha. This location enabled work in British India and also made convenient access to the kingdoms under indirect British rule. It was spearheaded by Lala Munshi Ram (1856-1926), better known as Swami Shraddhanand, one of the most important followers of Dayanand. The Shuddhi Sabha became particularly active around 1923, when it was supported by the Hindu Mahasabha that had received financial support from the industrial house of the Birlas.

Arya Samaj cadres worked in alliance with the Sanatana Dharma Sabha, targeting villages of Muslim Rajputs, Gujjars, Malkanas and Meos, all of them being groups whose identity could not be seen as exclusively either Hindu or Muslim. *Shuddhi* drew upon older conceptions within Hinduism of the *prayashchitta* (return to the Hindu fold following a purificatory rite signifying 'repentance'), but combined it with models of conversion available in Islam, Sikhism, and Christianity, endowing it with a new conceptual meaning that underlined the ritually impure status of the other (see Jones 1972: 129; Jaffrelot 1999). Body symbolism, involving the shaving of facial hair and the 'pork test' of eating food considered ritually transgressive for Muslims, and the endowment of a new name suggest that the emphasis was on repudiating Islam rather than on transforming individual consciousness or on a change of heart.[3]

The caustic attacks of the volunteers on Islam contributed to a deterioration of inter-community relations across north India. Tabligh became the counter-response to *shuddhi* in which a number of Islamic missionary organizations joined their *ulama*. These included the Jamiat-ul ulama-i Hind who claimed that they had taken up the duty of Tabligh after eight centuries; the Barelwis associated with the 'customary' veneration of sufis who established *madrasas* to educate the Malkanas; Dar-ul Ulum, Deoband; the Qadiyani Ahmadiyyas; and important *ulama* such as Maulana Ashraf Ali Thanawi (1863-1943), Sayyid Abul-Ala Mawdudi (1903-79), founder of the Jamaat-i Islami, and M. Abdul Bari (1878-1926) of the Firangi Mahall, *madrasa* of Lucknow. Sikand points out that Tabligh was not just about improving the Islamic consciousness of nominal Muslims, but grew into a project of the construction of a pan-Indian Muslim identity different from and defined against the Hindus. The involvement of lower and middle class Muslim artisans and shopkeepers in both Tabligh and Khilafat politics suggests how it tied in with their own quest for upward social mobility (Sikand 2002).

Subsequently Tabligh was organized by men in Delhi at the tomb-shrine of the Chishtiyya saint, Shaikh Nizamuddin Awliya, usually identified as a source of 'syncretic' Islam. Fierce polemics characterized the pamphlet exchanges of the two groups led respectively by Khwaja Hasan Nizami, *sajjada nashin* or custodian of the

Nizamuddin Dargah, and Swami Shraddhanand (Minault 1982; Thursby 1975). Competing groups worked in Rajasthan, Gujarat, Sind, Punjab and Kerala. Field accounts from the kingdom of Bharatpur, then under indirect British rule, give one a vivid sense of the making of boundaries. These were marked by the use of warlike metaphors: when the village of Sikri (Bharatpur) underwent *shuddhi*, the news went around, '*Sikrī kā gah tūtā*' (the fortress of Sikri has been breached). An Arya Samajist told me, 'We would shout slogans, *pat hojā hindu phir banegī khīr*' (become Hindu and we'll make rice pudding); or '*salan ved pahne lage ahle korān hoy jab masjid mai shruti gān*' (when the readers of the Koran study the Vedas, the mosques will resound with Vedic chants).'[4] The *maulvis* and the *mullahs* would also come and say, 'you stay with us, *khudā kī bāt mai akal kī dakhal nahī*' (reason has no role in the matter of God).[5]

Tabligh was reinstitutionalized by the TJ directed by the Islami Markaz. In 1927 M. Muhammad Ilyas al-Kandahlawi (1885-1944) launched an experiment on the Meos that was to become what is generally acknowledged as the most important Islamic movement of our times. Ilyas' special targets were what were considered the 'half Muslims' or 'border line Muslims' then being claimed by Shuddhi and Sangathan. Ilyas believed that only a grassroots Islamic religious movement could cleanse them of their Hindu accretions and educate them about their basic beliefs and rituals to save them from falling prey to Hindu proselytisers. Ilyas began his work recording that the Meos had Hindu names, Hindu deities, and worshipped Hindu festivals and could not even recite the *shahadah* (the belief in the unity and oneness of God). He established one hundred *madrasas* in Mewat, but was soon disillusioned by that approach (Ahmad n.d.). Ilyas' major contribution was to shift from the ulama as the mainstay of religiosity to the ordinary, even uneducated, Muslim; and to suggest that *dawa* (the Arabic term for proselytism) must be the work of all Muslims. This was a remarkable turn, given that the genealogy of the TJ is grounded in the rise of the Muslim service gentry of the Indo-Gangetic plain, and the rise and spread of the influence of Deoband, the largest Hanafi (indeed, Islamic) seminary in the subcontinent.

M. Muhammad Ilyas al-Kandahlawi was born in Saharanpur and educated in Deoband. He studied with M. Ashraf Ali Thanwi, known as Hakim-ul Ummah, to whom he took a *bayah* (oath of allegiance). M. Yusuf (1917-65), the son and successor of M. Ilyas, took over from him. After Yusuf's death the movement was led by Ilyas' nephew, Inamul Hasan al-Kandahlawi (1965-95). Known as Hazrat Shaikhul Hadis, even Yusuf was known to have consulted Inamul Hasan frequently. Subsequently M. Saad al-Hasan, Yusuf's grandson and M. Muhammad Zubair al-Hasan, Inamul Hasan's son, jointly led the organization. The alim Ihtisam al-Hasan al Kandahlawi was married to M. Ilyas' sister and one of his associates, Muhammad Zakariyya Kandahlawi (1898-1982) of the Mazahir al-Ulum, Saharanpur, produced the book used in TJ training called the *Tablighi Nissab*.[6]

The major institutional innovation of M. Ilyas was the Jamaat that consists of a small group oriented to teaching correct Islamic practice. It is based on the idea that each and every Muslim is potentially capable of communicating Islam, in particular the six principles of *kalimah*, *salaah* (prayer), *dhikr* (knowledge and remembrance), *ikram-i-momin* (respect for Muslims), *al-Ikhlaas* (sincerity), *al-khurooj fi sabeel-Allah* (travel for the preaching of Islam) to which others are invited to join. The contribution to this activity of at least forty days in a year and four months in a lifetime is advocated for each Muslim. Apart from this the acquisition of religious knowledge, the adoption of Islamic appearance and dress, the seclusion of women, the performance of the Islamic form of marriage, Islamic education, the adoption of Islamic belief and ritual, and the rejection of non-Islamic practices are also emphasized.

M. Muhammad Yusuf, Ilyas's son and successor, is credited with the internationalization of the TJ. This internationalization has occurred to the extent that the Conference volume on the TJ (Masud 1997) identified transnationalism and travel as the two major aspects of this movement. Yusuf consolidated the movement in South Asia after 1947, working across the border in both India and Pakistan. TJ was introduced in the Arab countries after 1948; in Western countries after 1950; in the Afro-Asian countries after 1956; and most recently in China and Central Asia (Gaborieau 1999). Members of Jamaats are often seen at railway stations and on roads, their bedding across their shoulders, and moving from door to door in villages, or sometimes addressing a mosque (*bayan*). Travel has a special significance comparable to the *hijrā* or Prophet's migration from Mecca to Medina and is also an inner journey from *dunyā* to *dīn*, a temporal withdrawal from this worldliness that is crucial. 'While going out, meeting others and speaking to them, one is urged to continually address oneself. Knocking at others' doors, one is expected to arrive at one's own doorsteps. The idea is to bring home the consciousness of a larger Muslim community that will transcend the limits of ethnicity, nation and gender' (Masud 2000). Sikand marks a shift after Ilyas' death and a concern with *ibadat* or personal piety to the exclusion of the *sharia* which generated some controversy (2002: 70).

It is important to stress the different styles of transnational religion. Metcalf refers to the TJ as a 'quietist, apolitical movement of spiritual guidance and renewal concerned with *dawa* or Tabligh (proselytising)'. She points out that the TJ is based on the central idea that *all* Muslims can convey the central Islamic values and in this process also heighten their own spiritual realization. During their *chilla* they are supposed to maintain an ascetic disposition and uphold a simplicity of language and dress; to refuse feasting and other invitations and cook their own food and bear their own expenses; to exemplify piety and service (*khidmat*); to emphasize gentleness, self-abnegation and modesty; and to cultivate an egalitarian, non-hierarchical ethos and discourse. Metcalf emphasizes the consequences for gender relations, since women assume leadership roles and address gatherings and men reported a change in their attitudes towards tasks such as cooking normally seen as womanly and inferior. She contrasts it with the political Islam of the Jamaat-i Islami that reinforces domesticity based as it is on nationalism's implicit public-private binary (Metcalf 1996).

What Metcalf, Ahmad, and others have ignored are the consequences of the spread of TJ ideology in local contexts, the chain of disputation, both inter-religious and intra-Islamic that has sometimes occurred in the wake of the movement of Jamaats. Clearly the very inception of the movement was rooted in politics and the competitive proselytism of the 1920s (Gaborieau 1999; Sikand 2002; Mayaram 1997).

What was the world of the nineteenth-century Meo? And what were the consequences of this intensified religious activity? Oberoi has come under increasing criticism for his description of the 'enchanted world' of the Punjabi villager (1994, Chap. 3). His critics point out that he has relied on colonial sources (see Nijhawan 2002). My own evidence comes from within the Meo oral tradition and it supports the general picture that Oberoi builds in the Punjab of shared sacred spaces and mythopoetic traditions that were common to communities across what are today presumed to be boundaries of religion.[7] The picture of regional religiosity, however, is a far more complicated one. Hardy refers to three different types of worship that comprise the religious culture of India, the *gramya*, *agamic* or *tantrika*, and the *vaidika*. The first, village religion (that relates to some four-fifths of the population of the subcontinent), involves the consumption of alcohol, smoking opium, shedding blood, killing animals, eating meat, and states of possession. The Vaidika Brahmin usually distanced himself from popular practice that Hardy refers to as the 'vulgarities of village cults' and also from 'the heterodox traditions of temple worship' (Hardy 1995).[8] The Meo, despite their 'conversion' to Islam that began in the fourteenth century were participants along with other castes in village religion and also in the cosmologies derived from the agamas and the puranas. Hence, for instance, the ubiquitous presence of the great yogi Gorakhnath who pops up in oral traditions everywhere whether relating to the Jats, Ahirs or the Dalits of Kannada-speaking region (Shivaprakash 2002), the special status of Krishna; and the reference to goddesses and their female force, the *yoginis*, and to the 330 million gods.

In Mewat castes that we now think of as Hindu and Muslim had the usual village guardian deities. Besides this, there were protectors of land and water (the Bhomiya or Kheradeva and Bhairu or Khwaja Khizr); gods and goddesses of disease and healing (such as the cooling goddess, Sitala, referred to as *mata* or mother) and those who were the guarantors of victory in war for the Meo Ksatriya warriors; ancestral deities and spirits; shared pilgrimages and shrines; and myths, meanings and realms of intersubjectivity.

Communities are usually seen in terms of a single religious culture, but what needs to be emphasized is the complexity of religious affiliation and identity within a single group such as the Meo. Meos were involved in varying degrees with several Islamic cultural universes. They were part of Muslim traditions stretching from the subcontinent to Persia and Central Asia. Many Meos were devoted followers of Salar Masud, the tenth century Indo-Islamic warrior saint, and sometimes clashed with adherents of the Madariyya Tariqa and the Chishtiyya Silsilah. Some Meos became involved with the Rasul Shahi order that had a significant presence in the eighteenth-century kingdom of Alwar. This was an ascetic order similar to that of the Qalandars, the wandering darweshes who considered the settled life of the *khanqah* sinful and came into conflict with Chishtiyya and Suhrawardiyya saints. The Rasul Shahis not only shaved facial hair, wore a loin cloth, and were given to mystic states of ecstacy induced by intoxicants, but were known for their rejection of social norms.

There were Meos who themselves became founders of sects. Shah Chokha, Chudh Sidh and Lal Das, for instance, initiated modes of worship that attracted other castes including Hindu merchants. Holi, Dussehra, and Diwali were festivals as important as Muharram, Id and Shabibarat (Powlett 1870: 38-9, 70). The harvest festival of Holi commemorated both the Abrahamic sacrifice as also that of Holika for her brother, Prahlada, both read as myths of the extraordinary devotion of Abraham and Prahlada, the great devotee of Vishnu. What were important then were not only multiple sectarian influences and textual models; but also the possibility of reinterpretations of texts in folk compositions such as of the great epic, the *Mahabharata*, and of ritual events such as Holi. This was no isolated and unchanging world, but one that was highly dynamic and marked by the mobility of ascetics, bards, genealogists, entertainers, wrestlers, and others. Religious identities were plural, multiple, and overlapping with several circles of belonging even as they could strive for singularity under influential sectarian movements. Skinner's work, the *Tashrīh-ul-Aquām* (Persian) of 1824 described the Meos as both Hindu and Muslim and as having one section with 'no religion' that included *darweshes*, *jogis*, *jangam*, *sevra*, *sannyasis*, and *paramhans*. Reverence and irreverence coexisted: one ethnographer remarked of the Meos and Gujars that they keep the feasts of both the Hindu and Islamic traditions, but the fasts of neither!

Sociality did not necessarily add up to 'harmony'. Ancestral deities themselves could be markers of difference as, for instance, when for one group of Muslims called the Khanzadas their *sayyids* (ancestor memorials) were seen as the consequence of sacrificial death and martyrdom of seven Khanzada brothers who were then battling the Meo in a prolonged feud. Conflicts over land, resources, women, and power were endemic among the groups that we today call Hindu and Muslim.

One of my favourite examples of cross-cutting alliances between regional castes and groups is a narrative from the Meo oral tradition because it illustrates so well the crossing of boundaries. This is a representative example of a frequent situation in which religious difference was overcome when overriding interests of power and state formation were at stake. It is a story of the alliance of a 'Mughal' Nawab and a Rajput Maharaja that involved revenue extortions from the Meo peasantry and the abduction of the two daughters of a Meo chief.[9] Religious symbols were invoked in the mobilization of both sides. In the story the armies of the Rajput-Nawab alliance threaten the goddess that they would destroy her temple unless she guaranteed their victory. But Jvala-Mukhi (the goddess in her form as flame-tongue) blessed instead the opposing alliance of Meo and non-Meo peasants endowing the Meo clan with the capacity to sustain a battle against the state for some forty years between 1796 and 1835.[10] A century later in 1930 the figure of Ali is invoked to mobilize all Meo clans to fight the cause of Rajput peasants and to intensify the Meo agitation against the state. The two instances indicate a very flexible use of religious motifs drawn from a large Hindu-Islamic pool of symbols.

This is the universe that was sought to be brought into 'Hinduism' and Islam by the respective cadres of Arya Samaj and TJ in the 1920s. To the Arya Samaj and its successor, the VHP, aspects of Meo/Merat belief and practice marked them as Hindu. What was required was the negative criterion of eating pork. On the other side, the TJ adheres to the ideology of Islamic universalism requiring Muslims to rid themselves of local and other 'deviations'. It insisted that villagers give up un-Islamic belief and practice; abandon their peasant dress in favour of what was described as Islamic clothing; and advised men to give up shaving beards. Their battle was as much with other Islamic sects since it was the Barelwi, Qalandariyya and Chishtiyya Islamic ideologies that had hitherto marked Meo Islamic practice.

Contemporary accounts suggest that groups subject to the competing cadres of Arya Samaj and Tabligh perceived them as somewhat comic. Malkana villagers, for instance, promised to adhere to either side in the presence of these cadres, and after their departure caricatured them and continued as before.[11] More recently, the French anthropologist Jamous describes the visit of the Jamaat (1990s) that reprimands Meos for their belief in spirits.[12] After their departure they revert to the usual practice. The Muslim *topi* or skull cap, asserts a Meo, is completely alien to our culture. What is wrong if we say namaz with our *sāfā* (turban) on? A woman's song collected by Jamous makes satiric fun of the Jamaat, holding it responsible for all the troubles of her village and household. There are many others, however, who have experienced a profound sense of spirituality, self-discovery, and social involvement in their participation as a member of a Jamaat.

The TJ has had long-term reverberations for religiosity and identity politics. The dramatic shift in allegiance for the Meos came about as a reaction to the politics of the 1940s when *shuddhi* squads made their rounds once again, this time with violent mobs. Die or undergo *shuddhi*, Meo villagers were told. Some did become Hindu, however temporarily, but for others the politics of genocide and forced conversion would result in a new singularization of identity: the Meo identification came to be with Sunni Islam, fostered by the Deoband school.

Certain Mewati *alim* are becoming increasingly sensitive to the fact that Tablighi criticism of the Meo performing traditions brought about an erosion of their collective, communal memory, the strong sense of their past, and the cohesive group identity that was grounded in the musical repertoire of the Mirasis. But they realized the larger advantage of de-emphasizing their Meoness *vis-à-vis* their Muslimness that has brought with it the security that comes from being a member of a larger 'minority', and access to networks through which local imbalances of power can be reworked and claims made to resources. For many Mewatis the TJ has meant a new sense of belonging to the Muslim *umma* and a sense of spiritual self-realization. One of my closest Mewati friends is a poor widow. A strong and articulate woman, she derives a subsistence livelihood from her small land-holding. The marriage of her several daughters took away any reserves that she might have had. Participation in women's Jamaats has given her a way of socializing with women from different backgrounds. It has deepened her understanding and knowledge of the Koran and its values of humility and equality.

VHP AND TJ AMONG THE MERAT

The region of Merwara is, if anything, an even more complex world. The Merat are a community who have been hitherto Muslim in respect to three practices, *khatna*, *garhna* and *halal* (or circumcision, burial and the eating of halal meat). But for the rest they shared the mytho-ritual world of two other regional groups, the Rawat and Chita. The three groups saw themselves as part of a larger brotherhood descended from the same ancestors and as part of a single kinship system in which they intermarried with each other. Some families told me how, until recently, they had been performing both the *nikaah* and the *pheras*, Muslim and Hindu marriage rites.

The totalizing categories of the colonial Raj were introduced to the Mer (as the entire group was then called) through their participation in the colonial Indian Army. These inaugurated a new awareness of being either Hindu and Muslim. Christianity had already come to them by the late nineteenth century with competitive proselytism between a series of Christian denominations followed shortly afterwards by the advent of the Arya Samaj. Conversion and reconversion and a new consciousness of difference in religious terms arose between the Rawat and the Merat. Religious boundaries further hardened following a new battle of identities between the TJ and the VHP beginning in 1975.

The VHP had been founded in 1964, among others by leaders of the militant Hindu nationalist organization, the RSS and Swami Chinmayanand. Its attempt was to promote Hindu nationalism, resist Westernization and globalization, and foster Hindu values while reaching out globally to all Hindus. It became active in the US after 1974, riding a major wave of immigration from India into the US.

After the conversions of Dalits to Islam in Meenakshipuram in 1981, the VHP became particularly active, intensifying what the Arya Samaj had begun much earlier. This organization and its affiliates have become purveyors of a political Hinduism that is also the attempt to define a Religion (in the upper case). This Hindu Religion defines a canon that is identifiable from the VHPs *paravartan* or 'reconversion' agenda. It establishes the ritual supremacy of the *yajna* or Vedic sacrifice and thereby of the *vaidika* authority in an area of hitherto little Brahmanical influence. Previously the 'low' castes conducted much of their own religious life through ritual specialists called Bhopas, who were non-Brahmins and could even be women or Muslim. The VHP substitutes these non-twice-born Bhopas with Brahmins. It relocates the dominant site of worship at temples, undermining the importance of the open shrine, the *thans* and the *dhunis*, shrines and hearths at which worship had been conducted. The VHP project of conversion privileges History, urging on the Hindu Merat and Chita, a sense of belonging in tune with their true history, as the Rajput descendants of Prithviraj, the last Hindu emperor before the Muslim conquest of India. Finally, it discounts local gods and goddesses in favour of what it describes as *pauranik* (pan-Indian, text-based) gods and goddesses and sanitized, de-eroticized readings of their mythologies. In other words, a packaged Purana-derived Hinduism is being superimposed over the religion of the Rawat, Merat, and Chita (for details, see Mayaram n.d.).

The TJ (as also *maulvis* affiliated to a variety of organizations) are equally active in Merwara. Members of a Jamaat might inform their followers about false gods who appear in forms seated, reclining or standing (referring to Shiva, the Buddha and Mahavira). Also about 'wrong' practices such as indulging in music, dancing and drumming during the holi festival of colours or playing *era khelna* (a popular hunting game). The Merat are instructed in offering namaz and in the need to fast on Ramadan and to give up their un-Islamic practices.

The actual work of both VHP and TJ is accomplished in the caste associations. Minor issues relating to the everyday—personal, familial and domestic—have become occasions for the struggle of religious world-views. Rites of passage such as succession to clan leadership and marriage are occasions for bitter contestation. Death and funerary rites are occasions for the play of identity politics rather than gatherings for the expression of loss, sorrow, or mourning. The battle over identities has cleaved households, clans, villages and groups. In a classic case, two brothers, called Zafar and Amar Singh, became the respective leaders of the two wings of the ethnicised community. The same issues recur: burial *vs.* cremation (to the extent that police protection is often required); images rumoured to have been broken by 'iconoclasts'; and cow killing by alleged beef-eaters who have supposedly thrown the bones into wells near a mosque/*madrasa*. In the nearby town of Beawar Muslims had lived in relative peace with Hindus. Worried about the new levels of anti-Muslim violence, a mosque in Beawar has put up a sign proscribing the entry of the TJ.

The VHP contributes to exacerbating and maintaining intense tension. It has inserted a series of new practices within local civil society, organized through programmes within educational institutions, and its presence in civic bodies including municipalities, panchayats, merchant and trader associations, trade unions, etc. High levels of mobilization of a 'Hindu' political community are achieved through religious and other processions, 'pilgrimages', and welfare.

Clearly the debate on conversion is one of the primary issues that links the local with the national and the global. The defence of the homeland's beleaguered Hinduism against Christian evangelization and Islamic *dawa* is what has won the VHP the support of the diasporic Indian—financial, technological, mobilizational, and other. The VHP, of course, denies that it is undertaking conversion at all and asserts that it is only reconverting. I have challenged this argument elsewhere and will only point out here that conversion is not just a rite. Under the VHP's elucidation it is a comprehensive category that signifies entry into Civilization and History, and not just Religion.

The moot point is whether the work of the TJ can be read as conversion. My own position is that the guidance (as distinct from governance) model of Islamicization that the TJ propagates entails implicit conversion. From 1927 to the present it has worked on the 'nominal' or 'half' Muslims, the term suggesting that the other 'half' was non-Islamic. The reading of the *kalima* symbolizes the abandonment of *jahilliyah* or backwardness that includes the worship of gods and goddesses, saints, spirits, ancestors, etc.[13]

Although it codes its own work as reconversion, the VHP seeks to incorporate the converted into a defined, bounded, and homogeneous national religion. It is grounded far more in the teaching of true 'history' than of theology. The Muslim Merat are, thus, told to recognize their 'genealogy' which traces descent from Prithviraj Chauhan, and their true 'history' of belonging to the Chauhan Rajput clan. One of the early Arya Samaj converts in rural Ajmer told me how his conversion had enlightened him about this true history.[14] His conversion did not represent a heightened spirituality or an inner awakening, but an entry into the time of the nation via history.

What does it mean for people to be brought into History? What happens when they come into Religion? (The upper case is used deliberately, because it is usually presumed in this discourse in Orientalist fashion that these are people who lacked history, and often religion). The irony is that the VHP has often ended up converting persons who have had more to do with the making and transmission of Hinduism than its own activists. Persons who are caretaker-priests of rural shrines and the gods of the byways are regarded by them as Muslim, hence, requiring a conversion to Hinduism. The story of conversion, however, is not one of passivity, a mere trickle down of religious ideologies. There is the question of human agency, particularly of individuals and caste associations seeking upward mobility in what is an agrarian ecology of extreme poverty.

RELIGION, GLOBALIZATION AND THE MAKING OF TRANSNATIONAL RELIGIOUS CIVIL SOCIETY

In a sense religion has always been marked by transnational flows. Religious visions, texts, and ideas have been carried across the seas and over the boundaries of nations by merchant-traders, militias, and missionaries. A marked departure occurred with the coming of print and education. The religious text and pamphlet went into mass circulation and religious doctrine could now be part of primary school curriculum. But clearly something dramatic has affected our times, altered with new information flows, the new media, and mass travel. The new possibilities of mobility make possible rapid communication, and the building of international networks adept at using modern technologies. M. Yusuf's walking Jamaats, for instance, are today more likely to be 'flying' Jamaats. There is also the possibility of distance-discourse, as gurus and saints address their audiences on TV. This has sprouted a series of gurus/movements, such as Asa Ram, the Brahma Kumaris and the Ahmadiyyas. The *communitas* is, in a sense, no longer that of the face-to-face community. The electronic revolution has made it possible for religious discourses to become available on cassette and video tape. They can now be downloaded from the worldwideweb. Theologies transcend distances of space and time through a variety of means. They constitute large new publics through relations of anonymity.

Simultaneously, the congregation that had always been an important feature of Christianity, has now become central to other world religions too. The TJ has paid detailed attention to institutional architecture, which is radically innovative. There has been a shift from the traditional religious institutions of the Islamic world, namely the *khanqah* (dargah)-mosque-*madrasa* to the *chilla*, Jamaat and *ijtima* (which is not to say that the mosque and *madrasa* have been rendered insignificant). TJ meetings in Pakistan and Bangladesh are known to attract one to two million persons. A figure of even three million has been suggested, and its conventions are said to offer prayers kilometres in length (Masud 2000). The TJ's annual conference is the second largest Islamic congregation after the Hajj. The VHP has deployed the idea of the Hindu congregation with regional and international Virat Hindu Sammelans in New York, 1984; Copenhagen, 1985; Singapore, Kuala Lumpur, Bangkok, The Hague, Nairobi and Nepal, 1988; Milton Keynes in England, 1989; the Global Vision Conference in Washington D.C.,1993, held in the post-Babri Masjid demolition period when it was banned.

Globalization aids the work of the TRMs even as they themselves are part of the phenomenon we describe as globalization. Intermediaries including professionals such as lawyers and management consultants, and specialists in media and cultural production have become involved in heritage creation the world over. Ironically, the construction of a national culture itself can come to depend on globalization. Organizations such as the VHP have made full use of new technologies. The global movement of its activists has been facilitated by the communications revolution and electronic and information technology that condenses spatial distance. The services of India's human resource of IT technocrats have been commandeered in building a certain version of 'Hindu' cyberspace (Lal 2003). New interdenominational and interreligious internet battles have substituted the pamphlet wars of the age of print. In contrast, the TJ has made relatively minimal use of both the electronic and print media and the worldwideweb, preferring conventional modes of oral communication.

TRMs demonstrate a remarkable capacity for organizing men and materials, which has enabled their transnationalism. The application of science can be seen in their extensive use of the geographer's map; the ethnographer's tools of writing and filing field reports; and the historians' attempt to construct a definite past as also to maintain their own record and archive it. They depend on modern, bureaucratized modes of governance, which involve training, organization, and technologies of control such as the *fatawa*. The period of *chilla* for a Tablighi begins with a training at the markaz, its central seminary. On the whole, however, unlike the VHP that has a high media profile, the TJ prefers not to interact with the media, or issue statements or communiques. Instead, communication is through word of mouth and there is little published material. As Gaborieau puts it, the movement is secretive, its inner core incommunicative, and indeed, quite inaccessible to outsiders. Most of the published sources are internal and in the form of biographies and hagiographies produced by the Nadwat-ul-ulama (Gaborieau 1999).

TRMs leave local contexts considerably altered and have very serious implications for cultural diversity. They work with and through local communities and individuals, empower and even capture tribal, caste and other local associations. They create boundaries within communities which they often divide into supporters and antagonists, collaborators and opponents. Obversely, they contribute to the unmaking of other boundaries as they work across borders of locality, region and nation. Undeniably they also enhance mobility, capabilities, and autonomy for their participants by providing possibilities of travel, and the experience of new horizons, places and persons.

TRANSNATIONAL RELIGIOUS MOVEMENTS AND THE STATE

The crux of globalized religion is the relationship between transnational religious civil society and the nation state. Writers such as Hannerz emphasize a distinction between globalization and transnationalism pointing out that the latter tends to be more decentred. In the case of transnationalism the actors are individuals, groups, movements, corporations, and not necessarily states as corporate actors as in the case of globalization (1996: 6).

The early phase of writing on globalization tended to valorize the postnational and the transnational in identifying the demise of nationalism, the (nation) state and sovereignty. Arjun Appadurai was representative of this celebratory position. He argued that emergent social forms such as refugee camps, peacekeeping forces, and international terrorist training camps, are already transnational, and therefore 'compel us to think post-nationally' (1996: 158). The more recent writing on globalization has tended to be more state-centric. Chatterjee argues that, on the contrary, we must necessarily speak from *within* the nation, even while recognizing that the nation-state is not necessarily our ally in the struggle for democracy (1998). His writings point out that we cannot prematurely supersede the nation or proclaim its demise (1993). Cheah and Robbins also recognize the importance of coming to grips with the national in the context of globalization, rather than merely celebrating transnationalism and diaspora (1998).

The role of the VHP and its obsession with state power is well known (Mathur et al. n.d.; McKean 1996; Bhatt and Mukta 2000; Mukta 2000; Mathew and Prashad 2000). In this case religion is used only instrumentally as a pool of symbols to be drawn upon; but it is also treated as an object to be moulded and reformatted, keeping political ends in mind. TRMs then can be sources of violence particularly when they are able to conjoin with state power, but they can also promote non-violent belief and action.

The relation of TJ to the state is more complex given its distance from electoral and party politics. For decades academic judgement pronounced the TJ apolitical (Metcalf 1993, 1993b, 1996; also Ahmad

1991). This is a view that has been challenged repeatedly (see, for instance, Gaborieau 1999; Mayaram 1997). Politics is not merely about the state and the ballot box. Sikand emphasizes the movement's political vision and how, through the various political roles that it plays, it is deeply engaged in questions of power and authority. If politics be seen 'in comprehensive terms, as the dynamics of power in society, the notion that anything can be apolitical in a political world strikes one as absurd. In this sense, the TJ can hardly be said to be apolitical' (2003: 42-3). Gaborieau argues that the dividing line is not between political and apolitical Islamic movements but between two ways of conceiving politics. While the Islamists work through the nation state, there are other groups who think beyond borders: 'putting politics most often in parentheses they first build individuals and institutions, which over time may exert a more lasting political influence' (Gaborieau 1999). Sikand argues that we shift methodological focus from TJ discourse to an analysis of the political roles the movement has played, as this demonstrates that it 'might well be impelled by a long-term political agenda'. To this, I would add that all spiritual visions necessarily incorporate visions of governance that are, after all, an aspect of a conception of a larger divine governance.

M. Ilyas had from the early beginnings of the movement emphasized its political character. This was explicit in its anticolonial posture. In 1908 when Ilyas joined the Dar-ul ulum *madrasa* in Deoband he took an oath of *jihad* against the British. Ilyas' diagnosis of the Indian Muslims' predicament was poised on the idea of their loss of power that he saw as deriving from their abandonment of the path of Islam. His departure from the Islamists lay in his emphasis on the reform of individual Muslims rather than the capture of political power. This inner change would lead to an Islamic society governed by an Islamic state. Sikand argues that reports of his interaction with other Muslim leaders suggest that Ilyas was concerned with the ultimate acquisition of political power in the future. He was 'not opposed to other contemporary movements struggling for Muslim political power [and] believed that the TJ and such Muslim movements were complimentary to each other'. 'There should be no competition or rivalry between them', Ilyas insisted. Sikand concludes, 'Ilyas' understanding of individual reform and his distance from matters related to the state can be read as reflecting an underlying division of labour—the TJ focusing on the individual, and other Muslim groups working in the political sphere.' Sikand cites the statement of an *alim* (whom he does not name) who claims that the TJs aloofness from overt political involvement is simply a temporary 'pious pragmatic policy' to enable it to promote 'Islamic consciousness'.

Both Ahmad and Sikand maintain that a shift followed Ilyas' death in 1944. With Muslims having become a minority in the aftermath of Partition and Independence, the TJ began presenting itself as completely apolitical. M. Yusuf believed that this was the only way in which the movement could remain active without provoking the animosity of Hindu groups. The adjustment with a secular state and non-Islamic rule was seen as provisional, until such day as Indian Muslims would be governed by an Islamic state. (This effectively was what happened in Bangladesh.) The movement's rejection of direct involvement in politics in independent India helped the TJ thrive in spite of an atmosphere of suspicion and hostility to Muslims. Sikand argues that the TJ sees the Muslim situation in India as akin to the Prophet's Meccan period when his followers were still learning the faith. After maturation they would be able to graduate to the Medinan period. The accommodation to secularism, he writes, is then 'ambiguous and not free from tension'. The TJ 'efforts at building a sense of Muslim identity, bringing Muslims all over the world together in a common mission, maintaining a strong sense of separate cultural identity and superiority, and condemning the popular culture that Muslims in local contexts share with others, has important political consequences in religiously plural societies'. Critics also allege the obverse that this has effectively depoliticized the Muslim community.

The TJ has had a differential impact across space.[15] Gaborieau points out that both in Pakistan and Bangladesh the TJ has an interface with the political establishment. In Pakistan its strengthening was encouraged by the army and administration to promote an activist vision of Islam, conducive to the growth of Islamist movements but also to counter the politically ambitious Jamaat-i Islami. In Bangladesh, it helped numerous Islamic activists escape state repression. Sikand cites Shamsul Alam, a TJ sympathizer, who refers to it as silently preparing Muslims all over the world for a goal akin to that of other Islamist groups: to engage in the 'lesser *jihad*', physical warfare against the 'enemies of Islam', and 'if occasion arises and if the policy is changed. . . . Tabligh is the Islamic movement which can call upon its dedicated followers not only to donate their time and money but also their lives to the cause of Islam'. A Tabligh supporter states on a website that the TJ has only been 'laying the groundwork for a much greater mission', which includes physical *jihad*, if necessary, and the struggle for the establishment of an Islamic polity. In Tabligh and *jihad* he finds a 'congruence of aims and objectives' since both are 'manifestations of the same impulse'. Tabligh activists have increasingly assumed more assertive political positions in Islamist organizations. These include Ghulam 'Azam, *amir* of Bangladesh's JII, Rachid Ghannoushi of the Tunisian Islamic Tendency Movement, and Farid Kassim of the Hizb ut-Tahrir in the UK. Islamists themselves are divided on the role of the TJ. While some are critical, others laud it for its role in promoting the awareness of Islam among Muslims and thereby assisting the long term strengthening of Islamist movements. A pro-Taliban website supports the TJ.[16] Critics point out the role of the TJ in the militant Pakistan-based Harkat ul-Mujahidin. Sikand cites a spokesman of the Harkat as claiming, 'our people are mostly impressed by the TJ. Most of our workers come from the TJ.'[17]

Tabligh activists have assumed important official roles and promoted the gradual Islamization of state structures and civil society. In Bangladesh, the TJ has a significant presence in the army. In Pakistan Rafiq Tarar has been President; Javed Nasir, a senior TJ activist, was chief of Pakistan's Inter-States Services Intelligence and responsible for the formulation of Pakistan's policy in the Afghan war; Mufti Mahmud, *khalifa* of the leading Tablighi ideologue, Muhammad Zakariya, was elected chief minister of Pakistan's Frontier Province and was in the forefront of the movement for a prophetic system that led to the deposition of Zulfiqar Ali Bhutto. Nawaz Sharif even got Tariq Jamil, the senior Tabligh leader, to address his cabinet on the 'responsibilities of rulers' and the need to 'enforce an Islamic system' similar to that in Afghanistan under the Taliban.

The 'local' gets reconfigured through historical processes associated with translocal and transnational religious ideas. Hence the enormity of cultural and political change in Mewat and Merwara in relation to ideas of universal Islam and Protestant and Nationalist Hinduism. The latter are in themselves hybrid outcomes of the transnational flow of ideas, in this case of nationalism, colonialism, and Christianity derived from Europe. Institutions activate local agency to work in local, translocal, or transnational contexts—hence the Mewati participant of the Jamaat or the neo-Hindu Merat VHP activist. Religious ideologies and movements as they work across borders are, in turn, themselves influenced by new national contexts. This is what explains the distinctiveness of Deoband in India from that in Pakistan or Afghanistan or of VHP India from VHP America.[18]

The religious vision of the TJ is grounded in the Deoband branch of the Sunni Islamic school of thought and given the close relation that has existed historically between the two it is important to recognise the shifts that have occurred in Deoband ideology across time and space. There is an extraordinary flexibility and malleability of the various sections of Deoband as it moves across the subcontinent. In India the Deobandi leadership had supported the anti-colonial struggle of Gandhi and the Congress and helped from the Jamiat-ul ulama-i-Hind (the Association of the Ulama of India). The latter fiercely contested the idea of a homeland for Muslims that it saw as the demand of a Westernized, secular leadership. It upheld the idea of India as a confederation of multiple faiths and religious communities. It continued to chart, post-Independence, a pragmatic policy with respect to the ruling group (Metcalf 2002).[19]

The rise of the Sangh Parivar and of Hindutva in India mirrors, in a sense, the radicalization of Deoband as also the Deobandization of Pakistan. A particular configuration of international and domestic politics including the search for legitimacy by the military regime of General Muhammad Zia ul-Haq (1977-88) led to a new prominence of Deoband and of its political institution, the Jamiat-i ulama-i-Islam (JUI). The Iranian Revolution intensified Shia activism in Pakistan that Saudi Arabia and Iraq attempted to counter by building a Sunni wall around Iran and strategically locating *madrasas* in Baluchistan and southern NWFP to block off Iran from Pakistan (Nasr 2000, 158; Zaman 1998). Saudi and Iraqi competition over the control of *madrasas* endowed these institutions with enormous financial resources, exacerbated factional conflicts and transformed *madrasas* from intellectual institutions into political ones. In effect, state policy and the international context 'helped create a whole new genre of *madrasas*—ones that were equally if not more concerned with *jihad* (holy war) than with religious scholarship' (Nasr 2000, 144).[20] Nasr maintains that within Deoband a new faction became assertive that comprised the followers of Husain Ahmad Madani who emphasized a politically activist role for the *ulama*. 'By posing as the protectors of Pakistan's Islamicity, the Madani group ensconced itself in Pakistan.' Nasr points out that militant expressions of Deobandis from the Sipah-i Sahaba Pakistan (SSP) to the Taliban to the Harakat ul

Ansar are offshoots of the Madani group. The SSP worked as an semi-autonomous faction of the JUI until its break in 1986 because of its advocacy of violence against Shias; but the two shared, and continue to share, many of their rank-and-file members and office-holders. It was known for its slogan, *agar Pakistan main musalman bun kar rahna hai, to Shia ko kafir kehna hai* (if you want to live in Pakistan as a Muslim you must call the Shia infidel). Its splinter group, the Lashkar-i Jhangvi, began to counter the assassinations by Shias with assassinations of Shias.

The JUI, in turn, became the teachers of the Taliban whose rise to power took place around 1994. The Taliban practised, as Ahmed Rashid puts it, 'an extreme form of Deobandism, which was being preached by Pakistani Islamic parties in Afghan refugee camps in Pakistan' (2000: 88). This drew upon a 'fairly narrow range of sharia law' characterized by an extreme severity. It was supported both by sections within the Pakistani State, the Arabs and by the United States (up to 1998) interested in the Central Asian oilfields. It was the Taliban with whom Osama bin Laden allied.

With the end of the Afghan war and decline in employment opportunities, the Pakistani state was unable to cope with demands of the various Islamic groups. The Afghan situation and Kashmir offered it a respite. Most guerrilla training bases run by the Jamaat-i Islami (JII) and the Hizb-i Islami were handed over to the Deobandi Taliban and the Harakat ul Ansar, reinforcing the political and military roles of the madrasahs and their graduates.

By 1996 the rising power of the SSP complemented the rise of the Deobandi Taliban in the NWFP and Afghanistan and the Harakat ul-Ansar in Kashmir, all of which replaced older guerrilla groups tied to the Jamaat-i Islami. Nasr comments, 'There appears to be a region-wide (transnational) radical Deobandi resurgence in the making—something akin to the Wahhabi explosion in the eighteenth-century Arabian peninsula—extending in the form of an arc from India through Pakistan and Afghanistan into Central Asia.'

Joshi points out that the Harkat ul-jihad-i Islami International (HUJI) was sponsored in 1980 by the JUI and the TJ of Pakistan to run relief camps for Afghan mujahidin. It was led by Maulvi Irshad Ahmed and supported by the Punjabi business community with JUI and TJ factions. The HUJI established links with the Pakistani intelligence agency, the Inter States Services Intelligence (ISI) and was sub-contracted to recruit and train mujahids. After the death of Maulvi

Irshad Ahmed, the HUJI split, and the Harakat ul-Mujahidin (HUM) emerged—this group used as its base the training camps in Afghanistan set up by the US–Saudi–Pakistani alliance against the Russians. The HUJI/HUM militias began work in Kashmir in 1992. Joshi maintains that in 1991 the Deobandi *ulama* of Karachi had asked the two Harkats to reunite to intensify the Kashmiri *jihad*, and the Harkat-ul Ansar was born in October 1993 (Joshi 1988, 1999). It continued until it was notified by the US government as one of thirty international terrorist organizations under the Anti-Terrorist and effective Death Penalty Act of 1996 and reverted to its original name of HUM. Joshi maintains that the HUA derives from the Deoband religious ideology and that its recruits came from the TJ (1999: 164, 178-9).

What implications this has for the TJ is not exactly clear. The TJ got a lot of bad press after 11 September 2002. This began with cases of recruitment for the Taliban through the TJ. The Western media, in any case, stamps terrorist over everything Muslim. At present, there is more conjecture than definitive evidence. There is speculation that the TJ is being used by *jihadi* groups as a cover and a source of recruitment. This is possibly because of an infiltration of the TJ by *jihadi* groups or there might be individuals and groups working within the TJ *in tandem* with militant organizations that are using it for their own ends (personal communication, Vali Nasr, 2003). In Pakistan, in particular, the majority of Tabligh participants belong to the frontier province adjoining Afghanistan. Allegations are rife that the movement there is covertly political.

Despite the speculation of its overt and covert politicization, Metcalf rightly points out that 'the a-political missionary tours, gatherings in local mosques and homes, and annual gatherings continue to be the routine of the movement, one that clearly offers meaning and dignity to many who participate' (2002: 17). Given the current debate on *jihad*, the TJ's foregrounding of the idea of the internal *jihad* as the greater *jihad* is extremely important. Indeed, the TJ is often welcomed by ruling elites, being seen as maintaining social order and curbing dissent and radical politics. It is also for this reason that the TJ is criticized by certain Islamist groups. A *fatwa* was actually issued *against* the TJ by Haji Abdalhaqq Sayf al-Ilm Bewley at the VI Conference on Islamic Fiqh, held at the Faculty of Science, Granada University, in Spain, on August 1992.[21] It maintained that the TJ misinterprets hadith pertaining to *jihad*, which they equate with *dawa,* and so have forgotten the real meaning of *jihad.* Instead they depend on weak hadith as is manifest in their key text *Tablighi Nissab.* The *fatwa* describes the TJ as deviant and responsible for the misguidance of millions of Muslims. It is alleged that the TJ emphasizes the private and moral aspects of revelation, omitting the legal and political aspects. Since the focus is individual, not institutional, it has depoliticized participants and impaired the work of groups such as the Jamaat-i Islami. The article points out that they need to teach their members the obligation of *jihad* against the *kuffar.* The irony, it states, is that there are more people who are Muslim than in any period of history, but nowhere in the world is there anyone who is guided by the Koran so that 'Islam does not exist anywhere'. The *ulama's* conspiracy with the British (an oblique reference to Deoband) led to the abandonment of *jihad* as the cornerstone of Islamic doctrine. The TJ is described as revisionist and modernist; as people who disturb worship at the mosque; who address only Muslims; and whose six principles neglect the very important aspect of *zakat* or the giving away of a portion of one's income as alms.[22] In some respects the critique of the TJ from the political Islam perspective reinforces the TJ's moral claims to a non-conflictual, non-violent, and hence superior way of addressing the question of being a Muslim in the world.

The criticism that the TJ needs to modify its hierarchical structure of religious authority is a far more salient one. For all its democratization with respect to the teaching of Islam, the leadership remains confined to a group that has significant mutual bonds, including those of kinship.[23] Sikand maintains that the shift from the *iqamat-i-din* to mere ritualism and passivity derives from the growing political importance of a conservative Gujarati bourgeoisie that has come to dominate the organization after M. Yusuf's death. Since their own economic interests are wired into 'un-Islamic' national and global economic structures, they have worked out an accommodation with secular politics that conveniently restricts religion to the private domain. This has overwritten M. Ilyas' own concern with establishing an Islamic polity. Ferozepuri points out that the TJ has become associated with wealth and power and neglects the poor, including those in the vicinity of its centre. This has dissociated it from ordinary Muslims and their lifeworlds. The emphasis is on the spectacle of mass conventions and on preaching, not practice; travel has become the measure of religiosity (Sikand 2002: 147-60).

Can the TJ and VHP be seen as bearers of new cosmopolitan projects (van der Veer 2001)? TRMs we know are significant for diasporas even as the latter also bridge the local and the global. Religion is particularly important for rural-urban and transnational migrants, faced with the insecurity of livelihoods, citizenship/refugee status, and belonging. It helps anchor and orient lifeworlds; provides fellowship, social assistance and networks; and suggests strategies for coping with the stranger. Transnational religion provides new forms of community for countries undergoing major economic and demographic transitions. Despite their spatial movement, migrants are introduced into new boundaries by these movements. Van der Veer acknowledges that these organizations promote religious enclaves of correct belief and behaviour (2001). Sometimes they provide a new language of politics for rapidly growing urban centers through which migrants can be integrated into urban social life.

Diasporas, in turn, suggest the counterinfluence of religion in the homeland, say, in the many uses of repatriated incomes of certain Gujarati Patels in India. In Pakistan the diaspora has funded *madrasas* and Islamic organizations (Nasr 2000, 145). The VHP's association with violence has become only too well known. In cities such as Ajmer it is currently contributing to the destruction of a cosmopolitanism that had grown around the city's development as a multi-religious centre associated with the sacred site of Pushkar and the most important Sufi of the subcontinent, Khwaja Muin-ud-Din Chishti (d. 1235). The TJ's effort at working on an agenda of moral regeneration has been far more sustained. But it would need to engage far more in dialogue and conversation with other groups, both Muslim and non Muslim, to qualify for being considered as furthering cosmopolitanism. And there is no reason why it cannot abandon its insularity and enter into an inter-faith dialogue such as is being undertaken by a variety of religious groups. A degree of openness and transparency would ease the criticism and suspicion that it presently engenders.

Rajagopal (2001) and van der Veer (2001: 6) emphasize the contrast between VHP India and VHP America. They point out that outside India, the VHP's anti-globalization propaganda is considerably toned down since its supporters favour liberalization and globalization of the economy rather than *swadeshi*. In India it is a nationalist movement, but in the US it is a global religious movement. Its focus there is on the reproduction of the cultural world of the Hindu family and its protection from pernicious, Western influence. But what these scholars ignore is how the discourse of conversion in the homeland connects with VHP operations worldwide. Ideas and images of the violent Muslim, of a shrinking Hindu demography, and of a Hinduism under siege bond VHP India and VHP America.

What is the impact of such TRMs on religious and cultural identities? Saberwal argues that there has been a growth of assertive, singular identities, specifically between Hindus and Muslims, in the Indian context beginning in the nineteenth century and continuing through the twentieth. The markers are all too well known and we have reviewed much of this religious institutional ground in this paper. But the faultlines that are being produced are intra-Islamic and intra-Hindu as much as they are inter-religious. Deoband is attempting to capture the debate on Islamism in Pakistan overtaking the Barelwi and the Jamaat-i Islami, not to speak of deepening the 'medieval' faultline against the Twelver Shia and the Ismaili Shia. The entire corpus of ritual life associated with Indian Sufism stands more or less discredited, except in its reformed version. And this relates to an extensive mytho-poetic literature, traditions of cultural performance, ritual healing and modes of worship. To the VHP and RSS for all their proclaimed 'tolerance', similarly unacceptable are practices associated with a range of cultural identities, including those of Rajputs, Gujars, Jats, Ahirs and other pastoral and peasant castes, Adivasis and Dalits. One wonders, is this Hinduism, that seeks the de-paganization of its cosmological imagination? That attempts to substitute the extraordinary intellectual and philosophical exploration associated with the Hindu with a Rambo version of Rama?

NOTES

1. Research accumulates debts to many persons for the journey of ideas that it contains. Many persons will find resonances of conversations with them in this work: Sudhir Chandra, Nasreen Fazalbhoy, Jan-Peter Hartung, Mushirul Hasan, T.N. Madan, Barbara Metcalf, Susanne and Lloyd Rudolph, Satish Saberwal, Alito Sequeira, Fr Christian Troll, Vali Nasr, Ziauddin Sardar and Iqbal Asaria. My thanks to all of them and to Abhay Dube of the Centre for the Study of Developing Societies for urging me to write on the subject of religion and globalization for the Centre's Hindi volume on globalization; to Ritesh Kumar and Saswata Ghosh for chasing research materials; and to Arvind, Anirudh, and Abhinav for being what they are. This paper has been presented to

several audiences through the various stages of its growth. An earlier version of this article was published in the *Economic and Political Weekly* 39 (1), January 2004, a special issue put together by the Centre for the Study of Developing Societies on the occasion of the World Social Forum in Mumbai.

2. There is the phenomenon of the globalization of charismatic Christianity. Jenkins points out that Christianity is assuming a fundamentally different character with its new dominance in the countries of the southern hemisphere such as Brazil, Mexico, Philippines, Nigeria, Congo, etc. This is a very different Christianity than what the European and North American experience has made familiar to us. It is far more concerned with the 'supernatural' as manifest in its dimensions of prophecy, visions, ecstatic speech, and healing. Indeed, there is a new syncretism of Christianity and paganism apparent in Africa and Latin America (Jenkins 2002). Pentecostalism and liberation theology have become major forces within the Christian world. Jenkins' critics point out, however, that the evidence indicates that world Christianity is conservative.
3. For a detailed discussion see Mayaram 1997, Chap. 3.
4. The lore of the *shuddhi* suggests Muslim 'otherness':

   swāmī pahuñche chauthe tabak par
   khudā kī shuddhī rahe hai kar dāhī
   katā kar chotī rakhā dī
   khudā dekhe tuka tuka
   Swami (Shraddhanand) reached the fourth stage
   performing the *shuddhi* of the Lord.
   Cutting beards he made them keep braids
   while the Lord watched helplessly.

   An activist of the period told me, 'After Swamiji was killed we would shout, *dahī katā kar swāmī pahuñche hai swarg mai*' (after getting beards shaved Swami has reached heaven). We would boycott Muslims until they became Hindu. The faqir used to come frequently to our house for alms, but now we said, '*miyāon kī jholī kardo band jarūr*' (don't give alms, close the bag of the Muslim). Shraddhanand's assassination by a Muslim provided the occasion for a large procession through the streets of Mathura shouting, '*Swamī kā balīdān kar gayā shuddhī ka ailān*' (the martyrdom of the Swami calls for *shuddhi*). Yes, it did create antagonism among Muslims.
5. Madan points out that in the case of the Arya Samaj the concern with political power is mute. My disagreement lies in his characterization of this as merely nascent rather than full-fledged fundamentalism (1998, 36).
6. For details of the movement see Nadwi (1952, 1983); Hasani (1989); Haq (1972).

7. For details see Mayaram forthcoming, Chap. 2.
8. The *vaidika* refers to worship deriving from the body of oral literature called the Veda or sacred knowledge that authorises the priesthood of the Brahmins as its protectors. The *śramana* traditions are usually referred to as non-*vaidika*. The *tantrika* refers to the yoga-centric tradition of transcendental praxis based on the *agama* literature composed after the tenth century.
9. According to Sikand it was Meo resentment against the Baniyas that led to their distancing from Hindu religious traditions. This is doubtful as this resentment was also against Rajputs, but invariably the Meos saw Hindu gods and goddesses coming to their defence against the Rajputs. Shahid Mahdi, Vice-Chancellor of Jamia Millia Islamia, told me the story of a similar feud in his village, personal communication, October 2003.
10. Sikand maintains that Meo resentment against the Baniyas led to their distancing from Hindu religious traditions. This is doubtful since such resentment also existed against Rajputs, but the Meos often also saw gods and goddesses coming to their defense against the Rajputs (2002: Chap. 3).
11. See, for instance, Ghazanfar Ali cited in Ahmad (1985: 33-4 n. 36).
12. Personal communication, Jaipur, January 1993.
13. *Jahiliyyah* (comes from *jahil*, meaning ignorant or untaught) and represents the time of ignorance deriving from pre-Islamic paganism prior to the revelation of Islam.
14. Surendra Singh, personal interview, December 1997.
15. This section draws on the excellent writing on Pakistan and Afghanistan including that of Metcalf, Nasr, Roy, Sikand and Zaman.
16. http://www.almadinah.org
17. Daghestan: Focus on Pakistan's TJ-background of TJ, http://www.saag.org/papers/paper80.html.
18. Recently following the coming to power of the BJP led coalition, the National Democratic Alliance, Deoband (India) issued a ban on cow slaughter on the occasion of Id.
19. Husain Ahmad Madani (d. 1957), the important leader of Deoband, as Metcalf's forthcoming biography of the leader tells us, identified himself as a follower of Gandhi and embraced the secular, democratic principles of the Indian nationalist movement. He saw himself as a staunch Indian nationalist to the extent that he was intolerant of anyone not wearing homespun *khadi*. An opponent of the creation of Pakistan, he supported the idea of a plural democracy.
20. Over a period the Pakistani political economy saw the rise of petty *ulama* who used rural mosques and *madrasas* to stake their own claim to power and wealth. Roy describes 'this dangerous class of religiously-inclined, militant, unemployed, frustrated, and half-

educated youth' as the 'lumpen intelligentsia' (Roy 1994). A new breed of militant *madrasa* graduates nominally *ulama* but jihadist in outlook displaced the older Shia and Sunni landed gentry-based *ulama* and preachers. Both militant activists and *madrasas* received support both from the state and from criminals involved in the drug trade. Mosques began to be used as arms depots rather than as centres of religious learning and instruction.

21. Http://www.geocities.com/altargospel/dar-al.htm.
22. Http://www.fatwas-online.
23. M. Rahmatullah's claim to succession was sidelined in favour of Inamul Hasan, Ilyas' sister's grandson and the son-in-law of Muhammad Zakariyya at the latter's intervention. The latter claimed to have received a command to this effect from Yusuf. M. Rahmatullah did not belong to the family of Siddiqui Shaikhs of Kandhala and is said to have belonged to the 'low' caste of oil-pressers (Sikand 2002: 157n).

REFERENCES

Ahmad, Mumtaz, 1991, 'Islamic fundamentalism in South Asia: the Jamaat-i-Islami and the Tablighi Jamaat of South Asia', in *Fundamentalism Observed*, ed. Martin E. Marty and R. Scott Appleby, 457-530, Chicago: University of Chicago Press.

———, 'The TJ', www.icna.org/tm/greatmovement3.htm.

Ahmad, Syed Nur, 1986 [1965], *From Martial Law to Martial Law: Politics in the Punjab 1919-1958*, Boulder and London: Westview Press.

Appadurai, Arjun, 1996, *Modernity at Large: Cultural Dimensions of Globalization*, Minneapolis, Minnesota University Press.

Bhatt, Chetan and Parita Mukta, 2000, 'Introduction: Hindutva in the West: Mapping the Antinomies of Nationalism', *Ethnic and Racial Studies* 23 (3): 442-66.

Chatterjee, Partha, 1993, *The Nation and its Fragments: Colonial and Postcolonial Histories*, Princeton: Princeton University Press.

———, Fall 1998, 'Beyond the nation? Or within?' *Social Text* (56).

Durkheim, Emile, 1915, *Elementary Forms of the Religious Life*, New York: Free Press

Gaborieau, Marc, 1999, 'Transnational Islamic Movements: TJ in Politics', *Institute for the Study of Islam in the Modern world Newsletter* 3 (99).

———, 2000, 'The Transformation of Tablighi Jama'at into a transnational movement under the leadership of Muhammad Yusuf, 1944-1965', in *Travellers in Faith: Studies of Tablighi Jama'at as a Transnational Movement for Faith Renewal*, ed. M.K. Masud, 3-43, Leiden-Boston-Cologne: Brill.

Hannerz, Ulf, 2000, *Transnational Connections: Culture, People, Places*, London: Routledge.

Hardy, Friedhelm, 1995, *The Religious Culture of India*, Cambridge: Cambridge University Press.

Hasani, M. Mohammad Thani, 1989, *Sawanih Mawlana Muhammad Yusuf Kandhelawi* (Urdu Biography of Maulana Muhammad Yusuf Kaṇdhelawi), Lucknow: Dar-ul uloom.

Haq, Anwarul Haq, 1972, *The Faith Movement of Mawlana Muhammad Ilyas*, London: George Allen and Unwin.

Jaffrelot, Christophe, 1999, 'Militant Hindus and the Conversion Issue (1885-1990): From Shuddhi to Dharm Parivartan', in *The Resources of History: Tradition, Narration and Nation in South Asia*, ed. Jackie Assayag, Paris: EFEO, 127-52.

Jenkins, Philip, 2002, *The Next Christendom: The Coming of Global Christianity*, New York: Oxford University Press.

Jones, Kenneth, 1976, *Arya Dharm: Hindu Consciousness in 19th Century Punjab*. Berkeley and Los Angeles: University of California Press.

Joshi, Manoj, 1988, 'Islamic reform and militancy in India', *Institute for the Study of Islam in the Modern World Newsletter* 1: 22.

———, 1999, *The Lost Rebellion: Kashmir in the Nineties*, New Delhi: Penguin.

Kepel, Gilles, 1985, *The Prophet and the Pharaoh: Muslim Extremism in Contemporary Egypt*. London: Al Saqi Books.

Khan, M. Wahiduddin, 1986, *Tabligh Movement* (trans. of *Tablighi Tahreek*), New Delhi: Islamic Center.

Khan, Dominique Sila, 1997, *Conversions and Shifting Identities: Ramdev Pir and the Ismailis in Rajasthan*, New Delhi: Manohar.

Lal, Vinay, 2003, *The History of History: Politics and Scholarship in Modern India*, New Delhi: Oxford University Press.

Mandaville, Peter, 2001, *Transnational Muslim Politics, Reimagining The Umma*, New York and London: Routledge.

Masud, Muhammad Khalid, ed., 2000, *Travellers in Faith: Studies of the Tablighi Jamaat as a Transnational Islamic Movement for Faith Renewal*, Leiden-Boston-Cologne: Brill.

Mathur, Chandana et al., n.d., 'Avasudhaiva kutumbakam: exploring the global dimensions of the Sangh Parivar', unpublished paper.

Madan, Triloki Nath, 1998, *Modern Myths, Locked Minds: Secularism and Fundamentalism in India*, New Delhi: Oxford University Press.

Mathew, Biju and Vijay Prashad, 2000, 'The protean forms of Yankee Hindutva', *Ethnic and Racial Studies* 23 (3): 516-34.

Mayaram, Shail, 1997, *Resisting Regimes: Myth, Memory and the Shaping of a Muslim Identity*, New Delhi: Oxford University Press.

——— (forthcoming), *Against History, Against State: Counterperspectives from the Margins*, New York and London: Columbia University Press.

———, n.d., 'Canonizing Hinduism: the politics of Vishwa Hindu Parishad Conversion', unpublished paper.

McKean, Lise, 1996, *Divine Enterprise: Gurus and the Hindu Nationalist Movement*, Chicago: University of Chicago Press.

Metcalf, Barbara, 1993, 'Living hadith in the TJ', *Journal of Asian Studies* 52: 584-608.

———, 1993b, 'Meandering madarsas: knowledge and short-term itinerancy in the Tablighi Jamaat', in *The Transmission of Knowledge in South Asia: Essays on Education, Religion, History, and Politics*, ed. Nigel Crook, 49-61, New Delhi: Oxford University Press.

———, 1994, 'Remaking ourselves': Islamic Self-fashioning in a Global Movement of Spiritual Renewal', in *Accounting for Fundamentalisms: The Dynamic Character of Movements* (vol. 4 of series), ed. Martin E. Marty and R. Scott Appleby, Chicago: University of Chicago Press, 1994, pp. 706-25.

———, 1996, 'Islam and women: the case of the TJ', SEHR, *Contested Polities* 5 (1).

———, 2002, 'Traditionalist' Islamic activism: Deoband, Tablighis, and Talibs', working paper, Institute for the Study of Islam in the Modern World.

Minault, Gail, 1982, *The Khilafat Movement: Religious Symbolism and Political Mobilization in India*, New Delhi: Oxford University Press.

Mukta, Parita, 2000, 'The Public Face of Hindu Nationalism', *Ethnic and Racial Studies* 23 (3): 442-66.

Nadwi, Abul Hasan Ali, ed., 1952, *Makatib-i-Hazrat Maulana Shah Muhammad Ilyas* (Letters of Hazrat Mawlana Shah Muhammad Ilyas), Delhi: Idara Ishaat-i Diniyat.

Nadwi, Abul Hasan Ali, 1983, *Life and Mission of Maulana Mohammad Ilyas*, Lucknow: Academy of Islamic Research and Publications.

Nasr, Seyyid Vali Reza, 2000, 'The rise of Sunni militancy in Pakistan: the changing role of Islamism and the ulama in society and politics', *Modern Asian Studies* 34 (1): 139-80.

Nijhawan, Michel, 2002, 'Dhadhi Voice and Agency: Performative Genres and the Public Sphere in the Panjab 1920-1935', unpublished paper presented to International Conference on Folklore, Public Space and Civil Society, Indira Gandhi National Centre for the Arts, New Delhi.

Oberoi, Harjot, 1994, *The Construction of Religious Boundaries: Culture, Identity and Diversity in the Sikh Tradition*, New Delhi: Oxford University Press.

Rajgopal, A., 2001, *Politics after Television: Hindu Nationalism and the Reshaping of the Public in India*, Cambridge: Cambridge University Press.

Rashid, Ahmed, 2000, *Taliban: Militant Islam, Oil and Fundamentalism in Central Asia*, New Haven: Yale University Press.

Robbins, Bruce and Pheng Cheah, 1998, 'Introduction', *Cosmopolitics: Thinking and Feeling Beyond the Nation*, ed. Pheng Cheah and Bruce Robbins, Minneapolis: University of Minnesota Press.

Roy, Olivier, 1994, *The Failure of Political Islam*, Cambridge, MA: Harvard University Press.

Seunarine, J.F., 1977, *Reconversion through Suddhi*, Madras: Christian Literary Society.

Shivaprakash, H.S., 2002, 'Manteswami and Madeshwara Kavyas: Critiques of Hegemonic World Orders', paper presented to International Conference on Folklore, Public Space and Civil Society, Indira Gandhi National Centre for the Arts, New Delhi.

Sikand, Y, 2002, *The Origins and Development of the Tablighi Jamaat (1920-2000): A Cross-country Comparative Study*, New Delhi: Orient Longman.

———, 2003, 'The TJ and Politics', *Institute for the Study of Islam in the Modern World Newsletter* 13: 42-4.

Skinner, James, 1824, *Tashrīh ul aquām* (Persian), London: British Museum.

Stein, S.J., 2002, 'The web of religion and violence', *Religious Studies Review* 28 (2): 103-8.

Thursby, Gene Robert, 1975, *Hindu-Muslim Relations in British India: A Study of Controversy, Conflict and Communal Movements in Northern India 1923-1928*, Leiden: E.J. Brill.

van der Veer, Peter, 2001, 'Transnational Religion', paper presented to Conference on Transnational Migration: Comparative Perspectives, Princeton University.

Zaman, Muhammad Qasim, 1998, 'Sectarianism in Pakistan: The Radicalization of Shia and Sunni Identities', *Modern Asian Studies* 32: 687-716.

14

Adivasi *vs.* Vanvasi: The Politics of Conversion in Central India

NANDINI SUNDAR

If adivasi lands and resources have come under sustained attack by the forces of organized capitalism over the past hundred or so years, their beliefs too have had to face a determined war of attrition by organized religions. The two processes, in fact, feed off each other, with a growing commodification of life seeming to require a portable, commodified religion.[1] However, unlike the 'adherent-centred view' adopted by much of the recent literature on conversion,[2] which seeks to explicate the multiple processes by which conversion occurs or its meaning in the life of those converted,[3] this paper studies the process as competing religions seek to establish hegemony on adivasi soil. Competitive proselytization is primarily a political phenomenon, aimed at expanding numbers and keeping alternative religions out. If converts find solace in religion, or if new forms of religious and social imagining emerge, this is quite incidental to the purpose for which programmes of conversion are undertaken Following Saberwal, the attempt here is to understand the ways in which resources and person-power are deployed to crystallize religious identities, and the implications of this process for adivasis in particular and for citizenship in India more widely, as the state reifies religious identity at the expense of other identities.[4]

Jashpur district in Chhattisgarh (on the border with Jharkhand and sharing a common culture and people) is a useful place for such a study, since it has one of the oldest and largest Catholic communities in central India. Not coincidentally, the RSS front, the Akhil Bharatiya Vanvasi Kalyan Ashram (henceforth VKA), was first established here, to counter Christian missionary activity and to 'awaken tribals to their true Hindu identity'. The population of Jashpur is predominantly Oraon, followed by a number of 'OBC' (Other Backward Classes) groups like the Rautia, Mahakul, Teli, and Gosain. Marwari, Jain, and Muslim traders dominate the district and block headquarters. In broad-brush terms, the Catholic church has its 'field' among Oraons, while the OBCs and upper castes form a potential Hindutva base. However, the RSS is also seeking to expand among unconverted adivasis. While the first half of the paper looks at the establishment of the Catholic church in Jashpur, its perceived connections with the demand for an independent Jharkhand state, the setting up of the Kalyan Ashram, and the politics of the Niyogi Commission, the second half of the paper examines the everyday working of the VKA.

Unlike conversion to Christianity, conversion to Hinduism has been much less studied, leave alone recognized,[5] except under the gradualist, anonymously authored processes termed 'the Hindu method of tribal absorption' or 'Sanskristization'.[6] For instance, both the Arya Samaj and the RSS describe their conversion merely as 're-conversion'—as *shuddhi* (purification) or *gharvapsi* (homecoming). Hindu conversions are helped by the unmarked Hinduism of the state which treats Hinduism as the default religion when it comes to classifying adivasis in the census or other government records. Both Christians and Hindus see Freedom of Religion Acts in MP and Orissa as targeted primarily at Christian conversion.[7] However, state practice is contradictory—in that judicial pronouncements on adivasi personal law have distinguished them from Hindus.[8]

Insofar as conversion is not just about a quantifiable change in religious belief, but a change of lifestyle, it is often hard to distinguish from other processes of change. Indeed, much change occurs through the process of 'uplift' or absorption into the 'mainstream', which are terms characteristic of state discourse towards adivasis. If the mainstream is defined as the path of capitalist development—Christianity in this area has long served to bring adivasis into the mainstream, through its emphasiz on education for a middle class lifestyle,[9] even as it owed its initial success to its stand on behalf of the adivasis against a mainstream represented by landlords and officials. When the VKA or other Sangh associates talk of the 'mainstream', however, they additionally define it in terms of Hindu religion and 'culture'. By equating nationalism with 'Hindutva', the RSS portrays conversion to Christianity as an 'anti-national' act, drawing spurious links between conversion to Christianity and separatism.

In every case, however, the real casualty is the pluralist idea of society and polity, in which adivasi religion and modes of resource use are celebrated and recognized in their own right. While a study of conversion would require a detailed description of the religion that existed before, my focus here is more on the politics of conversion campaigns than on actual processes of religious change. Adivasi religion, like any other, has never been static and what comes to us today as 'authentic' is necessarily filtered by a variety of influences and perspectives. For instance, much of Sarat Chandra Roy's classic study of Oraon religion and custom is taken up by trying to trace the various influences on Oraon religion from outside.[10] But in its bare bones, as described by Roy, Oraons had two main classes of deities—nature spirits and human spirits, and within them there were hierarchies. *Dharmes* or the Creator of the Universe, earlier known as *Biri-Belas* or the Sun-God, was the most important. In addition, Oraons made offerings to village tutelary deities and to spirits inhabiting particular rocks and trees. Each lineage or *khunt*, as also each household within the lineage, had its own ancestor spirits.[11] Oraons had no temples, except a shrine for *Devi Mai* (which Roy presumed was borrowed from the Hindus) and their deities were usually represented by stones or wooden pegs. A sal tree or grove known as *sarna* served as the site of worship. There was no separate priestly class and the *Pahan* performed the ceremonies. His office was hereditary in some villages, elected in others.[12]

The ongoing movement in Jharkhand to have adivasi religion recognized as *sarna dharm* or *adi dharm* and classified as such in the census, itself represents a systematization of a variety of practices. Yet it is perhaps the only alternative to the religious imperialism of both Hindus and Christians. Indeed, even when Hindus and Christians are willing to concede the existence of such a thing as a distinctive Adivasi religion, their descriptions involve acts of appropriation. A VKA pamphlet claims that adivasis are part of a wider Hindu family because Hindus also worship nature (Tulsi, Ganga, Nag, etc.).[13] Christian propagandists like John Lakra, on the other hand, argue that Oraon religion is similar to Christianity in that it too is founded on belief in *Dharmes* or one Supreme God.[14] Ultimately, all religions (like languages) are products of a particular politics of classification, and the recognition accorded to their gods depends on the economic and political power of a people.

COMPETING BIOGRAPHIES

THE ESTABLISHMENT OF THE JESUIT MISSION IN JASHPUR

> With a mission school there immediately follows a Sunday school and out of that grows a church. The history of many a Church in Assam can be traced back to an investment of say, forty dollars per year and the placement of a Christian teacher in an otherwise unevangelized village.[15]

The early histories of mission stations in Asia or Africa usually read as biographies of dedicated and self sacrificing priests who went out to the furthest corners of the world and liberated their benighted denizens from the spiritual and civilizational darkness in which they lived.[16] The first mission in the Jharkhand region was the German Gossner Evangelical Lutheran Mission in 1844, followed by the Anglican Mission or the Society for the Propagation of the Gospel in 1869, and then the Catholic Mission. All of them were first set up in Ranchi district.[17]

Internal Jesuit explanations for the phenomenal success of the Catholic mission[18] usually centre on the charismatic figure of Constant Lievens, a Belgian Jesuit who came to Chhotanagpur in 1885. Realizing that the main problem the Mundas faced was economic, he helped them fight their cases in court.[19] As his biographer Clarysse notes, while Lievens may have been more interested in the 'eternal happiness' of the Mundas, for them, the hope he held out for 'happiness in this life' by taking up their legal rights far overshadowed the other as a motive for conversion.[20]

Missionary entry into the princely states was faced with greater obstacles than in British India, in part because of the need to keep native rulers intact as figureheads, even as colonial administrations introduced changes in the tenurial system which meant higher rents, restrictions on access to forests and more forced labour (*begar*).[21] Conversion invariably involved a break in the traditional paternalist relations between rulers and their subjects, a relationship which was buttressed by the interpenetration of state ritual with local religion in the form of Dussehra celebrations, in which the king played a leading role. Being part of an alternative religious organizational structure emboldened Adivasis to protest against existing political and economic structures. Missionary activity thus often worked at cross-purposes with the colonial administration's need to maintain the *status quo*. Paradoxically, Independence and a constitutional right to propagate proved more congenial to Christian missionary activity (and even more so, of course, to Hindu missions) than was colonial rule.[22]

Caught between the need to maintain law and order in the states and a professed policy of religious neutrality, eventual outcomes usually depended on the predilections of particular colonial officials.[23] For Christian minded officers serving in Hindu ruled states, enforcing the 'freedom of religion' often translated as unofficial pressure on the rulers to allow Christian missionaries in.[24] In Jashpur, this resulted in the Raja being forced to allow the German Lutheran Mission and Catholics into the state in 1906-7, despite his fears of subversion. However, in later years, the missionaries were also warned not to allow their preachers to mobilize peasants against the king.[25]

Friction between the Raja and the missionaries continued until Independence, necessitating periodic government enquiries. In 1913, Blakesley, the Political Agent, found that most of the conversion was due to material incentives—the availability of easy loans, help with marriage expenditures, free legal services by the catechists and the belief among some Oraons that their land revenue would be settled and they would be free from *begar*, as in Chhotanagpur. However, the Central Provinces Government did not accept Blakesley's recommendations, and the Jesuits who were hitherto operating from Ranchi district now moved into Jashpur.[26] The colonial state's frequent application of the Defence of India rules to extern rebels or Congress protestors during the World Wars suggests that it did not subscribe to the freedom to propagate all ideologies in its territories. This also meant that those with economic grievances had no choice but to express them in religious terms.

Matters came to a head in 1922 when villagers in *Upargbat* (the portion of Jashpur state above the ghats), encouraged by Lutheran preachers, refused to perform *begar.*[27] Soon after, the movement spread to *Nichgbat,* with Lutherans playing the leading role, but both Catholics and non-Catholics joining in. Here too, the cause was excessive *begar* for zamindars and state officials which interfered with the peasant's own cultivation, the Raja's proposal to tax uplands and homestead plots, increases in rents, and oppression by state and police officials. Forest rights, e.g. contractor monopolies on lac, were another issue.[28] Large meetings were organized across *Nichgbat.* In one incident, a constable was killed, following which the Raja summoned forces from neighbouring Sarguja state. Several people were arrested and beaten, including twelve Catholic pracharaks. However, the Raja's demand for expulsion of the missionaries met with little success, and on the contrary, the joint outcry of the Lutherans and Catholics against 'human rights abuses' in Jashpur led to the Raja being deposed.[29]

The Belgian Jesuits maintained that they had nothing to do with the protests and had in fact asked their flock to keep away from such activities. Indeed, the Catholics opposed the total abolition of *begar* because it was a Lutheran demand, and as a report by Father Vandendriessche to the Archbishop of Calcutta shows, rejoiced when Lutheran meetings on the issue were a failure. On the other hand, one Tana Oraon of village Barangjori told the Diwan that the *bara padri* had allowed them to attend the meetings and told them that if they attended church regularly they would be let off *begar*. What perhaps was equally likely was that the Belgian fathers had lost control over both their local pracharaks and their converts: as one convert told Fr. D'Alcantara, 'Father, we shall remain Catholics of course, but with regard to these social affairs, we will no more listen to you because you are sitting with the Raja.' If the Jesuits allowed their flock to attend political meetings, it was so as not to lose them altogether.[30]

These 'disturbances' provide a clear sense of the way in which conversion was rooted in agrarian discontent as well as the extent to which Adivasi religious identity was as yet fluid, with individuals changing from one sect to another depending on the perceived benefits. Further, what European missionaries sanctioned and what their local preachers understood as the appropriate means and ends of conversion often exhibited significant divergences. We also get a sense of the schisms within Christianity—with both Catholics and Lutherans contesting for souls. Supporting peasants against the state was often less important than ensuring they did not fall into the clutches of the other church. Equally, we see how the Raja preferred to blame missionaries for incitement rather than address people's complaints regarding economic exploitation.

Similar pressure resulted in the Raja of Gangpur giving the Lutherans and Catholics extensive plots of land on perpetual lease.[31] First World War, however, ensured a Catholic advantage over the Lutherans. In W.G. Archer's words:

In the first place, the access which the Catholic Mission has achieved has been secured by the methods of commercial competition. It has undercut its rivals and has not hesitated to poach on other sportsman's grounds. Its main rival has been the Lutheran Mission, which prior to the War was a fighting alternative to the Jesuits. The War, however, sent the German missionaries into liquidation and although some of them returned when the hostilities were over, they found that the Catholics (mainly the Belgian Jesuits) had made similar annexations in the field of converts to those secured by the Allies in the German colonies.[32]

The mission question was revived in 1927 following reports of extensive proselytization in Khuria zamindari. The mission was found to run a virtually parallel administration, compounding minor offences and paying the fines into the mission account, concealing crimes, boycotting non-Christians, recruiting labour for the tea gardens, sugar plantations, and for the army, and running co-operative banks into which remittances were deposited.[33] Catholics were asked to attend mission schools rather than state schools,[34] and on occasion seem to have received preference in the land settlement.[35] In 1936, the Bishop of Ranchi asked for permission to erect schools and chapels in Udaipur state (neighbouring Jashpur), on the grounds that there was a huge demand for it. This was discovered to be somewhat fraudulent. It was a drought year, and people had heard that loans were easily available at Tapkara mission, provided they cut-off their top-knots. The numbers too were much fewer than the Bishop claimed: when one member of the family took a loan, the entire family was shown as having converted. The Bishop's justification, when confronted with this evidence, was a marvel of sophistry: 'the taking of loans is not a motive of conversion, but it is in the eyes of the Aborigines a sign of adherence and a pledge of earnestness and sincerity'.[36] The enquiry resulted in the missions being asked to maintain registers of converts, missionaries, and preachers, and to notify the government of changes, not unlike the measures required by the contemporary Orissa Freedom of Religion Act 1967 and the MP Dharma Swatantraya Adhiniyam 1968.

If in 1929 the Secretary of State could cite greater Christian sensitivity in England and America against bans on missionary activity,[37] by the mid-1940s various Hindu groups had become equally sensitive. Theble Oraon, the first president of the Chhotanagpur Kisan Sabha, who then joined Congress, and the Hindu Dharma Rakshak Sangh held meetings along the Ranchi-Jashpur border warning Adivasis about bible teaching by the missions.[38] In Mandla, another Adivasi-dominated area, Elwin had joined hands with his former adversary A.V. Thakkar of the Adimjati Sevak Sangh, to counter the Catholic mission's unethical practices and claimed that along with the Arya Dharma Seva Sangh and the Gond Seva Mandal set up by P.G. Vannikar, one of Thakkar's trusted aides, he had been able to shut down 25 mission schools.[39]

THE DEMAND FOR JHARKHAND

Through the late 1930s up to the mid-1940s, one of the issues of consistent concern to the colonial authorities in the Eastern States, was the agrarian unrest in Gangpur, which bordered both Jashpur and Ranchi district in British India.[40] Under a revised settlement in which lands reclaimed from the forest were taxed, rents went up by 44 per cent. Lutheran Mundas then embarked on a no-rent campaign, in some cases took forcible possession of lands from which they had been evicted, broke forest laws, held large meetings armed with bows and arrows, acknowledged Jaipal Singh as their leader, and refused even to listen to their pastors. The Catholics, although present in larger numbers in Gangpur, were not part of the campaign.[41] Although the movement was eventually suppressed, and counter meetings of 'anti-Adibasis' were organized in Gangpur, professing loyalty to the state,[42] the demand for Jharkhand was identified by Adivasis across the eastern states with a restoration of control over land and forests, and against the arbitrary power of *thekedars*, and forest guards.

Although non-Christian movements like the Tana Bhagats who operated along the Ranchi-Jashpur border also refused to pay rent, or obey forest laws, until they were persuaded to by Gandhi,[43] and both the Chhotanagpur Unnati Samaj and the Adivasi Mahasabha cut across religious boundaries, the movement for Jharkhand was identified by the RSS and the Congress government in Madhya Pradesh as a Christian inspired separatist movement similar to the Muslim demand for Pakistan.[44] A publication of 1993 of the Vanvasi Kalyan Ashram, titled *Friends or Foes of Adivasis and Dalits?* begins:

> The elements who had not reconciled to the nation's independence continued to conspire to weaken and fragment the country further. A little known event of those days was a conspiracy hatched by Christian missions to carve out, with the help of Mohammed Ali Jinnah and the Nizam of Hyderabad, an independent Christian country comprising Chhota Nagpur (Bihar) and parts of Madhya Pradesh, Orissa and West Bengal, which was

detected and foiled by our government. Because of this conspiracy the then State Government of C.P. and Berar was faced with a critical situation in the tribal areas of the province. The tribals, mostly Christian converts under the tutelage of Christian missionaries had revolted and the hostility of these tribals to India's new independence and the provincial government of the day was so strong that when late Pandit Ravi Shankar Shukla, Chief Minister (then known as Prime Minister) of the province toured the area, he was greeted with black flags and cries of 'Jai Jesus' in response to the slogan of Jai Hind raised from the dais.[45]

The founding narrative of the Vanvasi Kalyan Ashram takes off from this moment. Insulted on being greeted at Jashpur with slogans demanding Jharkhand and asking him to go back, Shukla asked the Gandhian, A.V. Thakkar, well known for his work among Adivasis and Dalits, for advice on tackling the 'missionary menace' and growing separatism. Thakkar advised taking the help of 'nationalist social service organizations' and on the recommendation of P.G. Vannikar, appointed Ramakant Keshav Deshpande of the RSS as Regional Director of the Tribal Welfare Department.[46] Deshpande's biographer, K.D. Sapre, comments on the irony of a Congress government about to arrest Deshpande as part of its sweep against the RSS after Gandhi's murder, sending him instead to Jashpur as a government servant.[47] Yet, this was not so surprising after all, considering that a strand of the Congress was sympathetic to the Hindu Mahasabha, and had been open to members of the RSS also joining the Congress.[48] The Madhya Pradesh branch of the Congress was dominated by the 'Hindu traditionalist faction' and Shukla, in fact, had been introduced to the Congress through Moonje of the Hindu Mahasabha.[49]

Indeed, Shukla's experience in Jashpur also forms the starting point for the Niyogi Commission.[50] In the chapter on 'The circumstances leading to the appointment of the committee', the Commission devoted several pages to the demand for Jharkhand as a Christian inspired separatist movement:

> In view of the political bias with which Christian missionaries had carried on proselytism during the last half a century in the merged territories and in view of their active support of the dangerous Jharkhand movement Government considered it necessary to put down the activities which led to fissiparous tendencies.[51]

Elsewhere of course (p. 50) the Commission recognizes that at least one strand of the movement was demanding merely merger of some states with Bihar rather than with the Central Provinces, or at most a separate Jharkhand state within India. Yet the treatment of the Jharkhand movement by the States Reorganization Commission and the Congress betrays total contempt for the right and capacity of adivasis to govern themselves, a right that they were happy to grant to much less culturally homogenous linguistic groups.

The Niyogi Commission

The Niyogi Commission was one moment when the interests of the RSS and the Congress government of Madhya Pradesh meshed rather well. Set up by the Shukla government in 1954 under the chairmanship of Dr. Bhawani Shankar Niyogi, retired justice of the Nagpur High Court, the Commission's mandate was to enquire into complaints that Christian Missionaries used force or monetary incentives to convert people. The Commission also ostensibly broadened the scope of its enquiry to look into complaints by Christian missionaries of harassment by local officials and non-Christians.[52]

However, both in terms of its composition—with only one Christian whom the Christians regarded as non-representative—and its mode of operation it was clear that the cards were stacked against the Christians. Sapre describes the close links that Niyogi and other Commission members like Ghanshyam Singh Gupta had with the RSS: Niyogi apparently took up the task only after Golwalkar re-assured him that the Vanvasi Kalyan Ashram and other RSS workers would represent the Hindus.[53] While the Commission toured 14 districts and visited a number of institutions, it also relied heavily on a 99-question survey, in which as the Catholics quite rightly complained, 'most of the questions were veiled accusations against the Missions'. Out of 385 replies to the questionnaire, 55 were from Christians and 330 from non-Christians, of which significant numbers were members of the Arya Samaj, or the RSS.[54] While noting that the activities of the Arya Samaj and RSS in countering missions had led to tensions, the Niyogi Commission blamed this on the 'objectionable methods followed by missionaries', who also initiated false complaints against others.[55] The Catholics argued that enumerating Adivasis under the Hindu column in the 1951 Census, when they had previously been classed as animists, was also a form of mass conversion to Hinduism.[56] Yet this cut little ice with the Commission who instead cited the problem faced by earlier census commissioners in distinguishing animists from Hindus.[57]

The Commission found that with Independence, American missionary evangelization increased,[58] and that the bulk of external money went towards paying pracharaks.[59] Methods of evangelization involved both coercion and inducement: changing the names of students to Christian names, holding compulsory Bible classes for non-Christians attending mission schools, giving witness, preaching in hospitals, moneylending and waiving interest if the borrower turned Christian, running orphanages, using Christians in government departments like the police, education or forest department, to hold meetings, organizing bhajan mandalis where Yeshu bhajans were sung and the *Yeshu Bhagwat* was recited, and abusing Hindu gods.[60]

The recommendations of the Commission—in response to what it pictured as a worldwide Christian conspiracy to 're-establish Western supremacy' and threaten 'the security of the state'[61]—were to ban all mission activity in labour recruitment, place controls on the entry of foreign missionaries and conversions, and increase government involvement in the running of orphanages, schools, hospitals, etc.[62] It also recommended, quite gratuitously, that the Indian churches establish a 'United Independent Christian Church in India without being dependent on foreign support', a suggestion later reiterated by the RSS after the then Prime Minister Vajpayee renewed the 'national debate on conversions'. And then in language that would be echoed by the RSS some 50 years later in its 2003 conference, the Commission noted, 'In the present secular state of India, the best safeguard any minority could have, is the goodwill of the majority community and the right attitude of the minority is one of trust and confidence in the fair sense of the majority.'[63]

Battling Christian Missionaries: Ramakant Keshav (Balasaheb) Deshpande

> Different kinds of activities are necessary for the all–round development of the country. The Sangh aims to cover all fields through its work. The Vishwa Hindu Parishad has its own distinct objectives—to bring all the Hindu sects onto a common Hindu platform and to revive all the temples that were destroyed and ruined. . . . The task of the Akhil Bharatiya Vidyarthi Parishad is to bring direction to the country's youth. The Bharatiya Janata Party is the political wing. . . . Today there is a

> concerted effort to separate the vanvasi samaj from the Hindu samaj and make them think they are not Hindus. Our effort is to awaken the vanvasi regions and remove this feeling of difference. For this we have to unite the Vanvasis. That is the Akhil Bharatiya Vanvasi Kalyan Ashram's work. That is its major role. We will do all sorts of work, and try and fill all kinds of gaps such as lack of health facilities or drinking water but at all times our objective must be clear.[64]

If Lievens was the heroic figure of Catholic perseverence in evangelizing the vast field that the Adivasis of Chhotanagpur represented, his RSS counterpart is Ramakant Keshav Deshpande, who, by setting up the Kalyan Ashram, stemmed the seemingly unstoppable march of the missionaries and reclaimed souls or bodies for the Hindus. Like Lievens, the inspiration for his presence in Jashpur came not from a curiosity about Adivasi life and conditions, or a desire to help, but from an organized system whose driving force lay elsewhere—in the RSS case, the establishment of a Hindu Rashtra, in which members of all other religious communities would have second class status.[65]

K.D Sapre's *Shri Balasaheb Deshpande: Jeevan aur Karya* (life and work), might be read as a classic Sangh biography of a classic Sangh figure. The hero of such biographies is inevitably born to a Sangh- or at least a conservative middle-class Maharashtrian family, has contact with the leading ideologues of the Sangh, is the innocent victim of police or government accusations, is arrested for terrorist and disruptive activities, acquitted for lack of evidence, and finally graduates to become a 'respectable' figure of society with wider acceptance among a Hindu public.

Born on 26 December 1913 at Amaraoti to Keshavrao Deshpande, a government karamchari, Ramkant was one of four brothers, all of whom did Law. His maternal cousin was Murli Deoras, the third RSS Sarsanghchalak. When visiting Nagpur, Deshpande attended *lathi* sessions, was introduced to Dr. Hedgewar and became a swayamsevak.[66] After finishing a BA and Law degree, Deshpande began a practice in Ramtek with his uncle. He also became the *karyavah* or leader of the Ramtek Sangh. In those days Golwalkar lived in Ramtek and had a library which Deshpande frequented. In this way, we are told, 'the stream of his life and that of respected Guruji met and Balasaheb's life of national service began.'[67]

Deshpande, says his biographer, was a dedicated freedom fighter, and patrolled the streets during the Quit India movement to maintain law and order, along with his band of RSS associates. Unfortunately, his sterling qualities were not recognized by the Muslim police officer in charge of Ramtek who arrested him and sent him to Nagpur for trial on charges of looting and arson. Despite extensive eyewitness evidence, he was acquitted because the Ramtek tahsildar, Harkare, who he had once saved from lynching by a mob, refused to testify against him. The elisions in this account are almost as fascinating as what Sapre actually tells us—such as the RSS's lack of involvement in the Quit India movement, or the strong likelihood that Deshpande was in fact engaged in communal and disruptive activities.

Deshpande then got married and got a job in the ration department, but soon resigned, ostensibly due to a stand against profiteering. He returned to law. After Gandhi's death, when the public was 'being incited' against the Sangh, Deshpande's house too came under attack. He was saved by the appearance of his brother. Soon after this, the incident at Jashpur with Ravi Shankar Shukla happened and Deshpande was posted to Jashpur as Director of the Tribal Welfare Department.

THE BATTLE OVER SCHOOLS

When Deshpande reached Jashpur, he found that the missionaries had a hundred primary schools. At once, so Sapre's story goes, he asked the government for permission to open a hundred government primary schools. Wherever there were mission schools, Deshpande set up one of his own, appointing teachers on the basis of their *chotis* (top-knots) and their physical strength. The teachers were warned that they would have to defend themselves. Some of them had only passed the fourth grade.[68]

In a remarkable section titled *Bhai Bin Hot na Preet* (without fear there is no love), Sapre approvingly recounts instances when Deshpande employed physical violence to cow the missionaries down, including filing court cases against them. For example, he went to a village which was a Christian stronghold, accompanied by eight or ten *lathi* wielding youth. Having gathered the villagers together he instructed them to say Jai Hind. When they allegedly replied Jai Ishu, he threatened to beat them all up. This tactic, Sapre tells us, worked wonders. But it was only after an incident when he beat up Fr Mews at the Ginabahar Catholic school, for ostensibly stopping an Ashram boy using the mission compound as a thoroughfare, that Deshpande claims he realized how important the schools could be as fighting centres.[69]

Given this unabashed account, the Catholic complaint that the teachers were not there so much to teach tribal students but to harass and threaten Christians, seems a reasonably correct one. In his reply to the Niyogi questionnaire, the President of the Raigarh Catholic Sabha explained why they refused to co-operate with the Adivasi Welfare Department:

> From the day of merger, the Madhya Pradesh Government declared a fierce war on our schools. All our Primary schools lost their recognition and none received a grant-in-aid. The Adivasi Welfare Department tried to open rival schools next to every Catholic school at least in areas that were not inaccessible. In these rival schools, teachers were paid fabulous salaries, at least three times the amount paid in our schools; the pupils were charged no fees, received books and stationary free, and also a daily meal into the bargain. And very severe pressure was put on non-Christian parents to induce them to withdraw their children from our schools.[70]

The Catholics sounded entirely aggrieved, complaining that the inspectors were failing their children.[71] However, their own reaction was of equal belligerence. Father Vermiere of the Jashpur Roman Catholic Mission wrote in a letter to one of his Superiors:

> You may have read in the Herald some very spirited answers purported to come from Jashpur Christian students against the vile slander by one who came with a large retinue to spy our institutions at Gholeng and Ginabahar. He dares call himself a member of the much esteemed Servants of India Society. He and his colleague have nearly wrecked the nascent Mission of the Norbertine Fathers in Mandla, District Jubbulpore. They were sent here by the Prime Minister, but if they hope to ruin this Mission, they are very much mistaken. Our Catholics are too advanced to be taken in, or frightened by such slanderers. Protest meetings against their vile report continue to be held, chiefly to wreck their treacherous machinations. As one of the two is a sort of Minister for the uplift of the backward people, he has a considerable government budget to dispose of. Their aim is more to prevent us from converting, than to care for the uplift of those they used to keep them in bondage [*sic*]. Just now they are starting 40 new schools for these backward adibasis. The third I hear of is in a village where we possess a school since 30 years. But knowing that many pagan children come to our schools and that we had sent a petition for a building to enlarge that school, they surreptitiously try and draw away the pagan children from us. But we are ready for them. Today my men are gone there to attend a big panchayat to draw up a protest, and get all the

pagans to refuse withdrawing their children from us. I am giving you all this for the sake of those in the community interested in Jashpur affairs.[72]

The Central Provinces Government, not surprisingly, came down on the side of the Tribal Welfare Department in the schools matter, noting that 'the duty of Government being to provide non-sectarian educational instruction for the people, no legitimate objection could be taken against it'.[73] Indeed, there could have been no objection, and given the sectarian nature of Catholic schooling, they would have had little right to complain if the schools run by the Tribal Welfare Department had been truly neutral. Instead, however, under Deshpande they functioned not merely as pro-Hindu but anti-Christian institutions.

Some fifty years later, the setting up of schools was still a matter of fierce competition, but this time, it was the VKA, that resisted government schools coming up in its vicinity. At a meeting in Chatori village in 2001, the headquarters of Manora block, inhabited primarily by Pahari Korwas, officially a 'Primitive Tribal Group', the Tribal Welfare Secretary from New Delhi, S.K. Naik, on inspection of the area, dusted down the teacher of the government school for having only three students while the Kalyan Ashram School had 62. K.P. Singh, General Secretary of the VKA, later told me that the government school had been set up by the Christian Tribal Welfare secretary of Chhattisgarh State in order to attract children away from the Kalyan Ashram school with the promise of midday meals. But the plan, he gloated, had backfired because the Hindu Tribal Welfare Secretary at the Centre decreed that the children in the Kalyan Ashram School should also get midday meals, because it didn't matter where they studied. The meeting at Chatori ended with Naik ordering more funds to be given to the Kalyan Ashram so that they could expand their hostel.[74]

Schools were not the only arena in which the Catholics and the Sangh clashed, and Deshpande seems to have been assisted by other Hindutva forces, in addition to the state. For instance, in its response to the Niyogi Commission, the Catholic Sabha of Jashpur had described the activities of the Arya Samaj, Deshpande's Ram Rajya Parishad and 'the All-India Vaidik Shuddhi Samaj of a certain Swami Ramanuj Saraswati' which involved 'spreading of the most shameless lies in the press and through fly sheets; for instance, that the Christians are gathering and hiding in the woods, arms and ammunition, against an eventual rising; frightening poor people into reconversion by threats of loss of land; also offering to give land; offering fabulous salaries to would-be converts to Hinduism.'[75] One Boko Sardar, under the guidance of Swami Ramanuj, urinated on the walls of a Christian chapel at Tangergaon and sang Hindu bhajans in another chapel.[76] The methods of the Christian missionaries, according to the Catholic Sabha, were in contrast, 'service of the neighbour, persuasion, never force or fraud'.[77]

Both sides disrupted intra-village relations, but each attributed this to the other. Deshpande's response to the Niyogi Commission emphasized the fact that Christian converts were not allowed to participate in village festivals and instead celebrated agricultural rituals like *nayakhani* in their churches. Dussehra was replaced by a festival called Jubilee. He also reported frequent village conflicts when Christians tried to bury their dead on *sarna* grounds or otherwise encroach on it. The Catholics, on the other hand, claimed that conversions made no difference to their way of life, other than renouncing idol worship and gram devatas ('we would deem it a grievous sin, if, knowing the one true God we went and gave worship to idols, devatas and bhuts').[78] Instead they blamed Deshpande for ruining relations between the two communities, which had hitherto been harmonious.[79]

THE VANVASI KALYAN ASHRAM

> We want the kind of vanvasi leadership which can bring Hindu unity. We need to erect a society which is proud of Hindutva. . . . Our work is to bring about awareness and create leadership.
>
> BALASAHEB DESHPANDE,
> *Sanstha, Shasan aur Karykarta*, 1990: 17

Deshpande resigned from government service after two years, because changing political exigencies meant that the government no longer gave him full support. While he had been successful at countering the Catholics, government rules prevented him from achieving his other major objective—giving tribal boys '*Hindutva sanskars*'.[80] He then set up the VKA along with another swayam-sevak, Morubhau Ketkar, and financial and moral help from the Maharaja of Jashpur.[81]

For a long time, no students came to the ashramshala. Sapre's narrative goes on to relate, in tones strongly reminiscent of Catholic primers on the lives of saints, how God's grace worked to bring students to the hostel. Just as Ketkar was about to give up, he dreamt of the RSS founder, Hedgewar, who advized him to carry on. By coincidence (read divine intervention), six boys came to the ashram to study that day and after this miracle, the ashram soon came into full swing.[82]

As Sapre tells it, local traders and sadhus played a significant role in the expansion of the Kalyan Ashram.[83] *Yajnas* and *Dharam Jagrans* were an especially useful occasion for mobilizing both—while traders contributed money and materials, local sadhus like Gahira Guru, Rambhikshuk Maharaj and Swarupanand helped in the 'dharm jagran'. One such event was the inauguration by Golwalkar of the new Kalyan Ashram buildings in Jashpur in 1963. Traders like Bhimsen Chopda, who felt threatened by the Jharkhand movement, introduced the Kalyan Ashram to larger magnates like Hanuman Prasad Poddar of Gorakhpur, who in turn helped them raise money from his Marwari contacts. Sympathetic government officials also helped. Thousands of Adivasis, according to Sapre, participated in these events, and Ramayan and bhajan mandalis were established in some 114 villages.

Relationship with Government

A significant part of the early history of the Kalyan Ashram centres on its uneasy relations with Congress governments. As with Christian missionaries under colonial rule, much depended on particular officers or politicians, and even as it officially eschewed dependence on government funding, efforts were/are constantly made to gain legitimation from senior politicians and functionaries as a 'non-political' organization doing 'good work' for 'Adivasi uplift'. In the process, links with the Sangh may be downplayed. In the early years, or so Sapre claims, both A.V. Thakkar and U.N. Dhebar accorded them significant recognition.[84] Later, when charged with a Jan Sangh association by Shankar Dayal Sharma (then Education Minister in the MP government), Deshpande reports telling him, 'If I had come to you with a white cap, you would have funded me. It is because we are far from politics that you don't want to fund me.'[85]

On the other hand, in pamphlets written for Kalyan Ashram workers, the organization emphasizes its Sangh identity:

> Once the Speaker of the Madhya Pradesh assembly Shri Ghanshyam Singh Gupt came to the Ashram. He said you are branded with the Sangh stamp, which is why you are not able to get government aid. So just change your board slightly. Put up an Arya Samaj board, but continue to do the same work. I'll make sure you get government aid. We said we are what we are. It is essential to retain our identity or the source of our inspiration will dry up and we will be able to do no work.[86]

The Ashram's official line is that dependence on government funding saps the spirit of voluntarism and restricts recruitment or the kind of work done, [87] and indeed, efforts are made to raise money from the 'public'. While locally, business families are a prime source,[88] non-resident Indians also contribute significantly through the US based India Development Relief Fund (IDRF), and the UK-based Hindu Swayamsevak Sangh.[89] Not all the donors are necessarily Sangh supporters. Following a critical investigative report on their activities, the IDRF attempted initially to deny that the VKA was a Sangh organization and later, when it was forced to admit this, tried to emphasize its 'service activities'.[90]

At the same time, it is undeniable that having the BJP in power at the Centre (1998-2004) involved substantial payoffs for such bodies.[91] K.P. Singh, General Secretary of the VKA, was appointed onto the board of CAPART for the eastern region, in-charge of funding NGOs, and Juel Oram ensured that funds from the Tribal Welfare Ministry he headed went to RSS NGOs.[92] Financial support from TRIFED, the Ministry of Tribal Welfare, the Ministry of Rural Development, and the Ministry of Youth and Sports, enabled the Kalyan Ashram to organize a Swadeshi Vanvasi Mela at the Nehru Stadium in Delhi from 11-14 February 2001. A seminar on Adivasi issues which was held on the premises was aimed at gaining public acceptability, with participants like the well known administrator turned activist B.D. Sharma or N.C. Zeliang of Nagaland speaking on the same platform as known RSS activists like Mahesh Chandra Sharma, BJP-appointed head of the Khadi Gramodyog Commission, Shree Basant of the Karigar Panchayat and K.P. Singh of the VKA.[93]

VKA Stand on 'Indigenous Peoples

The Kalyan Ashram is now trying to appropriate the concerns taken up by non-party social movements like land and displacement, though much of it appears instrumental. For instance, as Raghav of the VKA in Lohardaga (Jharkhand) confessed, a survey they conducted which raised the issue of restoration of alienated tribal land, was really aimed at Muslims, even though there are as many Hindu moneylenders.[94] Any contradictions that might arise between the BJP's support for multinationals or its base of exploitative traders and the VKA's constituency of Adivasis is reconciled by claiming to be two different organizations, by attributing it to the BJP's need to govern or get votes, and finally, by the understanding that ultimately the agenda is really the same—the building of a Ram temple and the establishment of a Hindu Rashtra.

At the same time, the VKA resists the terminology of 'indigenous peoples' and even the term 'adivasi', which grew out of the Jharkhand struggle. Instead, it prefers to call them *vanvasis* or forest dwellers as against *gaonvasis* (village dwellers) and *shahrvasis* (city dwellers), on the grounds, shared by many post-colonial critics, that the distinction between tribes and castes is a colonial product. Any attempt by Indian Adivasis to take their concerns to international forums on indigenous peoples is seen as contributing to the break-up of India. A letter from R.K. Deshpande to the Prime Minister, Narasimha Rao, warned the Government of India about the representations to the UN by the Indian Council of Indigenous and Tribal Peoples. After having pointed to the Church connections of some of the members of the delegation like Bishop Nirmal Minz, the memorandum warned of the 'nexus between the Church-backed separatists, insurgents and other disintegrationists like the ULFA, Khalistanis, Pak-aided Kashmiri militants and other similar outfits.'[95]

While the Kalyan Ashram blames Christian missionaries for changing Adivasi culture, it does little to protect it either, other than promoting their dances. Local languages are not forbidden in their schools and hostels but Sanskrit and Hindi are glorified. There is a real reluctance among Kalyan Ashram students to admit to knowing Kurukh and my attempts at getting assembled children in Chatori to sing a Pahari Korwa song while waiting for the Tribal Welfare Secretary were contemptuously discarded by one of their ideologues, Avadh Bihari, who asked them to recite a Sanskrit *shloka* instead.[96] However, if they see Christian competition in the use of local Adivasi languages, the VKA is not averse to using them either.

Although the Kalyan Ashram publicly claims that one-third to a half of its workforce is 'Vanvasi' and the ceremonial positions like that of the President and Vice-Presidents are filled by tribal people, the organizational positions which hold real control are in the hands of non-tribal, upper-caste RSS men. As of 2001, the VKA had 842 male and 210 female full timers, out of which approximately half were 'Vanvasis'.[97]

The VKA claims to have over 10,000 projects including satsang kendras and lok kala mandals, schools, ekal vidyalayas, bal sanskar kendras, libraries, dispensaries, hospitals, agricultural development and vocational training centres, and sports centres, and contacts with over 35,000 tribal villages.[98] However, as one ideologue put it, 'whatever we do is only a means to an end'.[99] There appear to be three major ends: 'dharm jagran' (lit. religious awakening) or conversion in order to expand numbers, recruitment of full time workers for the Sangh, and fomenting violence against minorities.

EDUCATION AS DHARM JAGRAN

Avadh Bihari: The main aim of Kalyan Ashram is Dharam Jagran. This is the cheapest and most effective way of mobilizing people. Schools and hospitals are just means towards this end. This is why VKA doesn't have too many schools and isn't entirely focused on education like the Ramkrishna Mission.[100]

Ramesh Upadhya: Dharam Jagran is the ultimate and real objective. Schools etc. are an easy way to draw people—the cheapest way to mobilize people is through Dharam, by running Bal Sanskar Kendras etc.

Rathi: The main difference between us and the Ramakrishna Mission is that they want perfection in what they do. We are not interested in horizontal achievement but in vertical spread. The more ground or people we cover the better.

NS: So your main aim is Dharm Jagran?

Rathi: Not even that. Our main aim is to keep Christians out.

Ramesh Upadhya: This was always the aim—that our numbers which had gone down due to theft by other faiths should go up again. But for strategic reasons, we don't want to do it publicly under the Kalyan Ashram banner. Swami Amaranand organizes the events and then calls Dilip Singh Judeo for publicity. Judeo gets lots of publicity which is good for his career, and we get his support.

Much of the media coverage of the VKA has focused on the public 'reconversion' ceremonies.[101] In Jashpur, these are organized by

Swami Amaranand who lives on the campus, and while the number of converts involved may be debatable, they are useful as public spectacles. VKA members simultaneously play on fears of increased conversion, as well as boast of having stemmed the tide.[102] In fact, as the above conversation shows, much more lasting conversion to Hindutva occurs through schools and hostels.[103]

Deshpande's early insight that schools could serve as incubators of physical violence was extended the use of hostels as nodal points for Sangh extension activities in the villages:

> We know that not all students of our chatravas [hostel] will become fulltime workers. But all of them will have received our sanskars. . . . of all our activities, the most important one is the running of the hostels. The rationale behind our hostels is different from the usual ones. We want to make our hostels the focus or center of attention for the region. Through this medium we want to bring about awareness in the whole region.[104]

Accordingly, a handbook for the private use of Kalyan Ashram workers notes that in addition to the hostel warden, an additional worker should set up a centre in or near the *chatravas* to keep in touch with a circle of 20-30 villages around and organize them through eklavya khelkud kendras, gram samitis, dramas, etc.[105] Children are trained to hold bhajan mandalis, satsang kendras, *shakhas* and other activities when they go home for the long summer vacations.

The hostels are in much demand and even some Christians apply.[106] Although the surroundings are shabby (especially in the girls hostel), and the food basic, these hostels provide a totalizing and intense experience. There is a proliferation of Hindu visual imagery, carefully planned to expose children to Hindu idioms.[107] The daily routine at both the girls and boys hostel stretches from early morning prayers to *shakha* attendance to an evening *shakha* followed by *arti* and bhajan, which appears to create an almost trancelike impact on the students. The students also read the *Hanuman Chalisa* or *Ramayan* path together in the mornings.[108] In addition there are weekly discourses on national events (from a Sangh point of view of course), annual days at which the leading people of nearby villages are invited, and celebrations of Hindu festivals. Girls are more involved in ritual activity than boys, especially on occasions like Janmashtami and Rakhee. Rakhee has a special meaning in the Kalyan Ashram calendar—with Vanvasi tying *rakhees* to non-Vanvasi, thus establishing a bond between the communities. In short, whatever time is spent away from studying goes into Sangh related activities. Needless to say, this routine is quite different from life at home. The prayers and the bhajans too are quite different from their own religious practices.

It is the everydayness of school and hostel life, however, and not just the exposure to rituals, which has the most lasting effects. Assi Zilya, from Kohima district studying in her final year of the BA degree in Raipur and living in the VKA hostel described how she only 'discovered' that she was really a Hindu when she came to the Ashram in Raipur:

Assi: Before that, we always thought we were different from Hindus. We worship the Sun God.
NS: So how did you know you were Hindu?
Assi: We also believe in the Sun, Hindus also believe in the Sun, and our ways of worship are similar. We also pray to God at sowing or harvest.

The North-East girls reported that when they go home, even if as Kalyan Ashram workers, they resume praying in their own languages and to their own local gods. But they say that a sense of identity with Hinduism—as against the locally dominant Christianity—remains.[109] A number of students in the Jashpur Chatravas had also been to mission schools at some point in their lives. Bima Bhunkar and Asha Chakris, two college going students at the girls hostel in Jashpur had both been at Mission schools. They told me they had not seen it as a problem then, but after coming to the Kalyan Ashram and learning about their Hindu dharm, they began to see how bad the Christians were for converting.

Apart from schools, the VKA runs pre-school centres for children ('balwadis' or 'bal sanskar kendras') to teach them the rudiments of reading, writing and '*sanskars*'. These *sanskars* include learning to say *pranam* instead of their own Adivasi greeting *johar*, touching the feet of their elders and shouting slogans like *Saraswati Mata ki Jai, Mahapati Ram ki Jai, Brindavan Krishna ki Jai*. Not every child understands what they are chanting and the littler ones often fall asleep, but sustained exposure to these centres inevitably inculcates respect for Sanskrit as a language worth knowing, and a belief that 'civilization' consists in Hindu markers of behaviour. More important than the actual information that children may or may not remember is the symbolic message.

'Keeping in mind the love of youth for sports' there are 'Eklavya khel kud centres' for older youth. The idea is 'through that medium to attract them to the Kalyan Ashram and Sangh' and having thus attracted them, 'to use the power of organized youth to bring about a change in society'.[110] Before and after the game children are expected to greet the motherland, shouting *Bharat Mata ki Jai.* The games are designed to be indigenous, with names like '*Agnikund*' and Ram–Ravan. Here, as in the *shakhas*, the referee calls out directions in Sanskrit, and while not all participants may be Sangh supporters, this enjoyable activity generates considerable goodwill for the ashram. Every four years the Kalyan Ashram holds an all-India sports event, and while there is an attempt to get children from schools other than just the Kalyan Ashram or RSS schools, Christian children are definitely discouraged.[111]

For older people, the VKA runs satsang kendras or religious gatherings in villages where villagers are taught Hindu bhajans and kirtans, and given discourses. Like the Catholics before them, who set hymns to local tunes, the Sangh may keep in references to the Singbonga or local gods, but Hindu gods like Ram and Krishna have pride of place. VKA newsletters also serve an important proselytizing function, especially in a situation where reading material and alternative sources of information are scarce. Each branch of the VKA brings out its own newsletter—for instance, the Jharkhand branch brings out *Ekal Varta*, the Jashpur unit brings out *Vanvasi Darshan*. One issue of *Vanvasi Darshan* had accounts of Christians who had 'reconverted' as well as an article on the universal importance of Lord Ram. They claimed this was shown by the fact that towns were named after him all over the world such as Rampside, Ramsbottom and Ramsgate in England, Ramtuel and Rambert Viliers in France.[112]

RECRUITMENT OF FULL-TIMERS

> The true test of how successful a hostel is the number of full-time workers it generates for the Sangh and the Kalyan Ashram—and only then does a hostel become meaningful.[113]

Judged by the standards of how many full-timers it generates, the Kalyan Ashram is a rather successful institution, with several of its hostellers going on to do *seva* for a couple of years before they take up normal lives and occupations. Some of these students go on to summer camps run by the RSS where, apart from more physical training, they also get ideological training.

When Avadh Bihari, an old pracharak and joint organizing secretary of the VKA, visited Jashpur he went on a recruitment round of all the hostels.[114] His discourses combined a grandfatherly interest in the futures of the children with inspiring examples of Sangh volunteers who had devoted their life to service. Each sermon ended with his asking how many students were willing to join the Sangh, warning them that they would have to give at least two years as full-timers after finishing their education. Each session generated some half a dozen volunteers from classes 11 and 12, and he encouraged them to write to him about their aspirations. At the girl's hostel, the conversation was appropriately tailored to his idea of female futures. After solving an internal hostel dispute, he claimed that this was the decade of women's empowerment and they should go forward just as 'Jijabai gave birth to Shivaji and Kaushalya to Ram. Behind every great man is a mother who gave the right *sanskars*, and sacrificed her life to bring the great man up.' He then told the girls the 'story of Itwari' who had been saved from being a nun and had joined the Ashram. Only one of the girls present had been to a Rashtriya Sevika Samiti camp, so the others were advised to join. Finally, Avadh Bihari asked how many of the girls wanted to do *samaj seva* (social work). At that point only one stood up but two others later said they had felt shy and asked for their names to be given to 'Dadaji'.

Much recruitment also happens through personal contacts in the villages. Somvari, a woman pracharak in Lohardaga, for example, comes from a family in Angul. She took quiet pride in the fact that her family knew Dara Singh, the killer of Graham Staines, and Jual Oram, the Tribal Welfare Minister. Male pracharaks used to come to their village to teach and she was attracted by the idea of doing *samaj seva* and *dharam raksha*. Somvari said she was also very keen to learn Hindi as it was the *rashtra bhasha*.

While Jashpur had no women pracharaks, Jharkhand had some 14 full-timers. Although the image of the ideal woman promoted by the RSS is of someone who takes care of the home and brings forth fighting children who will defend Hinduism, in practice the VKA women pracharaks are empowered women. While there is a clear internal gender hierarchy, the familial idiom in which the organization is run means the relationship between senior VKA men and the younger women pracharaks is a relaxed, even joking one. In part this may also be due to the fact that adivasi women are used to a relatively non-hierarchical structure in their villages. At the same time, the leadership of the VKA, as of the RSS more widely, is obsessed with sex—particularly the idea that 'Hindu' women are sexually exploited by Muslims and Christians and makes much of this propaganda in adivasi areas.

Living conditions in the Kalyan Ashrams are both spartan and egalitarian, providing a sense of community, with elders referred to in familial terms (Dadaji, Bhabhi, etc.). Workers are paid according to their needs —single pracharaks (male and female) get just enough to cover their living expenses, but men with families are paid on the basis of dependants. Unlike the 'Westernized' lifestyle of the Jesuit priests, which students in their schools are led to aspire to, the Kalyan Ashram purposely keeps its surroundings in tune with existing conditions.

Inciting Violence against Others

The Kalyan Ashram runs a variety of other programmes each of which is carefully described in the handbook. Yet even such a seemingly innocuous activity as organizing health workers in each village can serve as a means of mobilization against mission activities, as the following incident shows. A meeting of VKA village workers, balwadi workers and village level health workers at Sanna started off with Avadh Bihari asking questions on how many satsang kendras had been held and what kind of prayers had been conducted. The health workers were asked how many patients they had catered to and whether the patients were able to pay the five rupees charged per visit. The discourse then slowly shifted. They were told to look out for other organizations, which were evangelizing, and to inform the Kalyan Ashram so that it could be stopped. One by one, men got up to report the events in their area, mostly to do with religious issues—the visit of a 'German' preacher (from the German Evangelical Lutheran Church), a conflict in a village with the 'Adi Dharm party' (followers of original Oraon rituals). The Kalyan Ashram followers had prevented the Adi Dharm villagers from planting the karma in the *akhara* and they had taken the matter to the police. The villagers were told to go easy with the Adi Dharm as it was an internal fight between Hindus, and watch out for the Christians. Another man reported a dispute with a Christian farmer who owned a borewell but diverted water to the river instead of to others' fields—clearly a local quarrel which had little to do with religion. He was advised to get the villagers to sign a petition against the man. Differences with ordinary Christians were thus encouraged and turned into major religious difference, while differences between others, including Adi Dharm followers, were minimized.

While maintaining that they are a distinct organization from the VHP, in practice, relations are close, and while visiting the VKA in Lohardaga, I was taken to meet the RSS 'karjwa' there, who runs a sweet shop and coordinates all the RSS bodies in the area. Together the VKA worker and the RSS head told me of their activities during the Ramjanmabhumi shilanyas, when videos dramatizing the alleged destruction of the original temple, the construction of the Babri Masjid, and cow slaughter were taken around all the neighbouring villages. The VKA worker said he had taken part in the demolition of the Babri Masjid and had taken many people from Lohardaga.[115] There also appear to have been sporadic incidents of violence against Christian evangelists and some ordinary Christian villagers.[116]

Given the strength of the Catholic community in Jashpur, the priests there are less worried about the growing influence of the Kalyan Ashram there than elsewhere and tend to dismiss the 'reonversion' activities as vote building performances.[117] Most of the RSS envy and anger is directed at the Catholic Church, perhaps because its substantial buildings and estates visibly embody strength. Ironically, however, Catholic expansion in India has more or less levelled off and the Church is pre-occupied with maintaining its flock against the depredations of rival Christian denominations, particularly American evangelicals. Post Vatican II, the Catholic Church has also attempted to 'indigenize' itself, e.g. by reviving festivals like Sarhul which do not directly contradict Christian tenets, and using the Kurukh language.

While the Catholic Church and the Kalyan Ashram battle it out, a third force (the Parha Samaj) attempts to retain and strengthen the old Parha system and indigenous religion, but with little support from government or anyone else. As Sura Oraon, a Professor of Kurukh at the BS College Lohardaga and Secretary of the District Parha Sabha said 'Once the Christian missionaries had finished pulling us towards Christianity, the Kalyan Ashram began pulling us towards Hinduism.' There have been tensions between the Kalyan Ashram and the Parha Samaj over the holding of the Sarhul festival—with the Kalyan Ashram celebrating it with a *havan* instead of the traditional way, and holding it on a different day. In many ways, however, the Parha Samaj and the Kalyan Ashram share a common agenda; for instance, the Parha Samaj has also tried to take on Christian evangelicals, and one of their demands is that Christians should not get reservations, as they benefit doubly—from being minorities (with their own educational institutions) and being scheduled tribes.

CONCLUSION

While the sequence of the paper may seem to 'explain' the working of the Kalyan Ashram as a 'reaction' to Missionary activities, or appear to be drawing equivalence, this is not the case. The notion of a Hindu Rashtra has had an independent trajectory which makes it coeval with Muslim separatism and Christian conversion and not a mere consequence, much as the RSS would like us to think otherwise. The two forms of 'welfare conversion' cannot be equated in terms of their ultimate effects on adivasi society, at least in part because of the numerically marginal position of Christians within Indian society today.[118] It is also important to remember that the RSS is not simply converting people to Hinduism but to Hindutva, which is a political rather than spiritual affiliation. What does emerge clearly, though, is what Jaffrelot has identified as the key strategy of the RSS—'stigmatization' and 'emulation'.[119] Even while aiming to counter Christian missions, the VKA, not surprisingly, draws upon the organizational forms earlier developed and practiced by the Catholics.

In either case, it is the economic and political problems of the Adivasis coupled with state indifference, which have provided the ground for religious mobilization. High rents, *begar*, and restrictions on forest produce initially drew people to the Catholics and Lutherans, who offered a means of resistance; but in the post-colonial period, it is the Sangh's welfare activities in the field of education and health which draw people into its orbit. For many of those thus associated with the Kalyan Ashram, its discourse then begins to seem empowering, with its admission of 'neglect' by the Hindu upper castes, its call to primordial defence of religion, and its increasingly skilful use of mainstream development discourse on tribal land alienation and poverty.

The state's acts of omission and commission are central to the enterprise of religious mobilization. Quite apart from the unmarked religious practices of the state, both the colonial and post-colonial states have enabled conversion through their absence in the fields of education and health. But more subtly, the state also enables religions to convert by, on the one hand, refusing to recognise ordinary political protest as legitimate and, on the other hand, legitimizing religious violations as acts of conscience. In the past, while the colonial state routinely expelled people it thought guilty of political propaganda, it went out of its way to ensure freedom of conscience to those engaged in religious propaganda. In the present, state discourse through the media depicts the destruction of the Babri Masjid as something more than a pure act of vandalism, while political organizations fighting for the economic and political rights of workers or peasants are seen as terrorists. A demand couched in religious terms receives greater state attention than if it had been made in purely secular terms.[120] In other words, the Indian state has routinely privileged religious belief and identity over other forms of belief and identity, which inevitably has the circular and reaffirming effect of strengthening religious affiliation. Finally, insofar as the state, Christians, and Hindus share a vision of 'Adivasi uplift' that involves cultural change without accompanying access to economic and political power, they are all equally culpable for the obliteration of Adivasi identities.

NOTES

1. For instance, displacement and migration make it harder to worship spirits localized in particular natural phenomena.
2. For the term, see Sathianathan Clarke, 'Transformations of Caste and Tribe', in Rowena Robinson and Sathianathan Clarke, eds., *Religious Conversion in India: Modes, Motivations, and Meanings*, New Delhi: Oxford University Press, 2003, p. 218.
3. Recent studies have emphasized the political agency of converts, and conversion as the fashioning of new syncretic identities. See essays in Rowena Robinson and Sathianathan Clarke, eds., *Religious Conversion*; Gauri Visvanathan, *Outside the Fold: Conversion, Modernity and Belief*, Princeton: Princeton University Press, 1998; Richard M. Eaton, Comparative History as World history: Religious Conversion in Modern India', *Journal of World History*, 8 (2), 1997, pp. 243-71.

4. Satish Saberwal, 'Anxieties, identities, complexity, reality', in Mushirul Hasan, ed., *Will Secular India Survive?* Gurgaon: imprintOne, 2004, pp. 93-124.
5. For exceptions, see Sumit Sarkar, 'Hindutva and the Question of Conversions', in K.N. Pannikar, ed., *The Concerned Indian's Guide to Communalism*, New Delhi: Viking, 1999; Arvind Sharma, 'The Place of Conversion within Hinduism', *Contributions to Indian Sociology*, 11 (2), 1977, 345-54.
6. N.K. Bose, 'The Hindu Method of Tribal Absorption', *Science and Culture*, 8, 1941, pp. 188-94; for Sanskritization, see M.N. Srinivas, 'Hinduism', in *Encyclopedia Brittannica*, 12, Chicago, 1961.
7. In the Constituent Assembly Debates too, the 'right to propagate' was left in as a 'concession' to Christians.
8. Julian Saldanha, *Conversion and Indian Civil Law*, Bangalore: Theological Publications in India, 1981, pp. 47-56; see also Kumkum Sangari, 'Gender Lines: Personal Laws, Uniform Laws, Conversion', *Social Scientist*, 27 (5-6), 1999, pp. 17-61.
9. Fieldnotes on Loyola school, Kunkuri, January 2002.
10. S.C. Roy, *Oraon Religion and Customs*, Calcutta: Editions Indian, 1928, rpt. 1972.
11. Roy, *Oraon Religion*, pp. 11-12.
12. Ibid., pp. 4-8.
13. Surya Narayan Saksena, *Vanvasi Kalyan Ashram Kya or Kyon?*, Delhi: Akhil Bharatiya Vanvasi Kalyan Ashram, 1994, pp. 5-6.
14. John Lakra, 'Tribal Culture and Tribal Christians', *Sevartham*, vol. 25, 2000, p. 18.
15. *Senior Missionary at Kohima, 1937*, cited in Eaton, *Comparative History*, p. 254.
16. See accounts in Felix Padel, *The Sacrifice of Human Being*, New Delhi: Oxford University Press, 1995, pp. 199-206.
17. K.S. Singh, *Birsa Munda and his Movement 1874-1901*, New Delhi: Oxford University Press, 1983, pp. 20-1.
18. They numbered some 71,200 by 1900. Singh, *Birsa Munda*, p. 21.
19. L. Clarysse, S.J., 'Lievens and the Zamindari System', in *Sevartham*, 1985, p. 6.
20. Clarysse, *Lievens*, p. 15.
21. See Nandini Sundar, *Subalterns and Sovereigns*, New Delhi: Oxford University Press, 1997); H.S. Kamath, *Grazing and Nistar in the Central Provinces Estates: The Report of an Enquiry*, Bhopal: Government of the Central Provinces, 1941; R.K. Ramadhyani, *Report on Land Tenures & The Revenue System of the Orissa and Chattisgarh States*, Berhampur: Indian Law Publication Press, 1942.
22. See Padel, *Sacrifice*, p. 189, on post-Independence Christian

conversion of Konds; Frederick S. Downs, 'Christian Conversion Movements in North East India', in Robinson and Clarke, eds., *Religious Conversions*, pp. 381-400; Eaton, *Comparative History*; 'Move for North India Church Union', *Glasgow Herald*, 14 October 1948 which reports the Indian tour of Rev Dr. Nevile Davidson and the optimism of missionaries regarding their prospects under Independence.

23. File No. 268-P 1929, For. & Pol., National Archives of India, New Delhi (NAI).
24. File No. 233-P (S)/36, For. & Pol. Dept. (Pol. Branch), NAI. The bulk of this report is reprinted in the Report of the Christian Missionary Activities Enquiry Committee, Madhya Pradesh (henceforth referred to as the Niyogi Commission) Nagpur: Government Printing Press, 1956, vol. II, pt. B, pp. 325-74; see also Niyogi Commission, vol. I, pp. 46-7.
25. File No. 233-P (S)/36, For. & Pol. Dept. (Pol. Branch), NAI (henceforth referred to as Meek 1936, since his report forms the bulk of the file). Col A.S. Meek was Agent to the Governor-General, Eastern States Agency, which was established in 1933, covering the Chhattisgarh Feudatory States, Bengal, Bihar and Orissa States.
26. Ibid.
27. The account of 1922-3 is taken from R/1/1/1417, File No. 883-P(Sec) Part II, Disturbances in the Jashpur State and assumption of the management of the State by government, India Office Library and Record Room, London (IOL).
28. Ramadhyani, *Report on Land Tenures*, p. 35.
29. J. Connolly, Secretary to the Advisory Board of the GEL Church, Ranchi to Political Agent, 13 January 1923; B. Meuleman, Archbishop of Calcutta to Ley, 14 January 1923. Both in File No. 883-P(Sec) Part II, IOL.
30. File No. 883-P(Sec) Part II, IOL.
31. Meek, 1936, p. 331.
32. W.G. Archer, Christianity and Bihar, November 1935. Typewritten mss, in W.G. Archer papers Mss Eur/F 236/1, IOL.
33. Meek 1936, pp. 336-7; see also Fortnightly report for the Eastern States Agency (ESA), 1st half of November 1945, Acc. No. 352, Crown Representative Records (CRR), NAI.
34. Fortnightly report of the ESA, 1st half of July 1945, dated 20 July 1945, Acc. No. 352, CRR, NAI.
35. Fortnightly report of the Inspector General of Police and Police Advisor, ESA for the first half of February 1940, in F. No. 11(23)—P (S)/40 of 1940, Acc. No. 354, CRR, NAI.
36. Meek, 1936, pp. 326-8.

37. File No. 268-P 1929, For. & Pol., NAI (Proposed Legislation by the Gwalior Darbar of a law regarding change in religion).
38. Fortnightly report of the ESA, 1st half of July 1942, Acc. No. 354, CRR, NAI.
39. Undated typescript titled 'Bhumijan Seva Mandal', in Elwin correspondence, Bhulabhai Desai papers, Nehru Memorial Museum & Library, New Delhi. See also Nandini Sundar, 'Verrier Elwin and the Missionary Debate in Central India', in Tanka Subba, ed., *Verrier Elwin and the Tribal Question*, New Delhi: Orient Longman, forthcoming.
40. Fortnightly reports of the ESA, Acc. No. 352-57, CRR, NAI.
41. Fortnightly report, 2nd half of March 1938, ESA, Acc. No. 352. Also fortnightly reports from 1938-45, Acc. No. 352-57, CRR, NAI.
42. Fortnightly report of ESA, 2nd half of June 1942, Acc. No. 354, CRR, NAI.
43. Fortnightly report of ESA, 1st half of April 1945, Acc. No. 356, CRR, NAI; see also Agapit Tirkey, *Jharkhand Movement: A Study of its Dynamics*, New Delhi: AICFAIP, 2002, p. 57.
44. The Adivasi Mahasabha had got some help from the Muslim league. K.S. Singh, *Tribal Movements in India*, New Delhi: Manohar, 1982, pp. 4-5; Niyogi Commission vol. 1, pp. 9-15.
45. Surya Narain Saxena, *Friends or Foes of Adivasis & Dalits?*, Delhi: Publicity and Publications Bureau, Akhil Bharatiya Vanvasi Kalyan Ashram, 1993, p. 1.
46. K.D. Sapre, *Shri Balasaheb Deshpande Jeevan aur Karya*, Jabalpur: Van Sahitya Academy, 1999, p. 24.
47. Ibid., p. 25.
48. Bruce Graham, *Hindu Nationalism and Indian Politics*, Cambridge: Cambridge University Press, 1990, pp. 19-20, 24-5.
49. Christophe Jaffrelot, *The Hindu Nationalist Movement and Indian Politics*, New Delhi: Viking, 1996.
50. Niyogi Commission, vol. I, p. 9.
51. Ibid., pp. 13, 49-51.
52. The Catholics, especially in Jashpur, complained that Catholic candidates for government posts were asked to give up their religion, that they were not enrolled as home guards, their contributions to the Gandhi Memorial fund were not accepted etc. (Niyogi Commission, vol. I, pp. 15-16)
53. Sapre, *Shri Balasaheb*, p. 32.
54. Niyogi Commission, vol. IIA, p. 189.
55. Ibid., vol. I, pp. 18-19.
56. Ibid., vol IIA, p. 222.
57. Ibid., vol. I, pp. 28-9.

58. 236 out of a total of 480 foreigners working in Missions were American. Niyogi Commission, vol. I, 104.
59. Niyogi Commission, vol. I, p. 102.
60. Ibid., pp. 95-131.
61. Ibid., p. 132.
62. Ibid., p. 155.
63. Ibid., p. 158.
64. Balasaheb Deshpande, *Sanstha, Shasan aur Karykarta,* Delhi: ABVKA, 1990, pp. 8-9.
65. See M.S. Golwalkar, *We or Our Nationhood Defined,* Nagpur, 1939, p. 62.
66. Sapre, *Shri Balasaheb*, p. 11.
67. Ibid.
68. Ibid., p. 16.
69. Sapre, *Shri Balasaheb,* pp. 20-2.
70. Niyogi Commission, vol. IIA, p. 225.
71. Ibid., p. 226.
72. Reprinted in Niyogi Commission, vol. I, p. 9.
73. Niyogi Commission, vol. I, p. 14.
74. Fieldnotes, October 2001. After Naik's visit the VKA has been given funds to run the Pahari Korwa project for the 'uplift' of the Pahari Korwas. K.P. Singh proudly said that the Korwas stay in the ashram whenever they come to Jashpur for a court case—which is quite often because they get into trouble with the forest department, for cutting wood, or not supplying chickens, etc. Yet, there is no attempt by the VKA to challenge the authority of the Forest Department. It is also not clear how much of the money meant for Korwas or for their hostels is spent on these activities and how much on other propaganda activities for the Sangh.
75. Niyogi Commission, vol. IIA, p. 199.
76. Ibid., p. 213.
77. Ibid., p. 199.
78. Ibid., p. 218.
79. That this happened is also evident from Sapre's own account, *Shri Balasaheb*, p. 33.
80. Sapre, *Shri Balasaheb*, p. 25.
81. The Kalyan Ashram continues to have a mutually supportive if calculating relationship with the former Jashpur ruling family, enhanced by Dilip Singh Judeo's involvement in conversion ceremonies.
82. Sapre, *Shri Balsaheb*, p. 28.
83. It was later termed the Akhil Bharatiya Vanvasi Kalyan Ashram, under which state branches may have different names like the Vanvasi Kalyan Parishad in Gujarat and Rajasthan.

84. Ibid., pp. 27-8.
85. Deshpande, *Sanstha, Shasan*, p. 4.
86. Ibid., p. 6.
87. The decline in the Adimjati Sevak Sangh is blamed on the fact that they took 100 per cent government funding and therefore could not establish a hold in society (Deshpande, *Sanstha*, p. 5).
88. A fundraising event for the VKA's north-east girl's hostel in Raipur collected Rs. 51,000 in one afternoon. The audience seemed to consist mainly of Marwaris and Maharashtrian Brahmins. Fieldnotes, January 2002
89. South Asia Citizens Web (SACW) and Sabrang Communications *A Foreign Exchange of Hate*, published by SACW and Sabrang Communications, 2002.
90. Press Release of the Campaign to Stop Funding Hate, 5 March 2003.
91. See also D.K. Singh, 'Lost Tribes', *Communalism Combat*, 11 (102), October 2004, pp. 8-18 on the financial and legal help provided by the BJP ruled Rajasthan government to the Vanvasi Kalyan Parishad.
92. See also Akshaya Mukul, 'RSS Holds Key to "tribal treasury"', *Times of India*, 27 September 2003.
93. Fieldnotes, Vanvasi Mela, 11-14 February 2001.
94. Fieldnotes, October 2001; see also *The Hindu*, 28 February 2003 on the Kalyan Ashram's stand on the Muthanga firing in Kerala.
95. Saxena, ed., *Friends or Foes of Adivasis and Dalits?*, Delhi: ABVKA, 1993, p. 20
96. Fieldnotes, October 2001; January 2002.
97. Fieldnotes, October 2001; Akhil Bharatiya Vanvasi Kalyan Ashram, Statewise Activities at a Glance as on 23 September 2001. Information provided by the ABVKA, Jashpur.
98. ABVKA, ibid.
99. Saxena, *Vanvasi Kalyan Ashram kya aur kyun?*, Delhi: ABVKA, 1994, p. 11.
100. Avadh Bihari was then the Joint All-India Organizing Secretary of the VKA. Ramesh Upadhya is an old RSS worker, stationed at the Ashram in Jashpur, while Rathi was an old sympathizer also living in the Ashram. He has since died.
101. Raman Kirpal, 'Ghar Vaapasi—The great RSS Farce', *Indian Express*, 12 February 1999.
102. According to Ramesh Upadhya, 'when people decide to reconvert, Swamiji goes in procession for 3-4 km to the *mandap* in the village accompanied by dancers and *paltans* of Pahari Korwas with bows and arrows. Converts—husband/wife—are given a saree and dhoti and after prayer, Judeo washes their feet. This is seen as a great honour and helps their assimilation into society.'
103. For studies of the role of schools in Christian conversion, see Padel,

Sacrifice; Brendan P. Carmody S.J., *Conversion and Jesuit Schooling in Zambia*, Leiden: E.J. Brill, 1992; Carol Devens, '"If we get the girls, we get the race": Missionary Education of Native American Girls', *Journal of World History*, vol. 3, no. 2, 1992.

104. Balasaheb Deshpande, *Sanstha, Shasan*, p. 17.
105. Akhil Bharatiya Vanvasi Kalyan Ashram, *Keval Vyaktigat Upyog ke Liye*, Mumbai: ABVKA, ND; also Prasann Damodar Sapre, *Hamare Vanvasi aur Kalyan Ashram*, Lucknow: Lokhit Prakashan, 1991.
106. The rest of this section is based on fieldnotes, October 2001.
107. The VKA handbook prescribes how the hostel should look—it should be named after a famous Vanvasi man or woman, individual rooms should also be named after great peopie, there should be a cultural map of India and pictures of gods and goddesses or great men.
108. Some of them continue to read the *Hanuman Chalisa* even when they go home to their villages, although others also said that the pressures of work keep them from any kind of prayer at home.
109. The RSS penetration of the north-east is beyond the scope of this paper.
110. ABVKA, *Keval Vyaktigat*, p. 6.
111. Apparently, there was an internal debate on whether to allow Christian children to attend these sports events, with one school of thought declaring that they were the enemy while others argued that by introducing them to a Hindu environment they would perhaps 'reconvert'.
112. 'Duniya bhar mein Ram nam ke shahr', *Vanvasi Darshan*, May/June 2001, Year 17, vol. 3, p. 3.
113. ABVKA, Keval Vyaktigat, p. 2.
114. The rest of this section is based on fieldnotes, October 2001.
115. Fieldnotes, 22 October 2001.
116. See the film *Fishers of Men* which deals with the issue of conversions and reconversions and the killing of a Catholic man in Jashpur.
117. Fieldnotes, October 2001, January 2002.
118. The RSS argues that Hindus are numerically marginal in the world as a whole. It is true that American evangelism is growing and targeting India through the AD 2000 and Joshua Projects. See V.K. Shashikumar and Mayabhushan Nagvenkar, 'Preparing for the harvest . . .', in *Tehelka*, 7 February 2004, pp. 6-17. However, within India, Hindutva is a greater threat to the social fabric.
119. Christophe Jaffrelot, *The Hindu Nationalist Movement*.
120. See for example, 'Dalits Threaten to Convert if Displaced', *Times of India*, 22 December 1998.

LOOKING FOR ALTERNATIVES

Where then do we go from here? The papers of Mahajan and Dusche offer us comparative leverage in looking for ways to restrain unbridled religious belligerence. Locke, reflecting on a time of heightened Catholic-Protestant conflict in Europe, is Mahajan's point of departure for thinking for contemporary India. Dusche examines the recent German experience with Judaism and Islam for the kinds of response, by the state and by minority religious groups. These may well be emulated elsewhere.

Granting the fabled capacity of Hindu/Indian society to accommodate diversity, Gurpreet Mahajan holds that there is a 'distinction between tolerating differences and creating a tolerant society'. The Indian Constitution did provide for religious freedom, but it erred in circumscribing individual liberty—the freedom of speech and expression—'in the interest of public order, morality and national integrity'. These concerns have often been interpreted in terms reflecting the majority viewpoint. Looking for way forward, Mahajan turns to Locke's seventeenth-century reflections concerning a tolerant society in his European context, and finds the following principles: to recognize that state and church have distinctive functions; that the citizen's rights, and freedom of conscience, must be protected; that each religious authority should keep to its own flock; and that the state has to guarantee the arrangement overall on the basis of the equal status and liberty of all. While recognizing the vital role of the state, Mahajan proposes that the focus of our concern shift from the liberty of the 'individual' to that of a differentiated 'self and the other'.

We owe a study of the logic of assertive religious identities in contemporary, post-unification, Germany to Michael Dusche. Germany's extraordinary statutes enable diverse 'worldview-sharing' (read religious) groups to levy on their members 'taxes' to be collected by the state's taxation service. Visible engagement with organised religious institutions and practices has nevertheless been declining among Christians and even Muslims. It is in relation to Germany's two principal non-Christian religious categories, Jews and Muslims, that Dusche considers the questions of assertiveness and of a range of issues that arise where the state has to take a stand: Whom to engage on behalf of a religious category when the latter carries diverse orientations, and functions without Church-like institutions? Who should provide religious education in state schools for children of a small denomination? What sectarian practices to accept—Muslim girls'/womens' headscarves in schools, loudspeakers for calls to prayer in mosques—when these depart from wider public norms? The overall German effort, often mediated by law courts, has sought to devise arrangements that would be equitable and sustainable; and among the responses, on the Muslim side, has been the concept of Euro-Islam, that is, an Islamic religious practice that would function within the public norms that have evolved historically in Germany—and in Europe.

Appropriately for a volume loaded with contentious religious identities, we conclude with Nonica Datta on the experiences and the poetry of Amrita Pritam, the poet who began life in 1919, daughter of a man of letters, in an upper caste Punjabi Sikh family in Gujranwala and Lahore, now in Pakistan. She had chafed at the routines of commensal separation between Muslims and Hindus (and Sikhs) within her home and outside. Barely into her teens she had the separation abolished within her home; but blind furies were abroad, stoking religious passions and strife even as Amrita's closest friendships in Lahore were formed with Muslims. Animosities and violence were in the air; and the approach of Partition found her in Lahore, pregnant, and lost for medical help. In what she hoped would be only a temporary move, she came to Dehra Dun and Delhi, and then the possibility of return to her friends in Lahore closed. The searing experience of Partition, and the long tradition of transgressive love stories in Punjab, have given fire to her writing over the decades, as she has 'interrogate[d] the logic of Partition' in a hundred different ways.

15

In Pursuit of Tolerance: Why Liberty should Receive Priority

GURPREET MAHAJAN

INVOKING 'TOLERANT HINDUISM': THE PROBLEM

How can tolerance be nurtured and sustained in a culturally diverse society? In a world marked by increasing incidents of ethnic conflict and violence this question has once again become a central concern of liberal democracies the world over. In India it is the experience of sporadic but exceedingly brutal and focused violence against members of a targeted community that has compelled social scientists and political leaders to reflect on the issue of tolerance. In the face of intolerance, bigotry, and communal violence, two kinds of responses have structured the discussion. In the first instance tolerance is seen as a virtue that has existed in Indian society and culture for a long period of time. In the second, tolerance is specifically linked to the textual structure of Hindu religion. Here, tolerance is not treated just as a historically evident quality. Its presence is explained in terms of the attributes of the Hindu religion and way of life. In both cases tolerance is presented as a quality that is, or has been, a part of Indic civilization for centuries. This assumed tolerance has for some time formed the backdrop against which communal violence and the question of tolerance have been discussed in India.

It is indeed paradoxical that in a context where the experiences of communal violence are not uncommon, so many should speak so frequently of the tolerance of the majority community and societal culture. This is not to say that tolerance is a value that has no place in Indian society and culture. There is no doubt that in India, Hinduism co-existed with, and accommodated within its territory, 'Judaism . . . for nearly two thousand years, Christianity from the time before it went to Europe, and Zoorastrianism for over twelve hundred years' (Nandy 1998: 336). It is equally true that while much of Europe was torn by religious wars a far greater degree of religious difference existed in the Indian sub-continent and in the neighbouring empires. In the eighteenth century, Voltaire noted the peaceful co-existence of vastly different religious communities in the Ottoman Empire. Kant spoke more directly about the virtues of the Indian, or more precisely, the Hindu. Contrasting the latter with the Christians he wrote:

> It is a doctrine of the Indians (Hindus) that every nation has a religion of its own. Hence they compel no one to accept theirs. Whenever the Christian missionaries tell them about Christ, his teachings, his life, etc., they listen attentively and raise no objections. But afterwards, when they begin to narrate about their religion, and the missionaries get indignant over it and censure them, as to how they can believe such untruths, then the Indians resent it saying that they believed them everything they had said, even though they could not believe their stories, why then could they not likewise believe them. (quoted in Glasenapp 1973: 3-4)

Kant arrived at this judgement on the basis of an extremely limited acquaintance with Indians but the idea that the Hindu religion and its practitioners are quintessentially tolerant people has since gained stronger roots. In contemporary India, several analysts, cutting across ideological boundaries, make similar arguments. They refer to the structure of Hinduism and argue that it has no organized institutional hierarchy or sacred text that forms the basis of uncontested and supreme truth; while 'fixed' intellectual beliefs characterize each religion and separate one from another, Hinduism sets no such limits (Radhakrishnan 1926). 'Hinduism does not even have a theological unity. It is a mosaic of different and at times conflicting philosophical schools and religious practices. There is also an element of struggle between various traditions which are now commonly grouped together as Hinduism' (Deshpande 1985: 25). It is also not a proselytizing religion. As such, Hinduism is open, internally plural, and accommodative of diverse practices within. It is assumed here that a religion and people who live with a vast array of internal differences are tolerant; more specifically, that the presence and accommodation of plurality within implies respect for external differences. Although these conclusions do not all follow from the fact of internal heterogeneity, arguments of this kind at best challenge attempts aimed at homogenizing and canonizing Hinduism. They assume the existence of tolerance within society and take the presence of this value for granted. Instead of exploring ways of nurturing tolerance in a social world marked by ethnic and communal violence they assert the perceived virtues of the dominant community in the polity. The latter can perhaps help to assure vulnerable communities and victims that they may trust the 'other', and at the same time nudge the majority into reflecting upon its virtues; but they do not contribute significantly in sustaining practices that nurture tolerance and accommodation of difference in contemporary democracies.

Modern democracies rest on the premise of equality for all. While this value may not be fully realised in existing democracies, it is the commitment to promote equality of all citizens, irrespective of their ascribed identity, that sets contemporary democracies apart from other political systems. This is important because internal heterogeneity as well as respect for external differences can often be sustained more easily in situations of inequality. When, for instance, a community enjoys hegemony and unquestioned dominance in the public arena, it can readily accept the presence of others for they appear not to threaten its existence and dominance (Gupta 1996: 192-211). However, when that dominance is challenged or when a community has to accommodate and give equal space to another in the public domain, both contest and conflict surface more centrally. Consequently, what needs to be considered are frameworks that help to protect and promote tolerance in the context of a democratic political system committed to the principle of equality for all.

The context structures and configures the text; analyses that assume and assert the existence of an essential form and practice tend often to neglect this dimension. They tend also to forget that tolerance in a democracy denotes something more than the presence of differences. Certainly, in an environment of communal hatred and conflict, peaceful co-existence is itself prized. It is something to be attained and worked for; but what needs also to be noted and remembered is that the mere fact of peaceful living together, desirable as it is, is not a sufficient indicator of tolerance. The deepening of democratic consciousness demands that respect for difference must translate into our willingness to allow differences to be articulated, expressed, and asserted in the public arena (Leader 1966). Indeed it is this understanding of tolerance that has raised the further issue of the 'limits' of liberal tolerance. Without dwelling on that subject, let me reiterate here that assertions about the inherent plurality and tolerance of Hinduism, or, references to peaceful co-existence of communities in the past, do not adequately address the issue of tolerance. As was mentioned earlier, tolerance is not a matter merely of peaceful co-existence; it requires acceptance of equal status and liberty of all. Likewise, the presence of internal plurality is not also enough. In the case of Hinduism, for instance, the absence of an institutionalized religious structure co-existed with a rigid system of stratification and hierarchy. Hence, a multiplicity of forms is not itself a sufficient guarantor of tolerance or respect for differences. Indeed, articulations of plurality may be, and at times are, accompanied by sentiments of assimilation.[1] We need therefore to consider how in a milieu of increasing religious contestations and recurrent episodes of communal violence, a tolerant society may be nurtured and sustained in a democracy.

The framers of the Indian Constitution reflected on this problematic. They did not regard the accommodative spirit of Hinduism to be a sufficient condition for creating a tolerant and violence-free society. Instead, they set out to realize this ideal by devising a framework in which various communities and their members would be treated as equal. With a view of safeguarding, respecting, and accommodating differences in the public arena they provided liberty to all religious communities, and introduced provisions for protecting the social and cultural practices of identified minorities. While their commitment to constructing a multi-cultural and multi-religious democracy was unambiguous, they believed that the accommodation of differences in the public arena along with a formal recognition of differences would nurture a tolerant society. There is no doubt that a public accommodation of differences is a sign of tolerance and equality for all, and independent India was among the first few democracies to give constitutional recognition to differences. But these rights and liberties given to communities have not minimized communal conflict. While they have given a substantive content to what equality for all might entail in a democracy, they have not helped sustain tolerance and respect for differences. Above all, communal conflict and violence has increased and not diminished in independent India. It is this that compels us to reflect upon conditions that may help to foster tolerance and enable bearers of differences to co-exist as equals.

FROM RELIGIOUS INTOLERANCE TO TOLERANCE: THE EUROPEAN EXPERIENCE

Independent India pursued the path of tolerance by respecting diversity and protecting the liberty of communities. However, this is not the only route that liberal democracies have taken to build and create a tolerant polity. If we turn to Europe it is striking that prolonged religious wars and a high degree of religious intolerance and persecution marked the period between the fifteenth and eighteenth centuries. Each country had an officially recognized state religion; there existed a close and mutually supportive relationship between the official church and the state. The close alliance between the ruler and the recognized church meant that the believers of dissenting/non-recognized religions were deprived of whatever religious, political and civil liberty existed at that time (Mahajan 1998a: 20-3; 29-33). From this condition of extreme religious intolerance, secular and tolerant democracies were gradually constructed by guaranteeing the liberty of the individual.

In Europe tolerance flowed from policies that protected the liberty of the individual. Indeed, this task received primacy both in states that endorsed policies of separation and those that did not sever the link between religious institutions and state. In India, the importance of the liberty of the individual for sustaining tolerance has received relatively little attention. It is only the presence of diversity that is taken as a sign of tolerance. Diversity is an important value, particularly since its absence is often a mark of coercive homogenization. However, even as we cherish and protect diversity what needs also to be inserted is the need to give primacy to the liberty of the individual. This is of the utmost importance in a context where intolerance takes the form of targeted violence against an identified community and its members, and where the space for the expression of individual differences is also extremely limited (Mahajan 2002: 196-218).

The idea that privileging and protecting the liberty of the individual could lay the foundations for a tolerant society was perhaps understood and articulated most sharply in the writings of the seventeenth century English political philosopher, John Locke. The issue of religious tolerance occupied a central place in the intellectual discourses of the day. Although England, like many of the other European nations at this time, was neither a secular nor tolerant society, prevailing religious conflict and persecution was a matter that received some consideration. Even before the publication of Locke's *Letter Concerning Toleration*, the anonymously written *Vindiciae Contra Tyrannos (A Defence of Liberty Against Tyrants)* had been widely read and discussed (Laski 1924: 1-60). Locke's reflections on tolerance enriched ongoing debates and provided a perspective that would subsequently be owned by the liberals. In the seventeenth century, however, it exercised limited influence on public policy as religious persecution, exclusion, and intolerance remained the dominant order. But if we look back and ask how the transition from intense intolerance to tolerance was possible, it becomes evident that democracies in Europe made that transition by gradually affirming and upholding the liberty of the individual citizen.

LIBERTY AS THE CONDITION OF TOLERANCE: THE LOCKEAN FRAMEWORK

In defining the idea of liberty and relating it to tolerance, Locke was undoubtedly reflecting upon the social and historical context of his time. Ideas, as Quentin Skinner reminds us, need to be understood with reference to the context in which they emerge, but context-specificity is not to be confused with historical determinism (1969: 3-53). That is, while social and political thought addresses questions and debates of a given time, its content is not determined by that context. Locke shared in the intellectual and political concerns of his contemporaries but his response to these issues did not simply express the existing consensus or the operative policy. He envisaged and developed a framework that would endorse tolerance as a value in a diverse society and it is this that makes his insights significant for us.

In visiting Locke, one is not suggesting that England in the seventeenth century and contemporary India are similar in any relevant way or that there are lessons to be learnt from the English experience. Although such direct comparisons are sometimes made (see, for instance, Mitra 1995[2]), it is generally difficult to learn lessons from the past as historical situations are unique and to some extent non-replicable. Besides, the differences between seventeenth-eighteenth-century Europe and contemporary India are too vast to make comparison possible. European states had an official religion; India is avowedly a secular democracy. In most European countries there was formal legislation that limited the rights of dissenting faiths, both in the social and religious sphere as well as the political. Contemporary India, by contrast, acknowledges its religious minorities, gives them religious and cultural rights, and in the political sphere they have equal rights of participation. Yet that does not imply that views of tolerance that were expressed and debated in Europe then are of no relevance to us. As a political philosopher Locke reflected on the idea of tolerance and considered ways in which this value may be realized in political arrangements and institutional structures. Today, as we too seek to nurture tolerance in our society it is particularly important that we take note of these ideas and assess their relevance for us.

Of the many political theorists who deliberated on the concept of tolerance, this paper focuses on John Locke primarily because he delineates a framework of tolerance that may indicate what is missing in our understanding and pursuit of the same ideal in India. Tolerance, for Locke, was not simply a policy of 'live and let live'; it entailed respect for the individual and her liberty. Tolerance, in other words, was predicated not on the recognition of existing diversities but on the protection of individual liberty. At the most fundamental level, liberty implied absence of external interference and hindrances, and the ability to pursue one's own will. However, he noted that the pursuit of one's will is often restricted by two institutions in society: the state and the church (religious institutions/authority). Consequently, what was required to defend liberty and to promote tolerance is to restructure and define the functions and relationship of these institutions in a definite manner.

Locke accepted that both state and church perform important tasks within society. The state exists to ensure law and order; and, above all, to create conditions in which individuals can exercise and enjoy the rights that nature has bestowed upon them. In comparison to the state, which exists to promote material and physical well-being, the church is entrusted with the 'care of the soul' (Locke 1965: 172). Thus both perform valuable functions but if one institution encroaches upon the other or takes on its functions then liberty is necessarily curtailed and tolerance jettisoned. If the state stipulates religious beliefs and determines the content of religious doctrines it almost always minimises the religious liberty of the individual citizens. Likewise, if the church takes on the responsibilities of the state and appropriates, or amasses, instruments of coercion and force, it negatively impacts upon the liberty of its members and atheists. And when state and church (religious authority) join hands to pursue common ends, then intolerance and religious persecution become the order of the day. Consequently, if tolerance is to be nurtured and even cultivated, the most important thing is that each institution should be restricted to perform the functions for which it exists. And, even more importantly, each institution must accord primacy to individual liberty while executing its tasks and functions.

In the case of religious institutions (the church) according primacy to the liberty of the individual means that they must rely on persuasion and reasoning to convince members. Religious authorities must not use force to compel individuals to accept certain beliefs. Nor must they take the assistance of the state to enforce conformity in society or the community. The minimum requirement for tolerance, then, is the absence of force in the practice and promotion of a set of religious beliefs. But more than this, tolerance requires that religious institutions give individuals what may be called freedom of conscience, to decide what they regard to be acceptable. Individuals may choose to join a given religious institution and abide by its *diktats* or they may decide to exit. No religious institution can, or should, impose its will on individuals, particularly upon the congregation of another religion/ church. A religious institution may prescribe for its own members, who have joined the group voluntarily, a code of ethics and it may even punish and ex-communicate them if they do not abide by its belief. But even here the authority of the religious institution or community is not unrestricted. The church may, according to Locke, excommunicate its members but not deprive anyone of civil goods that he possessed formerly. In circumscribing the actions of the church, Locke maintained that the powers of the church, or any religious institution, cannot exceed those of the state. Just as the state power is curtailed by the prior existence of certain natural and inalienable rights of man, the church too must be limited in its actions by the same concerns. In both instances the rights and liberty of the individual curtail and restrict what the church may legitimately do. Indeed, Locke places an obligation upon the state to act to protect the rights of the individual if they were to be violated by the actions of the church as a religious institution.

Liberty of the individual, in the form of freedom of conscience, also implies that one church or religious institution must not interfere in the affairs of another. Each institution and community must be free to determine its own beliefs and practices. The only general limitation is that none should endorse or prescribe 'things that are not lawful in ordinary course of life, nor in any private house' (ibid.: 198). For Locke, things that are not considered permissible within the house or in everyday life cannot find acceptance in the 'worship of God, or in any religious meeting' (ibid.). Locke uses the example of human sacrifice to draw the boundaries of what may or may not be acceptable even in the name of religion. As the right to life is a fundamental right and a condition for enjoying liberty, human sacrifice is not, indeed it cannot be, accepted even if some claim it to be an essential part of religious belief. Locke argues that this is an action that finds no acceptance in the private or the social sphere of life. The responsibility, here again, falls on the civil magistrate—'one who has the responsibility for the care of the community, who holds the supreme power over all others and to whom, finally, is designated the power of constituting and abrogating laws' (ibid.: 212), to ensure that such violations of the norm do not occur even in the religious arena.

Promoting tolerance thus places obligations upon the state, or to use Locke's phrase, the civil magistrate. Further, the principle of liberty transforms the nature of religious institutions and authority. No longer is religious membership seen as a fixed variable, determined by virtue of one's birth; instead it becomes also a matter of choice. The church becomes a voluntary association that an individual may join or leave in favour of another. The important element is that the individual is not compelled to follow or be governed by the norms of a given community. Even when the individual willingly subjects himself to the authority of a given religious group the latter may not endorse practices that violate his/her basic rights and civil liberties. Either way, the liberty of the individual is primary; on the one hand this limits religious authority and, on the other, it places obligations upon the state.

Individual liberty mandates the right to exit from a community, but exit may be too heavy a cost to pay for expressing or holding on to differences. Locke therefore recommends what has since been called voice: that is, freedom to express dissent and difference while remaining within the community. Differences need to be accommodated internally and for this he suggests that the Church should be open in at least things that are 'indifferent' to religion. Locke makes a distinction between things that are essential to religion and things 'indifferent' to religion (ibid.: 193). Although this division is not entirely adequate as it is exceedingly difficult to separate the two in a clear and unambiguous manner. Nevertheless, the distinction is useful insofar as it suggests that while matters of religious doctrine may be treated as a subject essential to religion, there are other associated elements that may be involved in practice—such as, the time and place, habit and posture in worship—that may be placed in the category of things inessential. The church, or for that matter, all religious organizations, may be open to the expression of differences in such matters that are indifferent to religion and religious doctrine (ibid.: 194).

What eventually constitutes things that are considered to be 'indifferent' or 'inessential' to religion is a question that certainly requires further deliberation. The basis on which Locke draws the distinction may be less than adequate, and diverse communities co-existing in a society may need to dwell on what falls in each category. Yet what needs serious consideration is the idea that Locke is putting forward—that religious practice and activities may include aspects that are not drawn directly from the word of God. Consequently, each religion must accept, or create, space for the articulation of difference. This is necessary both for giving freedom, or 'voice', to members of the community within as well as for tolerating differences that exist outside.

In brief, then, Locke makes four crucial suggestions with regard to the promotion of tolerance: first, we need to have a clear understanding that state and church exist to perform different functions. Their tasks, and hence their powers and responsibilities, are different. The state comes into existence for ensuring the physical well-being of individuals while the church exists to promote spiritual well-being. Second, each institution, be it the state or the church, must function in a way that protects the basic rights and liberties of the individual.[3] The state must use its coercive power only to create a system of law that ensures the protection of the rights of man, and the church must treat its members as a voluntary congregation. Religious institutions and communities should, in other words, function in a way that is commensurate with freedom of conscience. Third, the state must shoulder the responsibility of ensuring that the life, liberty, and property of citizens is not encroached upon in the name of religion, its beliefs or practices. Last, given the presence of many different religious groups and churches, each religious authority must refrain from prescribing matters of religious belief and practice for the other. They must each respect the autonomy of the other. The prescribed religious beliefs and practices of all groups must respect the civil rights and liberties of the individual and the state has an obligation to ensure that all institutions, including the church, respects the liberty of all.

THE IDEA OF TOLERANCE AND LIBERTY REDEFINED

Locke, we have said, was concerned only with the question of generating tolerance as a value among competing churches. He did not consider a space for atheists or people of non-Christian faiths. Hence his 'tolerance' is fairly narrowly confined. However, the norms that he suggested for building tolerance in a society torn by religious strife need to be considered seriously, for they direct our attention to aspects of the idea and practice of tolerance that are relevant for many situations. In particular three ideas merit reflection. First, while it is customary to associate tolerance with respect for those who are different from the self, Locke suggests that there are two dimensions of tolerance, external and internal. The former denotes space for the existence of diverse religious communities, while the latter concerns expressions of difference within a community. A democratic polity needs to promote both kinds. Also, there is no necessity that tolerance at one level will necessarily usher in tolerance at the other. Indeed it is possible that different communities may co-exist within a society and show some degree of tolerance or indifference towards the other, but each may be rigid and hostile to the expression of differences internally. Likewise, a community may be willing to tolerate a range of plural practices within but it may be uncompromising towards the practices of another community. Hence, tolerance needs to be promoted at both levels. The basic rights of the individual receive and deserve primacy essentially for this reason. It is by privileging the rights and liberty of the individual that democratic polities can generate respect for different ways of life as well as create room for differences within.

Second, tolerance does not imply that 'anything goes'; nor is it simply a matter of 'live and let live'. Certainly it entails a respect for difference, but not everything can be accepted in the name of difference or just indifference to the other. While no community has a right to prescribe for the other, the democratic state has an obligation to ensure that difference does not sanction practices that violate the shared understanding of rights and liberties in a historical time and society. Locke had used the example of human sacrifice to highlight what may not be permitted in the guise of tolerance; we can extend the argument to include a range of practices that breach our understanding of what constitutes fairness and justice. This is particularly significant because tolerance is at times linked to the acceptance of practices that one is likely to find unacceptable (Raz 1988: 401-2).[4] Tolerance is, it is said, tolerance of that which our sensibilities find offensive. The advantage of privileging the liberty of the individual and using that principle for approaching the self and the other is that it subjects all practices to critical scrutiny and judgment. It does not unilaterally impose the perspective of the dominant community upon the other, and, at the same time, it does not sanction all that constitutes the self. I have argued elsewhere that modern democracies are assessed by their commitment to the value of non-discrimination (Mahajan 1998b: 1-20). It is by seeking to minimise and eliminate discrimination based on socially ascribed identities that liberal polities aver their identity as democracies. Consequently, within a liberal democracy all forms of practice and difference can in principle never be accommodated. Practices that disadvantage and discriminate against a section of citizens must necessarily be challenged and eradicated. There may be disputes about specific practices and whether they do in fact discriminate against some, but there is no shying away from this task in a democracy.

Third, while tolerance entails respect for differences, differences can best be respected by protecting the rights and liberties of the other. Locke had spoken of the liberty of the individual, but we need perhaps to add a caveat here. To promote tolerance between communities and tolerance within a community, the category of the individual needs to be replaced by the notion of self and the other. Intolerance in Europe stemmed from the fact that the individual whose liberty was being protected belonged to a specific community; others were often excluded from the category of citizens. However, once these forms of exclusion are abandoned and the assumption of homogeneity is also relinquished, then the protection of the liberty of the self and the other has the potential of nurturing tolerance. The limitation of the Lockean framework and much of later liberalism stemmed from a failure to postulate a heterogeneous public arena. Since the individual was conceived as an abstract and decontextualized self, it could variously eclipse differences or take on the attributes of the dominant community. It is therefore necessary that liberty that is defended is that of the self and the other. That is, it is more appropriate that the category of the undifferentiated individual be replaced by the notion of the self and other and then the liberty of each is protected and promoted.

DIFFERENTIATING THE FRAMEWORK OF LIBERTY FROM POLICIES OF SEPARATION

In India the growing intolerance in the polity is frequently explained as being a consequence of the increasing use of religion in politics. There is no doubt that mobilizations on religious and other community lines are today a common and visible feature of the Indian political system. But it does not follow from this that a separation of religion from politics can remedy the present situation of intolerance and religious discrimination. If we look at the experience of Europe and America, it is evident that complete separation is neither possible nor entirely desirable. As the Supreme Court of America noted, a policy of rigid separation would mean that 'Municipalities would not be permitted to render police or fire protection to religious groups. Policemen who helped parishoners into their places of worship violate the Constitution' (Zorach *vs.* Clauson, 343 US 312, quoted in Bedell et al. 1975: 77). A policy of separation might also result in the restriction of the liberty of some citizens. Denying state support and public facilities to religious groups and institutions could, in certain circumstances, disadvantage people who hold on to religious beliefs. If, to take one example, parents who sent their children to religious schools were ineligible for transportation subsidies that are provided to parents who send their children to public schools, then the former are penalized for the choices they make. The policy of separation would in effect discriminate against people who wish to hold on to their religious beliefs.

Policies of strict separation almost always present dilemmas of this kind. Hence the view that religious intolerance may be eliminated by pursuing policies of separation remains a bit of a non-starter. It is perhaps necessary to clarify here that it is not as if policies of separation pose a special difficulty in India.[5] The culture and historical experiences of India are significantly different from those of the West, but the point is that separation policies have posed serious difficulties even in Western liberal democracies. Indeed, there are very few countries that hold on to the policy of strict separation. To sustain an environment of tolerance it is therefore necessary to explore strategies other than those of separation. In fact what is being suggested is that it is by valuing and protecting the liberty of the self and the other that we may actually build and nurture tolerance.

What needs also to be emphasized is that endorsing the perspective of the liberty of the self and the other is different from invoking the principle of separation. When Locke developed the framework of liberty he began by distinguishing the basic functions of the state and the church. But in his case too what was sacrosanct was not a separation of the two domains. Rather, liberty and what Locke termed civil interests of the individual were the optic from which decisions about separation and intervention were to be taken. A distinctive aspect of the liberty framework was that it placed an obligation upon the state to intervene and act to ensure that liberty and rights of the individual were not infringed or contravened in the name of religion. Conditional privileging of the state within society was, Locke realized, a necessary condition of pursuing liberty.

It is of course possible that even a democratic state may not fulfil this obligation. In such situations it is individual citizens who have the responsibility of putting pressure on the state and making it accountable for its action and inaction. Either way it is the state that has to be pressured, for tolerance can only exist and be fostered when the state plays the necessary critical role of protecting the basic rights and liberties of the self and the other. If the state neglects this task, or adopts a policy of benign neglect, it is intolerance that is likely to take root. This is a further reason why policies of separation are not, and can never be, sufficient for sustaining tolerance. Tolerance requires a commitment from the state, and pressure from citizen groups, to ensure that the liberty of the self and the other is protected and stridently affirmed against all violations.

FROM RECOGNITION OF DIFFERENCES TO PROMOTING LIBERTY

A reason for the recurrent episodes of communal violence and the environment of intolerance in India is that the state has, time and time again, failed its obligation to secure the liberty of individuals of different communities. A policy comprising inaction, inefficiency, and neglect have all yielded room to sectarian and communal strategies that thrive on the politics of friend and foe. The state has relied much more on a recognition of difference and diversity than on affirming the liberty of individuals belonging to various communities. The rhetoric of tolerance has, as a consequence, been replete with references to the plural character of the Indian polity, the counting of different religions and languages, declarations of public holidays for different communities, and endorsing different forms of dress and address. Recognition of such differences is an important constituent of a frame of tolerance but it is by no means sufficient for building a plural and tolerant society. If there is one thing that the Indian experience has made evident it is that the social and public visibility of differences, desirable as it is, is not an adequate measure of the tolerance in a democratic polity. Were we to devise a scale to measure levels of diversity, India would score high compared to many other liberal democracies in the west, but this would be accompanied by an equally high score on inter- and intra-community violence.

It is not that cultural homogenization provides a better condition for sustaining tolerance but that the pursuit of diversity needs to be accompanied by an equally strong commitment to protecting the liberty of the self and the other. In the absence of these twin values tolerance can never be deeply entrenched in a democratic polity. Tolerance and intolerance manifest themselves at different planes in different ways. In Europe and America intolerance is expressed primarily through a reluctance to accommodate diversity in the social and public domain. In India, by comparison, intolerance is manifested more through inter-community violence. Thus, even though there was, at least in the past, some limited effort to include different communities in the narrative of the nation state, inter-community hatred and hostility persisted, and grew over time. It is in the specific context of India that we need to emphasize the importance of protecting and promoting the liberty of all citizens—the self and the other.

The framers of the Indian Constitution approached the issue of tolerance by seeking to protect the religious liberty of different communities. They believed that if the religious liberty of every community, particularly the minorities, was protected and constitutionally guaranteed, an environment of tolerance and respect for difference, would ensue. However, in the years that followed, the space for tolerance significantly shrank as elements associated with religious liberty in the Constitution, in particular, the right to propagate religion, came to be circumscribed. But that is not the only reason. The constitutional structure, even as it protects the religious liberty of all communities, has two limitations. One, the Constitution attempts to give religious communities some degree of liberty and autonomy in matters of social, cultural, and religious practices. But there is at every level a deep mistrust of the liberty of the individual. The latter is viewed as posing a threat to the nation state, and is not essential for sustaining a respect for difference. Hence, even as freedom of speech and expression were provided, they were severely restricted in the interest of public order, morality, and national integrity. Relative neglect of, and low priority to, the liberty of the self minimized the freedom of conscience, and this eventually eroded both the space for religious liberty of communities, as well as that of the individual within the community.

Two, guaranteeing religious liberty bestowed recognition upon different communities. It publicly acknowledged the presence of diverse religious groups, and within it, of diverse religious and cultural practices. The Constitution implicitly accepted that there may be occasions when these diverse practices may clash with each other and push in different directions. In all such cases it suggested that decisions be taken with a view to maintain public order; considerations of communal harmony could also be factored in. The experience of the last fifty years or more has shown that when concerns of order become the organizing principle, then the viewpoint of the majority tends to prevail. The balance is necessarily tilted in favour of the majority and it is the minorities who are expected to make the adjustment. Fairness would have required that the criterion of equal liberty be applied in all instances of conflict.

There is a distinction between tolerating difference and creating a tolerant society. It is the latter that liberal democracies should aspire to build and move towards. For differences may be tolerated under many conditions: a benevolent monarch may compel tolerance for people of different communities and fear of retribution may also yield a similar result. In another context, indifference or complete neglect towards the other may also permit differences to exist. The important thing in a democracy is that tolerance and the presence of differences must not depend upon generosity of some—the ruler or the majority; nor must it rely on fear of the other. Differences must exist by their own right. Making liberty of the self and the other the vantage-point through which relationships and institutions are negotiated enables us to make just this transition, from tolerating differences to constructing a tolerant society.

Too often in India we rely on the presence of tolerant individuals in positions of power and authority. We speak of the need to be tolerant; we ask individuals to give the benefit of doubt to others, or, to recognize that we are, and have been, a plural society. Every society must surely inculcate certain virtues in their citizens, but, as Hegel reminds us, individuals are likely to endorse and act by them if these also constitute the organizing principle of public and political life. If the latter are not organized in a way that expresses the same rationality, some individuals may be heroic enough to challenge the system and suffer the costs, but tolerance can not be nurtured and sustained by the virtues of a few. We need therefore to focus on creating and building a polity—in which the institutions are structured in a way that expresses and nurtures tolerance. It is to make this move from a tolerant self to a polity that the liberty of the self and the other needs to be prioritized in democracy.

NOTES

1. To illustrate this, note the following assertion. 'Hinduism is broad enough to give an honoured place to the Roman Catholics, Orthodox Greek Church, Protestants Christians of every variety including Jehova Witnesses and the Seventh Day Adventists etc. etc. Similarly, the Muslims —Sunnies, Shiyas, Sufies, Quadinies, Aghakhanites or any other variety —have sufficient space in the broad bosom of Hinduism. If our bretheren will only trace their respective ancestry, they will find that they have Hindu blood in them' (Ayyar 1968: 63). Here the assertion of the accommodativeness of Hinduism is easily linked to the idea that the members of these different religions and sects in India are essentially Hindu. Plurality vanishes, and all that is left is an essential identity with no legitimate basis for asserting your difference.
2. Mitra's concerns are of course somewhat different. He analyses the question—'Is India governable?' However, to explore this issue of governability, he makes a cross-cultural comparison. In particular he refers to popular discontent and disorder in late eighteenth-century England, and here suggests that 'The picture that we get . . . would be familiar to students of contemporary Indian politics. Rampaging crowds, corrupt state machinery and ineffectual government on a scale that is current in many parts of India today *were not altogether unknown in England two centuries ago'* (1995: 218.; emphasis added). Coupled with the argument that 'we can draw upon cross-cultural knowledge of coping mechanisms through which European states met popular discontent . . .' (ibid.: 220) he reinforces the suggestion that contemporary India bears a close parallel with eighteenth-century England. Also, that we might perhaps learn from the policies and strategies

adopted in England to see how similar situation can be dealt with and the desired result of governability achieved. Although this conclusion surfaces in many other accounts of India, Mitra's piece provides a cogent and systematic expression of it.

3. To quote Locke, 'neither single person, nor churches, nay, even commonwealth, have just title to invade the civil rights and worldly goods of each other upon pretense of religion' (ibid.: 183).
4. Tolerance is here linked to the notion of value pluralism. Insofar as value pluralism accords value to different, and often incompatible, ways of life, it is seen as establishing the desirability/value of tolerance. Within this broader framework, Raz argues that

   > Tolerance is a distinctive moral virtue only if it curbs desires, inclinations and convictions which are thought by a tolerant person to be in themselves desirable. Typically a person is tolerant if and only if he *suppresses a desire to cause to another harm or hurt which he thinks the other deserves*. The clearest case of toleration . . . *is where a person restrains his indignation at the sight of injustice or some other moral evil, or rather at the sight of behaviour which he takes to be of this character* (Raz 1986: 401-2; emphasis added).

5. It is sometimes argued that secularism, as a theory that advocates the separation of religion from politics, is inapplicable in India because of the distinct nature of her culture and society. In the words of T.N. Madan, the religions of South Asia are 'totalizing' and encompass all aspects of the follower's life; hence, they cannot be restricted to the private sphere (Madan 1987: 751 and 753). Secularism is here associated with Protestantism and seen as a peculiarly Western phenomenon that has little relevance in India.

REFERENCES

Ayyar, S.R. Narayana, 1968, *Wails of an Obscure Hindu*, Conoor, Madras: S.R.N. Ayyar, Devinilayam & Messrs Higginbothams.

Bedell, G.C., L. Sandon and C.T. Wellborn, 1975, *Religion in America*, New York: Macmillan.

Deshpande, G.P., 1985, 'The Plural Tradition', *Seminar*, 313, September, pp. 23-5.

Glasenapp, Helmuth von., 1973, *Image of India*, trans. S. Ambike, New Delhi: Indian Council for Cultural Relations.

Gupta, Dipankar, 1996, *The Context of Ethnicity: Sikh Identity in a Comparative Perspective*, New Delhi: Oxford University Press.

Laski, Harold J., 1924, 'Introduction' to *A Defense of Liberty Against Tyrants*, trans. by Junius Brutus, London: G. Bell.

Leader, Sheldon, 1966, 'Three Faces of Tolerance in a Democracy', *The Journal of Political Philosophy*, 4: 45-67.

Locke, John, 1965, *Treatise on Civil Government and A letter Concerning Toleration*, New York: Appleton-Century-Crofts.

Madan, T.N., 1987, 'Secularism in its Place', *The Journal of Asian Studies*, 46: 747-59.

Mahajan, Gurpreet, 1998a, *Identities and Rights: Aspects of Liberal Democracy in India*, New Delhi: Oxford University Press.

Mahajan, Gurpreet, ed., 1998b, *Democracy, Difference and Social Justice*, New Delhi: Oxford University Press.

Mahajan, Gurpreet, 2002, *The Multicultural Path: Issues of Democracy and Discrimination in Democracy*, New Delhi: Sage.

Mitra, Subrata K., 1995, 'Crowds and Power: Democracy and the Crisis of "Governability" in India', in Upendra Baxi and Bhikhu Parekh, eds., *Crisis and Change in Contemporary India*, New Delhi: Sage.

Nandy, Ashis, 1998, 'The Politics of Secularism and the Recovery of Religious Tolerance', in Rajeev Bhargava, ed., *Secularism and Its Critics*, New Delhi: Oxford University Press, pp. 321-44.

Raz, Joseph, 1986, *The Morality of Freedom*, Oxford: Clarendon.

Skinner, Quentin, 1969, 'Meaning and Understanding in the History of Ideas', *History and Theory*, 29: 3-53.

16

Asserting Religious Identities in the Federal Republic of Germany[1]

MICHAEL DUSCHE

ON PERSONAL AND GROUP IDENTITY, AN INTRODUCTION

Personal and group identity[2] formation is not a one-sided affair. Persons, like groups, develop their identity by engaging in a 'struggle for recognition'[3] with the surrounding social environment. This process involves a double image formation: Both, the individual will form an image of himself or herself, and correspondingly the world will form an image of the person. The individual is free, to a certain extent, to form a certain self-image and so are his or her social 'partners'. In the end, however, the two images have to match, at least partly, for the personal identity of the individual to achieve its purpose. For without the social environment recognizing it for what it purports to be, the society will not abide by the expectations that go with the individual's self-image.

The same holds true for the identity formation of a whole group of persons. A group may develop a certain perception of itself, but whether this self-perception is matched with a similar perception of it by the outside world is subject to an open process of negotiation. With social groups, the case differs in an important respect from that of personal identity formation. In the case of the individual, the world has to accept at least his or her actual existence. In the case of group identities, however, the social environment can both deny existence to a group, and force into existence a group of people who never thought of themselves as belonging together. For both cases, examples abound. An example of a group being denied existence is the Kurdish people in eastern Turkey. For a long time, the policy of the Turkish government has been to speak of them as 'mountain Turks'.[4] For the latter case, there are the recent examples of Serbians and Croatians in former Yugoslavia and of the Hutu and Tutsi in Rwanda. In both, people who thought of themselves as neither

Serbian nor Croatian, neither Hutu nor Tutsi, were forced to ally with either one of the two groups who were being whipped up against each other.

The social environment thus imposes certain limitations on the range of possible individual and group identity formations that derive from the prevalent world-view and the social norms of the time and place. In its general formulation, this proposition is probably a candidate for an anthropological constant. What has increased over time and with the growing complexity and differentiation in modern society is the number of different, disjunct social environments that a person is simultaneously exposed to in the process of its identity formation. With the ensuing anonymity, the identity that the individual conjures up for himself in various contexts is not checked across various social contexts. With family, work place, neighbourhood, nightclub, high school, university and various sub-cultures existing disjunct from each other, the individual is no longer confronted with a social environment where whatever he or she does in one context, will have repercussions in the others. Thus, somebody may be an obedient employee during the day and convert to a post-puberty rebellious hard rocker after 10 o'clock at night. There is no one to hold him accountable for any apparent inconsistency in his multi-faceted identity. It seems that it is never the whole human being which matters in any one social context. In fact, the pressures to conform to the expectations of one social environment exclusively may be so great that individuals are pushed to conjure up compensatory 'spare time' identities.

In the current literature of minority research and multiculturalism, a host of terms such as 'hyphen', 'plural', 'multi', 'patchwork' and even 'post-identities' have been coined. Yet others speak of 'fuzzy', 'liminal' or 'hybrid' identities. All of these terms stress the fact that identities are constructs; they reject the idea that underlying personal identity was some kind of an essence which governs individual or collective identity-genesis. The anti-essentialist assumption is that personal and group identity formation is an open process that includes the participation, and to a certain extent the conscious cooperation, of the subject concerned. The assumption is that, in spite of certain social constraints, the identity formation of any person or group involves some free choice.

Anti-essentialism can even explain why it is that some are under the impression that identity formation at the individual or group level involves some kind of a fixed pattern, a governing plan, that could be mistaken for an 'essence'. At the macro level it may seem as if the identity formation of any individual or group within the same social environment follows a regular pattern with the result that the ensuing identities bear certain similarities. This, however, according to anti-essentialism, is the result not of anything genetically inherent in the person or group, but of the similarity of the social environment, which has a similarly limiting impact on the range of choices each individual or group faces in constructing its identity.

At the micro level, an awareness of these limitations and possibly a reflection on how to overcome them may increase the scope for choice. This awareness has to be consciously created, for the more natural thing for anyone to do would be to internalize the perspective prevailing outside, and to adopt unreflectingly the roles that the society ascribes to its preconceived groups. This is how traditional identities are imbibed by successive generations. In the absence of a culture of awareness and critical self-reflection, social constraints that restrict the range of possible identity formations perpetuate themselves. Both essentialist and anti-essentialist cultural predilections have a tendency to become self-fulfilling prophesies as the first denies, whereas the latter cultivates, the reflective skills necessary for the subject to engage in a conscious quest for its own identity.

The macro-perspective, then, has a tendency to show more of the social constraints on identity formation; in micro-perspective the scope for choice is more apparent. Looking from without allows us to neglect the individual contribution of each person or group in the evolution and perpetuation of their identity. From this totalizing perspective, it is relatively easy to identify a person or a group solely with reference to certain discriminating features. A view from within, on the other hand, reveals a mosaic of different elements of individual or collective identity, with a subject that highlights each of these in proper circumstance. Some of these elements may seem strange to the observer, others familiar. The microscopic look thus reveals points both of common identity and of difference. It makes it difficult for the observer to totally identify with the other and also to completely reject him or her. To cultivate this look from within (to learn how to put oneself into the other's shoes, as it were) would be an important contribution in counteracting existing prejudice. It may be discovered, then, that whoever belongs to the 'other' in one respect can be part of the 'own' in another. Circles of identities and hence commonalities would seem to overlap in certain places and are not mutually exclusive as would appear from a totalizing point of view.

Processes of personal and group identity negotiation have an immediate impact on the potential of inclusion and thereby indirectly on the social cohesion of European and/or South Asian societies; thus its relevance for the viability of integration of Muslims in Europe and the mechanisms of inclusion and exclusion of Muslims in South Asia. Whereas the inclusion of a yet-to-be integrated minority is the order of the day in Europe, in South Asia, especially India, the case presents itself in reverse, with an already socially and politically integrated minority confronted with various strategies of exclusion under various schemes of ethnic or religious nationalism.

The circumstances of individual and collective identity formation are felt by some to be liberating, by others as a great burden. Some individuals enjoy the play with their self-images; others suffer from an apparent lack of inner coherence. Some are more, some are less, able to withstand the mutually exclusive demands of disparate social contexts. Some do not have the 'open mind' required to endure such stress on their subjective identity. They tend to develop an 'identity mania', as Thomas Meyer (2001) has called it, i.e. a craving for a unified social world in which a single community imposes a single set of norms on all individuals. In such a world, the individual would be spared the burden of balancing conflicting social demands since there is only one reference group with respect to which he/she forms his/her identity. Militant fundamentalism is an attempt to violently bring about such a unified, and simplified, social world and to deny, through violent means, or by means of forced hierarchization, what Rawls has called 'the fact of pluralism'.[5]

Due to its importance in the identity formation of important social groups, religion is receiving new attention of late by social scientists. While it was generally assumed throughout the 1960s and 1970s that religion as a social phenomenon would slowly fade away as it would become obvious to an ever-growing number of educated people that its tenets could not withstand the scrutiny of the scientific gaze, intellectuals in both regions note today that the debate around the role of religion in a secular state has re-emerged as a response to a new religious assertiveness amongst certain minorities. What are we to make of this? Did secularism fail, as some Indian intellectuals would maintain? Madan (1998) and Nandy (1998) blame the prevalence of an ideology of secularism in Indian statecraft for the emergence of religious fundamentalism, amongst both Hindus and Muslims. They call for a greater recognition of religion in the public sphere. In Germany, political analysts ask whether the re-emerging importance that is being claimed for religion in the public sphere is an indicator of an ever-growing politicization of religion with the aim of re-negotiating the boundaries between religion and politics.[6] They suggest that the more politics stays aloof from the religious aspirations of the majority, and the less it is able to provide for their spiritual guidance, the more religion will be politicised and established as an alternative source of identity and social praxis.[7]

The question thus arises as to whether, in the face of such threats, we have to re-think and possibly re-define the relation between state and religion. Such re-definition, of course, can go two ways. Either one follows the suggestions of the above-mentioned post-secularists, or one follows a strategy of further disinvestment of the state in the affairs of religious communities. The second option would involve a re-assertion of the fundamental principle of every liberal state and society according to which every individual and thereby everyone's religion and religious community are of equal value from the perspective of the state and its officials, no matter how well this religion is organized or not, or whether it is practiced visibly or invisibly.

Unlike in India, in Germany organized religion has steadily lost ground and continues to do so for a large part of the population. By organized religion I mean the classic church like organizations that exert a certain authority over their members and not, for example, the many individualistic forms of spirituality that seem to have gained in importance for an indefinite part of the population. Belonging to a religious organization of this kind also implies that one asserts one's religion visibly and publicly whereas the more individualized forms of religiosity are practised in private and are less visible. As I am concerned in this paper only with the interface of religion and state, and not with the phenomenon of religiosity as such, I am not interested here in a possible rise in religiosity if it does not lead to any new challenge for the liberal democratic state to re-think its relations with its religious communities. Thus religious assertiveness, for the purpose of this paper, is to signify the public assertion of religious identity. And it possibly has a political dimension as well. It is understood to include organized religion but is not restricted to it. Some religious minorities may be less organized but still very visible and their assertiveness definitely has a political dimension.

For Germany, the secularist prediction seems to have been validated to a certain extent as a growing third of the population professes no organized or publicly visible form of religion at all. The decline in religious affiliation, however, concerns mainly the two major Christian churches (the Protestant and the Roman Catholic). Amongst the smaller religious minorities, notably in the Muslim and Jewish minorities, a certain increase in public assertiveness and a growth of membership can be observed. In focusing on these two minorities, I would like to illustrate how in Germany the involvement of the state in the affairs of religious minorities can have a monitoring effect, moderating the politicization of religions, but also how state recognition of religious minorities can lead to a dilemma if it is based on the idea of a unified, church-like, organization serving as a model for non-Christian minorities. In Germany for instance, the possibility is being discussed of helping (or forcing) Muslims to form a unified organization that would serve the state as an interlocutor for its relations with the whole of the Muslim population. In France, similar attempts have already been made—and have been unsuccessful. In the following, I would like to cast some light on this debate as it takes place in Germany today. I begin with some data on the religious composition of the German population and about the German model of a secular state. In the remainder of the paper, I shall argue that the challenge posed by the new (and not so new) religious minorities should lead to a re-thinking of the relations between religious communities and the German state. The dangers lying in the conception of a unified representative body for every religious community will also become apparent, and I shall suggest that we abandon this idea in favour of a more pluralistic interface between state and religion in Germany.

THE RELIGIOUS COMPOSITION OF THE GERMAN POPULATION

The post-war division of Germany left roughly equal numbers of Roman Catholics and Protestants in West Germany. East Germany had five times as many Protestants as Roman Catholics. After more than four decades of socialist rule, the population of the eastern part of the country had become more areligious than the western part. Church representatives note that only 5 to 10 per cent of eastern inhabitants belong to a religious organization. There the authorities tried quite successfully to minimise the influence and authority of the Protestant and Roman Catholic churches. Although the Constitution theoretically provided for freedom of religion, the socialist state placed obstacles before those seeking to exercise that basic right. Pressure was exerted on citizens to renounce religion. East Germans who practised their religion outside the home were denied educational and professional opportunities, for example. Consequently, at unification the majority of East Germans were either not baptised or had left the church. In the 1990s, polls in the newly joined eastern federal states revealed that more than 70 per cent of East Germans did not believe in God. Young people were even less religious. Some polls found that only 16 per cent of East German schoolchildren believed in God.

In West Germany, freedom of religion was guaranteed by Article 4 of the Constitution (Grundgesetz), and the churches enjoyed a special legal status as bodies of public law. In theory, there was constitutional separation of church and state, but church finance complicated this separation. To support churches and their work, most West Germans paid a church tax, amounting to 8 or 9 per cent surcharge on income tax. Few West Germans formally withdrew from the established churches before the 1980s. Beginning in the 1980s, however, negative attitudes toward the churches and church tax became more common, and people began leaving the churches in significant numbers. Between 1980 and 1992, about 1 million Catholics and 1.2 million Protestants gave up their church memberships. A faltering economy and increased taxes caused many to withdraw for financial reasons. In a 1992 poll, approximately 42 per cent of those queried stated that the church tax was much too high; 64 per cent favoured abolishing the tax and supporting the churches through voluntary contributions. Fourteen per cent of those Roman Catholics and Protestants polled stated that they were likely to withdraw or definitely would withdraw from their church.

Since German unification in 1990, the visible practice of religion declined further. Attendance at religious services is falling. In 1990, there were nominally 30.2 million Protestants and 26.7 million Roman Catholics in united Germany, together about 71 per cent of the country's total population. According to the Federal Office of Statistics (Statistisches Bundesamt), the number of Catholics and Protestants shrunk by about 200,000 each between 1999 and 2000. More recent official data are not available but it is generally assumed that the trend of leaving the two major Christian churches is continuing.

In Germany today, roughly 30 per cent of the population profess no religion, 30 per cent are Protestant and 30 per cent are Roman Catholic. Amongst the remaining 10 per cent the Muslims form the largest group (3.5 per cent). Unlike amongst Christians where attendance of religious service has constantly decreased—according to the Catholic and Protestant churches in Germany, only 17.5 per cent of the Catholics and 4 per cent of the Protestants regularly attend religious service—32 per cent of the Muslim population attends service several times a week. Attendance is less amongst Muslim youth (22 per cent) but at the same time, there seems to be indication that religion plays an increasing role in the identity formation of Muslim youth.[8] A similar trend can be found amongst young Jews in Germany.[9] Thus, if we are looking for public religious assertiveness, with implications for re-thinking the relation between state and religion, the Muslim and the Jewish communities are the most likely candidates.

THE GERMAN MODEL OF A SECULAR STATE

To understand the nature of the relationship between state and religion in Germany, we have to look at the German State-Church-Law (*Staatskirchenrecht*) that regulates the relations between the central and federal states and diverse groups whose members share a common 'worldview' (*Weltanschauung*). Some perceive the German *Staatskirchenrecht* as the most sophisticated of its sort in all of Europe.[10] For one thing, the definition of 'worldview' is the widest conception in Europe of what forms a religious community. If a religious organization fulfils requirements such as assurance of permanence and a certain size, and if there is no indication that the organization's principles conflict with the Constitution or the European Human Rights laws, the organization may request that it be granted the status of a corporation under public law. Public law corporation status, among other things, entitles it to levy taxes on its members that the state collects for it and for which the organization pays a fee to the government.

Most religious organizations are registered and treated as non-profit associations and therefore enjoy tax-exempt status. State level authorities review these submissions and routinely grant this status. Organizations must register at a local or municipal court and provide evidence (through their own statutes) that they are a religion and thus contribute socially, spiritually, or materially to society. Among the religious organizations that have been granted public law corporation status are the Protestant and Roman Catholic Church, Judaism, and some smaller Christian denominations.[11] So far, Muslim communities in Germany do not qualify for this form of public recognition owing to their reluctance to recognize the right of their members to change or abandon their faith—which conflicts with the constitutionally guaranteed liberty of conscience and relevant Human Rights law at the European Union level.[12]

State governments also subsidise various institutions affiliated with public law corporations, such as church-run schools and hospitals. Most public schools offer religious instruction in cooperation with the Protestant and Catholic churches and the Central Council for Jews in Germany (CCJG). A non-religious course in ethics generally is available for students not wishing to participate in religious instruction. The issue of Islamic education in public schools is becoming topical in several states and at the federal level.

Relations between the various religious communities are generally amicable. However, following a rise in the incidence of anti-Semitic crimes and an increase in public criticism of the Israeli government's actions in the Middle East, Jewish community leaders expressed disappointment in the leaders of other religious communities, as well as in some local and national politicians, for not speaking out more forcefully against anti-Semitism.[13] Problematic is also the relation between public officials, government representatives or parliamentarians, and the non-religious section of the population. Leading politicians in Germany sometimes act as if the normative background consensus among the members of the society rested on the premise that the majority of the population subscribes to some religious faith. Thus, the president of the German parliament (Bundestagspräsident) Wolfgang Thierse fears that if the German society would become more '*secularised, then nothing remains, then the common ground would amount to nothing*'.[14] The non-religious part of the German population may find this alarming, for such remarks suggest that anyone who is not subscribing to any religion has no ethics and cannot be part of a decent political community. The fact that large numbers of the German population are turning their back on the traditional forms of organized religion is not to be taken as a '*total denigration and thereby annihilation of elementary . . . ethical fundamentals of society*', as Thierse would like us to believe. This would deny any ethical sensibility to those not practising any religion and turn a completely legitimate personal choice into an act of violence against society. The choice to abandon one's faith is a fundamental right that is just as constitutive of a liberal democratic society as the right to profess any religion.

I now come back to the main questions first, the question of public religious assertiveness in Germany and, subsequently, the question as to how a secular state should deal with it. We have located two instances of increased public religious assertiveness in Germany, that is, the Jewish and the Muslim community. By focusing on these two, however, I do not mean to suggest that the traditional churches are not equally assertive about their role in society. On the contrary, there appears to be a growing awareness amongst Christians in Germany that acceptance of their minority position could liberate them from the need to accommodate each and every one[15] and thus free them for a more partisan approach to the role of religion in public life. However, in terms of the need to rethink and possibly redefine the relationship between the liberal democratic state and the various religious communities, the Jewish, and particularly the growing Muslim community offer more controversial material for the debate since they conform less to the Occidentalist[16] view of how religious communities should be organized. In the following two sections, I will therefore try to give an impression of the controversial issues in these debates.

JUDAISM IN GERMANY

Surprisingly, at the moment Germany seems to be the number one destination for Jewish migrants in the world even in comparison to Israel. In the year 2002, more than 19,000 Jews, mostly from the former Soviet Union but also from Israel and North and South America immigrated to Germany (in the same year, only 18,700 Jews migrated to Israel[17]). This is particularly significant since between 1960 and 1990, only around 30,000 Jews lived in West Germany.[18] This population consisted in small part of Jews who had originally been born in Germany and for the most part of European Jews who had survived the Shoa (Holocaust) and who had found themselves as displaced persons in occupied Germany after the war. In post-war Germany, these Jews formed a Unified

Community (Einheitsgemeinde) uniting Jews of various traditions. In 1950, the Jewish communities in West Germany formed the 'Central Council of Jews in Germany' (CCGJ) as a common representation of Jews to the West-German government. Jewish communities built synagogues and community centres but their membership aged and shrank since many of the young members emigrated to Israel.

The turning point for Jewish life in Germany was the country's re-unification in 1990.[19] The last East-German government had established a policy allowing Jews from the former Soviet Union to emigrate to East Germany. After the collapse of the East-German government, re-unified Germany took over its foreign obligations and adopted the same policy with a sense of historic responsibility toward a European minority which had almost been extinguished under Hitler and which was facing anew anti-Semitic threats in the countries of the former Soviet Union. Today, after years of stagnation, Jewish life re-emerges in Germany. The result is an ever-growing diversity and dynamism prompting some observers to note that Germany had become the stage for a Jewish renaissance with repercussions for Jewish life worldwide.[20]

The main stage of this renaissance of Jewish life in Germany is the German capital itself. Berlin has the largest and most thriving Jewish community with currently 12,000 members, a Jewish high school, several synagogues, museums, theatres, online-magazines, and two weekly newspapers.[21] Among members of the Jewish students' organization (Bundesverband Jüdischer Studenten in Deutschland) it has been observed that—while it was fashionable among young Jews during the 1980s and 1990s to present themselves as 'secular'—today an increasing number of students grow more conscious of their religion and refuse to assimilate into the 'secular' mainstream.[22] In this sense, we can speak of a new public assertiveness of Jews in Germany today.

The climax of this development, for the time being, was the ratification on 6 June 2003 by the German legislative assembly (Bundestag) of a memorandum of understanding (Staatsvertrag) between the Federal Republic of Germany (FRG) and the CCJG. The MOU regulates the cooperation between the FRG and the CCJG in matters of common interest; it obliges the FRG to help preserve the German-Jewish cultural heritage, to help re-build a Jewish community in Germany, to help the CCJG with its social responsibilities, especially with the integration of Jewish immigrants from the former Soviet Union, and to help the CCJG to finance its administration.[23] The FRG obliges itself to help with an annual contribution of 3 million Euros 'in the awareness of the historical responsibility of the German people towards Jewish life in Germany'.

The new emergence of Jewish life as well as the reconciliatory spirit of the Staatsvertrag is welcomed in Germany. Controversies regarding the exclusiveness of the Staatsvertrag to orthodox Jews to the detriment of progressive Jews have been countered by the inclusion of a phrase that reminds the CCJG of its mandatory openness towards Jews of all denominations.[24] In the past, in spite of proclamations to the contrary,[25] the CCJG has often denied progressive congregations access to funds that are meant for all Jews.[26] German governments have often taken the side of the orthodox with the intention of upholding Jewish tradition.[27] However, in March 2000, the Federal Administrative Court (Bundesverwaltungsgericht) has obligated the CCJG to allow members of the Union of Progressive Jews in Germany, Austria, and Switzerland (UPJGAS) into their ranks and to receive the same benefits as orthodox Jews.[28]

The controversy, in the final analysis, amounts to the question as to how the secular state is to position itself with respect to inner religious controversies regarding the boundaries of the community. We will see below that similar controversies exist within the Muslim community. The question is, can we conceive of any neutral principle by which the state can define a religious community without getting entangled in theological issues? I will take up this question after a brief look at the situation of Muslims in Germany.[29]

ISLAM IN GERMANY

Whereas non-Muslim immigrants coming from other European countries were absorbed more or less easily, even after 40 years the Muslim population appears less integrated into German society than comparable minorities in other European countries. This is partly due to the fact that most Turkish migrants came from rural areas without technical skills and without any command of the German language whereas, for example, most Maghrebian Muslims coming to France knew French before coming and most South Asian Muslims coming to Great Britain knew English before. Another obstacle for integration was the old-fashioned descent based (*ius sanguinis*)

German immigration law that has only recently been amended by adding a right of the soil (*ius solis*) to it. Under the new law, children of migrants born in Germany can claim citizenship. Today, half of the 2.37 million people of Turkish descent living in Germany were born there.[30] Around half of these (700,000) chose German citizenship. The other half chose to retain their Turkish nationality.[31] A double German / Turkish citizenship is not available. A recent study carried out by the Essen-based Centre for Turkish Studies revealed that 57 per cent of Muslims feel 'at home in Germany'. At the same time, however, 71 per cent do not feel very close to Germans. More than half have apprehensions of 'becoming like the Germans'. This points to a dilemma in which many Muslims in Germany find themselves: they want to retain their traditional selves and at the same time integrate into the German society, thereby giving their own interpretation to the motto of a conference at Jamia Millia Islamia, 'living together separately' in December 2002.[32]

People of Turkish descent are comparatively worst off, economically, amongst all immigrant groups. In July 2003, 24.4 per cent of the Turkish immigrants were unemployed but only 18.5 per cent of the Italian and only 13.8 per cent of the Spaniard (the overall unemployment rate in Germany is around 10 per cent). One reason for their economical weakness is lack of education. Out of 417,000 Turkish school children only 22,000 (roughly 5.3 per cent) attend higher secondary school (Gymnasium).[33] Nevertheless, there is also an indication that a part of the Turkish population has begun to form a small middle class. In Germany, 59,500 people of Turkish descent run businesses and employ about 327,000 workers. 30,000 people of Turkish descent study in German universities, 80 per cent of whom have obtained their high school graduation from a German Gymnasium.[34]

Apparently, adverse social conditions and the competition with labourers from former East Germany have forced many Turks to shift from Germany to neighbouring countries like Belgium.[35] Nevertheless, the Muslim community in Germany appears to be growing through births and immigration. With an estimated 3 million adherents, Islam has become the third religion in the country. Several branches of Islam are represented, with a vast Sunni majority (2.2 million), large groups of Allevite (600,000) and a sizeable population of Shiites and Ahmadis (185,000).[36] The Allevites are generally not regarded as Muslims by the Sunni majority. Here again the question arises as to how the state, with its obligation to be neutral, is to position itself over such internal controversies.

In 2000, the German government published a comprehensive report on Islam in Germany[37] that examined issues concerning the Muslim minority in response to an inquiry from Parliament. The report acknowledges that Germany is still far from giving Islam its due place as the third largest religion as required by the Constitution.[38] The Grundgesetz (German Constitution) guarantees religious education in public schools to every sizable religious group,[39] a provision whose implementation in the case of Islam is still not satisfactory. The main controversy concerns who should be authorized to exercise this right. Since education is the prerogative of the federal states, the various states of the German federation have experimented with different models.

In 2000 the Federal Administrative Court upheld previous court rulings that the 'Islamic Federation' of Berlin qualified as a religious community and as a result must be given the opportunity to provide religious instruction in Berlin schools. The decision drew criticism from many other Islamic organizations not represented by the Islamic Federation, and the Berlin State Government expressed its concerns about the Islamic Federation's alleged links to Milli Görüs, a Turkish group classified as extremist by the Federal Office for the Protection of the Constitution (Verfassungsschutz). However, after another court decision in favour of the Islamic Federation in August 2001, Berlin school authorities decided to allow it to begin teaching Islamic religious classes in several Berlin schools starting in September 2001.

In many federal states, the teachers of Islam at public schools are recruited either from Islamic organizations in Germany or by the Turkish government. North Rhine Westphalia is the only state with its own public teacher-training programme for Islamic education. The programme has been worked out in collaboration with Muslim representatives in the state. The teachers are trained in Germany and the teaching medium is German as well. In a model experiment since 1999/2000, North Rhine Westphalia offers Muslim pupils a school subject called 'Islamic instruction in German' (Islamische Unterweisung auf Deutsch). The syllabus contains an introduction to Islam, and it also takes up problems that immigrant children face in the German host society.[40]

In other federal states, Muslim parents face a tough choice. They can opt for the religious instruction provided by the Turkish consulate, which would like to shape the children of Turkish immigrants into Turkish nationalists; they can opt for the religious education offered by Islamic Organizations which are often accused of being influenced by the Islamic fundamentalist organization Milli Görüs; or they can send their children to the afternoon schools run by mosques which are also not known for fostering a pro-German or pro-European Islamic identity.[41]

A second controversial issue regards the right of female Muslim pupils and teachers to wear headscarves in public schools. Unlike in France and England where female Muslim pupils are often barred from wearing headscarves at school, the same is accepted in German schools where no uniform dress code exists. The right of teachers to wear headscarves, however, is granted in some of the federal states (North Rhine Westphalia and Hamburg) and prohibited in others (in Lower Saxony and Baden Württemberg[42]).

The most noted case in this connection is that of the teacher Fereshta Ludin, a German citizen of Afghan origin whose right to wear a headscarf in front of her class was turned down by the regional board of education (Oberschulamt) in 1998 after the school where she had completed her training had denied her tenure. Subsequently, several courts have turned down her appeals: the Stuttgart Administrative Court of Baden Württemberg in 2000, the State Administrative Court in 2001, and the Federal Administrative Court in 2002. Now (24 September 2003), the Federal Constitutional Court (Bundesverfassungsgericht) has struck down the decision of the Federal Administrative Court on the ground that it lacked a legal basis. It has thereby referred the matter back to the state parliaments who are to enact a law which would regulate the dispute once and for all within the jurisdiction of the respective federal state.[43]

A third controversy discussed in the report surrounds the question as to how Muslims should be allowed to practise their religion in public. At times the presence of Muslims leads to societal discord, such as local resistance to the construction of mosques or disagreements over whether Muslims may use loudspeakers in residential neighbourhoods to call to prayer. The reasons behind such discord may in part stem from a widespread mistrust of Islam as a force with a tendency to disregard the constitutional set-up of the Federal Republic. The report, while acknowledging the danger of some Islamic organizations engaging in unconstitutional activities, however states that such a generalized mistrust is unwarranted. The degree of organization among Muslims in Germany is comparatively low: the three major Muslim organizations[44] taken together represent at most 15 per cent of the total Muslim population[45] and only from an even smaller percentage of this faction could potential danger emanate.[46]

In Germany and elsewhere in Europe, the concept of Euro-Islam is gaining wider currency. The idea has been popularized by the German International Relations scholar Bassam Tibi[47] and has recently been taken up by the German Commissioner for Foreign Nationals (Ausländerbeauftragte) Marieluise Beck[48] and by the president of the German parliament Wolfgang Thierse.[49] Tibi makes the simple observation, that historically there has never been a single unified Islam.[50] Islam has taken different shapes in Morocco and in Indonesia, in Africa and in India. It is thus to be expected that Islam in Europe will also be different from Islam in Turkey or the Arab world. In the same way, the liberal Imam of the Mosque of Paris, Dalil Boubakir, embraced the concept of Euro-Islam declaring that Islam would have no future in Europe without the recognition of the principle of the separation of religion and politics. Tibi demands that religious education in public schools be placed in the hands of the state to prevent radical Islamist organization from indoctrinating Muslim youth in a way that hampers their integration into German society by turning them hostile towards European civilization and its constitutional principles.

CONCLUSION

In conclusion, I return to the two questions that were raised at the outset of this paper. We have seen that the most interesting questions regarding the relationship between the state and various communities sharing a common world-view are raised by religious communities that somehow do not quite fit into the traditional scheme of church-state relations. We have seen that this is partly due to the fact that these communities lack the authoritative structures of traditional churches.

Here, an elite decided theological as well as political matters and the faithful were expected to follow suit. This model, having evolved in pre-democratic times, is seen as obsolete today even by many within the churches. Outside the Christian sphere, the model becomes completely untenable since in many non-Christian religious communities religious authority has always been diffuse and decentralized. Such a decentralized form of religious practice, however, seems more suitable for a democratic society then the authoritarian structures of the traditional churches. To force such religious communities into the unified framework of a church-like structure would do harm to this diversity and its inherent democratic spirit. It would necessarily lead to privileging some parts of the community over others. Such attempts have been made in France with respect to the Muslim community there and they are being discussed in Germany as well. So far, they have not proved feasible.

It seems that the lack of authoritative structures in other religious communities poses a new challenge to the liberal democratic state to redefine its relations with the growing number of religions claiming recognition in Germany. Here the state faces the following principal difficulty. The model of the State-Church-Law in combination with the concept of a unified religious community leads to the creation of a religious collective body with quasi-public functions. For the administration of church-tax revenues, the religious public body as the sole representative of the religious community has to decide whom it wants to count as its member. Thereby it can happen that the religious public body excludes a part of the religious community claiming to belong to the same faith. Seemingly, here, the state abdicates its obligation to benefit all citizens of a particular faith in favour of a corporation under public law that is granted a right to differentiate between members and non-members of that particular faith.

If this decision is left to the religious organization, the liberal democratic state abdicates its obligation to protect the religious autonomy of the citizen, for if an individual calls itself a Christian, a Muslim or a Jew without being recognised as such by the respective unitary organization, it should not be for the state or any other public body to decide whether this individual is justified in doing so. The decision cannot rest with the state lest it get entangled in theological controversies, nor can any public body be allowed to decide such matters on behalf of the state without the state sanctioning it. By sanctioning it, however, the state does take a stand in matters beyond its competence.

The only alternative left is to either abstain from creating or sanctioning such unified public bodies or to prohibit them from deciding on behalf of the state whether any individual should be counted as member of a particular religious community or not. Since the latter is no viable option for any religious community that wants to—and has a right to—define whom to count as its members, the concept of the unified pubic body is not a viable option for a liberal democratic state. There is an obvious way out. Abandoning the concept of a unified religious organization for religious communities, the faithful have the option of creating as many religious organizations as they need. Each can claim the same recognition and furtherance through the state, provided it abides by the Constitution and the European laws on Human Rights. Whether these organizations have to be bodies of public or private law is another matter. In any case, however, the same treatment has to be granted to organizations of all religions.

NOTES

1. This paper has grown out of a presentation for the international seminar titled 'Assertive Religious Identities' which was held at Jamia Millia Islamia, Academy of Third World Studies, 16-18 October 2003. I am grateful to the organizers, Satish Saberwal and Mushirul Hasan, for the invitation and to the participants for their useful comments. In particular, I thank Michael Brenner for clarifications regarding the Jewish community in Germany. Moreover, I thank Satish Saberwal, Margrit Pernau and Mollica Dastider for helpful comments and criticism regarding an earlier draft of this paper. The remaining shortcomings are entirely my responsibility.
2. I take personal as well as group identity formation as two kinds of social identity formation. Both follow similar patterns, the difference being that with group identity a general awareness is created amongst the members that everyone else is also part of the group. This awareness distinguishes a group from any random set of individuals that might share any given property. For further discussion Krappmann 1969.
3. Cf. Honneth, 1992 and 2001.
4. For details on Human Rights violations against the Kurds committed by the Turkish state, Kerr (2003).
5. Cf. Rawls, 1993.
6. Minkenberg and Willems, 2003: 6.
7. Ibid., 14.
8. Cf. Goddar, 2002a; Rollmann, 2002. The recent study of the Centre for Turkish Studies of the University of Essen, Germany, concludes that religiosity and marginalization are often correlated. Among the better integrated Muslims in Germany religiosity declines whereas the more

marginalized tend to be also more religious. While the study confirms our thesis that religiosity among Muslims, particularly after 11 September 2001, is on the rise, it also points to the fact that increase in religiosity is relatively low among young Muslims. Only 13 per cent of young Muslims in Germany rate themselves as traditionally religious. It could not be established whether the difference in rates of increase among different age groups is due to life-cycle, or to value change with future consequences. As one would expect, religiosity decreases with the degree of education and is consequently less frequent among educated professionals. Surprisingly, however, religiosity seems to positively correlate with duration of stay in Germany: the longer the stay, the more religious the person (Cf. Sen 2004).

9. Cf. Rollmann, 2003.
10. Cf. Etienne, 2002.
11. Mormons, Seventh-Day Adventists, Mennonites, Baptists, Methodists, Christian Scientists and the Salvation Army.
12. Cf. Etienne, 2002.
13. Beucker, 2001.
14. Luecke and Woehlert, 2002.
15. An aspiration dating from the time when religion was still the defining feature of an empire or, later, a territorial state.
16. In search for a European identity, conservative intellectuals sometimes allude to the old idea of the Christian Occident (Christliches Abendland) as a basis for such an identity (cf. Wehler 2002). The main thrust, here, is against the inclusion of Turkey in the European Union. Among the collateral damage, however, are many achievements of Western modernity which are at the basis of the constitutions of the EU member states: An equal standing of all religions, freedom of conscience, independence of the liberal democratic state from any of the religious organizations and a religiously neutral ethical justification for its legitimacy (cf. Dusche 2000).
17. Cf. Philipp, 2003; Bodemann, 2003.
18. Cf. Suchsland, 2003a.
19. An event that the CCJG supported even against objections from the Jewish World Congress (cf. Guttmann, 2003).
20. Cf. Bodemann, 2003.
21. Cf. Suchsland, 2003a; Goddar, 2003.
22. Cf. Rollmann, 2003.
23. Cf. Staatsvertrag, 2003, Art. 1.
24. 'Zentralrat der Juden in Deutschland . . . der nach seinem Selbstverständnis für alle Richtungen innerhalb des Judentums offen ist' (Staatsvertrag, 2003, Art. 1).
25. Cf. Braun, 2003.

26. Bremer, 2003.
27. I.e. the major (Oberbürgermeister) of Munich Christian Ude (cf. Bremer, 2003).
28. Cf. Bremer, 2003.
29. Cf. Dastider, 2001 for further details.
30. Cf. Weiland, 2003.
31. Cf. Bittner, 2003.
32. Cf. Sen, 2004.
33. Cf. Bitter, 2003.
34. Cf. Gaschke, 2003.
35. Cf. Geary, 2003, 5.
36. All numbers are rough estimates, cf. Weiland, 2003.
37. Bund, 2000.
38. Grundgesetz Art. 4 Abs. 1 & 2.
39. Art. 7 Abs. 3.
40. Goddar, 2002b.
41. Ibid., 2002b.
42. Cf. Weiland, 2003.
43. Cf. Klingst, 2003; Schmoll, 2003; Mueller, 2003a & b.
44. The Turkish Islamic Union ('Türkisch-islamische Union der Anstalt für Religion'), the Association of Islamic Culture Centres ('Verband der islamischen Kulturzentren') and the Islamic Community Milli Görüs ('Islamische Gemeinschaft Milli Görüs').
45. Cf. Weiland, 2003.
46. Further controversies are over the Muslims' right to provide religious chaplaincies in the military, in hospitals and in prisons. This is not dependent on the public law corporation status of a religious community. The Ministry of Defence is looking into the possibility of Islamic clergymen providing religious services in the military, although none of the many Islamic communities has the status of a corporation under public law.

    The right of Muslims to *halal* slaughtering procedures without the stunning required by the federal animal protection law was the subject of a court case that concluded in January 2002. In November 2000, the Federal Administrative Court ruled that the Islamic Community of Hessen was not a 'religious community' as defined in the animal protection law, which allows religious communities to apply for waivers of animal slaughtering regulations. As a result, Muslims could not apply for a waiver; however, the Jewish Community was granted a waiver shortly after the animal protection law first went into effect in order to slaughter animals by kosher procedures. The Muslim Community appealed the ruling, and in January 2002, the Federal Constitutional Court ruled that Muslim butchers could apply for waivers (cf. BVerfG, 2002).

47. Tibi, 1998; 2000, 325ff.
48. Cf. Goddar, 2002a.
49. Cf. Luecke and Waehlert, 2002.
50. Cf. Tibi, 2000, 330f.

REFERENCES

Bauer, Yehuda, 2003, 'Der dritte Totalitarismus', *Die Zeit* 31/07/03: 7.

Beucker, Pascal, 2001, 'Auf Bewaehrung frei', *Die Tageszeitung* 12/10/02: http://www.beucker.de/ 2001/taz01-10-12.htm.

Bhargava, Rajeev, ed., 1998, *Secularism and its Critics*, New Delhi: Oxford University Press.

Bodemann, Y. Michael, 2003, 'Die jüdische Identitaet in der Bundesrepublik hat sich fundamental gewandelt', *Das Parlament* 28/07-04/08/03: 10.

Braun, Stefan, 2003, 'Interview mit Meinhard Tenne, Leiter der Integrationskommission des Zentralrats der Juden in Deutschland', *Das Parlament* 28/07-04/08/03: 16.

Bremer, Joerg, 2003, 'Liberale Juden wollen teilhaben. Progressive Weltbewegung dringt auf gleiche Rechte in Deutschland', *Frankfurter Allgemeine Zeitung* 08/01/03: 3.

Bund, 2000, *Bericht der Unabhaengigen Kommission Zuwanderung*: http://www.bmi.bund.de/dokumente/Pressemitteilungen/ix_46876.htm.

BVerfG, 2002, *Pressemitteilung Nr. 2/2002 vom 15. Januar 2002*: http://www.bverfg.de/cgi-bin/link.pl?entscheidungen.

Dastider, Mollica, 2001, 'Racism in Germany: Double-Talk by Political Parties', *Economic and Political Weekly* 36: 1006-8.

Dusche, Michael, 2000, *Der Philosoph als Mediator. Anwendungsbedingungen globaler Gerechtigkeit*, Vienna: Passagen Verlag.

Etinenne, Bruno, 2002, 'La France multiconfessionnelle face a l'Europe plurielle', *Dialogues Politiques* 0 (April): http://www.la-science-politique.com/revue/revue0/france/

Gessler, Philipp, 2003, 'Interview mit Julius Schoeps', *Das Parlament* 28/07-04/08/03: 11.

Goddar, Jeannette, 2002a, 'Interview mit der Auslaenderbeauftragten Marieluise Beck', *Das Parlament* 18-25/01/02: 8.

———, 2002b, 'Islamunterricht in Deutschland: Was sollen 570·000 muslimische Schüler lernen?', *Das Parlament* 18-25/01/02: 8.

———, 2003b, 'Sprachrohr der Gemeinden: Der 'Aufbau' und die 'Juedische Allgemeine', *Das Parlament* 28/07-04/08/03: 15.

Guttmann, Micha, 2003, 'Der Zentralrat der Juden in Deutschland und der Staatsvertrag mit der Bundesrepublik Deutschland', *Das Parlament* 28/07-04/08/03: 1.

Habermas, Juergen, 1987, *Theorie des Kommunikativen Handelns*, Frankfurt am Main: Suhrkamp.

Honneth, Axel, 1992, *Kampf um Anerkennung*, Frankfurt am Main: Suhrkamp.

———, 2001, 'Recognition or Redistribution? Changing Perspectives on the Moral Order of Society', *Theory, Culture & Society* 18: 43-55.

Kerr, Stuart, 2003, 'On Trial in Turkey', *London Review of Books* 25 (18): 34-5.

Klingst, Martin, 2003, 'Feige Richter', *Die Zeit* 25/09/03: 7.

Krappmann, Lothar, 1969, *Soziologische Dimensionen der Identitaet. Strukturelle Bedingungen fuer die Teilnahme an Interaktionsprozessen*, Stuttgart: Klett-Cotta.

Luecke, Detlev and Thorsten Woehlert, 2002, 'Interview with Wolfgang Thierse', *Das Parlament* 18-25/01/02: 2.

Madan, T.N., 1998, 'Secularism in its Place', in: Bhargava, 1998: 297-320.

Meyer, Thomas, 2001, *Identity Mania: Fundamentalism and the Politicization of Cultural Differences*, New Delhi: Mosaic Press; German, 1997, *Identitaets-Wahn: Die Politisierung des kulturellen Unterschieds*, Berlin: ufbau Verlag.

Mueller, Reinhard, 2003a, 'Karlsruhe: Kein Kopftuchverbot ohne Gesetz', *Frankfurter Allgemeine Zeitung* 25/09/03: 1.

———, 2003b, 'Karlsruhe drückt sich', *Frankfurter Allgemeine Zeitung* 25/09/03: 1.

Nandy, Ashis, 1998, 'The Politics of Secularism and the Recovery of Religious Toleration', in Bhargava, 1998: 321-44.

Rawls, John, 1993, *Political Liberalism*, New York: Columbia University Press.

Rollmann, Annette, 2002, 'Islam in Deutschland: Alltagskultur und strenge Lehren bilden einen nicht ganz unproblematischen Gegensatz', *Das Parlament* 18-25/01/02: 9.

———, 2003, 'Im juedischen Studentenverband findet sich eine neue Generation', *Das Parlament* 28/07-04/08/03: 3.

Rothschild, Thomas, 2003, 'Juden ohne Gott oder die Suche nach der Normalitaet', *Das Parlament* 28/07-04/08/03: 4.

Schmoll, Heike, 2003, 'Karlsruhe stellt das Beamtenrecht auf den Kopf', *Frankfurter Allgemeine Zeitung* 25/09/03: 3.

Sattler, Karl-Otto, 2003, 'Die Zuwanderer stellen die deutschen Gemeinden vor Probleme', *Das Parlament* 28/07-04/08/03: 14.

Sen, Faruk, 2004, 'Entwicklung des Islam in der Migration', unpublished manuscript, Zentrum fuer Tuerkeistudien, Essen, Germany.

Staatsvertrag, 2003, 'zwischen der Bundesrepublik Deutschland und dem Zentralrat der Juden in Deutschland', cf. http://www.zentralratdjuden.de/down/staatsvertrag.pdf.

Suchsland, Ruediger, 2003a, 'Eindruecke aus der Israelitischen Kultusgemeinde Munchen', *Das Parlament* 28/07-04/08/03: 10.

———, 2003b, 'HaGalil-Online' ist das groesste juedische Internet-Magazin, *Das Parlament* 28/07-04/08/03: 15.

Tibi, Bassam, 1998, 'Der Euro-Islam ist die Loesung', *Spiegel-Spezial*, Hamburg: Spiegel Verlag.

———, 2000, *Der Islam und Deutschland—Muslime in Deutschland*, Stuttgart: Deutsche Verlags-Anstalt.

———, 2003, *Im Schatten Allahs: Der Islam und die Menschenrechte*, Frankfurt am Main: Ullstein.

Weiland, Severin, 2003, 'Stereotypen treffen nicht zu: Ein Gleichklang der Muslime gibt es nicht', *Internetausgabe Das Parlament* 01/08/03.

Wehler, Hans-Ulrich, 2002, 'Muslime sind nicht integrierbar', *Die Tageszeitung* 10/09/02: 6.

17

Transcending Religious Identities: Amrita Pritam and Partition

NONICA DATTA

In her recent autobiography, Amrita Pritam* discusses her 'inner journey'. She writes 'I realized and gathered what is the moot difference between a Brahmin and myself. Precisely that I'm not a Brahmin. That's also the difference between a Kshatriya and myself that I'm not a Kshatriya. Similarly, that's the difference between a Vaish and myself that I'm not a Vaish. And then it also dawned that there's a similar difference between me and a Hindu, Sikh or Muslim—that I'm not a Hindu, Sikh or Muslim.'[1]

Invoking the Sufi idiom, she refers to '*Main apne hujre ki mitti hun, main khuda ke shajre ki lakeer hun*'[2] [I'm the soil of Meditation, I am the line of divine hierarchy'].[3] Why was Amrita Pritam searching for *mein*, and what, indeed, led her to question her religious identity? What was the source of the anxiety that inspired her inner spiritual and creative journey? Amrita Pritam's life history reveals how she locates herself in family, community, and nation in the aftermath of Punjab's Partition. It suggests ways in which she attached inner meanings to religious languages. Her narrative problematizes the 'experience' of Punjabi women; as a witness and narrator, her account differs from narratives deriving sustenance from Punjab's religious and communal traditions.[4] Partition is the most crucial moment in defining her world-view; it enables her to forge a *kainaati rishta* (fraternal relationship) with the universe, and to create her world in accordance with Punjab's language, culture and social history.

GROWING UP IN LAHORE

Amrita Pritam was born into an Arora-Khatri Sikh family in Gujranwala on 31 August 1919. That year—of Rowlatt Satyagraha—Punjab tasted a major nationalist upsurge. The province experienced Hindu-Muslim-Sikh fraternization, a sequel to the Gandhian initiatives to cement inter-community amity. Amrita Pritam wrote a moving poem on the Jallianwala Bagh massacre. 'The earthen (*mitti*) smell', she recalls, 'is linked with birth, the first breath. The year I was born, that was the year of the bloodshed in Jallianwala Bagh. The air burning with pain was mixed with the smell of *mitti*.'[5]

But all this changed thereafter. Amrita Pritam notices the rapid transformation of the Punjabi landscape: 'when politics becomes manipulative, people are soaked in each other's blood in the name of religion. Until the eruption of violence I had not known that religion could be such a potent weapon to spread hate and to use ill-will for hatching political conspiracies.'[6] Again, 'what sort of shadowy tree was this, which was being infected with termite till its roots?'[7] Her sense of alienation was heightened by the drift in Punjab politics, especially after the Khilafat movement.

Though disillusioned with the political climate, the sacrifice of Bhagat Singh and his comrades is another important milestone in her political memories.[8] Reflecting on the execution of Bhagat Singh, she writes how, on the occasion of the death anniversary of Rajguru and Sukhdev on 23 March 1938, Tayar, Lahore's poet, sang Bhagat Singh's *ghori* (folk song). Even though the authorities had imposed restrictions, over a lakh of people gathered to pay their homage. Such was the poet's impact that people continued 'to sing and weep. . . . At that time Hindus and Mussalmans were one in raising their voice in favour of the liberation of the country. Many poets wrote songs for the independence of the country which were banned (*zabtshuda*). They were then patriotic, indifferent to the manipulations of high politics.'[9]

However, these were the years when divisive trends came to the fore. While visiting her mother's village in Gujranwala, she notices water being hawked at the railway platform as Hindu *pani* (water) and Muslim *pani*.[10] Renowned for its annual fair of Sultan Sakhi Sarvar, a 'syncretic' saint of Punjab,[11] Gujranwala faced polarization along religious lines. She questioned her mother—'is water also Hindu-Mussalman?' All that her mother, Raj Kaur, could say was: 'it happens here, God knows what all happens here'.[12] Amrita Pritam was a young girl when she heard her mother say so, and only eleven years old when Raj Kaur died.[13] But her message was not lost, as Amrita Pritam raised her voice against her grandmother, who kept separate utensils for use when her father's Muslim friends were visiting.[14] This was 'my first rebellion (*bagavat*) against religion',[15] she recalls:

I used to notice three glass tumblers kept away from all other pots and pans on a shelf in the corner of the kitchen. These were for use only when father's Muslim friends were offered tea or buttermilk when they came to visit him. After these tumblers had served their purpose they were scrubbed, and washed and put right back in their ostracized niche.

The three tumblers became a 'cause' for me, and the four of us put up a fight with grandmother. I was adamant, I would not drink from any other tumbler but one of those. Grandmother would rather see me thirsty than let me use them. The tale, inevitably, travelled to father. He of course did not until then have the faintest idea about such things. The moment he did, I succeeded in my revolt. Thereafter, not a single utensil was labeled 'Hindu' or 'Muslim'.[16]

'Neither Grandmother nor I knew then that the man I was to fall in love with would be of the same faith as the branded utensils were meant for', she adds.[17] Amrita Pritam's grandmother would have known of the *Qadamon-ka-mela* being celebrated in Lahore on the first Monday after the new moon in February. She may have made her offerings at the tomb of Sultan Sakhi Sarvar in Anarkali. She may have grown up with the legends of *Hir-Ranjha*, *Sassi-Punnun*, *Puran-Bhagat*, and *Sohni-Mahival*. And she may have subscribed to the pluralistic Sikh faith of the nineteenth century.[18]

And yet, her grandmother would have known that by the turn of the century pluralist trends were being assailed in different quarters. Two important processes were at work which exacerbated Hindu-Muslim-Sikh tension and led to widespread violence in Punjab. By constructing monolithic Hindu, Muslim, and Sikh communities, the colonial state had given legitimacy to new categories of religious identification and enumeration. Second, religious reformists and community leaders harped on imaginary homogeneous Hindu, Sikh, and Muslim communities with 'pristine' pasts. Consequently, community-based solidarities came to the fore in public and private arenas. And, cities, towns and countryside were flooded with *shuddhi* and *gauraksha sabhas*, with the Anujman-i-Islamia's *tabligh* and *tanzim* outfits. Thus fluid identities, multiple vocabularies, landscapes and inter-community solidarities were overshadowed by monolithic religious blocs. Not surprisingly, the Singh Sabha denounced the richness of nineteenth-century Sikh religious tradition as 'superstitious', and gave the vision of Tat Khalsa. As a result, Sikh resurgence made its presence felt in rural and urban spaces. It manifested itself in different ways: for example, in the objection of two Nihangs (a sect of Sikhs) to Amrita Pritam's father (Kartar Singh Hitkari), showing Sikh history slides on the large wall of the gurdwara. Armed with spears, the Nihangs shouted, 'Cinema is not going to be shown here'.[19] After this incident her father gave up trying to popularize Sikh history. She could not help asking him: 'Did that place belong to them? To those two individuals?' And, 'the religion you kept talking about, is that religion not theirs too?' Her father replied, 'The religion is mine, well for namesake it's theirs too, but if indeed it was theirs too, they wouldn't have unsheathed those spears.' And she bemoans, 'That big, black box [of slides] was never opened again. His ceaseless perseverance of countless years got locked in a box—forever. . . .'[20]

There are clear signs of the father and daughter, having lived in the composite ethos of Lahore, being aware of the divisive tendencies that had come to the fore in their otherwise peaceful environment. Her father ran a Punjabi monthly with Muslim, Hindu, and Sikh writers.[21] Having spent many years in Gujranwala, he was influenced by its pluralist ethos. This was after all the land of Waris Shah (*c.* 1736-90). Clearly, the world that Amrita Pritam related to was pluralist rather than religiously-oriented, and yet she was equally sensitive to the divisive trends appearing in Lahore society: 'before Partition there was a part of Lahore, where after sunset no Sikh was allowed to go. In an abusive way, they were called 'Sikhdas'. On the other side, lived the Hindus and the Sikhs, who called the Muslims, 'Muslahs'.[22] Hindus and Sikhs avoided passing through the lower-class 'Mussalmans' *mohallas* (neighbourhood). . . . During Holi, if by chance, any drop of colour was sprinkled on a Mussalman's clothes, a riot would immediately follow.'[23]

Though Amrita Pritam's world was isolated from such separatist tendencies, she did not subscribe to Lahore's *adabi* (literary) culture. For one, she never attended the meetings of the Progressive Writers' Association, which was quite strong in Lahore. Though she got to know the Urdu writers Krishan Chander and Rajinder Singh Bedi well, her world-view was principally rooted in the world of Sufi poets:

I only loved the Sufi poets, their *kalam* (poetry). *Hir Waris Shah* was the first book I read from my heart. My father introduced me to the Sufi poets. They were also part of my education—*vidvani* and *gyani.* I read Shah

Husain, Sultan Bahu and Bulle Shah in Punjabi. In fact, Punjabi, suffused with Urdu and Persian *alfaz* (words), was my language. It was part of everyday speech.[24]

Amrita Pritam's inner journey took a new turn in the tumultuous 1940s. She was keen to work in films, but her husband, Pritam Singh Kwatara discouraged her. She learnt the *sitar* and Bharatnatyam from Tara Chaudhary, even though her family disapproved of her public performances. Ultimately, she took a job with All-India Radio [Lahore] in 1945-6, and the first talk she gave was on Waris Shah. By this time she had also made two friends, who ultimately became her intellectual companions: Sajjad Haider [Urdu playwright] and Sahir Ludhianvi [well-known Urdu poet]. 'With Sajjad I had friendship. But Sahir who worked for *Adab-e-Latif* magazine, was my love.'[25]

1947, PARTITION

'In 1947, Lahore was turned into a graveyard', she writes. 'It was the politics of hate that swept Lahore in flames; at night one would see houses being in flames, hear cries of desperation, and witness long hours of curfew during the day.'[26] 'In Lahore, at night, I . . could hear those shrieks which got suppressed in the day-long curfew. . .'[27] 'Expecting my second child, I often went for a walk on the Mall road, an exclusive place in Lahore. There one day I saw a Sikh running around, with a knife pierced into his stomach. I immediately rushed back, and never stepped out of the house thereafter. At night, I would watch Lahore burning from my rooftop.'[28] The rise in the communal temperature reminded her of her father's persecution by religious bigots. She missed her father, who was no more, for he might have answered her 'never-ending' questions: 'does this land not belong to those who are born here? For whom are those spears flashing in their hands?'[29]

And yet, Amrita Pritam refused to forge a causal connection between the violence that rocked her Lahore and Punjab's Partition. She emphasizes, 'My Lahore was not entirely communalised.'[30] In fact, at the height of violence, Hindu women continued to frequent the *dargahs* (shrines) of *murshids* (preceptors), *pirs* (saints) and *faqirs* (mendicants), she says. While the city was swept in flames, and the news of women being abducted, raped and burnt alive in thousands reached her husband's home on Dhani Ram Road, Amrita Pritam thought it was a temporary madness. 'A storm of hatred', she calls it.

'This too will pass. It won't last. We will be able to come back.'[31]

But then disaster struck. With the issue of partitioning Punjab settled, Amrita Pritam, then 28 years old, immediately left with her husband and little daughter after the most horrific riots of March-April in Lahore. She was pregnant and needed regular medical attention, which was not possible in the riot-torn Lahore. Thinking that she would eventually return after the birth of her child, she would reunite with her two friends and repair her sense of short-term estrangement: 'I was expecting a child at that time. One would not find a doctor. One could not even get milk or medicine. That's why we left Lahore. One did not leave Lahore because of Hindu-Muslim *fasad* (riot).' She did not take her winter clothes, and left only with a red shawl. And 'my favourite *naurattan* (ornament with precious stones), I left in my cupboard.'[32] It was primarily her fear of losing her friends, Sajjad Haider and Sahir Ludhianvi, that haunted her on the fateful train journey from Lahore to Dehra Dun in early May 1947. She initially took shelter in Dehra Dun, and then in search of a livelihood, went to Delhi, and saw 'homeless people with a vacuous look—observed the land, where they were being labelled as refugees . . . in their own country—people without a country. . . .'[33] When winter arrived she did not have any clothes, and she cut that shawl into two pieces. 'One piece I took while the other piece was further cut into two parts to wrap up my children.'[34] Thus began her journey as a refugee.

'What memories? I was overtaken by a storm of hatred. Nobody realized that people would suffer so much—houses being burnt down, neighbours killing each other, and women being abducted and raped. I was haunted by what I saw at the railway station in Dehra Dun and Delhi. There was darkness all around. How could so many millions be dispossessed and displaced?'[35] From a running train, 'in the darkness outside, the mounds of earth seemed like the entire land is littered with graves. . . .'[36] 'The blowing breeze seemed to be moping over the darkness! At that hour, I recalled a composition of Waris Shah, who wrote a long, historic tale of Hir—and people memorized it in each and every home. I too conversed with Waris Shah. . . .'[37]As she records:

1947 . . . Uprooted from Lahore, I had rehabilitated myself at Dehradun for a while, but later went to Delhi for work and a place to live in. On my return journey, I could not get a wink of sleep on the train. The pitch-black darkness of the night was like a sign of the times. So piercing were the sighs the winds carried and echoed, it seemed we were back in mourning over this Watershed of History. The trees loomed larger and larger like sentinels of sorrow. There were patches of stark aridity in between like the mounds of massive graves. The words of Waris Shah, 'How'll the dead and departed meet again?' surged back and forth through my mind. I thought, a great poet like him alone could bewail the loss à Heer once had to bear. But who could lament the plight of millions of Heers today? I could think of no one greater than Waris Shah to chant my invocation to. In the moving train, my trembling fingers moved on to describe the pangs I went through.[38]

Thus while travelling from Dehra Dun to Delhi in 1948, she wrote the *nazm* (poem), 'Aj Akhan Waris Shah Noon', on a scrap of paper:[39]

Today, I call to Waris Shah—speak from your grave!
Today, open the next page in the book of love.
Once, a daughter of Punjab wept and you wrote an epic on her suffering
O Waris Shah! Today, tens of thousands of daughters of Punjab are weeping.

You, the friend to those in agony—rise up and look at your Punjab!
Today, corpses litter the pastures
And the Chenab river runs with blood,
Someone has poured poison into the five rivers
And those waters have drenched the fertile fields
So that every growing thing in this land has now turned poisonous
Every inch of every growing thing has turned blood red.
And worse, the curse of it has ripened.

The poisoned wind gusted into every single wood,
Transformed every bamboo flute into a serpent.
First, it bit the charmers and they lost the magic of their mantras
Then it bit whoever came their way
Its venom sealed the people's mouths
And then the poison spread
Soon all Punjab turned blue.
The song cut-off in every throat
Women friends who together once sat spinning parted
Threads on bobbins snapped
The humming spinning wheels fell silent.

The boatmen sank the boats with their own hands
The peepul trees broke the swings on their own branches
Where once piped melodies of love, the flute was lost
All of Ranjha's brothers had forgotten how to play.

The blood rained down upon the soil, seeping down even into the graves.
The princesses of love are weeping in their tombs.

Everyone became Kaidon (Hir's uncle), thieves of love and beauty
Where can I find another Waris Shah today?

I call to Waris Shah—speak from your grave!
Today, open the next page in the book of love.[40]

'I knew Waris Shah recognized the pain of this soil, and of a woman, a human being,' she explains. 'This story was inside me. After all, Waris Shah emotionalized the legend of *Hir-Ranjha* beautifully, for it is believed that he himself was in love with a Hindu woman, *Bhag-Bhari* (the fortunate one)', she adds, 'and he was, in fact, expressing his own love and suffering in the form of Hir' .[41]

This poem was recited everywhere. 'But there were also those who started showering abuse on me in newspaper columns, speculating on why I related to a Mussalman Waris Shah and dared to voice these sentiments. Those belonging to the Sikh faith asserted I should have related to Guru Nanak. And the communists asserted that I should have related to Lenin—not to Guru Nanak. . . .' [42] Such reactions only strengthened her resolve to steer clear of the politics of religiously-informed identity: 'writers are the *zamir* (conscience) of our own people. And can *zamir* be Hindu, Sikh, or Mussalman . . . Is the light of the sun also Hindu, Sikh or Mussalman?'[43]

'Do you know,' Amrita told me, 'that the poem is sung at the *mazar* (tomb) of Waris Shah in Multan (Pakistan) on the occasion of *Jashne Waris Shah*? People cried and sang when they heard the nazm over the radio.'[44] 'In camps, people, dispossessed and dislocated, tied this nazm into a knot, and wore it as an amulet.'[45] Surely, Waris Shah's popular appeal in Punjab's cultural landscape was the principal reason for the poem's popularity on both sides of the border.

By invoking Waris Shah, the eighteenth-century Sufi poet, Amrita Pritam draws upon the literary cultures of Punjab. More specifically, she uses the *qissa* tradition of which Waris Shah was one of the chief exponents. She thus reflects on Punjab's cultural topography and regional identity, and dwells on how worldly identities are repeatedly transgressed by love.[46] Central to the qissa genre is the theme of love between a Muslim and a Hindu. 'Such love is at once transgressive and assimilative', argues Christopher Shackle, 'for at the same point that Panjabi poets highlight it as illicit love, they also undermine the very categories Muslim and Hindu as oppositional and incommensurate.'[47] Crossing all dividing lines—of time and place, creed and class—the qissa genre did indeed forge a distinctive 'language of identity'.[48]

Amrita Pritam uses the Punjabi love stories, in verse, to cope with the painful religio-political reality of Partition. Waris' own affiliation to the Chishti order of Sufis, founded by Fariduddin Shakarganj (1173-1266) of Pakpattan,[49] profoundly nourished her creative and emotional self. Time and time again, Waris' message in Hir-Waris that it is because of Baba Farid that the Panjab remains free from sorrow and suffering gave her solace and hope. For Waris, 'the people' included both Hindu and Muslim Punjabis. Committed to the idea of 'the land of the five rivers', he was conscious of Punjab's distinct regional identity.[50] After all, 'few genres show a more powerful attachment to the specificities of place than the Punjabi verse romance called the qissa . . . which was largely the creation of Panjabi Muslim poets.'[51]

Though the *qissa* tradition was at its most creative in the period from 1650 to 1850,[52] it was strengthened *via* oral and print media in late nineteenth-century Punjab. The most popular ballads, *Mirza Sahiba ki Sur, Waris Shah ki Hir,* and *Sassi Punnun,*[53] were enacted in the streets and bazaars of Lahore. *Mirza Sahiba ki Sur* was a 'spirited story, well told, and its recital forms a part of every festive gathering.'[54] The same was true of the *Hir-Ranjha* story. They were popular partly because 'music, singing and dancing are all amusements much enjoyed by the natives'.[55] This form of story-telling was strengthened by the 'strong presence of the professional Mirasis or Bhats, a tribe of hereditary ballad singers, whose songs, ballads, and tales, recited at weddings and other festivities, are in reality the favourite literature of the day'.[56]

With the growth of the vernacular printing press, Lahore's burgeoning publishing industry turned into a leading centre of Punjabi literary creation.[57] Not surprisingly, Fazal Shah's (1827-90) version of *Sohni-Mahival* enjoyed immense popularity in the late nineteenth century.[58] He wrote five *qissas*: *Sohni-Mahival, Hir-Ranjha, Sassi-Punnun, Laila-Majanu* and *Yusuf-Zuleikha.* Kishan Singh Arif (1836-1900) penned the *Shirin-Farhad*, in 1873, in the traditional *bait* popularized by Waris. Other prominent *qissakars* were Ghulam Rasul Ghulam (1813-74), the author of *Sassi-Punnun* (1850) and Ghulam

Rasul (1849-92) who wrote the romance of *Yusuf-Zuleikha*. They were followed by Mohammad Buta Gujarati (1836-1919), whose greatest composition was Mirza-Sahiban's romance, and Joga Singh, whose *Hir* was printed in Lahore in 1889. Furthermore, Kahan Singh published *Hir* in 1883. Bhagwan Singh (1850-1902), too, composed romances of *Hir-Ranjha* (1886), *Mirza-Sahiban* and *Sohni-Mahival* (1891).[59] The continuing universal appeal of this unique literature is attested by the 'number of nineteenth-century manuscripts recording its compositions in Gurmukhi'.[60] Yet these qissas were not part of the 'Sikh literary heritage'; in fact, 'Sikhs were not only late comers to this well-established poetic tradition, but part of a Punjabi heritage which was being developed as a literary medium for the creation of superb verse by Muslim poets.'[61] Significantly, these love legends were not ensconced within any religious tradition,[62] but constituted the core of Punjab's literary cultural pasts expressed in Punjabi, a shared repertoire of Hindus, Muslims, and Sikhs. Though efforts were made to undermine the fluidity of *qissa* tradition, it continued to form an alternative space of shared culture, invoking multiple pasts, kept alive by scores of poets, writers, and cultural performers. Amrita Pritam was one of them.

At the time of Partition and amidst the horror of violence, Sufi poets became Amrita Pritam's companions. 'Somebody once asked me who were my contemporaries. I said Shah Hussain (1538-99), Sultan Bahu (1629-91), and Waris Shah (*c.* 1736-90)'.[63] In addition, she was deeply influenced by the Qadiri poet Bulle Shah's (1680-1757) famous invocation, 'Bulha, how should I know who I am?' His *kafi* (short mystical poem) opens with, 'Hindu, no! nor Musalman'.[64] Surely, Bulle Shah and other great lyricists of the late Mughal period derived their themes and symbols from the popular cultures and folk traditions incorporating Islamic, Hindu, and Sikh vocabularies.[65] Bulle Shah's use of the legend of Hir and Ranjha, in particular, reflects a synthesis of Krsnaite and Nath elements, and a commitment to the 'composite and often syncretic nature of Panjabi popular culture'.[66] Further, his mystical allegories demonstrate his affinity with the cultural universe of Punjabi people. Doubtless, such Sufi poets moulded a diffuse conception of South Asian religious identity.[67] Their thoughts were extremely diverse and manifested in many forms,[68] but their poetry appealed to audiences across religious boundaries.[69]

Amrita Pritam's 'literary inheritance' was symbolized in the 'fire of life' that 'burnt in the love legends of Sohni, Sassi and Heer', which she still carries within herself. The fire 'lit by the poet Waris', she inherited, she says in her autobiographical poem 'Akhar' (Words). And yet she laments, 'nobody nourishes fire in the city of stones.'[70] The fire motif commemorates that history and culture whose desecration she mourns. The tragic death of the legendary lovers signals her own disenchantment with societal, political, and communal pressures, and her creative rejection of an assertive religious identity. This was not all. By using the love legends of Sufi poets, she identifies with and appropriates a 'syncretic' Punjabi identity.

The amorphous Punjabi literary tradition enabled Amrita Pritam to interrogate the logic of Partition. 'There was no basis for Partition', she maintains. 'It had fragile foundations. Punjab's legacy is a shared one: our poetry starts with Baba Farid in the twelfth century. From then onward our language is common, and we share the same poets. After all, there was a *tehzibi rishta* (cultural relationship) between Hindus and Mussalmans.'[71] Punjab's literary cultures gave her a sensibility to respond to the violence and pain of Partition, and to cope with her anguish after her uprooting and displacement. As she narrates, 'the Partition of India continued to become a festered wound in the bosom of history. Nobody would ever know how the dreams of so many girls of this country were slaughtered. . . . Then I had written a long poem, *Tavarikh* (History), which echoes the voice of a young girl, who like thousands of other such girls, got lost somewhere.'[72] Here she compares Punjab's Partition with the anguish of an abducted woman:

I am the cursed daughter of Punjab
Just look at my fate.

How can I speak——
My tongue is cracked
My hands are tied together
And my feet are bound.

There is a narration of suffering:

What evil was done to me!
What a curse fell upon my head!
The lines of fate written on my forehead
Have turned into serpents.

The symbol of Sohni is central to the narrative:

I was the beauty of five rivers
And now look at my fate!
Storm, come
Flood the earth
So I can drown myself!

Further:

Who brought the unfired waterpot
And made me drown in the river?

An abducted woman cries out for her lost identity:

My destiny is sleeping, while the world is wide awake
Only I know what I am; only my faith knows
I tear the red *choli* (bodice) from my body
Take off my bracelets.
I break myself in pieces
And become mere threads.

Returning to her past, which she has lost, she cries:

Over there, rumours fly
The people who gave me birth are still alive
O traveller, just listen to me—
How can I walk when my knees and ankles are broken?
Where has my mother gone?

Using the symbols of Sohni and Punjab's great 'river of love',[73] the woman laments:

There is no boat, no oar
How can I cross the Chenab?

And the poet invokes her childhood memory:

I don't know where that courtyard is
Or where the toys I played with have gone.
I was sitting in my room
Who broke in through the wall?
Where was the doll I was playing with?
Where is the henna meant to be painted on my hands?
Where is my red wedding veil?
Nobody to make the tiny braids in my hair
Nobody to weave in the golden flowers,
To put a golden *chaunk* (mark) upon my head.
My hair has become wild.

Further:

Nobody to consult the stars
The honour of the house was crushed in the bazaar.
Where is the mother who is queen?
The father who is king?
Who has cursed the daughter?
Where are my own sisters, my own brothers?
Who has torn apart the ties of blood?

Where are the childhood friends, my own village?
Who can I tell what happened to me—
As if my limbs had been torn from my body?
Who brought the unfired waterpot
And made me drown in the river?

Where are those who gave me birth?
Where are the friends who wish me well?
I am the cursed daughter of Punjab
My eyes forever filled with tears.

The earth was broken apart
And no one cared.
Who separated blood from blood?—
Brutality and bloodshed without end.

Duty and faith were put on sale.
The women of the country were put on sale.[74]

Without using the categories of religion, community and caste, Amrita Pritam underscores a woman's experience of Partition as universal and irreparable. 'Who can sense the pain of such a girl—the youth of whose body is forced into motherhood.'[75]

My mother's womb was helpless
I too am a human being
I am the mark of that bruise
When Independence dealt its blow.
I am the symbol of that accident
Which left its mark upon my mother's forehead.
My mother's womb was helpless.

I am the curse of the human race
Born at a time when stars were falling
The moon lost its light
When the sun went out.
My mother's womb was helpless.

I am the scar of a wound
The blackened spot on my mother's body
I am the burden of that evil which my mother had to bear
Smelling the stench of her womb
Who knows how difficult it was
To grow such terror in the belly
When all the time her body's flesh and bones were smoldering.

I was the fruit of that time
When the trees of Independence were in bud.

My mother's womb was helpless.[76]

Amrita Pritam describes the trauma of rape through the metaphor of a mother's womb. The womb is a victim of Partition's madness: 'I am the symbol of that accident.' She identifies the birth of an accursed child from the womb with Partition. The 'evil in the womb' manifests itself in the division of Punjab into two parts, like the surgical operation on the womb. This was a helpless womb like a helpless Punjab, and it bore 'fruit', when, as she says, 'the trees of independence were in bud'. The course of 'independence' was torn asunder. The child that was born was in fact a 'blackened spot'. Her Punjab was, in many ways, a scar of the wound.

Amrita Pritam expresses her disillusionment with Independence, nation, and the newly drawn territorial boundaries that destroyed the rhythm and dreams of everyday. In her poem, 'The Story of Punjab', she writes, 'From out of nowhere Fate came galloping towards Punjab crushing Pothohar beneath the horses' hooves.'[77] She mourns that 'at year's end, a flourishing Punjab was cut down in its green age'. The poem poignantly captures the rural landscape and the shattering of everyday life amid the metaphor of changing year and months:

There in the high, broad fields
Were the green and red-ripe leaves
Someone threw a spark into the ready grain
The hayricks smoldered within
Then *Chetar* (the beginning of the new year) came
— with flames red-blazing and the sharpening of steel
The waters of the five rivers now ablaze with oil

They fanned the flames.
Look at the sport of destiny
While they were cutting furrows in the land, the seeds fell from their hands

While they sat at spinning wheels, their cotton flew to the ground
Ladles fell from pots
Ropes were lost in the well
Turbans were knocked from heads
And bangles were smashed right on their wrists
The belts on the spinning wheels snapped along with their cogs
And the bullocks smashed along with the seats on their circling waterwheels.

There is complete disillusionment with political parties and the state:

Deer died leaping
And the peacocks, dancing
How long can a tree survive?
How long the shade of a tree?
From its very roots, the slugs eat away at it
Who can I go and ask?
Who can I ask anything to?

Invoking folk legends:

What is this whistling wind which whirls around
What stories we told one another—
And the travellers lost their way.[78]

Again, she mocks the ruler:

O king, reigning over the land—
This is the month of *Vaisakh* (the month of early spring).
Ashes are blowing on the face of the new century
O king, reigning over the land—
What sort of *Jeth* (summer) has come?
No sky above our heads, no earth beneath our feet.

O king, reigning over the land—
The month of *Haar* (rain) has come
What's the use of talking?;
The fields have been eaten by the hedges.

O king, reigning over the land
What sort of a *Savan* (monsoon) has come?

We invited it in—this fate
Now, who can stop it?[79]

Amrita Pritam transcends the usual blame game of indicting political leaders and parties, and holds 'fate' to be responsible for the shattering of everyday life. By so doing, she not only expresses the helplessness of Punjab, but also makes a powerful statement about how Punjab was not responsible for its vivisection and the ensuing violence. Surely, for her Punjab was not communalized in its day-to-day life. True to the spirit of the Punjabi *qissa*, she repeatedly expresses her intimate attachment to Punjab's metaphorical and physical presence devoid of religious acrimony.

In the poem 'Divided', she conjures up the image of 'common motherland', and mourns the fracturing of the rural Punjabi landscape. Written for her friend Sajjad Haider in Lahore, the poet laments the loss of her neighbour, who was separated from her owing to Partition:

> You were driving away and away
> With your families,
> And your bag and baggage,
> Because our common motherland
> Has been dissected.
>
> 'One', they say, 'is Pakistan',
> 'The other', they tell us, 'is Hindustan'.
> . . .
> Beautiful neighbour!
> The Punjab was a single body
> The five rivers its blood-vessels,
> And the overflowing waters of those rivers
> The common blood.
> Today that body has been torn apart
> How will the blood pass
> Through the broken limbs!
>
> The skies under which
> I played kabbadi with your brothers,
> Joined the pageants with them,
> Sang Heer-Ranjha,
> Recited poems by Bulle Shah,
> Hymns from Guru Nanak,
> And listened to the folk songs of Mirza-Sahiban.
> Punjab is an ancient land
> Older than History itself
> It was once under foreign rule
> But now when we rule ourselves
> It stands divided.

Further:

> The compound where

You spun the wheels together,
And with the rhythm of folk dance
Sang the songs of the common soil,
We cannot walk there anymore.[80]

Amrita Pritam invokes many historically constructed pasts that have been embodied in the qissa tradition, as well in the cultural festivities, including *Qadamon-ka-mela*,[81] *Basant-ka-mela*,[82] *Chiraghon-ka-mela*[83] and *Bhadra-kali-ka-mela*[84] celebrated in and around Lahore. These symbolized shared cultures and multiple pasts embedded in the everyday life and dreams of Punjabis. More specifically, in her invocation of everyday one finds the influence of the well-known medieval Urdu poet Jawan, who composed the songs of twelve months. Translated into various dialects, their well-known rendering was in Punjabi by Ḫashim, the court poet of Ranjit Singh.[85] The poet describes the agony of a wife parting from her spouse who is starting on a journey to Central Asia, a metaphor of estrangement that continually permeates Amrita Pritam's poetry. In addition, her narratives are critical of the threat posed by the religiously exclusive languages to Punjab's literary cultures—though, interestingly, the Sufi saints she invokes are often devoid of their religious identity.[86]

And yet, Amrita Pritam constructs a powerful critique of assertive religious identities. In her poem 'Frenzy', religion is likened to a serpent's bite:

When religion goes to people's heads—
Steel is sharpened
People's tongues grow cruel
The tongues of love grow dull
Veins flowing with red blood, turn blue
At the black snake's bite.
From their hiding places behind every bush
Poisonous snakes come slithering out to bite
People walking on their way
And lips once beautiful to kiss begin to foam.
Vultures gather, their beaks tearing at the bodies
They don't care if it's the daughter or the daughter-in-law of the house.[87]

The poet condemns the politics of religious conversion and re-conversion promoted by *shuddhi* and *sangathan*, *tabligh* and *tanzim*:

Sheep of every flock coming upon strangers
Force scraps of flesh into their mouths

Or threads upon their necks.
They drag them into their own folds.
They gain merit, they gain virtue.
They serve up their good deeds to their religions
They raise the flag high
In bright daylight and in the pitch-darkness of night
Steel is sharpened.
Innocent children
Delicate women and strong young men
Are sacrificed at the altar of this passion.

The frenzy of religion goes to people's heads.[88]

In many scholarly works, Partition is a defining moment in shaping and strengthening communitarian consciousness. 'Sikhs, Muslims and Hindus,' argues Gyanendra Pandey, 'were all redefined by the process of Partition.'[89] Likewise, according to feminist writers, Partition subordinated 'other identities'—gender, class, caste, region—to an exclusive religious community.[90] And yet, as Amrita Pritam's life story suggests, not all Punjabis identified with a notion of a monolithic religious community in 1947. Women's experiences, in particular, were varied, multiple, fragmented, and historical.[91]Amrita Pritam's experience of Partition impels her to invoke a shared culture of cultural symbols and language, and to transgress and ultimately transcend the languages of religious and communal mobilization. In the process, she defines her selfhood and endeavours, to use E.M. Forster's expression, 'to connect' with *kainaat* (universe), and to establish an independent relationship between the self and universe. 'My whole life is a struggle, a study. Amrita Pritam is the name of a journey, from a small I to a big I; from word to meaning; from boundary to boundless.'[92]

PINJAR: A FINAL TESTIMONY

Pinjar (Skeleton) a novel about which a film has now been made, is the most compelling account of Amrita Pritam's experience of Partition. It serves as an enduring archive on inter-community relations in Punjab, and a Punjabi woman's ambivalent relationship to 'colonialism', 'nationalism', and 'communalism'. *Pinjar* is, I would say, Amrita Pritam's testimony to the Partition of Punjab.

At the centre of the story is Pooru, a survivor. Rashida, a Muslim of the neighbouring village, abducts her much before Partition.

Pooru's abduction illustrates patriarchical and religio-communitarian anxieties.[93] Her parents' refusal to accept her, after the abduction, suggests ways in which religiously-informed identities hardened barriers over the issues of women's 'honour' and 'purity'. Ironically, this point has been misread by a Hindu right-wing writer, Balbir K. Punj, in a recent article on the film *Pinjar*, where he absolves her parents of patriarchal control, and attributes their unwillingness to accept her to the fear of retribution from Muslim neighbours.[94] According to him, 'the behaviour of Pooro's parents isn't out of place and aptly reflects a fear of Muslim inbuilt in the mind of Hindus in those days.'[95] He juxtaposes the image of a cowardly Hindu with that of an aggressive Muslim. And, locating Pooru's abduction 'in the backdrop of the [Muslim] League's poisonous exhortations against the kafirs', he writes that 'the entire village, overwhelmingly Muslim, approves of the abduction and forced marriage. It does give us a peep into those troubled times'.[96] Punj clearly inserts his own prejudice into Amrita Pritam's nuanced narrative.

Contrary to Punj's interpretation, Pooru's travails are by no means those of a 'minority' Hindu in the Muslim-dominated area of undivided Punjab. Her plight is that of a woman with a fluid identity caught up in the crossfire of communal frenzy. Amrita Pritam, in fact, dilutes the stereotype of the Muslim as the Other, which had become the centerpiece of colonial and Hindu communitarian narratives in Punjab. For instance, she resists labeling Rashida as a 'Mussalman abductor', and, without justifying his action, offers a context for his having abducted Pooru. Here she highlights the economic reality of rural Punjab: for long, Pooru's Hindu Sahukar family had exploited Rashida's family of indebted Shaikh cultivators.[97] Pooru eventually transcends her bitter experience, becomes emotionally attached to her 'abductor', and overcomes her prejudice. She marries Rashida, acquires the name Hamida, but still maintains her fluid identity: 'She was neither one nor the other.'[98] This is in sharp contrast to Punj's reading which constantly harps on Hamida's 'encaged identity'.[99]

For sure, *Pinjar* recognizes the difference between Hindus and Muslims, and yet it suggests that Punjabi society was not polarized along communal lines alone. Punj, however, wrongly makes much of Pooru's abduction and conversion to Islam, interpreting it as a ploy to 'obliterate Pooro's Hindu identity'.[100] Amrita Pritam underscores the impermeability of communitarian identities, and ways in which gender erodes the barriers of religion and communitarian boundaries. For instance, Hamida and the low-caste Kammo transcend the bounds of religious communities to maintain their intimate friendship. Indeed, it is Amrita Pritam's own commitment to the idea of transcending religious difference that inspires her to juxtapose and to contrast religiously aggressive identities with individual and culturally defined ones.

The entry of a mad woman in the narrative stirs up the anxieties of masculinized and communalized groups. Her nakedness is a metaphor of her non-religious identity. It causes alarm, even though she harms no one. Amrita Pritam introduces a note of irony here. A communally divided society marginalizes the non-sectarian identity as 'mad, alarming and a source of terror'. The mad woman becomes pregnant, a further comment on a brutalized society. Ultimately, the mad woman dies giving birth to a boy. Was this the death of an individual's identity? The mad woman was conjured up from Amrita Pritam's own experience of having seen her in a Sheikhupura village, in the very land of Waris Shah, just before Partition. 'She was walking in the dust of Sheikhupura like dust itself', she remembers [101] Surely, Amrita Pritam had captured the tone of the times, for during the Partition violence the 'rational' voice of a mad woman was reported in the *Tribune*: 'In an atmosphere of choking communal madness in Multan, the only person talking sense on the road was a mentally-deranged woman, who was shouting near District Police HQs: "Oh God what has happened to these mad Hindus and Muslims! Why are they quarrelling and fighting like dogs?"'[102]

Hamida adopts the mad woman's child. Herein lay the rub. A *panchayat* of Hindus believes: 'The mad woman was a Hindu. The Muslims have grabbed a Hindu child. Under the very noses of Hindus, they have converted a Hindu child into a Muslim.' 'Are we sure that the mad woman was a Hindu?', asks one? 'With my own eyes I saw the sacred 'Om' tattooed on her left arm', asserts another. Hindu elders of the village snatch the child from Hamida, purify (*shuddh*) it, and give it to the water-carrier's wife for his upbringing. The boy on the brink of death is thrown back into Hamida's home. This is a powerful statement on the dominance of aggressive religious assertions and their impact on social relations before Partition.

In the final part of the story, Hamida refuses to return with her natal family, which had once ostracised her, to India, and decides to stay on in Pakistan. She belongs neither to India nor to Pakistan. In a way, Hamida and Amrita Pritam are orphaned daughters 'both of and in history'.[103] Hamida's inner being, amid the venomous assertions of monolithic religious formations, is split during the most tumultuous times in the subcontinent's history. The newly defined India and the resurgent Hindu community fail to bind her. 'My home is now in Pakistan.' '"Whether one is a Hindu girl or a Muslim one, whosoever reaches her destination, she carries along my soul also", Pooru said to herself and made a last vow by closing her eyes.'[104]

Ironically, Balraj Punj interprets Pooru/Hamida's decision to stay back in Pakistan as being shaped by her virulent Muslim identity. As he puts it, 'If Pooru's religious sensitivity, cultural moorings and family ties could alter within such a short time, say a year, is it unnatural for some of those converted for generations or centuries to disown their pre-Islamic past, hate it and eventually work for its destruction and turn into votaries of a fundamentalist Islamic state?'[105] In short, he interprets Pooru's abduction and conversion, and then her turning back on her parents as a sign of a convert's Muslim consciousness and identity. By so doing, he makes a larger point about the 'change of religion bringing about change of nationality'.[106] As the fear of 'abduction' and 'conversion' were at the heart of the Hindu communitarian anxiety, Punj interprets Pooru's identity through the prism of these two prejudices rooted in a Hindu's anxiety about Partition. As a Hindutva protagonist, he has unfortunately drawn *Pinjar* into the ambit of Hindu nationalist discourse, and has completely distorted the meaning of *Pinjar* and the conviction of its author.

Amrita Pritam shows how Pooru/Hamida defies patriarchal and territorial boundaries, and effectively uses her agency to critique the reality of Partition by choosing to stay on in Pakistan. Indeed, the issue of abduction is central to Amrita Pritam's concerns, but with a difference. For one, she situates it within the framework of Hindu identity and patriarchal anxiety. Here her world-view contrasts with the communal perspective that interprets abduction as an act of Muslim depravity and aggression, and singularly targets the entire Muslim community for its culpability.

Second, Pooru/Hamida's refusal to succumb to the state policy of recovering abducted women in 1947,[107] on the basis of their religion identification, resonates with the attitude of those women who resisted being 'recovered', and legitimized their cross-religious relationships.[108] Though her abduction predates Partition, her resistance to a return to her natal family after Partition makes a larger point about the attempts made by some women to secure citizenship by acting autonomously of religious community and state. While reflecting on her abduction, 'a sense of resentment surged in Hamida's mind. When it happened to her, religion had become an insurmountable obstacle; neither her parents nor her in-laws-to-be had been willing to accept her. And now, the same religion had become so accommodating!'[109] Indeed, in times when religious identity became a brutal blueprint of territorial boundaries and nationalism, Amrita Pritam and her female protagonist critique the elision of religious community with 'nation', highlight patriarchal hypocrisy and challenge nationalist obsessions.

In many ways, *Pinjar* is the story of a woman's liminal position in the face of hardening religious and national boundaries. Pooru/Hamida is a shining example of that liminality. Yet, she emerges as an active agent in shaping her destiny. Amrita Pritam shows that an abducted and raped woman is not a mere victim; her pain and anguish can be a source of powerful energy for her new identity. Surely, it is difficult not to read *Pinjar* as a highly autobiographical novel.

SUMMING UP

Amrita Pritam's emotional history takes us away from the familiar realm of elite manoeuvres and high politics to the world of life histories and Partition. Her narratives do, to some extent, resonate with recent historical perspectives, which sensitize us to the problem of the 'wide chasm between the historians' apprehension of 1947 and what we might call a more popular, survivors' account of it—between history and memory.'[110] Such historiographical interventions underscore alternative discourses and 'non-disciplinary accounts of 1947'.[111] Doubtless, Amrita Pritam's narratives identify with a different kind of 'national' past, a different notion of creative community, subjectivity and citizenry.[112] And yet, her account, though being that of a survivor's, does not 'assert a heroic sense of community in the face of all inherited senses of belonging and home.'[113] In many ways, she offers a different perspective on Partition, violence and community. Her narratives do suggest that survivors' accounts cannot be reduced to Partition as 'violence' alone.[114] In fact, survivors' recollections of Partition contain multiple narratives, stories and meanings. Above all, survivors' accounts of 1947 form part of their life histories.[115]

Defying the image of essentialized religious communities, Amrita Pritam's life history offers a variegated and creative experience of an individual with a 'community' forged around a complex weave of popular cultural norms and literary traditions of Punjab. She identifies with multiple alternative strands and spaces in Punjab's vibrant culture and history, and her perspective differs from those women and men who remained strongly entrenched in patriarchal and religio-communitarian solidarities.

This essay has tried to demonstrate the extent to which the politics of religious identity generated familial, communitarian, regional, and national anxieties, and yet there were possibilities of creativity, liberation, transgression, and transcendence in pre- and post-Partitioned Punjab. Amrita Pritam's life history reveals that many cultural identities and subjectivities existed along with religiously strident ones.[116] Loosely defined and expressed in a variety of ways, they often harked back to pre-colonial narratives and traditions for their sustenance, in times when efforts were made in several quarters to eliminate these. And yet, unlike religious solidarities, such cultural identities did not acquire wider political dimensions or territorial identifications. They were often fragile and fragmented in contrast to strident and sharp religious collectivities.

Amrita Pritam's idea of cultural community and identity testifies to a plurality in Punjab that was exemplified in cultural symbols, motifs, and landscapes. Partition liberated her from the bounds of her religious community, and helped her strengthen her fluid identity and subjectivity. Her life history problematizes the experience and consciousness of a 'refugee', a Partition victim. Clearly, she does not identify with national borders, which are political constructs and imagined projections of territorial power. For her, Partition was a destructive but also a creative moment. She comes into her own, even though she feels rootless, separated from her lover and homeland.

In short, Amrita Pritam offers an alternative voice in history. In many ways, her life history constitutes a counter-narrative to dominant histories of 1947 and it serves as an alternative archive of Partition.[117] Significantly, her relationship with her own religious community remains ambivalent, distant, conflictual. Amrita Pritam's life history informs us that a refugee's anguish is not necessarily rendered into a communalized consciousness, for it gave her the poetic sensibility to compose an ode to her undivided Punjab.

NOTES

* I owe a deep debt of gratitude to Amrita Pritam for sharing with me her life history over the years. Most of the translations in this paper are my own; including the interviews where Amrita Pritam spoke in Punjabi and Hindustani.

1. Amrita Pritam, *Shadows of Words*, New Delhi: Macmillan India, 2001, p. 106.
2. Ibid., *Aksharon ke Saaye: Atmakatha* (Hindi), Delhi: Rajpal, 1999, p. 123.
3. Ibid., *Shadows*, p.120. The Sufis had named their place of meditation as *Hujra*, where meditation of many years vibrates and vitalizes that place.
4. I have explored this theme in *A Daughter's Testimony and Punjab's Partition* (forthcoming); and 'Partition Memories: A Daughter's Testimony', in Mushirul Hasan and Nariaki Nakazato (eds.), *The Unfinished Agenda: Nation Building in South Asia*, New Delhi: Manohar, 2001, pp. 17-48.
5. Amrita Pritam, 'Mitti ka Muqaddar', in her *Dusre Adam ki Beti*, Delhi: Rajpal, 2000, p. 9. Hindi.
6. Ibid., p. 10.
7. Ibid.
8. Ibid., p. 9.
9. Ibid., p. 10.
10. Amrita Pritam, *Aksharon ke Saaye*, pp. 14-15.
11. His shrine in Dera Ghazi Khan was a 'resort of Hindus and Musalman mendicants'. See Jafar Sharif, *Islam in India or the Qanun-i-Islam*, revised by W. Crooke, Delhi: Orinetal Reprint, 1972, p. 143; 1st publ. 1921.
12. Amrita Pritam, *Shadows*, p. 7.
13. Ibid., *Raseedi Ticket* (Hindi), Delhi: Hind Pocket Books, 1998, Autobiography, p. 12.
14. Indu Arora, 'Waking Gods', *Amrita Pritam: A Living Legend*, Chandigarh: India Inter-Continental Cultural Association, 1995, p. 22.
15. Amrita Pritam, *Raseedi Ticket*, p. 10.
16. Ibid., *Life and Times*, Delhi: Vikas, 1989, p. 4.
17. Ibid., pp. 4-5.
18. H. Oberoi, 'From Ritual to Counter-Ritual: Rethinking the Hindu-Sikh Question 1884-1915', in Joesph T. O'Connell, Milton Israel, Willard G. Oxtoby (eds.), *Sikh History and Religion in the Twentieth Century*, New Delhi: Manohar, 1990, p. 137.
19. Amrita Pritam, *Shadows*, p. 5.
20. Ibid., p. 6.
21. Shahira Naim, 'An Interview with Amrita Pritam', *Amrita Pritam: A*

Living Legend, Chandigarh: India Inter-Continental Cultural Association, 1995, p. 44.

22. Ibid., p. 45.
23. Interview with Amrita Pritam, New Delhi, 10 January 2000.
24. Ibid., 12 January 2001.
25. Ibid.
26. Amrita Pritam, *Aksharon ke Saaye*, p. 14.
27. Ibid., *Shadows*, p. 7.
28. Interview with Amrita Pritam, 14 January 2001.
29. Amrita Pritam, *Shadows*, pp. 6-7.
30. Interview with Amrita Pritam, 10 January 2000.
31. Ibid., 14 January 2001.
32. Ibid.
33. Amrita Pritam, *Shadows*, p. 7.
34. Interview with Amrita Pritam, 14 January 2001.
35. Ibid., 10 May 2001.
36. Amrita Pritam, *Shadows*, p. 7.
37. Ibid.
38. Ibid., *Life and Times*, pp. 21-2.
39. Ibid., *Raseedi Ticket*, p. 24.
40. Ibid., 'Today I call to Waris Shah', translated from Punjabi by Arlene Zide and Amrita Pritam; Amrita Pritam, *Shadows*, pp. 8-9.
41. Interview with Amrita Pritam, 12 January 2001.
42. Ibid., *Shadows*, pp. 9-10.
43. Ibid., *Aksharon ke Saaye*, pp. 111-12.
44. Ibid., *Raseedi Ticket*, p. 26.
45. Interview with Amrita Pritam, 16 July 2001.
46. Christopher Shackle, 'Beyond Turk and Hindu: Crossing the Boundaries in Indo-Muslim Romance', David Gilmartin and Bruce B. Lawrence (eds.), *Beyond Turk and Hindu: Rethinking Religious Identities in Islamicate South Asia*, Delhi: India Research Press, 2002, p. 58.
47. Ibid.
48. Ibid.
49. According to Richard Eaton, 'shrines like that of Baba Farid made a universal culture available to local groups, enabling such groups to transcend their local microcosms'. Richard Eaton, 'The Political and Religious Authority of the Shrine of Baba Farid', Richard M. Eaton (ed.), *India's Islamic Traditions, 711-1750*, New Delhi: Oxford University Press, 2003, p. 280. Indeed, the appeal of Baba Farid was not lost to diverse local people in twentieth-century Punjab.
50. J.S. Grewal, 'The World of Waris', in Sudhir Chandra (ed.), *Social Transformation and Creative Imagination*, New Delhi: Allied, 1984, p. 114.

51. Shackle, 'Beyond Turk', p. 59.
52. Ibid., p. 64.
53. Syad Muhammad Latif, *Lahore: Its History, Architectural Remains and Antiquities, with an Account of Its Modern Institutions, Inhabitants, Their Trade, Customs, &c.*, Lahore: New Imperial Press, 1892, p. 267.
54. *Gazetteer of the Lahore District, 1883-84*, Calcutta, n.d., p. 50.
55. Ibid., p. 52.
56. Ibid., p. 49.
57. Ibid., p. 54.
58. Shackle, 'Beyond Turk', p. 66.
59. Sant Singh Sekhon, *A History of Panjabi Literature*, vol. 2, Patialia: Punjabi University, 1996, pp. 132-49.
60. Christopher Shackle, 'Some Observations on the Evolution of the Modern Standard Punjabi', J.T. O'Connell, Milton Israel and Willard Gurdon Oxtoby (eds.), *Sikh History and Religion in the Twentieth Century*, Toronto: University of Toronto, 1988, p. 106.
61. Ibid.
62. Oberoi, 'From Ritual', pp. 139-40.
63. Interview with Amrita Pritam, 12 December 2002.
64. On Bulle Shah, see Shackle, 'Beyond Turk', p. 57.
65. Denis Matringe, 'Krsnaite and Nath elements in the poetry of the eighteenth-century Panjabi Sufi Bulhe Sah', R.S. McGreggor (ed.), *Devotional Literature in South Asia*, Cambridge: Cambridge University Press, 1992, p. 190.
66. Ibid., p. 198.
67. Shackle, 'Beyond Turk', p. 57.
68. Ishtiaq Husain Qureshi, 'Projecting Sufi Thought in an Appropriate Context', L.F. Rushbrook Williams, *Sufi Studies: East and West*, New York: E.P. Dutton, 1973, p. 25.
69. For an alternative and somewhat limited perspective solely within the framework of Islamic tradition, see Mustansir Mir, 'Teaching of Two Punjabi Sufi Poets', Donald S. Lopez, Jr. (ed.), *Religions of India in Practice*, Princeton: Princeton University Press, 1995. On Sufism grounded not on theology, but on experience, see Qureshi, 'Projecting Sufi', p. 25.
70. 'Words', Amrita Pritam, *A Slice of Life: Selected Works*, Delhi: Vikas, 1990, p. 58.
71. Interview with Amrita Pritam, 22 January 2000.
72. Amrita Pritam, *Shadows*, p. 13.
73. One of the nineteenth-century poets Mian Qadir Yar (1803-92) composed a beautiful qissa of *Sohni-Mahival*, in which he identified the river Chenab as a river of love. Surinder Singh Kohli, *History of Punjabi Literature*, Delhi: National Book Shop, 1993, p. 112.

74. Amrita Pritam, 'I Am The Cursed Daughter of Punjab from History', translated from Punjabi by Arlene Zide and Amrita Pritam. Also Amrita Pritam, *Shadows*, pp. 13-14.
75. Amrita Pritam, *Shadows*, p. 12.
76. Amrita Pritam, 'Helplessness', translated from Punjabi by Arlene Zide and Amrita Pritam. Also Amrita Pritam, *Shadows*, pp. 12-13.
77. Amrita Pritam, 'The Tale of Punjab', translated from Punjabi by Arlene Zide and Amrita Pritam. Also Amrita Pritam, *Shadows*, p. 10.
78. In explanation, Amrita Pritam adds: 'Folk legends say that if you tell your stories during the day, travellers will lose their way.'
79. Amrita Pritam, 'Tale of Punjab'.
80. Ibid., 'Divided' (1947) Ramesh Mathur and Mahendra Kulasrestha (eds.), *Writings on India's Partition*, Delhi: Simant, 1976, pp. 35-6.
81. Latif, *Lahore*, p. 269; G.C. Walker, *Gazetteer of the Lahore District, 1893-94*, Lahore, 1894, p. 30.
82. *Punjab District Gazetteers*, vol. XXXA, Lahore district, with maps, Lahore, 1916, 84; Latif, *Lahore: Its History*, for its appeal to Hindus and Muslims alike, pp. 146 and 268-9. During Muharram, there was a substantial participation by Hindus. *Punjab District Gazetteers*, Lahore, 1916, p. 85.
83. *Punjab District Gazetteers*, 1916, p. 84; Latif, ibid., p. 268; Walker, *Gazetteer of the Lahore District*, p. 78.
84. *Punjab District Gazetteers*, Lahore, 1916, p. 84; Latif, *Lahore*, p. 272.
85. *Gazetteer of the Lahore District, 1883-84*, p. 55.
86. According to David Gilmartin, the *pirs* or *sajjada nashins* provided the vanguard of religious support for Pakistan in the 1940s. Amrita Pritam does not underscore the changing role that the Sufis and their shrines played in twentieth-century Punjabi society and polity. Instead, she celebrates their universal language that transcends religious boundaries. Sensitivities of Punjabis like Amrita Pritam's seem to escape Gilmartin's scholarly understanding of twentieth-century Punjab's society and polity. David Gilmartin, 'Religious Leadership and the Pakistan Movement in the Punjab', *Modern Asian Studies*, 13, 3 (1979), pp. 485-517. Also his *Empire and Islam: Punjab and the Making of Pakistan*, New Delhi: Oxford University Press, 1989.
87. Amrita Pritam, 'Frenzy', translated from Punjabi by Arlene Zide and Amrita Pritam. Also, 'Frenzy', Khushwant Singh (ed.), *Amrita Pritam. Selected Poems*, Delhi: Bharatiya Jnanpith, 1992, p. 101.
88. Ibid.
89. Gyanendra Pandey, *Remembering Partition: Violence, Nationalism and History in India*, Cambridge: Cambridge University Press, 2001, p. 18. Though Pandey makes an important point about Partition as a critical moment in the redefinition of religious identities, it needs

emphasizing that this process predates Partition. It is important to focus on the pre-history of Partition and to explore how religious identities were formed historically. After all, the Arya Samaj, the Singh Sabha and the Muslim Anjumans, followed by the Hindu Sabha, the Akali Dal, and the Muslim League, set the stage, so to speak, for the dominance of religious identity over other collectivities during Partition.

90. 'Introduction', Nighat Said Khan, Rubina Saigol, Afiya Shehrbano Zia, *Locating the Self: Perspectives on Women and Multiple Identities*, Lahore: ASR Publications, 1994, p. 5; Ritu Menon and .Kamla Bhasin, *Borders and Boundaries: Women in India's Partition*, New Delhi: Kali for Women, 1998, p. 257; Urvashi Butalia, *The Other Side of Silence: Voices from the Partition of India*, New Delhi: Penguin, 1998, p. 361.
91. This point is somewhat undermined in the gendered readings of Partition which represent women's experiences as unproblematically homogeneous. For instance, see Menon and Bhasin, *Borders*; Butalia, *Other Side*.
92. Interviews with Amrita Pritam, 12 May 2001, 10 January 2002.
93. Amrita Pritam, *The Skeleton and that Man*, New Delhi: Sterling, 1987, p. 6 [translated from Punjabi by Khushwant Singh]. Originally published 1950.
94. Balbir Punj considers Chandraprakash Dwivedi's film and Amrita Pritam's *Pinjar* to be the same. In fact, they are at crucial variance.
95. Balbir K. Punj, 'Do Skeletons Have a Soul', *Outlook*, 10 November 2003, p. 66.
96. Ibid., p. 68.
97. Amrita Pritam, *Skeleton*, pp. 7-8.
98. Ibid., p. 11.
99. Punj, 'Do Skeletons', p. 68.
100. Ibid.
101. Amrita Pritam, *Deewaron ke Saaye Mein*, Delhi: Rajpal, 1996, p. 34. Hindi; Interview with Amrita Pritam, 29 August 2000.
102. 'Mad Woman Talks Sense', *Tribune*, 14 March 1947.
103. I am borrowing the phrase from Antoinette Burton's reading of Attia Hosain's *Sunlight on a Broken Column*. Antoinette Burton, *Dwelling in the Archive: Women Writing House, Home, and History in Late Colonial India*, New Delhi: Oxford University Press, 2003, p. 135.
104. Amrita Pritam, *Skeleton*, p. 50.
105. Punj, 'Do Skeletons', p. 68.
106. Ibid.
107. A programme of recovery of abducted women was undertaken jointly by India and Pakistan on 6 December 1947. Known as the Central

Recovery Operation, it sought to 'recover' any woman who was seen to be in the company of a man of the other religion after 1 March 1947. Butalia, *Other Side*, pp. 143-4; Menon, *Borders*, pp. 123 and 256.

108. Ritu Menon, 'Reproducing the Legitimate Community: Secularity, Sexuality and the State in Postpartition India', Patricia Jeffery and Amrita Basu (eds.), *Appropriating Gender: Women's Activism and Politicized Religion in South Asia,* New York: Routledge, 1998, pp. 15-32; 24-5; Butalia, *Other Side*, p. 147.
109. Amrita Pritam, *Skeleton*, p. 39. Elsewhere, Amrita Pritam writes about the irony of the situation in 1947, 'Pooru was abducted much before Partition by a personal enemy, and her parents refused to accept her. This was one event, but during the time of Partition, there were many episodes like this taking place from home to home. Ironically, by this time, parents were looking for their abducted daughters.' Amrita Pritam, *Aksharon ke Saaye*, p. 24.
110. Pandey, *Remembering*, p. 6.
111. Ibid., p. 204
112. Ibid., p. 18.
113. Here her account appears to differ from Gyanendra Pandey's reading. According to Pandey, 'the undying valour of the community' is a theme that recurs very commonly and 'most forcefully' in the recollections of the survivors of 1947. Pandey, *Remembering*, p. 189.
114. On the relationship between violence and community in survivors' account of Partition, see Pandey, ibid., p. 175.
115. This aspect is somewhat missing in Gyanendra Pandey's pioneering work.
116. In several historical works, fluid identities appear to be transformed into monolithic ones in the colonial period. Seldom is a point made by historians about the coexistence of multiple identities, fragmented identities, and the need for their radical historicisation.
117. Burton, *Dwelling*, p. 134.

Contributors

RAZIUDDIN AQUIL is a Fellow in History at the Centre for Studies in Social Sciences, Calcutta. His book, on Religion and Politics under the Lodi and Sur Afghan rulers in north India in the late fifteenth and early sixteenth centuries, is likely to be published in 2006.

G. ARUNIMA teaches History at Lady Shri Ram College, University of Delhi. Her earlier work, *There Comes Papa: Colonialism and the Transformation of Matriliny in Kerala, Malabar, c.1850-1940* (2003) historicized the changes in matrilineal kinship amongst the Nayars of Kerala. She is currently completing a biography of O. Chandu Menon, the author of the first 'modern' Malayalam novel. This paper is part of her new work on religion in Kerala.

MICHAEL BRENNER is Professor of Jewish History and Culture at the University of Munich. After studies in Heidelberg and Jerusalem he received his Ph.D. from Columbia University, and taught at Indiana and Brandeis Universities, and as a visting profesor at the Universities of Mainz, Budapest, and Stanford. Among his publications are *Zionism: A Concise History* (German original 2002, English 2003) and *The Renaissance of Jewish Culture in Weimar Germany* (1996).

ANINDITA CHAKRABARTI is a senior Research Scholar at the Department of Sociology, University of Delhi. She is working on her dissertation, 'A Sociological Study of the Swadhyaya Movement'. She has done extensive fieldwork in Gujarat and Mumbai.

REKHA CHOWDHARY is Professor, Department of Political Science, University of Jammu. She did her M.Phil. from JNU and Ph.D. from University of Jammu. She worked extensively on the politics of Jammu & Kashmir and has published several articles in journals like *EPW, Seminar* and *Mainstream.*

NONICA DATTA teaches History at Miranda House, University of Delhi. She is the author of *Forming an Identity: A Social History of the Jats* (1999); and *A Daughter's Testimony and the Partition of Punjab* (forthcoming).

PRADIP KUMAR DATTA is interested in the interface between history, literature and politics. He teaches at a multi-disciplinary position in the Department of Political Science, University of Delhi. His publications include *Khaki Shorts Saffron Flags* (co-author) and *Carving Blocs*. He is currently at the Centre for Studies in Social Sciences, Calcutta.

MICHAEL DUSCHE taught at the School of Languages, JNU, until recently. He is now DAAD Research Fellow, Project Manager, Euro-Islam-Dialogue, Faculty of Philosophy, Universitaet Erfurt, Germany. He is the author of *Der Philosoph als Mediator* (2000).

AMAR FAROOQUI teaches history at University of Delhi. He is the author of *Smuggling as Subversion* (1998), *Early Social Formations* (2001), and *Opium and the Making of Early Victorian Bombay* (2005).

JAN-PETER HARTUNG is currently Post-Doctoral Research Fellow at the Chair of Islamic Studies, Erfurt University, Germany. His recent publications include *Viele Wege und ein Ziel: Leben und Wirken von Sayyid Abu l-Hasan 'Ali al-Hasani Nadwi (1913-1999)* (2004), and *Islamic Education, Diversity, and National Identity: Dini Madaris in India Post 9/11* (forthcoming).

MUSHIRUL HASAN, Vice-Chancellor, Jamia Millia Islamia, has introduced and edited a number of printed texts: *My Life: A Fragment* by Mohamed Ali, *Inside India* by Halide Edib, *Zakaullah of Delhi* by C.F. Andrews, *Regionalizing Pan-Islamism: Documents on the Khilafat Movement* (co-edited with Margrit Pernau) and *Negotiating with the West: Travels of Mirza Abu Talib* by Mirza Abu Talib (forthcoming).

PRALAY KANUNGO is Associate Professor at the Centre for Political Studies, Jawaharlal Nehru University. He taught at University of Delhi and was Fellow at Nehru Memorial Museum & Library, New Delhi. His publications include *RSS's Tryst with Politics: From Hedgewar to Sudarshan* (2002).

GURPREET MAHAJAN is Professor at the Centre for Political Studies, Jawaharlal Nehru University, New Delhi. Her publications include *Identities and Rights: Aspects of Liberal Democracy in India* (1998), *The Multicultural Path: Issues of Diversity and Discrimination* (2002) and *The Public and the Private: Issues of Democratic Citizenship in a Comparative Perspective* (ed.) (2003).

SHAIL MAYARAM is Senior Fellow, Centre for the Study of Developing Societies, Delhi. Publications include *Against History, Against State: Counterperspectives from the Margins* (2003); co-authored with Ashis Nandy, Shikha Trivedi, Achyut Yagnik, *Creating a Nationality: The Ramjanmabhumi Movement and the Fear of Self* (1995); co-edited with Ajay Skaria and M.S.S. Pandian, *Subaltern Studies*, vol. 12 (2005).

V. NAGENDRA RAO is Lecturer, Centre for Strategic and Regional Studies (CSRS), University of Jammu. He did his M.Phil. and Ph.D. from School of International Studies, JNU. Major research interest: Ethnicity and Nationalism. Apart from articles in leading journals, has co-edited *Central Asia: Present Challenges and Future Prospects* (2005). Edits the CSRS journal *Security and Society*.

SATISH SABERWAL was Professor of Sociology at the Centre for Historical Studies, Jawaharlal Nehru University. Current interests: social processes leading to the Partition of the Indian subcontinent and the long term historical experience of Chinese society, especially during the T'ang and Sung periods. Publications include *Wages of Segmentation: Comparative Historical Studies on Europe and India* (1995), *Roots of Crisis: Interpreting Contemporary Indian Society* (1996), and *Social Conflict* (1996, co-edited with N. Jayaram).

RANABIR SAMADDAR is Director, Calcutta Research Group, a research institute working on issues of rights, justice, and peace. Samaddar's wide range of critical studies and publications include contemporary issues of popular democracy, trans-border migration, community history, and technological restructuring. His recently published study of dialogues as part of war and peace politics, titled *The Politics of Dialogue* (2004) is a product of his long research on war and peace in South Asia.

NANDINI SUNDAR is Professor of Sociology at the Delhi School of Economics, University of Delhi. She has authored *Subalterns and Sovereigns: An Anthropological History of Bastar, 1854-1996* (1997); co-authored *Branching Out: Joint Forest Management in India* (2001), and co-edited *A New Moral Economy for India's Forests?: Discourses of Community and Participation* (1999).

SYED ZAINUDDIN wrote his Ph.D. thesis on Tablighi Jamaat in Orissa at Jamia Millia Islamia and teaches sociology at Aligarh Muslim University. His research and publications cover several aspects of the sociology of Indian Muslims. His current research focuses on *madrasa* education in India.

Index